# STRATEGIC MANAGEMENT

## From Confrontation to Transformation

Henk W. Volberda, Rick M. A. Hollen,
Joana R. Pereira, Jatinder S. Sidhu, Kevin Heij

1 Oliver's Yard
55 City Road
London EC1Y 1SP

2455 Teller Road
Thousand Oaks
California 91320

Unit No 323-333, Third Floor, F-Block
International Trade Tower
Nehru Place, New Delhi – 110 019

8 Marina View Suite 43-053
Asia Square Tower 1
Singapore 018960

Editor: Kirsty Smy
Development editors: Jessica Moran, Martha Cuneen and Sarah Turpie
Editorial assistant: Charlotte Hegley
Production editor: Nicola Marshall
Copyeditor: Catja Pafort
Proofreader: Tom Bedford
Indexer: C&M Digitals (P) Ltd, Chennai, India
Marketing manager: Lucia Sweet
Cover design: Francis Kenney
Typeset by: C&M Digitals (P) Ltd, Chennai, India
Printed in the UK

**Library of Congress Control Number: 2023933271**

**British Library Cataloguing in Publication data**

A catalogue record for this book is available from the British Library

ISBN 978-1-5297-7058-2
ISBN 978-1-5297-7057-5 (pbk)

At Sage we take sustainability seriously. Most of our products are printed in the UK using responsibly sourced papers and boards. When we print overseas we ensure sustainable papers are used as measured by the Paper Chain Project grading system. We undertake an annual audit to monitor our sustainability.

# DEDICATION

# BRIEF CONTENTS

# CONTENTS

# LIST OF TABLES AND FIGURES

## CHAPTER 1

## CHAPTER 2

## CHAPTER 3

# CHAPTER 4

# CHAPTER 5

# DIAGNOSTIC PART I

# CHAPTER 6

# CHAPTER 7

# CHAPTER 8

# CHAPTER 9

# DIAGNOSTIC PART II

# CHAPTER 10

# CHAPTER 11

# CHAPTER 12

# CHAPTER 13

# DIAGNOSTIC PART III

# CHAPTER 14

## CHAPTER 15

## CHAPTER 16

## CHAPTER 17

# DIAGNOSTIC PART IV

# LIST OF CASES, STRATEGIC FOCI AND KEY DEBATES

# CHAPTER 5

# CHAPTER 6

# CHAPTER 7

# CHAPTER 8

## CHAPTER 12

## CHAPTER 13

## CHAPTER 14

## CHAPTER 15

# CHAPTER 16

# CHAPTER 17

# PREFACE

Business leaders, managers and strategists are constantly confronted with disruptive changes and new realities. They are challenged to provide directions and lead their organizations, ensuring future success. This essential book on strategic management presents the original process to *Confront-Sense-Choose-Transform* – the CSCT protocol, which helps students of strategy to successfully address challenges of competition in the global marketplace. This book adopts a managerial perspective and presents the most widely used and trusted methods, tools and theories that enable the reader to confront blind spots and disruptive change, sense and interpret, choose generic strategies and make judgment calls, and to direct transformation. This novel perspective on the strategic management process focuses on the stages, concepts and strategic capabilities that help students of strategy to learn and practice how to confront new challenges, sense what matters, choose wisely, and transform structures, systems and operations. The process of *Confront-Sense-Choose-Transform* allows the strategy novice to find everything one needs to know about strategic management concepts and tools, and the knowledgeable reader to immediately find where to catch up on the cutting-edge knowledge presented in this book.

## What makes this book unique?

We live in a highly complex and dynamic world, with uncertainty and ambiguity being the norm. The rules that served strategists in growing economies of the past decades when the world was relatively simple, stable, clear and certain were fundamentally different to what is needed today. Part I of this book, Confront, acknowledges this great shift, and explores how new challenges question business leaders and strategists' ability to formulate and implement strategies. Making these strategy tensions explicit, this part helps to focus on the key strategic capabilities. Part II, Sense, enables readers to learn how to apply the analytical techniques and tools that provide an in-depth understanding of focal industries, competitors, complementors, customer segments, and, internally, an appreciation of capabilities. Part III, Choose, provides clarity of the numerous choices like the generic business-level strategies (e.g., cost leadership, differentiation, focus), diversification, internationalization, and alliance choices that need to be considered in terms of trade-offs. Part IV, Transform, presents how to carry the chosen strategy through to execution. Concepts and tools answering the critical questions on reorganization, strategic entrepreneurship, new business models, and strategic renewal are found here. Throughout the process stages, the action-oriented 'why-how'-structure helps students of strategy to understand what they need to know to cope with the new 'now'. Complementing the main text, in-text illustrations, and cases are 'pages of action', which will nudge readers to exercise their growing strategy muscles to apply what they found useful. Each chapter offers up-to-date theories of strategic management and best practices from businesses around the world, illustrations and material to trigger all five senses for active learning to allow readers' experience developing and implementing strategy in the real world.

*Strategic Management: From Confrontation to Transformation* differs from standard strategy textbook in several ways:

- Topics of growing importance include corporate purpose, disruptions, emerging (digital) technologies, business models, ecosystems, platforms, strategic change, organizational learning, digital transformation, and innovation. The comprehensive selection of concepts and methods in this book is biased; biased towards relevance. Phenomena of interest that businesses need to confront are centre stage in this book.
- Management education has increasingly seen diverse student bodies with growing numbers of international students. This book is designed and written to be taught for a global audience. This is manifest in the plenitude of iconic and original case studies from different continents: Europe, North America, Asia, and Oceania.
- The majority of courses, at all levels, take an approach that focuses on (and contrasts) the industrial organization and emergent models while highlighting, to varying degrees, critiques of this orthodoxy. This book focuses on the *Confront-Sense-Choose-Transform* process of strategic management, presenting theoretical perspectives when they are useful, not because they exist.
- Shorter case studies are popular for in-class discussion and illustrative purposes at undergraduate level and longer cases are used at postgraduate level (and, on occasion, for formative and summative assessment purposes at undergraduate level). This book, in print and on screen, offers brief vignettes and short case studies that help students to pick up the essence of concepts and methods. Additional case studies, offered online at **https://study.sagepub.com/volberda**, invite students to dig into in-depth cases to explore the reality of complex organization and learn about the intricacies of theories and tools' application.
- Particularly at MBA level, there is a shift away from 'theory followed by example'-delivery towards more active forms of learning, focusing on group work, skills and experiential exercises. Our book enables the new ways of learning – team-based, online, interactive and flipped – by providing in print and online experiential assignments, exercises and experiments, which we developed over the last decades.
- The challenge of what comes after defining the strategy remains an underexploited opportunity that we seek to seize in this book with much emphasis on strategy implementation/execution issues.

## Key characteristics

In contrast to traditional textbooks that follow the script of 'ODMAA' (one damned model after another), this book is not simply a string of models. We provide all the useful tools our readers expect and map them in an integrated process stage model to help understanding strategic management systematically and assist students in learning the foundations and cutting-edge concepts to move to the practice of confronting reality and creating solutions. We proceed from confront to sense, choose and transform. The process stages (*Confront-Sense-Choose-Transform*) allow for stepwise progression from strategy formulation to strategy development. Links between the interconnected areas of practical strategy development and execution are acknowledged in order to allow for fast and repeated learning cycles. Our strategic management process model helps students along on their own journey of discovering and learning how to develop and implement strategy while ensuring growing dexterity of essential skills to sense, choose and transform. Several characteristics of this book will enhance the student's learning opportunities:

- This book presents you with the most comprehensive and thorough coverage of strategic management that is available in the market. Various aspects of the strategy process are discussed in this book clustered around the four stages of confronting strategic issues, sensing new opportunities and threats, choosing proper strategies, and transforming the organization in the right strategic direction. *Confront* focuses on the changed reality that business faces. *Sense* details traditional as well as advanced analytical tools and techniques to gain insight. *Choose* explains how strategic decisions are made. *Transform* focuses on leadership and execution that brings strategy to life. Our strategic management process model provides a broad coverage of strategy formulation as well as strategy implementation.

- Moreover, this textbook not only addresses the most relevant theories and concepts in the strategy field, but, in contrast with most traditional textbooks, we also developed *diagnostic chapters* that describe various concrete tools for each stage of the strategy process: Part I: *Confrontrix*, Part II: *iSense*, Part III: *ChooseWell*, and Part IV: *Transformax*. The practical tools covered in each of these diagnostic chapters help students in strategic management to address and solve strategic problems, and provide important building blocks for strategy consulting.

- Our book presents you with many examples of how firms use the strategic management tools, techniques and concepts developed by leading researchers. Indeed this book is strongly *application oriented* and presents you, our readers, with a vast number of examples and applications of strategic management concepts, techniques and tools. Collectively, no other strategic management book offers the combination of useful and insightful theory and applications in a wide variety of organizations as does this text. Company examples cover a wide international range of large firms such as Adidas, Amazon, Apple, BMW, Coca-Cola, DSM, EY, Facebook, Google, Henkel, Hilton, IKEA, ING, McDonald's, Nestlé, Nintendo, Nokia, PepsiCo, Philips, Qualcomm, Shell, Tesla, and Volkswagen. We also include examples of successful younger firms such as Airbnb, Ben & Jerry's, Beyond Meat, Epic Games Store, Mindflow, Northvolt, PayPay, Protix, RealFevr and Stripe Inc.

- This new strategy textbook also covers several *new strategic themes* that have been mostly ignored in traditional textbooks. For example, in Chapter 2 we describe how strategy should be based on an authentic *Purpose*. Different from the taken-for-granted that a company basically has to create economic value, the notion of a purpose is based on the assumption that a company should also provide social value besides striving for financial gains. Chapter 3, which is devoted to *Stakeholders and Corporate Governance*, shows how firms' ability to simultaneously satisfy their stakeholders' different interests is critical to firms' success and has become an essential part of the strategic management process. Moreover, Chapter 5 discusses how various *Emerging Technologies* of the Industry 4.0 and Web 3.0 might affect future strategy-making and the emergence of new business models. Chapter 9 focuses on *Ecosystems and Platforms* and shows how strategy analysis of this higher level of analysis is fundamentally different from firm strategy. Chapter 13 covers a wide array of relevant interorganizational arrangements, and pays attention to strategic choices regarding both the alliance formation and post-formation stage. Chapter 16 covers *Business Models* as a reflection of the firm's chosen strategy and discusses several ways how to change the business model. Most firms fail to innovate their business model because they continue to do the same things that have made them successful in the past. Chapter 17 discusses how implementation of strategic actions may help firms to realize *Strategic Renewal* by transforming their core businesses, and seeking new avenues for growth.

- The research that underpins this book is drawn from the 'classics' as well as the most *recent contributions* to the strategic management literature, knowledge and practice. The historically significant 'classic' research provides the foundation for much of what is known about strategic management; the most recent contributions reveal insights about how to effectively use strategic management in the complex, global business environment in which most firms operate while trying to outperform their competitors.

- Focusing only on formulations of strategy is misguided. Strategy formulation is important, yet it is nothing without strategy implementation. This is especially important in the current global economic climate. With the dramatic changes that are unfolding, careful attention to the cyclical process of Confront-Sense-Choose-Transform enables companies to better adjust to the shifting context, making the implementation and renewal of strategy paramount for long-term success. Unlike many other textbooks, we devote four chapters to the *implementation of strategy*. No other book offers the formulation-implementation link in such clarity as presented here.

- We, the authors of this book, are also *active scholars*. We conduct research on a range of contemporary and challenging strategic management topics. Our passion for doing so is to contribute to the strategic management literature and to better understand how to effectively apply strategic management tools, techniques and concepts to create payoffs in organizational performance. Thus, our own research is integrated in the appropriate chapters along with the research of numerous other scholars and thought leaders.

## Structure of the book

This strategy textbook addresses the need of strategists to *confront* a fundamentally changed business landscape and a large variety of current and imminent strategic challenges that may arise over time, to *sense* – based on thorough analyses – what matters in relation to these confrontations, to make judgment calls and *choose* from a wide array of strategic options how to (re)act, and to ultimately *transform* the organization in pursuit of a sustainable or (at least) a transient competitive advantage and other desired outcomes of organizational activity. The book offers a novel managerial perspective on strategic management detailing these *Confront-Sense-Choose-Transform* process stages, which capture the essence of how to carry out strategic management in today's dynamic, ambiguous, complex and uncertain business landscape. The book is reader-friendly and does not assume prior strategy knowledge. It presents a variety of different tools, methods, concepts and theories that allow for stepwise progression from confrontation to transformation.

Following the general introductory chapter on strategy, the textbook is split up into four parts (I, II, III and IV), each of which consists of four regular chapters and one diagnostic chapter. These different parts and chapters are structured around the *Confront-Sense-Choose-Transform* logic, as visualized in our strategic management process framework, with Chapter 1 residing in the centre.

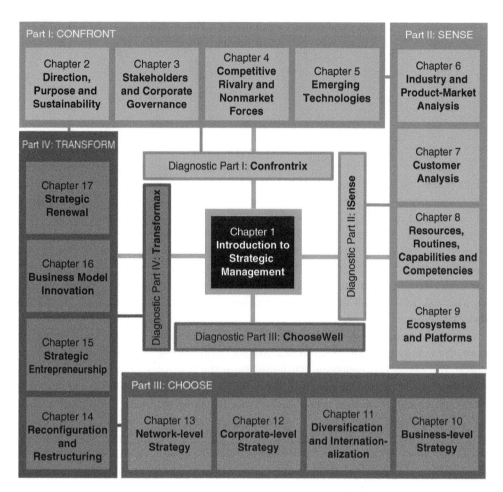

**FIGURE 0.1**   The strategic management process model: Confront-Sense-Choose-Transform

Framing the discipline and practice of strategic management, the introductory Chapter 1 allows the rookie student to understand the traditional linear narrative underlying strategy teaching. The bird's eye view in this chapter will be composed of a mix of traditional and emergent approaches in strategic management and end with an overall framework with different stages of the strategy process, which we examine in the remainder of the book. The reader will appreciate the challenges facing the strategists as tensions that typically arise in the strategy process.

From Chapter 2 onwards, we move clockwise through this framework. The regular chapters focus on the concepts and capabilities that help you learn and practice how to enable firms – and other types of organizations – to go through this iterative and dynamic process, allowing them to improve their strategic fit and progress towards prolonged above-average performance. The diagnostic chapters offer mainly practical and action-oriented tools and methods in relation to topics covered in preceding regular chapters. Although we cover the process of *Confront-Sense-Choose-Transform* in a sequential order, starting with confrontation, we see this process as dynamic and iterative, rather than as static and linear. Also, the chapters are highly interrelated – after all, as strategy is supposed to be a unifying and integrative approach, strategic choices, actions and commitments should be coherent and aligned with each other in pursuit of a firm's strategic goals and objectives. Next, we provide a bird's eye view of the different chapters of the book.

# Confrontation

Following the general introductory chapter on strategic management (Chapter 1), in which we delineate the field of strategy, along with presenting different perspectives on strategy formation, we arrive at Part I of the book, *Confront*. This part is structured around relevant changes and tensions that firms may face in relation to their mission, vision, purpose and their internal organization, market environment and broader environment. These changes and tensions and their consequences challenge strategists and demand that they confront their new realities. Letting go of deeply held, outdated, erroneous assumptions can unsettle managers because they understand how irrevocably altered the competitive arenas and surroundings have become. We present different concepts and tools that help to develop a better understanding of these changes and (sometimes unprecedented) challenges, which often give rise to tensions in the strategy process, and set the stage for the subsequent parts of the book.

One of the central tenets in Chapter 2 is the developing viewpoint that firms are there not only for economic value creation but also for contributing to the mitigation and fixing of social and ecological problems. Different from the taken-for-granted view that a firm basically serves an economic purpose, the notion of purpose is beginning to include the choices firms make regarding social ends besides striving for profit maximalization. The chapter also discusses how effective strategic management depends on a firm's mission, vision, core values and purpose cohering tightly with each other and with other strategic choices. The reality may be that this coherence is suboptimal, requiring firms to rethink their choices, commitments and actions. A firm may also be confronted with the situation that its overarching goals can no longer be met within its current industry or market scope, which could be a reason to change this scope.

Chapter 3 is where we look into a firm's stakeholders and then corporate governance, which revolves around balancing the interests of these stakeholders. Entities with which a firm engages are far-ranging, from investors to employees, regulators, local communities and activist groups, and they may bring conflicting expectations and demands to the table, which gives rise to tensions a firm must deal with. Also, these stakeholders may decide to exert pressure on the firm to change. Regarding corporate governance, the chapter indicates that ownership and control have been separated in many firms, which can lead to problems with misalignments that may arise over time. Besides that, firms may be confronted with inadequate corporate governance mechanisms with adverse effects on organizational functioning. Furthermore, the chapter points out potential dilemmas such as long-term versus short-term performance, shareholder versus stakeholder orientation, and the distribution of power between managerial and supervisory directors.

Chapter 4 discusses market dynamics and nonmarket forces and their impact on firms. Market dynamics refer to changes in a firm's competitive and operating environment, which is made up of competitors, customers, suppliers and complementors. These dynamics include, for instance, the entry of new rivals, changes in the degree and nature of competitive rivalry, disruption, the blurring of traditional industry boundaries, volatile customer demand, changing customer habits and preferences, supply chain dynamics, and the launch of complementary products by other firms. Nonmarket forces, in the form of political, economic, social, technological, ecological and legal factors shape the broader context in which firms compete and operate. Changes in this context as a result of nonmarket dynamics can have a significant impact on firms' strategic goals, activities and returns. This chapter stresses that we live in a highly dynamic and complex world, with uncertainty and ambiguity often being the norm. The rules that served strategists for a long time when the world was rather simple, clear and stable were fundamentally different to what is needed today. Increasingly, achieving transient or temporary competitive advantages is more feasible than sustaining a competitive advantage, especially when competing in fast-cycle markets, as we discuss.

Chapter 5 zooms in on a nonmarket force that deserves particular attention because it is so pervasive: emerging technologies, and technological progress in general. Think about internet technologies, artificial intelligence, machine learning, advanced sensor technologies, blockchain technology, cloud computing, nanotechnology, augmented reality, drones, robotics, and 3D-printing. These and other technological advancements push the increasing digitalization of the economy and play a significant role in the accelerated pace that most firms nowadays experience. Emergent technologies and the ambiguity of technology change bring unprecedent challenges, confronting firms' existing business models and the way they compete, collaborate and organize.

In *Confrontrix*, the diagnostic chapter of Part I, several tools and frameworks are introduced that can be used to recognize and anticipate environmental dynamics and changes and act on them.

## Sensing

When confronted with changing circumstances, firms have to analyze the short- and long-term need to take action and adjust to the new realities. Hence, a crucial part of the strategic management process is how you, as a strategist, are able to 'sense' the external and internal environment. Part II of the book, *Sense*, focuses on the concepts and analytical tools and techniques that help strategists conduct analyses to gain a broad and deep understanding of the key parameters, including both external and internal factors that influence strategic decisions. The analyses that are presented in this part include industry and product-market analysis, strategic group analysis, competitor analysis, customer analysis, internal analysis, and ecosystem analysis.

Chapter 6 focuses on the analysis of industries and product markets. As we elaborate further in this chapter, an industry is comprised of firms that produce similar products and compete for the same resources and consumers. An industry may consist of multiple product markets. A product market consists of products (good or services) with similar characteristics in terms of features, performance, intended use and price. Firms from different industries may compete in the same product market. This chapter enables you to conduct a three-dimensional analysis of firms' industries and product markets. The first dimension is the industry or product market as a whole, with attention to its boundaries, structure, life cycle and other characteristics. The second dimension concerns strategic groups, which are formed by firms that display similarities across a set of relevant dimensions. The third dimension is about rivals: their competitive behaviour and what drives this behaviour.

While most of the strategic management process emphasizes competition and rivals, one should not lose sight that customers are the ultimate source of income. Chapter 7 revolves around the analysis of the customer side of the market. As a business is run on revenue, and revenue comes from customers, it is critical to understand who a firm's current and potential customers are, what they need and want, when they buy, and how they choose among products. Market segmentation is a vital exercise to increase this understanding. Besides a focus on distinguishing different customer segments, this chapter draws on value disciplines and Blue Ocean strategy to analyze how firms can drive customer value in specific segments.

Chapter 8 switches attention from a firm's external environment to its internal organization. This internal environment encompasses tangible and intangible resources, routines, capabilities, and competencies that firms employ to create value. Firms that strive to accomplish sustained value creation need resources and capabilities that are valuable, rare, inimitable and non-substitutable. Moreover, firms should be able to adequately exploit them. The people who interact with and enact resources, routines and capabilities need to possess properties that allow them to help the organization excel. If resources, routines or capabilities turn inert, one needs to be able to change them. The chapter also points attention to the importance of understanding how the different activities of a firm are linked together and how they relate to its resources, capabilities and competencies.

An exclusive focus on analyzing industries, product markets, competitors, customers and internal factors would leave an analytical blind spot, as these analyses leave out complements and complementors from the overall picture. Catalyzed by advances in communication technology and digitalization, regulatory changes (which have opened up various product markets to more firms) and the blurring of industry boundaries, the last decade has witnessed a proliferation of business ecosystems. As covered in Chapter 9, these ecosystems comprise multiple organizations whose dynamic interactions, which are based on nongeneric complementarities instead of arm's-length relationships or hierarchical control, contribute to joint value creation. Many ecosystems are organized around a central platform (often a digital one) that serves as the principal foundation for firms to offer complements. Chapter 9 provides you with the basic insights to conduct an analysis of platform-centred ecosystems and other types of ecosystems.

In *iSense*, the diagnostic chapter of Part II, several practical tools and frameworks are introduced that support you in your endeavours to sense (internal) strengths and weaknesses and (external) opportunities and threats. Also, we show how the outcomes of different types of analyses can be put together in a SWOT overview that provides a basis for additional analysis.

## Strategic choices

Confronted with relevant changes and challenges in their environment, and fuelled with insights derived from external and internal analysis, strategists are challenged to give direction and lead their organizations towards future success. Part III of the book, *Choose*, is structured around sets of strategic choices that managers have to make. Making wise choices among promising options, which is at the heart of strategy, is difficult as this often involves trade-offs which we have to navigate. Also, potential synergies between choices need to be explored. This part of the book helps you to craft your own strategies on both a business unit and corporate level and, in addition to that, to formulate strategies regarding how to cooperate with other firms.

Chapter 10 covers business-level strategy (competitive strategy), which revolves around making choices on how to compete in a particular industry or market. One of these choices is which generic strategy to employ in pursuit of competitive advantage. Here, firms can choose between cost leadership, differentiation, focus (differentiation focus or cost focus), and a hybrid position. These generic strategies, which are explained in this chapter, represent strategic positions at the broadest and simplest level, and can be further specified by choosing the basis of these positions: customers' needs, the variety of a firm's product, or customers' accessibility. The recent proliferation of digital platforms has resulted in another 'generic' strategy: the leveraging of network effects. In addition to this, the chapter focuses on strategic decision-making in the context of competitive dynamics. A firm can decide to attack rivals in an effort to strengthen its competitive position, it may choose to fend off attacks of others in order to defend its current position, or it could decide to move away. Furthermore, firms may decide to be a first mover, a second mover or a later mover.

Before deciding on *how* to compete in a particular industry or market, you first need to decide on *where* to have a competitive presence: in what industries or markets? This 'where to compete' question is a fundamental decision that concerns the scope of a firm as a whole (including all component businesses). Chapter 11 zooms in on how this scope is shaped by choices concerning diversification and internationalization. We examine diversification and internationalization from both a growth perspective (i.e., the expansion of the firm's corporate scope to include new business areas and geographical areas) and a portfolio perspective (i.e., the firm's current levels of diversification and internationalization). In relation to the first perspective, we discuss different types and modes of diversification and internationalization, the reasons for these corporate expansions, and the associated challenges. In relation to the second perspective, we distinguish between different levels (or categories) of diversification and internationalization and examine how these relate to corporate performance. Also, we discuss trade-offs between a multidomestic, global, and transnational strategy.

Corporate-level strategy is not only concerned with what the corporate scope should be, but also with overseeing this scope. Chapter 12 deals with strategic choices regarding how to enhance the performance of a group of multiple divisions (or business units) that operate in different industries or markets. These divisions are overseen by a corporate parent whose choices regarding how to create value make up the corporate strategy. The chapter zooms in on the characteristics and functions of corporate parents and the roles they can play that allow them to achieve and sustain a corporate parenting advantage, which implies that more value is created than competitors would with the same businesses. The importance of some parenting roles over others depends largely on the intended degree of relatedness between divisions. In relation to that, the chapter zooms in on different type of interdivisional links that allow firms to achieve synergies. Synergy management is a corporate logic that stands in stark contrast to a capital orchestration logic, which goes hand-in-hand with unrelatedness among divisions. The chapter discusses both these logics. Furthermore, we pay attention to which factors corporate parents need to take into account when deciding how much to intervene, and what types of control mechanisms they can use.

Firms should not be seen as fully independently operating entities that strive to enhance their competitive and parenting advantage entirely on their own strength. After all, firms are typically embedded in networks of cooperative relationships with other organizations in their market environment. Accordingly, Chapter 13 focuses on making choices at the network level, where firms engage in cooperative arrangements to further their business-level and corporate-level goals and objectives. We zoom in on a variety of different forms of alliances from which firms can choose, including equity alliances, contractual alliances, and associational alliances, before moving on to discuss the choice of entering an alliance, the choice of alliance partner, and choices with respect to how to manage alliances in the post-formation stage.

In *ChooseWell*, the diagnostic chapter of Part III, several portfolio matrices are presented that can be used to support choices regarding how to prioritize the allocation of resources, where to cross-subsidize, which business to keep, divest or reposition, and how to achieve a balanced portfolio that benefits the corporation as a whole in the long term. In addition to this, the chapter points out how conducting the better-off test and ownership test, as well as viewing the corporation as a bundle of core competencies, can further improve business portfolio decisions.

# Transformation

The final part of this book, *Transform*, focuses on the concepts and tools that help achieve transformation and ultimately enhanced performance with the chosen strategy. Here, the reader will find chapters on reconfiguration and restructuring as well as strategic entrepreneurship that are mainly focused on evolutionary transformations. In contrast, the chapters on business model innovation and strategic renewal are focused mainly on more radical transformations involving the exploration of fundamental new business models and capabilities and competencies.

In Chapter 14, we discuss how the chosen strategies in Part III can be realized by various modes of reorganizing the company. Reorganization involves changing a firm's existing activities, resources or intraorganizational linkages or its underlying organizational and financial structure. Two main types of reorganization are discussed here, namely reconfiguration and restructuring, which are often related to each other. Reconfiguration is a change process that involves the adding, combining, transferring, splitting, or dissolving of business entities. We discuss both acquisition-based and divestiture-based reconfigurations, paying attention not only to the nature of these transactions but also the implementation process. Restructuring is a distinct change process, which involves alterations in a firm's underlying organizational or financial structure. Both organizational and financial restructuring are discussed in this chapter.

While Chapter 14 describes how to transform a firm by reconfiguration or restructuring, another way to transform a firm might be to start up de novo or starting something up in an existing context. Chapter 15 on strategic entrepreneurship is about transforming a firm by identifying and taking advantage of opportunities presented by the business environment to generate and capture value. Much of this chapter is on corporate entrepreneurship, an organization-wide nurturing of entrepreneurial initiatives through the introduction of new innovation-driven business. We describe how to boost entrepreneurship through internal and external corporate venturing, intrapreneurship and crowdsourcing. Moreover, we discuss several ways in which firms can boost business innovativeness through startup engagements that tap into new ideas such as corporate hackathons, corporate accelerators, or even corporate venture capital programs to systematically invest in new startups.

Sometimes reorganizing or exploiting entrepreneurial opportunities might not be sufficient, and a change of business model is required. Chapter 16 makes clear how firms can transform their business model and when they should do this (early warning signs). Most firms fail to innovate their business model because they continue to do the same things that have made them successful in the past. They listen carefully to customers, invest in existing business, and build distinctive capabilities, but tend to overlook disruptions in markets and technologies. In this chapter we identify several early warning signs of such a business model trap. Moreover, two modes of business model innovation are described, namely replication of the existing model and generation of a fundamentally new business model. Furthermore, the chapter presents the Business Model Innovation Matrix that helps to derive various transformation trajectories of how to change the business model.

For large, complex, and mature organizations, transformation requires often more than just reorganizing, strategic entrepreneurship or even changing the business model as discussed in the earlier chapters. A more integrated approach may be needed in those instances. Chapter 17 on Strategic Renewal describes how well-established firms can renew themselves by breaking out of path dependencies and adapting to their environment. For those firms to renew successfully and ensure long-term survival, two generic types of learning are required: exploratory and exploitative learning. We show different ways in which firms can achieve high levels of exploration and exploitation: contextual, structural, cyclical and reciprocal ambidexterity. Also, on the basis of different roles of top-, middle- and front-line management, several basic journeys of renewal are discussed: emergent ('follow the market'), directed ('top-management should be in control'), facilitated ('increase variety of renewal initiatives'), and transformational ('mobilize a company-wide renewal process').

In *Transformax*, the diagnostic chapter of Part IV, we provide you with several diagnostic tools and frameworks that can be employed in pursuit of transforming a firm. More specifically, these tools and frameworks may help you to plan for and conduct entrepreneurial activities, conceive of new business models (business model ideation), facilitate business model transformation, and achieve strategic renewal through the revitalization of the organization.

# ABOUT THE AUTHORS

**Henk W. Volberda** is Professor of Strategy & Innovation at the Amsterdam Business School of the University of Amsterdam and leads the Innovation & Digital group of the Strategy, Innovation & IB section. Moreover, he is Director of the Amsterdam Centre for Business Innovation. He obtained his Ph.D. *cum laude* in Business Administration at the University of Groningen. He has been a visiting scholar at the Wharton School at the University of Pennsylvania, Duke University's Fuqua School of Business, and City University's Bayes Business School in London. He holds various executive and advisory positions such as member of the supervisory board of NXP Semiconductors Netherlands and Apollo Tyres Netherlands, expert member of the World Economic Forum, and fellow of the European Academy of Management. Previously, he was, among other things, Vice-Dean of the Rotterdam School of Management of Erasmus University and Chair of the Strategic Management department. He is a member of the editorial board of, among others, the *Global Journal of Flexible Systems Management*, *Journal of Organization Design*, *Journal of Strategy and Management*, *Long Range Planning*, *Management and Organization Review* and *Strategic Change*. His research on technological disruption, digital transformation, coevolution, new business models, strategic renewal, strategic flexibility, and management innovation has led to an extensive number of publications in peer-reviewed journals including the *Academy of Management Journal*, *Journal of Management*, *Journal of International Business Studies*, *Journal of Management Studies*, *Management Science*, *Organization Science*, *Strategic Entrepreneurship Journal* and *Strategic Management Journal*. Moreover, he received numerous awards, including the Erasmus Research Award, the SAP Strategy Award, the EURAM best book award for *Reinventing Business Models: How Firms Cope with Disruption* (Oxford University Press, 2018), and the prestigious Igor Ansoff Strategic Management Award.

**Rick M.A. Hollen** is a senior lecturer and researcher at the Strategy, Innovation & IB section of the Amsterdam Business School, University of Amsterdam, and a managing research associate at the Amsterdam Centre for Business Innovation (ACBI). He has a mixed background in academia, contract research, and business (healthcare-related market intelligence services), and was affiliated to the Corporate Strategy department of the Port of Rotterdam Authority for over five years. He holds a PhD degree in management (specialization in strategy) from Erasmus University Rotterdam in the Netherlands, and took part in international study programs at the Wharton School (Pennsylvania, US), Pontificia Universidad Católica (Chile), HEC Montréal (Canada), and Copenhagen Business School (Denmark). At the University of Amsterdam he coordinates the MBA modules on competitive and corporate strategy, and teaches mostly strategic management and digital transformation. His current main research focus is on business ecosystems, cooperative strategy, corporate strategy, digital servitization, and innovation management. His work has been published in *European Management Review*, *Maritime Economics & Logistics*, and *R&D Management*, and in several books.

**Joana R. Pereira** is Lecturer in the Strategy and Organization group of Leeds University Business School (LUBS). Prior to joining LUBS, Joana earned a PhD in Management of Technology at the Chair of Corporate Strategy & Innovation (CSI) from École Polytechnique Fédérale de Lausanne (EPFL), Switzerland. Joana is interested among other things in collective, democratic, decentralized organizations that based on crowds or communities are able to engage in production and innovation activities, competing with bureaucratic organizations. She studies both traditional and modern collective forms of organizing, ranging from producer cooperatives to internet and blockchain-based crowds and communities. Her research has appeared in journals including *Technological Change and Social Forecasting* and *IEEE Transactions on Engineering Management*.

**Jatinder S. Sidhu** is Professor and Chair in Strategic Management and Organization at the University of Leeds (United Kingdom). He started his academic career at the Rotterdam School of Management, Erasmus University, to which he was affiliated as Associate Professor of Strategic Management. He earned his PhD degree at the Tinbergen Institute, Erasmus School of Economics. His research interests include the developing of better understanding of how companies manage and balance the demands and expectations of their shareholders and stakeholders, and with what consequences. He is particularly drawn to studying the impact of corporate leaders' gender, personalities and values on strategy and innovation in organizations. His research has appeared in a range of journals including *Journal of Management, Journal of Management Studies, Organization Science,* and *Organization Studies*. He serves on the Scientific Council of the European Academy of Management (EURAM) and as Editor for *European Management Review,* EURAM's peer-reviewed journal.

**Kevin Heij** is Senior Researcher of the Amsterdam Centre for Business Innovation, University of Amsterdam. He has an engineering degree of the university of applied sciences Rijswijk and achieved a PhD in management at Erasmus University Rotterdam. With his background in both business administration and engineering, he has worked with numerous corporations (such as Achmea and Siemens), industry associations (e.g., in care, construction and tech), foundations (e.g., Goldschmeding Foundation) and governmental agencies (e.g., Dutch Ministry of Economic Affairs, Province of Gelderland and Sportinnovator). His work – for which he received various awards – has been published in journals such as *Academy of Management Proceedings, European Management Review* and *R&D Management*. He is also co-author of many books including *Reinventing Business Models: How Firms Cope with Disruption*. Furthermore, he teaches strategy and digital transformation in various programs of the Amsterdam Business School, University of Amsterdam (MBA, executive program, master and bachelor levels).

# ONLINE RESOURCES FOR INSTRUCTORS

A selection of tried and tested online resources have been developed to accompany this text and support your teaching. Visit **https://study.sagepub.com/volberda** to set up or use your instructor login to access the following resources:

- **Teaching guide** providing ideas and inspiration for seminars and tutorials, including case study teaching notes and solutions, further reading suggestions, video links and more.
- **PowerPoint slides** for each chapter that can be adapted and edited to suit your own teaching needs.
- Online **case study bank** featuring additional case study material written by strategy lecturers.

# GUIDED TOUR

Each chapter in this book comes with a range of useful learning features to support you in your studies:

## Learning Objectives

a series of short bullet points outlining what you will gain from reading each chapter.

## Opening Case

a scene-setting case study showcasing a real-world business scenario at the start of each chapter.

## Introduction

a short overview of the topics covered in each chapter and their relevance.

## Strategic Focus

short boxes that shed light on contemporary phenomena or examples from multiple perspectives.

## Crack-the-Case

short case studies that can be analyzed using the models, frameworks and tools discussed.

## Key Debate

short boxes that outline opposing perspectives on key debates in the strategy field.

## Closing Case

an end-of-chapter case study that encourages you to apply what you have learned in each chapter to practice.

## Summary

a short recap of the key topics, themes and issues explored in each chapter.

## Review Questions

short answer questions to help you to reflect on and check your understanding of the content.

**Discussion questio...**

1. The notion of corporate purp...
   Why is this the case? Where d...
   companies in society?
2. Mission, vision, purpose, and ...
   foundation of strategic manag...
   foundational elements of strat...
   and cons of formulating and ...
   statements.

## Discussion Questions

long answer questions that can be used for discussion, library assignments and online projects.

## Experiential Exercises

scenarios that encourage you to engage actively with specific aspects of strategic management.

**EXPERIENTIAL EXERCI...**

Imagine you are the strategy officer of a...
can to the following questions:

1. What should the mission, vision, valu...
2. In the light of the foundational statem...
   objectives to be achieved in a two-y...
3. What strategies would you recomm...
4. In which quadrant of the purpose...
   journey would be appropriate f...

**Further reading**

Collins, J.C. and Porras, J.I. (200...
   New York, NY: HarperCollins...
Gartenberg, C., Prat, A. and Seraf...
   performance', *Organization Sc...*
Gulati, R. (2022), *Deep Purpose: T...*
   York, NY: Harper Business.
Henderson, R. (2021), *Reimagin...*
   PublicAffairs.
Mayer, C. (2021) 'The futur...
   *Management Studies...*

## Further Reading

relevant journal articles and/or book chapters to help you build your bibliography and expand your learning.

## Key Terms

short definitions of key terminology in reader-friendly language.

**Key terms**

**Corporate purpose** – the ...

**Dual-mode approach** – th...
non-economic goals are pu...

**Full-convergence approac...**
well as non-economic goal...

**Mission** – definition of t...
product(s), technolog...

...ial conve...

# ACKNOWLEDGEMENTS

This textbook is the outcome of a great team effort. The original idea of writing this fundamentally new textbook was developed by the first author Henk Volberda together with Robert Morgan and Patrick Reinmoeller. Unfortunately, Rob and Patrick had to step out because of new challenges at new business schools and competing time claims. Rick Hollen, Joana Pereira, Jatinder Sidhu, and Emre Karali stepped in. Unfortunately, Emre's new consulting position did not allow him to finish the job and we were lucky that Kevin Heij joined us in a later stage. With these members of this dream team we had many discussions on new developments in the strategy field, heavy debates on which topics to include, struggles on what cases to choose, and lively sessions how to better challenge and engage with our readers, students of strategy.

We have tested with students parts of this textbook over several years. Furthermore, this book has benefited greatly from the hands-on help of our colleagues and our students who have committed to many of these chapters. For this we thank especially:

- Omid Aliasghar, University of Auckland (Icebreaker case in Chapter 2)
- Sebastian Carter (Marks & Spencer case in Chapter 1)
- Hugo Elworthy (Northvolt case in Chapter 15)
- Liam Goodman (parts of Chapters 3, 4, 9 and Diagnostic Part I, the cases on Google and Stripe in Chapter 15, and the cases on Volkswagen, Qualcomm, and Shell in Chapter 17)
- Bram Huis in 't Veld (Axel Springer case in Chapter 1)
- Fiona Hurd, Auckland University of Technology (Icebreaker case in Chapter 2)
- Naadiya Ismail (EY case in Chapter 14)
- Emre Karali, Deloitte and Erasmus University Rotterdam (parts of Chapters 4, 8, and 10)
- Silvia Mateo Combarros (Tapestry/Capri Holdings case in Chapter 1)
- Raymond Meijnen (part of the first Strategic Focus in Chapter 6)
- José Miranda (RealFevr case in Chapter 5)
- Hakan Özalp, Amsterdam Business School, University of Amsterdam (parts of Chapters 9 and 10)
- Taghi Ramezan Zadeh, Amsterdam Business School, University of Amsterdam (Chapter 15 and part of Diagnostic Part IV)
- Max Rossmann (PayPay case in Chapter 9)
- Dennis Steur (part of Chapter 14)
- Jeroen Thorenaar (KPN case in Chapter 12)
- Pushpika Vishwanathan, Amsterdam Business School, University of Amsterdam (part of Chapter 2)
- Wieke Wagemans (Grocery retail and courier services case in Chapter 4)
- Luuk op de Weegh (KPN case in Chapter 12)
- Niels van der Weerdt, Amsterdam Business School, University of Amsterdam (part of Diagnostic Part IV)
- Joeri van der Wees (Hilton case in Chapter 12)
- Chrissy Welsh (Philips case in Chapter 12)
- Nick Ziats (Victoria's Secret case in Chapter 4)

The content of this book is enriched by the countless stimulating, challenging, though-provoking and always fun discussions we have had with current and former students in the bachelor, master, and MBA programs of the Amsterdam Business School and Leeds Business School. These class discussions, as well as the case presentations, have helped us to fine-tune our line of reasoning and forced us to convey our strategy frameworks in meaningful and manageable packets of learning. In addition, the many interactions with managers in the Fulltime and Executive MBA course Competitive & Corporate Strategy proved to be very useful in developing this book and further improving the strategy process framework.

Towers of strength in orchestrating our writing efforts to deliver this textbook were the secretarial offices, particularly Elsemieke Meijer from the Amsterdam Business School and our student-assistants, Liam Goodman, Roos Exterkate, Milo de Jong and Siem van de Kraats.

We also express our appreciation for the excellent support received from our editorial and production team at Sage Publications. We especially wish to thank our publisher Kirsty Smy and development editors Jessica Moran and Martha Cunneen. We are grateful for their patience, dedication, commitment and outstanding contributions to the development and publication of this book and its package of support materials.

The scientific debates we had with peers in the field, as well as comments from reviewers on previous work, served as the engine for progress. In particular, we are highly indebted to the reviewers of this strategy textbook:

- Torben Juul Andersen, Copenhagen Business School
- Maya Cara, University of Sussex
- Hemakshi Chokshi, London Metropolitan University
- Keith Halcro, Glasgow Caledonian University
- James Johnston, University of the West of Scotland
- Yiannis Kyratsis, VU University Amsterdam
- Joseph Lane, University of Reading
- John McCarthy, University of Limerick
- Deirdre McQuillan, University of Bradford
- Sorin Piperca, Birkbeck, University of London
- Misagh Tasavori, University of Essex
- Bilgehan Uzunca, ESADE Business School
- Karl Warner, University of Glasgow

Finally, we are grateful to our closest partners in this endeavour. Many days and evenings were spent on this book and too many weekends were sacrificed. This work would not have been accomplished without their unconditional support. We dedicate this joint work to them.

# 1

# INTRODUCTION TO STRATEGIC MANAGEMENT

## LEARNING OBJECTIVES

After reading this chapter, you should be able to:

- indicate what strategy is (not) about;
- specify what is meant by added value, above-average returns and competitive advantage;
- explain how firms can achieve above-average performance from both an industrial organization perspective and a resource-based perspective;
- indicate the difference between deliberate, emergent and unrealized strategy;
- distinguish between different prescriptive and descriptive schools of strategy formation.

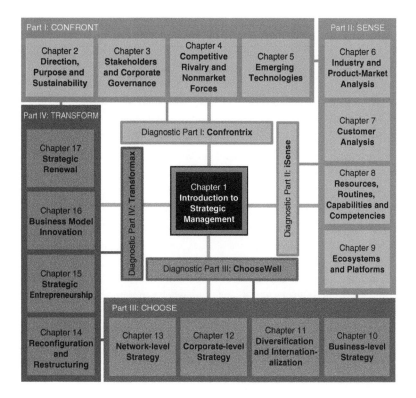

## OPENING CASE

Source: © T. Schneider (2021) / Shutterstock.

### Navigating the new frontier of the luxury fashion industry

In August 2023, Tapestry, Inc., a luxury fashion holding company recognized for its exclusive portfolio featuring Coach, Kate Spade, and Stuart Weitzman, made a significant announcement – the acquisition of its rival, Capri Holdings, renowned for its famous brands such as Michael Kors, Jimmy Choo (acquired in 2017 for $1.35 billion) and Versace (acquired in 2018 for $2.12 billion). The product mix of Capri Holdings, which relied heavily on brand loyalty, innovation and creativity, included accessories (representing just over half of group net sales), footwear, apparel, and licensed products. Horizontal diversification had allowed them to tap into the needs of different market segments and to offer different product categories in each of the brands, following the example of leading luxury firms like LVMH.

In 2023, luxury goods was a $355 billion industry worldwide, of which luxury fashion represented 31% of the global revenue.[1] The biggest markets are the US, followed by Japan, China, Germany, and Italy. Overall, it is a profitable industry with a composite net profit margin (for the 78 Top 100 firms that reported net profits) of 12.2% year-on-year in 2021. The top three players in the industry are the French firms LVMH (which includes Louis Vuitton, Tiffany and Christian Dior) and Kering (Gucci, Balenciaga), along with the US-based Estée Lauder Companies. There is a substantial degree of industry concentration, with the top ten firms – which did not include Capri Holdings (17th position) – representing over half of the total luxury goods industry revenue in 2022.[2] In 2016, older generations accounted for 73% of luxury purchases, however this is shifting. A 2020 study estimated that millennials will represent 40% of the global personal luxury goods market by 2025.[3] Hence, luxury fashion firms will need to transform to cater to the shopping habits and needs of newer generations born and raised in a more digital world. In 2020, various trends affecting the luxury market came to light[4]:

- <u>Conscious consumption and ethics:</u> consumers pay more attention to affordability and value for money, and they are increasingly more conscious about environmental and social issues, especially younger generations, asking for more responsible and purposeful brands.

- <u>Comfort and wellness:</u> self-care has become a key driver in purchase decisions, which favours sportswear and comfortable items.

- <u>Customization and local consumption:</u> consumers are looking for more personalized luxury goods and experiences and give higher relevance to domestic purchase.

- <u>Digital acceleration:</u> the huge growth of e-commerce, especially since the COVID-19 pandemic, has made firms invest in omnichannel strategies, revolutionizing the shopping experience by leveraging technological developments across all touchpoints.

One challenge faced by Capri Holdings was the relatively weak performance of its biggest brand, Michael Kors, which reported a 3.9% decrease in revenue in FY21 versus the year before, whereas both Versace and Jimmy Choo grew their revenues by 12.3% and 15.9% respectively. The group management explained this drop in performance as a brand positioning issue and identified the need to increase customer engagement.[5] This relates partly to the trend of digital acceleration, which presented another strategic challenge for the group. Consumers touch and feel offline but increasingly buy online for convenience. Firms are pressured to build an omnichannel approach that provides consumers a seamless shopping journey across key touchpoints. Such an approach implies leveraging technology to make the best of both the offline and online worlds. The thriving of online channels as the key touchpoint between brands and their customers is partly due to the preferences of newer generations but has been accelerated by the lockdowns during the COVID-19 pandemic and subsequent closure of physical stores. In 2018, online sales of luxury goods represented 10% globally, while they are expected to represent 25% by 2025.[6] Kering was even able to double its online sales in 2020 compared to pre-pandemic figures.[7] In parallel, physical stores suffered greatly because of pandemic-related restrictions: Offline sales inevitably declined as retail chains were forced to close stores. As customers got more used to online shopping, online sales remained on a high level also once most restrictions had been lifted.

In the period between the acquisition of Jimmy Choo and Versace and the first phase of the COVID-19 pandemic, Capri Holdings had focused on opening physical stores – at a remarkable rate of 22–30% YoY – as a strategy to boost revenues. 2021 was the first year to decrease the total number of stores versus the previous year (1,271 in 2020 vs 1,257 in 2021).[8] Although the opening of physical stores may have been a great strategy before the disruption of the industry, the acquisition of Capri Holdings by Tapestry raises questions about the company's readiness for success in the face of the changing luxury fashion market landscape.

## Questions

1. How could Tapestry strategically bolster the competitive standing of its Capri Holdings portfolio in the dynamic landscape of luxury fashion?
2. To what extent do you expect that (some of) the trends as listed in the case will also provide a challenge for firms in industries other than the luxury fashion industry?

## Introduction

As illustrated in the opening case, firms are confronted with new realities that challenge them to rethink their strategies. You may think about the emergence of digital platforms, disruptive new industry entrants, intensifying competition, changing expectations of dominant shareholders, more environmentally conscious consumption, new customer demands, shifts in demand across sales channels, regulatory changes, the emergence of artificial intelligence, geopolitical conflicts, and many other changes and dynamics that firms (and other types of organizational entities) may encounter. Their managers have to make adaptive choices to maintain a strategic fit in this new environment, and their firms may also actively shape this environment. As further detailed in the preface, this book addresses the fact that over time firms are confronted with – and contribute themselves to – a multitude of changes and challenges, requiring them to continuously sense and analyze what is going on, choose strategies to enable sustained value creation, and, when necessary, transform their organization in order to increase the odds of surviving and thriving in the face of new confrontations. This process of *Confront-Sense-Choose-Transform*, which is dynamic and iterative in nature, is at the core of contemporary strategic management. Chapters 2 to 17 zoom in on the different stages and elements of this process and their interlinkages. This chapter presents a general introduction to strategic management, which also services to anchor these follow-up chapters. We discuss what strategy and strategic management is (not) about, along with different perspectives on strategy formulation and formation.

## What is strategy?

Strategic management, strategic goals, strategic plan(ning), strategic investment, strategic initiatives, strategy consultant, strategist... Just a selection of the many different ways in which the term 'strategy' is used in today's business world. The term has been derived from the ancient Greek noun *strategos*, meaning '(military) general'. Alfred Dupont Chandler Jr., a former business historian at Harvard Business School, provided one of the first definitions of strategy in a modern business context:

> Strategy can be defined as the determination of the basic long-term goals and objectives of an enterprise and the adoption of courses of action and the allocation of resources necessary for carrying out these goals.[9]

Throughout this book we use the words firm, company, enterprise, and corporation inter-changeably to refer to a commercial organizational entity – that is, a for-profit business organization. Chandler's definition remains valid today and can also be used in the context of other types of organizations, such as public schools, research institutes, trade associations, trade unions, public clinics and hospitals, legal aid societies, charitable organizations, the armed forces and (semi-)governmental bodies. Although strategy is highly relevant for these 'other' organizations (see also this chapter's Key Debate), you will read in this book mostly about firms. In many instances, however, what you read is (largely) applicable to organizations other than for-profit business organizations as well.

**TABLE 1.1**   A selection of prior definitions of strategy

1. '[...] the determination of the basic long-term goals and objectives of an enterprise and the adoption of courses of action and the allocation of resources necessary for carrying out these goals'[10]

2. '[...] decision rules and guidelines [that] guide the process of development of an organization'[11]

3. '[...] the creation of a unique and valuable position, involving a different set of activities', and the creation of 'fit among [these] activities'[12]

4. '[...] an integrated, overarching concept of how the business will achieve its objectives.'[13]

5. [...] the process by which a firm deploys its resources and capabilities within its business environment in order to achieve its goals'[14]

6. '[...] an integrated and coordinated set of commitments and actions designed to develop and exploit core competencies and gain a competitive advantage'[15]

7. '[...] a set of goal-directed actions a firm takes to gain and sustain superior performance relative to competitors'[16]

8. '[...] the means by which individuals or organizations achieve their objectives'[17]

9. '[...] an integrative set of choices that positions you on a playing field of your choice in a way that you win'[18]

Table 1.1 provides some additional useful definitions of strategy, some of which include the word 'goals' or 'objectives' or both. A goal or objective in itself is not a strategy, but most strategies have one or more overall goals and more specific, actionable targets (objectives). The ultimate goal of any organizational strategy, regardless of the context in which it is carried out, is to sustain added value – that is, to sustain value creation.[19] What is considered 'value' typically depends on the type of organization and, partly related to that, on what type of stakeholder (such as customers, shareholders or society) the organization prioritizes over others (see Chapters 2 and 3). For instance, value can lie in profit maximization, the maximization of share- or stockholder equity, the maximization of societal benefits or a balanced satisfaction of multiple types of stakeholders. The verb 'sustain' signals the ability to continuously create value for an extended period of time. Strategists need to provide a coherent vision and high-level orchestration to achieve that.

## KEY DEBATE

### Strategy at nonprofit, not-for-profit and government organizations

Every organization needs a strategy for achieving its long-term goals, but not every organization has a primary focus on competing with and outperforming rivals. Think, for instance, about trade associations, trade unions, hospitals, and (semi-)governmental bodies, which usually do not have rivals because of the nature of their activities. Since the appearance of Porter's seminal work *Competitive Advantage* in 1985, however, strategy has often become synonymous with the pursuit of a sustained competitive advantage over rivals. The earning of above-average returns is frequently mentioned as a primary intended outcome of strategic endeavours. These returns are often expressed in terms of profitability ratios such as Return on Investment (ROI) and Return on Equity (ROE). There are multiple types of organizations, however, that are not driven by profits. These include nonprofit, not-for-profit, and governmental organizations. **Nonprofit organizations** have been formed to benefit the public good – for instance, by promoting a social cause or by advocating for the needs of certain social groups or communities. Most *non-governmental organizations* (NGOs), which typically focus on social welfare goals on a large (and usually international) scale, are nonprofit organizations. They are not commercially motivated but do often compete with other nonprofit organizations for members and external funding. Similar to nonprofit organizations, **not-for-profit organizations** do not earn profits for their owners, but, in contrast to the former, are not required to benefit the public good – instead, they can simply serve the collective goals of their members. Examples are trade associations and recreational sports clubs. Finally, **government organizations** are sovereign entities with authoritative power over other organizations in a certain state or area.

The term 'performance' does not necessary imply profitability – for example, think about a social return on investment (SROI) that reflects social or environmental factors. With that in mind, to what extent do the definitions of strategy in this chapter hold for non-commercial organizations?

In a for-profit context, added value equals competitive advantage.[20] Having a **competitive advantage** means that a firm is able to outperform its competitors, which commonly translates into above-average returns. Simply put, the term *return* usually denotes the money that is made (a *positive return*, which marks a profit, or financial gain) or lost (a *negative return*, which marks a financial loss) on capital, assets, equity, or another form of investment over a certain time period. Returns can be expressed either as a change in current monetary value (also known as nominal value), indicated in euros or another currency, or as a percentage return, commonly indicated in financial metrics such as Return on Investment (ROI), Return on Invested Capital (ROIC), Return on Assets (ROA) and Return on Equity (ROE). A firm is said to earn **above-average returns**, or *superior returns*, when it generates returns over a certain period of time in excess of what investors would expect to gain from alternative investments with a similar risk profile. The earning of above-average returns implies an **above-average performance**. One of the most rudimentary questions in strategy is why some firms outperform others. Firms that are outperformed by their rivals or whose returns are below the industry average have a **competitive disadvantage**. In between competitive advantage and competitive disadvantages lies **competitive parity**.

We can distinguish different levels and types of strategies, including functional-level strategies (for example marketing strategy and purchasing strategy), business-level strategy (also referred to as competitive strategy; see Chapter 10), corporate-level strategy (Chapter 12), and network-level strategy (also referred to as cooperative strategy; see Chapter 13). Although we discuss most of these strategies separately in individual chapters, they should not be viewed in isolation from one another. After all, the different strategic choices, commitments, and actions of a firm need to be aligned with one another in pursuit of its overarching strategic goals, including its purpose (see Chapter 2), which requires a certain level of orchestration. Also, strategists should adopt a unifying and integrated approach that combines sets of choices and actions and directs them towards this purposive endeavour. Hence, **strategy** can be defined as an orchestrated, unified, integrated, and purposeful set of choices, commitments, and activities directed at achieving and sustaining above-average performance. This set of choices can be divided into different domains, which can be seen as the principal elements of strategy:[21] arenas, differentiators, staging and pacing, vehicles, and the value creation logic (see Figure 1.1).

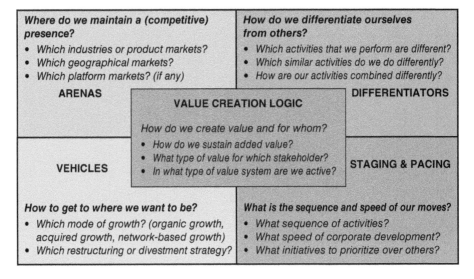

**FIGURE 1.1**   Elements of strategy

Source: adapted from Hambrick, D.C. and Fredrickson, J.W. (2001) 'Are you sure you have a strategy?' Academy of Management Executive, 15(4): 48–59.

In line with these five elements, a general strategy needs to provide compelling answers to the following interrelated questions:

- In what industries or markets do we have a (competitive) presence?
- How do we successfully differentiate ourselves from relevant others in these industries or markets?
- How do we get to where we want to be?
- How do we sustainably create value for which stakeholder(s)?

The last question lies at the heart of strategy – after all, without sustained added value, which, as previously discussed, translates into above-average returns, firms usually will not survive or thrive in the long term. It can be particularly challenging to sustain above-average returns for long periods of time when there is a high degree of market-related and technology-related turbulence; when firms are confronted with volatile markets, hypercompetition (see Chapter 4), or technological disruption (see Chapter 5), they might be able to achieve temporary competitive advantages at best.[22] As becomes clear from the above questions, strategy is about making choices about what to do and what *not* to do, which usually come with (sometimes very difficult) trade-offs.[23] Making clear trade-offs, and communicating these trade-offs to stakeholders, should constitute a key part of any strategic agenda.

## STRATEGIC FOCUS

### The history of the strategy field in brief

Strategy outside of a military context is a relatively young academic field. Its foundation can be traced largely to Alfred Chandler's 1962 publication *Strategy and Structure*,[24] as well as the seminal works of Edith Penrose and Igor Ansoff in the late 1950s and the 1960s.[25] These works had been inspired by the emergence of mass production in the 1920s and 1930s and the concomitant increase in average size of firms, introducing new type of challenges. In the 1960s, the Harvard Business School newly introduced a Business Policy capstone course with a focus on 'strategic' frameworks including the still widely used SWOT framework (see the *iSense* diagnostic chapter). The 1970s witnessed a proliferation of tools and frameworks in the area of business policy and strategy, partly driven by consultant firms, including the Boston Consulting Group and McKinsey & Company. These firms introduced various portfolio management matrices (see the *ChooseWell* diagnostic chapter) along with other tools to support strategizing in a world where this had become increasingly more complex partly due to increasing diversification (see Chapter 11), as studied by, among others, Igor Ansoff[26] and Richard Rumelt.[27] Also the agency theory of corporate governance (see Chapter 3) emerged in the 1970s.[28] Michael Porter's books on strategy, including *Competitive Strategy*[29] and *Competitive Advantage*,[30] resulted in an increasing focus on competitive advantage as the main cornerstone of strategic endeavours. The Five Forces Framework (see Chapter 6) and the notions of strategic positions and generic strategies (see Chapter 10) became widespread since Porter's work. In the 1980s and 1990s, the strategy field was further shaped by influential publications on the resource-based view of firms,[31] core competencies,[32] dynamic capabilities[33] (see Chapter 8), disruption,[34] and business models[35] (see Chapter 16). More recently, there has been an increasing focus within the strategy field on (digital) platforms[36] and ecosystems[37] (see Chapter 9). This overview is clearly far from complete (we would need another book), but it does provide a sense of how the field of strategy has developed over time.

To further clarify the concept of strategy, which has been described as 'an elusive and somewhat abstract concept'[38] by one of the founding fathers of the modern strategy field, Harry Igor Ansoff, it may be helpful to briefly discuss what strategy is *not* about. Michael Porter, another founding father, has stressed that 'operational effectiveness is not strategy'.[39] Operational effectiveness, including efficiency, revolves around realizing operational improvements. These improvements might result from employing management methods such as lean six sigma, total quality management (TQM), scrum, business process reengineering and benchmarking, and can be essential to above-average performance, as can strategy. However, although they typically are a necessary condition, operational improvements alone are not sufficient for firms to outperform other firms for an extended period of time. As Porter points out, these improvements imply performing *similar* activities *better* than competitors perform them, and hence are not based on any difference a firm is able to preserve during that time. Operational improvements are usually imitated relatively quickly and commonly culminate in a greater degree of homogeneity within industries. Strategy, in contrast, is concerned with achieving and sustaining above-average returns for an extended time period by performing similar activities in *different* ways (as compared to competitors) or performing *different* activities, and ensuring fit among these activities, which is generally more difficult for other firms to replicate successfully.[40]

A plan is not the same as a strategy either. Although managers can take a planned approach to strategy, as we will discuss further below, there are important differences between the two. Most notably, unlike a strategy, the set of activities that constitute a plan ('what are we going to do?') does not necessarily have to be coherent with other activities a firm decides to engage in and, moreover, revolves around how to spend certain resources, which by definition are under a firm's control. In contrast, a strategy specifies a desirable outcome – in terms of sustained above-average performance – for which it depends on other entities, most notably competitors and customers, which decide for themselves and are thus not under the firm's control.[41]

## Perspectives on strategy formation

The formulation (or articulation) and implementation (or execution) of strategy is jointly referred to as **strategic management**. Defined as such, just about everyone in an organization could somehow be involved in strategy. The classical perspective on strategy is that the strategic course of action of a firm is the main responsibility of the organization's CEO, executive board or owner, but strategy-making can instead involve a collective of different people, including those working at lower levels in the organization. For instance, middle-line managers may possibly be in a better position to make strategic choices about how to compete in a certain product market than senior managers. Hence, although strategy formulation can be a predominantly top-down process, it can also be more of a bottom-up process. Some firms are under the pressure of shareholders – or other types of powerful stakeholders – who are very dominant in enforcing certain strategies. Strategy formulation can be a largely analytical and rational exercise, based on facts, but instead it could also be based mainly on intuition of new market opportunities. A strategy could be formulated in a formal document or instead be more implicit, residing in people's minds. As these examples and the next few sections demonstrate, there exists a variety of perspectives on who should formulate a firm's strategy and how this is done, regardless of firm size and industry.

## How to earn above-average returns: I/O model versus resource-based model

How do firms select strategies that should enable them to achieve above-average performance? Let's compare two models that provide an alternative view of this: the industrial organization (I/O) model and the resource-based model (see Figure 1.2).

The underlying assumption of the **I/O model of above-average returns** is that the set of characteristics of the industries or industry segments in which firms choose to maintain a presence (see Chapter 6), and the degree to which their strategies consider or shape these characteristics,

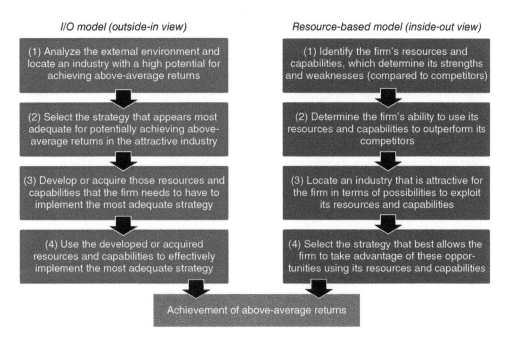

*I/O model (outside-in view)*

(1) Analyze the external environment and locate an industry with a high potential for achieving above-average returns

(2) Select the strategy that appears most adequate for potentially achieving above-average returns in the attractive industry

(3) Develop or acquire those resources and capabilities that the firm needs to have to implement the most adequate strategy

(4) Use the developed or acquired resources and capabilities to effectively implement the most adequate strategy

*Resource-based model (inside-out view)*

(1) Identify the firm's resources and capabilities, which determine its strengths and weaknesses (compared to competitors)

(2) Determine the firm's ability to use its resources and capabilities to outperform its competitors

(3) Locate an industry that is attractive for the firm in terms of possibilities to exploit its resources and capabilities

(4) Select the strategy that best allows the firm to take advantage of these opportunities using its resources and capabilities

Achievement of above-average returns

**FIGURE 1.2**   Comparing the I/O model and resource-based model of above-average returns

Source: authors, based on Barney (1991), Porter (1980a, 1985), Rumelt (1974), Wernerfelt (1984)

which change over time, is the main determinant of their performance. Therefore, according to this model, firms should take an outside-in approach to strategy formulation, meaning that the first thing they should look at is the external environment in which they are embedded, which includes both their market and nonmarket environment (see Chapter 4). Based on this external sensing, they should then locate those industries or industry segments whose structural characteristics seem to have the strongest potential for earning above-average returns. A firm then must select the type of strategy that is most adequate for exploiting this potential and focus on using those resources and capabilities (see Chapter 8) that are needed most to effectively implement this strategy. These resources and capabilities are already present in the organization or otherwise can be either accessed by engaging in an alliance (see Chapter 13), or acquisition (see Chapter 14) or developed internally (see Chapter 15). At a time when NXP, a Dutch semiconductor designer and manufacturer that had spun off from Philips in 2006, was not doing very well, its then-CEO Rick Clemmer decided that NXP should only invest in industries where the firm's market share was at least twice as large as its largest rival in those industries. The firm left many markets and strengthened its position in those markets where it was the market leader, which eventually resulted in above-average performance. This pacing rule for selecting attractive industries illustrates the logic of the I/O model.

The **resource-based model of above-average returns** alternatively assumes that it is in fact the set of resources and capabilities of a firm, in particular their uniqueness, and the degree to which the firm can successfully exploit these in one or more industries or industry segments, that determines its performance. Thus, instead of identifying general industry potential, this model is mainly about identifying the potential of organizational resources and capabilities for outperforming others. Firms should therefore – according to this model – take an inside-out approach to strategy formulation, meaning that the first thing they should look at are their relative strengths in terms of tangible and intangible resources (which are means of producing goods or providing services) and capabilities (which denote the capacity of an integrated bundle of resources to integratively perform certain activities) (see Chapter 8). Based on this internal sensing, firms should then determine their ability to use these strengths – while bearing in mind also their weaknesses – in a way that allows them to outperform others. This ability will be stronger in some industries or industry segments than in others. Once an industry or segment has been selected based on this consideration, a firm should select the strategy that puts itself in the best position to exploit its strengths in taking advantage of the opportunities in this industry or segment. Illustrative of this resource-based view is the fact that McKinsey & Company invests heavily in the unique skills and competencies of its consultants in particular knowledge areas and markets it wants to dominate.

Prior studies indicate that profitability is determined partly by the characteristics of the industry in which firms choose to compete but also by differences in their resource base and skill sets.[42] Firms would therefore be wise to not focus exclusively on a resource or I/O-based line of thinking – instead, a combination of these approaches is advised. A focus on one of these approaches at the expense of the other comes with significant risks. For instance, firms that demonstrate a very dominant resource-based approach run the risk of overdeveloping certain resources that they cannot sufficiently exploit in any market, while an exclusive focus on the I/O logic can result in an inability to sustain added value in certain industries because of a lack of resource distinctiveness.

## CRACK-THE-CASE
### Beyond Meat and Impossible Foods

Source: © Rblfmr (2019) / Shutterstock.

The alternative meat industry is moving full steam ahead and two firms stand out in terms of rivalry: Beyond Meat, founded in 2009, and Impossible Foods, founded in 2011. These US-based producers of meat substitutes are particularly known for respectively their Beyond Burger and Impossible Burger. The odds had been in favour of Beyond Meat – it has been around for longer so had wider recognition and market penetration. As Bloomberg Businessweek puts it, Beyond Meat is 'in more U.S. retailers (28,000 compared to Impossible's 20,000), more restaurants (42,000 in the U.S. vs. 30,000-plus), and more international markets (more than 80 vs. 5).'[43] But will things stay like that? Beyond Meat's large dependence on providing to sit-down locations has backfired due to the COVID-19 pandemic. Meanwhile, Impossible Foods' alternative meat got a boost, as they focused on pandemic-resilient takeout, drive-thru, and delivery options. Impossible Foods has also launched a price war, undercutting Beyond Meat in its prices for restaurants and grocery stores. During the pandemic, Impossible Foods increased its market share from 5% to 55% in plant-based patties that were sold in supermarkets. Despite these attempts by Impossible Foods, Beyond Meat still dominates the market and tries to keep things going through innovation design and sales,[44] as it seeks to enhance the taste of its alternative meat and its availability in stores and restaurants. The question is for how long the firm can maintain its position.

## Questions

1.  To what extent do Beyond Meat and Impossible Foods compete not only with each other but also with firms outside the alternative meat industry?
2.  What would be your main strategic advice to Beyond Meat or Impossible Foods?

## Strategy formation: Deliberate and emergent strategy

The I/O model and resource-based model of above-average returns entail that firms carefully select an appropriate strategy that – given certain industry characteristics and resource heterogeneity, respectively – should enable them to achieve above-average performance. Both models thus presume the presence of an **intended strategy:** a clear strategy that a firm intends to implement (see Figure 1.3). When this strategy is articulated explicitly, it is alternatively called a formulated strategy. Some parts of an intended (or formulated) strategy will possibly be abandoned along the way. These parts are collectively referred to as the **unrealized strategy.** The remaining parts of an intended strategy, which eventually are put into action, are collectively referred to as the **deliberate strategy.** In addition to – or even instead of – a deliberate strategy, there can be an **emergent strategy**, which is an internally consistent pattern of actions and reactions that arise spontaneously as a firm navigates within its operating environment (see again Figure 1.3).[45] Deliberate strategies (formed intentionally) and emergent strategies (formed spontaneously) can be seen as two ends of a continuum along which the firm's actual strategy formation lies.[46] This actual, real-world strategy formation (that is, what firms actually do) is also known as the **realized strategy.**[47]

By emphasizing the role of strategic choices in strategy formation over unplanned actions and reactions, deliberate strategy has received considerably more attention in the strategy literature than emergent strategy.[48] We provide a somewhat more balanced view. First, although Part III of this textbook ('Choose') revolves around strategic choices, we

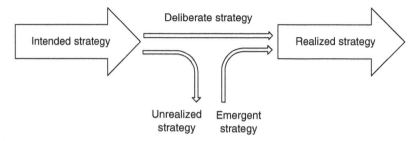

**FIGURE 1.3**   From intended to realized strategy

emphasize that these choices should be revisited regularly in the light of emergent strategy formation and, moreover, that they should go hand-in-hand with experimentation, learning, adjustment, a clear vision that provides guidance, and overcoming mental biases. Second, we explicitly zoom in on emergent strategy-formation processes in Chapter 15 (corporate entrepreneurial processes), Chapter 16 (emergent business model transformation) and Chapter 17 (emergent strategic renewal).

# Schools of strategy formation

The existing literature on the strategy formation process can be categorized by how this process is conceived. These categories have been labelled the **schools of strategy forma-tion**, or *strategy schools of thought*. As discussed next, we can distinguish multiple schools of strategy formation,[49] which are either prescriptive or descriptive in nature (see Table 1.2). Typically, none of these schools capture all of the strategy formation process at a certain firm over a specified period in time – often it is a combination of schools that comes closest to reality. Also, the applicability and dominance of some schools over others can change over time as, for instance, a firm or the industry in which it competes goes through dif-ferent stages.[50] The following overview of nine schools serves to present a more balanced view of how the strategy formation process may come about.

## Prescriptive schools of strategy formation

The design school, planning school and positioning school are **prescriptive schools of strategy formation,** in the sense that they prescribe how a strategy should be formed. They assume that strategies are formulated and not formed spontaneously, and that once they have been formulated they will eventually be realized. Prescriptive schools thus idealize the strategy formation process. This formation is associated with a top-down, analytical and fully rational decision-making approach. Although there is less variety in prescriptive schools than in descriptive schools, they are more pervasive in strategy textbooks as, in contrast to the latter, they come with different frameworks and analytical tools and techniques – many of which have been introduced by consulting firms – that enable analysis and measurement, which provides a more concrete and proactive basis for strategy forma-tion than describing emergent processes as they occur.

The **design school** perceives strategy formation as a process of achieving an optimal fit between a firm's strengths and weaknesses (compared to close competitors) at the one side, and opportunities and threats in its external environment at the other. The school's main

**TABLE 1.2** Stylized comparison between nine schools of strategy formation

| | School of strategy formation | Influential source(s) | Base discipline(s) | View of the strategy process | Essence of strategy | Central message | Central actor |
|---|---|---|---|---|---|---|---|
| Prescriptive | Design school | Selznick (1957), Andrews (1971) | none | process of conception | grand strategy | fit | CEO/top managers |
| | Planning school | Ansoff (1965, 1988) | cybernetics, systems theory | formal process | explicit planning | formalize | corporate staff |
| | Positioning school | Porter (1980, 1985) | industrial organization (I/O) | analytical process | generic strategy | position based on analysis | analysts |
| Descriptive | Cognitive school | Simon (1947), March and Simon (1958) | psychology, informatics | mental process | superior foresight | refine mental maps | CEO/top managers, brain |
| | Entrepreneurial school | Schumpeter (1934) | none | visionary process | superior vision | creatively destruct | (corporate) entrepreneur |
| | Learning school | Lindblom (1959), Weick (1969), Quinn (1980) | psychology | learning process | learning capacity | learn from trial and error | multiple (all levels) |
| | Cultural school | Johnson (1987, 1992), Pettigrew (1979, 1985) | anthropology (incl. ethnography) | collective process | collective perception | socialize | multiple (all levels) |
| | Power school | MacMillan (1978), Salancik and Pfeffer (1974, 1977) | political science | process of negotiation | power play | negotiate and persuade | multiple (all levels) |
| | Environmental school | Hannan and Freeman (1977), Meyer and Rowan (1977) | contingency theory | reactive process | passive | adapt | none (external environment is key) |

Source: authors, based on Mintzberg and Lampel (1999) and Mintzberg et al. (1998)

idea is that a firm's strategy should be designed based on this fit, which can be identified by performing an adequate SWOT-analysis (see the *iSense* diagnostic chapter). The design school states that the CEO, board or founder is the central actor in the strategy formulation process, expecting everyone else in the organization to work on implementing the 'grand strategy'. One implication of this approach is that it creates a separation of thinking (by the central actor) and action (by staff), which may result in a 'not-invented-here syndrome' and ensuing inertia or unwillingness to implement. Also, the articulation of a grand strategy entails commitments, which reduce flexibility. Moreover, this school assumes that structure follows strategy, which is not always the case. An additional critical note to this school is that the belief in an optimal strategy can be risky and may result in questionable strategies. In 1943, for instance, Thomas Watson Sr. is alleged to have said: 'I think there's a world market for maybe five computers'. A comparable statement was made in 1977 by Ken Olson, then chairman and founder of Digital Equipment Corp, at the World Future Society when he stated that 'There is no reason anyone would want a computer in their home'.

The **planning school**, which compared to the design school is a more nuanced school, perceives strategy formation as a formal process with a dominant emphasis on planning. It can be seen as a sort of cookbook for developing a great strategy: strategy according to this school is a detailed plan that is decomposed into steps, facilitated by checklists, awaiting implementation. For example, the planning may start with the setting of a firm's goals, followed by a review of the current situation (for which a SWOT-analysis or another analysis can be used), which might then be followed by several steps to formulate the strategy, decide on resource allocation (including, for instance, budget specification) and decide on how to monitor implementation. The CEO or the board is responsible for strategic thinking and for approving the overall plan, but most of the work is done by corporate planners who serve as strategic engineers and others that implement the formulated actions. When this school gained prominence, following the publication in 1965 of Ansoff's work on strategy, many firms created strategic planning departments. Strategic planning can work very well in changing but predictable environments, where it makes sense to develop a long-term, detailed plan. In environments that are not very predictable, however, the planning school may not work well. Other critiques of this approach are that it may lead to paralysis by analysis and that it can be very time-consuming to develop a sophisticated, detailed plan. Once the plan has been implemented, it may already have become outdated. Also, the separation between planning and execution may lead to issues comparable to that of the design school.

The **positioning school**, which is based largely on the work of Michael Porter,[51] perceives strategy formation as an analytical process. According to this school, which is most in line with the I/O model of above-average returns, a firm needs to identify and develop viable strategic positions. At the broadest level, these positions, which can be based on customers' accessibility, customers' needs or the variety of a firm's goods or services,[52] can be differentiation, cost leadership and focus (either a cost focus or a differentiation focus) (see Chapter 10). These positions are known as the generic strategies (see Chapter 10). A central premise of the positioning school is that the strategy formation process is mainly a matter of selecting an appropriate generic position in the industry, based on an adequate analysis of industry characteristics. One of the best-known frameworks that can be used for carrying out such an analysis is the Five Forces Framework (see Chapter 6). The central actors according to the positioning school are analysts that provide information, based on which the CEO or board makes decisions as to how to position the firm. Well-positioned firms are deemed able to exploit economies of scale, which results in diminishing costs, and to achieve a sustainable competitive advantage. However, this may not be feasible in circumstances where any competitive advantages are gradually eroded over time.[53] Another critique regarding the positioning school is that it is somewhat biased towards well-established firms and therefore less adequate for new industry entrants – for example, Virgin would possibly never have entered the airline industry, where it achieved success with Virgin Atlantic, if this decision would have depended on the outcome of a Five-Forces analysis.

## CRACK-THE-CASE
### Axel Springer: From near death to leading digital publisher

Source: © Mo Fotography Berlin (2022) / Shutterstock.

Axel Springer, founded in 1946, is a renowned German media conglomerate that holds the position of European market leader within the publishing industry. After the turn of the millennium, the firm found itself in a tough situation. Prior to this, it had always generated significant levels of sales volumes and profitability. However, an industry decline of advertising revenue in traditional print had a substantial effect on its earnings of 2001, suddenly turning the conglomerate into an industry midget.[54] Andreas Wiele, an executive at Axel Springer, even called it a 'near dead experience' for the firm.[55] At that point in time, digital technology and advertising started to take flight and for Axel Springer to survive it had to radically change its business model to meet the change in client needs. As a response, CEO Mathias Döpfner repositioned Axel Springer and envisioned the firm to become Europe's leading digital publisher, which meant that he went on to execute a bold move to cannibalize

*(Continued)*

the firm's traditional newspaper operations by populating its online media portfolio, prioritizing its digital media over its print media. This transformation towards a digital strategy in 2002 turned out to be fruitful. In 2018, digital media already accounted for 87% of the firm's complete advertising revenue.[56] Currently active in over 40 countries, with 16.000 employees and a total revenue of €3.1 billion,[57] Axel Springer has shown significant growth in the past decade. After its strategic transformation, the firm split its portfolio in three divisions. The News Media division is probably the most well-known and recognizable of the three. With numerous digital and print titles such as Bild, die Welt, Politico, and Business Insider, this division is also the largest in terms of revenue. The second division is Classified Media, whose portfolio predominantly revolves around online ad portals characterized by job, real estate, and auto advertising websites. Marketing Media, the third division, generates revenue from advertising clients by focusing on performance- and reach-based marketing.

Axel Springer tries to differentiate itself from competitors by providing quality content, which has been its prime profit driver since the start. However, capturing value by providing new digital news products proved to be challenging as in the perception of many people digital news should be free. Its News Media division implemented a 'freemium' pay-for-service model, believing that consumers are willing to pay for journalistic content in the digital world. Offering subscription-based services in News Media, monetizing content through advertiser revenue from selling Classified Ads, and its performance- and reach-based selling of advertiser space at Marketing has largely changed its revenue model from one end of the spectrum (print) to the other (digital). Axel Springer operates with a larger share of digital revenue than its 'traditional' competitors, such as Bertelsmann, Hubert Burda Media, and Ströer, and increasingly faces competition from technology giants such as Amazon, Google, and Meta on all fronts. Where news and content are shared across large platforms, it poses a revenue problem specifically to its media division. In a digitalized world, news and content is spread widely across multiple channels, shifting the needs of consumers and posing challenges for publishing firms. Governmental regulations have been introduced in some countries favouring the side of the publishing firms[58] and trust-related issues among social media could rule in favour of quality news brands[59] – however, this is not a given.

Another challenge for Axel Springer is that younger generations have weaker ties to traditional news media,[60] whereas since 1946 journalism has been Axel Springer's prime focus and is heavily embedded in its corporate cultural values. On top of that, nearly 46% of the firm's current revenue drivers come from Classified Ads and Marketing Media. Its News Media division has always been Axel Springer's prized possession, however in the past few years it has taken some serious beatings,[61] whereas Classified Ads and Marketing have been showing great promise. Axel Springer must decide on whether to continue focusing on expanding its paid subscriber base or pivot again and invest in profitable growth areas such as Classified Ads and Marketing where greater revenues are generated, but which may have implications for its corporate culture.

## Questions

1. What would you advise Axel Springer to do to secure the continuity of its operations?
2. How should a publishing firm such as Axel Springer deal with the influence of Big Tech (see also the Key Debate on Big Tech Platforms in Chapter 9)?

## Descriptive schools of strategy formation

The cognitive school, entrepreneurial school, learning school, cultural school, power school and environmental school, summarized next, are all **descriptive schools of strategy formation**, in the sense that they describe how strategies are activated. These schools each take a different point of view when it comes to what managers really do when they develop a strategy, instead of prescribing what managers 'ought' to do. Although it might be the case that managers in real life do what they ought to do according to the design, planning or positioning school, these descriptive schools assume otherwise and view strategy formation as a largely emergent process.

The **cognitive school** perceives strategy formation as a mental process that involves information processing, creative interpretation, knowledge structure mapping, and acquiring understanding through experience, thought and the senses. As such, this school assumes that strategies emerge from mental (or cognitive) maps that reside in people's minds.[62] Mental mapping, which is prone to cognitive biases, denotes how someone – or a collective of people – views and interprets the environment based on mental models or schemas, which include any dominant logics and the person's – or collective's – points of view and frames of reference that are based partly on prior experiences. This for instance means that a firm's competitive strategy for a certain business will be based partly on its experiences with its other businesses, if any. As a mental map represents a simplification of reality, all persons involved in strategic decision-making are inherently seen as boundedly rational (or cognitively limited), opposing the prescriptive schools' assumption of full rationality. Over time, people try to refine their mental maps, which are not only temporary and incomplete but also inert and hard to change. According to this school, we are only able to change our mental maps in situations of crises. This may explain why firms that face disruption first hold onto their existing competencies. A case in point is Kodak, which kept focusing on selling film for analogue cameras (see Chapter 16), as it could earn higher margins on that than on digital photography (which it had invented), for too long – its dominant cognition was that it had to stick to film as its core business. Groupthink that results in dysfunctional or irrational decision-making can be attributed to the sharing and unconscious matching of mental models.

The **entrepreneurial school** perceives strategy formation as a visionary process of what the economist Joseph Schumpeter called 'creative destruction'.[63] According to this view, strategy is based on a superior, forward-thinking vision by an entrepreneur or entrepreneurial director. This vision, in turn, is based largely on intuition and some experimentation, instead of leaning mostly on facts and figures, and on sensing opportunities where others primarily see risks and obstacles. For instance, Virgin Group, established in 1970 as a mail order record retailer, has become well-known for continuously venturing into territory previously unknown to the firm, such as the airline and telecom industry. The visionary director – Richard Branson in the case of Virgin – is often a transformational leader that creates room for entrepreneurial activities at lower levels in the organization and inspires employees to be creative, while maintaining close control over both strategy formulation and implementation. As the example of Virgin shows, the entrepreneurial approach to strategy is not restricted to startups. In the context of large, established firms, the label *corporate entrepreneurship* is used to refer to the creation of new products or businesses through entrepreneurial activities from inside the organization, which commonly involves both top-down induced strategic behaviour and bottom-up autonomous behaviour[64] (see Chapter 15).

The **learning school** perceives strategy formation as an emergent process that is based on learning capacity and capability. This school emphasizes that strategies are formed and change incrementally over time as a result of trial and error and the accompanying learning effects (that is, learning from mistakes) and retrospective sense-making. In other words, managers are just 'muddling through' and strategies are frequently altered based on what works and what does not. Illustrative of that view is the Twitter post that Elon Musk wrote two weeks after he took over Twitter for $44 billion and became the platform's new CEO: 'Please note that Twitter will do lots of dumb things in coming months. We will keep what works & change what doesn't'.[65] Learning takes place at different organizational levels, including the corporate, business division and functional level. Firms that act in line with the learning school tend to have mostly open-ended objectives and, in order to facilitate learning, keep open as many different pipelines of information as possible. Also, these firms try to successfully exploit learning by maximizing their ability to experiment, spot opportunities, learn quickly from mistakes and rapidly revise their market approach. A case in point is when Honda Motor Company decided to conquer the US motorcycle market in the 1960s, which was then dominated by US-based Harley-Davidson, UK-based BSA Motorcycles and Norton Motors, and Italy-based MotoGuzzi. At that time, motorcycles were primarily bought by the police and armed forces and a limited group of mostly leather and tattoo sporting civilians. In between 1959 and 1966, Honda managed to capture an impressive 63% market share. According to the Honda executives that had orchestrated its market entry, Honda had no strategy, other than the idea of seeing if they could sell something in the US. The firm targeted different market segments and focused on spotting new opportunities, such as small motorcycles for housewives, and on experimenting, learning from mistakes and revising design problems.[66]

The **cultural school** perceives strategy formation as a collective process that is rooted in organizational culture. This school highlights the importance of socialization, which results in common interests of organizational members, shared beliefs and understandings among these members, and a shared identity. It is not always clear to these members what underlies these beliefs, which could therefore be hard to analyze and question. Strategy, according to this school, predominantly takes the form of a (partly inexplicable) perspective. Strategic redirections tend to be largely in line with this perspective and its supporting resources and capabilities.

Whereas the cultural school emphasizes common interest and shared beliefs, the **power school** emphasizes the reverse: self-interest and fragmentation. The power school perceives strategy formation as a process of negotiation and influence that is rooted in power. This school has two branches: the micro power school and the macro power school. According to the *micro power school*, strategy formation results mainly from persuasion, bargaining, confrontation and playing office politics among different groups or individual actors, often with conflicting interests, inside an organization. The *macro power school* perceives strategy formation as resulting from a firm's efforts, possibly in conjunction with efforts by its alliance partners, to increase its control over others and exploit power asymmetries to its advantage. These two branches have in common that they emphasize the use of power play and politics to negotiate strategies favourable to certain interests at the expense of other interests.

The **environmental school** perceives strategy formation as a reactive process, which means that a firm's strategy is essentially determined by what the environment in which it operates imposes. In other words, executives and their organizations are considered passive actors that simply react to sets of general forces and pressures in their external environment. As these external developments set the managerial agenda, the degree of strategic choice is low to nonexistent – in that regard, we can hardly speak of strategy, considering our earlier definition. To deny such choice is at the opposite of attributing omniscient power to executives. Literature streams associated with the environmental school include contingency theory, institutional theory and population ecology theory.[67] *Contingency theory* describes how particular characteristics of the external environment, which can change over time, require a certain way of strategy-making – for instance, when the environment becomes less predictable, the firm should rely less on planning. *Institutional theory* describes how the set of strategic choices that executives have at their disposal is restricted by regulative rules, social rules, norms and shared conceptions of social reality. *Population ecology theory* postulates that firms must do as their environment dictates, or else are 'selected out' by this environment and thus cease to exist. Overall, the environmental school emphasizes the necessity to adapt to environmental demands in order to survive, which is particularly challenging when environmental conditions become hostile or resources scarce.

# The strategic management process: Confront-Sense-Choose-Transform

Following this introduction on what strategy is and on the various perspectives on strategy, we provide an integrated perspective of strategic management. This perspective, based on the *Confront-Sense-Choose-Transform* cycle, introduces strategic management as process stages that are essential when addressing strategic challenges. We present the most widely used and trusted theories, concepts, and tools that enable you to confront blind spots and disruptive change, sense and interpret, choose adequate strategies and make judgement calls, and to direct transformation. The textbook is therefore split up into four parts structured around the *Confront-Sense-Choose-Transform* logic as visualized in our strategic management process framework (see Figure 1.4). Each part consists of four regular chapters and one diagnostic chapter. From Chapter 2 onwards, we move clockwise through this framework.

The regular chapters focus on the theories, concepts and capabilities that help you learn and practice how to enable firms – and other types of organizations – to go through this iterative and dynamic process, allowing them to improve their strategic fit and progress towards prolonged above-average performance. The diagnostic chapters offer mainly practical and action-oriented tools and methods in relation to topics covered in preceding regular chapters. Although we cover the process of *Confront-Sense-Choose-Transform* in a sequential order, starting with confrontation, we see this process as dynamic and iterative, rather than as static and linear. Also, the chapters are highly interrelated – after all, as strategy has to be a unifying and integrative approach, strategic choices, commitment and actions should be coherent and aligned with each other in pursuit of a firm's overarching strategic goals.

Confront (Part I) explores how new challenges that firms face question strategists' and business leaders' ability to formulate and implement strategy, and highlights the delusions they may habour. This part starts with debunking some commonly held erroneous assumptions in strategic management: firms are on earth to provide economic value, the most important stakeholder is the shareholder, markets are predictable, new rivals are seriously limited by liabilities of newness, and firms can hold on to their existing technologies and competencies. This part focuses on the state of strategy and presents the different theories, concepts and tools – old and new – that help understand relevant changes and their

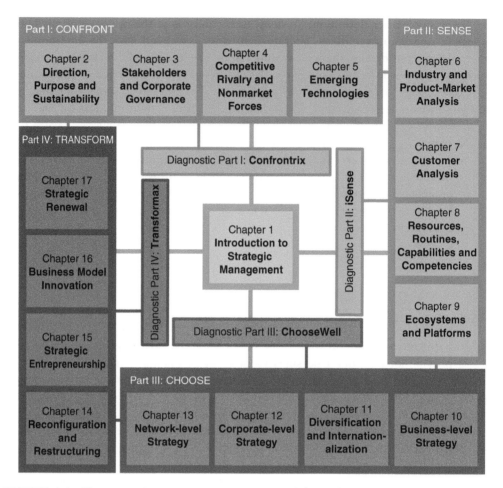

**FIGURE 1.4**   The strategic management process model: Confront-Sense-Choose-Transform

impact on the strategy process: how to define a purpose as the starting point for the firm's strategy that combines economic and social value (shared value), what kind of stakeholders to involve, how to formalize an adequate corporate governance model, how governments, activists and the general public can significantly influence market dynamics, how to spot potential rivals and disruptors, and what kind of frame-breaking technologies might impact the firm's existing business model. In the *Confrontrix* toolkit we provide you with several tools and concepts for starting such a Strategy Confrontation.

<u>Sense</u> (Part II) details analytical tools and techniques to gain insight. This part focuses on the analytical concepts, tools and techniques, classic and cutting edge, that help strategists to conduct analysis to better understand key parameters that influence strategic decisions. In-depth understanding of the firm's fit with its environment is key for strategy development and implementation. *Sense* challenges firms to analyze their resources and competencies (resource-based view), but also to see beyond their habits and routines by taking into account their industries, customers, and ecosystems. This part focuses on industry analysis (e.g., Five Forces), competitor analysis (e.g., Four Corners), customer analysis (e.g., market segmentation, value discipline analysis), resource analysis (e.g., VRINO analysis) and ecosystem analysis (e.g., Ecosystem Pie). Providing thus the essential tools to conduct inside-out and outside-in

analysis, this part relies heavily on industrial organization (I/O) theory, resource-based theory of the firm, and the dynamic capability theory of strategic management. Several practical tools to do these analyses are provided in the *iSense* diagnostic chapter.

Choose (Part III) explains how better decisions about strategies are made. Strategists are forced to improve their business, or they are forced out. This part builds on the analysis conducted in Part 2 and arrives at necessary choices among promising options. Among the classic concepts to develop options, we provide ideas about how to position the firm (e.g., generic strategies such as focus, differentiation and cost leadership), how to expand the corporate scope (e.g., vertical integration, horizontal diversification, conglomerate diversification, internationalization), how to achieve synergies (e.g., revenue, cost and financial synergies) in a multibusiness portfolio, and how to cooperate with other organizations (e.g., equity alliances, contractual alliances and associational alliances). In this part we also help you to craft your own strategies going beyond choosing between generic options; we explain various practical tools and approaches for refining multiple alternatives through iterations and learning. This part does not only provide a range of different strategies; the *ChooseWell* toolkit also helps you develop

**Confront**

- Rethinking the firm's mission, vision, values and purpose
- Redefining stakeholders and corporate governance models
- Re-assessing competitive rivalry and nonmarket forces
- Understanding the potential of emerging technologies

*Confrontrix Toolkit*

**Transform**

- Reorganizing through acquisitions, divestitures and restructuring
- Exploiting entrepreneurial opportunities
- Changing the business model
- Altering path dependencies and activating renewal trajectories

*Transformax Toolkit*

**Sense**

- Analyzing industries and product markets
- Studying customer groups
- Investigating resources, routines, capabilities, and distinctive competencies
- Exploring ecosystems and platforms and their effect on industry dynamics

*iSense Toolkit*

**Choose**

- Selecting competitive strategy
- Deciding about diversification directions and internationalization
- Choosing how to oversee and add value to multibusiness portfolios
- Selecting forms of cooperative relationship and alliance partners

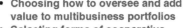

*ChooseWell Toolkit*

**FIGURE 1.5** The Confront-Sense-Choose-Transform cycle for stepwise progression from strategy formulation to strategy implementation

and internalize the 'algorithm' that helps to process these alternatives and deliver a successful strategy.

Transform (Part IV) focuses on execution that brings strategy to life. This final part of the book focuses on the concepts and tools that help achieve transformation and, ultimately, enhanced performance with the chosen strategy. Only a strategy that delivers transformation works. This part seeks to measure and ensure that the strategy comes to life and transforms organizations at risk into those that have better fit with the environment. You will find several ways to master transformation in times of dramatic growth or stagnant growth through acquisitions, divestitures, or restructuring. Sometimes transformation can be activated by exploiting entrepreneurial opportunities inside the company through intrapreneurship or outside the company by investing in startups. More radical transformations involve a change of business model or even strategic renewal by exploring new competencies and breaking out of path dependencies. *Transformax* is our label for the transformation toolkit. It helps to understand the areas, sequences and moves to conclude strategic initiatives (ranging from strategic entrepreneurship and business model innovation to strategic renewal) with transformation success.

Figure 1.5 provides a schematic presentation of the *Confront-Sense-Choose-Transform* cycle for addressing strategic problems. For each stage of the strategic management process, we describe the relevant strategic activities to perform. These activities are explained further in the chapters of each part to come, starting with Chapter 2 – the first chapter of the *Confront* part – in which we focus on developing and rethinking the mission, vision, value statements and purpose of the firm.

## CLOSING CASE
### Marks & Spencer's clothing and home division

Source: © Sorbis (2016) / Shutterstock.

The Marks and Spencer Group (M&S) is a major British retailer that sells general merchandise, most of which are own-brand products, such as clothing, home products and food. In 2023, the firm had around 64,000 employees, serving nearly 30 million customers each year.[68] Founded in 1884 as a market stall, M&S had close to 1,500 stores worldwide in 2023, more than 1,000 of which are in the UK.[69] It also operates online, selling general merchandise and wine through M&S.com, and food through a partnership with the firm Ocado.

M&S built a reputation for quality, and largely British products with exceptional customer service. Profits peaked in the late 90s, and it became the first British firm to make £1 billion in pre-tax profit in FY 1996–7. However, performance in the 21st century has been poor with the group facing a myriad of challenges. The historical policy of only selling British-made goods was revised far later than competitors, impacting profits and leaving M&S with an ineffective supply chain to this day. A similarly overdue loyalty card was launched in 2015 with little success. The extensive store network is increasingly problematic in the context of a rise in e-commerce. In modernizing the firm, the M&S reputation for quality has been tarnished and as such customer loyalty that spanned generations has been severely stretched. The group finished the financial year ending 2021 with a loss of £209.4 million before tax, the first loss recorded in the firm's 94 years as a public-traded organization.

Recent strategic decisions in the Food division have stabilized their contribution to the group and recorded £214 million profit. The unit increased the range of affordable convenience and undertook store refurbishment to revolutionize the food shopping experience. In addition, M&S entered a 50:50 partnership with the Ocado group in 2019 to offer M&S products for delivery through Ocado's platform and logistics. Adjusting for the impacts of COVID, the division saw underlying like-for-like growth of 6.9%. M&S now has a modern offering which is ahead of the competition. In contrast, the Clothing & Home division recorded a loss of £129 million, with revenues falling 32% from 2019/20. In fact, Clothing & Home revenues have decreased for 10 years in a row, a period where industry challenges have been met with lacklustre strategic innovation.

M&S has historically carried out a strategy of differentiation, targeting a broad market of adults throughout the UK who have some disposable income to purchase clothes as opposed to making themselves or purchasing budget clothing. This differentiation was achieved through:

- Quality, durability, and attractiveness of clothing products. This, with a historically strong marketing presence, led to an immense amount of value attached to the M&S brand.
- Exceptional customer service, characterized by the 1953 slogan, 'The customer is always and completely right!'[70]
- Accessibility and ease of purchase. The extensive store estate left few towns without an M&S store, the majority of which stocked a high proportion of the M&S range.

These elements led to a sustained competitive advantage that only increased over time: more products, more brand value, more stores. However, after decades of success and prominence, M&S' clothing and home division failed to explore and sufficiently adapt to a combination of key macro trends in fashion retail. These trends, beginning at the turn of the 21st century, have almost entirely eroded the historical advantage M&S once had:

*(Continued)*

- <u>Online shopping</u> – lowered footfall in stores and changed the marketing game. Redefining 'excellent customer service' away from human interaction, and to efficient and consistent logistics.
- <u>Fast fashion</u> with increasingly contrasted market segments – rapidly changing styles and desires from consumers, challenging the traditional seasonal cadence.
- <u>Emphasis on value</u> – enabled by cheap labour in the Far East, the consumer now expects quality clothing at a lower price.

While M&S has moved into e-commerce, the organization still to this day identifies itself as a 'bricks and mortar' business. As such, the domestic supply chain for e-commerce is underdeveloped. While competitors such as Next and Asos are able to offer same day delivery, M&S delivers to customers in 3-5 days. This leaves M&S with a Net Promoter Score of 81 in stores, rising from 2020, and a score of 51 online, falling from 2020. An overdue and badly executed move to suppliers in the Far East has left M&S with an expensive and disparate overseas supply chain that not only impacts their margin and the price that they are able to offer to consumers, but also constrains M&S to designing clothes over 6 months before they are to be sold. Firms such as Inditex's Zara are able to respond to consumer trends, from designer to sale, within 30 days, leaving them able to capitalize on the flavour of the moment.

Moreover, rather than recognizing that consumer tastes are changing, M&S designers have remained largely focused on a broad customer segmentation that is decades out of date. As such, M&S has lost relevance to its loyal generation and failed to capture the attention of a new one. Marketing strategies executed by competitors such as Boohoo have seen far greater success, for example partnering with TV programs and utilizing the growing 'influencer' social media marketing route.

Hence, there have been issues throughout the value chain; the firm finds itself in a position where it designs clothes that fail to capture the consumer's attention, it is unable to market or distribute those clothes in the way that a 21st century consumer desires, and it is weighed down by an outdated physical and cultural operating model. Cost efficiencies and quality marketing led to a resurgence in sales around 2010, but this turned out to be short-lived. As for the following years, returns have been in decline and M&S has not yet found an appropriate counterattack.

## Questions

1. From a positioning perspective, would you advise M&S to divest its clothing and home division? Why (not)? Would your advice be different when adopting a learning perspective instead?
2. If you recommend not to divest: what strategic actions could be taken by this division to help improve returns, taking into consideration macro-level trends as described in this case, and what strategic actions could be taken by M&S (the corporation)?
3. How could M&S find itself a market leader again in defining the role that 'bricks-and-mortar' plays in the 21st century omni-channel retail?

## Summary

- The ultimate goal of any organizational strategy is to sustain added value, which in a for-profit context translates into a sustainable competitive advantage.
- A firm is said to have a competitive advantage, which indicates above-average performance, when it is able to outperform its competitors, resulting in above-average returns.
- Strategy can be defined as a unified, integrated, orchestrated and purposeful set of choices, commitments and activities directed at achieving and sustaining above-average performance.
- Strategy is also relevant for organizations other than firms, such as nonprofit, not-for-profit, and governmental organizations.
- In general, a clear strategy should provide a compelling answer to each of the following questions: *where do we compete* (or add value), *how do we differentiate ourselves from others, how do we get to where we want to be, what is the sequence and speed of our moves,* and *how do we create value and for whom?*
- Strategy is not about pursuing operational effectiveness, nor should it be seen as a plan.
- Strategic management refers to the formulation and implementation of a strategy.
- The industrial organization (I/O) model and resource-based model of above-average returns can both be used to explain how firms can achieve above-average performance.
- Actual strategy formation lies somewhere on a continuum between a fully deliberate strategy and a fully emergent strategy.
- The strategy formation process can be conceived in different ways, which can be categorized into so-called 'schools of strategy formation'.
- A distinction can be made between prescriptive and descriptive schools of strategy formation.
- The design school, planning school and positioning school are prescriptive schools of thought.
- The cognitive school, entrepreneurial school, learning school, cultural school, power school and environmental schools are descriptive schools of thought.

## Review questions

1. What is the main goal of strategy?
2. Why is strategy distinct from operational effectiveness?
3. How do the I/O model and resource-based model differ in their view on how firms can achieve above-average returns?
4. Why is strategy formation not necessarily equal to strategy formulation?
5. What are the differences between prescriptive and descriptive schools of strategy formation?

## Discussion questions

1. What may have contributed to the fact that strategy is a relatively young academic field?
2. Why are there such large differences among firms with respect to who is involved in strategy?

3.  To what extent can the notions of competitive advantage and above-average performance be applied to a nonprofit context and a not-for-profit context?
4.  What are the main strengths and weaknesses of the mentioned schools of strategy formation?

## EXPERIENTIAL EXERCISES

1.  Choose a firm you admire or that you find interesting and explain clearly what its strategy is.
2.  Examine whether this strategy makes most sense from a resource-based perspective, an I/O-perspective, or a combination of both.
3.  Which school(s) of thought seem(s) to dominate the strategic formation process at this firm?

## Further reading

Duhaime, I.M., Hitt, M.A. and Lyles, M.A. (2021), *Strategic Management: State of the Field and its Future*. New York, NY: Oxford University Press.

Fréry, F. (2006) 'The fundamental dimensions of strategy', *MIT Sloan Management Review*, 48 (1): 71–5.

Hitt, M.A., Arregle, J. and Holmes, R.M. (2021) 'Strategic management theory in a post-pandemic and non-ergodic world', *Journal of Management Studies*, 58: 259–64.

Porter (1996), 'What is strategy?', *Harvard Business Review*, 74 (6): 61–78.

Volberda, H.W. and Elfring, T. (2001), *Rethinking Strategy*. London: Sage.

## Endnotes (references)

1.  Statista (2023) *Luxury Goods – Worldwide*. https://web.archive.org/web/20230730133359/https://www.statista.com/outlook/cmo/luxury-goods/worldwide; Statista (2023) *Luxury Fashion – Worldwide*. https://web.archive.org/save/https://www.statista.com/outlook/cmo/luxury-goods/luxury-fashion/worldwide
2.  Deloitte (2022) *Global Powers of Luxury Goods 2022: A New Wave of Enthusiasm in Luxury*. www.deloitte.com/content/dam/assets-shared/legacy/docs/analysis/2022/gx-global-powers-of-luxury-goods-report.pdf (accessed July 27, 2023).
3.  D'Arpizio, C. and Levato, F. (2020) 'The Millennial State of Mind', Bain & Company, May 18. www.bain.com/insights/the-millennial-state-of-mind (accessed May 30, 2023).
4.  Willersdorf, S., Hazan, J., Ricci, G., Prénaud, A., Bianchi, F., Seara, J. and Yang, V. (2020) *A New Era and a New Look for Luxury*. BCG, June. www.bcg.com/publications/2020/new-era-and-new-look-for-luxury (accessed July 18, 2023).
5.  Capri Holdings (2021) *Annual Report 2021*, May 26. https://s22.q4cdn.com/557169922/files/doc_financials/2021/ar/CAPRI-HOLDINGS-LIMITED-FY2021-ANNUAL-REPORT.pdf (accessed May 30, 2023).
6.  Smith, P. (2023) 'Number of Marks & Spencer stores from 2010 to 2023, by region', Statista. https://web.archive.org/save/https://www.statista.com/statistics/268649/marks-und-spencer-number-of-outlets-by-region
7.  Smith (2023)
8.  Smith (2023)
9.  Chandler, A.D. Jr. (1962) *Strategy and Structure: Chapters in the History of the Industrial Empire*. Cambridge, MA: MIT Press. p. 13.
10. Chandler (1962: 13)

11. Ansoff, H.I. (1988) *Corporate Strategy* (revised ed.). London: Penguin Books. p. 100.

12. Porter, M.E. (1996) 'What is strategy?', *Harvard Business Review*, Nov/Dec: 61–78. pp. 68, 75.

13. Hambrick, D.C. and Fredrickson, J.W. (2001) 'Are you sure you have a strategy?', *Academy of Management Executive*, 15 (4): 48–59. p. 48.

14. Rogers, J. and Rogers, J. (2009) 'Developments in Strategy', in J. Rogers (ed.), *Strategy, Value and Risk: The Real Options Approach* (2nd ed.). London: Palgrave Macmillan, 45–54. p. 45.

15. Volberda, H.W., Morgan, R.E., Reinmoeller, P., Hitt, M.A., Ireland, R.D. and Hoskisson, R.E. (2011) *Strategic Management: Competitiveness and Globalization*. Andover: Cengage. p. 7.

16. Rothaermel, F.T. (2021) *Strategic Management* (5th ed.). New York, NY: McGraw-Hill. p. 6.

17. Grant, R.M. (2021) *Contemporary Strategy Analysis* (11th ed.), Chichester: Wiley. p. 10.

18. Martin, R.L. (2022) 'A plan is not a strategy', Harvard Business Review YouTube Channel, June, 29. (1:11). www.youtube.com/watch?v=iuYlGRnC7J8 (accessed May 30, 2023).

19. Fréry, F. (2006) 'The fundamental dimensions of strategy', *MIT Sloan Management Review*, 48 (1): 71–5.

20. Adner, R. and Zemsky, P. (2006) 'A demand-based perspective on sustainable competitive advantage', *Strategic Management Journal*, 27 (3): 215–39.

21. Hambrick and Fredrickson (2001)

22. MacMillan, I.C. (1988) 'Controlling competitive dynamics by taking strategic initiative', *Academy of Management Executive*, 2 (2): 111–18.

23. Porter (1996)

24. Rumelt, R.P., Schendel D.E. and Teece, D.J. (1994) *Fundamental Issues in Strategy: A Research Agenda*. Boston, MA: Harvard Business School Press.

25. Penrose, E.T. (1959) *The Theory of Growth of the Firm*. New York, NY: Wiley; Ansoff, H.I. (1965) *Corporate Strategy: An Analytical Approach to Business Policy for Growth and Expansion*. New York, NY: McGraw-Hill.

26. Ansoff (1965)

27. Rumelt, R.P. (1974) *Strategy, Structure and Economic Performance*. Boston, MA: Harvard Business School; Rumelt, R.P. (1982) 'Diversification strategy and profitability', *Strategic Management Journal*, 3: 359–69.

28. Jensen, M.C. and Meckling, W.H. (1976) 'Theory of the firm: Managerial behavior, agency costs and ownership structure', *Journal of Financial Economics*, 3 (4): 305–60; Mitnick, B.M. (1975) 'The theory of agency: The policing "paradox" and regulatory behavior', *Public Choice*, 24: 27–42.; Ross, S.A. (1973) 'The economic theory of agency: The principal's problem', *American Economic Review*, 63 (2): 134–9.

29. Porter, M.E. (1980b) *Competitive Strategy: Techniques for Analysing Industries and Competitors*. New York, NY: Simon & Schuster.

30. Porter, M.E. (1985) *Competitive Advantage: Creating and Sustaining Superior Performance*. New York, NY: The Free Press.

31. Barney, J.B. (1991) 'Firm resources and sustained competitive advantage', *Journal of Management*, 17: 99–120; Wernerfelt, B. (1984) 'A resource-based view of the firm', *Strategic Management Journal*, 5: 171–80.

32. Prahalad, C.K. and Hamel, G. (1990) 'The core competence of the corporation', *Harvard Business Review*, 68: 79–91.

33. Teece, D.J. and Pisano, G. (1994) 'The dynamic capabilities of firms: An introduction', *Industrial and Corporate Change*, 3: 537–56; Teece, D.J., Pisano, G.P. and Shuen, A.

(1997) 'Dynamic capabilities and strategic management', *Strategic Management Journal*, 18 (7): 509–33.

34. Christensen, C.M. (2001) 'The past and future of competitive advantage', *MIT Sloan Management Review*, 42 (2): 105–9; Christensen, C.M., Raynor, M. and McDonald, R. (2015) 'What is disruptive innovation?', *Harvard Business Review,* 93: 44–53.

35. Amit, R. and Zott, C. (2001) 'Value creation in e-business', *Strategic Management Journal*, 22: 493–520.

36. Van Alstyne, M.W., Parker, G.G. and Choudary, S.P. (2016) 'Pipelines, platforms, and the new rules of strategy', *Harvard Business Review*, 94 (4), 54–62.

37. Adner, R. (2017) 'Ecosystem as structure: An actionable construct for strategy', *Journal of Management*, 43 (1): 39–58; Jacobides, M., Cennamo, C. and Gawer, A. (2018) 'Towards a theory of ecosystems', *Strategic Management Journal*, 39: 2255–76.

38. Ansoff (1988: 104)

39. Porter (1996: 61)

40. Porter (1996)

41. Martin, R.L. (2013) 'Don't let strategy become planning', *Harvard Business Review,* February 5. https://hbr.org/2013/02/dont-let-strategy-become-plann (accessed June 1, 2023); Martin (2022).

42. e.g., Bowman, E.H. and Helfat, C.E. (2001) 'Does corporate strategy matter?', *Strategic Management Journal*, 22: 1–23; Porter (1985).

43. Shanker, D. (2021) 'Impossible and Beyond slash prices as fake-meat market heats up', *Bloomberg*, April 16. www.bloomberg.com/news/articles/2021-04-16/beyond-meat-bynd-impossible-foods-battle-over-future-of-fake-meat-industry (accessed June 1, 2023).

44. Lucas, A. (2021) 'Beyond Meat unveils new version of its meat-free burgers for grocery stores', CNBC, April 27. www.cnbc.com/2021/04/27/beyond-meat-unveils-new-version-of-its-meat-free-burgers-in-stores.html (accessed June 1, 2023).

45. Slevin, D.P. and Covin, J.G. (2015) 'Emergent strategy', *Wiley Encyclopedia of Management* (vol. 3, Entrepreneurship). Hoboken, NJ: Wiley, 1-3.

46. Mintzberg and Waters (1985)

47. Mintzberg, H. (1987) 'Crafting strategy', *Harvard Business Review*, July: 66–75; Mintzberg, H. and Waters, J.A. (1985) 'Of strategies, deliberate and emergent', *Strategic Management Journal*, 6 (3): 257–72.

48. Mirabeau, L. and Maguire, S. (2014) 'From autonomous strategic behavior to emergent strategy', *Strategic Management Journal*, 35 (8): 1202–29.

49. Mintzberg, H. and Lampel, J. (1999) 'Reflecting on the strategy process', *Sloan Management Review*, Spring: 21–30; Mintzberg, H., Ahlstrand, B. and Lampel, J. (1998) *Strategy Safari: A Guided Tour Through the Wilds of Strategic Management.* New York, NY: The Free Press.

50. Mintzberg et al. (1998)

51. Porter (1980b, 1985)

52. Porter (1996)

53. MacMillan (1988)

54. WNIP (2017) 'How Axel Springer came back from the dead: It disrupted itself', *What's New in Publishing.* https://whatsnewinpublishing.com/axel-springer-came-back-dead-disrupting (accessed June 1, 2023).

55. DIS (2018) 'How Axel Springer came back from the dead', *DIS,* March 20. www.innovators-summit.com/news/detail/article/dis-2018-how-axel-springer-came-back-from-the-dead (accessed June 1, 2023).

56. Axel Springer (2018) *At a Glance: Axel Springer.* Berlin: Axel Springer. www.axelspringer.com/data/uploads/2018/06/ENG_Auf_einen_Blick_Doppelseiten.pdf (accessed June 1, 2023).

57. Axel Springer (2020) *Annual Report 2019*. www.axelspringer.com/data/uploads/2020/03/annual_report_2019.pdf (accessed June 1, 2023).

58. Rosemain, M. (2021) 'Google seals content payment deal with French news publishers', *Reuters*, January 21. www.reuters.com/article/us-france-google-publishers-idUSKBN29Q0SC (accessed June 1, 2023).

59. Jaworski, R. (2020) 'The renaissance of publications amid fake news and social media', *Trinity Audio*, December 21. www.trinityaudio.ai/the-renaissance-of-publications-amid-fake-news-and-social-media (accessed June 1, 2023).

60. Rosemain (2021)

61. Buck, T. (2019) 'German media group Axel Springer sees earnings fall in first quarter', *The Irish Times*, May 7. www.irishtimes.com/business/media-and-marketing/german-media-group-axel-springer-sees-earnings-fall-in-first-quarter-1.3883284 (accessed June 1, 2023).

62. e.g., Barr, P.S., Stimpert, J.L. and Huff, A.S. (1992) 'Cognitive change, strategic action, and organizational renewal', *Strategic Management Journal*, 13 (6): 15–36.

63. Schumpeter, J.A. (1934) *The Theory of Economic Development*. Oxford: Oxford University Press.

64. Burgelman, R.A. (1983) 'A process model of internal corporate venturing in the diversified major firm', *Administrative Science Quarterly*, 28: 223–44.

65. Musk, E. (@elonmusk) (2022) 'Please note…', *Twitter*, November 9. https://twitter.com/elonmusk/status/1590384919829962752 (accessed June 1, 2023).

66. Pascale, R.T. (1984) 'Perspectives on strategy: The real story behind Honda's success', *California Management Review*, 26 (3): 47–86.

67. Mintzberg et al. (1998)

68. Marks and Spencer (2023) *Reshaping M&S: Annual Report & Financial Statements 2023*. https://corporate.marksandspencer.com/sites/marksandspencer/files/2023-06/M%26S_2023_Annual_Report.pdf (accessed July 27, 2023).

69. Smith (2023)

70. Chislett, H. (2009) *Marks in Time: 125 Years of Marks & Spencer*. London: Weidenfield and Nicolson.

## Acknowledgements

The authors thank Sebastian Carter, Bram Huis in 't Veld and Silvia Mateo Combarros for their contribution to this chapter.

## Key terms

**Above-average performance** – performance that is above the market's or industry's average

**Above-average returns** – returns that are beyond the investors' expectations

**Cognitive school** – strategy formation as a mental process by analyzing how people perceive patterns and process information

**Competitive advantage** – the ability of a firm to outperform its competitors

**Competitive disadvantage** – a deficit in a firm's ability to outperform its competitors

**Competitive parity** – a rather similar overall performance of firm to that of its competitors

**Cultural school** – strategy formation as a collective and cooperative process rooted in a firm's culture

**Deliberate strategy** – parts of an intended (or formulated) strategy that are put into action

**Descriptive schools of strategy formation** – a group of perspectives that describe how strategies *are* actually formed

**Design school** – strategy formation as a process of designing a fit between a firm's internal strengths and weaknesses and external threats and opportunities

**Emergent strategy** – a strategy that arises from unplanned initiatives and actions within a firm

**Entrepreneurial school** – strategy formation as a visionary process of the founder or chief executive

**Environmental school** – strategy formation as a reactive process by responding to challenges in the external environment

**Formulated strategy** – an intended strategy that is articulated explicitly

**Government organizations** – sovereign entities with authoritative power over other organizations

**Industrial organization (I/O) model of above-average returns** – a logic where the external environment exerts a dominant influence on a firm's strategic actions

**Intended strategy** – a strategy that a firm hopes to execute

**Learning school** – strategy formation as an emergent process that occurs via small steps as a firm learns

**Nonprofit organizations** – organizations geared to benefit the public good

**Not-for-profit organizations** – organizations aimed to serve the collective goals of their members

**Planning school** – strategy formation as a formal process characterized by detailed planning

**Positioning school** – strategy formation as an analytical process to look at how a firm can improve its strategic position in an industry

**Power school** – strategy formation as a process of negotiation

**Prescriptive schools of strategy formation** – a group of perspectives that prescribe how strategies *ought* to be

**Realized strategy** – the strategy that a firm actually follows

**Resource-based model of above-average returns** – a logic where the uniqueness of a firm's resources and capabilities form the basis of its strategic actions

**Schools of strategy formation** – various perspectives on the strategy formation process

**Strategic management** – the formulation and implementation of strategy

**Strategy** – an orchestrated, unified, integrated, and purposeful set of choices, commitments, and activities directed at achieving and sustaining above-average performance

**Unrealized strategy** – abandoned parts of an intended (or formulated) strategy

# PART I
## CONFRONT

This part explores how new challenges question business leaders' and strategists' ability to formulate and implement strategy. Different theories, concepts and tools, old and new, are presented that help understand relevant changes and their impact on the strategy process: how to define a purpose as the starting point for the firm's strategy that combines economic and social value (shared value); what kind of stakeholders to involve and how to formalize an adequate corporate governance model; how governments, activists and the general public can significantly influence market dynamics; how to spot potential rivals and disruptors; and what kind of frame-breaking technologies might impact the firm's existing business model. In the Confrontrix toolkit we provide you with several tools and concepts for how to start such a Strategy Confrontation.

# 2

# DIRECTION, PURPOSE AND SUSTAINABILITY

## LEARNING OBJECTIVES

After reading this chapter, you should be able to:

- distinguish between the concepts of mission, vision, and values;
- appreciate the importance of mission, vision, and values statements for setting strategic objectives;
- understand the principle of company purpose and why a purpose statement matters;
- identify the challenges faced in becoming a purpose-driven organization;
- use mission, vision, values, purpose and strategic objectives for strategic management.

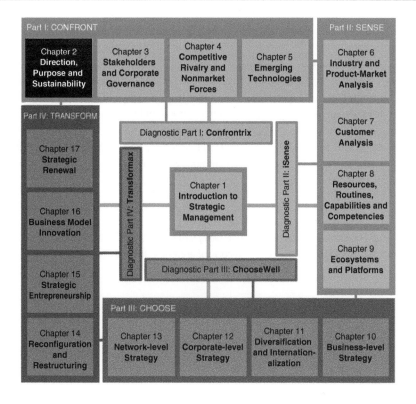

## OPENING CASE

### Ben & Jerry's does it differently[1]

"Baked Alaska" | Tasty-score (tm): 3.5 of 5 | Fredrik Ohlin | Flickr

Ben Cohen and Jerry Greenfield founded a pioneering company that ambitioned to achieve 'double dip': a framework that is attentive to business performance in the areas of profit and people. Ben & Jerry's started as an ice-cream shop in 1978 in a renovated gas station in the state of Vermont, US. Company values included offering a fair price to dairy farmers, being considerate to employees, and being environmentally friendly.

Source: original image © Fredrik Ohlin (2018) / Flickr. https://www.flickr.com/photos/fohlin/2380347141/

Values such as advocacy and activism still guide the company. Ben & Jerry's are not shy of taking a position on socially relevant issues, such as DEI (diversity, equity and inclusion) and the climate emergency. The company has played a role in the boycott of advertisements at Twitter and Facebook, because it felt that the social media giants had not acted firmly enough against racist messages. The company also got involved in helping thousands of migrants acquire a residence permit in Sweden. Activism is reflected, in fact, in many strategic and marketing decisions of the company. The launch of flavours with names such as Whirled Peace and Pecan Resist offer support to the DEI agenda.

Ben & Jerry's maintains that companies can use their influence to enable change: 'We believe that ice cream can change the world.' CEO Matthew McCarthy stated in an interview with *Forbes* that employees 'live our ice cream as well as our social mission every day'.[2] Many of the company's employees have an NGO or policy background, and the company collaborates with NGOs and hires professional activists. Ben & Jerry's involvement with socio-political issues has an economic dimension to it. It helps to build a strong connection with customers (or 'fans') who share the company's values. When taking a particular stance, the company is not afraid to alienate itself from stakeholders. McCarthy: 'a business or a brand that tries to be all things to all people – we know what happens to those folks, you usually tend to be not a whole lot to anybody'.[3] With customers increasingly finding it important for companies to have explicit opinions on societal topics, Ben & Jerry's regards its strong growth figures as reflecting its commitment to socio-political issues.

In 2000, Unilever purchased Ben & Jerry's, agreeing to let the company continue setting its own course. CEO McCarthy stated that 'businesses that do not deliberately try to do something good by addressing a specific social or environmental concern in their community, no matter how big or small, are going to find themselves irrelevant in the coming years'.[4]

### Questions

1. What conclusions can you draw about Ben & Jerry's mission, vision, and values?
2. For a company, what may be the pros and cons of engaging in socio-political activism?

# Introduction

Strategic management was introduced in Chapter 1 as a systemic process of confronting the firm with new challenges and tensions, sensing and interpreting these through rigorous analyses, choosing generic strategies and making judgement calls, and directing transformation. In Part I we focus on the first stage, *confrontation*, exploring how new challenges question business leaders' and managers' ability to formulate and implement strategy. As we cannot predict the future, there is considerable uncertainty regarding the expected payoffs or returns from the different strategic-decision options a company has and the specific strategic-decision choices it makes. Moreover, the set of options and expected returns typically changes over time, making coherent decision-making challenging. For decision-making under uncertainty, a company's decision-makers need a framework that can facilitate consistent strategy formulation and implementation. Such a framework is provided by a company's foundational statements of mission, vision, values, purpose, and strategic objectives.

Mission, vision, values, purpose and strategic objectives set the direction and thereby form the foundation of choosing and implementing strategies. As stated by Abell,[5] 'without these lighthouses to guide the way, enterprises and their management are likely to lose their way in the storms of change, and end up on the rocks'. Those foundational statements mirror a firm's philosophy or governing ideas as overarching goals, enabling one to see 'the big picture'. Ben & Jerry's double dip approach (see opening case) is just one example of that. They provide strategic guidance for a firm's journey by acting as powerful tools for managerial integration and control. In addition, they provide decision-makers a stable long-term template to guide strategic decisions. Against their backdrop, decision-makers can decide the objectives to strive for in the short term. Furthermore, they motivate employees and promote adaptive thinking: they spark a creative tension between where a firm currently stands and where it wants to be.

Notwithstanding their common ground, mission, vision, values, purpose and strategic objectives each have their own unique contributions in determining a firm's strategic course (see Figure 2.1). On reading this chapter, you will build your understanding of what these concepts mean in a business and organizational context, and how they connect with one another. In this regard, the view is forming that the purpose of companies should be more than profit maximization – it is also value creation for

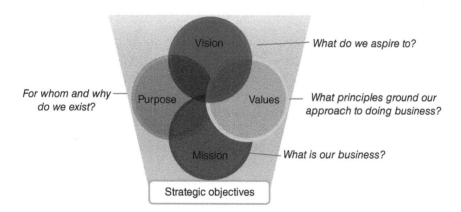

**FIGURE 2.1**  Interrelatedness of mission, vision, values, purpose and strategic objectives

their non-shareholder stakeholders and society at large. Companies, therefore, are facing increasing public and regulatory pressure to define their purpose more broadly to include the environmental and social goals they have set for themselves. Accordingly, companies are recognizing the notion of corporate purpose as an additional foundational element to consider, and have started formulating explicit purpose statements. In this context, the starting point of reflections on corporate purpose is often an engagement with environmental, social, and governance (ESG) issues, especially as articulated in the seventeen Sustainable Development Goals (SDGs) described by the United Nations. In this chapter, we systematically discuss corporate purpose, highlighting the challenges companies face in becoming purpose-driven as they strive to confront the realities of their business environment.

## Mission

The **mission** concept centres on what a company is in the business of, i.e. what lines of business, operations and activities are within the scope of the company, and which are outside. Specifying a company's mission amounts to demarcating the company's business domain. While a company's mission may seem obvious, this is almost never the case. Peter F. Drucker,[6] whose writings have contributed to the foundation of modern business corporations, went so far as to say that managerial neglect of the 'what business are we in'-issue is the number one cause of frustration and failure. Consider Eurostar, the train company which connects the UK with France, Belgium, and the Netherlands. Is the company's business domain the railway industry or the passenger transport industry? Depending on whether Eurostar defines its domain narrowly, as the railway industry, or broadly, as the passenger transport industry, is likely to determine the company's strategic decisions by affecting who it sees as its competitors and consumers, and the opportunities and threats it identifies.

When formulated explicitly, a company's mission statement describes the competitive arena the company has defined for itself and its business scope. The British Broadcasting Corporation (BBC), for example, articulates its mission as follows: '...serving all audiences through the provision of impartial, high-quality and distinctive output and services which inform, educate and entertain'.[7] Mission statements such as this one provide guidance for a company's strategic management. They offer a basis for industry and product market analyses by identifying a company's direct and indirect competitors (see Chapter 6). Moreover, they offer a basis for customer analysis by laying out the market segments a company will focus on and the customer needs it will serve (see Chapter 7).

The development of a mission statement requires deep understanding of a company and its context. As such, effective mission statements are those that are specific to a company – they are not off the shelf, general statements. Sometimes, in the case of smaller companies especially, the mission may not be written on paper. However, the benefit of a written statement is that it functions as a communication tool that can help avoid ambiguity about the business arena a company has defined for itself. A written mission statement should offer answers to the following questions (see also Figure 2.2):[8]

- <u>What does the company do?</u> This goes to the heart of the business function of a company – the generic customer need(s) the company exists to address.
- <u>How is the function performed?</u> This pertains to what is unique and valuable about the way the company performs the business function as compared to its rivals.

- <u>For whom is the function performed?</u> This concerns who the beneficiaries of the function would be and who would pay for it.

It is of value to answer the first question using a demand-side lens and not just a supply-side lens. Whereas the latter can clarify what the company does in terms of the technologies it employs and the products and services it offers, the use of the former is often more insightful as it reveals what customer need(s) the company satisfies. TikTok's mission 'to inspire creativity and bring joy' underscores the demand-side need the company fulfils and not the supply-side technology-product solution the company offers. Thinking in terms of technologies and products often tends to constrain attention to industry-level issues, blind-siding managers to emerging new ways of satisfying the underlying customer need with a completely different technology and product.

Because of the value of a demand-side perspective when articulating what a company does, mission statements are often customer-centric. L'Oréal's mission 'to offer each and every person around the world the best of beauty in terms of quality, efficacy, safety, sincerity and responsibility to satisfy all beauty needs and desires in their infinite diversity'[9] is just one of the many examples of such a customer focus. Determining the beneficiaries of a firm's function helps to define the company's market segments, which are customer groupings based on designated criteria such as age, education, and income levels. The answers to the above three questions should ideally bring out the firm's uniqueness by outlining its boundaries in terms of the customer needs and customer groups, and the technologies to be used. Figure 2.2a illustrates this point. Figure 2.2b shows how a producer of shared electric scooters may specify the company's mission using a three-dimensional framework.

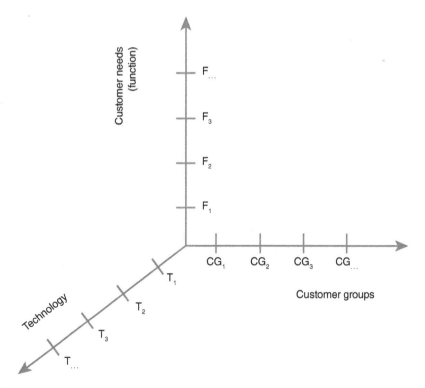

**FIGURE 2.2A**  Defining a company's mission

Source: inspired by Abell (1980)

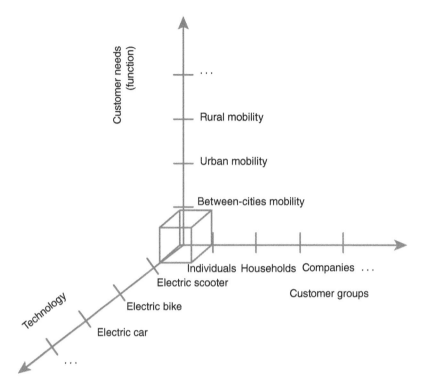

**FIGURE 2.2B**   Defining the mission of a producer of shared electric scooters

## Vision

In contrast to the mission concept, the notion of **vision** concerns the aspirations of a company: 'What do we wish to achieve?' given the context we face. The answer to this identifies the long-term ambitions and hopes of the company, the legacy it wants to build.[10] Vision statements often articulate not only aspirations concerning the focal company itself (internally-centred), but also aspirations regarding the kind of society or world that a company wishes to help build (externally-centred). Through the expression of these aspirations, vision statements are supposed to present bold but viable long-term expectations of the good a company hopes to do. A comprehensive vision statement has six characteristics:[11]

- Imaginable: creates an image of the intended future in the minds of the ones who read it.
- Desirable: appeals to the ones that are aiming to reach it and to customers.
- Feasible: brings together the feasible and the incredible.
- Focused: provides a concentrated direction for those who follow it.
- Flexible: broad enough in scope to allow modifications when needed.
- Communicable: easy to articulate to the audience.

Collins and Porras[12] suggest that vision statements act as a 'beacon' or a 'guiding star' in relation to what a company would like to accomplish.

When articulating its vision, a company must ensure its aspirations are achievable. Because although bold visions can motivate, unrealistic visions can engender cynicism. It is important to find the right spot between the vision being perceived as mundane versus the vision being perceived as unreal. There are many successful vision statements. Honda, for instance, envisioned a future in which society would attach more value to the environment. Guided by this vision, the company has become a pioneer in designing robots and fuel-cell cars that emit only water vapor.[13]

A vision statement complements the mission statement in providing guidance for a company's strategic management. As in the case of Honda's vision statement, it draws decision-makers' attention to the company's achievement priorities within the defined business domain. This helps to set up objectives and to make resource-allocation decisions. A vision statement can have additional positive influences. By inspiring and motivating personnel, it can contribute to their self-actualization. It can thus enhance the creativity and productivity of employees. It can also strengthen cooperation and smoothen coordination in the company by promoting the workforce's identification with a company. To quote Steve Jobs, the co-founder of Apple: 'If you are working on something that you really care about, you don't have to be pushed. The vision pulls you'.

To be appealing and inspiring, a vision should be expressed concisely and memorably, and abbreviations such as KISS ('keep it simple and straightforward') and BHAG ('big, hairy, audacious goals') can be used. If internal and external stakeholders cannot remember a company's vision, one can safely conclude that it is not successful in communicating the company's aspiration to its audience. In practice, vision statements vary greatly in terms of their orientation and other qualities such as clarity, pithiness, and memorability. Whereas some like those of Eskom Uganda Limited, 'to be the center of excellence in power concession management', and the Union Bank Philippines, 'to become one of the top three universal banks in the Philippines', are more internally oriented, others like those of IKEA, 'to create a better everyday life', and of Woolworths Holdings Limited (South Africa), 'to be one of the world's most responsible retailers', are more externally oriented.

It is also important to avoid a vision statement reading like a general slogan that does not communicate the company's individuality. Statements such as 'we want to be the best' and 'we want to be the number one in our market' are non-specific and fail to distinguish a company from others in its business domain. Thus, while there is value to having a crisp, concise vision statement, shortness should not be a goal in itself as it may reduce the statement's effectiveness, especially if the statement feels too generic. Moreover, a statement which does not have discriminatory power is unlikely to function as a source of enthusiasm and inspiration. Furthermore, a general statement will lack specificity to guide goal setting and the company's strategy.

A good practice is to develop a statement that is anchored in a company's culture and takes into account its external circumstances. This increases the likelihood that it will have a unique flavour to it and be perceived as more authentic. Sometimes, formulating a vision statement requires courage and entails risk. Internal discussions regarding the vision can generate tensions because people may hold different views. Still, to formulate a statement that has broad resonance, one must initiate an explicit conversation. As opting for one specific vision may mean the exclusion of alternative visions, the process needs to be managed with care and delicacy. Senior executives can seek to surface different perspectives, and then take the lead in synthesizing different viewpoints into a statement on which there is broad consensus.

# Values

The mission and vision of a firm require sufficient 'walk the talk', otherwise they are merely statements printed in some documents or hanging on a wall. **Values** and especially core values are closely tied to the mission and vision. They are a central embodiment of 'living' according to those statements in corporate reality.

The values concept refers to the ideals that guide conduct. Core values are a small set of guiding principles and ideals for the behaviours, thoughts and opinions that are widely shared throughout an organization. In a company, these guiding ideals pertain to the ethics and morals that are sacrosanct and the aesthetics and customs that underpin the business. When expressed in a written statement, they guide strategic management by providing decision-makers a grid of norms and principles that must be reflected in the business, the operations, and the products and services of the company. In the watchmaking industry, Breguet's values of craftsmanship and tradition, and Citizen's values of contemporary and future-looking, distinguish the two companies from one another. Values are non-negotiable for key decision-makers. For instance, based on the principle of 'fair taxation', PwC has let some customers go who were purely aiming for the lowest taxes and who did not make a real contribution to society.

An explicit values statement can help build a widely shared internal understanding of a company's values, which can be expected to facilitate the implementation of a formulated strategy. It is important when drawing up a values statement to include those values that are authentic to a company. Authenticity has to do with whether the stated values are consistent with the culture and history of a company. Although the enticement of impression management may suggest the articulation of lofty or showy values that are not genuine to a company, going down this path is more likely to do more harm than good. While authenticity energizes people and fosters cooperation and coordination, lack of it has the opposite effect. The authenticity element is a feature of Apple's value statement centring on the making of great products,[14] and Honda's value statement centring on creating intelligent products and bringing joy in people's lives.[15]

Like mission and vision statements, values statements are enduring. Indeed, authentic values are typically woven into the long-term fabric of a company. Regarding this, when presenting Heineken's manifesto of core values, an executive director explained that the company wanted to enunciate values that had been a cornerstone of the company for a very long time and would continue to be in the future.[16] Besides being perennial, effective mission, vision, and values statements inform and reinforce one another. Furthermore, it is important to reflect carefully on the number of values to articulate in a statement. A long list makes it difficult for insiders and outsiders to discern the company's core values.

As a rule-of-thumb, values statements should contain no more than three to five values. Exceeding this rule-of-thumb may suggest that some of them are not really core, because only a few can be actually at the core. For example, BASF, a chemical concern, enumerates four core ideals in its values statement: **c**reative, **o**pen, **r**esponsible, and **e**ntrepreneurial[17] – notice that the first letters of these four ideals form the word 'core'. TUI (Touristik Union International), a tourism company, communicates its values using words whose first letters lead to the acronym TUI: **t**rusted, **u**nique, and **i**nspiring.[18] To add to this, the articulated values may be expressed using single words as BASF and TUI do, or by using simple phrases that signal the values. For example, Patagonia expresses its values through phrases such as 'be just, equitable and antiracist as a company and in our community' and 'protect our home planet'.

## CRACK-THE-CASE
Protix[19]

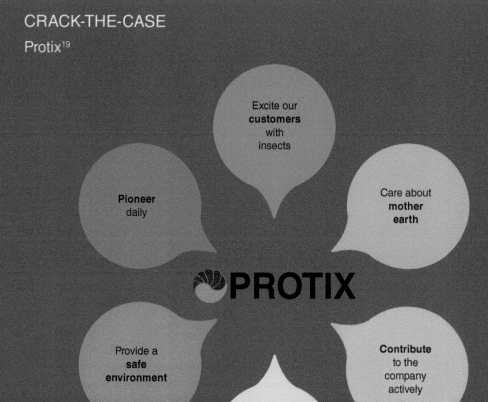

Source: Protix (2023)

https://protix.eu/protix-journey/

Protix, a pioneering company that uses insects to produce animal feed is an example of an enterprise in which there is tight interweaving of the mission, vision, values, and purpose of the firm. The idea at the heart of the company emerged back in 2009, as a vision experienced by Kees Aarts, the founder of the company. The vision was about a solution to the problem of overfishing. One day, when Kees Aarts went diving with his friends, he experienced dismay because there seemed so few fish left in the waters. Thinking about this led him to imagine a company whose overarching goal would be 'to bring the food system back in balance with nature'. He paired his vision for the company with the mission of producing fish and animal feed products in a non-conventional way. Whereas fish had been traditionally used to produce these products, the new company, Protix, would

(Continued)

use proteins derived from insects. In this way, the company could pursue profits as well as address the grand challenge of ensuring sustainable use of ocean, sea, and marine resources.

The story about the start of Protix is well known within the company. This has contributed to the ingraining of the company's values and purpose in the employees. The company has a set of six core values that provide an anchor to the company's operations and products: (1) excite customers with insects; (2) provide a safe environment; (3) pioneer daily; (4) care about mother earth (by pursuing a lower carbon footprint and learning from nature); (5) contribute to the company actively (by taking responsibility and becoming involved); and (6) enjoy life.[20]

## Questions

1. Do you deem the number and scope of Protix' core values appropriate given its mission and vision?
2. To what extent are Protix' core values likely to 'stand the test of time' if the company grows substantially?

# Purpose

Until quite recently, it has been common to regard economic value creation for the benefit of owners or shareholders as the core purpose of companies. This view is however changing. As the world faces a climate emergency and as inequalities around the globe continue to grow, it is important that companies participate actively in addressing the environmental and social challenges faced by humanity. In this regard, the view is forming that the purpose of companies should be more than profit maximization – it is also value creation for their non-shareholder stakeholders and the society at large. Accordingly, companies are recognizing the notion of corporate purpose as an additional foundational element to consider and have started formulating explicit purpose statements.

A **corporate purpose** can be defined as a concrete goal that goes beyond profit maximization and describes how the company contributes to solving problems of people and planet.[21] In a purpose-driven company, the social goal lies at the heart of the organization, and a profitable business model is placed at its service. A unique feature of corporate purpose is that it involves a firm's fundamental idealistic and moral motivations for performing its function by addressing problems of people and planet. This captures the 'soul' of a company. A case in point would appear to be Patagonia, a company whose purpose statement states that, '[We're] in business to save our home planet'.[22] Regarding this, Yvon Chouinard, Patagonia's founder, appears to hold the belief that profits should essentially be pursued as a means to battle climate change: 'Earth is now our only shareholder [...] Instead of "going public", you could say we're "going purpose". Instead of extracting value from nature and transforming it into wealth for investors, we'll use the wealth Patagonia creates to protect the source of all wealth'.[23]

A purpose thus captures the very essence of why a firm exists and elucidates the unique value or impact it provides for stakeholders such as customers, employees, shareholders and society at large. This differentiates a purpose from a mission and vision, because it describes the reasons *why* a firm does what it does and why it intends to head towards a certain future state.[24] The fundamental why-question is among the first questions in thinking strategically about business and without a clear answer it is hard to allocate resources intelligently. As such, discussions on the purpose typically start with questioning 'how would the world be worse off if we did not exist?'.[25]

A purpose statement communicates to audiences the aims of a company regarding how it will enhance societal well-being – that is, how it will make a positive contribution to the environment, the ecosystem, and the reduction of social disparities and difficulties in and across nations. As an aspirational, authentic and ambitious statement, it provides guidance for articulating specific strategic objectives and corporate decision-making. In so doing, a purpose statement can bring several benefits to a company. For instance, it can help to increase the social approval and legitimacy of a company, thus attracting financial and human resources that enable the realization of the company's mission and vision. Companies with a strong purpose engage with a broader range of stakeholders than just shareholders, have more motivated and productive employees, create a larger societal impact, achieve higher levels of innovation, and bring positive reputation effects to the firm. A purpose also has the power to attract, engage, and retain like-minded stakeholders to the company, including potential employees and customers. Anecdotal evidence indicates that Millennials and Generation Z entering the labour market prefer working for purpose-driven companies, which as a result are better placed when it comes to recruiting, engaging, and retaining capable personnel.

Of course, simply having a purpose statement is not enough. The substance of a statement and how it is presented is also important. Whether a statement is short or long, and whether it is abstract or concrete, may affect its impact. Whereas short, abstract statements allow the corporate purpose to be expressed pithily, longer, concrete statements may be seen as more sincere and genuine. An example of a short, abstract statement is that of ABN AMRO, a Dutch bank: 'banking for better, for generations to come'.[26] Although pithy, the statement does not convey any specific details regarding how the bank will make a positive contribution to societal well-being. It thus runs the risk of being ignored as a genuine purpose statement. An example of a longer but a more concrete statement is that of Philips, a Dutch HealthTech firm: 'improve people's health and well-being through meaningful innovation. [...] improve 2.5 billion lives per year by 2030, including 400 million in underserved communities'.[27] The statement links with one of the specific SDGs identified by the United Nations: ensuring 'health and well-being' for everyone on the planet (see the Strategic Focus on SDGs later in this chapter).

Notably, although a prime goal of a firm is often to be profitable, purpose statements typically do not mention such economic objectives. Somewhat 'dry and sterile financially oriented goals'[28] are less inspiring and motivational. Moreover, financial success is seen as a consequence of purposeful action rather than an end in itself. By keeping it short and concise, the purpose can be communicated and remembered more easily. For assessing whether a firm has articulated its reason of existence effectively in a purpose statement, it can be helpful to look at the following questions:[29]

- Is it relevant for the target audiences including (potential) customers?
- Is it clear whose lives and/or businesses ought to be improved in some way?
- Is the purpose unique, and what would happen if we disappeared?
- Is our firm the rightful owner of that purpose? For instance, does the firm have certain capabilities to address a societal challenge more effectively and efficiently than others?

It is important that the purpose statement of a company is consistent with and complements its mission, vision, and values statements. In this regard, it must be recognized that becoming a company with corporate purpose may be challenging at first. It is often difficult to seamlessly combine the pursuit of economic as well as environmental and social goals. One reason for this is that a company has many stakeholder groups, who press for greater attention to the pursuit of their specific interests and demands. We discuss this further in Chapter 3. In addition, the simultaneous pursuit of economic and non-economic goals is difficult because it often requires different administrative practices, mindsets, and structures. Companies that do manage it stand to benefit, as discussed next.

## STRATEGIC FOCUS
### Purpose, social responsibility and sustainability

While corporate purpose, corporate social responsibility (CSR), and sustainability all have to do with a company's engagement with the challenges facing society, the three are distinct from one another (see Table 2.1). One way to distinguish between them is to compare the three in terms of their (1) conceptual anchors, (2) aims, and (3) loci of attention.

The notion of CSR has conceptual roots in moral philosophy and business ethics. The advocates of CSR hold the view that companies and managers have a moral duty to improve the well-being of all stakeholders, not just shareholders. The aim or goal of CSR is for practice and practitioners to live up to their moral responsibility. As regards attention locus, CSR is often discussed in relation to environmental, social, and governance (ESG) issues. Attention to CSR, it is hoped, will ensure that business activities and operations contribute to ESG improvements.

Business and sustainability discussions, in contrast, are often conceptually anchored in systems science. It is held that because economic and ecological systems are bound to one another, companies should strive to reduce the negative impact of business activity on the environment. The aim or goal in this case is to ensure harmony between these systems so that major shocks or system malfunctions are averted. The locus of attention, not surprisingly, centres on reducing negative environmental externalities through, say, a lower carbon footprint, or on increasing positive environmental externalities through, say, planting of forests.

The notion of corporate purpose is moored in business studies, economics, and sociology. A shift from an economics-dominated approach to one that incorporates insights from sociology underpins

**TABLE 2.1**   Comparing corporate purpose with CSR and sustainability

|  | CSR | Sustainability | Purpose |
|---|---|---|---|
| **Conceptual anchors:** | moral philosophy, business ethics | systems science, planetary boundaries | business studies, economics, sociology |
| **Overriding aim:** | organizations and managers must live up to their moral responsibility for ESG improvements | establishment of harmony between economic and ecological systems | combining the pursuit of economic and social ends for the good of society |
| **Loci of attention:** | business activities should contribute to improving ESG issues | business activities should have positive impact on the environment | core business should increase firm value and social and planetary peace and prosperity |

the current thinking about corporate purpose. The aim in this case is the establishment of an optimal balance between the pursuit of economic and social ends. Regarding the specific social ends to focus on, companies are left free to choose based on their circumstances, expertise, resources, and preferences. In practice, the locus of attention is often some subset of the SDGs announced by the UN General Assembly in 2015.

Common to corporate purpose, CSR, and sustainability is the belief that for-profit businesses should participate in tackling the challenges society faces. In this respect, a company can commit to corporate purpose, CSR, and sustainability in parallel. For example, an energy company whose corporate purpose leads it to fund research on greener forms of energy is committing in parallel to CSR and sustainability.

## Balancing the pursuit of economic and sustainability goals

It is reasonable to ask whether the pursuit of non-economic goals may be a distraction for for-profit companies. Could it potentially imperil their long-term economic performance or, at the very least, reduce short-term bottom-line results by increasing expenses? For example, the costs of lowering a factory's carbon emissions can reduce net earnings. Or, the pursuit of non-economic goals may conflict with customer expectations, thus hurting a company through reduced sales. To illustrate, airline companies face the dilemma of reducing $CO_2$-emissions further at the risk of losing customers because of higher ticket prices.

Currently, most companies seem to be focused single-mindedly on pursuing economic goals. The results of a broad cross-sectional survey of Dutch companies[30] suggest that even when companies have an explicitly stated corporate purpose, it may amount to nothing more than words on paper because little effort is made to translate the words into actions. One explanation for why companies pay limited attention to environmental and social goals may be that they are under constant pressure to show profits every quarter and every year, whereas addressing grand challenges and the achievement of societal objectives is a longer-term endeavour. Interestingly, this survey also indicates that greater emphasis on economic goals only correlates with lower levels of profitability.

There are many though who believe that the pursuit of economic and non-economic goals can in fact be mutually reinforcing.[31] Statements such as 'doing well by doing good' reflect this viewpoint. The underlying thinking here is that the pursuit of ends regarded as important by society can lead to a more positive company image, greater social legitimacy, better reputation, and superior products and services that are environment friendly. Belief in this logic seems to underpin the efforts of Danone, Philips, Unilever, and many other companies to vigorously pursue environmental and social goals.

One reason why a company's economic performance may get better because of its environmental and social initiatives is the impact of these on its reputation. To illustrate, Zewa, a Hungarian brand of Essity, a hygiene and health company, started a campaign to tackle gender stereotypes in hygiene and care tasks. They contributed to SDG 5 ('gender equality') by developing a video to raise awareness about how gender stereotypes play out in household tasks and the impact it has on children who see these stereotypes from a very young age. The video showed a school obstacle race, designed to reveal the existing, unfair balance of family hygiene tasks between men and women. Zewa's campaign reached nearly

35% of Hungary's population and offered a platform to facilitate a wider societal discussion.[32] This case shows how taking leadership on a sustainability issue led to enhanced reputation and brand recognition, and consequently to the growth of the company's customer base. Ultimately, this may lead to a larger market share and profits.

Furthermore, environmental and social initiatives can improve financial results by strengthening stakeholder reciprocation. When stakeholders see that a company is taking their interests into account, they trust the firm more and reciprocate. For example, when a company provides detailed financial information in annual reports, shareholders tend to trust the company more and remain loyal investors even in the wake of economic setbacks. Similarly, when employees see that their company is putting extra effort into creating a safe work environment, they are likely to experience a stronger sense of commitment to the company, which can enhance productivity. Governments tend to reward companies that act in socially responsible ways; for example, by granting them more procurement contracts or refraining from imposing costly regulations. And companies that take the needs and interests of communities living near their production facilities into account usually encounter less resistance in the form of protests and negative media coverage. All these examples of positive reciprocal behaviour from stakeholders should contribute to better financial results.

In addition, both economic and non-economic goals can be pursued if strategy is based on exploiting opportunities that mitigate environmental, financial, and social risk. Risk can be reduced directly and indirectly. Direct risk reduction occurs because many environmental and social initiatives such as pollution prevention practices, employee safety and health programs, and fair-trade policies are specifically designed to reduce harm to stakeholders. Oil spills, worker injuries and death, and child labour, which are damaging to stakeholders, also have a detrimental effect on financial performance. Indirect risk reduction occurs when a company develops closer relationships with existing stakeholders and more elaborate stakeholder relationships outside the core business domain. Such relationships can help companies detect changes and threats in the environment earlier than competitors. When information is not shared and received on a timely basis, it can lead to major problems. In 2015, for example, engineers at Volkswagen used software that wrongly reported emission levels of diesel cars. The company had to pay a huge fine and saw its reputation take a tumble. An important reason why the issue was not detected internally was the culture of weak stakeholder relationship with employees, due to which employees were afraid to question the targets set or to share bad news with their superiors (see the Volkswagen case in Chapter 17).

When a company simultaneously pursues economic and non-economic goals, the attainment of both is facilitated further by the strengthening of the company's innovative capacity. Because engaging with environmental and social issues is new for companies, it compels them to rethink their product, operations, and value chain. This can trigger the development of new capabilities and major innovations. For example, environmental and social innovation at Danone, a food products multinational, enabled the complete transformation and renewal of the company. The company launched different base-of-the-pyramid projects, which are projects that enable those living in poverty to have access to products and services (SDG 1: 'no poverty' and SDG 2: 'zero hunger') they need. Danone gave its managers the room to spend time in developing countries to collaborate with local communities. This led to the development of new individual skills, which ultimately became collective organizational capabilities. Danone has now developed unique expertise in creating low-cost solutions to serve marginalized communities.

## KEY DEBATE

### Perspectives on purpose

Companies face increasing public and political pressure to articulate a purpose. But we do not yet have complete consensus on what the concept of purpose means. In particular, three views regarding purpose can be distinguished:[33]

- <u>Cause-based purpose.</u> Materializing to address a problem that will bring positive societal change – e.g., Tesla's purpose 'to accelerate the world's transition to sustainable energy'.[34]
- <u>Competency-based purpose.</u> Seeking to earn profits by satisfying a market need using proprietary knowledge and expertise – e.g., the 'First move the world' purpose of Mercedes-Benz Cars.[35]
- <u>Culture-based purpose.</u> The drive with which a company does business – e.g., the purpose of Zappos 'to live and deliver WOW'.[36]

We can also draw a distinction between goal-based and duty-based purpose. Goal-based purpose may be viewed as 'an organizational objective defined and chosen by the firm itself without necessarily recognizing the wider role of corporations in society as moral actors'.[37] Proponents of this view often equate purpose with mission and vision as discussed earlier in this chapter. In contrast, the notion of duty-based purpose incorporates a moral and ethical stance. Purpose is framed as an environmental or social imperative that a company addresses because of the moral obligation to do so. In this view, companies exist in a society, they are at the service of society, and so they must contribute to the resolving of problems faced by society.

### Questions

1. Which one(s) of the viewpoints summarized above come closest to your perspective on purpose?
2. What difficulties do you envisage should a company wish to adopt a duty-based view of purpose?

## Diverging versus converging purpose

One potentially useful way to classify firms that pursue both economic and environmental and social (E&S) goals is shown in Figure 2.3. Some companies' purpose orientation is supported by a **dual-mode** approach. In this case, economic and E&S goals are pursued separately, at arm's length. While the core activities are geared towards achieving economic ends, peripheral activities are dedicated to achieving E&S ends. Examples include companies such as AstraZeneca and JP Morgan, which have set up charitable foundations to pursue E&S ends. The activities of the charitable foundations are not directly related to these companies' core business.

There are also companies in which *some* of the core activities are focused on pursuing both economic and E&S ends. When this is the case, a company has a **partial convergence** approach. Heineken is an example. With respect to the production and marketing of so-called sustainable beers, which are based on the use of less water during the brewing process, and non-alcoholic beers, the company pursues both economic and E&S ends. However, in relation to alcoholic beers, whereas Heineken's focus is squarely on the attainment of financial goals, the focus of Heineken's Africa Foundation is on the attainment of E&S ends. Deft management is needed to ensure that differences in orientation of the different core activities do not produce tensions and frictions.

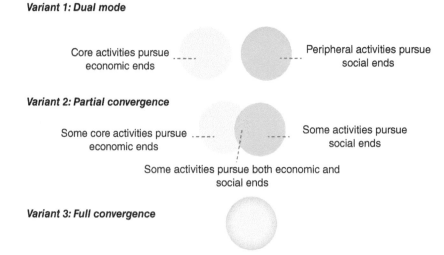

**Variant 1: Dual mode**

Core activities pursue economic ends

Peripheral activities pursue social ends

**Variant 2: Partial convergence**

Some core activities pursue economic ends

Some activities pursue social ends

Some activities pursue both economic and social ends

**Variant 3: Full convergence**

All activities pursue economic and social ends

**FIGURE 2.3**    Dual-mode, partial-convergence and full-convergence approaches

Source: based on Volberda et al. (2022)

Lastly, there are companies that have a **full convergence** approach, such that all core activities are oriented similarly towards pursuing economic as well as E&S ends. The pursuit of the two ends is seen to go hand-in-hand and to be mutually reinforcing. Philips, for example, pursues both economic and E&S ends through the provision of healthcare solutions that are based on digital technology.

## STRATEGIC FOCUS

### The purpose map[38]

Why do companies differ in regard to being purpose-driven? Why do some adopt a dual-mode approach to pursue economic and social ends, while others embrace a full-convergence approach? The factors responsible for the differences can be internal as well as external. Internally, important actors, such as the founder(s), CEO, executive and non-executive directors, and coalitions of employees can influence a company's purpose orientation. Moreover, organization-level factors, such as company history and culture, may affect the purpose-drive. Externally, the expectations of customers, shareholders, and the public would seem the most significant factors. In addition, governmental institutions play an important role by passing legislation related to ecological and societal themes.

The purpose map (Figure 2.4) shows that if we plot the internal and external factors on the vertical axis and the divergent versus convergent pursuit of economic and social ends on the horizontal axis, four types of companies can be identified:

- Reactive divergent type. Companies in which there are goal frictions and which face pressure from outside to become purpose-driven.
- Proactive divergent type. Companies in which there are goal frictions, but internal drivers encourage them to become purpose-driven.

- Reactive convergent type. Companies in which there is goal convergence and which face pressure from outside to become purpose-driven.
- Proactive convergent type. Companies in which there is goal convergence and internal drivers encourage them to be purpose-driven.

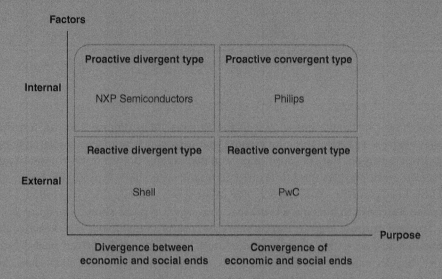

**FIGURE 2.4** Purpose map

Source: Volberda et al. (2022)

In proactive divergent type companies, CEOs and top management teams appear to play a particularly important role. At NXP Semiconductors, a CEO change was the catalyst that resulted in the company's shareholder-oriented focus changing to a broader interest in all stakeholders. In such companies, employees tend to value social goals and are involved in initiatives towards this end. In addition, corporate culture also drives the companies' purpose disposition. Their proactiveness notwithstanding, these companies may experience tension between the pursuit of economic and social ends. More focus on one may impact adversely the focus on the other, compelling a company to work on the realization of goal harmonization. As in the case of a proactive divergent type, internal drivers are an important force behind the drive of a proactive convergent type. Firms in this latter category, however, have figured out how to realize goal harmonization. By carefully crafting balanced policies, guidelines, and targets vis-à-vis their different stakeholders, they succeed in creating synergies between the pursuit of economic and social ends. Philips is one example of such a company. It is effective in combining profitability through the provision of healthcare solutions with achievement of social ends that have positive impact on the wellbeing of Philips' stakeholders and the wider community. In such companies, the pursuit of social ends may in fact contribute to the better achievement of economic ends. However, when the wellbeing of stakeholders or the wider community is negatively affected due to Philips' inadequate quality procedures in producing sleep apnea devices, it can lead to a decline in economic performance.

As regards a reactive divergent type, there is a strong external push compelling such a company to become purpose-driven. It may face pressure from governments and industry regulators to be more attentive to societal or ecological issues. In addition, it may be urged to pursue social ends by

*(Continued)*

its customers and shareholders. Given this type's focus on economic ends, it may see and experience the quest to combine achievement of economic ends with the achievement of social ends as a trade-off and hard to achieve. Shell is an example. Reactive divergent companies find it difficult to thread the needle of doing business in a societally acceptable way while keeping shareholders satisfied.

Reactive convergent types also experience pressure from outside to become purpose-driven. In contrast to the reactive divergent type, though, a reactive convergent company is able to harmonize the pursuit of economic and social ends. PwC is an example. Although the company's drive towards becoming purpose-driven has been compelled by external factors, including pressure from the Dutch Authority for Financial Markets, the company is comfortable in combing the pursuit of economic and social ends.

## Purpose journeys

The four types of companies shown in the Purpose Map (Figure 2.4) can transition to a different type over time. One may assume that companies would want to transition to the proactive convergent type because of potential synergies between the pursuit of economic and social ends. Markets tend to reward companies that have a profitable business model and also have positive social impact. The other types of companies can follow one of two **purpose journeys** to become a proactive convergent type as shown in Figure 2.5.

The first purpose journey can be characterized as an inside-out one. Reactive divergent companies may seize the initiative and embark on an internally driven push-for-purpose. Rather than let external forces decide their engagement with social ends, they can themselves formulate a purpose statement that fits with their history, culture, mission, vision, and values. As the next step, they can devote effort to putting in place structures, administrative systems, and governance practices that facilitate a balanced and harmonious pursuit of economic and social ends.[39] Randstad, the biggest private employment agency in the Netherlands, is on this purpose journey. Going back to the time of its founding by Frits Goldschmeding, Randstad has retained the idea of being valuable to society as part of its culture. In the light of the changing social context, Randstad has become more proactive in defining its purpose by drawing inspiration from the company's ethos and philosophy.

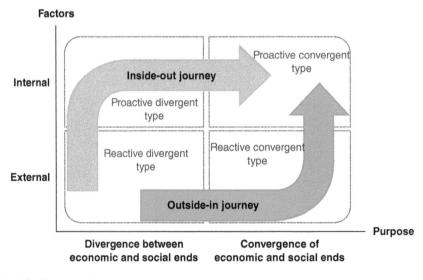

**FIGURE 2.5**   Purpose journeys

Source: Volberda et al. (2022)

The company is now working on developing a business model that can achieve both economic and social ends simultaneously.

The second purpose journey can be characterized as one that is outside-in. In this case, a reactive divergent company, driven by external factors, develops a business model that sets it up as a convergent type. The journey is effectively a pull-to-purpose by external motivators. Companies take this path when they respond to stakeholders' wishes and look for ways to attend to stakeholders' varied interests in a balanced fashion. In contrast to the first path, where the primary drivers for change were internal, in this path the alignment of purpose with internal values is only of secondary importance. ABN AMRO is on this purpose journey. Facing increasing scrutiny from customers, socially oriented investors, and industry financial analysts about the bank's commitment to sustainability, the company has started to work on changing aspects of its core businesses with a view to facilitate the achievement of both economic and social ends. In this context, conversations that were unlikely to take place in the past, such as whether to finance businesses in controversial industries (e.g., tobacco and weapons manufacturing), are quite the norm today.

## CRACK-THE-CASE

### H&M: Building a sustainable fast-fashion future

Source: © Basel Al seoufi (2021) / Shutterstock.

https://www.shutterstock.com/nl/image-photo/hm-fabric-24recycled-polyester-20-cotton-1987764668

Until 2017, H&M was considered the most valuable brand in the fast-fashion sector. However, it has lost its leadership to Zara, which has been gaining ground in terms of speed to market, customer average expenditure, and profitability. However, H&M is planning to reinvent itself and the fast-fashion sector, and sustainability (particularly, 'responsible consumption and production' – SDG 12, one of the SDGs espoused by the United Nations) is a key element of its repositioning. H&M's initiatives include the following:

<u>Building sustainability from the top.</u> H&M's strong commitment towards sustainability starts with the top managers. The company has created a Sustainability department,

*(Continued)*

nominating a head of sustainability who reports directly to the CEO of the group. Over 2300 people across H&M have sustainability as their core task. Sustainability is progressively becoming part of everyone's roles and is integrated into performance evaluation.

Recycled and sustainably sourced materials. At present, 64.5% of the firm's products are made from sustainable or recycled materials, but H&M aims to reach 100% by 2030. Today, H&M already uses cotton that is recycled, organic, or sourced through the Better Cotton Initiative (BCI). H&M also uses Agraloop Biofibre, a natural fibre made of food crop waste (in this case, oilseed hemp waste). Another H&M target is to decrease its environmental footprint. This will be achieved by applying innovative low environmental impact dyeing techniques, using biotechnology, plant-based pigments, and closed-loop systems, to die the textiles used in their production processes.

Collaborations and partnerships. H&M is building a collaborative network with suppliers who develop sustainable materials and use innovative dyeing techniques. H&M has worked with Colorifix – the first company to use a natural, biological process to produce and fix pigments into textiles. Similarly, H&M also advertises its collaboration with Agraloop's brand owner Circular Systems. H&M further announced a partnership with Maisie Williams, a British actress, who will lead a worldwide initiative towards a more sustainable fashion future, where reusing, remaking, and recycling are key to closing the fashion loop.

Closing the loop in fashion. To close the loop in fashion, H&M is developing two main initiatives: the Looop Machine and clothes renting service. The first initiative entails recycling old clothes into new ones through the Looop Machine. This is the world's first in-store recycling machine, turning old garments into new ones. No water or dye are used. H&M is also developing a clothes renting business in some locations. For instance, in its Sergels Torg flagship store in Stockholm, H&M made carefully selected dresses and skirts from their premium line available for renting. Another initiative has been launched in the US, where customers can rent a suit for a job interview; this is known as the ONE/SECOND/SUIT initiative.

Sensibilization and education. H&M wishes to educate and inspire customers with sustainability initiatives and empower them to make meaningful decisions, creating a community of Change Makers. Thinking about future generations, the brand launched a global initiative to help empower young civic, environmental, and social role models making progress on sustainability.[40] Through the initiative, H&M will tell the stories of young changemakers from around the world. As part of their sensibilization plan, H&M aims to connect digitally with younger generations. The H&M Looop Island was launched in Nintendo's hugely popular game Animal Crossing. H&M Looop Island has been designed with an overarching sustainable theme.

H&M hopes to change the fashion industry from a linear into a circular business model. Accordingly, it has developed a range of resources and capabilities to implement sustainable strategies. However, public opinion still believes that sustainability principles clash with fast-fashion business model principles, accusing the company of greenwashing. The question remains whether fast fashion will ever be profitable when implementing sustainable practices.

## Questions

1.  Are the fast-fashion business and sustainability compatible?
2.  Do H&M's sustainability initiatives reflect an inside-out purpose journey or an outside-in purpose journey?

# Strategic objectives

The mission, vision, values and purpose represent various types of overarching goals. They form the foundation for a firm's strategic objectives. Objectives and goals (including sub-goals) are described as '"targets" (or "end-points") which a firm is striving to achieve'.[41] **Strategic objectives** are specific goals that are applied to operationalize the mission, vision, values and purpose. They are also known as key performance indicators (KPIs).

Strategic objectives are more specific and relate to a more well-defined timeframe. This allows one to measure those objectives in order to control and monitor them. Setting those objectives is also associated with having SMART goals (which is made of the first letter of the following words), which are:

- **S**pecific (a precise indication of the desired outcome) or **s**tated (a concrete target);
- **M**easurable (it can be measured sufficiently if a target is achieved);
- **A**chievable (the reachability of the target);
- **R**elevant (the relevance of the target in a specific context) or **r**ealistic (the challenge is doable); and
- **T**argeted (factual specification) or **t**ime-oriented (temporal specification).

Strategic objectives provide guidance on how a firm can move towards or fulfil its mission, vision, values and purpose; they show a strong relationship with its performance results. In the light of the set objectives and observed performance, the firm can evaluate its strategic options and decide on the strategies that seem most appropriate. In the context of strategy formulation, strategic objectives form a bridge between the abstract essence of a firm and its operational strategies. The short-term direction-providing role strategic objectives play supplements the general, long-term direction provided by the foundational statements. They act as signposts that mark the path towards an envisaged future state of the firm.

Next to their role of providing orientation and guidance (e.g., for resource allocation decisions), goals have a control function to evaluate firm success (comparison of realized results with goals), and they act as a motivator for managers and employees (e.g., link incentives to goals). In the context of strategy implementation, whether a firm's strategies are effective can only be meaningfully assessed and corrective actions taken if there are clear objectives against which to evaluate performance. Strategic objectives, thus, are very important to the strategic management process.

Historically, strategic goals are mainly quantitative yardsticks (often financial ones), allowing a firm to judge strategic options and alternatives. Those yardsticks are, for instance, in the area of sales, market share, profitability, return on investments, and market capitalization (i.e., the total value of a firm's shares of stock). They may also include non-financial metrics such as employee and customer satisfaction. For instance, strategic objectives of the Volvo Group are about 'having leading customer satisfaction for all brands in their segments', 'be the most admired employer in our industry' and 'have industry leading profitability'. Volvo's objectives allow the firm to work towards its vision 'to be the most desired and successful transport and infrastructure solution provider in the world'.[42]

In recent times, with more attention being paid to company purpose, businesses have also started to formulate specific objectives connected to the sustainability goals they seek to pursue. Philips, for instance, has introduced non-financial strategic objectives that are aligned with its purpose, such as on sustainability and the number of human lives that are improved. NXP Semiconductors has formulated a goal that by 2030 30% of its workforce must be women. Danone has developed a set of nine strategic objectives for 2030 such as 'deliver superior sustainable profitable growth' (with priorities on accelerating growth, efficiency, and resource allocation) and 'impact people's health locally'.[43]

Those strategic objectives relate to its mission, vision, values and purpose regarding the acceleration of the food revolution by 2030 and each of those objectives are connected to at least one of the SDGs of the United Nations.

Companies often use the SDGs as a starting or reference point to identify which sustainability values or goals are most relevant for them. The SDGs were introduced in 2015 as a global call for action to address by 2030 the foremost environmental and social grand-challenges facing humanity. The 17 SDGs are depicted in Figure 2.6. They are 'no poverty' (SDG 1), 'zero hunger' (SDG 2), 'good health and wellbeing' (SDG 3), 'quality education' (SDG 4), 'gender equality' (SDG 5), 'clean water and sanitation' (SDG 6), 'affordable and clean energy' (SDG 7), 'decent work and economic growth' (SDG 8), 'industry, innovation, and infrastructure' (SDG 9), 'reduced inequalities' (SDG 10), 'sustainable cities and communities' (SDG 11), 'responsible consumption and production' (SDG 12), 'climate action' (SDG 13), 'life below water' (SDG 14), 'life on land' (SDG 15), 'peace, justice and strong institutions' (SDG 16), and 'partnerships for the goals' (SDG 17).

**FIGURE 2.6**   The 17 Sustainable Development Goals (SDGs)[44]

Source: United Nations (2023). https://www.un.org/sustainabledevelopment/. The content of this publication has not been approved by the United Nations and does not reflect the views of the United Nations or its officials or Member States.

An increasing number of companies embrace ESG goals in addition to the pursuit of profit. Most of these non-financial targets relate to sustainability targets (i.e., the E for 'environmental'). The more social targets often relate to employee satisfaction, diversity, or safety (the S for 'social'). The 'G' in ESG goals refers to 'governance', such as characteristics of a firm's decision-making and compensation of senior executives. The ESG goals can be used to screen investments and to encourage a firm's responsible behaviour. Facebook's misuse of data and Volkswagen's emission test scandal illustrate cases of a strong emphasis on profitability at the expense of ESG goals.

The overall corporate strategic objectives can be further translated 'down' into the organization: to specific divisions, functions (e.g., human resources, marketing, procurement, and production), and even at the level of individual organizational members. Such sub-goals further clarify the relevance of overarching goals, and they are typically more specific and reflect the day-to-day activities of the particular group more closely than their overriding goals. The implications of Heineken's overarching goals can be found, for instance, in 'greening' its production processes and in its marketing campaigns. The beer brewer aims to increase traffic safety by including former Formula 1 drivers in its 'when you drive, never drink'-campaigns. With its brand Tecate the company actively highlighted the issue of domestic violence in Mexico.[45]

In setting up such a system of goals, it is important that a sub-goal (let's say in human resources) contributes to achieve the overriding corporate strategic goals. Ideally, such goal complementarity (also known as goal harmony) should also apply between various sub-goals. For example, a harmony might be found between the goals of reducing production costs and reducing sales prices. However, there are occasions that various goals conflict (also known as *goal competition*), whether it is deliberate or not. For instance, goals on reducing advertising expenditures and increasing the customer base may conflict. Such goal conflicts can be designed to encourage employees to think out-of-the-box. In case of goal neutrality (goal indifference), the realization of one goal does not have an impact on realizing other goals, at least initially. This may apply, for instance, to the goal of introducing a certain language as the corporate language.

Strategic goals have profound implications for the design of a firm's strategy – for instance, whether it wishes to pursue a profit or growth strategy and where it wishes to operate (and where not). In addition, they serve as motivations for organizational members in executing specific strategies. Having the right set of strategic goals in place also allows a firm to evaluate the success of a certain strategy, something which may drive a firm towards a different strategy.

## CLOSING CASE

### Icebreaker: A new direction?

Source: © Kym McLeod (2019) / Shutterstock.

*(Continued)*

As a true New Zealand success story, the Icebreaker tale has been told many times. Founder Jeremy Moon's passion for merino wool began in 1994 when farmer Brian Brackenridge showed him prototypes of merino wool underwear, dubbed Ice Breakers. The 24-year-old recent commerce and marketing graduate was intrigued, and after wearing them, was hooked on the lightweight, silky soft natural fiber. He quit his job, mortgaged his house to buy the business concept from Brackenridge, and locked himself in his room to figure out how to build the company. His first step was to understand the fiber better – 'I started staying on merino sheep farms, and I was amazed at the relationship between the families and the land, and the animals. There was this symbiotic relationship going on. So I had to put a meaning around that garment'. That meaning formed the centre of the company: symbiosis and kinship with nature, essentially pulling together what New Zealand is known for.[46] This focus has evolved into the following vision statement: 'Icebreaker is about ice-breaking: we explore the relationship between people and nature. It's about kinship, not conquering. Nature is our hero'.[47] The current purpose of the organization is articulated as 'Driven by the belief that nature has the solutions, we provide natural performance alternatives to synthetic based apparel to create a healthier more sustainable future for our species and the planet.'[48]

The product was initially made by local suppliers, but the first production runs were far from perfect. One batch turned out a strange yellow, which Moon tried to sell as 'buttercup' colour. It also became evident that the raw merino wool varied in quality. In response to these production issues, Moon established close, long-term partnerships with farmers that produced New Zealand's best quality merino wool. The relationships with suppliers are of the upmost importance. 'We work with 180 families who run merino […] there are approximately 500,000 merino that are part of our team.'[49]

Icebreaker began exporting in 1998 and by 2002, international sales exceeded sales in New Zealand for the first time. Initially the company targeted Europe, locating potential distributors by exhibiting at a large international trade show for sports equipment and sportswear in Germany. The distributors, who also stocked other complementary brands, sold to specialist sports equipment and clothing retailers. As of 2022, the company has partnerships with third-party distributors in Chile, Israel, Japan, the Netherlands, South Africa, Taiwan, and the UK. As international sales scaled, in the early 2000s, production was moved to China. This move initially raised some criticisms about whether large-scale international manufacturing was at odds with Icebreaker's natural, sustainable image.[50] However, since these early days, Icebreaker has worked to balance the economic advantages of international manufacturing and remaining true to values, with significant emphasis on supply chain transparency and long-term relationships with manufacturers,[51] mirroring the relationships formed with wool suppliers.

In 2002, Icebreaker entered the US market by signing a deal with a manufacturer of a non-competing outdoor clothing line, who undertook to establish and sell Icebreaker as an independent brand. Sales were disappointing, however, and in 2006 Icebreaker set up its own subsidiary in the US, selling to retailers. To help boost their efforts, Icebreaker hired the head of sales for Adidas in the US, and in their German subsidiary they hired the head of North Face for Europe. Its international success soon gained the attention of international players, with Icebreaker being sold in 2018 to the American retail giant VF corporation, whose other brands include The North Face, Timberland, and SmartWool. Moon said: 'Our partnership with VF provides us with the largest platform in the world to tell our story, access new markets and reach new consumers at an accelerated pace'.[52]

With success and growth came increased challenges to maintaining the core values, however. The new parent company, VF Corporation, has recently been linked to unethical labour practices,[53] while Icebreaker had spent the 2017 year improving value chain practices, being awarded the Ethical Fashion Report's 'most improved brand' award, moving the brand into number 5 of 407 global brands for ethical practices.[54] Icebreaker described the key improvement as follows: 'The big learning for us last year was that it wasn't enough just to be confident in our own processes, we needed to get better at talking to our customers about our supply chain'.[55] Competition was also becoming challenging, with merino products readily available, including from top athletics apparel brands Adidas and Nike. These companies have far greater capacity and distribution reach, and capital to invest in design capabilities. What they do not have currently are the relationships with New Zealand merino farmers. New Zealand merino wool is still considered the premium material.

## Questions

1. How are Icebreaker's vision and purpose connected to its home country, and to its entrepreneurial development story?
2. How can Icebreaker retain its core values, and work towards sustainable practices, within the context of global growth and competition?

## Summary

- Mission, vision, values, purpose, and strategic objectives are foundational statements, which enable strategic management. They provide decision-makers with the necessary framework for consistent strategy formulation and implementation.
- The mission concept is concerned with the business domain of a company, i.e. what lines of business, operations, and activities are within the scope of the company, and which are not. A mission statement thus delineates a company's competitive arena.
- The notion of vision concerns the aspirations of a company. Accordingly, a company's vision statement discloses the long-term ambitions and desires of a company. Vision statements can enthuse and inspire.
- The corporate purpose concept captures the idea that a company exists for pursuing economic goals for owners or shareholders, as well as for pursuing environmental and social goals considered important by society. A purpose statement identifies the specific environmental and social goals a company has set itself.
- The drivers to formulate or alter a corporate purpose can be located within and outside of the firm. Such a variety in the drivers for purpose (mainly internal versus external drivers) and the purpose approach (duality versus convergence in societal and economic goals) form the dimensions of the purpose map. A transition from one quadrant in the purpose map to another is called a purpose journey. Two dominant purpose trajectories (purpose journeys) are the inside-out journey (push for purpose) and the outside-in journey (pull for purpose).

- Values refer to the ideals that guide conduct. In a company, these guiding ideals pertain to the ethics and morals that are inviolable and the aesthetics and customs that underpin the business. When expressed in a written statement, they guide strategic management.
- Strategic objectives are targets which a firm is striving to achieve in order to fulfil its mission, vision, values and purpose. They operationalize the vision, mission, values and purpose in specific targets (financial and non-financial ones) with a well-defined timeframe to enable strategy formulation and implementation. Corporate-level objectives typically provide the framework for setting business-level objectives, which in turn form the backdrop for setting functional- and individual-level objectives.

## Review questions

1. What are the key characteristics of mission, vision, and purpose statements?
2. How do mission, vision, value statements and purpose complement one another?
3. When is a values statement more likely to play an effective role in strategy formulation and implementation?
4. How do strategic objectives relate to foundational statements and what is their relevance for strategic management?

## Discussion questions

1. The notion of corporate purpose has received a lot of attention in recent years. Why is this the case? Where do you stand as regards the debate about the role of companies in society?
2. Mission, vision, purpose, and values statements, and purpose are viewed as the foundation of strategic management. However, not all companies have these foundational elements of strategy in a written form. What are the potential pros and cons of formulating and implementing strategy without explicit foundational statements.

## EXPERIENTIAL EXERCISES

Imagine you are the strategy officer of a HealthTech firm of your choice. Try to respond as best as you can to the following questions:

1. What should the mission, vision, values, and purpose of the firm look like at the firm?
2. In the light of the foundational statements you have formulated, identify two corporate-level objectives to be achieved in a two-year period.
3. What strategies would you recommend for the firm?
4. In which quadrant of the purpose map would you place the firm and why? Which purpose journey would be appropriate for the company and why?

# Further reading

Collins, J.C. and Porras, J.I. (2005), *Built to Last: Successful Habits of Visionary Companies*. New York, NY: HarperCollins.

Gartenberg, C., Prat, A. and Serafeim, G. (2019) 'Corporate purpose and financial performance', *Organization Science*, 30 (1): 1–18.

Gulati, R. (2022), *Deep Purpose: The Heart and Soul of High-Performance Companies*. New York, NY: Harper Business.

Henderson, R. (2021), *Reimagining Capitalism in a World on Fire*. New York, NY: PublicAffairs.

Mayer, C. (2021) 'The future of the corporation and the economics of purpose', *Journal of Management Studies*, 58 (3): 887–901.

# Endnotes (references)

1. Volberda, H.W., Sidhu, J.S., Vishwanathan, P., Heij, K. and Kashanizadeh, Z. (2022) *De winst van purpose: Hoe ondernemingen het verschil kunnen maken*. Amsterdam: Mediawerf.

2. Fromm, J. (2019) 'The purpose series: Ben & Jerry's authentic purpose', *Forbes*, June 4. https://www.forbes.com/sites/jefffromm/2019/06/04/the-purpose-series-ben-jerrys-authentic-purpose/ (accessed June 7, 2023).

3. Fromm (2019)

4. Fromm (2019)

5. Abell, D.F. (2006) 'The future of strategy is leadership', *Journal of Business Research*, 59 (3): 310–14. p. 312.

6. Drucker, P.F. (1974) *Management: Tasks, Responsibilities, Practices*. New York, NY: Harper & Row.

7. BBC (2019) 'Mission, values and public purposes', *bbc.com*. https://www.bbc.com/aboutthebbc/governance/mission (accessed June 7, 2023).

8. Abell, D.F. (1980). *Defining the business: The starting point of strategic planning*. Englewood Cliffs, NJ: Prentice Hall. Sidhu, J.S. (2004) 'Business-domain definition and performance: An empirical study', *SAM Advanced Management Journal*, 69 (4): 40–6.

9. L'Oréal (n.d.) 'Create the beauty that moves the world', *loreal.com*, https://www.loreal.com/en/group/about-loreal/our-purpose/ (accessed June 7, 2023).

10. Collins, J.C. and Porras, J.I. (1996) 'Building your company's vision', *Harvard Business Review*, 74 (5): 65–77.

11. Kotter, J.P. (1996) *Leading Change*. Cambridge, MA: Harvard Business School Press.

12. Collins and Porras (1996)

13. Nonaka, I. and Zhu, Z. (2012) *Pragmatic Strategy: Eastern Wisdom, Global Success*. Cambridge: Cambridge University Press.

14. Interview with Steve Jobs, YouTube video fragment on core values (published on September 29, 2019) is accessible through: https://www.youtube.com/watch?v=JHXp1kTZMys&t.

15. Honda (2023), *About us: Honda Services & Quality Cars*. https://web.archive.org/web/20230701172637/https://www.honda.com/about (accessed July 27, 2023).

16. Kashanizadeh, Z., Volberda, H.W., Vishwanathan, P., Sidhu, J.S. and Heij, K. (2022). On becoming a purpose-driven firm: practices and drivers of corporate purpose, *EURAM Annual Conference 2022*, June 16, Winterthur.

17. BASF (2023) 'Who we are', *basf.com*. https://www.basf.com/global/en/who-we-are/strategy.html (accessed June 7, 2023).

18. TUI (2023) 'Vision and values', tui.com. https://careers.tuigroup.com/our-dna/tui-values (accessed June 7, 2023)

19. Volberda et al. (2022).

20. Protix (2023) 'Values', protix.eu. https://protix.eu/protix-journey/values (accessed June 7, 2023).

21. Henderson, R.M. and Van den Steen, E. (2015) 'Why do firms have "purpose"? The firm's role as a carrier of identity and reputation', *American Economic Review*, 105 (5): 326–30.; Mayer, C. (2021) 'The future of the corporation and the economics of purpose', *Journal of Management Studies*, 58 (3): 887–901.

22. Chouinard, Y. (2023) 'Earth is now our only shareholder', *patagonia.com*. https://eu.patagonia.com/gb/en/ownership/ (accessed June 7, 2023).

23. Chouinard (2023)

24. Fitzsimmons, A.B., Qin, Y.S. and Heffron, E.R. (2022) 'Purpose vs mission vs vision: Persuasive appeals and components in corporate statements', *Journal of Communication Management*, 26 (2): 207–19.

25. Knowles, J., Hunsaker, B.T., Grove, H. and James, A. (2022) 'What is the purpose of your purpose? Your *why* may not be what you think it is', *Harvard Business Review*, March–April: 36–43. p. 38.

26. ABN AMRO (2023) 'Our purpose and strategy', *abnamro.com*. https://www.abnamro.com/en/about-abn-amro/purpose-and-strategy (accessed June 7, 2023).

27. Phillips (2023) 'About us', *phillips.com*. https://www.philips.com/a-w/about.html (accessed June 7, 2023).

28. Bart, C.K. and Baetz, M.C. (1998) 'The relationship between mission statements and firm performance: An exploratory study', *Journal of Management Studies*, 35 (6): 823–53. p. 846.

29. Blount, S. and Leinwand, P. (2019) 'Why are we here?: If you want employees who are more engaged and productive, give them a purpose – one concretely tied to your customers and your strategy', *Harvard Business Review*, 11: 1–9.

30. Volberda et al. (2022)

31. See, for instance, Henderson, R.M. (2021) 'Changing the purpose of the corporation to rebalance capitalism', *Oxford Review of Economic Policy*, 37 (4): 838–50; Vishwanathan, P., van Oosterhout, H., Heugens, P.P., Duran, P. and van Essen, M. (2020) 'Strategic CSR: A concept building meta-analysis', *Journal of Management Studies*, 57 (2): 314–50.

32. Nudging for Good (2019) 'Awards finalists 2019', September 13. http://www.nudgingforgood.com/2019/09/13/hygiene-has-no-gender-carewelllivewelltogether/ (accessed July 19, 2023).

33. Knowles et al. (2022)

34. Clifford (2019) 'Elon Musk: This is the 'why' of Tesla', *CNBC*, 4 February 2019. https://www.cnbc.com/2019/02/04/elon-musk-on-the-why-and-purpose-behind-tesla.html (accessed July 17, 2023).

35. Mercedes-Benz (n.d.) 'The purpose of Mercedes-Benz cars', *mercedes-benz.com*. https://www.mercedes-benz.com.vn/en/passengercars/the-brand/mbv.pi.html/the-brand/mbv/journey/vision/purpose (accessed June 7, 2023).

36. Zappos (2023) 'About us', *zappos.com*. https://www.zappos.com/c/about (accessed June 7, 2023).

37. George, G., Haas, M.R., McGahan, A.M., Schillebeeckx, S.J.D. and Tracey, P. (2021) 'Purpose in the for-profit firm: A review and framework for management research', *Journal of Management*. 49 (6): 1–29. p. 3.

38. Volberda et al. (2022)

39. Battilana, J., Obloj, T., Pache, A.C. and Sengul, M. (2022) 'Beyond shareholder value maximization: Accounting for financial/social trade-offs in dual-purpose companies', *Academy of Management Review*, 47: 237–58.

40. H&M (2021) 'H&M launches global initiative to support today's real role models: kids', press release April 27, https://about.hm.com/news/general-news-2021/h-m-launches-global-initiative-to-support-today-s-real-role-mode.html (accessed July 27, 2023).

41. Bart and Baetz (1998: p. 829)

42. Volvo (2023) 'Strategy', *volvo.com*. https://www.volvogroup.com/en/about-us/strategy.html (accessed June 7, 2023).

43. Danone (2018) 'Extra-financial performance towards Danone's 2030 goals', *danone.com*. https://iar2018.danone.com/performance/extra-financial-performance-towards-danones-2030-goals/impact-peoples-health-locally/ (accessed June 7, 2023).

44. United Nations (2023) 'The 17 goals', https://sdgs.un.org/goals (accessed July 27, 2023). See the following link for a figure suitable for print and web, as provided by the United Nations: https://www.un.org/sustainabledevelopment/news/communications-material/

45. Heineken (2017) 'TECATE, for a Mexico without violence against women', *thebeinekencompany.com*, December 14. https://www.theheinekencompany.com/our-sustainability-story/our-progress/case-studies/tecate-mexico-without-violence-against-women (accessed June 7, 2023).

46. New Zealand Story (2022) *Building a Nation of Storytellers*. www.nzstory.govt.nz (accessed June 7, 2023).

47. Icebreaker (2023a) 'Philosophy', *icebreaker.com*. www.icebreaker.com/en-nz/our-story/philosophy.html (accessed June 7, 2023).

48. Icebreaker (2023a)

49. Osborne, B. (2015) 'Behind the brand: Icebreaker's Jeremy Moon', *mountainlifemedia.ca*, December 28. https://www.mountainlifemedia.ca/2015/08/behind-the-brand-icebreakers-jeremy-moon (accessed June 7, 2023).

50. Burstyn, B.S. (2006) 'Buy Kiwi-made', *Scoop*, August 29. www.scoop.co.nz/stories/HL0608/S00351.htm (accessed June 7, 2023).

51. Icebreaker (2022b) 'Supply chain', *icebreaker.com*. www.icebreaker.com/en-us/our-story/supply-chain.html (accessed June 7, 2023).

52. VFC (2017) 'VF Corporation announces definitive agreement to acquire Icebreaker®, a New Zealand-based outdoor and sport apparel brand', *vfc.com*, November 2. https://www.vfc.com/investors/news-events-presentations/press-releases/detail/1636/vf-corporation-announces-definitive-agreement-to-acquire (accessed June 7, 2023).

53. Underhill, J. and Mandow, N. (2018) 'Icebreaker buyer used sweatshop labour', *Newsroom*, May 4. www.newsroom.co.nz/2018/05/03/107106/icebreaker-buyer-used-sweatshop-labour (accessed June 7, 2023).

54. RNZ (2018) 'Kiwi companies in best and worst of ethical fashion report', *RNZ*, April 18, www.rnz.co.nz/news/business/355393/kiwi-companies-in-best-and-worst-of-ethical-fashion-report (accessed June 7, 2023).

55. RNZ (2018)

## Acknowledgements

The authors thank Pushpika Vishwanathan, Omid Aliasghar and Fiona Hurd for their contribution to this chapter.

## Key terms

**Corporate purpose** – the environmental and social goals a company has set for itself

**Dual-mode approach** – the company's core activities pursue economic goals, while non-economic goals are pursued through peripheral activities

**Full-convergence approach** – the company's core activities seek to pursue economic as well as non-economic goals

**Mission** – definition of the business domain of the company, which delineates its product(s), technology, and market scope

**Partial convergence approach** – company in which only a part of its core activities are focused on pursuing both economic and non-economic goals

**Purpose journey** – the path a company can follow in transitioning from one purpose type to another on the purpose map

**Strategic objectives** – specific (financial and non-financial) targets that a firm strives to achieve

**Values** – the ideals that guide strategic management of the company

**Vision** – aspirations and desires concerning the future state of the company

# 3
# STAKEHOLDERS AND CORPORATE GOVERNANCE

## LEARNING OBJECTIVES

After reading this chapter, you should be able to:

- distinguish between different stakeholder types and assess their power;
- understand the challenges of balancing the pursuit of interests of different stakeholders;
- articulate and discuss the importance of effective corporate governance for value creation;
- recognize the limitations of internal and external mechanisms of corporate governance;
- acknowledge current trends in corporate governance.

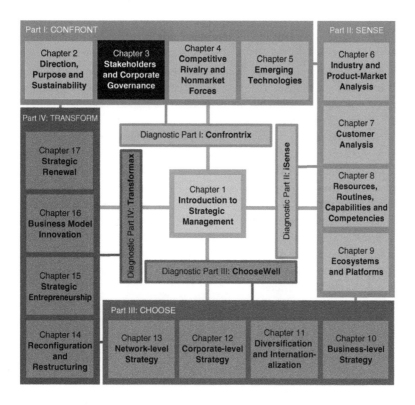

## OPENING CASE

Source: © Gofra (2021) / Shutterstock.

### Tesla's Berlin Gigafactory hits speed bumps[1]

Elon Musk, one of the wealthiest people in the world in 2022, overcame a significant hurdle in March that year. His company, Tesla Inc., finally began operations at its Berlin factory. Out of excitement, Musk started dancing in the assembly hall filled with press and employees to celebrate the opening of the Berlin plant that had been delayed by almost a year. This delay cost Tesla precious time as it tried to hold on to its lead in the electric vehicle segment. The delay was not due to Tesla's market strategy, resulting instead from stakeholder issues involving environmental groups and the local government. Did Tesla fail to choose an appropriate approach to deal with its stakeholders – or was a delay of this magnitude inevitable?

In early 2022, Tesla's stock market value exceeded $1 trillion. This made the former Texas-based startup more valuable than its five largest competitors combined. Yet the road to this success has not been a paved one. In 2007, Tesla began delivering its first vehicle through a production contract with Lotus Group, which would handle the vehicle's manufacturing minus the electric drivetrain. By 2012, Tesla had moved production in-house, and in 2016 Tesla began production at its first large factory: Gigafactory 1. The factory is based in Nevada and employed roughly 7,000 workers as of 2019. Building the factory and starting production played out to be a strenuous task. When discussing the scaling up of production for its Model 3 car at the factory, Musk described the process as 'production hell'. Car manufacturing processes have proven to be some of the most optimized and complex production processes. Musk's lofty production targets only further increased the pressure. Yet, after months of hardship, Tesla succeeded in rapidly scaling up its production at its Nevada factory. Once the factory was operational, Tesla shifted its attention to the next move: building additional factories overseas.

The first overseas vehicle manufacturing expansion came in 2019 when Tesla opened its Shanghai Gigafactory. Then later that year, in November, Musk unveiled his plans for a Gigafactory in Berlin. The manufacturing plant was set to supply the European market with its popular Model Y car. German officials had convinced Tesla that it was the ideal location for its European Gigafactory, beating out other nations such as the Netherlands, over which Germany had certain advantages such as access to relevant knowledge and talent due to its powerful car manufacturing sector.

The discussion surrounding Tesla's Berlin Gigafactory initially centered around the fact that it would be in the backyard of its German competitors: Volkswagen, Mercedes-Benz, and BMW. Yet, headlines would soon shift to concerns outside Tesla's competitive landscape. Environmentalists warned of the factory's dangers to local biodiversity and groundwater levels. Musk disregarded these concerns initially as the German government cleared environmental concerns in May 2020. Following the decision, Tesla began clearing the forest and commencing production. Later, in August 2021, Musk was again asked about the factory's threat to groundwater levels by reporters. Musk burst out in laughter and called the notion 'completely wrong' as he pointed his finger at the surrounding water areas.[2] Yet, six months later, Tesla was in a German court over the factory's threat to local water supplies. While Tesla eventually emerged victorious the lawsuit took up precious time for the car manufacturer.

Almost a year after its intended opening date, Gigafactory Berlin finally opened in March 2022. Yet the fight may not be over as environmental activists continue to target the factory, and the powerful unions in Germany are gearing up for more confrontation over labour conditions.

### Questions

1.  Which type of stakeholder did Tesla overlook?
2.  What actions could Tesla have undertaken to better handle the factory opening?

# Introduction

As indicated by the opening case of this chapter, stakeholders potentially have the power to disrupt a company's strategy and thus scuttle its efforts to create and sustain competitive advantage. To have stakeholders' support, companies need to meet their expectations and further their interests – after all, companies exist to serve the stakeholders. While Chapter 2 highlights that companies' purpose is to pursue profits for shareholders as well as to create value for stakeholders, in Chapter 3, we take stock of the different types of stakeholders that companies have, and their potential influence on their strategic decisions. On reading this chapter, you will develop appreciation of the different types of stakeholders and their power in order to successfully manage them. The power of stakeholders refers to their ability to influence the mission, vision, purpose, and strategic objectives of a company. The chapter recognizes that effective stakeholder management is crucial for successfully confronting the threats and opportunities in the competitive landscape.

This chapter will also help build your grasp of corporate governance, which refers to the oversight system of the executive function as it manages a company on behalf of its shareholders and stakeholders. The value of good corporate governance is perhaps best illustrated by referring to well-known failures of corporate governance, such as the downfall of Enron at the turn of the century, the 2007–2009 global financial crisis, and the 2022 collapse of the FTX cryptocurrency exchange. Within companies, the most potent mechanism of corporate governance is the board of directors, which monitors and supports executives as they formulate and implement strategy. Corporate boards have the power to question, discuss, and vote on the actions proposed by the executive function, and they have the duty to evaluate executives, set executive compensation, and replace executives when an incumbent is dismissed or retires. Besides developing your knowledge of the shareholder and stakeholder governance models, the chapter will also contribute to your understanding of the different internal and external mechanisms of corporate governance. The chapter further discusses the reasons why governance systems vary across nations and how corporate governance is evolving worldwide as our collective understanding of companies' purpose changes, and shareholder and stakeholder activism increases.

# Stakeholders

Every company has individuals and groups who have a stake in it and with whom it has exchange relationships.[3] The exchange relationships imply mutual interdependence, such that a company relies on its stakeholders for resources and legitimacy that enable the company's existence, operations, and growth; the stakeholders, in turn, expect the company to fulfil their goals and expectations. **Stakeholders**, who have a decisive influence on the mission, purpose, objectives, and strategies of a company, support it when the company's conduct and performance meet their expectations. When expectations are not met, however, stakeholders seek to effectuate change, as the Tesla opening case illustrates. As stakeholders are important to a company, their expectations and interests must be considered when making strategic decisions (see Figure 3.1). Herein lies a major challenge though – the wishes of different stakeholder groups can be contradictory. Therefore, as part of careful **stakeholder management**, it is important for a company's executives to prioritize stakeholder groups by identifying the ones with more power and respective expectations and find mutually acceptable solutions in order to meet them and avoid frictions.

**FIGURE 3.1**    Stakeholder groups

The different groups or types of company stakeholders can be divided into two broad categories: primary and secondary stakeholders.[4] Primary stakeholders are those who have direct exchange relationships or transactions with a company. Thus, customers, employees, and suppliers are usually a company's primary stakeholders. Secondary stakeholders are those who have indirect exchange relationships or transactions with a company. For example, the communities in the physical neighbourhood of a company's facilities and the government indirectly contribute with resources to the company and are affected by its actions. The primary stakeholders of a company can be further divided into those who are internal and those who are external. As shown in Figure 3.2, examples of internal primary stakeholders include employees and shareholders; examples of external primary stakeholders include banks, which provide credits and loans, as well as customers and suppliers. While

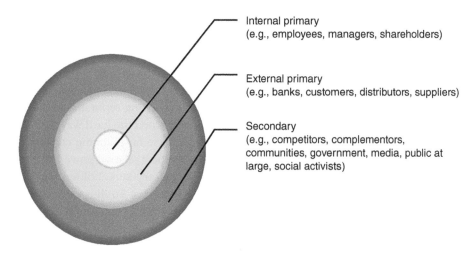

Internal primary
(e.g., employees, managers, shareholders)

External primary
(e.g., banks, customers, distributors, suppliers)

Secondary
(e.g., competitors, complementors,
communities, government, media, public at
large, social activists)

**FIGURE 3.2**  Primary and secondary stakeholders

the shareholder-stakeholder bifurcation is sometimes pedagogically handy, shareholders are in fact a type of stakeholder.

It is possible that individuals may belong to different stakeholder groups shown in Figure 3.2. For example, managers may also be shareholders in a company, or customers may also be employees of a company. Furthermore, it is not necessary that one or more of the stakeholder groups will usually be the most powerful, and hence the most important from a stakeholder management perspective. Although companies have tended to pay the most attention to their shareholders and the least attention to social activists,[5] this is now gradually changing. The most important stakeholder groups may vary across companies, situations, and contexts. For example, local communities affected by air and noise pollution levels may be a very important stakeholder group for Heathrow Airport but not for Barclays Bank. Companies, therefore, need to ascertain on an individual basis which of their stakeholders groups' expectations to prioritize, with a view to incorporate these accordingly into the company's strategic decisions.

## Stakeholder management

As a firm has many primary and secondary stakeholders, it can be arduous for it to accommodate fully the expectations and interests of all stakeholders at a single point in time, or in relation to a single strategy or event. Companies usually prioritize the demands of their various stakeholders serially. Thus, which stakeholders to pay attention to at each point in time is an important issue for companies. Primary stakeholders, despite having a direct exchange relationship with a company, may not necessarily line up as the ones whose demands must get priority over those of secondary stakeholders. As the Tesla case indicates, secondary stakeholders may at times need more attention than primary stakeholders. Secondary stakeholders can obstruct a company's plans, directly or indirectly, when they perceive a company's actions to be at odds with their objectives. As an example of direct obstruction, secondary stakeholders can file a legal claim against the company. As an example of indirect obstruction, they can taint the reputation of the company. In 1996, the magazine *Life* published a report on child labour at factories that Nike did business with. The report included a photo of a 12-year-old Pakistani child sewing a Nike soccer ball, which triggered international outrage and resulted in long-lasting reputational damage for Nike.[6] Nike, the world's largest sportswear manufacturer, learned the hard way that ignoring secondary stakeholders, social activists in this case, can have far-reaching consequences.

To prioritize stakeholders, it is important to consider their relative power. The sources of power of stakeholders may differ. For instance, secondary stakeholders may control strategic resources that are essential for a company's operations. To illustrate, social activists may determine whether a company enjoys moral legitimacy or not, a key resource for a company to attract the support of other primary and secondary stakeholders. As another illustration, product, service, or network complementors may determine whether a company benefits from critical network resources as in the case of e-commerce companies like Alibaba and eBay and social media companies like LinkedIn and TikTok. As regards primary stakeholders, their power may reside in the knowledge they possess, as in the case of employees, or their willingness to engage with a company's products, as in the case of customers. Like secondary stakeholders, primary stakeholders can also have a disruptive effect. For example, following the killing of more than 20 people by a gunman, Walmart's employees staged a walkout to pressure the company to cease selling firearms.[7] Besides the power of stakeholders, a company should also consider the urgency of satisfying a particular stakeholder group.[8] To illustrate, in today's socio-political climate, automobile manufacturers such as Hyundai and Mahindra may find it more urgent to address

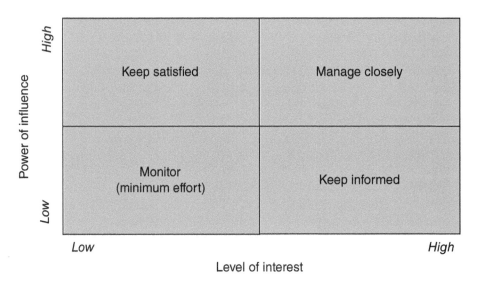

**FIGURE 3.3**   Power-interest matrix

the demands of secondary stakeholders centering on sustainability as compared to the demands of primary stakeholders centering on higher product quality and profit margins.

A tool that companies can potentially use to manage their stakeholders is stakeholder mapping. A well-known way for doing so is the *power-interest matrix* (also referred to as the power-interest grid as shown in Figure 3.3). This entails a simple two-dimensional visualization of whether the power of a stakeholder group is low or high and whether the urgency of attending to a stakeholder group's expectations is low or high. Having mapped different stakeholders on the power-urgency dimensions, the company can then decide the best course of action in terms of stakeholder engagement. This last can take different forms ranging from incorporating stakeholders' wishes directly into the company's strategy, to relationship-enhancing dialogues that keep stakeholders informed and engaged with the company. In addition, a company's corporate governance system, the topic we turn to next, should seek to keep an eye on and address stakeholder expectations and needs.

A complementary approach to the power-interest matrix regarding stakeholder mapping is the materiality matrix. This matrix illustrates the 'materiality' of themes, meaning the extent to which they impact a business and its stakeholders (see Figure 3.4). Figure 3.5 shows Randstad's materiality matrix. In the diagnostic chapter *Confrontrix* we will further discuss the materiality matrix.

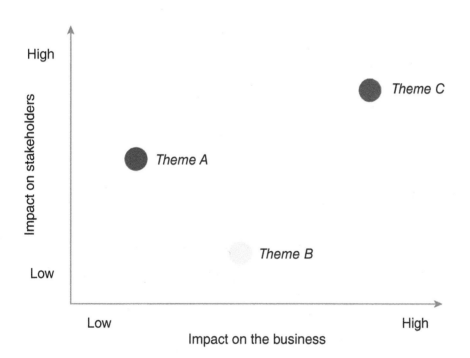

**FIGURE 3.4**   Materiality matrix

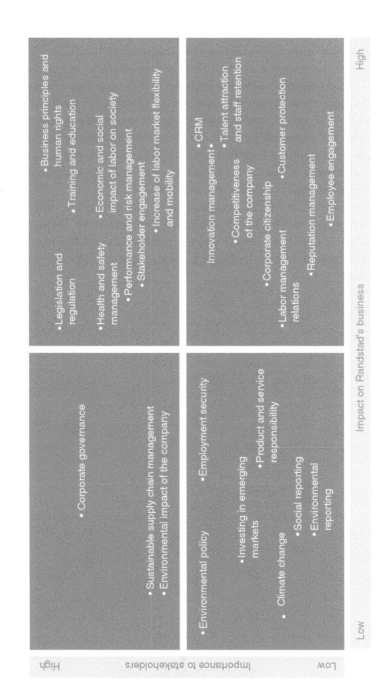

**FIGURE 3.5** Materiality matrix Randstad

Source: Randstad Holding (2016), Annual Report 2016, p25.

## KEY DEBATE

### ESG: Positive change or window dressing?

The use of the acronym ESG (which stands for environmental, social, and governance) is quite common nowadays in current business literature and news. Companies – confronted with greater pressure from governments, investors, lenders, insurers, and other stakeholders to do more to address the grand challenges that society faces – are finding it in their interest to report their ESG performance in addition to reporting their financial performance.[9] The ESG idea came to life in 2005 and, 15 years later, it has become a global phenomenon representing $35.3 trillion in assets under management.[10]

Many organizations, including Bloomberg and Dow Jones & Company, provide ESG ratings for companies. A problem with these ratings and self-furnished ESG scores by companies is that they entail subjectivity and are not readily verifiable. An important reason for this is the absence of universal standards for ESG reporting. One study, which analyzed more than 1,000 academic papers, found that 'studies use different scores for different firms by different data providers'[11]. With the ESG term being defined and measured inconsistently, it is difficult to establish whether a company is truly ESG compliant. Some regard ESG to be a vague term and fear that this ambiguity may lead to window dressing, such that companies present themselves as ESG compliant simply to improve their public appearance. Greenwashing, for example, is the expression used to refer to the practice of making misleading claims that a company and its products are environmentally friendly.

To bring some measure of uniformity to ESG reporting, policy makers and regulators in countries around the globe have made efforts to disseminate and enforce guidelines concerning non-financial ESG disclosures by companies. In 2020, the European Union published its 'Taxonomy for sustainable activities', which set out to remove significant ambiguity.[12] Yet, as Christopher Merker of the CFA Institute notes, 'Like it or not, integrative ESG, which considers non-financial factors as risks to stock prices, is investment management. And as with active management, some approaches will work better than others. So, the ambiguity and the associated concerns about greenwashing will remain.'[13] With the world facing a climate emergency, business leaders are not willing to wait for researchers and others to figure out the best way of implementing, measuring, and reporting ESG practices. Instead, all stakeholders are taking a leap of faith together and expecting each other to play their role in ensuring appropriate ESG compliance.

### Questions

1. What do you consider to be the strengths and weaknesses of the EU's Non-Financial Reporting Directive?
2. As a business leader, how would you seek to ensure that your company's ESG reporting is not mis-characterized as greenwashing?

## Corporate governance

Market systems around the world are organized in a way that the owners, such as shareholders, of public companies, but also those of private companies and family businesses, delegate the responsibility for the day-to-day activities and operations of their companies to professional managers. As discussed earlier in the chapter, shareholders are only one group of stakeholders in a company. Because shareholders and other stakeholders are not directly involved in the managing of a company, a misalignment can easily arise between their interests and those of the managers who run the company. Keeping the interests of these different parties united is the central concern of corporate governance. Whereas past definitions of corporate governance tended to lay emphasis on aligning the interests of shareholders and managers, this is now changing. With a growing public consensus that companies have both an economic and a social purpose,[14] as discussed in Chapter 2, the definitions of corporate governance are changing as well. One holistic definition suggests that 'corporate governance is the system of checks and balances, both internal and external to companies, which ensures that companies discharge their accountability to all their stakeholders and act in a socially responsible way in all areas of their business activity'.[15]

At its core, **corporate governance** is about having a system which ensures that the strategic decisions taken by the company's executives contribute to increasing the economic value of the firm and to attaining social goals. It is about confronting and addressing the varied demands and expectations of different stakeholder groups in an ever-changing business context. Effective corporate governance is not easy. One set of difficulties has to do with the fact that the interests of different stakeholders rarely coincide neatly.[16] For example, the payment of higher dividends to shareholders and the incurring of higher costs to meet sustainability objectives often means less resources for improving employee's welfare through higher wages, work-life balance programs, and capability-enhancing trainings. Moreover, there is the issue of the short-term versus the long-term goals. Executive decisions that benefit some stakeholders in the short-term (e.g., activist investors and creditors) may not contribute to long-term value creation that would benefit other stakeholders (e.g., dedicated institutional investors and individual investors). For example, regulatory practices supposed to ensure a better check on the actions of the executive function have been found to reduce risk-taking and innovation, which are important for long-term value creation.[17]

While corporate governance plays a crucial role in companies, in the wake of numerous corporate frauds, scandals, and value-destroying strategic decisions by executives, much of the public interest in corporate governance has centered on its shortcomings and how to fix them. The 2001 collapse of the US giant Enron Corporation and, with it, Arthur Andersen (see the next Crack-the-Case), the 2003–2005 Parmalat financial scandal in Italy, the 2008 Satyam fraud in India, the 2007–2009 global financial crisis, the 2018 fall of Crillion in the UK, and the 2022 bankruptcy filing by the FTX Cryptocurrency Exchange registered in the Bahamas, are all instances of disasters that corporate governance was supposed to prevent. Following every crisis, policy makers and regulators around the world have sought to strengthen corporate governance frameworks by reforming the codes of practice. Their efforts have centered on improving, for example, the internal auditing of companies, risk management practices, incentive structures, board independence through appointment of non-executive directors, and boardroom ethics.

## Models of corporate governance

Two theoretical frameworks are used often to study corporate governance, namely, agency theory and stakeholder theory. The starting points of the two frameworks differ, reflecting different views regarding the purpose companies serve. The *agency theory* framework refers to the first emergence of stock markets and the idea of limited liability through the dispersed ownership of shares of joint stock companies[18] to highlight the agency problem arising from the separation of ownership and control of companies.[19] The crux of the agency problem is that when the owners or shareholders (also known as the 'principals' of a company) delegate management to professional executives (also known as the 'agents'), the agents may not act in the best interests of the principals. Whereas principals want to maximize the return on their investment in the company, the agents may be inclined to pursue their personal goals, such as geting the highest possible compensation package, enhancing status and prestige among their peers, and improving the prospects of a lucrative future position elsewhere. This goal conflict may mean that instead of focusing on long-term value creation, agents may take (risky) strategic decisions aimed at increasing short-term profits, from which agents stand to gain but which will not necessarily benefit the principals.

Much of the corporate governance thinking that is informed by *agency theory* emphasizes better monitoring and control of the executive function (i.e., the senior-most managers) to ensure that the goals of the principals and agent are aligned. The quality of monitoring and control depend on knowledgeable, well-informed principals and incentive systems that encourage agent behaviours and decisions that serve the principals' interests. One key mechanism by which principals can monitor and control agents is through the exercise of their voting rights. For example, principals can vote at a company's annual general meeting to decide the composition of the company's **board of directors**, a mandatory organ that companies are required to have as part of the system of checks and balances to keep an eye on the executive function and to support executives in the discharge of their responsibilities.[20] In addition, principals can seek to influence the executive function through shareholder resolutions that lobby the company regarding decisions and matters that shareholders are discontented about.[21] Furthermore, institutional shareholders have the possibility to exercise oversight through direct meetings with executives.[22] The more the principal-agent alignment, the less the likelihood of managerial opportunism and, thus, excessive risk-taking and fraud.

The *stakeholder theory* approach to corporate governance maintains that a company's executives are not only accountable to shareholders but to all the company's stakeholders. The basis of this view lies in recognizing that the success of a company rests on the contributions of all those having an exchange relationship with the company,[23] including creditors, customers, employees, local communities, suppliers, taxpayers, and the general public. This perspective underpins the public and regulatory pressure on companies to demonstrate that the executive function is working on creating value for shareholders as well as other stakeholders. For example, companies these days face tremendous pressure to show their commitment to the exercise of corporate social responsibility (CSR).[24] In this regard, both social and regulatory demands are leading to more voluntary and mandatory disclosure of non-financial data for use by stakeholders, such as data indicating the environmental, social, and governance (ESG) performance of companies. This trend can be expected to continue as we enter an era in which consensus is shifting towards a position that besides serving an economic purpose, companies also serve a social purpose.

As compared to the shareholder-centric model of corporate governance, a potential advantage of the stakeholder model of corporate governance is that it may curb excessive risk-taking by the executive function. The reason being that stakeholders, such as creditors and employees, are typically more risk-averse than shareholders, because the former focus on value creation through less risky projects. Moreover, when corporate governance focuses on all stakeholders, it is likely to counter the incentive of executives to focus on short-term profits to please investors, stimulating them to take actions that contribute to longer-term value creation. On the other hand, it is possible that a stakeholder orientation may lead to lower returns on investment and reduced innovation as executives become reluctant to take risks and forego lucrative projects that do not contribute to attaining social goals. At any rate, corporate governance systems that ensure that the expectations of all stakeholders are met are not easy to implement. The alternative according to some is an approach that gives priority to the interests of shareholders but also considers stakeholder expectations.[25] Table 3.1 summarizes the key differences between the shareholder and stakeholder models of corporate governance.

TABLE 3.1    Shareholder and stakeholder models of corporate governance

|  | Shareholder Model (Agency theory) | Stakeholder Model (Stakeholder theory) |
| --- | --- | --- |
| Focus on | Shareholder | All stakeholders |
| Goal of the firm | Maximising shareholder value | Creating value for all stakeholders |
| Chief concern | Countering agency problems | Balancing stakeholder desires |

Source: adapted from Volberda et al. (2022)[26]

## CRACK-THE-CASE
### The downfall of Enron[27]

In the early 2000s, Enron Corporation was one of the largest corporations in the United States. Then, almost overnight, it disintegrated. Thousands of workers lost their jobs, and shareholders lost billions as Enron's share price fell dramatically. The spectacular demise of Enron tells a cautionary tale on corporate governance and regulatory oversight.

Enron Corporation was a US energy, commodities, and services firm headquartered in Houston, Texas. The firm was created as the result of a 1985 merger between InterNorth and Lay's Houston Natural Gas, two regional energy firms. Enron expanded aggressively in new domestic markets and overseas in the subsequent 15 years. On the outside, Enron's financials looked stellar. Fortune magazine named Enron 'America's most innovative firm' for six consecutive years from 1995 to 2001. By 2001, the firm employed nearly 30,000 individuals and boasted a valuation exceeding $60 billion. The firm received widespread praise from investors and employees alike, praising its strong finances, exceptionally effective management, and robust pension scheme.

On the first of January 2001, Enron appeared as a healthy titan of corporate America. Less than 12 months later, the firm would no longer exist. The demise of Enron began in early 2001 when a set of accounting irregularities in the 1990s were revealed. Enron and its auditor, Arthur Andersen, were implicated in actions that bordered fraud. In the subsequent days, it emerged that Enron was using special-purpose entities in much of its operations. Through this corporate structure, Enron hid most of its debts off the books, making the firm seem far more profitable than it truly was. It was discovered that Enron's recorded assets and profits were inflated, fraudulent, or non existent. As the scandal unfolded, Enron's share price dropped from $90.56 in the summer of 2000 to just $0.26 by the time it filed for bankruptcy on December 2, 2001. At the time, the default represented the largest ever in American history, wiping out $11 billion in shareholder value.

The scandal rippled through the markets, where it also took down Enron's auditor, Arthur Andersen. The firm, at the time one of the world's top five accounting firms, was found guilty of crimes regarding their auditing of Enron. As a result, Arthur Andersen was compelled to surrender its Certified Public Accountants license. While the court finding was overturned in 2005, the damage to Arthur Andersen was so great that it never was able to rebuild its business. The firm was left near defunct, with only 200 employees remaining from around 28,000 in 2002. Interestingly, in what appears to be sheer luck, Andersen Consulting was granted independence from Artur Anderson months before the Enron scandal began. Today this spin-off is known as Accenture – one of the world's largest professional services firms.

The story of Enron shows the importance of strong corporate governance. The executive arm of Enron did not face sufficient scrutiny from shareholders, and auditors do not always succeed in detecting or communicating fraud and accounting irregularities. This shows that strong corporate governance does not simply mean frequent audits and inspections. Instead, it is primarily viewed as implementing robust procedures that produce checks and balances for the executive arm of a firm – focusing on preventing fraud instead of detecting it later on.

## Questions

1. Why did shareholders not scrutinize Enron over its excessively optimistic finances?
2. What procedure can you conceive that could have prevented Enron's management fraud?
3. Why did Arthur Andersen fail to inform shareholders of Enron's irregular accounting practices?

The Enron case illustrates the importance of effective corporate governance mechanisms. In the absence of adequate checks and balances, those who hold power in a company can engage in reckless risk-taking and outright fraud. The Volkswagen emissions scandal, which saw the company deceiving regulators about the emissions of its diesel engine cars, provides another illustration of this. Volkswagen was penalized due to its lack of rigorous governance mechanisms and had to pay more than four billion euros in fines across the world.[28]

## Corporate governance mechanisms

Effective corporate governance that prevents excesses by the executive function but also supports it to enable value-creating strategies is vital for companies. In this regard, both weak and overly strong corporate governance can be detrimental to the health of a company. Whereas weak governance can result in fraud and extreme risks, strong governance can interfere with strategic decisions essential for innovation and performance. Finding the right balance is challenging. The effectiveness of corporate governance depends on many factors, including a nation's institutional environment and regulatory framework that affect the mechanisms of corporate governance. Broadly, the mechanisms to monitor, control, and support the executive function can be divided into two categories: internal and external. Whereas internal mechanisms include the board of directors, executive compensation, and ownership concentration, the external mechanisms include the market for corporate control and the market for executives.

## The board of directors

The board of directors or the (corporate) board is a crucial corporate-governance mechanism. Typically, boards are made up of *executive directors*, who are senior managers within a company, and *non-executive directors* (NEDs) who have no managerial role within the company. The NEDs are also referred to as outside or independent directors, who are supposed to contribute to an objective perspective vis-à-vis the monitoring and guidance of the executive function. Boards potentially have the power to control the executive function as they have the mandate to set **executive compensation**, and to select, evaluate, and dismiss executives, including the chief executive officer (CEO). Besides exercising oversight, boards are also a source of knowledge and information and thus can provide valuable advice and counsel to the executive function.[29] As board members are elected by the shareholders of a company and may represent different stakeholders, the board as a collective body serves as the governing instrument of those with a direct interest in the company.

Corporate governance systems differ across the world. While some countries have one-tier boards, others have two-tier boards. On a **one-tier board**, both executive and non-executive directors are jointly responsible for monitoring and guiding the executive function on behalf of the stakeholders. In a **two-tier board** system, the executive directors and non-executive directors serve on two formally separated boards that have different roles. Executive directors oversee the day-to-day operations of the firm, and non-executive directors are responsible for supervising the executive function and providing advice and guidance to it. In the context of a one-tier board, research indicates that a greater proportion of NEDs produces stronger governance.[30] Moreover, many authoritative works suggest that corporate governance would be well served if different individuals hold the positions of board chair and company CEO.[31] Studies in this field also show that the quality of corporate governance, firms' strategies, and value creation also depend on the diversity of experiences, knowledge, and relational networks of board members.[32]

It is important to note that too many NEDs on a board can be counterproductive. Outside directors are not well versed with the firm's day-to-day operations and typically do not have the information needed to effectively evaluate managerial decisions and initiatives. Boards with more insider directors tend to be better informed about the best strategic options and the potential payoffs associated with them.[33] Without this type of information, outsider-dominated boards may emphasize the use of financial controls as opposed to strategic controls, which shifts more of the risk to the executives, who, in turn, may make decisions to maximize their interests and reduce their employment risk.[34] Reductions in R&D investments, additional diversification of the firm (see Chapter 11), and the pursuit of greater levels of compensation are some of the results of managers' actions to achieve financial goals set by outsider-dominated boards. Additionally, boards can make mistakes in CEO-succession decisions because of the lack of important information about candidates as well as specific needs of the firm. The foregoing implies that the ratio of executive to non-executive directors needs to be well balanced.

Because of numerous instances of failures of corporate governance systems, the performance of boards and of individual board members is under a great deal of scrutiny these days. Given the demand for greater accountability and improved performance, many boards have initiated voluntary changes, such as the strengthening of management and accounting control systems and the establishment of formal processes to evaluate the board's performance. In addition, there is a trend towards the inclusion of a 'lead independent director' position on boards, which has many powers associated with it.[35] Furthermore, outside directors are being increasingly required to own significant equity stakes as a prerequisite to holding a board seat. Some studies indicate that firms perform better if outside directors have equity stakes; the trend is towards higher pay for directors with more stock ownership but with fewer stock options.[36] However, other studies suggest that too much stock ownership may be counterproductive as it can reduce outside directors' independence.[37]

## STRATEGIC FOCUS

### Where have all the good directors gone?[38]

The global financial crisis from 2007 to 2009, largely the result of extremely poor strategic decisions made by top-level managers in the financial services industry, laid bare the holes in the global corporate governance systems. In particular, the outcomes showed that many boards of directors were very weak. Boards of directors had suffered significant criticism for the failures in monitoring executive actions in the likes of Enron, Ahold, Parmalat and others in the 2000s. As board failures continue, with the collapse of the FTX Cryptocurrency Exchange in 2022 as an example, boards face substantial public anger and scrutiny. It is difficult for people to understand how boards can allow company executives to take extreme risks that eat away corporate value when the debt burden becomes too heavy for firms.

The seemingly reckless behaviour of executives in many companies continues to add fuel to the enduring debate regarding excessive executive compensation. Many contend, especially in the wake of the 2007–2009 financial crisis, that there seems to be no clear connection between corporate performance and executive pay, and that excessive risk-taking by CEOs is rewarded by high salaries. In this regard, following the financial crisis, the first measure against the 'reckless behaviour' of executives was to regulate the bonus system in the financial industry. Moreover, there was a global effort to regulate the bonuses of bankers.

As a result of the economic meltdown following the global financial crisis, which was also a consequence of poor strategic decisions and boards' inability to prevent these decisions, many corporate boards around the globe have had to change. Old board members resigned and were replaced by new members. In the case of the Royal Bank of Scotland (RBS) Group, the CEO, Fred Goodwin, resigned in 2008. Goodwin was held accountable for RBS's loss of £24.1 billion, the biggest loss in UK corporate history. There was also public outrage about his pension plan worth £700,000 a year. In the case of the Dutch pension fund PME, the board structure had to change as a direct result of the financial crisis. The Dutch National Bank claimed that the PME executive board was incompetent and insisted on downsizing the board from 14 to six executive directors.

Research suggests that smaller boards may be more effective than larger ones in governing companies. In line with this, Candover, a British private equity firm, announced the resizing of its board after being hit by the financial crisis. In general, researchers, policy makers, and regulators are constantly looking for ways to improve the monitoring of the executive function by boards of directors. Both board composition (e.g., the ratio of executive to non-executive directors and the diversity of directors) and board structure (e.g., board size and the roles and responsibilities of board sub-committees such as the audit and compensation committee) are aspects that are often looked at to ensure the best possible monitoring of the executive function. Furthermore, national financial regulatory authorities and other governmental agencies often recommend the introduction of new rules and regulations to increase board effectiveness. For instance, the Financial Reporting Council in the UK introduced a revised version of the Combined Code (a corporate governance template used by investors and listed companies) following the financial crisis.[39]

(Continued)

## Executive compensation

The executive compensation package, comprising salary, bonuses, and stock options, offers a further mechanism to align the interests of stakeholders and executives. Whereas salary is the fixed component of executive pay, bonuses are the varying component, comprising a backward-looking portion to reward attained results and a forward-looking component, such as stock options, to encourage strategies and performance that create value for stakeholders. A critical consideration when designing compensation packages is how to balance long- and short-term incentives to align stakeholder value and managerial wealth creation. Designing a balanced executive compensation package is a difficult task for several reasons. First, strategic decisions are complex, unpredictable, and often difficult to measure. The tendency is to link executive compensation to observed financial performance rather than future performance. Second, many factors affect a firm's performance, it is difficult to ascribe poor or good performance to the executive function and design compensation packages accordingly. At best, executive compensation is a blunt instrument for addressing the agency problem. Nevertheless, executives may manipulate long-term incentive plans to their own advantage.[40] Third, while long-term incentive plans encourage value-creating risk and innovation, they increase executives' exposure to risks associated with uncontrollable events such as market fluctuations and industry decline, necessitating higher compensation than otherwise.[41]

## Ownership concentration

Ownership concentration is an internal mechanism of corporate governance that relies on shareholders who hold a sizable fraction of a company's stock. Such shareholders, sometimes referred to as large *blockholders*, could be institutional investors (e.g., banks, insurance firms, and public or private pension funds) or business families. When there is more ownership concentration (i.e., a greater percentage of a company's stock is held by large blockholders), closer monitoring of the executive function can be expected because of blockholders' considerable stake in the company. Indeed, large blockholders may be able to elect their representatives as NEDs on boards. Moreover, because blockholders, such as Berkshire Hathaway, tend to have interest in stable, long-term investment rather than risky ventures, more ownership concentration is likely to restrain excessive risk-taking by executives.[42] However, as blockholders' interests may not overlap with those of other investors and stakeholders, more ownership concentration may hinder across-the-board principal-agent alignment.[43]

## Markets for corporate control and for executives

The **market for corporate control** (MCC) is an external governance mechanism that refers to the potential threat of external takeover of a business by other companies or individuals. It implies expert buyers looking to identify and buy firms that are not man-aged well.[44] Poorly managed firms have a relatively low market value (i.e., price of stock) compared to their book assets. The takeover of Twitter by Elon Musk illustrates the principle of MCC. Because external takeover puts the executives of a company in a bad light and because new owners are likely to replace them, the executives have a strong interest in their company not being taken over. As such, when the MCC operates effec-tively, the disciplining effect of potential takeover ensures that the executives work in the best interest of a company's stakeholders to have their support and a strong market valuation.[45] The government has an important role to play in relation to the presence of an effective MCC. It must ensure that the regulatory policy and legal frameworks allow the takeover of underperforming firms without delay and difficulties. At any rate, MCC is not a very precise instrument for the purpose of corporate governance. For instance, incumbent executives may be able to hide poor performance for a long time, rendering MCC ineffective. There is also no guarantee that the external buyers of a poorly perform-ing company will be able to effectively turn it around for the benefit of stakeholders, instead of stripping its assets to make profits for themselves.

The market for executives is another external mechanism of corporate governance. Executives can be expected to do more to further stakeholders' interests in the presence of an effective labour market for executives, which has the necessary information to reward or sanction them for their past performance in managerial positions. When executives have built up a positive reputation through actions valued by stakeholders, they stand to gain in the labour market through future job offers. For example, executives who have built up standing as champions of CSR or for innovation that creates long-term value are likely to find it easier than others to be offered leadership positions in other companies. However, this instrument again is a blunt one. For instance, executives can hide their role in the poor past performance of companies they have worked at.

## STRATEGIC FOCUS

### Blockchain-based corporate governance[46]

A central issue in corporate governance is the agency relationship between the owners (i.e., the principals) and executives (i.e., the agents) of a company. In recent years, blockchain technology (see Chapter 5) has begun to offer new ways of organizing this relationship. A firm can remove interme-diary agents through cryptography, peer-to-peer networks, and blockchain-based collaboration.[47] Corporations continue to be the most popular governance structure for large firms. Yet little has been done to address the major limitations of this model. Now, with the power of blockchain and, more fundamentally, cryptography, there are possible remedies to addressing the main drawbacks of the corporate model. Central to this is the reduction of agency problems. In recent times, firms have tried to better align executives' incentives with those of shareholders by tying executive compensation to specific targets set by the board of directors. Yet, the impact of this development has been limited. Experts hope blockchain technology can lead to more transparency and substantial alignment between the shareholders' and executives' interests. When using a blockchain-backed transaction, so-called guarantees require that all parties fulfil specific parameters, which are subsequently verified with a consensus algorithm. Experts hope that with blockchain-backed transactions and other cryptographic

*(Continued)*

tools, more robust and transparent solutions can be developed to align principal-agent interests, which would reduce agency problems.

## Questions

1. How can the additional transparency of blockchain-backed transactions decrease the principal-agent problem?
2. Which party or parties would most benefit from the suggested advantages of blockchain-based governance?

## Corporate governance internationally

Systems of corporate governance differ across nations. The reasons for this are manifold, including differences in culture and history, governmental policies, legal systems, and corporate ownership structures. Multinational corporations (MNCs) seek to understand these different systems in order to confront the threats and opportunities they present internationally. It is important to note that corporate governance systems are not rigid entities – they are fluid, continuously adapting to economic, political, and social changes. There are also efforts underway to achieve greater global convergence in corporate governance systems. MNCs with foreign subsidiaries, integration of national capital markets, increasing foreign investments, and activist institutional investors, such as CalPERS and Elliott Management, represent some of the forces driving the convergence. This notwithstanding, there are notable differences in systems across the globe (see Table 3.2).

The corporate governance in the UK and US is similar in key respects and is labelled as the Anglo-Saxon system. With reference to the shareholder and the stakeholder models of corporate governance discussed earlier in the chapter, the UK and US systems approximate more to the shareholder model. As companies in these countries depend primarily on the stock market to finance themselves, shareholders are a central player in the system, appointing the board of directors to monitor and advise the executive function on their behalf. A feature of the Anglo-Saxon system is the one-tier corporate board, which arguably has an advantage over two-tier boards. Because executive and non-executive directors (NEDs) are both members of the same board, the NEDs direct involvement in decision-making is greater. NEDs are also more likely to have access to detailed information on a timely basis, allowing them to participate more effectively. As such, one-tier boards' quality of decision-making may be better than that of two-tier boards.

In contrast to the UK and US, in Germany and other European Union countries, banks play a major role in financing companies and are, thus, a key player in the corporate governance system. They participate in monitoring and advising the executive function through their representatives on the supervisory boards of companies' two-tier board system. Bank representatives, along with other NEDs, representing employees and shareholders, vote on appointing executives to the management board of the two-tier boards. Banks similarly are also important in the corporate governance system in Japan. Furthermore, as in Germany, in Japan too employees and other stakeholders, such as creditors, customers, and suppliers, have customarily more influence on the oversight of the executive function as compared to the shareholder dominated Anglo-Saxon system. As such, the corporate governance systems in Germany and Japan correspond more to the stakeholder model than the shareholder model.

In China, corporate governance has been evolving as the country moves from a system of state-owned enterprises (SOEs) to a more liberal market system. Although stock markets now play a greater role in the financing of businesses and there has been extensive privatization of SOEs, central and state governments still hold substantial ownership stakes in companies and have considerable influence on strategic decisions through their representatives on supervisory boards. The supervisory boards oversee the executive-director boards in China. Inasmuch as the central and state governments represent the interests of various stakeholders, the corporate governance system is of the shareholder-model type. One issue with the system, however, is that because of state ownership and involvement, shareholder protection is weak, and shareholders do not have much power to monitor and influence the executive function.[48]

**TABLE 3.2**  Corporate governance models

|  | UK, USA | Germany, Japan | China |
|---|---|---|---|
| Financing | Stock market | Banks | Government, stock market |
| Primary focus | Shareholders' property rights | Shareholders' and stakeholders' interests | Government and shareholders' interests |
| Ownership structure | Dispersed | Concentrated | Concentrated |
| Management | One-tier board | Two-tier board | Two-tier board |

## CRACK-THE-CASE

Source: original image "Satyam, Chennai" © Venkiteswaran Ramaswami (2006) / Flickr.

### The Satyam fraud and corporate governance failure[49]

In 2008, Satyam was India's fourth largest IT company, well known and respected. The firm provided IT services to more than one third of the Fortune 500 companies and had clients all over the world. The Founder and CEO, Ramalinga Raju, was named, in September 2008, the Ernst & Young Entrepreneur of the Year, and awarded, in December 2008, with the Golden Peacock Award for Corporate Governance and Compliance. Soon thereafter, however, his term as CEO started to unravel.

On December 17, 2008, Raju announced plans to acquire two companies, Maytas Infra and Maytas Properties, both of which were owned by members of his family. The rationale offered was to diversify Satyam's business portfolio to avoid being overly tied to the IT-services market. However, the stockholders initiated major protests over these acquisitions. They contended that while Raju and his family would benefit from the acquisitions, Satyam would not.

On December 23, 2008, the World Bank announced that Satyam was barred from doing business with the bank because of alleged malpractices in securing previous contracts (e.g., paying bribes). In turn, Satyam requested an apology from the World Bank. Shortly afterwards, the price of Satyam's stock declined to a four-year low. Furthermore, on

*(Continued)*

December 26, three important non-executive directors resigned from Satyam's corporate board. Worsening the situation, on January 7, 2009, Raju sent a letter to Satyam's board of directors and India's Securities and Exchange Commission. In this letter, he admitted his involvement in overstating the amount of cash held by Satyam on its balance sheet. The overstatement was indicated to be approximately $1 billion. Furthermore, Satyam had a liability of $253 million, which was arranged for Raju's personal use, and the company's September 2008 quarterly revenues were overstated by 76% and quarterly profits by 97%. This disclosure sent shockwaves through corporate India and through India's stock market. Not only did Satyam's stock price suffer greatly, declining by 78%, but also the overall market declined by 7.3% on the day of the revelation.

Ironically, Satyam means 'truth' in Sanskrit. While Raju was arrested and charged, others worked hard to save the company. And corporate governance in India took a big hit.

## Questions

1. What factors might explain the Satyam scandal despite India's sound corporate governance framework and strong legislation? (You may have to look up further information on this case online.)
2. Do you think that the various corporate governance mechanisms discussed in this chapter could have prevented the Satyam scandal?

## Global trends in corporate governance

In the past, corporate governance systems had mainly focused on facilitating growth and maximizing shareholder value. However, this is now changing as pressure on companies grows to focus on long-term societal value creation instead of short-term shareholder returns.[50] The catalyst for this development is the changing view of the purpose of companies (see Chapter 2). The growing social sense that a shareholder fixation may be responsible for the neglect of sustainability issues has pushed policy makers and regulators to encourage companies to adopt a broader stakeholder orientation that addresses the social and environmental challenges that humanity faces. Also, many institutional investors[51] and corporate leaders, such as Larry Fink, the CEO of BlackRock, the world's largest asset management company, are pressing for greater attention to ESG issues in corporate governance. This change can be anticipated to affect firms' missions and the strategic choices going forward. For instance, companies are spinning off some of their business lines to mitigate potential environmental liabilities.[52] DuPont's spin-off of its specialty chemicals business is a case in point. As another example, banks in the Netherlands are adopting the strategy of discounted mortgages for purchase of properties that are more energy efficient.

The growth in recent years of shareholder and stakeholder activism can be expected to continue. These two forms of **activism** will exert different pressures on executives and on corporate boards. Whereas shareholder activism will push for strategic decisions that create shareholder value through cost-cutting measures and divestments of unrelated businesses, stakeholder activism will push for strategic decisions that address societal problems. As stakeholder activism gains relevance, it is more difficult for firms to ignore it. Consider in this regard the numerous activists' demonstrations in 2022 targeting famous art works to draw attention to the climate emergency.[53] Employee activism is on the rise as well. It can be expected that activism will have an impact on strategic decisions as executives try to act first to avoid being targeted by activists. Overall, long-term value creation is set to become the priority for corporate boards, meaning that they will be monitoring and advising executives for attention and commitment to issues and outcomes that concern not just shareholders but also other stakeholders.

## CLOSING CASE

### L'Oréal and the white knight[54]

Source: © Patcharaporn Puttipon (2020) / Shutterstock.

When the French president Georges Pompidou died suddenly in 1974, it was likely that left-leaning François Mitterrand would come into power. Eugene Schueller, founder of cosmetics firm L'Oréal, and his daughter Liliane Bettencourt, who inherited the firm in 1957, were known to be strong supporters of the French far right. Bettencourt feared that her firm, which had gone public, would be nationalized if Mitterrand were elected. As a pre-emptive move, she decided to sell 30% of L'Oréal to Nestlé (in return for a small stake in the latter), thinking that the government would be less likely to nationalize L'Oréal if it was owned partly by a Swiss firm. It would also protect against hostile takeovers. Right-leaning Giscard d'Estaing eventually won the election, but Nestlé's (passive) 'white knight' stake in L'Oréal

*(Continued)*

remained untouched. The ties between Nestlé and L'Oréal intensified when they established the joint venture Galderma (in 1981), which provides skin care products and treatments, and founded Laboratoires Innéov to produce cosmetic nutritional supplements (in 2002).

Fast forward to June 25, 2017, and US-based hedge fund Third Point, which had invested over $3.5 billion in Nestlé, including options, sent out an eight-page letter to Nestlé shareholders. It pled for divesting the firm's stake in L'Oréal as part of a strategic overhaul. This stake, which had been reduced to 23.29% in 2014 as part of a buyback agreement, was worth around $25 billion (10% of Nestlé's total market capitalization). In the letter, it stated that 'having L'Oréal in the portfolio is not strategic and shareholders should be free to choose whether they want to invest in Nestlé or some combination of Nestlé and L'Oréal'.[55] The activist investor also urged Nestlé to improve its productivity, return capital to shareholders, and reshape its portfolio, which included more than 2,000 brands spread over a variety of food, beverage, and health science categories. The sprawling portfolio included cereals, chocolate, confectionery, ice creams, frozen meals, pet food, coffee, bottled water, dairy, medical lozenges, and medical nutrition. Nestlé shares had underperformed most of their European and US peers on a three- and ten-year total shareholder return basis. Third Point requested Nestlé to strategically reduce exposure to businesses that were not central pillars of future growth and to consider accretive, bolt-on acquisitions in advantaged and high growth categories.

At a Nestlé investor seminar three months later, Ulf Mark Schneider, Nestlé's CEO as of January 2017, articulated Nestlé's Nutrition, Health, and Wellness (NHW) strategy with food and beverages at its core. He also stressed the necessity of active portfolio management, with an important role for acquisitions and divestments that would be based on the criteria of strategic fit, category attractiveness (in terms of growth and margin), and the ability to win. Following up on this, within a few months, Nestlé announced it would reorganize its infant nutrition business, extend its consumer healthcare portfolio by acquiring Atrium Innovations, and divest its US confectionary businesses. Regarding the L'Oréal stake, Schneider announced some impressive figures: it had had a 42-year annual total return on investment of approximately 12%. In the last ten years, when this annual return on investment had gone up to 14%, the L'Oréal dividends had contributed 9% of Nestlé's earnings per share over the last ten years.[56] Third Point remained unsatisfied and sent out a new letter on July 1, 2018, addressed to Nestlé's chairman and board of directors. The letter communicated that Nestlé management was not moving quickly enough to exit non-strategic (non-NHW) and underperforming businesses. It also reiterated that the L'Oréal stake should be sold, stating that 'the Board remains unable to articulate a compelling long-term strategic rationale for its continued ownership'.[57]

In February 2018, five months before the second letter, L'Oréal had publicly underscored its readiness to buy back the 23.29% stake held by Nestlé, and Nestlé was requested to clarify its strategic intent concerning L'Oréal. Schneider was faced with a dilemma. The white knight investment had provided excellent returns and there were no signs that this would be any different in the future. Third Point, however, argued that this investment confused Nestlé's corporate identity and that the right strategic path would be to sell the stake and use the proceeds to engage in expedited share buybacks, enhance productivity, and make acquisitions in core businesses. What would be the best thing to do? Laboratoires

Innéov had ceased to exist in 2014, and in the same year, Galderma became a wholly owned subsidiary of Nestlé. Should Schneider also cut the remaining ties with L'Oréal by selling its stake in the company? Nestlé sold Galderma in 2019, and in 2021 Nestlé announced that it would further reduce its stake in L'Oréal to 20.10%;[58] however, as of 2023, the firm was still keeping its strategic options open regarding this remaining stake.

## Questions

1. If you were Mark Schneider, what would be your decision concerning Nestlé's stake in L'Oréal, and why?
2. Third Point is one of Nestlé's largest shareholders. Yet, Nestlé's CEO has so far refused to fulfil Third Point's wishes. Why do you believe this is the case? What, if any, stakeholders' interests might be at odds with those of Third Point?

## Summary

- The stakeholders of a firm are individuals and groups who have an exchange relationship with it. Whereas primary stakeholders such as customers, employees, and shareholders have a direct exchange relationship with a company, secondary stakeholders have an indirect relationship with it.
- Because a company has many stakeholder groups and their expectations and interests may not coincide, careful stakeholder management is necessary. This should take into account the relative power of different stakeholder groups and the urgency of attending to their demands.
- Corporate governance is a system of internal and external checks and balances to ensure that the executive function of a company conducts itself in a socially responsible manner and takes strategic decisions that further the interests of a company's stakeholders.
- The board of directors of a company is a very important internal mechanism of corporate governance. It monitors and advises the executive function. Board members include executive directors and non-executive directors from outside the company.
- Corporate governance systems vary across nations because of differences in corporate ownership structures, governmental policies, legal systems, culture, and history. One manifestation of these differences is variation in the structure and composition of corporate boards, with some countries having one-tier boards and others two-tier boards.
- Corporate governance in the future is likely to focus more on the creation of long-term societal value and not just short-term returns for shareholders.

## Review questions

1. What are the different types of stakeholders a company has?
2. Why are companies increasingly focusing on meeting the expectations and interests of non-shareholder stakeholders?

3. Explain the agency problem arising from the separation of ownership and control of companies. What does agency theory suggest regarding the resolution of this problem?
4. Compare and contrast the shareholder and stakeholder models of corporate governance.
5. What is a board of directors? Why do some companies have one-tier boards and others two-tier boards, and what are the advantages and disadvantages of each type?
6. What is the market for corporate control? What factors are likely to influence the effectiveness of this market as a corporate governance mechanism?

## Discussion questions

1. Activist stakeholders tend to draw a great deal of attention to their cause. Discuss the potential implications of this for non-activist stakeholder groups.
2. Governments put a lot of effort into revising and improving corporate governance frameworks and codes. However, executive misconducts and poor decisions are still not a thing of the past. Why do you think this is the case and what might be the best solutions to the problem?
3. Consider the latest developments regarding the corporate governance system in the country you are located. Debate the pro and cons of these developments with your classmates.

### EXPERIENTIAL EXERCISES

1. Identify a company of your interest. Looking at its different stakeholder groups, identify the more and less powerful group(s). Based on this, what recommendations do you have for the company regarding stakeholder management?
2. Pick a social-media company that you find interesting. Try to establish whether internal or external corporate governance mechanisms are likely to be more effective in aligning the interests of the company's stakeholders and executive team.

## Further reading

Aguilera, R.V., Judge, W.Q. and Terjesen, S.A. (2018) 'Corporate governance deviance', *Academy of Management Review*, 43 (1): 87–109.

Alvarez, S. and Sachs, S. (2022) 'Where do stakeholders come from? Positive vs. subjectivist worldviews', *Academy of Management Review*, 48 (2). https://doi.org/10.5465/amr.2022.0328

Finkelstein, S., Hambrick, D.C. and Cannella, A.A. (2009) *Strategic Leadership: Theory and Research on Executives, Top Management Teams, and Boards*. Oxford: Oxford University Press.

Freeman, R.E. (2018) *Stakeholder Theory: Concepts and Strategies*. Cambridge: Cambridge University Press.

Shi, W. and Hoskisson, R.E. (2021) *Understanding and Managing Strategic Governance*. Hoboken, NJ: John Wiley & Sons.

# Endnotes (references)

1.  Tesla (2023) 'Electric cars, solar & clean energy, corporate website'. https://web.archive.org/web/20230629171948/https://www.tesla.com/giga-berlin (accessed June 7, 2023); Rothaermel, F.T. (2021) *Strategic Management* (5th ed.). New York, NY: McGraw-Hill Education; Shead, S. (2022) 'Elon Musk breaks out the dance moves as he opens new Tesla factory in Germany', *CNBC*, March 22. https://www.cnbc.com/2022/03/22/gigafactory-berlin-tesla-ceo-elon-musk-opens-electric-vehicle-plant.html (accessed July 28, 2023); Trudell, C. and Cantrill, A. (2021), 'Elon Musk laughs off concern Tesla German plant will sap water supply', *Bloomberg*, August 13. www.bloomberg.com/news/articles/2021-08-13/musk-laughs-off-concern-tesla-german-plant-will-sap-water-supply (accessed July 20, 2023).

2.  Trudell and Cantrill (2021)

3.  Freeman, R.E. (1984) *Strategic Management: A Stakeholder Approach*. Corydon: Pitman Press.

4.  Freeman (1984)

5.  Vasi, I.B. and King, B.G. (2012) 'Social movements, risk perceptions, and economic outcomes: The effect of primary and secondary stakeholder activism on firms' perceived environmental risk and financial performance', *American Sociological Review*, 77 (4): 573–96.

6.  Cushman, J. H. Jr. (1998) 'Nike pledges to end child labor and apply US rules abroad', *The New York Times,* May 13. www.nytimes.com/1998/05/13/business/international-business-nike-pledges-to-end-child-labor-and-apply-us-rules-abroad.html (accessed June 12, 2023).

7.  Bhattarai, A. and Bensinger, G. (2019) 'Walmart employees stage a walkout to protest gun sales', *The Washington Post*, August 7. www.washingtonpost.com/business/2019/08/07/walmart-employees-staging-walkout-protest-gun-sales (accessed June 12, 2023).

8.  De Bakker, F.G.A. and Den Hond, F. (2008) 'Introducing the politics of stakeholder influence', *Business and Society*, 47: 8–20.

9.  Stolker, J., Keskin den Doelder, B. and Sidhu, J.S. (2020) 'Climate-related reporting by publicly listed companies in The Netherlands: An attention-action mapping', *Maandblad voor Accountancy en Bedrijfseconomie*, 94 (7/8): 285–92.

10. GSI Alliance (2020) 'Global Sustainable Investment Review', *gsi-alliance.org*. www.gsi-alliance.org/wp-content/uploads/2021/08/GSIR-20201.pdf (accessed June 12, 2023).

11. Whelan, T., Atz, U., Van Holt, T. and Clark, C. (2021) *ESG and Financial Performance,* ICGN. https://www.icgn.org/sites/default/files/2021-08/ESG%20and%20Financial%20Performance%20Uncovering%20the%20Relationship%20NYU%20Stern.pdf (accessed June 12, 2023).

12. European Commission (2020) 'EU taxonomy for sustainable activities', European Commission. https://finance.ec.europa.eu/sustainable-finance/tools-and-standards/eu-taxonomy-sustainable-activities_en (accessed June 12, 2023).

13. Merker, C. (2020) 'The ESG debate heats up: Four more challenges', *Enterprising Investor,* February 4. https://blogs.cfainstitute.org/investor/2020/02/04/the-esg-debate-heats-up-four-more-challenges (accessed June 12, 2023).

14. Murray, A. and Meyer, D. (2022) 'Shareholders are putting more pressure on firms over environmental and social issues', *Fortune,* February 15. https://fortune.com/2022/02/15/shareholders-proxy-proposals-esg-conference-board-esgauge-ceo-daily (accessed June 12, 2023).

15. Solomon, J. (2021) *Corporate Governance and Accountability* (5th ed.). Hoboken, NJ: Wiley. p. 6.

16. Grosman, A., Aguilera, R.V. and Wright, M. (2019) 'Lost in translation? Corporate governance, independent boards and blockholder appropriation', *Journal of World Business*, 54 (4): 258–72.

17. Gao, H. and Zhang, J. (2019) 'SOX section 404 and corporate innovation', *Journal of Financial & Quantitative Analysis*, 54 (2): 759–87.

18. Berle, A. and Means, G. (1932) *The Modern Corporation and Private Property*. New Brunswick, NJ: Transaction.

19. Jensen, M.C. and Meckling, W.H. (1976) 'Theory of the firm: Managerial behavior, agency costs and ownership structure', *Journal of Financial Economics*, 3 (4): 305–60.

20. Boivie, S., Bednar, M.K., Aguilera, R.V. and Andrus, J.L. (2016) 'Are boards designed to fail? The implausibility of effective board monitoring', *Academy of Management Annals*, 10 (1): 319–407.

21. Semenova, N. and Hassel, L.G. (2019) 'Private engagement by Nordic institutional investors on environmental, social, and governance risks in global companies', *Corporate Governance: An International Review*, 27 (2): 144–61.

22. Rubach, M.J. (2021) *Institutional Shareholder Activism: The Changing Face of Corporate Ownership*. Abingdon: Routledge.

23. Freeman (1984)

24. Reid, E.M. and Toffel, M.W. (2009) 'Responding to public and private politics: Corporate disclosure of climate change strategies', *Strategic Management Journal*, 30 (11): 1157–78.

25. King, M. and Atkins, J. (2016) *Chief Value Officer: Accountants Can Save the Planet*. Abingdon: Routledge.

26. Volberda, H.W., Sidhu, J.S., Vishwanathan, P., Heij, K. and Kashanizadeh, Z. (2022) *De winst van purpose: Hoe ondernemingen het verschil kunnen maken*. Amsterdam: Mediawerf.

27. Bondarenko, P. (2016, February 5) 'Enron scandal – Downfall and Legislation', *Encyclopedia Britannica*. www.britannica.com/event/Enron-scandal (accessed June 12, 2023); Federal Bureau of Investigation (2016) 'Famous cases & criminals: Enron', *FBI*. www.fbi.gov/history/famous-cases/enron (accessed June 12, 2023).

28. Lynch, D.J (2017) 'VW admits guilt and pays $4.3bn emissions scandal penalty', *Financial Times*, January 11. www.ft.com/content/d998b804-d81a-11e6-944b-e7eb37a6aa8e (accessed June 12, 2023).

29. Bosboom, B., Heyden, M.L. and Sidhu, J.S. (2019) 'Boards of directors and strategic renewal: How do human and relational capital matter?', in A. Tuncdogan, H. Lindgreen, H.W. Volberda, and F.A.J. Van den Bosch, (eds), *Strategic Renewal: Core Concepts, Antecedents, and Micro Foundations*. Abingdon: Routledge, 119–40.

30. Hooghiemstra, R. and Van Manen, J. (2004) 'the independence paradox: (Im)possibilities facing non-executive directors in The Netherlands', *Corporate Governance: An International Review*, 12 (3): 314–24.

31. Solomon (2021)

32. Sidhu, J.S., Feng, Y., Volberda, H.W. and Van den Bosch, F.A. (2021) 'In the shadow of social stereotypes: Gender diversity on corporate boards, board chair's gender and strategic change', *Organization Studies*, 42 (11): 1677–98.

33. Shen, W. and Cannella, A.A. (2002) 'Power dynamics within top management and their impacts on CEO dismissal followed by inside succession', *Academy of Management Journal*, 45: 1195–208.

34. Zorn, M.L., Shropshire, C., Martin, J.A., Combs, J.G. and Ketchen, Jr, D.J. (2017) 'Home alone: The effects of lone-insider boards on CEO pay, financial misconduct, and firm performance', *Strategic Management Journal*, 38 (13): 2623–46.

35. Krause, R., Withers, M.C. and Semadeni, M. (2017) 'Compromise on the board: Investigating the antecedents and consequences of lead independent director appointment', *Academy of Management Journal*, 60 (6): 2239–65.

36. Shen, W. (2005) 'Improve board effectiveness: The need for incentives', *British Journal of Management*, 16: S81–9.

37. Deutsch, Y., Keil, T. and Laamanen, T. (2011) 'A dual agency view of board compensation: The joint effects of outside director and CEO stock options on firm risk', *Strategic Management Journal*, 32 (2): 212–27.

38. Volberda, H.W., Morgan, R.E., Reinmoeller, P., Hitt, M.A., Ireland, R.D. and Hoskisson, R.E. (2011) *Strategic Management: Competitiveness and Globalization*. Andover: Cengage.

39. Financial Reporting Council (2018) *The UK Corporate Governance Code*. London: The Financial Reporting Council. https://www.frc.org.uk/getattachment/88bd8c45-50ea-4841-95b0-d2f4f48069a2/2018-UK-Corporate-Governance-Code-FINAL.pdf (accessed June 12, 2023).

40. Kalyta, P. (2009) 'Compensation transparency and managerial opportunism: A study of supplemental retirement plans', *Strategic Management Journal*, 30: 405–23.

41. Meulbroek, L.K. (2001) 'The efficiency of equity-linked compensation: Understanding the full cost of awarding executive stock options', *Financial Management*, 30 (2): 5–44.

42. Connelly, B.L., Tihanyi, L., Certo, S.T. and Hitt, M.A. (2010) 'Marching to the beat of different drummers: The influence of institutional owners on competitive actions', *Academy of Management Journal*, 53 (4): 723–42.

43. Hoskisson, R.E., Hitt, M.A., Johnson, R.A. and Grossman, W. (2002) 'Conflicting voices: The effects of institutional ownership heterogeneity and internal governance on corporate innovation strategies', *Academy of Management Journal*, 45 (4): 697–716.

44. Gemson, J. (2021) 'Private company acquisitions in the market for corporate control: A comparison between private equity and corporate acquirers', *The Quarterly Review of Economics and Finance*, 81: 342–57.

45. Stringham, E. and Vogel, J. (2018) 'The leveraged invisible hand: How private equity enhances the market for corporate control and capitalism itself', *European Journal of Law and Economics*, 46 (2): 223–44.

46. Kaal, W. (2021) 'Blockchain-based corporate governance', *Stanford Journal of Blockchain Law & Policy*, 4 (1). doi.org/10.2139/ssrn.3441904

47. Kaal (2021)

48. Yeh, Y-H., Shu, P-G., Lee, T-S. and Su, Y-H. (2009) 'Non-tradeable share reform and corporate governance in the Chinese stock market', *Corporate Governance: An International Review*, 17 (4): 457–75.

49. Volberda et al. (2011)

50. Dallas, L.L. (2017) 'Is there hope for change? The evolution of conceptions of "good" corporate governance', *San Diego Law Review*, 54(3): 491–564.

51. Kavadis, N. and Thomsen, S. (2022) 'Sustainable corporate governance: A review of research on long-term corporate ownership and sustainability', *Corporate Governance: An International Review*, 31 (1): 198–26.

52. Baker, A.C., Larcker, D.F. and Tayan, B. (2020) 'Environmental spinoffs: The attempt to dump liability through spin and bankruptcy', Rock Center for Corporate Governance at Stanford University Closer Look Series: Topics, Issues and Controversies in Corporate Governance No. CGRP-87. https://papers.ssrn.com/sol3/papers.cfm?abstract_id=3727550 (accessed June 12, 2023).

53. Gayle, D. (2022) 'Just Stop Oil activists throw soup at Van Gogh's Sunflowers', *The Guardian,* October 14. www.theguardian.com/environment/2022/oct/14/just-stop-oil-activists-throw-soup-at-van-goghs-sunflowers (accessed June 12, 2023).

54. Business Wire (2018) 'Third Point publishes presentation on "#NestléNOW"', *Business Wire,* July 1. www.businesswire.com/news/home/20180701005073/en/Third-Point-Publishes-Presentation-on-%E2%80%9CNestl%C3%A9NOW%E2%80%9D (accessed June 12, 2023); Galderma (2019) 'Galderma to become the world's largest independent global dermatology company after completion of CHF 10.2 billion carve-out of Nestlé Skin Health', *Galderma,* October 2. www.galderma.com/news/galderma-become-worlds-largest-independent-global-dermatology-company-after-completion-chf-102 (accessed June 12, 2023); Jolly, D. (2014) 'L'Oréal begins to untangle its bonds with Nestlé', *The New York Times,* February 11. www.nytimes.com/2014/02/12/business/international/loreal-says-it-will-buy-back-8-of-its-shares-from-nestle.html (accessed June 12, 2023);. Naik, G. (2019) 'Attention shifts to Nestlé's $29B L'Oréal stake after sale of skin health unit', *S&P Global,* July 18. www.spglobal.com/marketintelligence/en/news-insights/latest-news-headlines/attention-shifts-to-nestl-233-s-29b-l-oreal-stake-after-sale-of-skin-health-unit-52918238 (accessed June 12, 2023); Nestlé (2014a) 'Strategic transaction approved by boards of Nestlé and L'Oréal', Nestlé, February 11. www.nestle.com/media/pressreleases/allpressreleases/nestle-loreal-galderma (accessed June 12, 2023); Nestlé (2014b) 'L'Oréal and Nestlé announce the project to end the activity of their joint venture Innéov', *Nestlé,* November 27. www.nestle.com/media/pressreleases/allpressreleases/loreal-nestle-end-joint-venture-inneov (accessed June 12, 2023); Nestlé (2017a) 'Nestlé reorganizes infant nutrition business, announces changes to Executive Board', *Nestlé,* November 15. www.nestle.com/media/pressreleases/allpressreleases/infant-nutrition-business-management-changes (accessed June 12, 2023); Nestlé (2017b) 'Nestlé extends consumer healthcare portfolio by agreeing to acquire Atrium Innovations', *Nestlé,* December 5. www.nestle.com/media/pressreleases/allpressreleases/nestle-acquires-atrium-innovations (accessed June 12, 2023); Nestlé (2018) 'Nestlé agrees to sell US confectionary business to Ferrero', Nestlé, January 16. www.nestle.com/media/pressreleases/allpressreleases/nestle-agrees-to-sell-us-confectionery-business-ferrero (accessed June 12, 2023); Nestlé (n.d.) 'What is the nature of Nestlé's relationship with L'Oréal?', *Nestlé.* www.nestle.com/ask-nestle/our-company/answers/nature-of-nestles-relationship-with-loreal (accessed June 12, 2023); Schneider, M. (2017) 'Nestlé: Strong foundation, clear path forward, bright future', Nestlé, September 26 (presentation Nestlé Investor Seminar 2017). www.nestle.com/sites/default/files/asset-library/documents/library/presentations/investors_events/investor-seminar-2017/mark-schneider.pdf (accessed June 12, 2023); Subramanian, R. (2019) *Nestlé and L'Oréal: The "Elephant in the Room".* London, Ontario: Ivey; The Economist (2009a) 'In pursuit of beauty; L'Oréal and Nestle', *The Economist,* 390 (8615), January 22. https://www.economist.com/business/2009/01/22/in-pursuit-of-beauty (accessed June 12, 2023); The Telegraph (2006) 'History of L'Oréal', *The Telegraph,* February 20. www.telegraph.co.uk/finance/2932582/History-of-LOreal.html (accessed June 12, 2023); Third Point (2017) 'Third Point letter to Nestlé's investors', *Third Point,* June 25. www.thirdpointpublic.com/wp-content/uploads/2017/06/Third-Point-Nestle-Letter.pdf (accessed June 12, 2023); White, S. and Vidalon, D. (2018) 'L'Oréal ready to buy Nestle stake in cosmetics leader', *Reuters,* February 9. www.reuters.com/article/us-loreal-results-nestle-idUSKBN1FT101 (accessed June 12, 2023).

55. Third Point (2017)

56. Schneider (2017)

57. Business Wire (2018)

58. Nestlé (2021) 'Nestlé reduces stake in L'Oréal to 20.1%, initiates new CHF 20 billion share buyback program', press release, December 7. www.nestle.com/media/pressreleases/allpressreleases/loreal-stake-new-share-buyback-program (accessed July 30, 2023).

## Acknowledgements

The authors thank Liam Goodman for his contribution to this chapter.

## Key terms

**Activism** – efforts by a company's stakeholders to push for change that is expected to promote environmental and societal well-being

**Board of directors** – an internal mechanism of corporate governance to monitor and advise the executive function

**Corporate governance** – the system of checks and balances to ensure alignment between the interests of the principals of a company (i.e., its owners and stakeholders) and their agents (i.e., senior executives)

**Executive compensation** – a corporate governance mechanism that focuses on the executive compensation package to align principal-agent interests

**Market for corporate control** – an external corporate governance mechanism, which depends on the threat of external takeover of poorly performing companies

**One-tier board** – a corporate board whose members include executive as well as non-executive directors

**Stakeholder management** – the sequential prioritization of different stakeholders' expectations and interests and the maintenance of a productive relationship with stakeholders

**Stakeholders** – individuals and groups who have an exchange relationship with a company

**Two-tier board** – a system consisting of an executive board and a supervisory board. While the executive board is comprised of executives only, the supervisory board is comprised of representatives of stakeholders

# 4

# COMPETITIVE RIVALRY AND NONMARKET FORCES

## LEARNING OBJECTIVES

After reading this chapter, you should be able to:

- understand the relevance of external-environment analysis for strategic management;
- appreciate why blurring industry boundaries are making competitor analysis more challenging but also more important;
- identify a company's rivals using different criteria;
- conduct systematic and comprehensive macro-environment analysis;
- make use of scenario planning to inform decisions about strategy.

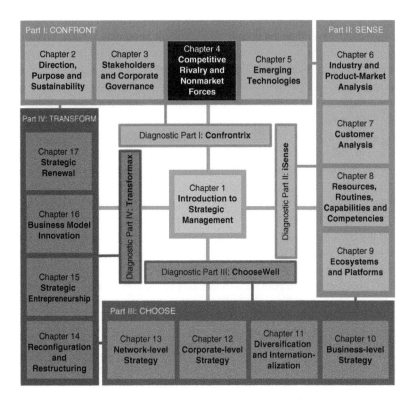

## OPENING CASE

Source: © Metamorworks (2023) / Shutterstock.

### Troubles in streaming paradise

Netflix was founded in 1997, in a time when people still watched videos they rented from their nearest Blockbuster store. Streaming had yet to be discovered. Netflix started with the promise that if it did not have stores, but only warehouses which mailed out videos, it would be able to provide more convenience and variety. Netflix successful pushed this desire out to the public, and since then the amount of Blockbuster stores has decreased from 9,094 stores in 2004 to just 1 in 2020 (a franchised store located in Bend, in the US state of Oregon, that was featured in the 2020 documentary film 'The Last Blockbuster'). In 2007, Netflix launched the first version of the streaming service we know today. Although they were the first, they certainly were not going to be the only player in this area. Many video streaming services have come forward since then, but the one that seems to be really keen on stealing Netflix's throne is the animation powerhouse Disney. For a long time, it seemed The Walt Disney Company was merely a supplier to Netflix rather than a rival. But then things changed.

In 2009, Disney made its first steps into video streaming with Hulu. While this was an important development, Netflix had little to fear – Disney intended to supply its productions to Hulu but was still supplying to Netflix too. Also, Hulu was relatively modest in size, scope and growth. However, Disney shifted gears when it launched sports streaming service ESPN+ in 2018 and a streaming service that would primarily focus on Disney franchises, Disney+, in 2019. Its franchises streamed on Netflix were scheduled to be pulled from that platform. In that same year, 2019, Disney announced that it would bundle its three streaming services for a price much lower than the price of Netflix's single streaming service.[1] Unlike Netflix, Disney is not just relying on its streaming income for its survival – it has many more divisions it can count on for compensating income, such as its theme parks, resorts, merchandise sales, and franchise income. Assessing the aggression and size with which Disney has entered the streaming industry, as of today, Disney arguably is Netflix's most feared rival and the question is whether it is just a matter of time before Disney takes Netflix's crown.

In the same year that ESPN+ was launched, the mobile video firm NewTV was formed, which soon changed its name to Quibi, short for *Quick bites of content*. In April 2020, Quibi launched a streaming platform that would only host short-form video of up to 10 minutes on mobile devices.[2] By doing so, Quibi hoped to portray itself as a new and different kind of streaming service. If it succeeded, Quibi would have had nothing to fear from the likes of Netflix, Disney, and Amazon. Yet, Quibi shut down after just a few short months in December 2020. It was not able to lure viewers away from the traditional streaming services. Quibi's business model depended on viewers wanting to watch short videos on the move, say, when commuting or waiting for an order. The idea was that people in such situations would have insufficient time for watching traditional content, and ten-minute videos would work in these time-limited situations. What Quibi forgot to account for was that due to the COVID-19 pandemic, people would be mainly at home, where they would favour bigger screens and longer videos over mobile device screens and shorter videos. The rest is history. A similar streaming service, called GAIN, was launched in Turkey in January 2021. They seem to have learned from Quibi's mistakes, because only months after their launch they opened up GAIN for bigger screens. Only time will tell whether GAIN will become more successful than Quibi.

## Questions

1. Do you think that Netflix can stay ahead, even though its cash balance and profitability are much lower than that of Disney? Can Netflix's single service compete with a cheaper Disney bundle? Netflix has sports documentaries, original programming, and non-Disney animation offerings, but will all of this be enough to maintain the edge? If you were the CEO of Netflix, what would be your concerns?
2. To what extent have nonmarket forces such as advances in digital technology and the outbreak of COVID-19 had an effect on the performance of Blockbuster, Netflix, Disney's streaming business, and Quibi?

# Introduction

All entities and happenings outside a firm's boundaries are collectively referred to as the 'external environment'. Think about the actions and activities of individual actors, other firms, and institutions, but also about events and trends around the world. Together the outside entities and developments shape the business environment that a firm must contend with. To consistently deliver value, firms need to be aware of their external environment and react appropriately to external changes when required. This is true for multinational corporations as well as small businesses. Thus, firms of all types and sizes need to be aware about what is happening around them through active engagement with their environment. Firms that fail to look outward may be overwhelmed by setbacks they could have noted and possibly avoided.

For a systematic analysis of a firm's external environment, it is helpful to disaggregate it into the micro-environment and the macro-environment (see Figure 4.1).[3] The **micro-environment** refers to the external organizations and individuals – and their actions and activities – in direct contact with the firm, such as customers, suppliers, distributors and competitors. All other entities and factors residing in the external environment are part of the **macro-environment**.

The most important part of the micro-environment is the **market environment**, commonly referred to as the market, which is the place where the firm and its competitors interact with and compete for customers. A firm may compete in just one market or in multiple markets. As elaborated further in this book, a distinction can be made between product markets (such as the streaming market and the video rental market) and geographical markets (such as Turkey and the US state of Oregon). Firms that compete simultaneously in multiple products markets, such as the Walt Disney Company, are commonly referred to as *multibusiness firms*, while firms that compete in multiple geographical markets outside their home country are often referred to as *multinational firms* (see Chapter 11).

This chapter is divided into two main parts. In the first part, we zoom in on competitive rivalry in the market and on changes in rivalry that a firm is confronted with – for instance, as a result of blurring industry boundaries. The second part of the chapter is about *non-market* forces. It discusses the broader forces that affect the market and the firm, such as governmental regulation and the state of the economy. We focus particularly on nonmarket forces in the macro-environment, which are most pervasive.

While it is analytically helpful to disaggregate the external environment into a micro and a macro component, it is important to note that competitive rivalry in the micro-environment

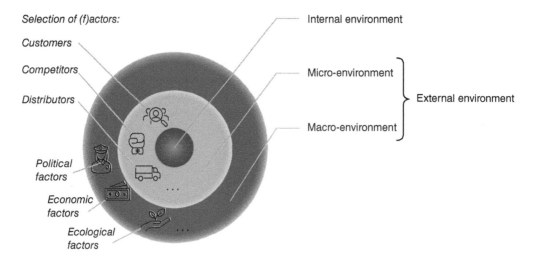

**FIGURE 4.1**   Classification of a firm's environment

is influenced by events in the macro-environment.[4] In addition, although this chapter discusses the external environment separately from the internal environment, the two are in fact deeply intertwined. An external event may impact the firm on any level at any time. Robust organizational structures are needed to ensure firms are aware of and act upon significant developments in their environment. Procedures are required at all relevant levels, whether for a marketing manager who wants to differentiate a firm's product from that of rivals, or for an operations manager who must remain mindful of sourcing issues for a firm's raw materials, or for a public affairs representative who needs to be aware of any government policy that may inhibit firm operations. Achieving this requires firms to have excellent environmental awareness (see Chapter 2) and good stakeholder management (see Chapter 3).

## Competitive rivalry

As elaborated further in Chapter 6, **competitors** are firms that operate in the same industry or product market, offering similar products (in the form of a good or service), and targeting the same customers.[5] Competitors have an impact on the position of a firm, because they can affect its profitability, market share, and other performance metrics. Note though that a fashion retail giant like Inditex's Zara is unlikely to pay much attention to a small family business around the corner, even though the two are technically competitors. As this example illustrates, being a competitor is one thing, and **competitive rivalry** (in short, rivalry) is another. This subtle yet significant difference is often overlooked. Rivalry implies confrontation. Imagine you are hired as the lead strategist for an established firm. Which companies are your firm's rivals? Sorting this out is important for deciding how to allocate your firm's resources to confronting rivalry. By knowing its rivals, the firm minimizes inefficiency, while maximizing the effectiveness of use of time, funds, and people. Additionally, it will be better able to make positioning decisions, will have greater chance of anticipating relevant developments in its market(s), and is less likely to be taken by surprise by potential competitive attacks on its business(es).

A firm that seeks to understand who its **rivals** are needs to first examine its market commonality with other firms in its business domain. Such commonality can pertain to a range of factors, such as pricing, product quality, and level of customer service. Second, it needs to assess whether its resources and capabilities (see Chapter 8) will allow it to effectively compete with firms with which it has market commonality. We focus next on these two dimensions of competitive rivalry.

## Market commonality

The basis of successfully engaging in rivalry from an outside-in view (see Chapter 1) is analyzing your competitors' market position.[6] Not every competitor is a rival. Therefore, not every market position should be of concern and draw attention. For a firm's market position to set off the alarm bells it should overlap with your firm's own, which is referred to as **market commonality**.[7] As the next few sections will clarify, market commonality is multidimensional: there can be commonality with respect to, for instance, current or prospective products, price-quality balance, location, and sales channels. Moreover, it is prone to changes and shifts as firms enact strategic actions.[8]

Rivalry starts with how your *products* overlap with your rivals. Any product that has an impact on your firm's competitive position is a competitor. But to be rivals, a high potential level of impact on one's competitive position is needed. The sale of electric bikes, for example those of Giant Bicycles, will affect sales of Hyundai cars, even if it is only of minor impact and the two are not rivals. The most impact to a firm's competitive position will stem from a firm that has products that are as closely related as possible – think about, for instance, Mercedes and BMW. Firms should also take into account rivals' prospective products: is it likely that a firm that is not yet a rival may become one through launching a new product? A relevant example is Apple, which became a rival to Blackberry and Nokia only after it introduced its first iPhone. Until that point it was only seen as a rival to firms in the computer and music player industries.

Any firm operates in a business landscape with competitors widely ranging in their *price-quality* balance. To give an example, the fashion retail industry includes a wide range of firms in terms of their price-quality combination. Each one of these firms will claim a piece of the fashion retail industry pie. In the end, all of them are competitors. Yet, all of them cannot be rivals, because rivalry changes are substantially based on the offered balance between price and quality. Quality generates demand, yet comes with a cost. Higher prices can cover more unit costs but will often also decrease unit demand. Higher quality products also require different types of resources and capabilities than lower quality products, as the production and design process have to be different in terms of material used, skills utilized, and technologies applied. A firm, unless a corporation with specialized business units, cannot engage with every type of cost structure at the same time, cannot master every type of production and design, and cannot utilize every type of technology. Even if it is theoretically possible, it will not be viable from an income and expenditure point of view. Hence, rivalry entails understanding how the price-quality balance of a firm relates to that of its competition. The more related it is, the likelier it is that it should see that competitor as a rival.

Another important factor to take into account when judging which firms are your rivals, besides the current or prospective type of product offering and price-quality balance as discussed above, is their *geographical presence*. Which parts of the world are you competing in and who else is there? Sometimes firms choose to focus only on a neighbourhood – think about a local bakery. Other times firms are active almost all over the world, such as international fast-food chains. Even if a firm offers a similar price-quality balance, it will not count as your rival unless you operate in the same geographical market. The extent to which a firm's geographical market overlaps with that of another firm will increase the likelihood with which it should treat this other firm as a rival. Firms are in flux and where you will operate tomorrow, or where a competitor will operate tomorrow, should be taken into account when making the decision of who your rivals are. This requires being sufficiently forward-looking when you craft your own firm's strategy, and anticipating competitors' moves even when they are not yet in close proximity.

A fourth relevant factor in analyzing competitors in market positioning stems from understanding the overlap of current and prospective *sales channels*, which denote the path that a firm takes to reach its customers – for instance, directly via a mobile app or a physical market stall or indirectly via a wholesaler or retailer. Firms can choose from different sales channels, and, over time, they can change or modify their choices. Understanding a competitor's current and prospective sales channels means that you understand what type of customer this firm wants to appeal to. Asos, the online-only fashion retailer, clearly taps into a different type of customer pool than Primark, the bricks-and-mortar fashion retailer. Similarly, Ocado, a British online supermarket, taps into a different type of customer pool than traditional supermarkets like Lidl, Carrefour and Tesco. It is important to take into account that an online-only firm can choose to open a physical shop, just like Amazon once upon a time was online-only. Similarly, a supermarket can choose to open an online shop, just like Tesco has.

## Resource and capability similarity

It is crucial for a company to understand whether its competitors pose a threat in terms of the resources they possess and their capabilities to use these effectively. The resource-based view (see Chapter 1) regards **resources** to be the principal building blocks of a company, which are fundamental to its strategy and provide the wherewithal to compete with rivals.[9] The rivals of a firm are companies that have a potential similar to its own by virtue of having comparable resources and capabilities. For the analysis, a firm's resource base needs to be evaluated as widely as possible. Both *tangible resources*, such as buildings, plants, and equipment, and *intangible resources*, such as experience, goodwill, and proprietary technologies, should be documented. Of vital importance are the resources that directly serve the achievement of strategic goals and objectives (see Chapter 8). Rivalry can be better assessed through an examination of commonality of strategic resources in research and development (R&D), technological infrastructure, patents, financial reserves, and the management team. A company having similar types and quantities of resources as the focal firm is more likely to pose a significant competitive threat. Furthermore, the quality of the resources is also important. The following four questions need to be asked in this regard: How valuable are the resources of my competitors and what potential income can they generate? How rare are these resources and does our firm have the same resources? If not, can our firm imitate the resources of competitors to counter disadvantages from not having these resources? Is it possible for our firm to substitute the resources of competitors with alternative resources?[10]

Resources by themselves do not have any value unless they are used, which is where capabilities come in.[11] **Capabilities** are the competencies that harness resources to execute strategies that enable a company to achieve its goals (see Chapter 8). To illustrate, in order to innovate a single manager must usually combine their knowledge and skills with those of other employees, knowledge databases, and technological infrastructure. The competency to coordinate and direct the efforts of human and capital resources effectively is an example of a capability. There are a variety of capabilities. For instance, *operational capabilities* support the enactment of daily activities, while *dynamic capabilities* allow a firm to change its operational capabilities or resource base. To decide whether a competitor should be classified as a rival, it is important to consider the type of capabilities they possess and the strength of these capabilities. A firm that has weak operational capabilities cannot hurt the focal firm's competitiveness through daily events. Such competitors will lack efficiency or effectiveness, say, in relation to attracting away the focal firm's customers through marketing events. Firms with weak dynamic capabilities will have a hard time following the changes the focal firm makes in its products and operations. Such competitors are unlikely to leapfrog the focal firm and thus pose a low risk.

Rivalry is dynamic. A competitor may not be the focal firm's rival today but may become so tomorrow. Likewise, a rival today may not remain a rival tomorrow. Resources and capabilities need to be frequently changed in the face of environmental dynamism,[12] for example to prevent resources from turning obsolete.[13] In addition to this, a firm's resource base can grow over time, through either the acquisition or accumulation of resources. The resource base may also shrink because of divestitures (see Chapter 14). To understand the extent to which competitors are rivals, firms must consider how their resource base and capabilities develop over time. This means keeping track of what resources and capabilities are acquired and accumulated.[14] *Tradeable resources* can be acquired. A competitor may hire a new top manager or may acquire a startup to integrate its new product development capability. *Non-tradeable resources*, such as reputation, need to be accumulated. Resources and capabilities can also be grown – for instance, a machine can be built through periods of R&D that include trial-and-error learning, and a digital marketing capability can be developed through education. Another dynamic is that resources and capabilities may become obsolescent. Rivals' sluggishness, overconfidence, or myopia may withhold them from investing in keeping resources and capabilities from turning obsolete.

## CRACK-THE-CASE
### Grocery retail and courier services in post-pandemic times

Grocery retailers commonly operate in highly competitive, small margin markets, which underwent significant disruption during the COVID-19 pandemic. The shopping habits of consumers changed as people became hesitant to go to physical stores and started ordering groceries online. The convenience of online shopping sped up a structural shift from bricks to clicks. The established supermarket chains were initially reluctant to invest in home-delivery since it was generating losses and would cannibalize their profitable brick-and-mortar stores. As supermarket chains lagged in fully meeting the needs of consumers, the super-fast grocery delivery industry had room to grow. Initially, the industry had mostly local players, such as Cajoo in France, Dija and Weezy in the UK, and GoPuff in the US. However, Germany-based Flink internationalized to France and the Netherlands, while

*(Continued)*

Gorillas, which also started in Germany, expanded into Denmark, France, the Netherlands, and Spain before being acquired by Turkey-based Getir in December 2022. Prior to that acquisition, Getir had moved into France, Germany, Italy, the Netherlands, Portugal, Spain, the UK, and the US. GoPuff was introduced in London in the UK. In addition, the market also now includes firms such as Uber and Glovo, which specialize in meal delivery or not-so-fast grocery delivery but could decide to increase their presence in the fast grocery-delivery space. Finally, Netherlands-based Crisp and Picnic, Finland-based Wolt, and UK-based Ocado are online supermarkets, which for now do not compete on the basis of delivery speed but may in the future.

Supermarket retailers and other traditional grocery retailers, thus, do not only compete with each other, they also compete against new online supermarkets and super-fast, on-demand grocery delivery firms. The pandemic accelerated the growth of these competitors. Some super-fast grocery delivery firms have attracted enormous capital investments. Also, they do not need to be profitable for a while; their main goal is to enlarge their market share. The online grocery ordering systems of most traditional grocery retailers have high order values and relatively long delivery times. In contrast, many of the new entrants deliver groceries faster than people can shop themselves, targeting customers who desire convenience. The prices of groceries that are ordered via these services are somewhat higher than brick-and-mortar retail prices, but convenience-preferring customers are fine with paying the higher price. Also, Generation Z and millennials who have grown up in the online-possibilities world are changing the way we buy and sell, forcing firms to examine how they do business.[15] The super-fast delivery firms mostly use dark stores (i.e., a warehouse or retail outlet used exclusively to fulfil orders placed online), and do not need to house supermarkets in expensive shopping center locations and employ a large staff. Goldman Sachs has estimated that online parties will have increased their total European market share in 2040 by between 25% and 30%.[16] From an environmental perspective, the growing use of electric transport for delivering multiple-orders is improving the image of grocery home-delivery as a sustainable alternative to individual shopping.[17]

The lower operational costs and convenience to customers make on-demand grocery shopping a serious threat to brick-and-mortar retail. The new entrants deliver fast, are tech-driven and asset-light, and thus more adaptable, and have access to large sums of capital. How should traditional grocery retailers whose revenue models have come under pressure cope with this confrontation?

## Questions

1. Why did supermarket retailers not start offering the type of service being offered by the super-fast grocery delivery providers?
2. How should supermarket retailers respond to the proliferation of super-fast grocery delivery providers?

# Blurring industry boundaries

While knowing one's rivals is always important, it is even more so when boundaries between industries begin to blur, and it is difficult to map the competitive landscape (see Figure 4.2). In such contexts, instead of regarding all incumbents in the firm's focal industry as rivals, the criteria of market commonality and resource and capability similarity offer a more suitable method for identifying a smaller set of true rivals. Delineating industry boundaries is becoming an ever more difficult task in today's market economy. One reason for this is that companies are increasingly engaged in activities in different industries, which impacts the structure of value creation within and across industries. Furthermore, the blurring of industry boundaries is fueled by the extension of firms' activity mix to include those that were previously performed by other industries.[18] While the blurring-boundaries phenomenon can offer a plethora of opportunities, creating new industries and product markets, it also represents a challenge for incumbent firms. These firms need to extend their competency base beyond their existing expertise and accumulate new competencies that will allow them to compete with boundary-spanning rivals. Therefore, companies with strong innovation competencies, acquisition capabilities, and ability to establish fruitful strategic alliances seem better placed to deal with the challenges and pitfalls of blurring industry boundaries.

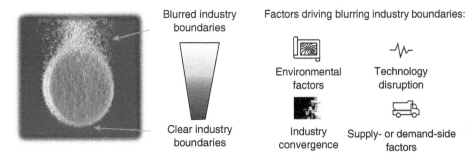

**FIGURE 4.2**   Visualization of blurring industry boundaries: A tablet dissolving in water

Research points to four main factors why boundaries between industries are becoming fuzzy in many cases (see again Figure 4.2): environmental factors, technology disruption, industry convergence, and supply or demand factors.

Environmental factors. The current business environment is characterized by unprecedented volatility, uncertainty, complexity, and ambiguity (VUCA), which is increasing the speed, scale, and scope of changes in the competitive landscape. Variables such as political regulation or deregulation, globalization, scientific breakthroughs, and the pervasiveness of information and digital technologies are contributing towards the blurring of industry boundaries.[19]

Technology disruption. Technology disruptors are causing industries to emerge, disappear, and merge. This happens when firms from outside an industry use new technologies to challenge industry incumbents' positions. Usually, such new technologies attempt to change the industry standard by satisfying an existing customer need with a new product or by offering the same product at a lower cost and better functional performance, breaking the standard cost-quality barrier. Additionally, even if a new entrant's product complements existing products, the way that value is distributed and captured in the industry value chain may change substantially.[20]

Industry convergence. This can occur because of technology convergence. Technology convergence happens when the breadth and depth of interactions between different technologies increases over time, leading to the co-evolution of these technologies to perform similar tasks.[21] Technology convergence tends to lead to industry convergence, which means that previously distinct industries converge to a single industry. Some suggest that industry convergence processes start with the convergence of scientific fields, followed by the convergence of technologies, and finally, industry convergence.[22]

Supply-side or demand-side factors. Changes in the supply side or the demand side can also contribute to the blurring of industry boundaries. One such change is the growing interest in satisfying multiple needs with one transaction or through a single product. Such a trend has led suppliers to increase the scope of their products, sometimes offering products that were traditionally offered by suppliers from different industries. Customers also increasingly favour multifunctional products such as the smartphone and the smart TV, which bring together functionalities that were once delivered by separate products from distinct industries.

The telecommunications industry exemplifies well the blurring of industry boundaries. Before the emergence of digital technologies, the boundaries of the industry were defined to include telephone companies such as AT&T, telephone equipment manufacturers who produced the physical devices for consumers, and auxiliary equipment manufacturers who produced the physical infrastructure to allow communication. However, digital technologies have changed the nature of information transmitted (from voice to multimedia data) and also the devices that send and receive the data (from a single device to a range of devices).[23] As a result, the boundaries of the telecommunications, IT, and electronics industries have become blurred over the years. In a similar vein, the boundaries of the chemicals industry, which has benefited from scientific developments in physics and biotechnology, have also become blurred. Other examples include the convergence between the pharmaceutical and cosmetics industries, which has resulted in the cosmeceuticals sector, and the convergence between the food and pharmaceutical industries, which has given birth to the nutraceuticals and functional foods sector.[24]

Also, there are the digital native companies that do not fit in any single industry and compete simultaneously in multiple areas. One example is Rakuten Ichiba, which is the largest online retail marketplace in Japan. In addition to its retail business, it also provides e-money services, issues credit cards and offers other financial products and services including mortgages and securities brokerage.[25] Another example is Amazon, which started as an online marketplace for books, and now offers a massive range of services including online advertisement, streaming services, and cloud computing among many others. Uber is another example, which started as a ride-hailing platform focused on transportation, but has since expanded to food delivery and freight services. Such multi-sector tech giants are shifting the nature of competition, offering a wide range of products through a single gateway and making industry boundaries fuzzier and more fluid than ever.

## KEY DEBATE

### How to foresee blurring industry boundaries

A question that remains unanswered is how to foresee or detect blurring or fading industry boundaries. Researchers have suggested using patent-data analysis for this. Patents function as precursors of technological developments, before a new technology has reached the mainstream market. The degree of convergence between new patents and existing patents and publications can anticipate the direction that the industry is taking, revealing industry convergence trends.[26] However, not all industries are patent-intensive – services industries and digital platforms are a case in point. What, then, might enable the prediction of whether industry boundaries will blur?

## Nonmarket forces

Developments in the macro-environment, possibly because of stakeholder actions (see Chapter 3) can significantly influence market dynamics and the ability of firms to create and capture value. As these developments are external to the market environment, they are commonly referred to as nonmarket forces. While these forces can sometimes be beneficial for companies, for example, if they create an economic boom, at other times they can produce an unfavourable context, for example, an armed conflict – however, for businesses in the defense industry armed conflict generates revenues and profits.

Nonmarket issues with which firms are confronted may play out in various settings – from courtrooms, through social media, to the national parliament. The arena in which a nonmarket issue unfolds can affect which interest group or actor is successful. The arena can also shift. For example, when losing in the courtroom, a coalition of actors may shift its focus to social media and news media, where it may be able to get the upper hand. Nonmarket conflicts can occur in different arenas – for instance, in the legislative, executive, judicial or public arena. Within these different arenas, actors need to be aware of the characteristics of each arena. In a political arena such as the parliament, it is essential to know which parties hold power, in which areas, and how to engage in corporate political activity (see also the last Strategic Focus in this chapter). Every political system has its own unique set of institutional norms, formal protocols, and informal rules that must be considered. Furthermore, arenas also differ across regions and countries. For example, whereas German courts tend to take a balanced position between employees and employers, American courts tend to side with employers. Nonmarket information frequently plays a decisive role in deciding who emerges victorious in an issue.[27] This can be true for all arenas. The most crucial information for winning an issue may differ across arenas. To win an issue in court frequently requires a different information set than trying to win the issue in the political arena. This underscores that holding the right information for the right nonmarket arena is vital.

## STRATEGIC FOCUS

### Scenario planning: An explanation and real-life example[28]

With the business environment having become more volatile and unpredictable, making it difficult to anticipate how the future will unfold, firms are increasingly turning to scenario planning.[29] **Scenario planning** is a tool to develop alternative scenarios of the future competitive context to inform the company's strategy.[30] In contrast to forecasting, which relies on quantitative data from the past to make exact predictions about the future (see the *Confrontrix* diagnostic chapter), scenario planning makes use of qualitative data and gut-feelings to encourage out-of-the-box thinking that envisions plausible general models of the future.[31] Traditionally, scenario planning has been used by firms operating in capital intensive industries, such as energy and aerospace.[32] Shell has been one of the pioneers of scenario planning, using it since the 1970s to guide its decision-making.[33]

Source: © Gabo_Arts (2022) / Shutterstock.

Another company that uses scenario planning to respond to growing uncertainty in the global markets is Rolls-Royce. Known initially for its iconic luxury automobile, Rolls-Royce no longer produces cars. The company started in 1884 as an electrical and mechanical business established by Henry Royce, who later teamed up with Charles Rolls to build a range of vehicles sold exclusively by CS Rolls & Co. At the start of the First World War, Royce designed his first aero engine called *the Eagle*, which powered approximately half of the Allied aircraft, thus leading the company into the aviation industry. Rolls-Royce sold the rights to the Rolls-Royce car name and brand to BMW in 1998. Today it focuses on three core business areas: civil aerospace (where it is a prominent manufacturer and service company for aeronautical engines), power systems (where the company focuses on producing engines used for non-aviation purposes), and defense (where the company makes engines for military transport, patrol, and combat aircraft). Rolls-Royce has customers in more than 150 countries. In 2022, it generated an annual revenue of roughly £12.7 billion and an operating profit of £652 million, while its gross R&D expenditure was nearly £1.3 billion. In 2020, the firm joined the *UN Race to Zero* campaign, pledging to achieve net-zero greenhouse gas emissions by 2030, and aims to play a fundamental role in enabling sectors in which it operates to achieve net-zero carbon by 2050.

Since 2016, Rolls-Royce has incorporated scenario planning into its strategic planning and risk management procedures.[34] Scenario planning is not used to prepare forecasts or business projections but to explore the future and prepare the firm to deal with plausible, alternative future states. Climate-related scenarios take established climate-change science and apply these projections in a business context to explore their potential impact. As a firm operating in carbon-intensive sectors, climate change[35] will have a material effect on Rolls-Royce's business strategy and model. Consequently, the firm has developed three distinct scenarios tailored to Rolls-Royce's business circumstances to help assess the potential impact of climate change on its business strategy and model. Each of these scenarios includes a spectrum of transition risks and longer-term risks pertinent to the firm, such as the impact of temperature rise on the safe operating parameters of the equipment it produces, responses from international policies, carbon pricing, and variables such as the global oil price and changing societal perceptions concerning air travel.

The findings of the exercise on climate scenario planning at Rolls-Royce identified a range of potential plausible impacts on its business model and strategy because of climate change. Many of these findings relate to what Rolls-Royce identifies as known principal risks, such as supply chain disruption, business continuity, and talent retention. However, climate change was found to intensify or accelerate this risk. As a result of the scenario planning process, Rolls-Royce now considers climate change as a principal risk in its own right. It is interesting to note that the climate scenario planning process at Rolls-Royce not only identified business risks but also significant business opportunities for the firm because of the transition to a low carbon economy – namely, opportunities to address the demand for low and zero-carbon technologies to facilitate and accelerate this transition. The opportunities include the introduction of aerospace and marine engines powered by electrical (battery) or hydrogen sources and the development of Small Modular Reactors for nuclear energy generation.

## PESTEL-segments

The macro-environment, which confronts firms with a large variety of nonmarket developments, can be divided into six interrelated segments named after their nature: **P**olitical, **E**conomic, **S**ocio-cultural (often simply referred to as social), **T**echnological, **E**cological and **L**egal. The six segments together make up the PESTEL-framework shown in Table 4.1. A firm must assess which of these six segments have the most significance for their operations and whether it is sufficiently aware of the events and trends in relation to each segment. The *Confrontrix* diagnostic chapter provides some practical guidelines on how the PESTEL-framework can be used to derive relevant insights which, as explained in the *iSense* diagnostic chapter (featured in Part II of this book), can subsequently be used as input for an adequate SWOT-analysis.

### Political

Political factors are about how and to what extent a government intervenes in and influences a particular industry. This can include government policy, political stability or instability, tax policy (see also the Crack-the-Case on the tobacco industry), corruption, foreign trade policy, trade restrictions, and funding schemes. These are all factors that need to be considered when analyzing the political segment. Some industries are highly impacted by politics, such as the pharmaceutical industry in the UK.[36] The budget allocated to healthcare in the UK is a highly discussed topic nationwide. As the government is a big buyer of drugs, changes

**TABLE 4.1**    Forces of the macro-environment with examples

| P | E | S | T | E | L |
|---|---|---|---|---|---|
| *Political* | *Economic* | *Socio-cultural* | *Technological* | *Ecological* | *Legal* |
| Political stability | Economic growth | Demographics | Digitalization | Climate (and climate change) | Antitrust laws |
| Government policy | Disposable income | Life expectancy | Automation | Weather | Discrimination laws |
| Corruption | Interest rates | Career attitudes | Robotization | River and sea levels | Consumer protection laws |
| Trade policy and restrictions | Inflation rates | Traditions | Mass media advances | Natural disasters | Employment laws |
| Tax policy | Exchange rates | Cultural norms and barriers | Technological standards | Recycling standards | Intellectual property laws |
| Internal political issues | Unemployment rates | Lifestyle attitudes | Technological awareness | Animal welfare | Health and safety laws |

in its healthcare budget will directly influence pharmaceutical firms and medical technology suppliers. For some firms, political factors can represent an opportunity. Consider the field of renewable energy. Governments in many countries have put significant efforts in shaping and leveraging the development of this field,[37] which has been achieved partly through providing subsidies. For renewable energy firms, such subsidization schemes represent an opportunity.

## STRATEGIC FOCUS

### Corporate political activity

Companies often attempt to shape government policy in ways favourable to them. These efforts are referred to as corporate political activity (or CPA).[38] CPA can be of two types: proactive CPA and reactive CPA.

### Proactive CPA

Proactive CPA includes informing government decision-makers about the impact of possible legislation, actively promoting the reduction of regulations, and lobbying – either through trade associations (see Chapter 13) or alone. Firms may also employ other novel approaches to proactive CPA. However, what connects proactive activities is that they are all focused on actively trying to influence the legislative and regulatory processes. Proactive political actions can take various forms. A very common action is to seek ways to reduce the regulation of the firm. Firms can employ different tactics to influence policy makers. The most mundane process is to inform legislators of the unfavourable impact a government regulation is having or may have when implemented. When policy makers remain undeterred, a firm may also decide to play out the battle in the court of public opinion. Here, firms launch marketing campaigns to sway public opinion in their favour. The firms hope that public support will secure support among legislators. Lastly, a firm may win influence over the legislative process through lobbying.

## Reactive CPA

Reactive CPA includes activities of a passive or anticipatory nature, such as tracking the development of legislation and regulations. Reactive political actions center around compliance. Firms may track the legislative process to see which regulations may be revoked, changed, or implemented. By doing so, firms hope to be well prepared to comply with rules and regulations. Furthermore, a firm may choose to exceed compliance. While seeming unnecessary, exceeding compliance can have three distinct benefits. First, it may increase the odds that a firm can keep its business processes intact because it exceeds the compliance standards coming into effect. Second, it may see this as a unique selling point to attract potential customers. For example, Volvo is long known for exceeding compliance standards and building exceptionally safe vehicles. Third, exceeding compliance can serve as a strategy to prevent the tightening of regulations in the future. When an industry shows exceedingly high standards, legislators may have less incentive to create laws to codify additional compliance rules.

## Economic

Economic factors concern an economy's performance. They include economic growth (or decline), the gross domestic product (GDP), customers' disposable income, inflation rates, wage rates, exchange rates, interest rates and unemployment rates. The factors, expressed as economic indicators, influence demand and supply dynamics and customers' purchasing power. They also therefore affect the sales, pricing, product offering, and profitability of firms. The growth of industries is frequently linked to the growth of an economy, which can be measured through growth in GDP. When firms evaluate the potential of certain geographic areas to invest in, they often look to this indicator, which varies across regions and countries. With the COVID-19 pandemic, many countries saw a downturn in economic growth, forcing firms to revise their growth rates.

## Socio-cultural

The socio-cultural segment captures the demographic characteristics, norms, customs, and values of the population in which a firm is located. Demographic characteristics include population growth, birth and death rates, age and gender, life expectancy rates, income distribution, social stratification and inequality, education levels, and ethnicity. Geographic indicators include population density and distribution across cities and rural areas. Lifestyle markers encompass career attitudes, health consciousness, well-being, work-life balance, sustainability concerns, and attitudes towards government, work, and savings. Social factors are crucial to understanding customers' wants and the desires of a firm's workforce. For example, the increased concern about sustainability has compelled firms to change their practices regarding the consumption of resources and the treatment of production waste.

Similarly, an increase in health consciousness has prompted food firms to invest in organic, vegetarian, vegan, light or zero-sugar product categories. These categories, some of which are more healthy than alternative categories only in the mind of consumers, have grown immensely in advanced economies.[39]

## Technological

Technological factors pertain to infrastructure and innovation related indicators that affect how firms operate. They refer to technology investment incentives, R&D activity, internet and communication infrastructure, patent activity, productivity improvements, startups per capita, technology life cycles, and the amount of technological awareness that a market possesses. These factors affect firms' investment decisions in specific locations as firms operate on the top of technological infrastructures. For example, technology-oriented firms tend to establish themselves in innovation hubs like Silicon Valley, Beijing, Bengaluru, London, New York City, Shanghai, Singapore, Tel Aviv or Tokyo.[40] These tech hubs display well-developed IT infrastructures, substantial investment opportunities, an ecosystem of business partners, and a network of investors that allow firms to increase their return on R&D.

## Ecological

Ecological factors include, among others, weather, temperature, climate change, sea levels, water and air pollution levels, natural disasters, pressures from NGOs, recycling standards, and renewable energies. Ecological factors are increasingly recognized as very important due to the increasing scarcity of raw materials used by firms in their operations, pollution and carbon footprint targets set by governments, and increasing customer awareness of and attention to the environmental practices of firms. Some industries, such as agriculture, insurance, and tourism, depend significantly on ecological factors. For these industries, changes in ecological factors can dramatically affect profitability. The growing societal awareness about global warming and environmental protection affects how firms operate in these industries and which products they offer. This has led to many firms becoming more responsive and transparent regarding sustainability and corporate social responsibility (CSR) (see Chapter 2). Such trends have impacted car manufacturers, creating an opportunity to score big by developing electric cars and hybrids.

## Legal

Legal factors include specific laws, such as discrimination laws, antitrust laws, employment laws, customer protection laws, copyright and patent laws, and health and safety laws. When firms compete in several markets, they need to be familiar with different legislation systems. It requires moderate investment to acquire such knowledge and adapt to each reality. For example, Uber experienced several licensing issues in Germany, the Netherlands, and the UK because the legislation in these countries had not taken ride-sharing business models into account.[41] In Denmark, Uber was banned following a new taxi legislation.[42]

## CRACK-THE-CASE
The tobacco industry facing nonmarket challenges[43]

Source: © Hayati Kayhan (2023) / Shutterstock.

How do you lobby a government to make a cancer-inducing product more profitable? This is a question that tobacco firms have asked themselves for years. During the last century, the tobacco industry found itself in a very different situation. The adverse effects of smoking had not yet been fully recognized and cigarette brands were advertised on national television, with actors even portraying doctors in the commercials. This all has changed in the last decades as the health risks of tobacco have become irrefutable. Many countries have tightened regulations around tobacco to reduce consumption and the associated ill effects on people's health. In the wake of this, the tobacco industry has had to think about how to deal with this important nonmarket-environment issue.

For years, the tobacco lobby in many countries has followed a two-pronged approach: studies highlighting the negative health impacts of tobacco were discredited, and tobacco regulation was framed as being authoritarian. It was only when the health risks of smoking became incontrovertible that the lobby decided to change its strategy. The public increasingly began to regard smoking as a bad habit, which was expensive and unhealthy. Also, various nations moved to ban lobbying by the tobacco industry. In 2008 the World Health Organization approved Article 5.3, which outlined that government officials may only interact with the tobacco lobby for technical communication. The Netherlands became one of the initial nations to adopt the framework. While the framework does not ban parliamentarians from interacting with the lobby, many politicians see the tobacco lobby as toxic. Affiliating or merely talking with the tobacco lobby could be used against politicians by their rivals.

*(Continued)*

With the public being aware of its harm and politicians unwilling to talk with the lobby, the tobacco industry in the Netherlands considered launching a campaign to equate tobacco with alcohol. The lobby felt that the public opinion may soften on tobacco when it was highlighted that alcohol continued to be widely accepted in society despite having numerous adverse health effects. The idea was however abandoned while still in development.

Later, the lobby implemented a new two-pronged nonmarket approach. First, it started to promote CSR to the extent that it could. In the Netherlands, it became common to see three messages on the websites of tobacco companies: do not start smoking; if you are a smoker, stop smoking; and if you cannot stop smoking, consider using less harmful cigarette types such as e-cigarettes.[44] This was an interesting approach – encouraging customers to stop using their product. But this was the only communication the industry could employ to promote itself as responsible. Second, the tobacco lobby found a compelling issue to center its political activity around: border effects. Each time a country raised taxes on tobacco, the retail price of the product would increase relative to other nations. When two adjacent countries levied different taxes on cigarettes, a border effect emerged, such that people could buy the product in the country where taxes – and, thus, retail prices – were lower. This dynamic has been the foundation of the Dutch tobacco lobby's political activity in recent years. The lobby keeps up the effort to convince policy makers at all levels to not increase taxes on tobacco as this will not reduce consumption – it would only incentivize smokers to buy cigarettes in a neighbouring country where taxes are lower. Tax increases, the lobby argues, will not contribute to public health in the Netherlands, but would harm the economy and small retailers.

As of 2020, 85% of the price of a cigarette sold in the Netherlands is essentially the tax on the product, which is comparable to 83% of the price being the tax in Belgium.[45] These tax rates are significantly higher than the 69% tax in Germany. While experts argue that raising taxes further is the best way for the Dutch government to dissuade smoking, the government has not done so for years. Instead, the government has opted for other approaches, such as banning smoking areas inside clubs and requiring grocery stores to hide cigarette packs from sight. The lobbying effort appeared to be bearing fruit, but in May 2022 Dutch government officials proposed a gradual increase in taxation to the tune of 500% of the selling price. This proposal would slowly change the price of a pack of cigarettes from around €8 to €40 over 11 years. This level of taxation would make smoking as expensive as in Australia, reaching a price point at which most smokers would no longer be able to afford the habit. However, a member of the largest party in the government coalition (the liberal party) has criticized the proposal. The parliamentarian argued that such a hefty price increase creates unrest and does not solve the underlying issue. The politician continued by noting that the law proposed by the government does not account for border effects. One may wonder, will the government backtrack on its policy, or will the tobacco lobby's nonmarket approach go up in smoke?

## Questions

1. What developments in the macro-environment have been most confrontational for tobacco firms?
2. Describe the corporate political activity (CPA) tactics employed by the tobacco lobby over time.

## Interrelatedness between PESTEL-factors

Although the PESTEL-factors have been discussed separately here, in practice they can be highly intertwined. For instance, some argue that at its root the COVID-19 pandemic is an ecological issue. It is suggested to be linked to an unprecedented destruction of nature, which has brought wildlife and human activity into close proximity and made wildlife-to-human transmission of diseases more likely.[46] The issue of deforestation is related to rapid population growth and urbanization, which are developments in the socio-economic domain. Governments worldwide took a variety of restrictive measures to curb and halt the spread of the COVID-19 virus, varying from making it mandatory for citizens to maintain sufficient distance between each other and to wear a face mask in public spaces, to more drastic measures including the imposing of near-complete economic lockdowns. These political and legal factors, in turn, had a significant effect on both the socio-cultural domain, as people had to live in isolation from each other, and the economic domain in the form of reduced economic activity. These social and economic issues have largely been resolved because of the development of COVID-19 vaccines, which can be seen as part[47] of the technological domain of the macro-environment. All these different developments, pertaining to different domains of the macro-environment, have had large effects on firms. Take Adidas, for instance, one of the world's largest manufacturers of athletic shoes and apparel. In early 2020, customers could not visit 70% of the stores that were closed due to the pandemic. During its first-quarter earnings call with investors in 2020, the CFO of Adidas announced a 96% decrease in net income.

## Shaping and managing the nonmarket context

When opportunities are controlled by the market, as in the case of the consumer electronics industry, it is normal for a firm's strategy to take cue from market variables (see Chapter 10). However, when the government controls market opportunities, as is often the case in relation to the defense industry, a nonmarket strategy becomes important. A firm's **nonmarket strategy** refers to the activities undertaken to shape or manage the institutional or societal context in which the firm competes to achieve business-level and corporate-level goals.[48] These activities typically entail interactions with secondary stakeholders, and may range from public politics (e.g., lobbying) to private engagement (e.g., engaging with activists). Nonmarket strategy lies at the confluence of two complementary types of activities: CPA, as described in the Strategic Focus above, and CSR, as discussed in Chapter 2. Together, CPA and CSR are complementary nonmarket strategies.

Research suggests that engaging in CPA benefits firms, leading to better performance.[49] Research on CSR has yielded mixed results,[50] but consistently finds that responsible business conduct does not negatively impact firm performance. The effectiveness of a firm's nonmarket efforts depends on the firm's unique context and factors such as firm size. For instance, small and mid-sized firms may not have the power to exert political pressure. As such, these firms are more likely to bargain collectively, whereas large firms are more likely to go at it alone.[51] Other factors that tend to be associated with nonmarket efforts include a firm's age, its degree of diversification (see Chapter 11), its dependence on government contracts, and the availability of cash. Foreign ownership has been identified as a factor linked to less nonmarket activity.[52]

## CLOSING CASE

Unlocking the revival of Victoria's Secret

Source: © Sorbis (2014) / Shutterstock.

Founded in 1977, Victoria's Secret had a humble beginning after founder Roy Raymond felt embarrassed purchasing lingerie for his wife, Gaye, at a traditional department store.[53] With $80,000 secured for funding from their family and bank, Roy and Gaye opened the first Victoria's Secret store in Palo Alto, California with a Victorian-era theme to invoke sophistication.[54] The Raymond family soon thereafter sold Victoria's Secret to billionaire investor Les Wexner in 1982 for $1 million, which turned out to be quite the bargain. Under Wexner's leadership, Victoria's Secret flourished in the 1990s and 2000s. By the early 1990s Victoria's Secret had become the largest lingerie retailer in the US with more than 300 stores nationally and revenue surpassing $1 billion.[55] By the 2000s Victoria's Secret was firing on all cylinders with a host of world-famous models (which were dubbed as *Victoria's Secret Angels*) and a line-up of fly-off-the-shelf products led by Wonderbra and Wonderbody,[56] sculpting the standard of what sexy should look like. By 2015, Victoria's Secret was operating in more than 80 countries, with over 1,200 stores globally, and total revenue approaching $8 billion.[57] However, in 2016, Victoria's Secret's fortunes began to change.

Several factors played a role in Victoria's Secret fall from grace. First, Victoria's Secret was slow to adapt to new trends. While Victoria's Secret continued to push their padded and push-up bras, women were increasingly choosing comfort over appearance, shopping for bralettes, sports bras, and 'athleisure' clothing instead of the typical products that Victoria's Secret offered.[58] Second, the rise of online shopping led to a sharp decline in foot traffic at shopping malls. This directly impacted Victoria's Secret because nearly all their stores are located in shopping malls. The firm has responded by decreasing their store count and focusing on e-commerce offerings, but their online shopping experience was sub-par. According to a study conducted by the Baymard Institute, Victoria's Secret's e-commerce user interface ranked 'mediocre'. Victoria's Secret ranks particularly poor in product listing and specifications, according to this study. With an insufficient e-commerce platform, Victoria's Secret was caught off guard and was forced to play 'catch-up' to the rest of the prolific e-commerce retailers.

Another relevant factor was the rise of the 'Me Too' movement. Although initially coined in 2006, this movement took centre stage in 2017 because of the sexual assault allegations against Harvey Weinstein. Women all over the globe began to speak out about their own experiences of abuse, spreading their stories with the hashtag: #MeToo. The movement brought forth wide-ranging issues in society, one of them being the topic of body positivity. The image of what sexy should look like had been crafted by male CEOs, and created a standard of what men found sexy, not necessarily one that women found sexy themselves. Furthermore, Victoria's Secret's product offering was limited for women of smaller and larger sizes. This further narrowed the standard of what sexy was, subconsciously implying that if a woman did not fit within Victoria's Secret's standard, then they were not considered sexy. The emphasis on body positivity began to change this narrative. Instead of trying to fit into this social construct of beauty, more women began to focus on loving their body no matter the shape or size. Victoria's Secret brand reputation was damaged by this because they were seen as the anti-body-positive corporation, negatively weighing on customer sentiment. As a result, Victoria's Secret market share of lingerie declined from 32% in 2016 to 16% in the spring of 2020.[59]

In recent years, Victoria's Secret has tried to change their faltering brand reputation. The firm introduced a more casual and comfortable line of clothing, featured a more diverse and inclusive line-up of models in their advertisements and website, increased their focus on body positivity, and reconfigured their board of directors to include a majority of women. Nonetheless, sales have yet to recover. In fact, sales have declined every year, except for one, since 2016.[60] Customers might feel that Victoria's Secret's strategic changes are disingenuous – they have implemented several strategies that give off the appearance of a changed firm, but their product offering is still limited to the same old sizes and shapes. And even if Victoria's Secret was genuine with their changes, it still might not be enough to change customer perception of the brand and products. Could Victoria's Secret make even greater changes in order to reverse their looming demise? What should they do to turn around their fortunes?

## Questions

1. Which of the factors that played a role in Victoria's Secret's fall from grace do you deem most important, and to what extent do you think that this fall could have been foreseen?
2. Which choices could be most appropriate for Victoria's Secret in the context of the challenges, as described in the case, for making a successful comeback?

# Summary

- Whereas the micro-environment of a firm refers to actors who are in direct contact with the firm, such as the firm's customers, suppliers, distributors, and competitors, the macro-environment refers to general contextual factors that have bearing for all firms in the industry and even those outside the industry.
- The general contextual factors that make up the macro-environment can be segmented into the political, economic, socio-cultural, technological, ecological, and legal categories.
- An important part of the micro-environment is the market environment, commonly referred to as the market, which is the place where the firm and its competitors interact with and compete for customers. A firm may compete in just one market or in multiple markets.
- Identifying a firm's rivals must happen through both the outside-in approach and the inside-out approach (see Chapter 1 for a discussion of both approaches). Both go hand-in-hand.
- Market commonality refers to a situation when two firms operate in the same market. Market commonality and similarity in the resources and capabilities of firms can help identify rivals.
- The boundaries between many industries are blurring due to environmental factors, technology disruption, industry convergence, and supply and demand dynamics.
- Scenario planning is a tool to facilitate decisions regarding strategy based on the envisioning of alternative scenarios about the future using qualitative data and out-of-the-box thinking.
- Nonmarket strategy refers to activities to improve a firm's performance by engaging with and managing the institutional and social context of the firm.

# Review questions

1. What does market commonality mean and why is it important for understanding rivalry?
2. What are the factors that underlie the blurring of many industry boundaries in today's business context?
3. What are the different segments of the macro-environment of a firm?
4. What is the firm's nonmarket environment and why is it important to analyze it on an ongoing basis?
5. How can nonmarket strategy be used to improve firms' performance?

# Discussion questions

1. Firms like Apple and Google, which compete in multiple lines of business, may have market commonality with respect to several of these. To what extent is this likely to increase or decrease their rivalry?
2. How might scenario planning be useful for informing strategic decisions in a context in which industry boundaries are blurring?

3.  Besides the tobacco industry, the fast-food industry is also facing some stigmatization because of the apparent ill effects of fast food on health. What nonmarket strategy would you recommend for firms in the fast-food industry? Discuss its pros and cons.

## EXPERIENTIAL EXERCISES

1.  Take a firm you have affinity with. Who are its main rivals? To what extent is it well equipped to deal with prominent social trends?
2.  Imagine you are the CEO of a major fossil-fuel company, and that most of your shareholders are pressing you to prioritize short-term shareholder value creation. However, there are also some shareholders who are asking you to consider moving towards renewable energy. What type of nonmarket strategy would you employ to address the expectations of both shareholder groups?

## Further reading

Capron, L. and Chatain, O. (2008) 'Competitors' resource-oriented strategies: Acting on competitors' resources through interventions in factor-markets and political markets', *Academy of Management Review*, 33: 97–121.

Chen, M. (1996) 'Competitor analysis and interfirm rivalry: Toward a theoretical integration', *Academy of Management Review*, 21 (1): 100–34.

Ramirez, R. and Wilkinson, A. (2018) *Strategic Reframing: The Oxford Scenario Planning Approach*. Oxford: Oxford University Press.

Withers, M.C., Ireland, R.D., Miller, D., Harrison, J.S. and Boss, D. (2018) 'Competitive landscape shifts: The influence of strategic entrepreneurship on shifts in market commonality', *Academy of Management Review*: 43 (3): 349–70.

## Endnotes (references)

1.  Reuters Staff (2019) 'Disney to bundle Disney+, Hulu, ESPN+ at popular Netflix price', *Reuters*, August 7. www.reuters.com/article/us-walt-disney-streaming-idUSKCN1UW2JB (accessed June 14, 2023)
2.  Alexander, J. (2020) 'Quibi is coming, with the worst – or maybe best – timing', *The Verge*, April 5. www.theverge.com/2020/4/5/21202564/quibi-launch-streaming-short-form-video-date-price-jeffrey-katzenberg (accessed June 14, 2023).
3.  Kotler, P.T. and Keller, K.L. (2016). *Marketing Management* (15th ed.). Harlow: Pearson Education.
4.  Castrogiovanni, G.J. (1991) 'Environmental munificence: A theoretical assessment', *Academy of Management Review*, 16 (3): 542–65.
5.  Chen, M. (1996) 'Competitor analysis and interfirm rivalry: Toward a theoretical integration', *Academy of Management Review*, 21 (1): 100–34.
6.  Porter, M.E. (1980b) *Competitive Strategy: Techniques for Analysing Industries and Competitors*. New York, NY: Simon & Schuster.
7.  Chen (1996)

8.  Withers, M.C., Ireland, R.D., Miller, D., Harrison, J.S. and Boss, D. (2018) 'Competitive landscape shifts: The influence of strategic entrepreneurship on shifts in market commonality', *Academy of Management Review*, 43: 349–70.

9.  Barney, J.B. (2001) 'Is the resource-based "view" a useful perspective for strategic management research? Yes', *Academy of Management Review*, 26 (1): 41–56; Wernerfelt, B. (1984) 'A resource-based view of the firm', *Strategic Management Journal*, 5: 171–80.

10. Barney, J.B. (1991) 'Firm resources and sustained competitive advantage', *Journal of Management*, 17: 99–120.

11. Collis, D.J. (1994) 'Research note: How valuable are organizational capabilities?', *Strategic Management Journal*, Winter Special Issue 15 (S1): 143–52.

12. Teece, D.J. (2007) 'Explicating dynamic capabilities: The nature and microfoundations of (sustainable) enterprise performance', *Strategic Management Journal*, 28 (13): 1319–50.

13. Capron, L. and Chatain, O. (2008) 'Competitors' resource-oriented strategies: Acting on competitors' resources through interventions in factor-markets and political markets', *Academy of Management Review*, 33: 97–121.

14. Maritan, C. and Peteraf, M.A. (2011) 'Building a bridge between resource acquisition and resource accumulation', *Journal of Management*, 37: 1374–89.

15. Goldman Sachs (2021) 'Millennials infographic', *Goldman Sachs*. www.goldmansachs.com/insights/archive/millennials (accessed June 14, 2023).

16. Braaksma, J. (2021) 'Thuisbezorgen boodschappen ontpopt zich als lieveling van investeerders', *Financieel Dagblad*, September 27. https://fd.nl/bedrijfsleven/1413875/thuisbezorgers-boodschappen-ontpoppen-zich-als-lieveling-van-investeerders (accessed June 14, 2023).

17. Weijer, C. (2021) 'De zegen van thuisbezorging', *Financieel Dagblad*, October 22. https://fd.nl/tech-en-innovatie/1416430/de-zegen-van-thuisbezorging (accessed June 14, 2023).

18. Szalavetz, A. (2022) 'The digitalisation of manufacturing and blurring industry boundaries', *CIRP Journal of Manufacturing Science and Technology*, 37: 332–43.

19. Atluri, V., Dietz, M. and Henke, N. (2017) 'Competing in a world of sectors without borders', *McKinsey Quarterly*, 3: 32–47.

20. Szalavetz (2022)

21. Agarwal, N. and Brem, A. (2015) 'Strategic business transformation through technology convergence: Implications from General Electric's industrial internet initiative', *International Journal of Technology Management*, 67 (2–4): 196–214.

22. Szalavetz (2022)

23. Nicholls-Nixon, C.L. and Jasinski, D. (1995) 'The blurring of industry boundaries: An explanatory model applied to telecommunications', *Industrial and Corporate Change*, 4 (4): 755–68.

24. Curran, C.S., Bröring, S. and Leker, J. (2010) 'Anticipating converging industries using publicly available data', *Technological Forecasting and Social Change*, 77 (3): 38595.

25. Atluri et al. (2017)

26. Curran et al. (2010)

27. Baron, D.P. (1995) 'Integrated strategy: Market and nonmarket components', *California Management Review*, 37 (2): 47–65.

28. Ramírez, R., Churchhouse, S., Palermo, A. and Hoffmann, J. (2017) 'Using scenario planning to reshape strategy', *MIT Sloan Management Review*, 58 (4). https://sloanreview.mit.edu/article/using-scenario-planning-to-reshape-strategy/ (accessed June 14, 2023); Rolls-Royce (2022) 'Climate change'. https://web.archive.org/save/https://www.rolls-royce.com/sustainability/approach/climate-change (accessed July 30, 2023).

29. Harris, S. and Zeisler, S. (2002) 'Weak signals: Detecting the next big thing', *The Futurist*, 36 (6): 21–9; Holopainen, M. and Toivonen, M. (2012) 'Weak signals: Ansoff today', *Futures*, 44 (3): 198–205; Grant, R.M. (2003) 'Strategic planning in a turbulent environment: Evidence from the Oil Majors', *Strategic Management Journal*, 24: 491–517.

30. Ringland, G. (1998) *Scenario Planning: Managing for the Future.* Hoboken, NJ: Wiley.

31. Lindgren, M. and Bandhold, H. (2009) *Scenario Planning.* London: Palgrave Macmillan.

32. Accenture (2016) 'Scenario-based planning: Exploring the best chance on success', *Accenture Insights,* April 22. www.accenture.com/nl-en/blogs/insights/scenario-based-planning-exploring-the-best-chance-on-success (accessed June 14, 2023).

33. Shell (2022b) 'Shell scenarios', *shell.com.* www.shell.com/energy-and-innovation/the-energy-future/scenarios.html (accessed June 14, 2023).

34. Rolls-Royce (n.d.) 'Climate scenario planning', https://www.rolls-royce.com/~/media/Files/R/Rolls-Royce/documents/sustainability/climate-scenario-planning-for-publication.pdf (accessed July 30, 2023).

35. Adapted from Rolls-Royce (n.d.)

36. Walley, T., Earl-Slater, A., Haycox, A. and Bagust, A. (2000) 'An integrated national pharmaceutical policy for the United Kingdom?', *British Medical Journal*, 321 (7275): 1523–6.

37. International Energy Association (2021a) *Global EV Outlook 2021.* Paris: IEA. www.iea.org/reports/global-ev-outlook-2021 (accessed June 14, 2023); International Energy Association (2021b) *Renewables 2021.* Paris: IEA. www.iea.org/reports/renewables-2021 (accessed June 14, 2023).

38. Hillman, A., Keim, G. and Schuler, D. (2004) 'Corporate political activity: A review and research agenda', *Journal of Management*, 30 (6): 837–57.

39. Euromonitor International (2020) 'The rise of vegan and vegetarian food', November, www.euromonitor.com/the-rise-of-vegan-and-vegetarian-food/report (accessed June 14, 2024); Jones (2020) 'Veganism: Why are vegan diets on the rise', *BBC News*, January 2. www.bbc.com/news/business-44488051 (accessed July 27, 2023).

40. KPMG (2021) *Technology Innovation Hubs.* https://web.archive.org/web/20230503192511/https://www.kpmg.us/industries/technology/tech-hubs.html (accessed July 27, 2023).

41. Reuters Staff (2021) 'Factbox: Uber's legal challenges around the world', *Reuters*, February 19. www.reuters.com/article/us-uber-britain-factbox-idUSKBN2AJ1N7 (accessed June 14, 2023).

42. Skydsgaard, N.R. (2017a) 'Uber to end services in Denmark after less than three years', *Reuters*, March 28. www.reuters.com/article/us-uber-tech-denmark-idUSKBN16Z10G (accessed June 14, 2023).

43. European Commission (n.d.) 'Taxes in Europe Database v.3' https://ec.europa.eu/taxation_customs/tedb/taxSearch.html (accessed June 14, 2021); Nationale Smokkel Monitor (2022) 'De illegale tabakshandel compleet in kaart', Nationale Smokkel Monitor. https://smokkelmonitor.nl (website in Dutch, accessed June 14, 2023); Lester, T. (2020) 'How Philip Morris is planning for a smoke-free future', *Harvard Business Review online*, https://hbr.org/2020/07/how-philip-morris-is-planning-for-a-smoke-free-future (accessed July 30, 2023); Philip Morris International (2022) 'Our smoke-free vision'. https://web.archive.org/web/20221013130817/https://www.pmi.com/our-transformation/our-smoke-free-vision (accessed June 14, 2021); WHO (2012) *Technical Resource for Country Implementation of WHO Framework Convention on Tobacco Control Article 5.3 on the Protection of Public Health Policies with Respect to Tobacco Control from Commercial and Other Vested Interests of the Tobacco Industry.* Geneva: WHO. www.who.int/publications/i/item/9789241503730 (accessed June 14, 2023).

44. Philip Morris International (2022)
45. European Commission (n.d.)
46. WWF (n.d.) 'Nature and pandemics'. https://www.wwf.org.uk/nature-and-pandemics (accessed July 27, 2023)
47. Adidas (2020) 'Adidas nearly doubles e-com sales in challenging second quarter', press release August 6, www.adidas-group.com/en/media/news-archive/press-releases/2020/adidas-nearly-doubles-e-com-sales-challenging-second-quarter (accessed July 27, 2023); Belvedere, M.J. (2020), 'Adidas says first-quarter profits fell more than 90% due to coronavirus store closures', *CNBC*. www.cnbc.com/2020/04/27/adidas-q1-2020-earnings.html (accessed July 27, 2023).
48. Baron (1995); Lux, S., Crook, R. and Woehr, D.J. (2011) 'Mixing business with politics: A meta-analysis of the antecedents and outcomes of corporate political activity', *Journal of Management*, 37: 223–47; Mellahi, K., Frynas, J.G., Sun, P. and Siegel, D. (2016) 'A review of the nonmarket strategy literature: Toward a multi-theoretical integration', *Journal of Management*. https://doi.org/10.1177/0149206315617241; Wrona, T. and Sinzig, C. (2017) 'Nonmarket strategy research: Systematic literature review and future directions', *Journal of Business Economics*, 88: 253–317.
49. Hillman et al. (2004)
50. McWilliams, A. and Siegel, D. (2000) 'Corporate social responsibility and financial performance: Correlation or misspecification?' *Strategic Management Journal*, 21 (5): 603–9.
51. Hillman et al. (2004)
52. Getz, K. (1996) 'Politically active foreign-owned firms in the US: Elephants or chickens?', in D. Woodward and D. Nigh (eds), *Beyond Us and Them: Foreign Ownership and US Competitiveness*. Columbia, SC: University of South Carolina Press, 837–57.
53. Business Insider Nederland (2020b) 'The rise and fall of Victoria's Secret, America's biggest lingerie retailer', *Business Insider,* May 5. www.businessinsider.nl/victorias-secret-rise-and-fall-history-2019-5 (accessed June 14, 2023).
54. Campbell, H. (2021) 'The surprising origin story of Victoria's Secret', *The List,* June 2. www.thelist.com/427006/the-surprising-originstory-of-victorias-secret (accessed June 14, 2023).
55. Business Insider Nederland (2020b)
56. Business Insider Nederland (2020b)
57. Business Insider Nederland (2020b)
58. Bhattarai, A (2020) '5 factors that led to Victoria's Secret's fall', *The Washington Post,* February 21. www.washingtonpost.com/business/2020/02/20/5-factors-that-led-victorias-secrets-fall (accessed June 14, 2023).
59. Ell, K. (2021) 'The comeback continues at Victoria's Secret', *WWD*, February 25. https://wwd.com/fashion-news/intimates/victorias-secret-l-brands-earnings-1234743370. (accessed June 14, 2023).
60. Smith, P. (2023) 'Net sales of Victoria's Secret worldwide from 2010 to 2022', *Statista,* May 19. https://www.statista.com/statistics/255806/net-sales-of-victorias-secretworldwide (accessed May 30, 2023).

## Acknowledgements

The authors thank Emre Karali, Liam Goodman, Wieke Wagemans and Nick Ziats for their contribution to this chapter.

## Key terms

**Capabilities** – the competencies that harness resources to execute strategies that enable a company to achieve its goals

**Competitive rivalry** – the existence of active competition between firms

**Competitors** – firms that offer similar products and target the same customers

**Macro-environment** – the set of general contextual factors that matter for a company

**Market commonality** – participation by firms in the same market

**Market environment** – the place where the firm and its competitors interact and compete for customers

**Micro-environment** – the external actors that a company has direct contact with

**Nonmarket strategy** – activities to manage the firm's institutional and societal context

**Resources** – the principal building blocks of a company, which are fundamental to its strategy and provide the wherewithal to compete with rivals

**Scenario planning** – a tool for envisioning alternative scenarios about the future competitive context

# 5

# EMERGING TECHNOLOGIES

## LEARNING OBJECTIVES

After reading this chapter, you should be able to:

- analyze the stage of a technology using different technology life-cycle frameworks;
- identify the different technologies that culminated in Industry 4.0 and Web 3.0 revolutions;
- understand how Industry 4.0 is affecting existing industrial business models;
- assess how Web 3.0 is impacting internet-based business models;
- discern the different ways of collaborating and of organizing enabled digital technologies.

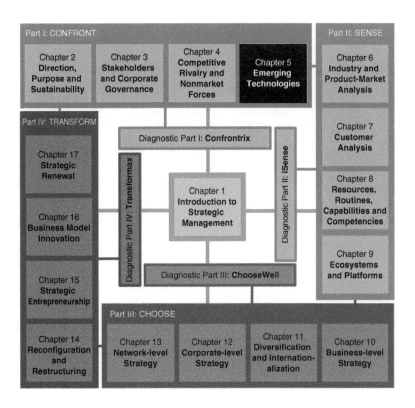

## OPENING CASE

### RealFevr: The fantasy leagues fever (Part I)

#### The inception

RealFevr was born on José Miranda's couch, while he was playing American basketball fantasy leagues. Fantasy leagues allow anyone to be the 'virtual' owner and/or coach of a football team and compete against friends' teams. Fantasy leagues are based on the on-field performance statistics of real-world players, and owners and coaches win or lose games based on those statistics. Born and raised in a football fan family, José always questioned why there were no good football fantasy leagues in Portugal, and in Europe more broadly. José, then, decided to create RealFevr, a football fantasy league that had two main distinguishing factors: a draft model and realistic statistics (see Figure 5.1). In the classic fantasy leagues, users have a budget to create their teams and they can acquire any player as long as they have the budget for it. This means that in the classic fantasy leagues, players are not unique, and users can have the same players and even alike teams. In the draft model, users always have different teams as players are unique and can only belong to a single virtual team. This small difference makes the fantasy leagues more engaging and challenging for users. The other distinguishing factor of RealFevr is more accurate and robust statistics. In the classic fantasy leagues, the statistical models were simplistic and often resulted in users feeling unsatisfied and disappointed. In RealFevr, the statistics are refined and improved, which considerably enhances the fantasy league's accuracy, directly impacting users' motivation and engagement with the game.

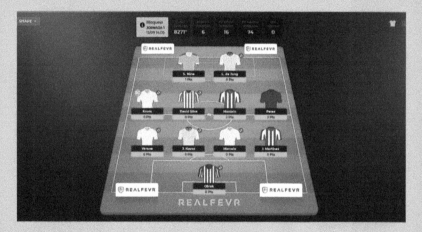

**FIGURE 5.1**   Example of team planning from RealFevr fantasy league app

#### The growth phase

With a distinctive model in mind, José convinced two friends to form a team and develop RealFevr in their spare time. In 2014, they were able to launch the RealFevr fantasy league beta version, which in a few months generated a couple of million visualizations and more than 1,500 registered users, without any structured marketing plan or investment. Not bad for a hobby! The dream team decided to run for funds: it was about time to get seed capital. After a couple of rounds of pitches, they found a potential investor who was a specialist in online traffic management and online advertising monetization models. The investor seemed the perfect partner to help RealFevr grow and prosper. The idea was to generate traffic towards the fantasy league and monetize it through online advertisement.

In 2015, the RealFevr team started to dedicate itself full time to the project, implementing an aggressive growth plan that encompassed the Portuguese Football league (100,000 users), the Brazilian league (60,000 users), and the 2018 World Cup (250,000 users), confirming the success of the RealFevr fantasy league model in attracting users. While the user base was showing a steady growth, the bottom line was displaying a different reality. Despite its growth, RealFevr did not have enough scale to be profitable: a problem that has become usual in online advertisement business models. At this point in time, RealFevr was web- and app-based and the traffic was spread across the two platforms, not having enough scale to monetize the traffic on either platform. The team needed to face the reality: RealFevr's user traffic was not big enough to win the online advertisement game.

## The options for the future

At this point, the RealFevr team and investors were pondering three different options for the future. The first option entailed shifting the business model from online advertisement to a software-as-a-service business model. In such a model RealFevr would sell the fantasy league service to official leagues from different countries. The official football leagues would pay a fee, and the estimated breakeven point would be around nine contracts. The main setback of this plan would be fierce competition from parties that had also shifted towards this business model all across Europe.

The second option centered on implementing a freemium business model, such that users would pay a fee to have access to premium features. It was estimated that about 3% of the registered users would pay the fee to access premium features. To break even, RealFevr would need to have around 1,000,000 registered users, which would require a sizable investment to launch and market several leagues simultaneously in different countries.

The third option entailed transition to a token-based business model in which RealFevr would adopt blockchain technology and create a cryptocurrency (tokens). This was the riskiest option of all in view of the team's lack of understanding of this emergent technology and the uncertainty surrounding the potential application of blockchain to the business.

The RealFevr case shows that sometimes even good products that are successful among users are difficult to monetize because they may not reach the scale necessary to be profitable. However, the RealFevr team still believes that the business could be reinvented. For them, the game is not over yet! (Read this chapter's Closing Case *RealFevr: Reinventing the business model from Web 2.0 to Web 3.0 (Part II)*.)

## Questions

1. Identify the technology trends adopted by RealFevr.
2. Analyze the pros and cons of the three business models that RealFevr is pondering for the future.

# Introduction

**Emergent technologies** are playing a key role in the accelerating pace of change firms are having to contend with. One consequence of this pace of change is that firms' positions of competitive advantage are becoming transient or temporary. Emergent technologies are either completely new technologies or advancements in existing technologies whose potential applications are still to be realized. These emergent technologies, and technology progression more generally, have the potential to revolutionize existing standards. For firms, emergent technologies and the ambiguity of technological change present unprecedented organizational and managerial challenges, which have bearing on their business models and the way they cooperate with others.

Emergent technologies play a decisive role in affecting a firm's cost and quality advantage, thereby affecting optimum output levels, customer satisfaction, and profitability. While the embracing of new technological developments allows firms to adapt their business models (see Chapter 16) and thus improve their prospects of survival and growth, it also implies the taking of risks and facing potential failures. A key challenge for firms is to build for the future without completely undermining their present position.

To equip you with the tools to identify the technology-development stage a firm is facing, this chapter discusses the technology-cycle models, specifically the S-curves cyclical model and the Gartner Hype-cycle model. The chapter also discusses how emergent technologies, especially the **Industry 4.0** and **Web 3.0** technologies, are impacting industrial and digital business models. Furthermore, the chapter describes how digital technologies are changing the way firms and individuals cooperate and organize through crowdsourcing, online communities, and decentralized autonomous organizations (DAOs).

# Technology life-cycle models

Emergent technologies can disrupt existing business models, transform value chains, create new markets, and crush entire industries. While it is impossible to fully predict the timing and impact of disruptive technologies, managers and investors can seek to identify and forecast their current and future rate of performance and expected value. In this regard, two models can help strategists evaluate the stage of the emergent technology, namely the S-curves cyclical model, and the Gardner Hype-cycle model.

## S-curves cyclical model

The emergence of a new technology can overturn the existing competitive landscape, creating new leaders and new losers. Therefore, it is of major importance that strategists understand and identify the life-cycle stage of a specific technology. The technology life-cycle evolutionary model,[1] also known as the **S-curves cyclical model**, serves as a good basis for identifying the performance and social acceptance dynamics of a new technology. The S-curves cyclical model centers on social and technological dynamics during eras of *ferment* and *incremental* change. The authors propose that a technological breakthrough, or discontinuity, triggers an era of intense technical variation and selection, culminating in a dominant design. Then follows a period of incremental technical progress, which may be interrupted by another technology breakthrough, which again creates a discontinuity[2] (see Figure 5.2). The model builds on Schumpeter's theory of creative destruction, which describes the incessant process of the dismantling of existing technologies, which creates space for the emergence of new, improved ones that increase productivity and revolutionize the economic structure.[3]

Technology discontinuity. The first stage of the technology life cycle, called technology discontinuity, represents the emergence of a new technology. It is anticipated that technology discontinuity can dramatically advance the industry, pushing the price-performance frontier. Usually, a technology discontinuity allows firms to either satisfy the same customer need but in a fundamentally different

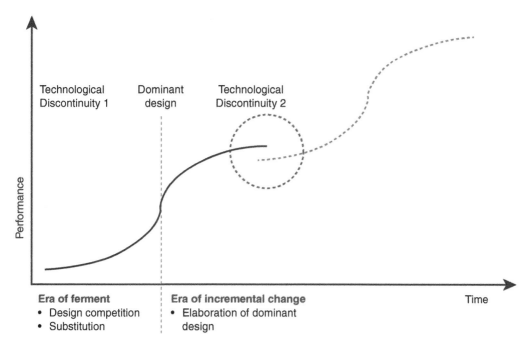

**FIGURE 5.2**  S-curved Model

Source: adapted from Anderson and Tushman (1990)

way, or address a new customer need with a new product architecture. In the discontinuity phase, firms often see their existing competencies being destroyed and their current expertise being rendered obsolete.

Era of ferment. In the era of ferment, many technological applications and design versions emerge. This is an experimentation phase, which can also be called the variation and selection phase, in which firms present a variety of designs and the market selects the best. The competition for achieving design dominance is fierce during this phase. The duration of this phase may vary depending on the degree of the newness of technology.

Dominant design. The era of ferment culminates when a dominant design is selected by the market. The dominant design is a single product architecture that has established dominance in the market. The dominant design is eventually adopted by all manufacturers in the industry. Industry sales normally peak after the dominant design has emerged and there is mass adoption of the design.

Era of incremental change. This is a phase during which a range of design and functional features are added to the products, such as different colors and increased capacity. These additions represent updates that do not fundamentally change the product. The focus is on increasing the product performance and decreasing costs.

If one considers the technological evolution of how people have stored and listened to music over the last 20 years, at least three technology discontinuities can be identified (see Figure 5.3). Around 20 years ago, consumers used to store and listen to music using MP3 players, whose storage capacity improved from hundreds of megabytes to tens of gigabytes. The next technology discontinuity was introduced by smartphones, which integrated MP3 players' features with equivalent storage capacity and sound quality. Then followed the music streaming services, which allowed users to access their music tracks across devices by subscribing to streaming-music service providers, such as Amazon Music, Deezer, iTunes, or Spotify. Before the MP3 players, the technology for sound storage and listening had gone through several technology discontinuities – think, for instance, about cassette tapes and portable cassette players, and compact discs and CD players.

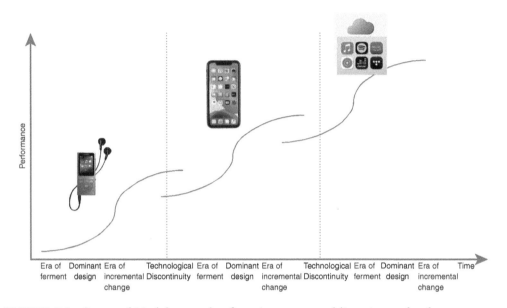

**FIGURE 5.3**   S-curved Model example of music storage and listening technology

The S-curves cyclical model calls attention to the different development stages a technology tends to go through, highlighting that managers should take decisions beyond the current technology stage, considering the future developments of the technology in terms of performance and social acceptance through time. Such a model can support strategists in anticipating price-performance evolution, estimating R&D expenditure, and forecasting cash-flows. Nevertheless, the model is not without its flaws. The timing of the technology discontinuity and the duration of the eras are crucial information for strategists that escape the model predictions. So, it is hard to conclude when to invest in an emergent technology or when to dispose of current technologies. Furthermore, while the model adopts a linear fashion, it is indeed possible to have new and old technologies co-existing. For example, online commerce did not replace physical shops; they continue to exist in parallel.

## Gartner Hype-cycle model

Another useful framework to analyze and forecast emergent technologies is the **Gartner Hype-cycle model**. Developed in 1995 by Gartner Inc., a US-based technological research and consulting firm, the Hype-cycle model explains a general path that technology takes from emergence to extinction in terms of expectations or visibility of the value (y-axis) through time (x-axis). The Hype-cycle model encompasses different stages (see Figure 5.4), including the ones described next.[4]

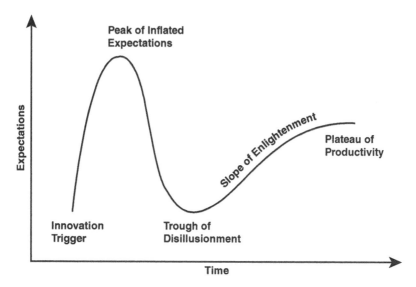

**FIGURE 5.4** Gartner Hype-cycle model

Source: Fenn and Raskino (2008)

<u>Innovation trigger.</u> In the innovation trigger phase, the potential of the technology is recognized by a minority that invests in it and develops a proof of concept. At this stage, some public interest starts to arise following technology utility demonstrations. Some venture capitalists start to invest aiming at gaining first mover advantage, despite the fact that very few usable products exist, and the commercial viability of the technology still raises doubts.

<u>Peak of inflated expectations.</u> The next stage, the peak of inflated expectations, is characterized by high expectations, few success cases and many failures. At this stage, a small group of firms decide to take action even if they do not have a clear strategy, while the vast majority decide to wait to see how the technology evolves.

<u>Trough of disillusionment.</u> The trough of the disillusionment phase arrives when some unsuccessful cases become public, failing to deliver performance and revenue expectations. The technology survives this phase if investment continues, and survivors can improve the use cases and satisfy the needs of the early adopters. The hype this time tends to be negative and spreads rapidly across media.

<u>Slope of enlightenment.</u> The slope of enlightenment is the next phase as experiments start to pay off and new use-cases start to emerge, demonstrating market acceptance. The potential of the technology starts to crystallize and the knowledge about the technology is more widely diffused and understood. Second- and third-generation products start to emerge in the market and more firms decide to invest, regaining confidence in the technology.

<u>Plateau of productivity.</u> Finally, there is the plateau of productivity phase, in which the technology is adopted by the mainstream and starts to be realistically valued. The criteria for technology viability are clearer and better understood, and one can distinctly see applicability and benefits. The technology is no longer limited to a niche market, and mass adoption and continued development starts to take place.

The Gartner Hype-cycle model is often used at the industry or market level, allowing strategists to position the different technologies that are currently impacting or that will influence the market in the future across the phases. For example, in digital marketing, the customer digital twin is a technology currently at the innovation trigger stage. This technology allows marketing firms to create virtual representations of customers to simulate and anticipate their behaviour. At this stage, only a few digital marketing firms recognize the importance and applicability of such technology, while the majority have doubts about its utility. Another example is artificial intelligence (AI) for marketing, which is currently at the peak of inflated expectations stage. The application of AI to digital marketing allows the creation of algorithms that change and adapt on demand in order to increase effectiveness and efficiency of marketing initiatives. At this stage there are high expectations about this technology, and a few firms have started to invest in it while the majority wait to see how the technology develops. In contrast, multichannel marketing hubs, which entail email automation and personalization, have reached the plateau of productivity stage, being considered a mainstream technology.

Despite its popularity and wide adoption by large technology firms, the Gartner Hype-cycle model is considered to be flawed by many. Researchers point to the model's lack of scientific background; the terms and phases lack objective definitions, which makes it difficult to identify the stage of a technology. Additionally, the model does not offer action guidelines, being mainly descriptive. Researchers also point out that hype dynamics can capture the existing life-cycle models and S-curves through the identification of peak, disappointment, and recovery patterns.[5] Nevertheless, the Gartner Hype-cycle model is known for being widely used by practitioners and venture capitalists.

## Technology impact on firms' business models

The last decades of technology developments led to the rise of two megatrends in the industrial and digital arenas, namely Industry 4.0 and Web 3.0. Below we describe these megatrends and discuss the main technologies that have empowered such trends. These two revolutions have the potential to create new industries and also to transform existing ones, impacting firms' business models in terms of production flexibility, efficiency, and productivity.

### Industry 4.0

The first industrial revolution, in the 18th century, was led by steam and water power that allowed companies to produce for the masses. The second industrial revolution culminated in the 19th century with the use of oil, gas, and electric power, allowing some level of production automation. In the 20th century, the development of computers and communication technologies marked the rise of the third industrial revolution, characterized by the digitalization of production processes. In the 21st century, the rapid technology change enabled by interconnectivity and automation has led to the rise of a new industrial revolution, coined by Klaus Schwab of the World Economic Forum as Industry 4.0. As in previous industrial revolutions, the change was not brought about by a single technology but by a group of interdependent emergent technologies, such as AI, machine learning, robotics, 3D printing, and the industrial internet of things (IIOT), among others (e.g., Big Data analytics, cloud computing, cybersecurity, augmented reality, drones, GPS, RFID, simulation, and digital twins), that enable interconnectivity and automation. Such technologies are changing the way companies manufacture and distribute their products through increased automation, predictive maintenance, self-optimization of processes, and, above all, new levels of efficiency and customer responsiveness not possible before.[6]

## Machine learning and artificial intelligence

Machine learning and artificial intelligence is a computer science subfield that emphasizes the creation of computer systems able to perform tasks normally requiring human intelligence, such as visual perception, speech recognition, decision-making, and translation between languages.[7] Such computer systems are usually fed with large volumes of data (*Big Data*), learning to distinguish patterns and making reasonable predictions. Machine learning and artificial intelligence are driving the development of self-driving cars, intelligent routing, simulations, and complex data interpretations. At an industrial level, intelligent machines can help firms to take advantage of Big Data collected through devices and sensors. The resulting insights can improve predictability and automation of processes and operations, enabling predictive maintenance and higher efficiency.[8]

As an example, IBM Watson is one of the leading firms in offering machine learning and artificial intelligence services to their customers. IBM Watson services allow customers to predict outcomes, automate complex processes, and optimize internal processes. One client of IBM Watson is Korean Air, South Korea's largest airline, which uses IBM Watson to use structured and unstructured data about airplane maintenance from multiple sources. Watson's natural language and content analytics allows Korean Air to uncover previously hidden defect and failure patterns, showing probable causes, and recommending solutions that help maintenance crews diagnose and solve problems 90% faster.[9]

## Robotics

While machine learning and artificial intelligence have ambitions to imitate human cognitive functions, robotics attempts to imitate human actions. Robotic machines, or robots, are designed to substitute, help, and assist humans, replicating human actions. Artificial intelligence and robotics are often intertwined. In Industry 4.0, robots can sense the environment, comprehend, act, and learn, and hence are able to conduct self-adapting processes. The development of robotics at the industrial level helps to automate manufacturing, optimize the operation line, and allows machine-to-machine interconnectivity. Robots allow the production of higher quality customized products with high accuracy in less time.[10]

ABB Robotics is one of the world leaders in robotics, machine automation, and digital services. ABB find its clients mainly in manufacturing industries such as automotive or electronics, but also logistics. Their highly automatized robots are mainly used for arc and spot welding, materials handling, painting, picking, palletizing, and assembling, among other activities that in the past required intense human intervention.[11] One of the leading users of robots is the automotive industry. The assembly lines of firms in this industry are populated with various types of robots, from fully and semi-autonomous, to robots that work side-by-side with human workers, assisting them in more detailed processes.

## 3D printing

One of the trends of Industry 4.0 is 3D printing, also known as additive manufacturing. With 3D printing, firms can create three-dimensional objects using geometrical representations (computer-aided design, or CAD) and layering processes. As such, an object is created through successive layers of a material, such as plastics, composites, or even biomaterials. 3D printing allows creating and mass-producing objects with complex shapes, allowing on-demand manufacturing, low stock levels, and shortened prototype and production cycles. While in the beginning 3D-printing technology was mainly used for prototyping, nowadays such technology is being used for mass production and customization in several fields, such as consumer goods (e.g., eyewear, footwear, design, furniture), agriculture, healthcare (prosthetics, dental crowns and dentures, implants), automotive (spare parts, tools, out-of-production parts), and construction, among others.[12]

3D Systems invented 3D printing back in 1989, and it is one of the leading firms in the industry nowadays. 3D Systems offers a wide range of 3D-printing technologies, such as selective laser sintering, multi-jet printing, film-transfer imaging, colour jet printing, direct metal printing, and plastic jet printing. The company sells 3D printers, software, and materials for the printers, and also support and consulting services. One of the main use cases of 3D printers is the aerospace industry, which uses additive manufacturing to design and produce parts on-site to create airworthy parts with reduced weight and improved performance in shorter periods of time, improving their return on investment by 60%.[13] Other industries that use 3D technology include automotive, consumer technology, jewelry, healthcare, semiconductor, and shipbuilding.

## IIOT (industrial internet-of-things)

We live in an era in which various types of devices are connected through the internet, in what we call the internet of things (IoT). IoT is a vital component of smart factories, in which sensors (i.e., devices that generate and transmit real-time data from physical stimulus) enable machines to connect with other web-enabled devices, such as machines, computers, or mobile phones. Such 'smart objects' require minimal human intervention, remotely collecting and analyzing data that can be used to increase efficiency and efficacy of the manufacturing system. Specifically, in IIOT, the data collected and shared across components and systems allows tracking historical trends, identifying patterns, and taking more efficient resource planning and production decisions. The data collected also ensures real-time visibility of manufacturing processes, allowing predictive maintenance to minimize equipment downtime. Overall, IoT devices in smart factories lead to higher productivity and improved quality.[14]

Rockwell Automation is one of the leading providers of IIOT services. Its InnovationSuite service combines data analytics, machine learning, and IIOT, applying them to industrial operations. InnovationSuite service maximizes the potential of information and operational technologies from existing equipment and systems to collect, organize, and analyze large and multiple data streams to provide and recommend actionable insights in a centralized dashboard. With such connected and contextualized information, clients can combine, compare, and analyze information in real-time across machines, lines, processes, and facilities. One use case of IIOT is the life sciences industry, which encompasses pharmaceuticals, medical devices, and biotech firms. Around 95% of the Fortune 500 life sciences firms use Rockwell Automation services to improve product quality, increase personalized medicines feasibility, decrease the number of supply chain disruptions, and accelerate speed to market.[15]

## CRACK-THE-CASE

Lectra in the era of smart services[16]

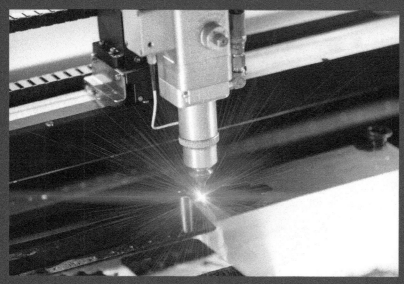

Source: © Aumm graphixphoto (2023) / Shutterstock.

Lectra is a global leader in integrated technology solutions (software, CAD/CAM hardware, and associated services), offering high precision cutting technologies for clients that use textiles, leather, and other industrial fabrics in their products. Lectra clients are from diverse industries, such as fashion, automotive, and furniture, among others. Lectra preserves long-term relationships with customers from more than 100 countries, supporting them in automating, streamlining, and accelerating product design, development, and manufacturing. However, Lectra has not always been what it is nowadays. In what follows, we will dive into Lectra's story of transitioning from a technology supplier to a smart service provider and, finally, to a digital transformation partner.

## From a technology supplier to a smart service provider

Lectra has traditionally been seen as a supplier of cutting room technology, however, Lectra knew that they could offer more to their clients. As machines become increasingly digital, Lectra could help their customers to use and analyze the data to improve their production efficiency and quality. Therefore, Lectra shifted its market approach from a product to a service-centered positioning. The core selling point of Lectra services, which were called 'smart', was that in addition to selling the technology, Lectra would also help customers with machine maintenance and prevention during the entire installed machine's operating life.

*(Continued)*

In that way, customers achieve higher returns on investments and, consequently, Lectra gains a stable long-lasting revenue stream, turning every trade into a partnership.

Clients could benefit from Lectra's Smart Services choosing one of the four available packages that would vary in their customization levels: PowerFlex, PowerPlus, PowerMax, and, finally, PowerPro, which is the most customized solution. The first two packs focus on the core service, mainly on maintenance and prediction. The last two packages present a higher level of customization, incorporating extensions and adaptations to satisfy customers' specific needs. In the negotiation process, Lectra would use the information available to negotiate based on quality and benefits, rather than on price.

## From a smart service provider to a digital transformation partner

Lectra smart services were quite successful among customers who over the years were increasingly digitalizing their production processes. Lectra saw again an opportunity to support their clients in that transition, helping them to accelerate their digital transformation and embrace the Industry 4.0 revolution. Lectra took a step forward from providing smart services to digital transformation consulting and implementation services, offering a range of hardware and software solutions across the value chain. Instead of pre-defined packages, Lectra now presents a spectrum of services that can be adapted to the reality of each client and help them to digitally transform their businesses, integrating and analyzing data streams across the value chain.

Lectra does not only offer world class cutting vector machines and maintenance and predictive services (smart services) that support clients during the production phase, but also offers solutions for product development, e-commerce, and competitive intelligence. In the product development phase, Lectra offers digital solutions that allow clients to estimate fabric consumption, evaluate product viability, forecast procurement needs, and control activity peaks, which allows clients to accelerate the whole product development process. Lectra also offers digital solutions that cover more downstream activities of the value chain through e-commerce solutions that accelerate direct-to-consumer digital retail activities. Finally, Lectra also offers competitive intelligence solutions with accurate and real-time data that allows comparison with competitors and acceleration of the go-to-market process (price, assortment, discount, etc.).

Lectra wants to support clients in aggregating and storing the data flows generated across the entire value-chain in a single platform that encompasses all product-related data from their first sketch, production, to sales.

## Questions

1.  How did Lectra help clients to transition from Industry 2.0 to 3.0, and to 4.0?
2.  What are the technologies that support Lectra's evolution to Industry 4.0?

## Web 3.0

While in Web 1.0 people could access websites without much interaction in a read-only fashion, in Web 2.0, people could also read and write, consuming and creating content through platforms. Compared to Web 2.0, Web 3.0 is a paradigm shift because people not only read and write but also own their data. Web 3.0 is an evolution of Web 2.0 towards decentralization, which allows users to own and exchange value securely and transparently without centralized intermediaries that control and own the information. In Web 2.0, internet users need to trust platforms to save their data and to deliver a service they promise. In Web 3.0 however, digital assets are registered on blockchains, and instead of trusting centralized platforms, users put their trust in the underlying algorithms, following the so-called 'trustless' model. Web 3.0, as any other evolution, is a culmination of several technological developments, specifically blockchain, decentralized applications (DApps) and non-fungible tokens (NFTs), among others.[17]

## Blockchain

Blockchain is the foundational technology behind Web 3.0, which empowers decentralization. Blockchain is a distributed ledger technology (DLT), meaning a public database, where data is written in 'blocks of information' that are cryptographically linked to the previous blocks, forming a secure chain of blocks. Cryptography is a method to protect information and transactions through the use of secure codes that prevent third parties or the public from reading private messages. To function, blockchain uses a peer-to-peer network, in which network nodes must agree upon each new block that is added to the chain (and also on the whole previous chain of blocks). In this way, the blockchain is not owned by a single entity but by the users, being secured by a network of nodes that compete to provide the best service to users. Blockchain platforms may integrate tokens (also known as cryptocurrency) that are used to incentivize users and nodes to use and maintain the network; and also Smart contracts, which are code lines stored in the blockchain that trigger transactions automatically when certain conditions are met, without the need for intermediaries or centralized platforms. On top of decentralization, blockchain technology offers security, immutability, cost-efficient auditing of transactions, and improved tamper proofing and reliability.

The first widely known attempt to implement blockchain technology was Bitcoin, a digital cryptocurrency founded in 2009; however, other projects have built blockchain platforms with their own tokens and smart contracts.[18] This is the case of Ethereum, launched in 2015, which is a decentralized application platform with smart contract functionality that allows anyone to use their technology to create DApps that interact with users. At present, there are 210 million Ethereum addresses owned by users interacting with around 3.000 Ethereum-based DApps.[19]

## DApps (decentralized applications)

Web 3.0 users can interact using a variety of blockchain platforms and also using DApps that are built on top of these protocols. DApps are open-source, automated, and decentralized applications that run on a specific blockchain protocol. DApps differ from other web or mobile applications because they run on a peer-to-peer network (blockchain) and use smart contracts, which automatically trigger transactions without intermediaries. In addition to smart contracts, DApps usually have their own cryptocurrency/tokens that can be exchanged inside the application (users can buy, spend, earn, send and receive tokens) or outside the application through exchanges that allow users to swap tokens from different DApps. Thousands of DApps are being created on different blockchain protocols (e.g., Ethereum, Binance Smart Chain) across several categories, such as gaming, marketplaces, decentralized exchanges (allows the exchange of different tokens), decentralized finance (token-based financial instruments), gambling, social media, and collectables (NFTs).[20]

## NFTs (non-fungible tokens)

NFTs are cryptographic assets registered in the blockchain with a single identification that makes them unique. While in fungible tokens, like Bitcoin, one Bitcoin is equivalent and indistinguishable from any other Bitcoin, in the case of non-fungible assets, all tokens are different – hence, 'non-fungible'. NFTs allow exclusive ownership of a digital asset that can be a piece of art, a collectable, music, video, text, digital artefact or a piece of land in the metaverse, among others. Creators and owners can prove the existence and ownership of the asset and track its trade history because it is registered in a blockchain. NFTs' convenience, tradability, liquidity, and interoperability have made them a promising intellectual property solution for digital assets.[21] Capitalizing on these features, several DApps are offering services that sell, create, and exchange NFTs, such as OpenSea, Rarible, LookRare, and RealFevr.

## STRATEGIC FOCUS

### The saga of parallel metaverses: Web 2.0 versus Web 3.0

The metaverse is a network of 3D virtual immersive worlds on the internet. In a metaverse, people can use avatars to perform an ever-growing list of activities, such as buy land, play games, gamble, trade digital assets, work, and socialize. We are seeing not only the rise of multiple worlds inside the metaverse but also the emergence of parallel metaverses that build on different technologies and ideals: Web 2.0 and Web 3.0.

In Web 2.0, users use centralized platforms that are likely to be controlled by tech giants such as Meta, NVIDIA, Microsoft, Apple, Roblox, and Epic Games. In this model, platforms make money by selling digital services, products, and advertising space, serving their extensive user base. Such Web 2.0 giants will use their customer experience, existing ecosystem, and internal resources (e.g., financial and technical) to offer complete and immersive experiences to users. However, such tech giants have not grown without controversies, such as censorship, data leakage, expropriation, and privacy risks – problems that can be magnified in the metaverse.

In Web 3.0, the main players are startups that adopt token-based business models to build blockchain-enabled products, meaning digital services and assets that run on the blockchain, following the ideals of decentralization, community ownership, immutability, and transparency. Web 3.0-native projects, such as Decentraland or The Sandbox, were able to raise a huge amount of funding and are building business models that allow decentralization, digital ownership, and cross-platform interoperability that have the potential to rocket scale. However, while Web 3.0 promises to create a 'better' internet where customers own their data and products, creating and appropriating the value they create, those Web 3.0 native projects still face significant barriers, such as low-quality customer experience and potential attacks and hacks that may frighten mainstream users.

While Web 2.0 and Web 3.0 metaverses look distant in their ideals and technologies, the future might hold scenarios with a dominant metaverse. This might happen if Web 2.0 giants (e.g., Meta, Roblox, Epic Games) integrate blockchain and Web 3.0 technologies; or if Web 3.0 native-projects (e.g., The Sandbox, Decentraland) achieve rapid growth in terms of offer and scale, dominating the market. The future will tell if Web 2.0 and Web 3.0 metaverses will exist in parallel or if they will converge at some point in time.[22]

# Emergent technologies' impact on the way entities collaborate and organize

Emergent technologies affect not only firms' industrial and digital business models but also how entities (individuals or firms) cooperate with each other, leading to the emergence of new organizational and collaborative forms. Next, we discuss different emergent organizational forms that are enabled by the development of information technologies, namely crowdsourcing, online communities, and DAOs.

## Crowdsourcing

Bill Joy, the founder of Sun Microsystems, once said that 'no matter who you are, most of the smartest people work for someone else' (Joy's law).[23] **Crowdsourcing** allows firms to access the knowledge of these 'smart people' that may work for someone else and that can be located anywhere in the world. Therefore, crowdsourcing is a collaborative organizational form in which an entity opens a call to the crowd to solve a problem. Crowdsourcing, in its different forms (tournament-based and collaborative-based), has been used by firms to access knowledge that may lie beyond their boundaries[24] (see also how crowdsourcing may boost entrepreneurship and open innovation as described in Chapter 15).

There are two main types of crowdsourcing: tournament-based and collaboration-based. In tournament-based crowdsourcing, a sponsor, which can be an individual, a firm, or an institution, opens a call with a specific goal and anyone can answer the call. In such cases, participants (or groups of participants) submit their solutions and, at the end of the tournament, the best idea is rewarded with a prize. An example of tournament-based crowdsourcing is Innocentive, an innovation intermediary platform, where firms post problems that they have, and large crowds propose solutions. In the case of collaboration-based crowdsourcing, crowd members provide a part of the solution and the crowdsourcer aggregates the different parts to achieve their goal. One example of a collaboration-based crowdsourcing platform is Zooniverse, which is a platform that hosts science projects that source volunteer contributors to analyze, interpret, or categorize large datasets that are difficult for computer algorithms but, when modularized, are relatively easy for general crowds.[25]

Crowdsourcing thus, allows firms to collaborate with vast crowds distributed around the world, and to access innovative and sometimes unexpected solutions for complex problems. Through the different forms of crowdsourcing, firms can access a wider pool of knowledge and diverse thinking, thus achieving faster problem-solving.

## Online communities

Another form of collaboration enabled by digital technologies is online communities. While in the case of crowdsourcing, members tend to be anonymous and isolated (rarely interacting with each other), in online communities, members communicate often, creating strong ties over time, and sharing information, knowledge, and assistance. **Online communities** are collaborative forms of organizing in which members interact over the internet, sharing common interests, values, and norms. The 'purpose' of such online communities can be more localized, for example creating Legos, or it can be more elevated, like responding to a 'grand challenge' such as climate change or creating a free, open-source operating system (e.g., Linux). In either form, online communities rely on collaborative goal setting, where members can voice opinions, learn, and contribute.[26]

In recent years, there has been a rise of varied forms of online communities including customer communities, open-source software communities, user communities, and online-learning communities. These and other online communities allow bottom-up collaborations across intra- and inter-firm networks and among individuals located all over the world. Research on online communities shows how such collaborative organizational forms enrich process-oriented businesses in idea-searching and selection, harnessing bottom-up innovation capacity.[27]

## STRATEGIC FOCUS
### Online communities' problems and perils

While online communities offer the promise of worldwide distributed members collaborating and exchanging knowledge at very low cost, they also face some problems. The first problem relates to difficulties attracting members and fostering members' repeated contributions. This may happen because self-selected members do not have the right set of skills or are not engaged enough to generate an interesting amount of content and interactions.[28] The second problem relates to conflicts among members. When online communities manage to attract a large and diverse collective of members able to foster innovation and creativity, they may end up facing the challenge of coordinating widely dispersed knowledge from large collectives of individuals. Conflicts may emerge due to perceived differences and disagreements about resource allocation, beliefs, values, or practices.[29] The third problem relates to the collective action problem, or the free rider problem. If there is no way to exclude an entity from accessing the benefits of a product resulting from collective action, actors may have little incentive to contribute to that collective product. If all participants decide to free-ride (i.e., they use the product without contributing to it), this will lead to increased degradation of the collective good and the so-called 'tragedy of the commons'.[30] The fourth problem relates to appropriation issues. Over time, members tend to manifest concerns about intellectual property and value appropriation, which may lead to diminishing incentives to participate in online communities.[31] Community sponsors need to be aware of the problems and perils of creating and maintaining an online community that can enhance their innovation processes. If creating and nurturing an online community brings such problems and perils, why should companies create them in the first instance?

## DAOs (decentralized autonomous organizations)

The emergence and development of blockchain technology and Web 3.0 brought new organizational forms called DAOs. **DAOs** are blockchain-based systems that enable members to coordinate and govern themselves following a set of self-executing rules that run without the interference of a central authority.[32] DAOs are owned and governed by members, through contributions, voting, and other participation schemes. In Web 3.0, people not only own their data, but they also can own the DApps they use through buying tokens and participating in the decisions about their future. One of the first examples of a DAO was Bitcoin, a cryptocurrency based on blockchain (distributed ledger) technology designed to allow people to securely transact and exchange value at a global scale without the need for costly intermediaries.[33] With the purpose of creating an independent financial system, Bitcoin is sustained by a crowd able to validate transactions and co-create and implement code updates, which translates into new functions without the interference or orchestration of a central sponsor. Since Bitcoin, more sophisticated DAOs have emerged with systems that allow members to suggest and vote on proposals, using a range of on-chain or off-chain schemes that facilitate collective participation. *On-chain* means that the transactions, in the case of DAOs proposals and votes, are registered in the blockchain and are visible to all nodes in the network; *off-chain* means that the transactions are not registered in the blockchain.

DAOs have been emerging in different areas such as decentralized finance (e.g., Uniswap), media (e.g., Global Coin Research and Forefront), gaming (e.g., Decentraland), art and culture (SuperRare and Rarible), and investment funds (e.g., BitDAO and MetaCartel). While DAOs might be a native governance form of DApps (decentralized applications that run on the blockchain), not all DApps are DAOs, as they may display different levels of governance decentralization and automation.[34]

## KEY DEBATE
### Adopting Industry 4.0

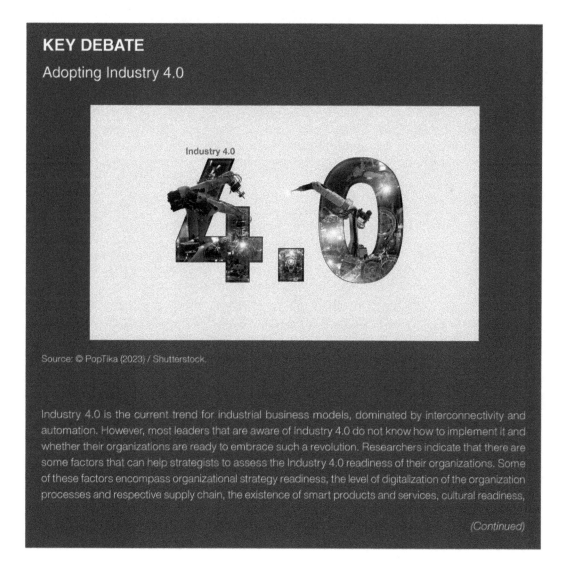

Source: © PopTika (2023) / Shutterstock.

Industry 4.0 is the current trend for industrial business models, dominated by interconnectivity and automation. However, most leaders that are aware of Industry 4.0 do not know how to implement it and whether their organizations are ready to embrace such a revolution. Researchers indicate that there are some factors that can help strategists to assess the Industry 4.0 readiness of their organizations. Some of these factors encompass organizational strategy readiness, the level of digitalization of the organization processes and respective supply chain, the existence of smart products and services, cultural readiness,

*(Continued)*

and employees' and top managers' level of involvement.[35] On the other side, practitioners indicate that assessing the readiness of the organization for Industry 4.0 is a difficult task, that it will be mainly based on self-assessment and managers' judgement, and that some industries might never be ready for such a transformation. Additionally, while scholars mostly see the advantages of Industry 4.0,[36] such as increased efficiency, efficacy, and product quality, many practitioners mainly highlight the disadvantages, such as large investment, a lack of skills, absolute dependence on machines, and a cultural gap.

## Questions

1.   Do you think that scholars and practitioners' views are antagonistic or complementary? Explain why.
2.   Further elaborate on the list of advantages and disadvantages of adopting Industry 4.0.

## CLOSING CASE

### RealFevr: Reinventing the business model from Web 2.0 to Web 3.0 (Part II)

RealFevr is a Portuguese company specializing in football fantasy leagues. RealFevr users create 'virtual' football teams, winning or losing games based on on-field performance statistics of the real-world players. RealFevr was able to show steady growth in the number of users in the first years, attracting venture capitalists. However, while the generated traffic looked good for a fantasy league, it was not enough to achieve the breakeven point. Everyone inside RealFevr was on the same page: they needed to reinvent their business model (read this chapter's Opening Case *RealFevr: The fantasy leagues fever*).

### The transformation from a Web 2.0 to a Web 3.0 business model

RealFevr has shown that they like to take risks, and together with the venture capitalists, the team decided to transform their business into a token-based model, transitioning from Web 2.0 to Web 3.0 technologies. To proceed, they would need to hire Web 3.0 specialists as their business model was dominantly on Web 2.0. In their search, they found Fred Antunes, a blockchain enthusiast and specialist who agreed to lead the RealFevr transformation plan as CEO; and Pedro Febrero, an experienced blockchain consultant and writer, who assumed the head of blockchain position. Fred and Pedro knew that transforming the RealFevr business into a token-based model would mean a profound restructuring and that it would take time to win the hearts and minds of RealFevr team members and users.

   NFTs are unique digital tokens that provide a certificate of ownership that can be bought and sold. NFTs can comprise digital creations as files, art, music files, videos, video game items, and other creative work. Inspired by the US-based NBA Top Shot, a project where customers can acquire and trade NFT collectables of basketball players' iconic moments, RealFevr decided to adopt a similar model with two distinguishing factors: decentralization and football collectables. The first difference relates to the fact that NBA Top Shot uses a private blockchain to store the NFTs, which is a controversial decision among Web 3.0 enthusiasts who demand decentralization and self-sovereignty. Therefore, RealFevr decided to use a public blockchain (Binance Smart Chain) to store the NFTs in which the users would be the 'real' owners of the digital collectables. The second biggest difference is that RealFevr NFT collectables are football videos, in which the users buy packs of videos that may range from common to unique. To complement this model, RealFevr created a token, called *Fevr*. To acquire and trade the NFT collectables inside the RealFevr marketplace (see Figure 5.5), users need to acquire Fevr in the first place. With such moves RealFevr had a full business model based on tokens, NFTs, and blockchain, entering in the Web 3.0 era for good.

**FIGURE 5.5**  RealFevr NFT collectables marketplace

## Rising from the ashes

The RealFevr IDO (Initial DEX Offering), in which RealFevr sold their Fevr tokens to the public through a decentralized exchange (DEX), sold out in one minute, which was considered a tremendous success at global scale by Web 3.0 specialists. The next step was to launch the NFT collectables drops. The first drops encompassed unforgettable football moments like the first goal of Cristiano Ronaldo and Bruno Fernandes, and other spectacular football moments that now can belong to the users' collections. The first drop sold out in 24 hours and the second in 28 hours, confirming the success of the business model. RealFevr has already performed three drops, with the last one featuring the Torino league (Italian football Serie A league), showing their ambition to internationalize.

*(Continued)*

RealFevr is already a reference in the Web 3.0 and NFT industry at global scale, however, they want more, they want to be in more football leagues, and maybe cover other sports. Will they keep ahead of competition in the Web 3.0 arena? The future will tell...

## Questions

1. Identify the Web 3.0 technologies that RealFevr implemented in their business model.
2. Identify and analyze the main opportunities and threats that RealFevr may face in the future.

## Summary

- Emergent technology is a concept used to describe new technologies whose potential applications are largely unrealized yet.
- Strategists use two main models to identify the current stage of technology development: the S-curves cyclical model and the Gartner Hype-cycle model.
- The S-curves cyclical model of technological change focuses on social and technological dynamics during eras of fermentation and incremental change.
- The Gartner Hype-cycle model explains a general path that technology takes from emergence to extinction.
- Industry 4.0 is the fourth industrial revolution characterized by interconnectivity and automation.
- Web 3.0 is the third internet evolution characterized by decentralization, transparency, and disintermediation.
- Emergent technologies can also transform the way firms collaborate and organize, some examples being crowdsourcing, online communities, and decentralized autonomous organizations (DAOs).
- Crowdsourcing is a collaborative organizational form in which one opens a call to the crowd to solve a problem.
- Online communities are collaborative forms of organizing in which members interact over the internet, sharing common interests, values, and norms.
- DAOs are blockchain-based systems that enable members to coordinate and govern themselves following a set of self-executing rules.

## Review questions

1. What are the different phases that a technology goes through according to the S-curves cyclical model and the Gartner Hype-cycle model?
2. The technological revolutions result from multiple interlinked technological developments that converge towards few trends. How could you characterize in a few words the Industry 4.0 and Web 3.0 revolutions?

3. Digital technologies allowed the emergence of new ways of collaborating and organizing. What are the fundamental differences between crowdsourcing, online communities, and DAOs?

## Discussion questions

1. The Gartner Hype-cycle model has been widely used by practitioners, while the S-curves cyclical model is mostly used by scholars. Scholars point out that technological developments can be captured by existing life-cycle models and the S-curves cyclical model. Do you agree that existing models are able to represent hype dynamics as peak, disappointment, and recovery? If yes, how do they do that?
2. To what extent have digital technologies that have emerged in the last five years fundamentally changed how firms compete?

## EXPERIENTIAL EXERCISES

1. Use the Gartner Hype-cycle model and respective stages (innovation trigger, peak of inflated expectations, trough of disillusionment, slope of enlightenment, and plateau of productivity) to position the following technologies and trends: flying vehicles, autonomous cars, Big Data analytics, 5G, 3D printing, Emotion AI, the Metaverse.
2. Thousands of DApps are being created every day across several categories such as gaming, marketplaces, decentralized exchanges (allowing users to exchange different tokens), decentralized finance, collectables, gambling, and social media, among others. Such DApps build on existing blockchain protocols such as Ethereum, BNB chain, or Solana, among many others. Investigate the following DApps and identify which blockchain protocol they use (you can use DappRadar to find the DApps): Uniswap, PancakeSwap, Solend.

## Further reading

Brabham, D.C. (2013) *Crowdsourcing*. Cambridge, MA: MIT Press.

Faraj, S., Jarvenpaa, S.L. and Majchrzak, A. (2011) 'Knowledge collaboration in online communities', *Organization Science*, 22 (5): 1224–39.

Monrat, A.A., Schelén, O. and Andersson, K. (2019) 'A survey of blockchain from the perspectives of applications, challenges, and opportunities', *IEEE Access*, 7: 117134–51.

Sony, M. and Naik, S. (2019) 'Key ingredients for evaluating Industry 4.0 readiness for organizations: A literature review', *Benchmarking: An International Journal*, 27 (7): 2213–32. doi.org/10.1108/BIJ-09-2018-0284.

Taylor, M. and Taylor, A. (2012) 'The technology life cycle: Conceptualization and managerial implications', *International Journal of Production Economics*, 140 (1): 541–53.

# Endnotes (references)

1. Anderson, P. and Tushman, M.L. (1990) 'Technological discontinuities and dominant designs: A cyclical model of technological change', *Administrative Science Quarterly*, 35: 604–33.
2. Anderson and Tushman (1990)
3. Schumpeter, J.A. (1942) 'Capitalism, socialism and democracy', *Social Science Electronic Publishing*, 27 (4): 594–602.
4. Fenn, J. and Raskino, M. (2008) *Mastering the Hype Cycle: How to Choose the Right Innovation at the Right Time*. Boston, MA: Harvard Business Press.
5. Steinert, M. and Leifer, L. (2010) 'Scrutinizing Gartner's hype cycle approach', in *PICMET 2010 Proceedings*. New York, NY: IEEE, 254–66.
6. IBM (2022) 'What is Industry 4.0?' *IBM*. www.ibm.com/topics/industry-4-0 (accessed June 15, 2023).
7. Oxford Reference (2023) 'Artificial intelligence', *oxfordreference.com*. www.oxford reference.com/display/10.1093/oi/authority.20110803095426960 (accessed June 15, 2023).
8. Ongsulee, P. (2017) 'Artificial intelligence, machine learning and deep learning', in 15th *International Conference on ICT and Knowledge Engineering* (ICT&KE). New York, NY: IEEE, 1–6.
9. IBM (2019) 'Maintenance done 90% faster'. https://web.archive.org/save/https://www.ibm.com/watson/stories/airlines-with-watsonWatson (accessed July 30, 2023).
10. Goel, R. and Gupta, P. (2020) 'Robotics and Industry 4.0', in A. Nayyar and A. Kumar (eds), *A Roadmap to Industry 4.0: Smart Production, Sharp Business and Sustainable Development*. Cham: Springer, 157–69.
11. ABB (2022) 'ABB Robotics'. https://web.archive.org/web/20230509170420/https://new.abb.com/products/robotics/robots (accessed June 15, 2023).
12. Shahrubudin, N., Lee, T.C. and Ramlan, R. (2019) 'An overview on 3D printing technology: Technological, materials, and applications', *Procedia Manufacturing*, 35: 1286–96.
13. 3D Systems (2022) 'Additive manufacturing for aerospace & defense', July 12. www.3dsystems.com/additive-manufacturing-aerospace-defense?ind=aerospace (accessed June 15, 2023).
14. Boyes, H., Hallaq, B., Cunningham, J. and Watson, T. (2018) 'The industrial internet of things (IIoT): An analysis framework', *Computers in Industry*, 101: 1–12.
15. Rockwell Automation (2022) 'Life science manufacturing', *Rockwell Automation*. www.rockwellautomation.com/en-gb/industries/life-sciences.html (accessed June 15, 2023).
16. Lectra (2022) 'Lectra services', Lectra. www.lectra.com/en/products/lectra-services (accessed June 15, 2023); Pereira, J.R. (2011) 'Best practices benchmarking of smart services: The Lectra case', MSc dissertation, Universidade Católica Portuguese, Lisbon. https://repositorio.ucp.pt/bitstream/10400.14/7770/3/7770.pdf (accessed June 15, 2023).
17. Ethereum Foundation (2022a) 'Introduction to Web3', *ethereum.org*. https://ethereum.org/en/web3/ (accessed June 15, 2023).
18. Febrero, P. and Pereira, J. (2020) 'Cryptocurrency constellations across the three-dimensional space: Governance decentralization, security, and scalability', *IEEE Transactions on Engineering Management*. https://ieeexplore.ieee.org/document/9254134 (accessed June 15, 2023).
19. Ethereum Foundation (2022b) *Ethereum White Paper*. https://ethereum.org/en/whitepaper (accessed June 15, 2023).
20. DappRadar (2022) 'Top Blockchain Dapps', *dappradar.com*. https://dappradar.com/rankings (accessed June 15, 2023).

21. Ali, M. and Bagui, S. (2021) 'Introduction to NFTs: The future of digital collectibles', *International Journal of Advanced Computer Science and Applications*, 12 (10): 50–6.

22. Liquin, C. and Dogan, A. (2022) 'A Tale of 2 Metaverses'. https://builtin.com/ blockchain/metaverse-web2.0-vs-web3 (accessed June 15, 2023).

23. Manville, B. (2015) 'How to get the smartest people in the world to work for you', *Forbes*, July 24. www.forbes.com/sites/brookmanville/2015/07/24/how-to-get-the-smartest-people-in-the-world-to-work-for-you (accessed July 30, 2023).

24. Afuah, A. and Tucci, C.L. (2012) 'Crowdsourcing as a solution to distant search', *Academy of Management Review*, 37 (3): 355–75.

25. Barbosu, S. and Gans, J.S. (2022) 'Storm crowds: Evidence from *Zooniverse* on crowd contribution desig', *Research Policy*, 51 (1): 104414; Cox, J., Oh, E.Y., Simmons, B., Lintott, C., Masters, K., Greenhill A., Graham, G. and Holmes, K. (2015) 'Defining and measuring success in online citizen science: A case study of Zooniverse projects', *Computing in Science & Engineering*, 17 (4): 28–41.

26. Adler, P.S. (2015) 'Community and innovation: From Tönnies to Marx', *Organization Studies*, 36 (4): 445–71; Franke, N. and Shah, S. (2003) 'How communities support innovative activities: An exploration of assistance and sharing among end-users', *Research Policy*, 32 (1): 157–78.

27. Majchrzak, A. and Malhotra, A. (2020) *Unleashing the Crowd.* Cham: Springer; Von Hippel, E. (2005) 'Open source software projects as user innovation networks – no manufacturer required', in J. Feller, B. Fitzgerald, S. Hissam, and K. Lakhani (eds), *Perspectives on Free and Open Source Software.* Cambridge, MA: MIT Press, 267–78.

28. Ma, M. and Agarwal, R. (2007) 'Through a glass darkly: Information technology design, identity verification, and knowledge contribution in online communities', *Information Systems Research*, 18 (1): 42–67.

29. Adler (2015)

30. Ostrom, E. (1990) *Governing the Commons: The Evolution of Institutions for Collective Action.* Cambridge: Cambridge University Press.

31. Boudreau, K.J. and Lakhani, K.R. (2015) '"Open" disclosure of innovations, incentives and follow-on reuse: Theory on processes of cumulative innovation and a field experiment in computational biology', *Research Policy*, 44 (1): 4–19.

32. Hassan, S. and De Filippi, P. (2021) 'Decentralized autonomous organization', *Internet Policy Review*, 10 (2): 1–10.

33. Nakamoto, S. (2008) 'Bitcoin: A peer-to-peer electronic cash system', *Decentralized Business Review*: 21260.

34. DeepDao (2022) 'Organizations', deepdao.io. https://deepdao.io/organizations (accessed June 15, 2023)

35. Sony, M. and Naik, S. (2019) 'Key ingredients for evaluating Industry 4.0 readiness for organizations: A literature review', *Benchmarking: An International Journal*, 27 (7): 2213–32. doi.org/10.1108/BIJ-09-2018-0284.

36. For instance, Brozzi, R., Forti, D., Rauch, E. and Matt, D.T. (2020) 'The advantages of Industry 4.0 applications for sustainability: Results from a sample of manufacturing companies', *Sustainability*, 12 (9): 3647; Javaid, M., Haleem, A., Singh, R.P., Suman, R. and Gonzalez, E.S. (2022) 'Understanding the adoption of Industry 4.0 technologies in improving environmental sustainability', *Sustainable Operations and Computers*, 3: 203–17.

37. DappRadar (2022)

## Acknowledgements

The authors thank Pedro Febrero and José Miranda for their contribution to this chapter.

## Key terms

**Crowdsourcing** – a collaborative organizational form in which one opens a call to the crowd to solve a problem

**DAOs** – blockchain-based systems that enable members to coordinate and govern themselves following a set of self-executing rules

**Emergent technologies** – new technologies or developments of existing technologies, the potential applications of which are largely unrealized yet

**Gartner Hype-cycle model** – a general path that technology takes from emergence to extinction in terms of expectations or visibility of the value (y-axis) through time (x-axis)

**Industry 4.0** – an industrial revolution that focuses on interconnectivity and automation, enabled by the development of artificial intelligence, machine learning, robotics, 3D printing, and IIOT technologies

**Online communities** – collaborative forms of organizing in which members interact over the internet, sharing common interests, values, and norms

**S-curves cyclical model** – model of technological change that focuses on the social and technological dynamics during the eras of ferment and incremental change

**Web 3.0** – an internet evolution towards decentralized platforms, which encompasses blockchain, DApps, and NFT technologies, among others

# Diagnostic
# Part I
## CONFRONTRIX

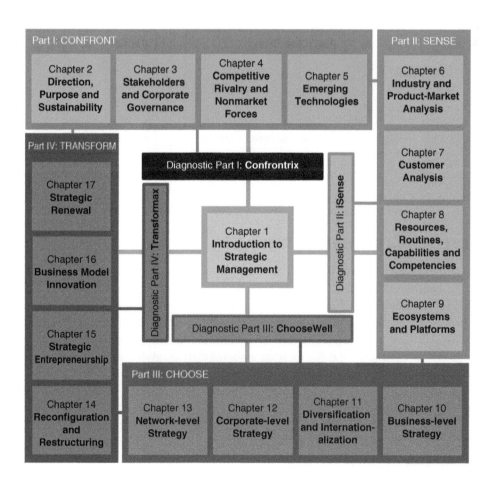

# Introduction

Before you can assess the competitive position of a firm and subsequently formulate its strategy, it is necessary to understand the general environment. Creating this bird's eye view of the environment is what we discussed in Chapters 2 to 5. Building on these chapters, this *Confrontrix* diagnostic chapter introduces tools and frameworks that allow you to apply the discussed concepts in the real world. The tools raised to confront the firm with challenges in its business environment follow a sequential process. First, we introduce frameworks that aid in understanding the general environment. Second, we discuss several approaches to plan for changes in this environment. Last, we consider tools for the corporation's governance in relation to its environment. The tools in this diagnostic chapter, as listed in Figure A.1, aid in building an understanding of the organization's environment and how you can confront it.

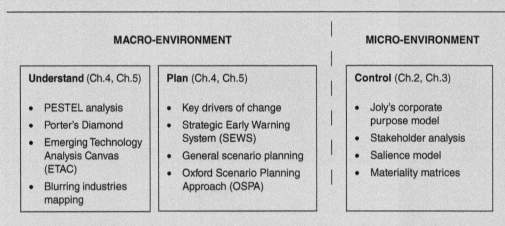

**FIGURE A.1**   Confrontrix aggregate framework

# Macro-environmental analysis

The macro-environment is the broader environment in which a firm finds itself (see Chapter 4). Here, we consider the societal forces that shape a firm's 'playing ground'. Special attention is given to two factors which are currently especially present. First, emerging technologies have played a central role in shaping society (see Chapter 5). Excellent awareness of this technological force will help organizations retain or improve their competitive position. Second, macro-environmental forces such as deregulation, globalization, and technological breakthroughs have ushered in a new era of competition (see Chapter 4). In the 2020s, traditional industry boundaries continue to blur. To confront this, organizations need to be aware of their new landscape.

## Understand

Analyzing the macro-environment can be a daunting task. The PESTEL model can guide you through the various dimensions of the macro-environment. Here, you can use a tool such as worksheets to systematically analyze and evaluate the organization's environment. The PESTEL analysis can be complemented by focused frameworks that address a single environmental factor in depth. Here, Porter's Diamond provides insight into the competitiveness of nations, the Emerging Technology Analysis Canvas helps to understand new technologies, while the blurring industries mapping can aid in understanding the blurring of traditional economic sectors.

## PESTEL analysis

The PESTEL framework (also known as PESTLE) comprises an analysis of political (P), economic (E), socio-cultural (S), technological (T), ecological (E) and legal (L) factors that have or may have an impact on the way a company operates (see Chapter 4). This framework attempts to capture all the relevant dimensions of the macro-environment to ensure that important events affecting firms' activities are not ignored. The forerunners of this framework, which evolved over time, were ETPS (not including ecological and legal aspects)[1] and STEP (Strategic Trend Evaluation Process),[2] STEPE (Social, Technical, Economic, Political, Ecological) and PEST (Political, Economic, Socio-cultural, Technological).

Some PESTEL factors are more critical than others or even irrelevant to a focal organization. The analyst must use critical thinking when considering the factors to be included or excluded based on relevance and impact on a firm's activities and profitability. If you desire to structure further the PESTEL analysis, Figure A.2 proposes a configuration in which each force is classified as an opportunity or threat, with high or low impact. For example, in the pharmaceutical industry the socio-cultural trend towards ageing population represents an opportunity to the industry with high positive impact in the future. Contrarily, an economic recession (economic factor) represents a threat, as consumer available income might suffer and impact pharmaceuticals' sales negatively.

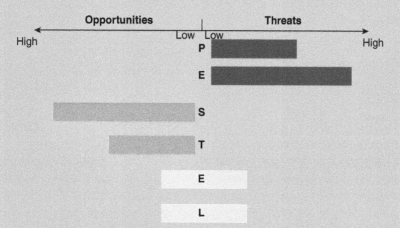

**FIGURE A.2**   PESTEL factors classified as opportunities or threats for a pharmaceutical company

The PESTEL framework provides a flexible starting point for a comprehensive environmental analysis. Using a worksheet, you can review how macro-environmental forces are shaping your organization. Figure A.3 provides an example of such a worksheet. To achieve the maximum value, you may write down the events per factor in order of significance to the organization.

| | Parties affected | | | |
|---|---|---|---|---|
| | Organization | Industry competitors | Rivals | Customers |
| **Political** | | | | |
| Strict regulatory frameworks | X | X | X | |
| Raising government interest in regulating medicines prices | X | X | X | |
| **Economic** | | | | |
| Economic recession and decreasing purchasing power | X | X | X | X |
| Growing healthcare spending (individuals and governments) | X | X | X | X |
| **Sociocultural** | | | | |
| Ageing population | X | X | X | |
| Trend towards being more health conscious | X | X | X | |
| **Technological** | | | | |
| Biotechnology industry growth | X | X | X | |
| Digital direct advertisement tools | X | X | X | X |
| **Ecological** | | | | |
| Carbon footprint | X | X | X | |
| **Legal** | | | | |
| Patent laws | X | X | X | |
| Increasing number of lawsuits against pharmaceutical companies | X | X | X | X |

**FIGURE A.3**   PESTEL worksheet example for a pharmaceutical company

## Porter's Diamond

Porter's Diamond, or the Porter Diamond Theory of National Advantage,[3] is used to understand a nation's competitive advantage in the international market. Porter considers national competitiveness to be a function of productivity. In a competitive nation, firms ruthlessly pursue improvements, consistently innovate, and remain steadfast in seeking competitive advantage. With this model, you can consider the competitiveness through four broad attributes of nations (see Figure A.4):

- Factor conditions: the nation's position in factors of production such as skilled labour or infrastructure.
- Demand conditions: The kind of home-market demand for products and services.
- Related and supporting industries: the presence in the nation of competitive supplier industries and associated industries.
- Firm strategy, structure and rivalry: the conditions in the nation that determine how firms are created, organized, and managed, as well as the level of domestic rivalry.

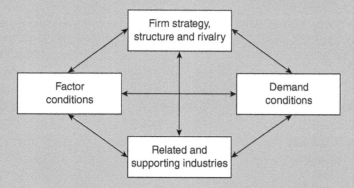

**FIGURE A.4**   Porter's Diamond Theory of National Advantage diagram

Source: Porter (1989) *The Competitive Advantage of Nations*

## Emerging Technology Analysis Canvas

Evaluating an emerging technology and its potential ramifications for an organization can be a daunting challenge. To aid in this, Perera and colleagues[4] adapted the Business Model Canvas (see the *Transformax* diagnostic chapter) of Alexander Osterwalder for emerging technologies. The Emerging Technology Analysis Canvas (ETAC) combines aspects of PESTEL analysis and SWOT analysis (see the *iSense* diagnostic chapter) to create a single framework for assessing the opportunities and threats an emerging technology may have for an organization (see Figure A.5).

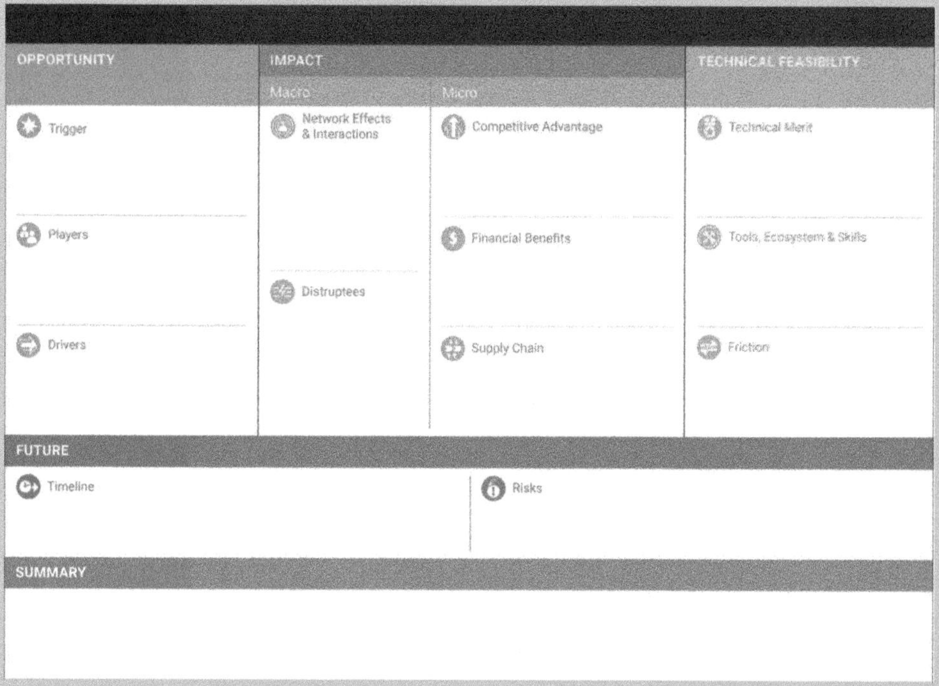

| OPPORTUNITY | IMPACT | | TECHNICAL FEASIBILITY |
|---|---|---|---|
| | Macro | Micro | |
| ⭐ Trigger | Network Effects & Interactions | Competitive Advantage | Technical Merit |
| 👥 Players | | Financial Benefits | Tools, Ecosystem & Skills |
| | Disruptees | | |
| Drivers | | Supply Chain | Friction |

| FUTURE | | |
|---|---|---|
| Timeline | Risks | |

| SUMMARY |
|---|
| |

**FIGURE A.5**   Emerging Technology Analysis Canvas

Source: Perera et al. (2022)

In the ETAC's <u>opportunity</u> section, the analyst needs to explain the trigger (the problem that the technology solves), the players involved (other firms and organizations that are already using the technology to solve problems), and the drivers (external factors impacting positively the technology). The PESTEL framework could be used for identifying the drivers. The <u>impact</u> part of the ETAC framework is divided into macro and micro impacts. The *macro-level impact* covers potential network effects and interactions (i.e., positive feedback loops in technology adoption), and who are the *disruptees* (i.e., which industries and technologies will be affected by the new technology). The *micro-level impact* encompasses competitive advantage (i.e., how technology can bring advantage over competitors), financial benefits (i.e., bottom line impact), and the supply chain (more specifically, changes required in the supply chain to adopt the technology). New technologies' *technical feasibility* is another important dimension to consider when analyzing an emergent technology. Dimensions such as technical merit (breakthroughs and limitations), tools, ecosystems, skills (available skills to support the technology implementation and development), and friction points (technical and nontechnical risks) can help in assessing the feasibility of the emergent technology. The future section (i.e., future prospects) comprises the *timeline* (milestones for technology readiness) and *risks* (the big question marks regarding the future of the technology). Furthermore, the ETAC framework encompasses a summary section that resumes the main points of the ETAC analysis.

A possible summary of the ETAC framework applied to the Blockchain technology would allow concluding that the technology has the potential to revolutionize financial and non-financial sectors; however, it faces technical gaps related to scalability, weak developer tools, and a lack of verification methods.

## Blurring industries mapping

As industry lines blur, your organization may find itself navigating not only its primary sector but various other sectors. To assess the actors and the sectors the organization is confronted with, blurring industries mapping, which consists of the following four stages, can provide a guiding hand:

1. Define what the value proposition is to which the focal organization contributes.
2. Consider all stages a purchaser (e.g., consumer) goes through with this product. For example, a buyer of an electric car may go through the following steps: searching for a car, acquiring the car, using the car, maintaining the car, interacting with others by offering the car on a car-sharing app, and selling the car (see Table A.1).
3. For each stage, you list the activities the purchaser goes through, and which organization is involved (e.g., in the acquisition stage, the purchaser obtains insurance from a financial insurance firm).
4. Classify the activities and their provider in each stage according to their primary industry (e.g., the main industry of the financial insurance firm is the financial sector).

# Plan

Once you understand the firm's macro-environment, you can start planning to confront the firm with key drivers, discontinuities and strategic surprises, and possible scenarios. Tools such as the key drivers of change, strategic early warning systems (SEWS), general scenario planning, and OSPA can assist you with this.

**TABLE A.1** Sectors engaged across various stages (from search to sell) within personal mobility

| | Search → | Acquire → | Use → | Maintain → | Collaborate → | Sell → |
|---|---|---|---|---|---|---|
| **Retail marketplace** | Search dealers and test drive at dealer | Purchase or lease vehicle | Purchase gas (not in case of EV's) or gain/use rewards points | Purchase accessories and auto parts | Purchase accessories and auto parts | Sell car |
| **Service marketplace** | | Purchase service terms | Access maintenance, cleaning and vehicle tracking services | | Use apps for carsharing and monetization (e.g., ridesharing) | |
| **Information marketplace** | Research vehicles | | Use mapping or GPS | | | List car for sale on seller-buyer connecting platforms, and research car value considering model, mileage, condition, etc. |
| **Energy** | | Requests for placement of charging stations | Using charging infrastructure to power EV's (if applicable) | | Collaborate with energy providers for grid stability | Find second-life applications for batteries |
| **Finance** | Search and receive finance terms | Obtain financing | Dynamically adjust finance terms to market changes | | | Benefit from new purchaser's ability to finance |
| **Insurance** | | Obtain insurance | Adjust insurance dynamically based on driving history | Dynamically adapt insurance to car condition | | Transition insurance coverage to next vehicle |
| **Government** | Governmental stimulus of alternative mobility | Calculate taxes and registration fee, register vehicle, and pay taxes | Schedule inspections and update registration | | Adjust licensing if using car as rideshare driver | Register sale |

Source: Adapted from Panorama by McKinsey (2017)

## Key drivers of change

Macro-environments are constantly changing; some trends can represent tremendous opportunities for businesses, while others are serious threats. The drivers of change have a structural effect across many societal layers, inevitably affecting business environments. Therefore, it is crucial to understand the main drivers of change in the macro-environment and how those can affect a focal organization. Examples of broadly defined key drivers of change are globalization, regionalization, industrialization, and digitalization. One way to structure such analysis is to (1) rank the key drivers of change considering their relevance to the focal organization; (2) name and (3) explain them in broad terms; (4) evaluate if the driver constitutes an opportunity or threat for the organization; (5) assess if its impact will be in the short, medium or long term; and, finally, (6) list the required business adjustment to take advantage of the opportunity or mitigate the threat (see Figure A.6).

| Rank | Key driver of change | WHAT (broad definition) | HOW (opportunity or threat) | WHEN (short, medium, or long term) | Required adjustments |
|---|---|---|---|---|---|
| 1 | Globalization | The world is increasingly interdependent and interconnected. | *Opportunity* – Potential to connect and sell to customers all over the world. | Medium term | • Develop own e-commerce platform<br>• Expand distribution channels |
| 2 | Digitalization | Digital technologies are changing how companies do business. | *Threat* – Digital platforms are dominating several industries | Medium term | • Collaborate with online platforms<br>• Cooperate with other ecosystem actors |
| 3 | Industrialization | Increasing dominance of industrial activities in countries' economies. | *Opportunity* – Reduced average costs due to mass-production | Short term | • Improve machinery efficiency<br>• Increase factory automation |

**FIGURE A.6**   Illustrative ranking of key drivers of change

Source: authors

## Strategic early warning system

Formally known as the SEWS, this model assists organizations in detecting discontinuities and strategic surprises.[6] The model suggests that threats to an organization do not appear without warning signs. Yet, these warning signs are often weak and ignored by those in control of strategic planning. An organization should institute procedures to detect these weak signals to limit surprises. This process is a subsection of environmental analysis (see Chapter 4). A SEWS ideally consists of three phases (see Figure A.7):

- <u>Scanning</u> – In the first phase, you gather data on early warning signs. This process primarily relies on quantitative data such as financial and media sources.
- <u>Monitoring</u> – In the second phase, you scrutinize the data gathered to discover trends and patterns. This process will indicate bubbling problems that are not apparent yet.

- Assessing – In the final phase, you prioritize the threats and formulate strategies to confront them.

**FIGURE A.7**   Strategic early warning system (SEWS) phases

Source: authors

## General scenario planning

Scenario planning has a long history; it was initially developed by RAND for the American Airforce and has gone through many iterations.[7] Scenario analysis is a dynamic framework that allows for building possible developments or events (scenarios) that could take place between the present time and a certain point of time in the future (see Chapter 4). The future is full of uncertainties, and organizations should explore different possibilities to prepare contingency plans. Here, we will consider the general steps to scenario planning. Separately, we will consider OSPA, a modern approach to scenario planning that provides a well-defined process.

To conduct a general scenario planning analysis, there are three broad steps:

1. Identify relevant factors affecting the business operations. Such factors usually result from the PESTEL analysis and other models from the 'Understand' section.
2. Evaluate the trajectories of such factors (e.g., increase, decrease, radical or minimal change, positive or negative outcome).
3. Name the different scenarios and predict the possible outcomes and implications.

Figure A.8 shows an example of a scenario planning developed by a consumer goods company. Two factors that may affect its business are transportation costs and consumer purchasing power. The name of the scenarios reflects the impact of each scenario on the firm's sales. Finally, different colors may signal the impact – for example, red signals a threat and green an opportunity for the business.

## Oxford Scenario Planning Approach (OSPA)

One of the latest versions of scenario planning is the Oxford Scenario Planning Approach (OSPA). The OSPA is also known as strategic reframing,[8] as it is principally concerned with supporting a cycle of prospective sensemaking that involves framing and reframing future contexts. This process subsequently aids in improving leadership judgement. The model considers a more focused scope of the external environment. Instead of assessing the entire range of macro-environmental factors (see PESTEL analysis), the OSPA engages with TUNA conditions (Turbulence, Uncertainty, Novelty, and Ambiguity). There are five central characteristics of the Oxford Approach to scenario planning:[9]

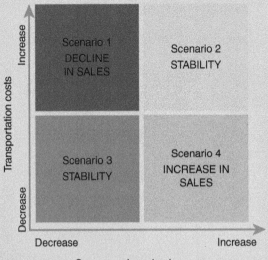

**FIGURE A.8**   Example of scenario planning of a consumer goods company

Source: authors

1. When planning, you must make explicit what is framed in and what is framed out when setting a strategy.
2. A limited number of scenarios should be proposed to enable organizations to re-perceive current and plausible future contexts effectively.
3. The scenario planning process relies on iterative reframing and re-perception.
4. Everyone involved in and affected by the procedure should play a role in the process.
5. The scenario planning process is designed to explore different types of weak signals.

# Micro-environmental analysis

The micro-environment considers the actors in direct contact with the organization, such as competitors, suppliers, and customers. The micro-environment can be further divided into actors that support the organization and those that challenge the organization (see Chapters 3 and 4). Next, we concentrate on corporate governance, also known as 'control'. This encompasses managing the firm within the context of the external environment and the handling of its stakeholders.

## Control

In an era where firms' negative impact on society is under a magnifying glass, they must show that they are not the problem but an essential part of the solution to make the world a little better. Firms with a purpose choose a social goal as the foundation of the enterprise and put a profitable business model at its service. Joly's Corporate Purpose Model aids in defining the corporation's purpose. Yet this is only the first step. The control of a corporation is primarily concerned with governance aspects such as stakeholder management. Here, the following frameworks play a central role: the Stakeholder analysis, the Salience model, and Materiality matrices.

## Joly's Corporate Purpose Framework

Defining an organization's purpose can be an obscure task. It is easy to formulate a purpose statement that is either too general or not comprehensive enough. To orientate strategists on the organization's purpose, Joly[10] finds that it can be located at the intersection of four areas: *societal needs* (what the world needs), *the organization's strength* (what the firm is uniquely good at), *value creation* (how the firm can create economic value), and *workforce passion* (what people at the firm are passionate about) (see Figure A.9). Once the organization's interests have been written down, one needs to position them on the Purpose Framework. Interests closest to the intersection of the four circles can be seen as contenders for the organization's purpose. After using the Purpose Framework for orientation, strategists may pick one or several interests most central to the organization and brainstorm with the team. These can subsequently be evaluated across five criteria: meaningful, authentic, credible, powerful, and compelling. Finally, one may select the best-suited purpose statement.

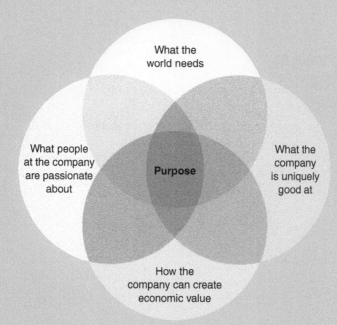

## Looking for your company's purpose
It lies at the intersection of these four circles.

**FIGURE A.9**   Joly's Purpose Framework

Source: Joly (2021) *The Heart of Business: Leadership Principles for the Next Era of Capitalism*

## Stakeholder analysis

As discussed in Chapter 3, understanding who a firm's stakeholders are and prioritizing their needs is the first step in conceiving an effective stakeholder management strategy. As further described next, an adequate stakeholder analysis consists of four phases: (1) identify the stakeholders, (2) prioritize the stakeholders, (3) understand key stakeholders' needs, and (4) assess shifting stakeholders.

1.  <u>Identifying your stakeholders</u> – Identifying stakeholders can be done by writing up a simple list of parties involved with the organization. To gain insight during this phase, it is helpful to identify the actors and structure them among two dimensions. With the two-dimensional Stakeholder Grid (see Figure A.10) you can create a clear overview of your stakeholders and their relation to your organization. The *Stake*-dimension defines the actor's involvement concerning the organization, whether that is equity ownership, other economic transactions, or influencers. Here, the prior two form the primary stakeholders, and influencers form secondary stakeholders. *Power*, the grid's second dimension, indicates what kind of power relation the organization has with the actor (see Figure A.10).

| Stake/Power | Formal or Voting | Economic | Political |
|---|---|---|---|
| **Equity** | • *Stockholders*<br>• *Directors*<br>• *Minority interests* | | |
| **Economic Transactions** | | • *Customers*<br>• *Competitors*<br>• *Suppliers*<br>• *Debt holders*<br>• *Unions* | • *Foreign governments* |
| **Influencers** | | | • *Consumer advocates*<br>• *Government*<br>• *Trade associations* |

**FIGURE A.10**   Stakeholder Grid

Source: adapted from Rosen (1995) *Strategic Management: An Introduction* [11]

2.  <u>Prioritizing your stakeholders</u> – After completing a stakeholder mapping in Phase 1, you have an initial idea of which stakeholders to watch. This consideration is materialized in Phase 2, where the stakeholders can be visualized in a Power-Interest Matrix that comprises a stakeholder's level of power (influence) and the stakeholder's interest in the organization (see Figure A.11).

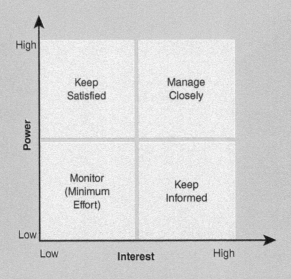

**FIGURE A.11**   The Power-Interest Matrix

Source: Ackermann and Eden (1998) Making Strategy: Mapping Out Strategic Success [12]

3.  <u>Understanding key stakeholders' needs</u> – After completing Phases 1 and 2, you will have a better sense of who the organization's stakeholders are, and who to prioritize. Subsequently, you should consider which stakeholder needs are most pressing by considering the stakeholders that rate high in the Power dimension (see Phase 2). Firms should understand their stakeholders by evaluating them systematically. This can be done by asking questions such as:

    - What interest do stakeholders have in the achievement of the firm's strategic aims? Is it positive or negative?
    - What motivates them?
    - What information do they want, and what is the best way to communicate this?
    - What is their current assessment of the firm?
    - Are there third parties that influence stakeholder's views, and should the firm also consider their needs?
    - How can the firm gain or maintain support from them?
    - How does the firm manage the stakeholders if it cannot gain their support, or if their interests are incompatible with the firm's strategic objectives?

4.  <u>Assessing shifting stakeholders</u> – When an organization adjusts its strategic objectives, its new direction may cause existing stakeholders to disappear or new ones to appear. When considering new strategic options, it is essential to review the stakeholder analysis by repeating Phases 1 to 3 and reviewing the results of this new assessment before deciding on implementing new strategic objectives.

## Salience model

The Salience model is an alternative to the Power-Interest Matrix.[13] The model is represented by a Venn diagram with three dimensions: *Legitimacy* (A), *Power* (B), and *Urgency* (C). The eight regions of this model (see Figure A.12) each represent a stakeholder group.

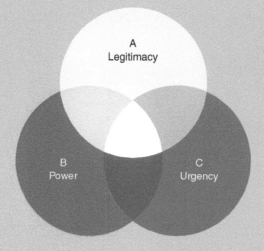

**FIGURE A.12**   The Salience model for stakeholder classification

Source: Mitchell, Agle and Wood (1997) *Toward a theory of stakeholder identification and salience*

1.  <u>Discretionary stakeholders:</u> stakeholders with little urgency and power. While they have legitimate claims, they are unlikely to pressure the focal organization (Yellow region).

2. <u>Dormant stakeholders:</u> stakeholders with power but no legitimacy or urgency. They are unlikely to become heavily involved with the organization (Blue region).
3. <u>Demanding stakeholders:</u> stakeholders with little power or legitimacy. However, they may show disruptive behaviour to achieve their demands, such as racketing (Red region).
4. <u>Dominant stakeholders:</u> stakeholders with power over the organization and legitimacy, yet without urgency. These stakeholders tend to have expectations that must be met (Green region).
5. <u>Dangerous stakeholders:</u> stakeholders with power and urgency but no formal association with the organization (Magenta region).
6. <u>Dependent stakeholders:</u> stakeholders which have urgent and legitimate involvement but little power. These stakeholders may depend on other stakeholders to support their desires (Orange region).
7. <u>Definitive stakeholders:</u> stakeholders with power, legitimacy, and urgency. These stakeholders have the highest salience and are key to the organization (Central white region).
8. <u>Non-stakeholders:</u> stakeholders with no legitimacy, power, or urgency (region outside circles A, B, and C).

## Materiality matrices

Environmental, social, and governmental (ESG) standards have recently gained prominence in finance (see Chapters 2 and 3). Financial institutions primarily rely on ESG ratings such as MSCI (Morgan Stanley Capital International Index) for evaluating a firm's performance regarding ESG.[14] Yet a second important disclosure of ESG performance is the annual reports that corporations publish. A common approach to displaying ESG performance is through a materiality matrix (see Figure A.13). This diagram showcases ESG factors along certain dimensions, such as the importance to stakeholders and the influence the factor has on the firm achieving its strategic objectives. Companies often employ third-party firms, such as accounting firms, to conduct the research for these diagrams. However, you may also perform the analysis internally.

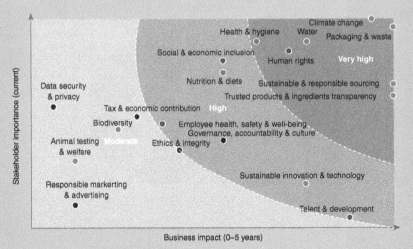

**FIGURE A.13**   Materiality Matrix of Unilever plc 2019–2020

Source: Unilever (2022a)[15]

# Endnotes (references)

1. Aguilar, F.J. (1967) *Scanning the Business Environment*. New York, NY: Macmillan.
2. Brown, A. and Weiner, E. (1984) *Supermanaging*. New York, NY: McGraw-Hill.
3. Porter, M.E. (1989) *The Competitive Advantage of Nations*. New York, NY: Palgrave.
4. Perera, S., Fremantle, P., Leymann, F. and Jenkins, J. (2018) *Emerging Technology Analysis Canvas (ETAC)*. https://www.researchgate.net/publication/328172070_Emerging_Technology_Analysis_Canvas_ETAC (accessed June 15, 2023).
5. Atluri, V., Dietz, M. and Henke, N. (2017) 'Competing in a world of sectors without borders', *McKinsey Quarterly*, 3: 32–47.
6. Ansoff, H.I. (1975) 'Managing strategic surprise by response to weak signals', *California Management Review*, 18 (2): 21–33.
7. Ramírez, R., Churchhouse, S., Palermo, A. and Hoffmann, J. (2017) 'Using scenario planning to reshape strategy', *MIT Sloan Management Review*, 58 (4). https://sloanreview.mit.edu/article/using-scenario-planning-to-reshape-strategy/ (accessed June 14, 2023).
8. Ramírez, R. and Wilkinson, A. (2016) *Strategic Reframing: The Oxford Scenario Planning Approach*. Oxford: Oxford University Press.
9. Ramírez et al. (2017)
10. Joly, H. (2021) *The Heart of Business: Leadership Principles for the Next Era of Capitalism*. Cambridge, MA: Harvard Business Review Press.
11. Rosen, R. (1995) *Strategic Management: An Introduction*. Lanham, MD: Pitman.
12. Ackermann, F. and Eden, C. (1998) *Making Strategy: Mapping Out Strategic Success*. London: Sage.
13. Mitchell, R., Agle, B. and Wood, D. (1997) 'Toward a theory of stakeholder identification and salience: Defining the principle of who and what really counts', *Academy of Management Review*, 22 (4): 853–86.
14. Giese, G., Lee, L., Melas, D., Nagy, Z. and Nishikawa, L. (2019) 'Foundations of ESG investing: How ESG affects equity valuation, risk, and performance', *The Journal of Portfolio Management*, 45 (5): 69–83.
15. Unilever (2022a) 'Materiality Matrix 2019/20', Unilever. https://www.unilever.com/files/0acda6a5-c6af-44a6-a803-485346cd6b67/unilever-materiality-matrix-2019-2020.pdf (accessed June 16, 2023).

# Acknowledgements

The authors thank Liam Goodman for his contribution to this chapter.

# PART II
## SENSE

This part focuses on the analytical tools and techniques, classic and cutting edge, that help strategists to conduct analysis to better understand key parameters that influence strategic decisions. It challenges firms to analyze their resources and competencies (resource-based view), but also to see beyond their habits and routines by taking into account their value network, industry and ecosystem. This part focuses on industry and product-market analysis, customer analysis, internal analysis, and ecosystem analysis, and their interlinkages. Providing the essential tools to conduct inside-out and outside-in analysis, this part relies heavily on industrial organization theory, resource-based theory of the firm, and the dynamic capability theory of strategic management. Several practical tools to conduct these analyses are provided in the iSense toolkit.

# 6

# INDUSTRY AND PRODUCT-MARKET ANALYSIS

## LEARNING OBJECTIVES

After reading this chapter, you should be able to:

- appreciate the three dimensions of industry and product-market analysis;
- assess industry and product-market attractiveness and competitiveness;
- identify strategic groups across a set of strategic dimensions;
- determine the intensity of rivalry between firms and their likely reactions to a rival's actions.

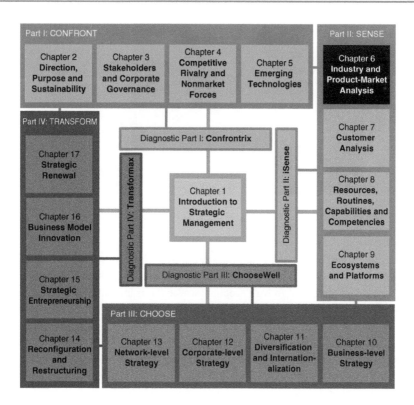

## OPENING CASE

### Thriva and the rugged competitive landscape of the e-Health market (Part I)[1]

Thriva is a London-based at-home blood-testing company founded in 2015 that allows people to do health check-ups, testing for a range of internal blood markers associated with good/bad health, including cholesterol levels and kidney and liver function. Thriva's business model is simple. First, customers acquire a finger-prick kit with clear instructions (see Figure 6.1). Second, customers take the blood sample and mail it to Thriva's partner lab. Finally, the results are received through Thriva's platform with professional counselling and recommendations, explaining what lifestyle changes customers should make to improve their health. While Thriva's business model may look simple, its competitive landscape is rugged. Thriva faces growing competition from e-Health competitors and other healthcare-related companies.

The e-Health market is growing and attracting new players specializing in different niches. Some examples are Medichecks, Forth, LetsGetChecked, and Living DNA (see Closing Case: The e-Health market: Identifying the strategic groups (Part II)). At this stage, customers' switching costs are low, at least while they do not hook up with subscriptions and accumulated health data; therefore, customers are expected to bargain for lower prices and higher service quality.

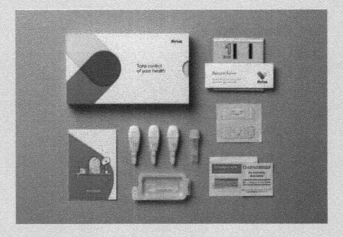

**FIGURE 6.1**   Thriva sends the blood testing kits by post

Second, considering the broader healthcare industry in the UK, Thriva may also compete with the National Health Service (NHS). The NHS is a competitor with a different dimension, value chain, and a broad range of healthcare services that are out of Thriva's scope; however, it has invested tremendously in preventive health check-ups and e-services. While the NHS can provide such services for free or at a low price, which is convenient for price-sensitive customers, it is also increasingly challenging to access, which increases the chances that customers opt for Thriva's services.

Third, Thriva does not perform the blood tests nor produce the take-home testing kits; instead, Thriva relies on business partners that take over such activities, such as registered laboratories and healthcare suppliers. Such suppliers are highly specialized and differentiated, being fundamental to sustaining Thriva's business model. However, these laboratories and healthcare suppliers display strong bargaining power and prominent financial resources. Thriva needs to consider the possibility that they forward integrate and step into the e-Health market themselves.

Thriva is trying to seize an uprise in demand for e-Health services and convenient at-home health check-ups. However, it competes in a very uncertain competitive environment where boundaries are blurred, and competitive threats come from all fronts.

## Questions

1. How would you map the competitive landscape of Thriva?
2. Identify the life-cycle stage of the healthcare industry, the e-Health market, and the at-home blood-testing market.
3. Identify the main forces affecting the healthcare industry.

# Introduction

In the chapters of Part I (*Confront*) of this book we discussed several emerging challenges and tensions firms are being confronted with. How to contribute to economic goals as well as social-environmental goals? How to engage with a broad set of stakeholders with conflicting demands? What changes in rivalry is the firm confronted with and how to shape the broader institutional environment? And what are the emerging technologies the firm is confronted with? In this Part II (*Sense*) we continue with the next stage of the strategy process and consider how to further analyze and make sense of these business challenges and tensions. We particularly focus on analyzing the implications for the firm's industries and product markets (Chapter 6), its customers (Chapter 7), its resources, routines, capabilities and competencies (Chapter 8), and the ecosystems and platforms the firm is participating in (Chapter 9). This part ends with the *iSense* diagnostic chapter, providing several tools and analytical techniques for an in-depth understanding of focal industries, customer segments, competitors, complementors, and, internally, an appreciation of resources and capabilities. We start here with Chapter 6 on analyzing and making sense of industries and product markets.

An **industry** is a group of firms producing similar products and competing for the same resources and customers in the marketplace. Industry analysis has its roots in the Industrial Organization (I/O) model of above-average returns (see Chapter 1), considered by many the application of microeconomics to the analysis of firms, markets, and industries. I/O scholars have focused on the impact of industry structure on competition and of competition on prices, investment, and innovation.[2] Such scholars highlight the importance of analyzing the industry in which a firm competes because different industries can display different levels of competitive intensity, consequently impacting firms' performance. Researchers interested in industry effects conclude that the industry in which a firm competes tends to explain around 20% of its performance.[3]

While in the past, researchers and analysts tended to study firms' competitive environment adopting an industry-level unit of analysis, nowadays, industries have become more complex, comprising different types of products and heterogeneous competitors, and displaying blurry boundaries (see Chapter 4). It might, therefore, be necessary to analyze the competitive landscape using the product market as the unit of analysis. A **product market** includes goods or services with similar characteristics in terms of features, performance, intended use, and price. Instead of considering all the players in an industry, the product-market perspective considers those competitors that offer similar goods or services across a range of characteristics.

Considering the importance of industry and product markets, it is thus essential to understand how managers and analysts can assess the competitive environment where a firm is located. In this chapter, we suggest three dimensions of analysis: industry and product-market boundaries, strategic groups, and rivalry. In the first dimension, we will understand how to delineate the industry and product-market boundaries, analyzing their structure, life cycle, forces, profit pools, and value networks. In the second dimension, we will identify the different strategic groups within an industry or market using a range of strategy-related dimensions. Finally, in the third dimension, we will zoom in to the strategic group to identify a focal firm's direct rivals (see Figure 6.2).

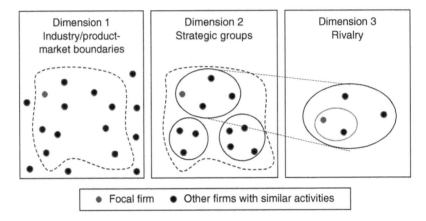

**FIGURE 6.2**   The three dimensions of industry and product-market analysis

## Industry and product-market boundaries

When analyzing an industry, the first step is defining its boundaries. However, setting industry boundaries is not always easy, and mistakes can result in strategic misfits and disappointing results. The first issue when delineating industry boundaries is defining them too broadly, encompassing firms that compete in different product markets or serve different market segments, making the analysis too complex. In these situations, managers can consider disaggregating the level of analysis, narrowing it down to product markets (see Chapter 11) or market segments (see Chapter 7). Some industries can be disaggregated into multiple product markets. For example, the PC industry comprises several complementary products, such as hardware, software, and peripherals, each one representing a product market. Furthermore, industries, or even product markets, may also comprise different market segments. Market segments adopt a customer perspective and entail identifying specific groups of customers that react similarly to market stimuli. These market segments, also known as customer segments, are delineated using geographic, demographic, and psychographic, among other criteria (see Chapter 7). In the PC industry, each product can have different market segments based on their purchasing and usage profile. For instance, the 'corporate' segment buys in bulk and uses computers professionally, while the 'gamer' segment buys a single powerful unit for recreational purposes. This example shows that industries or even product markets can be further disaggregated into market segments.

## STRATEGIC FOCUS

### Industries and product markets

The difference between an *industry* and a *product market* depends on the context. In some contexts, they are one and the same. In some other contexts, a product market is a subset of an industry. And in yet other contexts, the product market can be a superset, meaning that firms from different industries compete in the same product market.

To illustrate the fact that a product market can be a subset of an industry, consider the centrifugal pump industry, a $31 billion industry.[4] Large players in this industry are Grundfos, Ebara, Flowserve, ITT Goulds, Kirloskar, KSB, Pentair, Sulzer, Weir, Wilo, and Xylem. There are also many small players, which mostly serve a niche based on specific offerings regarding materials and applications. Centrifugal pumps are offered in a variety of sizes. For instance, Grundfos' pump portfolio is built on a standard range of very small (capacity<1[m³/h]) to medium-sized pumps. Others, like Pentair, Flowserve and Kirloskar, have a mix that ranges from small sized pumps up to very large pumps (up to 180,000[m³/h]). The markets for small pumps are very different from the markets for large pumps. In that regard, one could say that this industry consists of two main product markets. Volumes (quantity of units sold) is inversely related to pump size. This means that for small pumps, large volumes can be sold and for large pumps, limited numbers can be sold. As small pumps are needed in large quantities, supply chain strategies that are closer to a 'ship-to-stock' (STS) strategy, which implies standardized activities within the firm's value chain, are assumed better suited. But for large pumps, a higher degree of customization is requested, because of the operational cost advantages it can bring during a pump's complete life cycle. After all, larger pumps generally have a very long technical life span – if maintained well, life spans of more than 80 years are possible. This means firms supplying these larger pumps often opt for an 'engineer-to-order' (ETO) strategy, implying customization throughout their value chain. Hence, a different market approach and supply chain strategy is optimal for small versus large pumps. For instance, Grundfos has a standardized product range and allows its customers to select pumps and to find information by offering an openly available web-based advanced product configurator. Others, like Pentair, have a mixed approach, where smaller pumps are offered in a more standardized portfolio and basic-level selections and information can be found by a low-level online pump selector. However, for its large pump offerings, customers must always contact the company to request more information.

To illustrate that a product market can be a superset, consider the market for beverage-holding containers. These containers can be made from, for instance, steel, aluminium, carton, plastic, and naturally biodegradable, compostable materials. The firms producing these containers, which may be considered substitutes by the customer, come from different industries – such as the steel industry (production of steel containers) and the aluminium industry (production of aluminium containers).[5] In this case, different industries come together in a single product market.

Identifying the industry, product market, or even market segment boundaries is a complex and multidimensional exercise, and different levels of analysis might be required in different contexts. The question is whether to perform several separate analyses (e.g., focusing on the industry and on different product markets and market segments) and end up with a complex assessment or simplify the study to a single unit of analysis and miss out on variations that might be relevant for strategic planning. Defining industry or product-market boundaries is even more complex in hypercompetitive environments where the competitive landscape changes constantly, boundaries are blurring, and market players cross the boundaries of several industries. There is no rule of thumb for delineating the industry or product-market boundaries in these and other contexts. A useful exercise to pick the right level of analysis is to review how firms historically identify the nature of their business. Some focus on the characteristics of their product line (e.g., airline companies, machine-tool companies, automobile companies), while others describe themselves by the technology or resources they use (e.g., steel companies, aluminium companies, and glass companies). Another exercise is to try out broader and narrower industry/market boundaries to ensure that no important actors or forces are overlooked.

Defining the boundaries is a stepping stone for assessing the nature of competition in a specific industry or product market. It is followed by the assessment of industry or product-market competitiveness, dynamics, and attractiveness. In this section, we present various theoretical perspectives that serve such purposes, namely market structure, industry or product life-cycle, market forces, profit pools, and value networks.

## Market structure

The market structure concerns the composition of the marketplace in terms of the number of companies competing for the same resources and customers, and producing the same product or service. Market structure elements include the degree of market concentration (the number of competitors and their size), the extent to which products are differentiated (differentiated or similar products), and how easy it is for firms to enter the market (barriers to entry).[6] Industry and market concepts are often used interchangeably in the literature, as this analysis holds for whole industries and also for different product markets and market segments.

Historically, market structure analysis builds on Bain's structure-conduct-performance (SCP) paradigm. Such a view postulates a relationship between market structure (concentration), firms' conduct (e.g., independent or collusive price-setting behaviours, investment in R&D and marketing), and economic performance (efficiency, profitability). According to the SCP view, high market concentration and high barriers to entry buffer market participants from intense competition. In a nutshell, the SCP paradigm states that firms in more concentrated markets earn higher profits than those in less concentrated markets.[7] The neoclassic theory of the firm discusses four main types of market structures: monopoly, oligopoly, monopolistic competition, and perfect competition (see Figure 6.3).

In a <u>monopoly</u>, also referred to as a monopolistic structure, only one firm exists in the market; therefore, market concentration is high, and competition is non existent. Governments can impose monopolies through licenses and by increasing the barriers to entry in a particular market. However, monopolies may also emerge naturally when high investment levels are required to enter the market, and only a single player can raise the amount of capital needed. Electricity, gas, and water companies in many countries reflect a monopolistic market structure.

In an <u>oligopoly</u>, or an oligopolistic market structure, a few firms compete in the marketplace – when only two firms compete in the marketplace, the market is referred to as a duopoly. In such markets, barriers to entry tend to be medium-high, and competition intensity is low. The worldwide shipping carrier market is an example of an oligopoly, in which the leading competitors at the global scale are FedEx, UPS, and DHL.

In <u>monopolistic competition</u> many firms compete in the market, but they have differentiated products. The market concentration is low, and barriers to entry are medium, which leads to a medium-high competition intensity. An example of such a market is the tech hardware industry, in which key players include Apple, Samsung, Dell, Sony, HP, Lenovo, LG, and Cisco.

In <u>perfect competition</u> markets, many undifferentiated firms operate in the same market, displaying low concentration, minimal product differentiation, and low barriers to entry. In such a market, competition intensity is high. Such a market structure is typical in commodity markets such as the markets for milk and sugar.

| | Monopoly | Oligopoly | Monopolistic competition | Perfect competition |
|---|---|---|---|---|
| Market concentration | High (one firm) | High (few firms) | Low (many firms) | Low (many firms) |
| Product differentiation/ similarity | N/A | Similar or differentiated | Differentiated products | Similar products |
| Barriers to entry | High | Medium | Medium | Low |
| Competition intensity | Low ⟶ | | | High |

**FIGURE 6.3** Market structure

While the SCP paradigm provides essential information for analyzing industry or market competitive intensity, scholars have recognized that such a paradigm fails to predict industry competitiveness and firms' performance accurately. Indeed, a range of other factors besides industry concentration can play a role in explaining industry competitiveness, such as: the industry development stage, because growing industries are different from declining ones in terms of competitive intensity (see section on Industry structure); the strength of competitive forces as affected by buyers, suppliers, substitutes, and new entrants (see section on Industry forces); the different profit pools comprising the industry (see section on Profit pools); and the value networks that determine how sets of suppliers and buyers create value together (see section on Value networks). Another limitation of the SCP paradigm and the industry structure analysis is that, in practice, it is not easy to find pure representatives of the industry structure types. Industries are multidimensional constructs and may have different structures for different markets or geographies. Nevertheless, it is helpful to have broad categories in mind to compare the attractiveness of markets and likely broad patterns of competitive behaviour within them.

## Industry and product-market life-cycle

One of the main criticisms of market structure and the SCP paradigm is their static nature and inability to explain how industries, products, and firms change over time. The Organizational Ecology school aimed at addressing this gap, introducing the concept of the life-cycle, which emphasizes the importance of technological disruptions and developments for industry and market emergence and fading.[8] The **life-cycle model** charts the evolution of a market from introduction to decline. This model suggests that industries or product markets tend to be relatively small in the introduction phase, then go through a period of rapid growth, culminating in a period of maturity, and then decline. Each stage of the life-cycle displays differences across competitive intensity, product differentiation, and key success factors[9] (see Figure 6.4).

In the <u>introduction</u> phase, firms attempt to develop customers' interest in the product. This is also an experimentation phase, typically with few players and a low competitive intensity, where competitors develop highly differentiated products. Prices might be high in this phase; however, profits might be low due to the high investment requirements.

In the <u>growth</u> phase, new competitors are attracted to the industry/market, and competition starts to increase; however, there are plenty of opportunities in the market as demand grows at a good pace. Barriers to entry are still relatively low, and companies may start to be profitable in this phase due to product differentiation and high prices. At this stage, the critical success factors are product quality and reliability and marketing investment to increase firms' reputation and attract customers.

When growth slows down, the market reaches the <u>maturity</u> stage. Each company competes harder for market share, and the market tends to be fragmented. Barriers to entry tend to increase, as established players control the distribution channels and achieve economies of scale. In this phase, products tend to be standardized (low differentiation), and competition is based on price, advertising, and branding.

The last phase is when sales start to <u>decline</u>. This stage is characterized by extreme rivalry, leading to a 'dog-eat-dog' type of competition. Customers select on price, and there is fierce price competition and cost control.

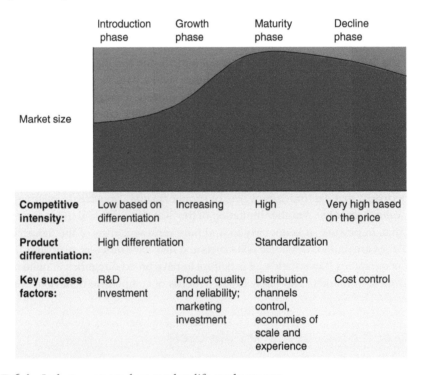

**FIGURE 6.4**   Industry or product-market life-cycle stages

The life-cycle view draws and summarizes critical information from different schools, providing practical advice and predictive power that can be applied at the industry, product- market, or market segment levels. Additionally, it highlights the advantages of an early entry into the market, as first movers tend to gain substantial strategic advantage over time. The life-cycle perspective also calls attention to the 'maturity mindset', in which managers are complacent with the decline, calling for efforts to reinvent products, services, and strategies to rejuvenate the market.[10] Finally, this framework highlights the cyclical nature of market development and demand, noticing that markets' competitiveness and attractiveness vary across the different phases.

The main limitation of the life-cycle perspective is its simplistic and oversimplified description of stages and firms' behaviour across these phases. For example, some industries or product markets may have few/many competitors across all stages of the life cycle. Others may even miss some stages of the life cycle, as is the case of fast-fashion products that grow and decline quickly without going through the maturity phase. Another problem is the duration and characteristics of the stages that may vary across markets. For example, revitalized markets sharply decline and then grow again, as happened with the photography market after the introduction of digital cameras. Finally, the life-cycle view assumes that companies are takers and have no impact on the market stages, which is only sometimes true. Companies can indeed shape the market development and the shape of the life-cycle curve.[11]

## Market forces

Industry (or product-market) structure and life cycle are two important perspectives that help to analyze competition intensity. However, competitive intensity is not always a predictor of market attractiveness (i.e., profitability). There are instances when very competitive markets are attractive, and also instances when markets with low competitive intensity are not attractive at all. Michael Porter proposes a more holistic perspective on industry competitiveness and attractiveness, capturing dimensions that are not covered by the structure and life-cycle views. Porter suggests that five main forces can influence an industry's attractiveness, namely, the threat of new entrants, the threat of substitute products, buyers' bargaining power, suppliers' bargaining power, and the intensity of competitive rivalry[12] (see Figure 6.5).

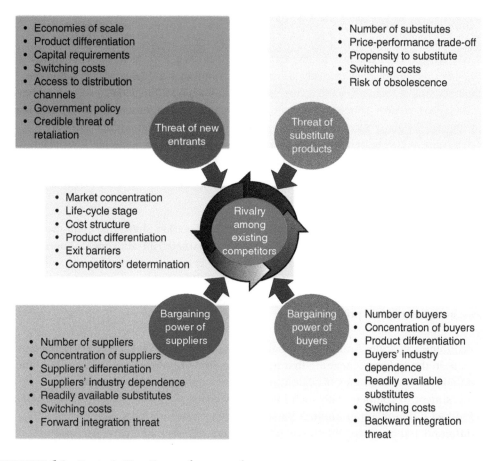

**FIGURE 6.5** Porter's Five Forces framework

## Rivalry among competitors

Building on Industrial Organization (I/O) theory, Porter proposes that the higher the rivalry among competitors within an industry, the lower the attractiveness of that industry. The competitive intensity among firms operating in the same market can be assessed not only through market concentration and life-cycle stage (see sections on Market structure and Industry and product-market life-cycle) but also by analyzing competitors' cost structure, product differentiation, exit barriers, and determination.

- Market concentration: When market concentration is low, and many competitors of similar size are fighting over each other's market share, competition intensity tends to be high. In contrast, when there are few large players competing in the market, competition intensity tends to be low.
- Life-cycle stage: The maturity of the market is another indicator of rivalry intensity. The further along the industry or product market is in the life-cycle, the higher the number of competitors, the pressure over margins, and, therefore, the rivalry intensity.
- Cost structure: Another dimension that helps to assess rivalry intensity is firms' cost structure. Players with high fixed costs tend to cut prices to conquer market share and gain scale to cover such costs, intensifying competition.
- Product differentiation: Product differentiation level is another indicator of rivalry intensity. When differentiation is low, rivalry concentrates around price competition, intensifying competition. Contrarily, high product differentiation buffers competitive intensity.
- Exit barriers: The existence of exit barriers, which can happen when companies invest in highly specialized assets or costly licenses, also contributes to higher rivalry within the market. In this situation, some companies tend to remain in the market, even when they display low returns or negative margins, with the ambition to retrieve the investment made.
- Competitors' determination: Rivalry can also be intense when competitors are determined, committed, and have leadership aspirations. In some markets, clashes of egos and historical rivalries can escalate competition.

## Threat of new entrants

New entrants bring extra capacity and desire to gain market share that puts pressure on competitors' margins, reducing industry (or product-markets') attractiveness. Therefore, the more barriers to entry there are, the more difficult it is for new entrants to put competitive pressure on the market. Barriers to entry can have different sources, such as economies of scale, product differentiation, switching costs, capital requirements, distribution channels' access, and government policy.

- Economies of scale: An important barrier to entry is the existence of economies of scale in the industry, meaning that incumbent firms produce at a large scale and low unitary costs. Economies of scale can deter new entrants as they require massive investment to compete with such low unitary costs.
- Product differentiation: Another barrier to entry can result from incumbents' differentiated products. When competitors have differentiated products, strong brands, and high customer loyalty, it is more difficult for new entrants to gain market share, as this would require a substantial investment.

- Switching costs: Switching costs comprise the expenses that the customer incurs to change between two products. The higher the customers' switching costs, the more difficult it is for new entrants to gain customers in the market.
- Capital requirements: The level of capital required to compete in a certain industry can also be a barrier to entry. The need to invest significant financial resources (e.g., facilities, inventories, branding) to compete in a market may limit the pool of likely entrants.
- Distribution channel access: New entrants need to make their products available to customers to compete in the market; therefore, the ease of accessing distribution channels is fundamental to them. When new entrants can access distribution channels easily, the barriers to entry in the market decrease. In contrast, when the distribution channels are monopolized by incumbents, the barriers to entry increase.
- Government policy: Finally, restrictive government policies can function as a barrier to new entrants as governments may protect specific industries through licensing, restrictions on foreign investment, or strict regulation. However, government policies can also function as an enabler for market development through, for example, subsidies.

## Bargaining power of suppliers

Powerful suppliers can capture part of the value created by charging higher prices or limiting supplies quality and availability, thus squeezing profit margins. Therefore, the higher the suppliers' bargaining power, the lower the market attractiveness. Dimensions such as the number and concentration of suppliers, suppliers' differentiation, the existence of substitutes, and forward integration threat can help to assess suppliers' power.

- Number and concentration: Suppliers can be powerful if they are few and more concentrated than the industry they sell to, exerting their power and bargaining for higher prices. In contrast, when there are many available suppliers in the market, their bargaining power tends to be low.
- Suppliers' differentiation: If suppliers are differentiated, they also have more control over buyers, as buyers cannot easily replace them. Contrarily, if the suppliers are not differentiated, their bargaining power decreases during the negotiation process.
- Existence of substitutes: If there are no available substitute suppliers or the switching costs of changing suppliers are high, the suppliers tend to display a high bargaining power over buyers.
- Forward integration threat: Finally, if the industry is attractive and the barriers to entry are low, suppliers can forward integrate, replacing the buyer. If such a threat is credible, suppliers tend to have higher bargaining power, decreasing industry attractiveness.

## Bargaining power of buyers

The flip side of powerful suppliers is influential buyers that can also capture a considerable slice of value, forcing prices down and demanding higher quality and availability. Therefore, markets in which buyers' bargaining power is high tend to be less attractive. Factors such as buyers' number and concentration, product differentiation, and backward integration threat may influence the power that buyers hold when negotiating product price and availability.

- Number and concentration: The primary source of buyers' bargaining power is their number and concentration. When there are many dispersed buyers, they tend to have low bargaining power, as none of the individual buyers can negotiate prices. However, if buyers are few, concentrated, or buy large volumes, they tend to have higher bargaining power as suppliers depend on them.

- Product differentiation: The level of product differentiation can also dictate buyers' bargaining power. When products are differentiated, buyers cannot find an equivalent elsewhere, which reduces their bargaining power. The same happens with high switching costs that mitigate buyers' bargaining power.
- Backward integration threat: Finally, the bargaining power of buyers increases if they can credibly integrate backwards and replace the supplier.

## Threat of substitutes

Substitutes are products that fulfil the same customer need as the focal product but belong to a different industry. For example, trains are substitutes for cars, plastic for aluminium, and video conferencing for face-to-face meetings. While substitutes exist almost always, they are easy to overlook. However, they can reduce industry attractiveness, squeezing prices and margins. The threat of substitutes can be assessed through, among others, the analysis of price-performance trade-off, switching costs, and the risk of obsolescence.

- Price-performance trade-off: The threat of substitutes is high when alternative products offer an attractive price-performance trade-off relative to the industry product. In this case, buyers can easily substitute the product or service, which decreases industry attractiveness.
- Switching costs: If customers find switching from one product to its substitute easy and cheap, then the threat of substitutes is high. Otherwise, if customers face relevant costs if they switch to a product substitute, the threat of substitutes is low.
- Risk of obsolescence: Substitute threats may emerge from developments in other industries. For example, the technological advancements in plastic materials allowed the substitution of steel products in many sectors, mainly automobile components. Nevertheless, improvements within the industry can also offer exciting opportunities to substitute other products in different sectors.

Porter's Five Forces framework offers a structured and straightforward approach to analyze industry or product-market attractiveness. Overall, the 'Porterian' view highlights the importance of buyers' and suppliers' bargaining power and their ability to squeeze margins in the industry. It also encourages companies to look beyond the immediate competitive landscape, looking for substitute products and services in other industries.

   On the limitations side, Porter's Five Forces model is static, in that it provides a snapshot of the market at a point in time. It is useful for short-term strategic decisions but less useful for developing long-term strategy. Another problem that may arise when applying the Five Forces model is the difficulty of delineating industry or market boundaries. As discussed, companies sometimes straddle different industries and compete in different product markets; in other cases, the boundaries between industries are blurring due to globalization and rapid technological development. Under such conditions, defining the boundaries can be challenging, compromising the applicability of such analysis. Finally, the model ignores the role of alliance partners (i.e., co-operators) and complementors. Given that companies compete in increasingly complex collaborative ecosystems (see Chapter 9), ignoring such actors may compromise a firm's ability to compete.

## STRATEGIC FOCUS

### Smart connected products and the nature of competition

The development and proliferation of information technologies have revolutionized hardware production that has migrated from mechanical and electrical parts to complex systems that combine hardware, sensors, data storage, microprocessors, and software. These 'smart connected products' display new opportunities, functionalities, interconnections, and capabilities that force companies to rethink how they compete, create, and capture value. Such new competition requires coordination and integration among suppliers, channels, and customers across platforms and geographies. Smart connected products are reshaping the industry and market boundaries, encompassing related products and interconnected systems. The focus changed from a product to the performance of a broader system that is interoperable with other systems in a big network of systems.[13] In this scenario, market players need to compete and cooperate simultaneously, but how can they build interdependent and trustworthy relationships while aspiring for market dominance?

## Profit pools

After analyzing the market structure, life-cycle, and the five forces, the next thing to pay attention to is the firm's bottom line by looking at the market shares of different products and services and the profitability levels. As discussed in the industry and product-market boundaries section, some industries aggregate several product markets or/and market segments; however, the success of firms is often evaluated based on their overall market share in terms of sales, which is an incomplete indicator and sometimes a misleading one. The profit pools perspective invites us to look to the bottom-line to understand the market profit structure.[14]

The profit pools perspective identifies core and secondary profit generator activities and seizes their profit margins. For example, in the PC industry, PC makers sell various products such as PCs, software, peripherals, microprocessors, and other components and services, such as software training, repairs, and data recovery (see Figure 6.6). These products have different operating margins, representing different profit pools. For example, PCs represent the most significant share of industry revenues (around 40%); however, it is the product category with the lowest operating margin (about 3%), while microprocessors represent the lowest revenue share (around 5%) but the highest operating margin (approximately 35%).

The profit-pools perspective highlights that companies may have different sources of profits, and that the first movers in creating and exploring activities that bring disproportional profitability will be better prepared to capture a good share of industry profits in the medium/long term. It also highlights that market share alone is an insufficient measure of performance. Sometimes, firms with high market shares are not the most profitable ones. For example, margins tend to be very low in the car renting market, and customers make decisions based on price that is easily comparable through online platforms. However, insurance and equipment rental (e.g., GPS) are complementary services that display healthy margins. Thus, it is misleading to evaluate competitors' performance based on sales of car-renting only, as the most profitable segment are the complementors. While the analysis of profit pools seems obvious, managers intuitively pursue strategies that look for revenue growth and increasing market shares in hopes that profits will follow. However, endorsing such strategies in hypercompetitive markets is dangerous because profit pools change fast, and firms need systematic and updated information on the different profit pools to succeed.

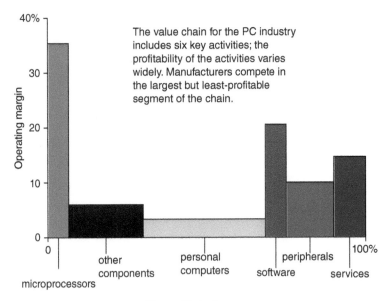

**FIGURE 6.6**  PC industry profit pools

Source: Gadiesh & Gilbert (1998)

Analyzing how profit pools change over time can also help firms to seize growing product markets or market segments, or to identify the ones that are declining and act accordingly, redirecting their strategic focus.

## Value networks

The value networks perspective is based on the axiom that 'the value that any party can capture from engaging in transactions with a given set of parties is bounded by the value each of them can add to parties outside the set'.[15] This axiom means that actors have different choices regarding whom to create value with, switching customers or suppliers with the ambition to create more value. Therefore, there is always a comparison between the value created with an actor and the value that could be created with an alternative actor. In the value capture view, each player, either a customer or a supplier, experiences a single force of competition: suppliers compete for customers, and customers compete for suppliers.

A value network comprises a core and a periphery. The core encompasses the focal firm, its suppliers, and customers, while the periphery comprises the available actors with whom the focal entities can transact alternatively. To map a value network and evaluate the competition intensity, managers need to consider its suppliers and customers, which are part of the network's core, and the periphery actors as they compete for the same suppliers and customers. For example, in Figure 6.7, Firm A sells a product to Customer B; however, Customer W would also be interested in buying from Firm A. Then, Customer W is an alternative buyer in the periphery of Firm A, increasing competition in this value network. The same applies to the other actors' value networks. For instance, Supplier C sells to Firm A, but Customer X could also be an alternative customer. Similarly, Customer B buys from Firm A but could also buy from Supplier Z, which is in the periphery of Customer B. On the one hand, the fact that Customer B and Supplier C have available options in their peripheries erodes Firm's A ability to appropriate value. On the other hand, Firm A also has options on its periphery, increasing its ability to appropriate value

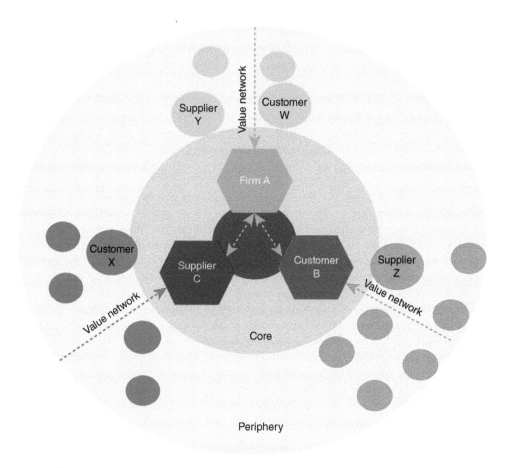

**FIGURE 6.7** Value network map of Firm A (hypothetical example)

from its suppliers and customers. If no alternative opportunities to create value exist beyond the network itself, there is no competition; therefore, the higher the number of options in the actors' periphery, the higher the competition.

While the value network perspective is enriching, it might be challenging to apply. Mapping a value network requires collecting data about all suppliers and customers that belong to the system's nucleus. Such groups of suppliers and customers can be very diverse, belonging to different industries and competing across varied markets. Such suppliers and customers may also display a diverse set of suppliers and customers in their periphery, which requires collecting a large amount of data that may not be available. Even though the value network perspective is based on simple premises of collective value creation and a single competition force (suppliers compete for customers, and customers compete for suppliers), its implementation can result in cluttered maps that are difficult to interpret.

## Strategic groups

The industrial organization assumption that firms in the same industry are homogeneous and de facto competitors has been challenged by the **strategic group** literature. This literature argues that industries consist of different groups of competitors, such that companies within a group are homogeneous and companies across groups are heterogeneous when their strategic attributes are compared. Thus, the strategic group perspective suggests an intermediate level of abstraction between the firm and industry levels.[16] While strategic group scholars mostly focus on finding groups within an industry, it also can be applied to product markets, mainly when such product markets comprise a large group of competitors with different market positionings.

Strategic groups scholars created a framework, the *strategic group map*, that allows its users to visually organize the different groups of firms that compose the competitive landscape. A strategic group map analysis entails first, finding relevant competitive dimensions that distil the competitive landscape into a few strategic dimensions; second, grouping the firms into meaningful clusters; and finally, interpreting the results to extract relevant information for strategic analysis.

1.  Finding the dimensions. The first step in designing a strategic group map is identifying the relevant competitive dimensions for a particular industry or product market. This can be difficult as there are many competitive dimensions that may be relevant.[17] To help in this task, researchers have identified three main categories of measures that can help in identifying the key strategic dimension of an industry or product market: *competitive positioning*, the *scope of activities*, and *resource commitment* (see Figure 6.8). Competitive positioning reflects the basis of the competitive advantage of a firm in an industry or market, for example, cost-leadership, differentiation, mass-market, and premium, among others. The scope of activities reflects the spread of activities across the product portfolio, geographical areas, market segments, or distribution channels. Finally, resource commitment refers to firms' size and capacity to invest. Selecting the relevant strategic dimensions in a certain industry or product market entails a detailed competition analysis. A good starting point can be identifying the market's main success factors, which are likely to be relevant competitive dimensions.

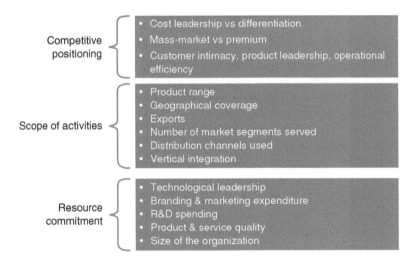

**FIGURE 6.8**   Strategic dimensions to form strategic groups

2.  Grouping the competitors. The second step in building a strategic group map is dividing the competitors into groups that reflect meaningful organizational categories. This exercise can be theoretical, using pre-existing categories, or empirical, using statistical or subjective approaches.

    •   Theoretical approach: The theoretical technique uses pre-existing categories such as Miles and Snow's strategic types (prospectors, defenders, analyzers, and reactors)[18], Porter's generic strategies (differentiators, cost-leaders, and focused, as discussed in Chapter 10)[19], or even Treacy and Wiersema's value disciplines (firms focused on customer intimacy, product leadership, or operational efficiency).[20]

- Empirical statistical approach: The empirical statistical approach entails rating the competitors within the industry or product market across multiple dimensions and then performing factor analysis, to identify groups of correlated dimensions, and cluster analysis, to aggregate the strategic groups based on the factors identified in the previous step. Other, more sophisticated statistical methods may entail multi-dimensional scaling[21] and latent class regressions.[22]

- Empirical subjective approach: Finally, the empirical subjective approach is based on common sense and context expert knowledge. In this method, competitors are grouped based on a few dimensions, which tend to be the key success factors of the market, and group composition is checked for coherence in an interactive process. One strategy is mapping the top performers (by revenues, sales, or growth) and comparing them with low performers. Another tactic can be identifying the direct rivals within the market, grouping them and reverse engineering to draw the dimensions that may explain such differences/similarities between/within groups.[23]

The rule of thumb is that the appropriate number of groups is between two and five. Having a high granularity, meaning high number of strategic groups, will add too much noise to the map and make it difficult to interpret. Otherwise, having very few groups might not provide in-depth information about the competition structure of the market, making the analysis irrelevant. A good example of a strategic group analysis is the grocery retailing market (see Figure 6.9), in which price and product range allows one to identify the different groups in the market. Specifically, *supermarkets* offer a wide range of food products at a relative medium price. In contrast, *hypermarkets* combine supermarkets and department stores under the same roof, selling food, appliances, and clothing, among other products, displaying a high product range at lower prices. *Premium supermarkets* offer a medium range of products but focus on higher quality and price products. Another strategic group in the grocery retailing market is the *discounters*, who focus on a smaller product range but at low prices. Finally, *convenience stores*, which are small retail stores that stock a small range of everyday products, sell them at a relatively higher prices than supermarkets.

3. Interpreting the results. Strategic group maps can be used to identify many aspects of the competitive environment of an industry or product market, such as mobility barriers, performance differences and rivalry intensity between and within groups, untapped niches, outliers, and dynamic effects.

- Mobility barriers: Strategic group maps help to identify mobility barriers, which prevent a firm from easily changing group membership. Mobility barriers may exist because firms within a group share characteristics that cannot be easily imitated by other firms or because firms within a group are likely to collude to build mobility barriers around the group.[24]

- Performance differences: within and between groups. Some scholars argue that one can identify higher-performance and lower-performance groups through strategic group analysis. Group members' similar competitive and cooperative strategies may help to explain such differences in performance between groups.[25] However, more recent studies found that performance differences between groups may not exist, focusing instead on inside-group performance variation between 'core firms' and 'secondary firms'. While 'core firms' identify and follow the group strategy closely, 'secondary firms' are loosely aligned

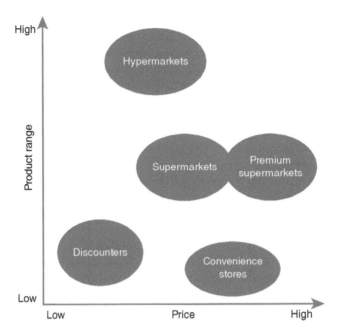

**FIGURE 6.9**   Strategic groups in the grocery market

with a multi-firm group main strategy. Although 'core firms' may benefit from legitimacy and decurrent privileged access to resources, 'secondary firms' beneficiate from building a strategic distinctiveness in the market, displaying higher profitability levels when compared to 'core firms'.[26]

- Rivalry intensity within and between groups: It is expected that firms within the same strategic group experience a higher competitive intensity than firms from different groups. Within-group rivalry intensity may depend on (1) the degree of membership similarity that may intensify rivalry or (2) the existence of collaboration or collusive behaviours that may alleviate within-group rivalry. Strategic group maps can also help in analyzing between-group rivalry intensity. The closer the groups are on the map, the greater the rivalry and interdependence among groups.[27]

- Untapped niches: The strategic group map framework can also help identify attractive market segments that are untapped or under-occupied by current competitors. In the grocery market example, such 'unoccupied' space could be the 'discount hypermarkets' that would offer a high product range at a low price (see Figure 6.9). However, such 'white spaces' in the competitive landscape can also represent 'black holes', which are noncompetitive positionings due to intractable industry cost-quality trade-offs and technology limitations.

- Outliers: Outlier groups or firms may indicate exceptionally successful or extremely unsuccessful players that might be on their way out of the market. In the first case, outliers, or solitary firms, can challenge the standard cost-quality trade-offs of the industry, find unique market positions, and develop resource sets that best serve a segment of the market. Interestingly, research shows that 'secondary firms' within a strategic group may display higher performance than solitary firms that do not belong to any strategic group, indicating that strategic group membership may have positive performance implications after all.[28]

- <u>Dynamic effects:</u> A dynamic analysis of strategic group maps allows for assessing the importance and persistence of mobility barriers within the industry. It can also help to identify future market trends by spotting the trajectories of both new entrants and industry incumbents. The analysis of within-groups position changes, from secondary to core members or vice versa, can also provide important information on firms' individual competitive trajectories.

While the strategic group perspective can help companies to better understand their competitive landscape, many questions remain open in the literature. The firms' performance implications between and within groups is a major point of disagreement among researchers, who report contradicting results.[29] A source of such contradiction comes from the fact that there is no single way to construct a strategic group map, and different studies may employ different methods. Additionally, the whole exercise of finding the dimensions and grouping the firms assumes that industry and product-market boundaries are stable, and competitors can be easily identifiable, which is not always the case. Identifying strategic groups and mapping them can be a truly complex exercise, mainly in contexts where industry boundaries are blurring, and competitors compete across multiple industries and product markets.

# Rivalry

While the focal firm's industry or a product market encompasses the full set of potential competitors and its strategic group a smaller number of direct competitors, only some of these direct competitors may be its rivals. Competitive dynamics has historically focused on rivalry, specifically on inter-firm action-response dyads, seeing competition as a dynamic process rather than a static one.[30] This research school examines the causes and consequences of firm-level competitive behaviours, using competitive actions, such as new products, promotions, pricing, and market signaling, as a unit of analysis. For competitive dynamics scholars, firms are interdependent; therefore, a firm's performance is a function of its strategies and rivals' actions.[31]

One of the main points of interest for competitive dynamics scholars is the antecedents of rivalry, precisely, the dimensions that predict the likelihood that two competitors experience competitive tension. Ming-Jer Chen, one of the most influential scholars in the competitive dynamics field, suggested that two firms are likely to experience competitive tension if they display high market commonality and resource similarity (see also Chapter 4). On the one side, **market commonality** entails the number of markets where rivals compete simultaneously, the importance of the shared market to each firm, and the strength each rival has in the markets where they overlap. On the other side, **resource similarity** captures the extent to which competitors possess comparable strategic assets and capabilities. Assessing resource similarity is essential because firms with similar resource portfolios are likely to have similar strategic capabilities, competitive vulnerabilities, and also similar competitive behaviours. Following how competitors acquire and develop their resources and capabilities over time is essential to understand rivals' trajectories in the marketplace.[32]

Competitive dynamics scholars also suggest that even when rivals compete in the same markets (market commonality) and display similar resources (resource similarity), they still may not pose an equal threat to each other, as perceived rivalry tends to be asymmetrical. For example, in the airline market, Hawaiian Airlines, a smaller geographically focused airline, would find both American and United, two large carriers, its primary rivals due to market overlap. However, Hawaiian Airlines is not considered a significant rival by American and United, as Hawaiian Airlines' market overlap is small for them. Asymmetrical rivalry highlights that the degree of perceived rivalry might not be reciprocal between two direct competitors. Therefore, rivalry analysis is performed from a focal firm perspective as each firm will experience rivalry differently towards different actors. Some frameworks can support companies in studying their rivals in terms of drivers of competitive behaviour (Awareness-Motivation-Capability framework) and behavioural profile (Porter's Four Corners).

## Drivers of competitive behaviour

The Awareness-Motivation-Capability framework (AMC) is another central construct of competitive dynamics literature. This framework delineates the behavioural drivers influencing firms' decision to attack or respond to the opponent. The AMC perspective predicts that a focal firm is likely to attack or respond to a rival if it is aware of competitors' initiatives, motivated to act, and capable of doing so. While it looks obvious that a company shall follow rivals' actions and responses, empirical studies showed that fewer than 1 in 10 managers tracked rivals' moves systematically.[33] The AMC framework can help structure such analysis.

### Awareness

Awareness is a prerequisite to investigating a rival's response in the market. Intuitively, one can understand that if a focal firm did not notice a rival's move in the market, it would not respond to it. However, some rivals' competitive moves are more visible than others. For example, when a rival launches a new product or campaign, direct competitors will notice it immediately. However, other competitive moves might be taken internally, and competitors will not be aware of them until the information is made public. For example, an investment of strategic importance in a new product or service or in a new technology that has not yet materialized. On top of action visibility, the size and relevance of the rival that initiated the move might also influence the focal firm's awareness. A focal firm is more likely to notice competitive moves from large rivals that display high resource similarity and market commonality since such rivals' competitive moves tend to influence the focal firm's market performance.[34]

### Motivation

Although a firm may be aware of moves made by rivals, it may not be motivated to respond due to the perceived gains and losses that the response may trigger. Market commonality, also known as multiple-point competition, influences firms' motivation to attack or respond to a rival. While it would be expected that firms with high market commonality are more likely to respond to rivals' attacks to defend their markets, this might not always be the case. Research shows that rivals interacting in multiple markets would be less motivated to compete aggressively to avoid retaliation across markets. By contrast, a lack of multimarket contact may lead to a higher motivation to attack or respond to rivals' attacks.[35]

### Capability

A focal firm might be aware of and motivated to respond to a rival attack; however, it might lack the resources needed to respond to it. Therefore, capability translates into the focal firm's operational and resource-deployment ability to contest and challenge the market rival.

Resource similarity is one of the main dimensions influencing the attack or response capability of firms. If rivals display similar resources and capabilities, the focal firm is likely to be able to match rivals' competitive moves. However, if resource similarity is low between the rivals, it will be time-consuming and costly for the focal firm to respond to or attack the opponent. Therefore, the higher the resource similarity between rivals, the higher the likelihood that the focal firm is capable of attacking or responding to the rival.[36]

While the market commonality and the resource similarity concepts are intimately related to the AMC framework, they entail a subtle but important difference. While market commonality and resource similarity predict whether two market players are likely to experience competitive tension, the AMC framework foresees whether two market players will actually attack or respond to each other. This difference is important because a focal firm may experience competitive tension with a rival and opt not to attack or respond to that rival. This might happen when the focal firm lacks the motivation or capability to do so, as explained in the AMC framework.

## Behavioural profile

Porter recognized that firms are mutually dependent, feeling the effects of each other's actions.[37] Therefore, when analyzing the competitive landscape, firms look at the aggregate (industry and product-market) level and also at the individual firm level, closely examining the rivals that are more likely to affect their performance. Porter's *Four Corners framework* serves that purpose, assessing rivals' behavioural profiles. Such a tool helps to understand rivals' mindsets and assumptions and helps determine how they will react in a given situation. Understanding rivals' motivations and actions can help build a strategy that focuses on blind spots, taking advantage of rivals' weaknesses. The model is composed of four corners, which are drivers, motivation, strategy, and capabilities (see Figure 6.10).

- <u>Drivers: What is their goal?</u> Understanding rivals' motivation, drivers, and goals can provide insights into their course of action. Drivers entail understanding what rivals are looking for, their intentions, and what they pursue. A significant gap between a rivals' drivers may lead to attack strategies, while a narrow gap may produce defensive strategies.
- <u>Motivations: What are their assumptions?</u> Mapping rivals' perceptions and assumptions helps to understand the course of their strategy. Rivals perceived strengths and weaknesses, culture, and beliefs help predict what they will do next. The questions here are what rivals take for granted and how they perceive themselves and the industry.
- <u>Strategy: What are they doing?</u> A firm can map all rivals' visible competitive moves in the market and classify them across a range of dimensions, such as action or response, response speed, strategic or tactical, and type (e.g., price change, marketing campaign, investment or new products). Understanding how each competitive move affects rivals' performance is essential to determine whether they will remain in the same action course or change it soon.
- <u>Capabilities: What can they do?</u> Rivals' capabilities determine their capacity to respond to external forces or change their course of action. Under external threats or performance gaps, companies tend to rely on their strengths to respond to market pressures, such as their distribution network, financial resources, and innovation capabilities. The question here is, what are the rivals' strengths and weaknesses, and how are these resources being used to gain competitive advantage?

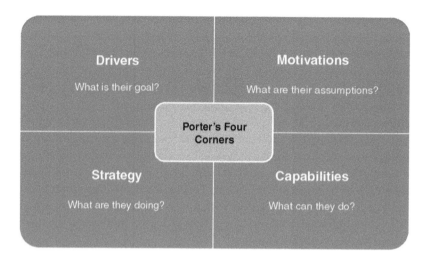

**FIGURE 6.10**   Porter's Four Corners model

Porter's Four Corners model links rivals' goals, strengths, and weaknesses to their assumptions and beliefs. While companies usually understand rivals' strategies, strengths, and weaknesses, they tend to underestimate rivals' motivations and drivers. A motivated competitor can create more competitive pressure than a larger rival that is not very motivated. This model sheds light on the role of implicit factors, like culture, beliefs, mental framings, and assumptions, in explaining rivals' competitive behaviours. The disadvantage of Porter's Four Corners model is that it focuses too much on rivals, which may keep a company from thinking of creative ways to be different and unique. Being obsessed with competition consumes essential resources that could be allocated to guaranteeing customer satisfaction.

## CRACK-THE-CASE

### PepsiCo versus Coca-Cola Company: A longstanding rivalry[38]

Source: © Monticello (2020) / Shutterstock.

PepsiCo and Coca-Cola Company, whose most famous products are Pepsi and Coca-Cola, respectively, are two reputable food and beverages multinationals whose market reach and influence seem to know no boundaries. Throughout the years, these iconic rivals have fought numerous battles across market segments and geographical regions. If you are a Coca-Cola fanatic or a Pepsi devotee, this case will have a special taste for you.

PepsiCo knows its rival, Coca-Cola Company, very well, using detailed information (such as market share, product and pricing strategy, financial performance) to attack it on different fronts. PepsiCo knows that Coca-Cola Company's biggest driver is its ambition to be the most popular drink in the world. A powerful supply chain, a valuable brand reputation, and strong financial resources have leveraged such driving ambition. Coca-Cola Company's strategy was to associate its brand with happy moments because 'whenever there's fun, there's always Coca-Cola' (from Joey Diggs' lyrics 'Always Coca-Cola'). Aligned with this strategy, Coca-Cola internationalized the Santa Claus Imaginarium, associating the brand with Christmas and joyful family moments. Its reputation and impressive history allowed Coca-Cola Company to lead the beverage market worldwide.

Paying attention to Coca-Cola's behavioural model, PepsiCo developed a strategy to address the blind spots in the competition to grow its market presence. Even though PepsiCo started as a beverage company, it has diversified its product portfolio across snacks, like Lays, Doritos, and Cheetos, and other beverages, such as Lipton, 7up, Aquafina, and Gatorade. Nowadays, beverages represent 46% of PepsiCo's portfolio, being number two worldwide; and snacks represent the remaining 54%, being a clear leader worldwide. The main difference between PepsiCo and Coca-Cola Company is that the latter is solely a beverage company, while PepsiCo is a beverage and snacks company. PepsiCo attacked the niches that the Coca-Cola Company ignored, and nowadays, Coca-Cola soda might still be the most popular drink in the world but PepsiCo, as a group, is bigger than Coca-Cola Company. PepsiCo's annual revenue has been around twice Coca-Cola's in the last few years. No one knows how the future will unfold, but PepsiCo is a clear winner for now.

## Questions

1. Imagine that you are PepsiCo's manager. Apply Porter's Four Corners framework to Coca-Cola Company.
2. How has PepsiCo explored Coca-Cola's weaknesses to become one of the biggest food and beverages companies in the world?

## KEY DEBATE

### The usefulness of analysis and planning

Competition analysis relies on the assumption that the past is essential to predict the future, explaining why strategy modules give a fair share of attention to external analysis in general and industry and product-market analysis in particular. However, strategy is essentially about the future and learning from the past may lead to framings, beliefs, and assumptions that may no longer apply to future scenarios.

*(Continued)*

Perhaps the future is a combination of past events and new and unknown conditions; however, this makes us question the usefulness of extensive and sometimes bureaucratic analysis and planning. Management scholars have questioned this already, and some examples are Henry Mintzberg[39] and Roger Martin[40]. Their works discuss the importance of emergent strategies and the need to focus more on customers' needs than on competition analysis and planning. According to Roger Martin, the future is unpredictable and extensive analysis and planning can be a waste of resources; instead, firms shall take bold decisions, detached from the past, to define their future.

## Questions

1. Discuss how extensive industry and product-market analysis can support or prevent successful strategies.
2. Under which market conditions would it make sense to perform extensive analysis and planning?

## CLOSING CASE

### The e-Health market: Identifying the strategic groups (Part II)[41]

Source: © Zaozaa (2023) / Shutterstock.

The e-Health market is growing worldwide, with a projected $233 billion in 2022 and $981 billion by 2032.[42] This market encompasses electronic medical records, software systems, and health-related applications. Applications providers are growing in number and the variety of services offered is increasing. A growing segment in the e-Health market is the at-home blood-testing segment, which allows customers to collect their blood at home through kits, send it through the post, and receive the results online or through an app. The critical success factors of this segment are the reliability and convenience of the at-home blood-collection kits, specialized and unique blood markers, and data-based algorithms that can increase the accuracy and automation of the diagnosis. Thriva (see opening case: Thriva and the rugged competitive landscape of the e-Health market (Part I)), Medichecks, Forth, LetsGetChecked, and Living DNA are the most prominent players in this segment.

Thriva is a London-based at-home blood-testing company founded in 2015 that offers packages focused on longevity, energy levels, sleeping patterns, mood, fitness, weight management, diabetes, anaemia, thyroid, and high cholesterol. The packages include GP reports, evidence-based advice, customized recipes, directed articles, podcasts, and access to a mobile app. The base price is £21, plus tests that range from £5 to £19. The ready-to-buy packages' prices vary from £65 to £104 and have around five blood markers.

Medichecks is another at-home blood-testing company founded in 2001. Medichecks offers a wide range of tests adapted for women and men, sports performance, wellness, and health conditions. The blood tests cover hormones, health checks, sports performance, nutrition, fertility, energy levels, thyroid function, antibodies, vitamin D, iron, anti-Müllerian hormone, progesterone, stress cortisol, and cholesterol, among many others. In total, Medichecks can offer tests for 90 different blood markers. In Medichecks, customers select the tests they want, and the price ranges from £31 to £199; however, most of the tests are in the £31 to £60 range.

Forth is specialized in nutrition and well-being. Forth's customers are looking for ways to improve their health and well-being. Forth combines scientific data and expert advice to help customers navigate a path to better health. Their packages cover well-being, women's and men's health, nutrition, COVID-19, mental health, and sports. Forth's packages range from £39 to £324, and the average value per blood marker is around £7.

LetsGetChecked is another personal health test company founded in 2015 in New York. LetsGetChecked offers packages on STIs (sexually transmitted infections), women's and men's health, wellness, and COVID-19. It enables customers to order, manage and track their own clinical outcomes through a personal online account and a mobile app. LetsGetChecked offers packages for both individual customers and businesses. It offers more than 30 test markers, and packages' prices range from £59 to £209, with an average value per blood marker of around £19.

Living DNA is a UK-based company with facilities in the US and Denmark. It is specialized in DNA and well-being. They claim that they own the world's most advanced ancestry test that helps customers to discover their family and ancestors, using a unique process of analysis and linked DNA. Living DNA offers three ready-to-buy packages, ranging from €69 to €99.

The at-home blood-testing segment is growing fast, and new players are experimenting and offering a range of different services with varied pricing, as well as different levels of specialization.

*(Continued)*

### Questions

1. Build a strategic group graph using the information provided about the main players competing in the at-home blood-testing segment, identifying the main strategic groups.
2. Identify under-occupied areas on the graph. Discuss whether these under-occupied areas represent an attractive untapped area or an uncompetitive 'black hole'.

## Summary

- An industry is composed of companies that produce similar products and compete for the same resources and customers in the marketplace.
- Industry analysis can be disaggregated into product markets and market segments.
- Industry and product-market analysis entails three dimensions: boundaries, strategic groups, and rivalry.
- Industries and product markets can have different structures, ranging from monopoly to perfect competition. Knowing the market structure can help to predict competition intensity.
- The industry or product-market life cycle helps to understand whether the market is in the development, growth, maturity, or decline stage. The life cycle can help to predict competition intensity, product differentiation level, and key success factors at each life-cycle stage.
- The Porter's Five Forces framework encompasses suppliers' and buyers' bargaining power, the threat of new entrants and substitutes, and rivalry.
- The profit pools perspective looks at the market bottom line, understanding the different sources of profits and revenues.
- The value network view highlights that firms are integrated into a network of customers and buyers, creating value together.
- Strategic groups are sets of competitors that display similarities across strategic dimensions.
- The competitive dynamics school focuses on inter-firm rivalry, studying the antecedents and consequences of rivals' action-response dyad.

## Review questions

1. Why do some companies analyze the competitive environment using the industry as the main unit of analysis while others use product markets?
2. What are the main frameworks that assess industry or product-market competitive intensity? What are the main differences across such frameworks?
3. What are the differences and similarities between the concepts of strategic groups and rivalry?

# Discussion questions

1. What are the benefits and risks of focusing on value creation instead of competition? What are the pros and cons of each view?
2. What is the role of digitalization and emergent technologies in industry boundaries blurring? Can you provide examples?

## EXPERIENTIAL EXERCISES

1. Virtual reality (VR) is a technology that aims to offer a simulated immersive and sensorial experience to customers worldwide and across many sectors. With an estimated market size of $84 billion by 2028, VR finds use cases in entertainment, such as gaming, e-sports, live events, and corporate training across various industries such as automotive, retail, healthcare, aerospace, military, and education.[49] VR is also gaining popularity in the education sector, where universities are exploring new ways to deliver remote teaching. It is expected that 11 million headsets will be shipped for education institutions in 2026, representing $20 billion in total market revenue. Analyze the higher education VR market structure, life-cycle, and main forces in Europe.
2. The automotive industry is one of the largest worldwide by revenue, encompassing companies that design, develop, manufacture, and sell motor vehicles. The leading players in the automobile industry are Volkswagen (Germany), Toyota (Japan), Daimler (Germany), Ford (US), Honda (Japan), General Motors (US), SAIC (China), BMW (Germany), Nissan (Japan), and Hyundai (South Korea). Identify the main strategic groups in the automotive industry and profile Toyota's main rival(s) using Porter's Four Corners framework.

# Further reading

Gadiesh, O. and Gilbert, J.L. (1998) 'How to map your industry's profit pool', *Harvard Business Review*, 76: 149–66.

Kothandaraman, P. and Wilson, D.T. (2001) 'The future of competition: Value-creating networks', *Industrial Marketing Management*, 30 (4): 379–89.

Meilich, O. (2019) 'Strategic groups maps: Review, synthesis, and guidelines', *Journal of Strategy and Management*, 12 (4): 447–63.

Porter, M.E. (2008) 'The five competitive forces that shape strategy', *Harvard Business Review*, 86: 79–93.

Smith, K.G., Ferrier, W. and Ndofor, H. (2005) 'Competitive dynamics research: Critique and future directions', in M. Hitt, R.E. Freeman and J. Harrison (eds), *Handbook of Strategic Management*. London: Blackwell, pp 309–54.

# Endnotes (references)

1. O'Hear, S. (2016) 'London-based Thriva offers a home finger-prick blood test to quantify your bad self', *TechCrunch*, June 19. https://techcrunch.com/2016/06/19/thriva (accessed June 16, 2023); Statista (2021d) 'eHealth – Worldwide | Statista market

forecast', *Statista,* www.statista.com/outlook/dmo/digital-health/ehealth/worldwide (accessed June 16, 2023); Thriva (2021a) 'Thriva – Track and improve your health', https://thriva.co (accessed June 16, 2023).

2. Schmalensee, R. (1988) 'Industrial economics: An overview', *The Economic Journal,* 98 (392): 643–81.

3. Hansen, G. and Wernerfelt, B. (1989) 'Determinants of firm performance: The relative importance of economic and organizational factors', *Strategic Management,* 10: 399–411.

4. Frost & Sullivan (2020) 'Strategic outlook of the global pumps market', Frost & Sullivan. https://store.frost.com/strategic-outlook-of-the-global-pumps-market-2020.html (accessed June 16, 2023).

5. Ansoff, H.I. (1988) *Corporate Strategy* (revised ed.). London: Penguin Books.

6. Lipczynski, J., Wilson, J. and Goddard, J. (2009) *Industrial Organization: Competition, Strategy, Policy* (3rd ed.). Hoboken, NJ: Prentice Hall.

7. Bain, J.S. (1967) *Industrial Organization* (2nd ed.). New York, NY: John Wiley & Sons.

8. Peltoniemi, M. (2011) 'Reviewing industry life-cycle theory: Avenues for future research', *International Journal of Management Reviews,* 13 (4): 349–75.

9. Klepper, S. (1996) 'Industry life cycles', *Industrial and Corporate Change,* 6 (1): 119–43.

10. McGahan, A. (2000) 'How industries evolve', *Business Strategy Review,* 11 (3): 1–16.

11. Dhalla, N.K., and Yuspeh, S. (1976) 'Forget the product life cycle concept', *Harvard Business Review,* 54 (1): 102–12.

12. Porter, M.E. (1979) 'How competitive forces shape strategy', *Harvard Business Review,* 57 (2): 137–145; Porter, M.E. (1980b) *Competitive Strategy: Techniques for Analysing Industries and Competitors.* New York, NY: Simon & Schuster.

13. Porter, M.E. and Heppelmann, J.E. (2014) 'How smart, connected products are transforming competition', *Harvard Business Review,* 92 (11): 64–88.

14. Gadiesh, O. and Gilbert, J. (1998) 'Profit pools: A fresh look at strategy', *Harvard Business Review,* 76 (3): 139–48.

15. Ryall, M.D. (2013) 'The new dynamics of competition', *Harvard Business Review,* 91 (60): 80–7.

16. Caves, R.E. and Porter, M.E. (1977) 'From entry barriers to mobility barriers: Conjectural decisions and contrived deterrence to new competition', *Quarterly Journal of Economics,* 91 (2): 241–61; McNamara, G., Deephouse, D. and Luce, R. (2003) 'Competitive positioning within and across a strategic group structure: The performance of core, secondary, and solitary firms', *Strategic Management Journal,* 24 (2): 161–81.

17. Cattani, G., Joseph, F.P. and Howard, T. (2017) 'Categories and competition', *Strategic Management Journal,* 38 (1): 64–92.

18. Miles, R.E. and Snow, C.C. (1978) *Organizational Strategy, Structure and Process.* New York, NY: West.

19. Porter, M.E. (1985) *Competitive Advantage: Creating and Sustaining Superior Performance.* New York, NY: The Free Press.

20. Treacy, M. and Wiersema, F. (1993) 'Customer intimacy and other value disciplines', *Harvard Business Review,* 71 (1): 84–93.

21. DeSarbo, S., Grewal, R. and Wang R. (2009) 'Dynamic strategic groups: Deriving spatial evolutionary paths', *Strategic Management Journal,* 30 (13): 1420–39.

22. Murthi, B.P.S., Rasheed, A. and Goll, I. (2013) 'An empirical analysis of strategic groups in the airline industry using latent class regressions', *Managerial and Decision Economics,* 34 (2): 59–73.

23. Meilich, O. (2019) 'Strategic groups maps: Review, synthesis, and guidelines', *Journal of Strategy and Management,* 12 (4): 447–63.

24. Caves and Porter (1977)

25. Dranove, D., Peteraf, M. and Shanley, M. (1998) 'Do strategic groups exist? An economic framework for analysis', *Strategic Management Journal*, 19 (11): 1029–44.

26. McNamara et al. (2003)

27. Cool, K., and Dierickx, I. (1993) 'Rivalry, strategic groups and firm profitability', *Strategic Management Journal*, 14 (1): 47–59.

28. McNamara et al. (2003)

29. McNamara et al. (2003)

30. Scherer, F.M. and Ross, D. (1990) *Industrial Market Structure and Economic Performance* (3rd ed.). Boston, MA: Houghton-Mifflin.

31. Smith, K.G., Ferrier, W. and Ndofor, H. (2005) 'Competitive dynamics research: Critique and future directions', in M.A. Hitt, R.E. Freedman and J.S. Harrison (eds), *The Blackwell Handbook of Strategic Management*. Oxford: Blackwell, 309–54.

32. Chen, M. (1996) 'Competitor analysis and interfirm rivalry: Toward a theoretical integration', *Academy of Management Review*, 21 (1): 100–34.

33. Montgomery, D.B., Chapman Moore, M. and Urbany, J.E. (2005) 'Reasoning about competitive reactions: Evidence from executives'. *Marketing Science*, 24 (1): 138–49; Coyne, K. and Horn, J. (2009) 'Predicting your competitor's reaction', *Harvard Business Review*, 87 (4): 90–7.

34. Chen, M. and Miller, D. (1994) 'Competitive attack, retaliation and performance: An expectancy-valence framework', *Strategic Management Journal*, 15 (2): 85–102.

35. Baum, J. and Korn, H. (1999) 'Dynamics of dyadic competitive interaction', *Strategic Management Journal*, 20 (3): 251–78.

36. Smith, K., Grimm, C., Gannon, M. and Chen, M. (1991) 'Organizational information processing, competitive responses, and performance in the US domestic airline industry', *Academy of Management Journal*, 34 (1): 60–85.

37. Porter, M.E. (1980a) 'Industry structure and competitive strategy: Keys to profitability', *Financial Analysts Journal*, 36 (4): 30–41.

38. Dorn, M. (2020) 'The PepsiCo stock: Fizzy profits with dividend topping?', *Dividend Stocks,* November 11. https://dividendstocks.cash/blog/the-pepsico-stock-fizzy-profits-with-dividend-topping (accessed June 16, 2023); PepsiCo (2022) 'Our products', *PepsiCo.* www.pepsico.com/our-brands/creating-smiles/our-products (accessed June 26, 2023); Ridder, M. (2021) 'PepsiCo's net revenue worldwide from 2007 to 2020', *Statista,* May 30. www.statista.com/statistics/233378/net-revenue-of-pepsico-worldwide (accessed June 16, 2023); Team, T. (2019) 'Can Coca-Cola bridge its revenue gap with PepsiCo?', *Forbes,* December 18. www.forbes.com/sites/greatspeculations/2019/12/18/can-coca-cola-bridge-its-revenue-gap-with-pepsico (accessed June 16, 2023); The Coca-Cola Company (2019) 'FAQ: Did Coca-Cola create Santa Claus?', December 5. www.coca-colacompany.com/faqs/did-coca-cola-invent-santa (accessed June 16, 2023).

39. Mintzberg, H. and Waters, J.A. (1985) 'Of strategies, deliberate and emergent', *Strategic Management Journal*, 6 (3): 257–72.

40. Martin, R.L. (2014) 'The big lie of strategic planning', *Harvard Business Review*, 92 (1/2): 78–84.

41. Forth (2021) 'Ultimate health test', *Forth.* www.forthwithlife.co.uk/health-tests/wellness/ultimate (accessed June 16, 2023); LetsGetChecked (2021) 'LetsGetChecked UK: Health tests from home & enterprise wellness solutions'. www.letsgetchecked.co.uk (accessed June 16, 2023); Living DNA (2021) 'Living DNA | DNA test kits | Bring your DNA to life'. https://livingdna.com/eu (accessed June 16, 2023); Medichecks (2021) 'Immunity health checks and blood tests – B2C medichecks', https://medichecks.com/collections/immunity (accessed June 16, 2023); Thriva (2021b)

'Support mood | Mental health', *Thriva*. https://thriva.co/goals/improve-mood (accessed June 16, 2023).

42. Global Market Insights (2023) 'Digital health market', March. https://web.archive.org/web/20230730113849/https://www.gminsights.com/industry-analysis/digital-health-market (accessed July 27, 2023).

43. Fortune Business Insights (2021) 'Virtual reality (VR) market to reach USD 84.09 billion by 2028; Acquisition of NextVR by Apple Inc. to incite business development', *globenewswire.com*, August 19. www.globenewswire.com/news-release/2021/08/19/2283207/0/en/Virtual-Reality-VR-Market-to-Reach-USD-84-09-Billion-by-2028-Acquisition-of-NextVR-by-Apple-Inc-to-Incite-Business-Development-Fortune-Business-Insights.html (accessed June 16, 2023).

# Key terms

**Industry** – a group of companies producing similar products and competing for the same resources and customers in the marketplace

**Life-cycle model** – charts the evolution of a market from introduction to decline

**Market commonality** – the extent to which two firms compete in the same markets

**Porter's Five Forces framework** – summarizes the main forces that help explain the industry's level of attractiveness

**Product markets** – goods or services with similar characteristics in terms of features, performance, intended use, and price

**Resource similarity** – the extent to which competitors possess comparable strategic assets and capabilities

**Strategic groups** – are formed by firms that display similarities across a set of strategic dimensions

# 7
# CUSTOMER ANALYSIS

## LEARNING OBJECTIVES

After reading this chapter, you should be able to:

- grasp the significance of customer-orientation for strategy formulation;
- perform market segmentation using a range of criteria;
- appreciate the importance of operational excellence, product leadership, and customer-intimacy value disciplines;
- understand the importance of Blue Ocean thinking and plot a value curve.

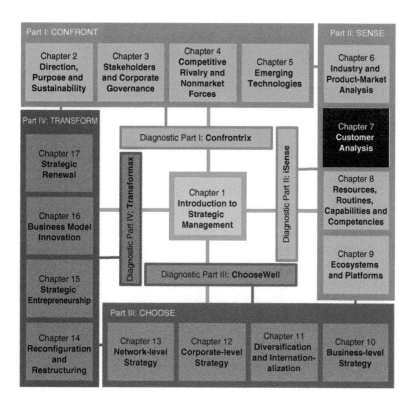

## OPENING CASE

### The gaming console war: PlayStation 3 versus Nintendo's Wii (Take I)[1]
### Nintendo turns the tables

Source: © Gam13it (2010) / Shutterstock.

Since the original PlayStation launch in 1994 and throughout two generations of PlayStation hardware, Sony has dominated the video console industry. Before 2006, with declining market shares and shrinking margins, Nintendo was among the top three companies in the game console industry, after Sony and Microsoft. However, this changed on Christmas day 2006, when Nintendo launched Wii, a console with a three-axis accelerometer controller able to measure players' movements in three dimensions. Nintendo's new console allowed a simple and intuitive way of playing, with players moving to swing a tennis racket or toss a ball.

Traditionally, gaming console companies focused on addressing the needs and tastes of the core-gamer segment, i.e., males between the ages of 18 and 65 who are passionate about game sequels, more realistic and faster graphics, improved technology, and higher diversification of games. With Wii, Nintendo unfurled a new market segment, the non-gamers. This segment comprises people between the ages of 9 and 65 who are looking for playful, easy, and fun games with no tricks or complex stories. For the non-gamer segment, existing video game systems are too complicated and time-consuming. But Nintendo's Wii console was easy to use, and even video game novices could learn how to play within minutes.

Despite the inferior technology as compared to competitors' consoles – namely, Sony's PlayStation 3 and Microsoft's Xbox 360 – Wii was fun, user-friendly, and relatively cheap to produce. Nintendo understood that the main barrier for new users was the games' complexity, not the quality of existing graphics. Nintendo avoided the hardware and graphics performance competition by removing that barrier and enhancing the fun factor, expanding its market and growing a profitable business. Nintendo was playing a different game. In 2007, Nintendo had sold 6.4 million units of Wiis, nearly as many as the combined sales of PlayStation 3 and the Xbox 360.[2]

### Is the game over for Sony?

Nintendo Wii's entrance into the video console industry in 2006 disrupted the market. At the time, the president of Sony America stated: *'If you look at the industry, any industry, it doesn't typically go backwards technologically. The controller is innovative, but the Wii is basically a repurposed GameCube. If you've built your console on an innovative controller, you have to ask yourself, is that long term?'* Sony had planned to launch a new version of PlayStation in 2013 and had to decide whether to wait until then to respond to Wii's market leadership or to react immediately. In 2006, these were the main options on the table:

1. Cut PlayStation 3's price to increase sales and keep the focus on the core gamer segment for 2013's launch.
2. Copy Nintendo's controller to fit with PlayStation's existing hardware to target the non-gamer segment.
3. Focus on the 2013 launch and invest in disruption (whether related or not to motion-sensing games or virtual reality).

*(If you want to know what happened, read the end-of-chapter case: The gaming console war goes on: PlayStation 4 vs Nintendo Switch (Take II))*

## Questions

1. List the pros and cons of Sony's three options to attack Nintendo Wii's position.
2. Which option would you recommend to Sony and why?

# Introduction

While most of the strategic management process emphasizes competition and competitors, companies should not lose sight of the fact that customers are the source of a company's income. As a business is run on revenue, and revenue comes from customers, it is critical to understand customers' needs and wants. Whereas in the past companies could hope to sustain their competitive advantage over extended periods of time, in today's hypercompetitive environment competitive advantage tends to be transient. This makes it important to understand customers and their changing needs for maintaining market leadership and continued competitive advantage.[3]

Back in the 1960s, Levitt speculated whether companies' main reason for failing was because they were more product-oriented rather than customer-oriented.[4] As shown in the opening case, the Nintendo Wii's revolutionary technology changed the rules of the gaming console market, unleashing new market segments and addressing customers' emergent needs. Even though the technology behind Wii was inferior, it brought a fun factor that the customers appreciated. Sometimes, winning the market is not about focusing on technology and the product but listening to customers' needs and changing the foundations of competition. In customer-oriented companies, every function of a company addresses customer satisfaction and retention. A customer-driven strategy is a way to enhance customer satisfaction and, consequently, companies' profitability.

Market segmentation is vital to understanding who a company's customers are, what they want, when they buy, and how they choose among products.[5] In the opening case, for example, PlayStation and Wii addressed different customer segments. While PlayStation focused on the core gamer segment, Wii targeted the non-gamer segment. In this chapter, after discussing market segmentation and the assessment of the viability of customer segments, we turn our attention to examining value disciplines and the concept of Blue Ocean strategy. This discussion provides insight into how a company can increase customer value in a specific segment.

# Market segmentation and segment viability

In 1956, Wendell R. Smith introduced the concept of market segmentation. Instead of focusing on making products more appealing than those of competitors, Wendell proposed that a company should divide its customers into segments and adapt its products to address the needs of those segments. **Market segmentation** entails identifying groups of customers that tend to react differently to various product offerings and marketing stimuli.

This exercise of narrowing down a larger market into smaller groups allows companies to craft effective customer-value propositions and communication strategies. Market segmentation is usually accompanied by a segment viability assessment to evaluate whether a segment is sustainable in terms of size, growth, and profitability.

## Market segmentation

Market segmentation can help a company to establish the differential advantage it has vis-à-vis competitors (see further Chapter 10).[6]

### Who are they?

There are two main customer types, namely business-to-business (B2B) and business-to-customer (B2C). B2B type customers are thus other companies and B2C customers individuals who may or may not be the final consumer. B2C customer segments are delineated based on geographic, demographic, socio-economic, psychographic, and behavioural criteria. As summarized in Table 7.1, B2B segments are defined based on demographic characteristics, purchasing approach, situational factors, company characteristics, and value-added by customers. Companies that serve B2B or B2C segments have entirely different market approaches, as these two groups of customers behave fundamentally differently and have distinct selling points. For example, for B2C segments the selling points tend to be prompt availability, pricing, branding, and product quality, and for B2B segments they tend to be one-to-one sales, performance measures, cost, and service quality.

Besides identifying the primary customer type, i.e., B2B or B2C, companies also need to understand the role of the individual who is effectively buying the product. For example, the *initiator* identifies the need for a product; the *influencer* has information or preference input into the decision; the *decider* makes the final decision through budget authorization; the *purchaser* buys the product; finally, the *user* consumes the product. While in some situations, the roles overlap in one individual, in others, the purchasing process involves different individuals with different functions. For example, in B2C segments, adults are often the *purchasers* in buying cereal and toys, among others, but the *users* are children. In B2B segments, the *user* and *influencer* can be an engineer concerned about performance, but the *buyer* is a salesperson concerned about price and delivery. Understanding the different customer roles can help companies adapt their communication and selling techniques to close the deal.[7]

### What do they want?

Different customer segments have different needs and look for different benefits. Understanding what customers want and their purchasing patterns is important data companies must collect and analyze. Such data may encompass how recently and how frequently the customer bought the product. Companies should also collect information about other products and brands that customers buy, how they use the product, and where they consume the products to understand the entire customer experience. This information allows companies to evaluate how valuable each customer segment is.

**TABLE 7.1** Segmentation criteria

| Segment | Criteria | Examples |
|---|---|---|
| B2C | Geographic | Region, city, population density, climate |
| | Demographic | Age, sex, education, family size, religion, nationality |
| | Socioeconomic | Income, occupation, social class |
| | Psychographic | Lifestyle, personality, interests, activities |
| | Behavioural | Buying occasion and location (specialist store, gas station, etc.), benefits, user status, usage rate, loyalty status, attitude |
| B2B | Demographic | Industry, size, location, sector (public, private, cooperative, nonprofit) |
| | Purchasing approach | Centralized, decentralized purchasing department, power structure (engineering or financial oriented), existing relationship (long or short term) |
| | Purchasing policies | Leasing, service purchase, purchasing requirements (value quality, price, or service) |
| | Situational factors | Urgency on the purchase, specific application, level of adaptation, order size |
| | Company characteristics | Mission and values, attitudes towards risk (risk-taking or risk-avoiding), loyalty towards suppliers, innovativeness, lead users (like to buy first and try new things) |
| | Value added by customers | Source of competitive advantage (price, service, etc.), emphasis on R&D and innovation |

## When do they buy?

Customers can buy at a different time of the year (e.g., summer or winter), month, or day. For example, food companies know that their customers may consume their products at breakfast, dinner, or lunch. Similarly, beachwear companies see their demand increase during summer. Usually, companies look for more consumption occasions or ways to even out demand across the year. For example, breakfast cereal companies now also sell cereal bars as daytime snacks. Similarly, beachwear companies can enter markets in different hemispheres to keep production and sales stable during the year.

While in some industries companies can predict sales variations, in others, market demand is more difficult to predict, sometimes due to unexpected events. For example, medicines to alleviate cold symptoms usually have more demand in colder months; however, with the COVID-19 pandemic, there was a run to stockpile medicine out of season. Understanding when customers use the product is essential to adapt the sales channels and firm's operations to ensure that customers can buy the product when they need it.

## How do they choose?

Customers follow a decision process before buying a product or service. Overall decision processes can be emotional, holistic, automatic, or spontaneous. In any case, before buying a product, customers collect information about the product. The more traditional information sources are advertisements, in-store ads and staff recommendations, brochures, internet search, and other customers' reviews. Further details on the decision process encompass the attributes that customers value the most, the customer perceptions and the relative importance of the different features. Such information can be acquired through customer observation, and focus groups, surveys, and interviews.

## Segment viability

Once companies identify the relevant customer segment for their business, they evaluate the viability of the segment in terms of identification, size, profitability, competition, and growth.

- Identification. Market segments that are difficult to identify are even more challenging to reach. Therefore, companies need to be able to identify the market segment to take strategic decisions about product development, operations, marketing, and advertising to reach customers.
- Size. Setting the customer base too narrow or too broad can be a mistake. There is a distinction between the immediate customer base (e.g., those travelling by railway) and the broader customer base (e.g., those travelling by public transport, railway, aircraft, buses, etc.). Companies should start by adopting a wide view of who the customers are to ensure that a full range of potential customers and competitors are identified but then, they shall adopt a narrower view of immediate customers to establish an addressed offer.
- Profitability. Some segments are more profitable and attractive than others. For example, some segments might be larger but less profitable and others smaller but more attractive in profit margins. Companies need to identify segments that are broad enough to be profitable.
- Competition. Distinct segments might experience different competition intensity. For example, specialist segments might have a lower number of competitors than mass-market. Ideally, companies should position themselves in less competitive segments as those tend to be more profitable.
- Growth. Some segments are expanding and growing, while others are shrinking and dying. It is essential to understand a segment's life-cycle stage to plan for medium- and long-term sources of profitability. Companies also need to profile not only the current customer base but also future customers. Companies that focus only on present customers' needs might see their medium-term sources of profitability compromised.

## Market segmentation in the digital era

The emergence of Big Data and analytical tools is revolutionizing the way companies perform market segmentation. Companies are moving towards a more personalized one-to-one marketing strategy, achieving very high levels of individualization. Instead of broad customer categories, companies can access information on individual customer needs and wants, increasing from a few segments to many segments.

One-to-one digital marketing strategies entail advanced data analytics, artificial intelligence, machine learning tools, and cloud technology. These tools allow data collection on customer profiles with transactional and behavioural information, predicting customer needs, detecting shifts in demand through time-series data, and tracking customers' buying journeys to utilize this information for future campaigns. All together, these tools allow companies to collect customer data, identify specific sub-segments, and create campaigns, cutting lead times from weeks to hours. Modern data collection and segmentation tools complement traditional market segmentation strategies, allowing marketeers to go from a broad segment to thousands of sub-segments.

## CRACK-THE-CASE

### Airbnb multiple-segmentation[8]

Source: © Ink Drop (2017) / Shutterstock.

Airbnb is a global hospitality service platform that works as a marketplace for peer-to-peer lodging and experiences services. Airbnb was founded in 2008 in San Francisco, US, and since then has collected more than 6 million listings in more than 191 countries worldwide, where more than 500 million guests have stayed. The company's mission is to provide lodging options that are local, authentic, diverse, inclusive and sustainable.

Airbnb displays a multisided platform business model, creating value by intermediating interactions between customers and suppliers (guests and hosts), and collecting revenue through commission (9% to 15%). With this business model, Airbnb revolutionized the accommodation industry without owning any properties itself but by instead orchestrating the resources of a pool of hosts spread worldwide. Airbnb became profitable in 2017, with a profit of $93 million.

*(Continued)*

On top of an unconventional business model, Airbnb also approaches market segmentation differently. They target multiple segments, offering different service packages to each one. The Airbnb packages include cost-effective apartments for more cost-conscious customers, 'plus' packages for customers that look for quality and design, and, finally, luxurious offers to customers looking for five star accommodations.

Airbnb follows behavioural segmentation, dividing the travelers' market into two groups: business and leisure. Business travelers want to save some expenses, get more space and comfort than standard hotel rooms, and feel at home with a kitchen to cook and other household amenities. The leisure segment encompasses money-savers, globetrotters, and family travelers. Money-savers are cost-sensitive travelers looking for a simple and cheap place to stay on their road trip. Globetrotters like to stay local and know more about unique cultures; they like to interact with locals and have authentic local experiences. Family travelers find it difficult to find a big place to stay at a lower cost.

As a multisided platform business, Airbnb needs to segment both sides of the market: guests and hosts. Airbnb hosts tend to be young people looking for extra money who like to interact with people from all over the world and companies that manage Airbnb places.

In addition to addressing multiple segments of guests and hosts, Airbnb also explores new market segments continuously, launching services that start with low turnover but have potential in the medium and long term. For example, the launch of adventure packages, such as 'Around the world in 80 days' or 'Becoming a beekeeper'.

## Questions

1. Identify and characterize the main Airbnb segments using demographic, socio-economic, psychographic, and behavioural criteria.
2. Identify the main competitors for each segment.

# Value disciplines

Michael Treacy and Fred Wiersema, two American strategy consultants, developed the different value disciplines that market leaders follow to provide superior value for their customers: product leadership, operational excellence, and customer intimacy. The value disciplines represent different customer value propositions in the market, describing the benefits that customers can expect from companies' products and services. For instance, firms pursuing product leadership provide the most advanced technological solution; companies that seek operational excellence ensure adequate solutions at the lowest cost; finally, firms that invest in customer intimacy deliver the most customized solutions (see Figure 7.1).[9]

The value disciplines view argues that to compete effectively, companies should narrow their focus to one of the three value disciplines while meeting industry standards on the other two. In this way, companies can gain a lead that competitors find it hard to catch upto. However, achieving leadership in these different value disciplines is difficult and requires companies to align their business model (see Chapter 16 – Business Model Innovation), value chain (see Chapter 8 – Resources, Routines, Capabilities and Competencies), and culture, processes, and management systems.

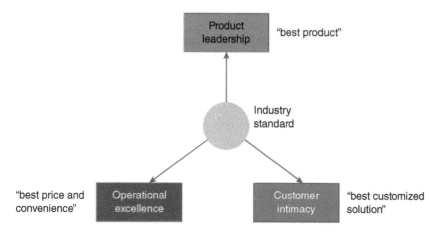

**FIGURE 7.1**   Value disciplines

Specific value disciplines tend to be more common in specific industries and at specific stages of technology maturity. For example, in technologically mature markets, it is more common to find companies that pursue operational excellence and customer intimacy, as companies seek the exploitation and adaption of existing technologies. In markets that are more dynamic in technological terms, product leadership value positioning tends to be more common.[10]

## Operational excellence

Companies that achieve **operational excellence** focus on offering reliable products at competitive prices, delivered with minimal difficulty or inconvenience. These organizations focus on optimizing business processes to cut costs and waste, eliminating intermediate steps and transactions costs, and improving products' convenience, reliability, and efficiency. Their goal is to make products better and cheaper and to serve existing customers through technology exploitation. Some examples of systems developed by operational excellence-focused companies are automated inventory, invoice-less payments, integrated information systems, and lean and efficient operations.

Companies that focus on operational excellence focus on exploitation, which implies improving existing technology and product platforms based on their customer knowledge. Maintaining lasting relationships with channel partners and customers and having profound knowledge about market conditions are essential for these companies. The main issue of operational excellence-focused companies is their inertia towards new technologies.

The quest for operational excellence makes companies develop different production models; most of them are associated with Lean production and Agile manufacturing. *Lean thinking* is a management system designed in the 80s inspired by the Toyota Production Line, characterized by a high-volume repetitive manufacturing environment. The Lean management system follows the principles of relentless pursuit of reducing waste, higher quality, lower cost, and shorter lead time.[11] While Lean thinking is more focused on cutting costs and reducing lead times, *Agile manufacturing* emphasizes the need for flexibility and responsiveness to customers' needs and market changes while still controlling costs and quality.[12]

## Customer intimacy

Companies that pursue **customer intimacy** target particular segments and then tailor offerings that match segments' individual needs, providing personal attention and anticipating customers wants. They combine detailed customer knowledge with operational flexibility to respond quickly to almost any customer need, from customizing a product to fulfilling special requests. These companies move beyond single transactions to deep, long-lasting customer relationships, experiencing high customer loyalty levels. Such companies tend to implement computer systems that collect customers' information, give personalized service, and keep profile information over time. In terms of human resources management, customer intimacy-focused firms implement hiring, training, and rewarding policies that enhance employees' empowerment to work close to the customers.

To create value, customer intimacy-focused companies need to develop adaption capabilities, using existing technology to adjust products and services to meet customers' needs perfectly. These companies use their close relationship with customers to collect information to add and refine products' features. They typically do not experiment with new technologies but rather optimize existing routines. Customer intimacy-focused companies often fail to recognize that customization success ultimately depends on the costs involved, which restrains them from searching for more efficient alternatives.

The way firms achieve customer intimacy has evolved over time: from handcrafting to mass customization, personalization, mass intimacy, and, nowadays, collective intimacy (see the Strategic Focus 'Collective intimacy and Big Data'). The proliferation of the internet allows companies to develop new methods to connect with customers that before were not possible. Firms can not only nurture digitally mediated relationships with customers but also collect a massive volume of data about them. Companies that invest in business intelligence, Big Data, and sophisticated algorithms can describe and predict customers' behaviour and needs, and tailor ads, discounts, and suggestions to different customer groups. Online mediated customer intimacy strategies allow companies to create more profound and long-lasting customer relationships, translating into customer loyalty, higher revenues, or even market leadership.

## Product leadership

Companies that focus on **product leadership** concentrate on offering cutting-edge products and services that constantly enhance customers' usage or application, thereby rendering rivals' goods and services obsolete. These companies strive to produce state-of-the-art goods, focusing their operations and business processes on accelerating innovation and ideas commercialization. Product leadership-focused companies always look for the next technology, continuously scanning for innovations in design, engineering, and user experience to create best-in-class products and introduce radical innovations to the market.

To create value, product leadership-focused companies need to develop exploration capabilities. Such capabilities entail developing new products through processes of experimentation and variation to leverage the most updated technologies. Product leadership-focused companies would rather invest in launching new products and tapping new segments than extending existing products. However, constant exploration may lead to chasms and initiative fatigue, and product leadership focusers may risk losing the focus and facing flops.

## Value disciplines, hypercompetition and ambidextrous organizations

**Hypercompetition** theory challenges the argument that companies should primarily invest in one of the three value disciplines. Hypercompetition results from intense and rapid competitive moves, in which competitors attack quickly with unexpected and unconventional competitive actions and responses. In hypercompetitive markets, companies should integrate elements of different value disciplines, and often change their value proposition to surprise competitors and gain competitive advantage (at least until the next competitors strike). Such 'hypercompetitors' continuously create new competitive advantages that destroy or neutralize the industry leader's edge, leading to constant industry disequilibrium and disarray. Hypercompetition teaches that strategy is about creative destruction and that in highly competitive markets, the sources of competitive advantage are vulnerable and relatively short-term. Indeed, focusing on sustaining the competitive advantage may prevent companies from developing new ones and surprising competitors. In such markets, to cope with such a fast-moving pace, companies need to co-optimize multiple value disciplines, often changing the basis of their value proposition for the market.[13]

How can companies constantly change the source of competitive advantage? This question is answered by organizational ambidexterity scholars. Just as being ambidextrous means using both the left and right hand equally well, organizational ambidexterity requires organizations to be adept at both exploration and exploitation (see Chapter 17). In hypercompetitive market spaces, companies need to be ambidextrous to migrate quickly from one competitive position to another, nurturing different value disciplines simultaneously or at different times.[14]

## STRATEGIC FOCUS
### Collective intimacy and Big Data

While customer intimacy entails collecting knowledge about an individual customer and meeting their needs, collective intimacy involves mass data collection and aggregating and analyzing information to nurture deep relationships at scale with *all* customers. Such scale also involves developing computing excellence to save and process a massive amount of information efficiently while conserving customers' privacy.[15] Collective data collection and analysis on customer behaviours and preferences is core for businesses such as Amazon and Netflix and to many others that are yet to discover the value-added that collective intimacy can bring to their businesses. For example, Amazon and Netflix use information across customers to feed the algorithms which give customers recommendations on what to watch or buy next, adding value to their services. In this case, collective intimacy allows companies to offer extra value to customers through an extraordinary service and level of guidance. Is collective intimacy, rather than customer intimacy, the new standard in the digital era? Which industries can take advantage of collective intimacy? Does it make sense to invest in collective intimacy across all industries or only in specific ones?

## Blue Ocean strategy

W. Chan Kim and Renée Mauborgne, professors at INSEAD, proposed the concept of the Blue Ocean strategy. This framework helps companies think creatively and find uncontested market spaces, so-called 'Blue Ocean spaces', where competition is minimal.

The **Blue Ocean strategy** theory emerged as a critique of existing literature that considered competition as the single most important element for deciding company strategy. Kim and Mauborgne suggested, in contrast, that companies should not focus on the competition but make competition irrelevant, arguing that 'competing in overcrowded industries is no way to sustain high performance. The real opportunity is to create Blue Oceans of uncontested market space'.[16]

Blue Ocean strategy is the pursuit of differentiation and low-cost positions simultaneous with the ambition to create new markets where competition is minimal or non existent. A Blue Ocean strategy enables a company to create an uncontested market space, as opposed to competing in a Red Ocean full of sharks. Red Oceans are well-defined industries where competition is intense, and boundaries are known. In Red Oceans, the goal is to beat competitors to get higher market share and exploit existing demand. In contrast, Blue Oceans are new marketplaces where competition does not exist yet. Companies that create Blue Oceans reinvent the industry boundaries and look for unique needs to serve with a view to ensure a high rate of profitability. They break the value-cost trade-off, pursuing differentiation and low cost at the same time.[17]

## Strategy canvas

A strategy canvas is a Blue Ocean strategy tool created to help companies reinvent their value proposition in the marketplace. It compares competitors across an industry's critical success factors (CSFs) to create Blue Oceans. Designing a strategy canvas involves three steps:

1. Identify the critical success factors. The first step is to identify the industry CSFs. The *CSFs* are industry factors or product features that customers value. For example, in the wine industry, the CSFs may include price, international prizes, wine quality, taste complexity, vineyard prestige and legacy, ageing, and marketing. In the mobile phone market, the CSFs could include processor speed, screen size and quality, weight, storage, and camera quality.
2. Eliminate-Reduce-Raise-Create factors. Companies need to reflect on their value proposition across the industry CSFs, reducing, raising, eliminating, and creating factors. To create a Blue Ocean, companies need to: (1) eliminate factors taken for granted by the industry; (2) reduce factors below industry standard; (3) raise factors above industry standard; and (4) create factors that are brand new to that industry.
3. Plot the value curves. After identifying the industry CSFs and reflecting on which factors the company wants to eliminate, reduce, raise, and create, the value curves can be plotted. As shown in Figure 7.2, the value curve is a graphic representation of the company's and competitors' value offerings across the CSFs. If a company's value curve converges to other competitors', it means that its value position is undifferentiated and hard to communicate (see Company 2 and Company 3 in Figure 7.2). In contrast, a company has a Blue Ocean strategy when its value curve diverges from competitors' ones (see Company 1 in Figure 7.2).

## The benefits and risks of Blue Ocean thinking

The Blue Ocean view is simultaneously a theoretical and an action framework that helps companies rethink how they create value for customers. It can help in identifying a way to achieve differentiation and low cost simultaneously, breaking the industry standard

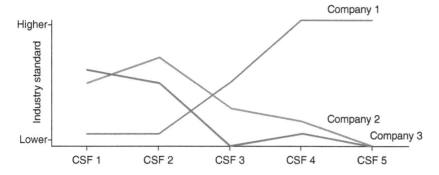

**FIGURE 7.2** Strategy canvas

value/cost trade-off. The framework also raises awareness that companies tend to over-focus on raising and creating new factors, instead of reducing and eliminating features, often offering costly over-engineered products and services.

While a Blue Ocean strategy sounds promising on paper, it is difficult to achieve by most companies. First, finding a Blue Ocean requires high investment in analysis, research, development, and organizational structures. Companies need to find an unmet need, define the market segment, develop a new product, and often redefine their internal structure, culture, and business model. On top of this, finding Blue Oceans requires confidence, persistence, and patience, as results will not become visible immediately. Second, even if a company manages to find an untapped market segment, there is the possibility that the company is too early to the market. When technology or products are brand new, customers might not understand their utility and usage immediately, such that the demand may be low initially. The Apple Newton (very early version of a tablet) and the first Microsoft Tablet PCs were the right ideas, but a couple of years too early. Finally, even when a company finds a new market segment that is profitable and the customers are ready for the product, other companies will also be attracted by the market opportunity. Therefore, companies still need to find ways to defend their Blue Oceans through superior execution speed, brand power, and technology investment.[18]

## KEY DEBATE

### Viability of Blue Ocean strategy

Blue Ocean thinking involves companies pursuing untapped market segments where competition is non existent. However, finding a Blue Ocean requires a high level of investment and entails the risk of arriving too early, when customers may not be ready for the product. Additionally, when a company finds a Blue Ocean and starts to explore it with a commercially viable product, other firms become aware of the opportunity. Thus, even before a first mover knows it, other sharks may have smelled the opportunity and may be exploring ways to enter the market and establish dominance by capitalizing on their existing knowledge and technologies. If the opportunity exists and its potential is mensurable, other entrepreneurs could enter with a lower level of investment. Knowing this, how realistic is it to think that a Blue Ocean strategy presents a viable way forward in today's markets?[24]

## Blue Ocean and the Red Queen effect

Blue Oceans are desirable markets; however, the higher the attractiveness and profitability of a particular market or segment, the higher the likelihood that other companies will respond and launch competing products. This is called the Red Queen effect, which describes a situation in which companies escalate efforts to protect their market (see also Chapter 17). The Red Queen effect is named based on a line in Lewis Carroll's novel *Alice Through the Looking Glass*, in which the Red Queen tells Alice: 'Here, you see, it takes all the running you can do to keep in the same place. If you want to get somewhere else, you must run at least twice as fast as that!'[19] The Red Queen hypothesis maintains that any strategy that is effective is likely to be met by a reaction because competitors will learn about the opportunity and will take steps to undermine the first-mover's advantage. Organizational learning theorists and evolutionary scholars argue that companies do not win on a permanent basis, they can only have short-term victories. As Alice did in the Lewis Carroll novel, firms need to run faster and faster to maintain their edge over others and to protect their position. The smartphones market illustrates this effect. Even though Apple wiped out many mobile phone makers in the market, a few years later, new competitors emerged, vying with Apple for market leadership. Over the years, the time-to-market of new smart phones shrank as the innovation and imitation pace of the industry increased. This example highlights that before too long, a company's Blue Ocean could be full of sharks.[20]

## STRATEGIC FOCUS

### Design-thinking: Human-centered creative process

Design-thinking is a human-centered problem-solving method that focuses on having a deep understanding of customer needs, generation of ideas, and rapid prototyping. It puts together a product that is desired by customers, is technologically possible, and is economically viable. In design-thinking, cross-functional teams engage directly with individual users, develop empathy with them, and observe how they behave. This creative method often uncovers surprising ideas that make people's lives better, and have potential to unleash Blue Ocean segments.[21]

IBM is one of the leading firms in using design-thinking as a methodology to improve user experience. IBM assembles teams for its products consisting of designers and engineers who follow the design thinking process: first, define objectives; second, engage people throughout the process; third, propose a solution; fourth, start over again. IBM claims that its business units that used the design-thinking approach most intensively grew their revenues by double digits.[22] Nonetheless, for many, design-thinking is no more than a list of boxes to check that reduces creativity to a contained and linear process, bringing no value added to companies that are customer-driven. What, then, are the differences between customer-driven strategies and design thinking?

## CRACK-THE-CASE

### NFTs and digital art[23]

NFTs are unique and unreplaceable non-fungible tokens. They are cryptographically generated, one-of-a-kind units of data recorded on a shared ledger known as a blockchain (see Chapter 5 – Emerging Technologies). While Bitcoin is a digital currency with fungible tokens such that one bitcoin equals another bitcoin, NFTs are unique digital tokens that provide a certificate of ownership that can be bought and sold. NFTs can comprise digital creations such as files, art, music files, videos, video game items, and other creative work.

One of the most successful NFTs is a digital art piece called *Everydays: The first 5000 days* created by Beeple (Mike Winkelmann) and sold by Christie's auction house for $69 million (see Figure 7.3). Even though the image has been copied and shared countless times, the buyer of the NFT owns a token that proves that they hold the original work. While this expensive art piece called the world's attention to NFTs, there are collectable NFTs that can be afforded by the average person, for example, CryptoKitties cards. CryptoKitties was one of the first attempts to create NFTs, consisting of a collection of unique cards with virtual cats that cost something between a few cents and $300,000. Another example of a successful NFT collection is the NBA Topshot that sells players' clips of iconic moments.

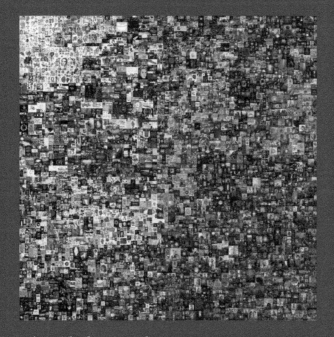

**FIGURE 7.3**   *Everydays: The first 5000 days*

Source: created by Beeple (aka Mike Winkelmann)

NFTs can be copied like any other art piece – just as anyone can have a copy of the Mona Lisa painting in their drawing room, there will only ever be one original Mona Lisa. The NFT gives the owner a certificate of ownership that guarantees the uniqueness of the digital asset. It is arguable whether NFTs entail more or less security costs than material pieces of art. Just as security is needed for material artifacts, it is also needed in the digital arena because a computer can be hacked. However, NFTs are certainly more convenient as they are easier to transport and store and do not deteriorate over time. NFTs are also unbreakable or impossible to damage and easier to transact.

*(Continued)*

Additionally, since an NFT is a digital asset, it is possible to link such an asset with other cryptocurrency tools, as is the case with DeFi (decentralized finance). DeFi is a system in which token-holders can bank tokens (equivalent to depositing money in a bank), and these tokens can be borrowed by other people while rendering a yield to the owner.

You might think that such multimillion NFTs are out of reach for most of us, like the Mona Lisa is, or that they are valuable only for people that own crypto. However, considering that we live in an increasingly digitalized world, why would art escape this trend?

## Questions

1. Identify the main CSF in the industry of material and digital art.
2. Plot the value curves of digital art NFTs versus traditional material art.

## CLOSING CASE

### The gaming console war goes on: PlayStation 4 vs Nintendo Switch (Take II)[25]

As stated in the opening case of this chapter, in 2006 Nintendo launched the Wii console with a user-friendly and innovative technology that disrupted PlayStation's leadership of the game console market. Nintendo sold 101 million consoles and unfurled a new market segment of people who like simple and fun games – they found a deep Blue Ocean of non-gamers and secured leadership of the console game market for a while.

PlayStation did not let its market leadership slip away easily. The first response of PlayStation was to decrease the price of PS3 by $100 (to $499) to boost sales. With this move, Sony suffered losses on its hardware (PS3) sales but hoped to make profits by selling the games (Opening case – Option 1). Sony's second move was the launch of PlayStation Move, a controller set with a motion-sensing system for PS3 (Opening case – Option 2). The most significant difference between the PlayStation Move controller and the Wii was the price; PlayStation's offer alone cost $100. Critics said that PlayStation Move was a copy-cat of Wii. The Sony solution had a higher definition on TV, but precision was lower. This was the case because Sony had adapted a controller to an existing console that was not initially designed for it.

In 2013, Nintendo launched an updated version of the Wii, the Wii U, which only sold 10 million consoles. This product flop showed that the motion-sensing technology was a fad. Such failure inspired PlayStation to launch, in 2013, the PS4 and the PlayStation VR set (Opening case – Option 3). The launch had better graphics and exclusive blockbuster games and sequels, such as *Uncharted 4: A Thief's End*, *Horizon Zero Dawn*, and *Bloodborne*. PlayStation kept its focus on the core-gamers, the most profitable and loyal segment. PlayStation's responses paid off, and in 2017, PS4 sold more than 102 million units, more than double the sales of its direct competitor, Microsoft's Xbox One. However, long-term competitive advantage is difficult to maintain in this market, and in 2017 Nintendo struck again.

Nintendo launched the Switch, a console that can be transformed at home to a portable system in a snap. The Nintendo Switch came together with new entries in Nintendo's big hit series, Super Mario and The Legend of Zelda. In addition, Nintendo Switch had augmented reality integrated into it, called Nintendo LABO (see Figure 7.4). Nintendo LABO consists of a cardboard Toy-Con that offers an enjoyable and engaging building process and creative programming tools. Players can use the cardboard to be a robot, a piano player, or even a fisherman. Nintendo Switch has been an enormous success – with sales of 20 million units in the first ten months, it has had the fastest market penetration ever in game console market history. Between 2017 and 2023, Nintendo Switch sold 125 million units. The increasing adoption of Nintendo Switch by women, families, kids, and teenagers, as well as the COVID-19 pandemic, which forced people to stay at home and spend more time playing, contributed to this enormous success.

**FIGURE 7.4** Nintendo Switch LABO Robot Kit

As Nintendo explores new segments, Sony has kept investing in the core players, with their much-anticipated PS5, in which 'Play has no limits'. This PlayStation is a next-generation machine with improved graphics and performance and exclusive games. It is also compatible with a VR headset and comes with the option to play games both through disc and digitally. PlayStation is also investing in their PlayStation Plus subscription service, with access to buy and store games online in the cloud. From November 2020 to February 2021, PS5 sold 5.2 million units, very similar figures to PS4. However, Sony was incurring losses selling its hardware, hoping to either achieve economies of scale or to make profits with games.

The game console industry is a highly competitive market where players cannot sustain a competitive advantage for too long. History shows that the rivalry between Sony and Nintendo is a game with multiple sequels.

## Questions

1. How would you describe PS5's and Nintendo Switch's segment positioning?
2. Identify the CSFs of the game console industry, and, using the Blue Ocean value canvas, plot PS5's and Nintendo Switch's value curves.

# Summary

- Market segmentation involves identifying distinct customer groupings which react differently to marketing stimuli and product offerings.
- Market segmentation centers on throwing light on who the company's customers are, what they want, when they buy, and how they choose among different product offerings.
- There are two main types of customers: business-to-business (B2B) and business-to-consumer (B2C). To serve B2B and B2C segments, companies need different approaches because the two have distinct selling points.
- Value disciplines – product leadership, operational excellence, and customer intimacy – are pathways that can be followed to provide superior value to customers.
- Firms that pursue product leadership focus on producing a continuous stream of innovative goods and services.
- Operational excellence is a pathway that focuses on the elimination of unnecessary production steps and the optimization of business processes with a view to offer customers the best price and convenience.
- Firms that focus on customer intimacy shape and adapt products to fit customers' needs.
- Blue Ocean thinking is an idea that helps companies think creatively to find uncontested market spaces where competition is minimal.
- The strategy canvas is a framework to facilitate thinking about the critical success factors a company should eliminate, raise, reduce, or create to strengthen its competitive position.

# Review questions

1. Why is market segmentation important and how are digital technologies changing the way companies segment the market?
2. Scholars often advocate that companies should focus on a single value discipline. Practitioners, however, report that this is difficult. Why do scholars put emphasis on focusing on a single discipline?
3. Ideally, companies would find Blue Oceans that are full of opportunities and minimal market competition. This is different than Red Oceans, where competition is fierce. What are the main dimensions that distinguish Red from Blue Oceans?

# Discussion questions

1. In which industries may a focus on Blue Ocean strategy be more rewarding?
2. Big Data and advanced analytical tools are revolutionizing market segmentation practices. Moreover, companies are moving towards a personalized one-to-one marketing strategy, achieving very high levels of individualization. To do so, companies collect data on every online click of a customer. However, this massive data collection raises some important issues. Are customers fully aware of the ways their data is being collected, by whom, and how it is being exchanged among internet firms? What if there is a security breach? Who will be held responsible? Where does the line between customer intimacy and intrusion lie?

## EXPERIENTIAL EXERCISES

1. Social network apps allow people to interact, communicate, and build personal relationships by engaging in different types of interactions (e.g., resharing, commenting on, and (dis)liking posts). However, beyond the social component, social network apps are a multi-billion dollar market that generates revenues through targeted advertising, brand promotion, and in-app purchasing. Identify the critical success factors (from a customer perspective) of this market and plot the value curves of Facebook, Instagram, Twitter, and TikTok. Which of these players, if any, is following a Blue Ocean strategy?

2. Ride hailing apps, which connect passengers and local drivers, conquered the transportation market. Uber, Lyft, Didi Chuxing, and BlaBla Car are among the biggest players in the market. Identify the value disciplines followed by Lyft, Uber, Didi Chuxing, and BlaBla Car. Do they use a single value discipline or a mix? Do value disciplines make sense for multisided platform businesses?

## Further reading

Agnihotri, A. (2016) 'Extending boundaries of blue ocean strategy', *Journal of Strategic Marketing*, 24: 519–28.

Burke, A., Van Stel, A. and Thurik, R. (2010) 'Blue ocean vs. five forces', *Harvard Business Review*, 88 (5): 28–9.

Derfus, P.J., Maggitti, P., Grimm, C. and Smith, K. (2008) 'The Red Queen effect: Competitive actions and firm performance', *Academy of Management Journal*, 51 (1): 61–80.

O'Reilly III, C.A. and Tushman, M.L. (2013) 'Organizational ambidexterity: Past, present, and future', *Academy of Management Perspectives*, 27 (4): 324–38.

Payne, A., Frow, P. and Eggert, A. (2017) 'The customer value proposition: Evolution, development, and application in marketing', *Journal of the Academy of Marketing Science*, 45 (4): 467–89.

## Endnotes (references)

1. Christensen, C.M. (2007) 'What should Sony do next?', *Forbes,* August 1. https://www.forbes.com/2007/08/01/sony-games-innovation-lead-cz_cc_0802christensen.html (accessed June 19, 2023); Wolverton, T. (2010) 'Sony's PlayStation move can't quite challenge Wii', *Phys.org*, October 1. https://phys.org/news/2010-10-sony-playstation-wii.html (accessed June 19, 2023); Mack, S. (2017) 'Wii – Nintendo's change of video game experience', May 5. https://web.archive.org/web/20230730115434/https://www.cbs.de/en/blog/wii-nintendos-change-of-video-game-experience (accessed July 27, 2023).

2. Alsop, T. (2022) 'Unit sales of game consoles in the United States by platform from 2007 to 2018', *Statista*, February 8. https://web.archive.org/web/20230730120404/https://www.statista.com/statistics/685117/us-game-consoles-unit-sales (accessed July 29, 2023).

3. D'Aveni, R.A. (1994) *Hypercompetition: Managing the Dynamics of Strategic Management.* New York: Free Press.

4.  Levitt, T. (1960) 'Marketing myopia', *Harvard Business Review*, 38 (4), 24–47.

5.  Lehman, D. and Russel, W. (2008) *Analysis for Marketing Planning* (7th ed.). New York, NY: McGraw Hill.

6.  Smith, W.R. (1956) 'Product differentiation and market segmentation as alternative marketing strategies', *Journal of Marketing*, 21 (1): 3–8.

7.  Lehman and Russel (2008)

8.  Dudovskiy, J. (2019) 'Airbnb segmentation, targeting & positioning', September 10. https://research-methodology.net/airbnb-segmentation-targeting-positioning (accessed June 19, 2023); Guttentag, D., Smith, S., Potwarka, L. and Havitz, M. (2018) 'Why tourists choose Airbnb: A motivation-based segmentation study', *Journal of Travel Research*, 57 (3): 342–59; Simpson, D. (2021) 'Why do we use Airbnb?', *CABI Market segmentation study*, May 15. www.cabi.org/leisuretourism/news/25588 (accessed June 19, 2023).

9.  Osterwalder, A., Pigneur, Y., Bernada, G. and Smith, A. (2014) *Value Proposition Design: How to Create Products and Services Customers Want.* Hoboken, NJ: John Wiley & Sons; Treacy, M. and Wiersema, F. (1993) 'Customer intimacy and other value disciplines', *Harvard Business Review*, 71 (1): 84–93.

10. Zacharias, N.A., Nijssen, E. and Stock, R. (2016) 'Effective configurations of value creation and capture capabilities: Extending Treacy and Wiersema's value disciplines', *Journal of Business Research*, 69 (10): 4121–31.

11. Krafcik, J.F. (1988) 'Triumph of the lean production system', *Sloan Management Review*, 30 (1): 41–52.

12. Powell, D.J. and Strandhagen, J.O. (2012) '21st century operational excellence: Addressing the similarities and differences between Lean production, Agility and QRM', In *2012 IEEE International Conference on Industrial Engineering and Engineering Management.* Washington, DC: IEEE, 449–53.

13. D'Aveni (1998)

14. O'Reilly III, C.A. and Tushman, M.L. (2013) 'Organizational ambidexterity: Past, present, and future', *Academy of Management Perspectives*, 27 (4): 324–38; Jansen, J.J.P., Tempelaar, M.P., Van den Bosch, F.A.J., and Volberda, H.W. (2009) 'Structural differentiation and ambidexterity: The mediating role of integration mechanisms', *Organization Science*, 20 (4): 797–811.

15. Weinman, J. (2013) 'How customer intimacy is evolving to collective intimacy, thanks to Big Data', *Forbes*, June 4. www.forbes.com/sites/joeweinman/2013/06/04/how-customer-intimacy-is-evolving-to-collective-intimacy-thanks-to-big-data/?sh=331d3db25dbc (accessed June 19, 2023).

16. Kim, W.C. and Mauborgne, R. (2004) 'Blue Ocean Strategy', *Harvard Business Review*, October: 71–79. p.71.

17. Kim, W.C. and Mauborgne, R. (2015) *Blue Ocean Strategy, Expanded Edition: How to Create Uncontested Market Space and Make the Competition Irrelevant.* Cambridge, MA: Harvard Business Review Press.

18. Agnihotri, A. (2016) 'Extending boundaries of blue ocean strategy', *Journal of Strategic Marketing*, 24 (6): 519–28; Sheehan, N.T. and Bruni-Bossio, V. (2015) 'Strategic value curve analysis: Diagnosing and improving customer value propositions', *Business Horizons*, 58 (3): 317–24.

19. Carroll, L. (1960) *The Annotated Alice: Alice's Adventures in Wonderland and Through the Looking-glass.* New York, NY: New American Library.

20. Barnett, W.P. and Hansen M. (1996) 'The red queen in organizational evolution', *Strategic Management Journal*, 17 (1): 139–57; Derfus, P.J., Maggitti, P., Grimm, C. and Smith, K. (2008) 'The Red Queen effect: Competitive actions and firm performance', *Academy of Management Journal*, 51 (1): 61–80.

21. Ideo, U. (2021) 'What is design thinking', *Ideo U.* www.ideou.com/blogs/inspiration/what-is-design-thinking (accessed June 19, 2023).

22. Cutler, A. (2016) 'IBM Design Thinking: A framework to help teams continuously understand & deliver', *LinkedIn,* January 21. www.linkedin.com/pulse/ibm-design-thinking-framework-help-teams-continuously-adam-cutler (accessed June 19, 2023).

23. BBC (2021) 'What are NFTs and why are some worth millions?', December 16. www.bbc.com/news/technology-56371912 (accessed June 19, 2023); Christie's (2021) 'Beeple's Opus', *Christie's.* www.christies.com/features/Monumental-collage-by-Beeple-is-first-purely-digital-artwork-NFT-to-come-to-auction-11510-7.aspx (accessed June 19, 2023); Dale, B. (2020) 'The inevitable marriage of yield farming and NFTs, explained', *CoinDesk,* September 28. www.coindesk.com/tech/2020/09/28/the-inevitable-marriage-of-yield-farming-and-nfts-explained (accessed June 19, 2023); Nguyen, T. (2021) 'NFTs, the digital bits of anything that sell for millions of dollars, explained', *Vox,* March 11. www.vox.com/the-goods/22313936/non-fungible-tokens-crypto-explained (accessed June 19, 2023).

24. Kim, W.C., and Mauborgne, R. (2004) 'Value innovation: The strategic logic of high growth', *Harvard Business Review*, 82 (7/8): 172–80.

25. Mendoza, N.F. (2021) 'PlayStation rakes in $2.6 billion in PS5 sales', February 25. https://web.archive.org/web/20230315225822/http://www.techrepublic.com/article/playstation-rakes-in-2-6-billion-in-ps5-sales/ (accessed June 19, 2023); Minotti, M. (2019) 'PlayStation 4 sales surpass Wii and the original PlayStation', *Gamesbeat,* October 30. https://venturebeat.com/2019/10/30/playstation-4-sales-surpass-wii-and-the-original-playstation (accessed June 19, 2023); Wang, A. (2017) 'The follow-up story of Nintendo Wii', *Medium,* November 23. https://medium.com/@wangilex/the-follow-up-story-of-nintendo-wii-798923db7909 (accessed June 19, 2023); Webster, A. (2020) 'The Nintendo Switch has been the US's bestselling console for 23 straight months', *The Verge,* November 13. www.theverge.com/2020/11/12/21562530/nintendo-switch-lite-sales-october-2020 (accessed June 19, 2023).

## Key terms

**Blue Ocean strategy** – the simultaneous pursuit of differentiation and low-cost position to create new markets in which competition is non existent or minimal

**Customer intimacy** – centers on adapting products to fit customers' needs

**Hypercompetition** – when competitors attack one another quickly with unexpected and unconventional competitive actions and reactions

**Market segmentation** – identifying customer groupings that react differently to marketing stimuli and product offerings

**Operational excellence** – a value discipline that centres on optimizing business processes

**Product leadership** – producing a nonstop stream of innovative products

# 8

# RESOURCES, ROUTINES, CAPABILITIES AND COMPETENCIES

## LEARNING OBJECTIVES

After reading this chapter, you should be able to:

- appreciate the importance of a firm's resources for sustained value creation;
- understand the meaning of routines and whether they can be changed;
- describe different types of dynamic capabilities;
- understand the meaning of core competencies;
- describe the conditions under which resources, routines, capabilities and competencies may act as sources of competitive advantage, and when ad hoc problem solving is more suitable.

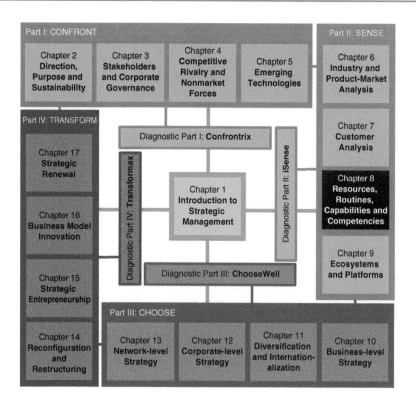

## OPENING CASE

### Formula 1's formula for success[1]

Source: © Image Craft (2023) / Shutterstock.

Formula 1 is a well-known, well-attended, and lucrative industry. Annually, it takes around 23 races across the world to determine which one of ten teams and 20 drivers will emerge as the winner. On average, every Grand Prix race has an audience of about 87 million people, with Formula 1 being the second fastest growing major sports league globally. The winning driver and team collect huge salaries, bonuses, and prize moneys, which may be in the range of tens of millions of dollars. While all this sounds amazing, there is more to the Formula 1 industry.

While lucrative, Formula 1 is a very expensive industry. Maintaining a Formula 1 team therefore requires having a group of people who are the best in what they do. Every team needs the best engineers, because a Formula 1 car is based on cutting edge technology and innovation. Indeed, Formula 1 technology has spurred advancements in many other domains, including the automotive industry, sailing, public transportation, safety, and sustainability. Furthermore, every team seeks to recruit the best drivers. It is no secret that a great car does not deliver great results without a great driver. Formula 1 is dominated by powerful companies, such as Mercedes-Benz Group AG, Red Bull GmbH, and Groupe Renault, and is sponsored by behemoths such as UBS, AMD, Walmart, and Shell. The best engineers and drivers tend to go to the teams that have the greatest resources.

The marketing aspect of Formula 1 is key as well. Formula 1 as an industry is dominated by teams that are either owned or backed by diversified companies, who participate in Formula 1 to promote the sales of their products in other lines of business. Skilled marketing professionals, besides victories on the racetrack, determine the reach of a Formula 1 team, which in turn determines the companies willing to sponsor a team, which then completes the cycle by influencing the recruitment of skilled professionals and track victories. It is evident that the Formula 1 industry is very attractive to some companies as there is a very lucrative aspect to participating in it. However, the industry is not characterized by uniformity. The industry dynamics depend on what happens at the company level – how each company acts and how this feeds into the next round of competition. It is this never-ending, ever-recurring question that contributes to the popularity of Formula 1.

### Questions

1.  What are the key resources a Formula 1 team has and how do resources matter for a team's performance?
2.  How can a Formula 1 team outperform other teams if all teams have access to a similar amount and quality of resources?

# Introduction

The strategic management discipline is concerned with how a company can achieve superior returns as compared to others in its business domain. Building on the resource-based view (RBV) of the firm introduced in Chapter 1, in this chapter we examine how the resources, routines, and capabilities of a firm, and the competencies to deploy these, matter for the firm's competitive position. The RBV and the related knowledge-based view of the firm and the dynamic capabilities perspective hold that competitive advantage arises from having the right resources and deploying them at the right time. In line with this, this chapter's opening case suggests that whether a Formula 1 team is victorious or not hinges on the resources a team has access to. On reading this chapter further, you will develop appreciation of why strategy formulation and implementation should be founded on the resources, routines, capabilities, and competencies of a firm.

As outlined in Figure 8.1, this chapter will help develop your understanding of the concepts of resources, routines, capabilities, and competencies. This chapter explains why resources need to be valuable, rare, inimitable, and non-substitutable to enable unique strategies that generate competitive advantage. Recognizing that competitive advantage often tends to be transient in today's business environment, the chapter highlights that the maintenance of positions of competitive advantage depends usually on altering the firm's resource base through the creation, modification, and extension of resources. In relation to this, routines and (dynamic) capabilities play an important part. Furthermore, the chapter looks at ad hoc problem solving as a mechanism to deal with the issue of change.

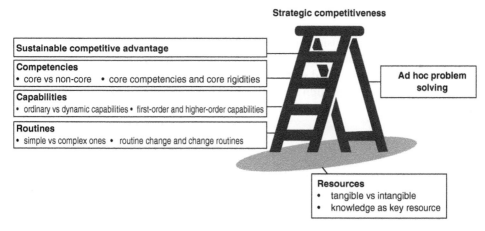

**FIGURE 8.1** Simplified visualization of the resource-based strategy

Source: © Frederic Legrand - COMEO (2019) / Shutterstock

# Resources

The **resources** of a firm are all the assets tied to the organization on a relatively permanent basis.[2] The land owned by a company, access to raw materials, borrowing capacity, specialized production facilities, knowledge, trade secrets, brand name, and reputation are all examples of resources. While a property on the Avenue des Champs-Elysées in Paris can be a valuable asset for boutique shops, having talented personnel can be a valuable asset for an IT company. In the digital era, data has received increased attention as an asset. Because resources can often be valued, the term 'capital' is also sometimes used instead of 'resources' – for example, human capital.

Resources can be either tangible or intangible. **Tangible resources** are assets that can be observed, are measurable, and can be traded relatively easily. Examples include plant and equipment, inventory, and securities like stocks and bonds. They can be grouped into physical resources (e.g., machinery and vehicles), financial resources (e.g., cash reserves), administrative resources (e.g., an inventory management system), and technological resources (e.g., patents). To illustrate, the tangible resources of the Danish shipping company Maersk include its shipping vessels, its cash reserves, and its logistics coordination systems.

**Intangible resources**, in contrast, are assets that do not have physical substance. These resources are therefore generally more difficult to quantify and trade. Intangible resources may be tied to the firm's workforce (e.g., knowledge and loyalty of employees), administrative and organizational aspects (e.g., innovative organizational culture), and market relationships (e.g., name recognition and positive reputation). Also data is commonly considered an intangible resource. Often, intangible resources accumulate over time, which make it more difficult for competitors to acquire or develop quickly. For example, the knowledge and reputational resources of Apple and Disney have been built over time, giving these companies a competitive edge over potential challengers who cannot get these resources instantly.

Among the intangible resources of a firm, knowledge is held to be a particularly important resource that can provide a competitive advantage over others who do not possess it.[3] The unique knowledge a firm possesses may be embedded in its intellectual property (e.g., artwork, designs, and patents) or reside in the individual and collective expertise of its employees (e.g., specialized knowledge and skills to collectively accomplish a task). According to the knowledge-based view of the firm, a company may be viewed as a unique, knowledge-bearing entity. In this view, because employees are an important repository of knowledge, retaining and developing them is regarded as a crucial task.

The knowledge-based view attaches much importance to knowledge acquisition and knowledge sharing. The acquisition of knowledge can happen in diverse ways, ranging from the recruitment of individual employees to the acquisition of complete businesses. Acquired knowledge needs to be integrated with existing knowledge to be useful. Knowledge sharing in a company can happen through informal and formal interactions.

## CRACK-THE-CASE
### Amazon's turnover

Source: © Frederic Legrand - COMEO (2019) / Shutterstock.

Amazon is globally known for its successes in e-commerce through its website, its streaming service through Twitch, Prime Video, and Amazon Music, its cloud computing through Amazon Web Services, its virtual assistant technology in the form of Alexa, and so much more. Having started off as an online bookstore, Amazon today has become a giant that sells and provides just about anything. While its synergetic diversification has led to one of the most valued companies on the planet, has this success perhaps come at a cost?

An important challenge that Amazon faces today is that it struggles a lot with its employee base. Many Amazon workers are not happy with their wages and working conditions and feel discouraged by the absence of unions. They believe that the only way they can get a decent raise is by quitting their job at Amazon and then joining the company again. This reality, and the massive pressure to perform, may explain the high rates of employee burnout at Amazon. Another downside of a dissatisfied workforce is that Amazon is losing about 3% of its workforce weekly, or 150% annually.[4]

Some turnover is always good, in the sense that in a free market, employees should have the flexibility to respond to better offers or to explore new opportunities. Also, a company may prefer to have employees leave if their performance is unsatisfactory. The problem with Amazon's turnover rate however is that it tends to be rather high as compared to the industry norm. By contrast the annual average turnover in transportation, warehousing and utilities was 49% in 2021 and in retail it was 64.6%, less than half of Amazon's turnover. Moreover, those leaving Amazon are oftentimes skilled employees who cannot easily and cheaply be replaced.

A loss of employees means the loss of tacit knowledge. The employees who leave take with them their expert knowledge as well as their knowledge about a company and task organization and execution. Rivals, therefore, could potentially benefit from recruiting ex-Amazon employees. Even otherwise, if an employee leaves Amazon, the time and money invested by the company in employee development is lost, necessitating a reinvestment in the training of new employees.

Amazon has always been a frugal company that seeks to economize on costs. As turnover is always costly, Amazon stands to benefit from a decrease in the turnover rate. The question is, how can Amazon accomplish this?

## Questions

1. What would be your recommendation to Amazon regarding the company's employee turnover rate?
2. What may be the implications of Amazon's employee turnover rate for the company's stock of tangible and intangible resources?

---

Resources can be a source of competitive advantage, but they can also be a source of inertia.[5] A problem with most resources is that they can become obsolete over time. Products, technologies, and even knowledge can become dated in the face of new science and alternative solutions to address customer needs. The replacement of horse carriages with automobiles offers a classic illustration. The once-successful knowledge and products of companies can engender inertia in the face of change. Consider the decline of Kodak, a dominant player in the analogue camera and film business before the advent of digital technology and digital cameras, including those embedded in smartphones.

To continue to be a successful company, it is important that the company's strategy breaks free of inertial forces, which can be cognitive (e.g., dominant mental models of decision-makers), organizational (e.g., unsuitable administrative structures and practices), or resource linked (e.g., dated knowledge and technology). An important element in overcoming inertia is the recognition of the need to adapt the firm's existing resource base by acquiring or developing new resources and abandoning or selling off redundant resources. In relation to the alteration and adaptation of the resource base, routines, capabilities, and competencies play an important role (see Figure 8.2).

Routines, capabilities, and competencies are shaped over time through the accumulation of knowledge. They emerge and crystallize as managers take repetitive, coordinated actions to compete efficiently and effectively in the market. Technical and contextual knowledge is the key building material of routines, capabilities, and competencies.

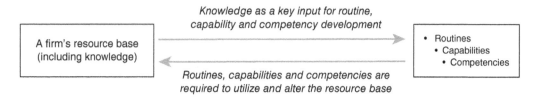

**FIGURE 8.2** Visualization of the relationship between resources (left) and routines, capabilities and competencies (right)

## KEY DEBATE

### Cognition and knowledge-based strategy[6]

Strategic management entails decisions about strategy formulation and implementation. However, different managers may arrive at different decisions even if they have the same data, information, and knowledge. Differences in managerial cognition are a decisive factor in this regard. People's cognition and mental frames vary because they notice and interpret things differently. When combined with people's bounded rationality (i.e., limited ability and time to gather and process information relevant for decision-making) decision-makers' cognition and mental frames are very consequential for the resource base of a firm.

Should a shared cognition develop in a company, a dominant logic begins to rule. Such a dominant logic reflects the collective belief of those in the company regarding the current and future competitive context and key success factors. Because the dominant logic tends to be difficult to change, it can produce tunnel vision and inertia. This can be a problem when the dominant logic is not an accurate reflection of objective reality. While a dominant logic usually emerges as the result of working together and socialization processes, managers may purposively seek to generate or alter a dominant logic through recruitment, training, and alterations in business scope of the company.

### Questions

1. How can a dominant logic develop even though people differ in their cognition?
2. What is the likely consequence of a dominant logic on the resource base of a firm?

# Routines

A **routine** can be defined as a pattern of actions which involves multiple actors and that is repetitive and recognizable.[7] To illustrate, when a patient arrives at a hospital, the diagnostic routine involves a recurrent pattern of actions by nurses and doctors to establish the cause of the patient's ailment. Chemical companies such as BASF, LyondellBasell, and Sabic have, for example, safety routines encoded in company handbooks. The numerous routines in a company often interact with one another, giving rise to bundles or clusters of routines.

Routines have also been described as habits, heuristics, scripts, or standard operating procedures that foster efficiency by minimizing the discretionary role of the individual. These descriptions of routines have in common that they regard routines to be automatic structures that embody knowledge of past organizational successes and failures. By functioning as repositories of past knowledge that reproduce successful patterns of action, routines reduce uncertainty and provide organizational stability.[8]

In addition, routines facilitate path-dependent innovations that depend on past knowledge. However, if the environment changes and past knowledge and path-dependent innovations are no longer of value, the inertia of routines can be a problem, resulting in a misfit between the company and its changing environment. To avoid misfit, a change of routines is required to ensure that the organization is adaptive and aligned with the environment. However, as routines are embedded in a company, their self-reinforcing nature makes them hard to change.[9]

It is suggested, however, that sometimes routines do gradually change through the adaptation of actors' actions.[10] The adaptations, if they perform well, are retained and replicated, leading to routine change. Such routine change could occur during trial-and-error learning as actors attempt to address imperfections in operations. Toyota is a well-known example of a company where imperfections are addressed by frontline employees and routines are adapted. Furthermore, routines may change by engaging organizational members in different types of routine work to either flex or stretch the routine. They may also change by inventing a new routine that might be better able to cope with a particular situation. This can spark creativity, improvisation, and novelty.

Some of a firm's routines may also center on introducing change. Such routines, which monitor for signs of decreasing competitive advantage by keeping an eye on crucial parameters, can provide important informational input for broader change. Change routines can be found at Toyota's production unit, where hands-on improvements by frontline employees are translated into quality and productivity gains over time. A firm may also possess innovation routines that can drive change at the organization level. These routines can help foster innovations by, for example, providing input for assembly routines.[11]

Routines can vary in their degree of complexity, ranging from simple to complex.[12] Simple routines are labelled as simple rules, rules of thumb, and heuristics. Such routines often depend on a single resource, for instance, a highly capable individual. As indicated in Table 8.1, there are many such simple routines. Their semi-structured nature provides firms with much more room for improvisation than allowed by more complex routines. Accordingly, simple routines provide the potential to direct the firm's activities towards new directions. However, an overemphasis on simple routines may move a firm towards chaos over time and may conflict with the demands of a firm's operating systems.

Simple routines may become more extensive and complex over time as new activities mature. Complex routines span different people, professions, and departments. They may

**TABLE 8.1**    Different kinds of simple routines

| Type of simple routine | Logic | Example |
|---|---|---|
| **How-to rules** | Key features of how a process is executed | Customer service processes (e.g. at Akamai): every question must be answered in the first call or e-mail |
| **Priority rules** | Ranking the accepted opportunities | Allocating manufacturing capacity (e.g. at Intel): allocation is based on a product's gross margins |
| **Timing rules** | Synchronization of management, other parts of the firm and emerging opportunities | Product development (e.g. at Nortel): project teams must know when a product has to be delivered to the leading customer to win, and product development time must be less than 18 months |
| **Exit rules** | Decide when to pull out of yesterday's options | Pulling the plug on projects in development (e.g. at Oticon): the project is killed if a key team member – manager or not – chooses to leave the project for another within the company |

Source: adapted from Eisenhardt and Sull (2001)[13].

involve many interactions between members and may require the integration of many different ideas, skills, and knowledge. The total quality management routine, a company-wide approach to improving business processes, is an example of a complex routine. The complexity of changing such routines produces stability within a company. As such, the balance between simple and complex routines underpins the balance between stability and change.

# Capabilities

Firms develop capabilities as they utilize their resources. Thus, a firm's **capability** can be defined as an ability to deploy a company's resources in order to achieve a desired end result.[14] Firms deploy resources as they perform a particular activity or process in a reliable and – at least minimally – satisfactory manner.[15] To compete in the marketplace, organizations develop capabilities related to product design, supply-chain management, production, customer service provision, and marketing, among others. For instance, companies such as Amazon, FedEx, and ING aim to deploy technology-related resources (such as drones in the case of Amazon) to improve their customer service-related capabilities. Similarly, the increased attention to sustainability forces companies to acquire new resources and develop sustainability-related capabilities. This is the case of construction firms that are acquiring capabilities related to the assessment of control of nitrogen emissions at construction projects, for example.

Organizational capabilities do not exist on their own. They are a result of bundles of routines, which are patterns of actions. Routines are the building blocks of capabilities; however, routines and capabilities are not synonyms.[16] By combining bundles of coordinated routines, capabilities allow firms to respond to a variety of technological and market changes, having a strategic intent.[17] This difference is evident in their definitions, as capabilities aim at achieving a 'desired end result,' being focused on ends, while routines are 'patterns of actions,' focusing mainly on means.

Capabilities bring together sets of routines with a strategic intent that can be functional- or activity-based. Some capabilities are developed in functional areas such as operations management, supplier relationship management, or human resource management. At a micro level, a well-known representation of a firm's main functional activities is depicted in Porter's generic **value chain** (see Figure 8.3). This model views a firm as a chain of sequential value-creating activities, allowing managers to visualize the firm's primary and support activities and respective capabilities.

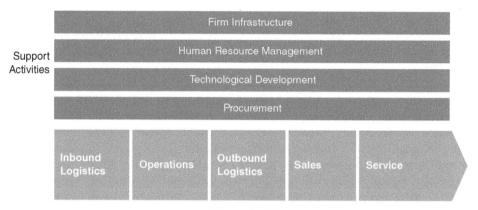

**FIGURE 8.3** Porter's generic value chain

Source: From COMPETITIVE ADVANTAGE: Creating and Sustaining Superior Performance by Michael E. Porter. Copyright ©1985 by Michael E. Porter. Reprinted with the permission of The Free Press, a division of Simon & Schuster, Inc. All rights reserved.[18]

Primary activities are the ones that directly add value to the end product. They involve all the activities to transform inputs into outputs till the interface with customers. Five primary activities are distinguished in that value chain:

- Inbound logistics: Activities that relate to receiving, storing, inventorying, and controlling the raw materials that will be incorporated in the final product.
- Operations: Operations entail all the processes involved in transforming raw materials into finalized products. It encompasses production, packaging, and assembly.
- Outbound logistics: Outbound logistics encompass all the steps taken to make the product available to customers, including warehousing, transportation, inventory control and distribution.
- Marketing and sales: Marketing and sales encompass activities that support customers during purchasing, comprising shops, promotions, and all other activities related to retail management.
- Services: Services entail all the support that proceeds the product acquisition, specifically after-sales, customer service, repair services, installation, training, spare parts management, upgrading, and other activities designed to enhance or maintain a product's value.

On top of primary activities, firms also perform support activities. Support activities assist the primary activities, improving their efficiency and efficacy; they add value through important interactions with primary activities. Firm infrastructure, human resource management, technology development, and procurement are the traditional support activities that firms undertake to implement their strategies:

- Firm infrastructure: The firm infrastructure comprises the general management team, the structure of the firm, and its various departments such as finance, accounting, legal, among others.

- <u>Human resource management:</u> Human resources management relates to people recruitment, development, retention, motivation, and compensation.
- <u>Technology development:</u> Technology development comprises all activities that aim at improving the processes in terms of efficiency and automation, encompassing also activities related to R&D and design.
- <u>Procurement:</u> Procurement activities guarantee that the firm purchases all the necessary inputs for the production process, such as raw materials, services, buildings and machines.

In practice, the length and weight of primary and support activities differ greatly across business types. For some companies, information and communication technology (ICT) or research and development (R&D) may actually be a primary activity, while for others, inbound logistics may be a support activity, for example. If a company decides that a value chain activity is not of primary nature and can be done by another party in a cheaper and/ or better way, it may decide to outsource this activity, meaning that the firm contractually agrees with this other party to perform the activity. Contrastingly, when a company believes that outsourced activities are primary and important, it may decide to insource the activities to preserve or enhance its competitive edge. Out- and insourcing activities change a firm's scope in its supply chain.

## STRATEGIC FOCUS

### An internal and a broader perspective on the value chain and supply chain[19]

Strategists can analyze value chains from two main perspectives: an internal (firm-level) perspective and a broader perspective (commonly at the industry level). From a firm-internal perspective, the value chain aggregates processes and activities performed within company boundaries. Porter's generic value chain ties into this perspective. This internal value chain forms part of a larger stream of consecutive value-adding activities, which is frequently referred to as a *value system*[20] or *industry value chain*. Value chain analysis conducted from this broader perspective allows a firm to spot where it and other companies are situated along a chain of consecutive value-adding activities that is relevant to the firm, and how it should position itself.

The value chain and supply chain concepts are often used interchangeably. Although highly related, they are not identical. A supply chain is defined as a set of entities (organizations or individuals) that are involved, through upstream (e.g., suppliers) and downstream linkages (e.g., distributors and customers), in different activities and processes to move a product from supplier to customer (see Figure 8.4). This can go all the way from raw materials up to meeting a particular customer need. The value chain notion extends the supply chain concept by including demand planning, customer requirements, and market definition. In short, the value chain view focuses on how value is added along the supply chain.

supplier → focal firm → customer

**FIGURE 8.4** Simplified illustration of a supply chain

The supply chain and value chain views also differ in their underlying assumptions. The supply chain view emphasizes the importance of ensuring linear, sequential flows of materials and information with minimal disruption to enhance the added value. This concurs with the traditional view where customers are located at the end of the chain and where the better the chain is in servicing those customers the more value is created. Contrarily, the value chain view highlights that improvement of a firm's competitive position can be achieved by considering the value streams in which firms operate as well as other parallel streams that use similar supply chains (or certain parts of those chains).

These different underlying assumptions have profound strategic implications. Firms are aware that the strength of a chain depends on the strength of each link and the breaking of one link may collapse the entire chain. Therefore, firms traditionally have sought to own multiple stages and links of the supply chain – also known as *vertical integrated firm* – or move towards that direction (for instance via *insourcing*, as opposed to outsourcing), integrating activities either upstream, downstream or both (see Chapter 11). Oil, gas and energy firms such as BP and Shell are renowned for their vertical integration strategy (from source to the filling station). However, the business world evolves, and customers are increasingly involved in value-creating activities (e.g., as designers and evaluators at LEGO) instead of just being the consumers of a product. This requires the re-thinking of firms' value propositions, devoting sufficient attention to both existing and potential value streams to come up with appropriate strategies that enhance value creation and delivery.

Vertically integrated firms often own a variety of resources, routines and capabilities as they need to possess or control resources, routines and capabilities related to a range of activities and processes within the supply chain (e.g., extracting raw materials, production and wholesale). They also need to have resources, routines and capabilities for the integration, alignment and coordination across those various activities and processes.

## Questions

1. Select a firm of your choice. What does the value chain of that firm look like? Describe the main primary and support activities of that firm by using Porter's generic value chain.
2. What are the main resources, routines, and capabilities of that firm?
3. Adopting a broader perspective, what would the supply chain of that firm look like?
4. How would that value chain and those main resources, routines and capabilities be different if that firm performs vertical integration?

Capabilities can display varying levels of complexity. More complex capabilities encompass numerous, interlinked activities across the entire value chain, such as integration, short product development, and process innovation capabilities. Firms can map their capabilities using an *activity-system map* (see Figure 8.5), which links activities (the light colored circles in Figure 8.5, such as 'in-house design focused on cost of manufacturing') to their strategic intent (the dark colored circles, such as 'low manufacturing costs'). When crafted well, an activity-system map can show (1) how discrete activities are linked to and affect each other; (2) how clusters of (tightly) linked and tailored activities relate to one another, forming firms' capabilities; and (3) which capabilities are in place or are needed to align various activities. Furthermore, activity-system maps allow the assessment of whether each activity is consistent with the strategy, whether activities or groups of them can further reinforce each other, and whether changes in one activity reduce the importance or even the presence of other activities.

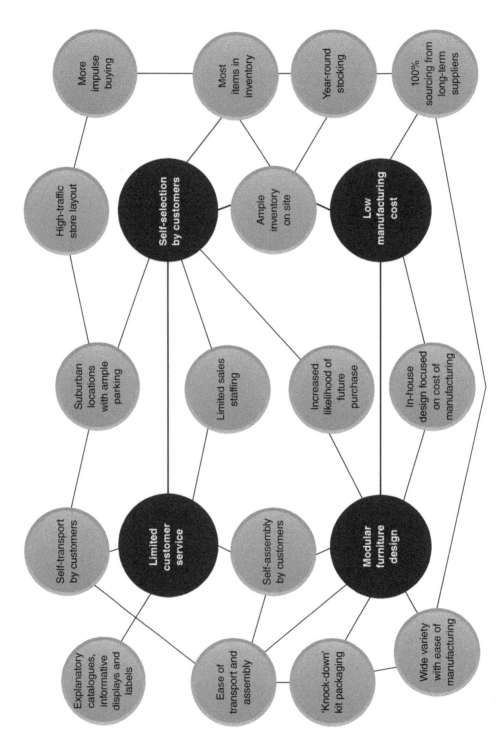

**FIGURE 8.5** Activity systems map in case of IKEA

Source: Porter (1996)[21]

The linkages between a firm's activities can also reflect the type of fit between them. Three types of activity fit are:[22]

- First-order fit (simple consistency): the activities are aligned with the overall strategy.
- Second-order fit (activities are reinforcing): various activities reinforce each other in such a way that a combined set of activities contributes more strongly to the overall strategy than the sum of the contribution of those activities when viewed in isolation.
- Third-order fit (optimization of efforts): there is coordination and information exchange across activities to eliminate redundancy, minimize wasted efforts and potentially to eliminate certain activities.

## Dynamic capabilities

The capabilities that reflect a firm's capacity to perform its basic activities are also known as operational, ordinary or zero-order capabilities. These capabilities are short-term oriented and enable a firm to utilize its existing resource base and routines. However, long-term firm success typically requires creation, modification and/or extension of the resource base and routines. Many strategic actions and transformations are difficult to routinize intentionally. Even if firms possess change or innovation routines, those routines typically have a very specific and operational nature rather than a deliberate strategic component. Altering a firm's resource base with a strategic intent requires other type of capabilities: dynamic capabilities. **Dynamic capabilities** are about a firm's capacity to create, extend and modify[23] organizational resources in order to perform activities in a repeatable, satisfactory, purposeful, and reliable manner.[24] They utilize bundles of change routines for structurally changing the resource base. Because of their ability to develop the most adequate resource base over time, dynamic capabilities alter the way in which an organization makes its living.[25]

The word 'dynamic' in dynamic capabilities may thus refer to changes or renewal in a firm's resource base and routines. Doing so, however, also involves changes in a firm's capabilities. For instance, dynamic capabilities can change mature capabilities, either to further benefit from them, or to cut the damage that they are doing.[26] Specifically, dynamic capabilities can renew capabilities (or their features) to enhance their effectiveness, redeploy or replicate capabilities to different geographic markets or product markets, and recombine separate capabilities into new ones, benefiting from the synergies. Dynamic capabilities can also be utilized to retrench capabilities, when they are less utilized or needed, or retire them when changing events occur (e.g., legislation, bans, or inside strategic decisions).

Dynamic capabilities are not 'something' that can be turned on or off nor can they be purchased off the shelf. Instead, they must be built internally, requiring time to identify, nurture, and leverage them. Therefore, skill acquisition and learning become fundamental issues for firms that want to develop dynamic capabilities.[27] These firm-specific and path-dependent characteristics make dynamic capabilities intangible (mainly when compared to resources), hard to quantify and value, and quite difficult to imitate by competitors.

Dynamic capabilities can be further disentangled into first-order and higher-order types. First-order dynamic capabilities operate to change ordinary capabilities and operating routines. Those first-order capabilities may be found at product development, strategic decision-making or alliancing. For instance, the first-order capabilities deployed at the announced merger between the airlines Air India and Vistara alter ordinary capabilities and operating routines by consolidating routes, stations, and staff.

Higher-order dynamic capabilities – also known as *meta-capabilities* – translate into the ability to transform first-order dynamic capabilities. They relate to learning-to-learn capabilities because they result from organizational learning to alter or create lower-order dynamic capabilities.[28] Such higher-order capabilities can be found at Valve Corporation, which began as a game company in 1996 and evolved into a digital distribution platform. Its handbook for new employees offers some hints towards those higher-order dynamic capabilities, such as 'the company is yours to steer towards opportunities and away from risks', 'you have the power to green-light projects', and 'you were not hired to fill a specific job description, you were hired to constantly be looking around for the most valuable work you could be doing'.[29] Instead of prescribing what exactly employees need to do, they are guided and challenged in the quest for new projects, choosing the teams they want to join. In doing so, organizational members may learn, reflect, and potentially alter first-order capabilities.

## Competencies

Whereas a firm's capabilities are about its ability to utilize (and alter) its resource base for a desired end result, a firm's **competencies** can be defined as sets of behaviours instrumental to delivering desired results or outcomes.[30] They enable the performance of tasks that require a collective effort, and they result from activities that are being performed, either repetitively or quasi-repetitively. As such, competencies integrate and coordinate capabilities. For instance, the competency of developing successful new products may draw from a variety of underlying capabilities around management and information systems, marketing, research and development, and production.

A firm's competencies can be grouped in various ways, including:

- Technological or functional competencies: attributes (such as attitudes, knowledge and skills) associated with technology or functional expertise needed to perform the role or profession.
- Managerial competencies: attributes required to mobilize, organize, plan and utilize various resources.
- Human competencies: attributes to develop, motivate and utilize human resources.
- Conceptual competencies: ability to think at abstract levels, visualize the invisible and to plan future business.

Competencies can be core or non-core to a firm. Although non-core competencies may be less prominent on the managerial radar, they might move towards the core over time. This happened for instance at DSM where former periphery competencies on chemistry and penicillin, for instance, moved towards the core. This suggests that the strategic value of non-core competencies should not be underestimated. Nonetheless, a firm's strategic direction is often organized around its **core competencies**.[31] They refer to elements of behaviour that are imperative for nearly all organizational members to possess and indicate what makes a firm more successful than its competitors for a rather sustained period. In doing so, they reflect a firm's 'personality' (i.e., unique characteristics) and form sources of competitive advantage that last longer. The explicit presence of a specific competitive advantage is also what differentiates a core competency from a capability. Capabilities on just-in-time delivery, for example, may enable or be a prerequisite to develop a competitive edge via a core competency regarding delivering low-cost solutions. A core competency overarches regular competencies in that it spans the competencies across departments or business units. They are widely shared and collectively learned, and with that, can be found all around the organization. If new product development goes beyond a new product development department, it may qualify as a core competency, as it would be a competency that would require cross-company collaboration and integration. To be classified as such, core competencies must meet three basic characteristics[32]:

- They provide access to a wide variety of markets (product and geographical).
- They contribute substantially to the end product benefits.
- They are difficult to imitate by competitors.

The value chain (see also Figure 8.3) and activity-based mapping (Figure 8.5) can also be used as tools to identify and build core competencies, for instance by portraying how they contribute to end product benefits. The unique nature of core competencies rests on a set of functions and activities, and those tools provide a template that firms can use to analyze and identify their competitive position on a set of certain functions or activities and to identify one or multiple means of how to develop core competencies.

Some examples of core competencies are about miniaturization (Sony), organizing information (Google), and lithography system architecture (high-tech company ASML). Its rather lasting nature also pinpoints that a core competency typically transcends an individual product or service: it can span multiple products and markets, as Google illustrates with its diversifications into, for instance, home automation and navigation. This suggests that the opportunity to leverage core competencies is more important for a firm than merely possessing them, as it is not an end in itself just to have them. Although outcomes of competencies (e.g., increased reputation) have received quite some attention in discussions on competency, it is important to differentiate between a competency and the outcome created or sustained by it. The outcome cannot be managed directly: the competencies to deliver those outcomes can be managed. The skills and experience to design, produce and market their offering provide companies such as Ferrari to enjoy a reputational advantage.

However, changes in a firm's environment including innovations (either from the focal firm or other actors in a market) can be competency-enhancing or competency-destroying. In the first case, a firm can build further on and reinforce its existing competencies. In this scenario, a firm can continue to leverage its core competencies. Competency-destroying changes, on the contrary, render existing competencies obsolete. In that case, the existing competencies are substantially different from the required ones, making them less valuable and potentially handicapping a firm to respond properly.[33] Under these circumstances, core competencies may turn into core rigidities.[34] Core rigidities occur when a firm is overdependent on its existing core competencies, for instance because of past success with those competencies. Firms then stick to them for too long and do not pay proper attention to renewal of their competencies, resulting in situations where competitors with new and better competencies overtake them (see Chapter 17). This happened for instance at some newspapers and retailers that were overtaken by competitors possessing digital competencies.

## Sustainable competitive advantage

A firm's core competencies thus need to be different from those of its competitors to be classified as such. As with resources, routines, and capabilities, (core) competencies are of greatest value if they can be a source of sustainable competitive advantage. This requires them to be valuable, rare, inimitable, non-substitutable, and organized.[35] Figure 8.6 depicts the *VRINO framework* including what the competitive position is if a firm does not meet certain criteria.

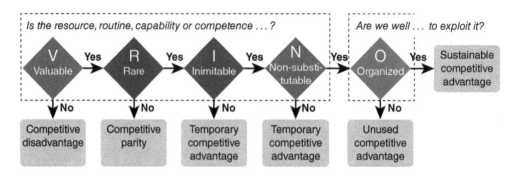

**FIGURE 8.6** VRINO Framework

Source: authors, based on Barney (1991, 1995) and Barney and Hesterly (2010)[36]

The first requirement to be a source of sustainable advantage is that a resource, routine, capability, or competency is *valuable*. This means that they enable a firm to consider or implement strategies that enhance its effectiveness and efficiency by exploiting opportunities or neutralizing threats. Such a resource can be, for example, an executive, a device, or a technology. Elon Musk, for example, was indispensable in tapping into space transportation via SpaceX. Similarly, valuable proprietary knowledge enables pharmaceutical companies to develop effective medicines. A resource, for instance, that is not valuable is possibly a source of competitive disadvantage.

Second, to deliver sustainable competitive advantage, a resource, routine, capability, or competency should be *rare*, meaning that not every organization should (be able to) possess or control it. For example, since a particular well-known and exceptional player is only hired by one sports organization at a time, that organization has access to the rare assets and capabilities of that player. If many firms operating in the same market or industry have the same resources, routines, capabilities, and/or competencies, then they can exploit them in the same way, leading to common strategies. Rare resources will translate in (parts of) routines and capabilities being rare as well, adding to the rarity of the organization's sources of competitive advantage (see also Figure 8.2). A certain valuable resource, routine, capability, or competency (or bundles of them) has the potential to generate a competitive advantage if the number of organizations that possess them is less than the required number of firms for having perfect competition. Firms enjoying first or early mover advantages may have an advantage in meeting this criterion, especially until competition on it starts to move in.

Third, resources should be *inimitable*, meaning that competitors should not be able to copy them easily. A resource, routine, capability, or competency is harder to imitate if their generation is socially complex, the ability to obtain them depends on unique historical conditions, and/or the link with a firm's sustainable competitive advantage is causally ambiguous. For various other towers around the world that mimic Paris' Eiffel Tower it is nearly impossible to imitate the unique historical and social dimensions of the original one in Paris. To reduce the chances of imitation, and with this to extend the time window of competitive advantage appropriation, companies tend to use intellectual property protection, such as patents and trademarks. However, raising excessive high imitation barriers may drive substitution as competitors may be more inclined to circumvent it via alternative equivalents.

Fourth, they should be *non-substitutable*. Even if a resource, routine, capability, or competency meets the first three criteria, a competitor may substitute it, just like tea and coffee both fulfil the need for a hot drink. While substitutes are not identical, they are able to deliver a similar outcome. Substitution may lead to equivalent strategies via a similar resource, routine, capability, or competency (e.g., when competitors copy the idea of having a unique top management team by creating their own unique one) or a different one (e.g., visionary leadership versus planning systems that may lead to similar strategic outcomes). A resource, routine, capability, or competency that is hard to substitute has the potential to be a source of sustainable competitive advantage.

Finally, a resource, routine, capability, or competency should be *organized*, meaning that a firm is able to exploit them to reap their benefits. Having them just laying unused on the shelves does not provide a firm a competitive advantage, even if they are valuable, rare, inimitable, and non-substitutable. This happened for instance at Nokia where knowledge and capabilities on a mobile phone with internet, email, and apps was just lying on the shelves for years. Its management did not believe that there was a market for 'fun' products. In 2007, Apple introduced the iPhone which contained those functions. Important factors are how well the organizational structure enables their utilization, whether management control systems give sufficient insight into how well strategy is being executed, and whether compensation policies sufficiently incentivize employees towards the goals of the organization.

## Ad hoc problem solving

Not all actions in an organization flow from routines or capabilities, nor should they. Routines and capabilities are expensive, in that they need to invested in. After all, for a routine and capability to make sense, it needs to reliably ensure a minimum level of effectiveness, and this requires investment in people, artifacts, and the functioning of the routine or capability altogether. Yet sometimes a company utilizes resources for a single time. Think of crises that are expected to never again occur, or for occasions that are not expected to occur in the near future. To maintain a capability, an organization needs to invest in it. A dynamic capability requires an organization to have routines that recur and ideally are generative so that they do not have to be changed all the time, which is yet another struggle. A dynamic capability requires an organization to invest in education, networking and breaking through dominant logics.

For ad hoc problem solving, such investments are not needed. Their costs largely disappear if there are no problems to solve. **Ad hoc problem solving** is a category of change behaviours that are non-routine and do not depend on dynamic capabilities. Those behaviours are largely non-repetitive, not highly patterned, though intendedly rational. Ad hoc problem solving is a kind of 'firefighting mode' characterized by a contingent, opportunistic, high paced and possibly creative search for suitable alternative behaviours.[37]

These characteristics are quite the opposite to those of change routines and dynamic capabilities, making ad hoc problem solving an alternative way of implementing change. Ad hoc problem solving may be a necessity when routines and capabilities fail to deliver necessary change. It is, therefore, often utilized in situations that an organization had never encountered before, does not know how they will play out, and thus is uncertain about.

The COVID-19 pandemic was a situation where many organizations went for ad hoc problem solving, for instance on how to make the workplace 'COVID-19 proof' and how to sell products when shops were forced to close their doors for a while.

Ad hoc problem solving can be too reckless when change routines or dynamic capabilities are up to the task. Those change routines or dynamic capabilities are much more efficient, because they are readily deployable. They are also much more reliable in the sense that they have been proven to deliver a certain minimum level of outcome, because they recur frequently. With ad hoc problem solving, while an organization economizes on investment costs, it also does not know whether the capacity for ad hoc problem solving within the organization will be enough when it is called upon.

A firm holds a repertoire of various routines, capabilities and competencies to facilitate its daily operations. They can act as sources of sustainable competitive advantage when they are – just as resources – valuable, rare, inimitable, non-substitutable and organized. Next to that repertoire, a firm ought to possess a portfolio of change routines, dynamic capabilities, and ad hoc problem solving to alter the way in which it makes its living. Long-term success requires that firms need to find a delicate balance between, on the one hand, continuing along their existing resource bases, routines, capabilities, and competencies, and, on the other hand, changing their resource bases, competencies, routines, and dynamic capabilities.

## CRACK-THE-CASE
### Hitting back at war[38]

Source: © Istanbulfotograf (2018) / Shutterstock.

ING, a Dutch bank, is one of the leading banks in Europe. ING Bank serves around 38 million clients in over 40 countries. In 2021, ING Bank had a net income of €4.7 billion, which is up to par with pre-pandemic levels. Its size, success and ambitions have come with a liability, however. ING Bank has among European banks some of the largest exposure to the Russian economy. It has been around since 1993, is seen as one of the most reliable banks in Russia and has about €4.5 billion of loans outstanding. Until recently, ING's position in Russia was actually a seized opportunity, as the bank profited from the fast growth of the Russian economy and utilized possibilities in the areas of energy and sustainability. Yet, as Russia invaded Ukraine, ING was directly and indirectly hit by sanctions that were imposed on Russia. About €700 million of loans were directly hit by sanctions, the bank said, while ING has a total of €6.7 billion outstanding to companies that are Russian or have a Russian owner. It does not stop there though. Additionally, Russian organizations and individuals were cut off from the international banking system called SWIFT, which basically intermediates and executes financial transactions between its members worldwide. An extended effect of these sanctions is that, because ING has a strong presence in Eastern Europe, its clients may be affected by the sanctions, and with that, their creditworthiness. Another challenge for ING has been societal pressure to voluntarily stop doing business with Russia and Russians. Though ING has a decades-long presence in Russia, it announced its support for Ukraine. It vowed not take on new Russian clients and is said to be restricting lending for deals involving movement of commodities from Russia and Ukraine. This will halt ING's expected growth, as the Russian market has been a fast-growing one. ING's exposure of about €600 million to Ukraine is also important to note, as is the exposure of its clients to businesses in Ukraine that may turn into financial problems.

Bringing all this together, one can see that ING faces certain challenges. Its financial resources will take a hit in the short run, due to sanctions and societal pressure, with an additional risk in the mid-to-long run due to bankruptcies. ING will need to change how it has been looking at the set of procedures by means of which it guards its financial health. Additionally, ING will have to rethink its technological infrastructure. ING vowed to support its current client base, so it will have to find a way to do so without the SWIFT system. Then, ING will have to work on its image. The bank has always prided itself on being honest, responsible, and ethical. The bank will be challenged by its stakeholders on whether it actually upholds these values and principles. Therefore, ING will need to engage in the massive task of rethinking its corporate communication division.

## Questions

1. What kind of dynamic capabilities would you recommend to ING for coping with these challenges and what should these capabilities look like?
2. How may ad hoc problem solving help the bank in responding quickly to those challenges?

# CLOSING CASE
## Pandemic

Source: © Wut_Moppie (2020) / Shutterstock.

The COVID-19 pandemic ruptured the lives of many. On the one side, people were restricted because of legal and political factors. Lockdowns forced people to stay home, fully or partially, and prevented people from behaving as freely as they always had. On the other side, the pandemic affected people psychologically. Fear of the unknown, in combination with (social) media interaction, illnesses, diseases, and the legal and political changes, meant for many that they were worse off psychologically due to a state of chaos.

A combination of policy and psychology affected customer behaviour tremendously, and with this, affected businesses' health. Many companies went bankrupt, as the pandemic led people to consume differently and less. Differently, in that people did not want to attend to crowded shops, or abandoned physical shopping entirely for some periods. Less, in that people were unsure about how the pandemic would play out, and because of this wanted to preserve financial resources just in case additional money would be needed in the near future.

Altogether, this has meant that many companies went bankrupt. Some lacked the financial reserves to divert the pandemic blow. As the pre-pandemic era was one of relative calm and prosperity, many organizations never thought of holding sufficient financial resources to divert a blow. Financial resources have also been important from the perspective of investment. Many organizations that went bankrupt during the pandemic did not invest properly in digital infrastructure or change mechanisms. This is related to the dominant logic inside the organization and essentially how these companies used to cope with inertia. To invest, an organization needs to acknowledge shortcomings. When organizations are stuck in a particular cognitive frame, they simply may not see that certain challenges may arise or that certain problems are structural and therefore need to be solved. Also, when resources, routines and capabilities have not changed for too long or have not been designed for change, even if the company wants to change, it may be too late.

Not every company went bankrupt. Others continued operations, but surprisingly faced a huge spike in employee turnover rates. This is particularly strange because one might assume that people would hang on to their jobs in turbulent times, due to risk aversion in terms of lost income. Yet, the pandemic made people realize they were undervalued and underpaid. They also came to realize their potential more, in that people started thinking about what they wanted to do with their lives and chose a career that suited that desire more closely. The pandemic also accelerated the demand for and supply of online work, allowing people to leave their in-person jobs.

All in all, the pandemic changed the business landscape dramatically. Many companies that lacked the necessary resources, routines, capabilities and competencies have disappeared, while labour forces have changed drastically.

## Questions

1. How did the COVID-19 pandemic affect the resource base of companies described in this case, focusing especially on monetary resources and knowledge?
2. In addition, how did reduced levels of operations affect their routines and capabilities?
3. How could dynamic capabilities and/or ad hoc problem solving have helped those companies in dealing with the consequences of the COVID-19 pandemic?

## Summary

- The resources of a firm are about valuable assets that are tied into the firm in a relatively permanent fashion. They can be tangible (i.e., observable and quantifiable) and intangible. Knowledge especially is considered a key resource.
- A routine is a pattern of actions, involving multiple actors, that is repetitive and recognizable. Routines can vary from simple to complex. Change routines can change aspects of an organization. Changing routines can be a daunting task and can be driven from within (endogenous) and/or outside (exogenous) of the firm.
- A firm's capability is about its capacity to deploy resources for a desired end result. That result can be functional and activity based. Dynamic capabilities are about a firm's capacity to create, extend and modify organizational resources in a repeatable, satisfactory, purposeful and reliable manner. While first-order dynamic capabilities operate to change ordinary capabilities and operating routines, higher-order dynamic capabilities are capabilities that transform first-order dynamic capabilities.
- A firm's competencies are its sets of behaviours that are instrumental in the delivery of desired results or outcomes. A firm's competencies can be non-core or core, (i.e., elements of behaviour that are imperative for organizational members to possess and indicate what makes a firm more successful than its competitors). Competency-destroying changes may turn core competencies into core rigidities.

- A firm's resource base is utilized and altered via certain routines, capabilities and competencies, but a firm's resources and in particular knowledge also form the foundation of those routines, capabilities and competencies. Routines constitute capabilities and capabilities constitute competencies.
- Criteria for a resource, routine, capability and competency to be a source of sustainable competitive advantage is that it is valuable, rare, inimitable, non-substitutable, and organized.
- Ad hoc problem solving is a category of change behaviours that are largely non-repetitious, not highly patterned though intendedly rational. It is an alternative way of change when routines and dynamic capabilities are not suitable, such as in uncertain and unfamiliar situations.

## Review questions

1. What are a firm's resources, routines, capabilities, and competencies, and what are various types of each of them?
2. What are the implications of changes in routines, capabilities, and competencies for a firm's resource base?
3. How do routines, capabilities, and competencies relate to each other?
4. What is a firm's value chain and what does it consist of?
5. What are criteria for a firm's resources, routines, capabilities, and competencies to act as sources of sustainable competitive advantage?
6. What is ad hoc problem solving and under what conditions might it be superior to a firm's routines and capabilities?

## Discussion questions

1. Can you think of organizations that have demonstrated dynamic capabilities and ad hoc problem solving successfully and unsuccessfully? What do you think were the reasons for this?
2. How do the topics discussed in this chapter (i.e., firm's resources, routines, capabilities, competencies, and ad hoc problem solving) complement the topics discussed in Chapters 6 and 7 to achieve superior returns?

## EXPERIENTIAL EXERCISES

1. Sberbank, a Russian bank, was hit by a multitude of sanctions due to the Russian-Ukrainian war. Among the most important of these were the bank's exclusion from the international messaging system for banks, called SWIFT, an asset freeze, a restriction in its scope of operations, a loss of reputation, and an increased risk that its clients will not be able to pay back the loans outstanding. What would you do if you were the CEO?

2. Zoom benefitted a lot from the COVID-19 pandemic, as it gained a lot of traction due to an increased demand for video conferencing. Today, as the pandemic's effect on human behaviour bounces back, there are questions about Zoom's future, particularly considering strong competition from Google and Microsoft. How would you advise Zoom to change?

# Further reading

Fainshmidt, S., Wenger, L., Pezeshkan, A. and Mallon, M.R. (2019) 'When do dynamic capabilities lead to competitive advantage? The importance of strategic fit', *Journal of Management Studies*, 56 (4): 758–87.

Gerhart, B. and Feng, J. (2021) 'The resource-based view of the firm, human resources, and human capital: Progress and prospects', *Journal of Management*, 47 (7): 1796–819.

Hernandez-de-Menendez, M., Morales-Menendez, R., Escobar, C.A. and McGovern, M. (2020) 'Competences for industry 4.0', *International Journal on Interactive Design and Manufacturing*, 14: 1511–24.

Volberda, H.W., Khanagha, S., Baden-Fuller, C., Mihalache, O.R. and Birkinshaw, J. (2021) 'Strategizing in a digital world: Overcoming cognitive barriers, reconfiguring routines and introducing new organizational forms', *Long Range Planning*, 54 (5): article #102110.

Wenzel, M., Danner-Schröder, A. and Spee, A.P. (2021) 'Dynamic capabilities? Unleashing their dynamics through a practice perspective on organizational routines', *Journal of Management Inquiry*, 30 (4): 395–406.

# Endnotes (references)

1. Austen-Hardy, P. (2021) 'F1 prize money 2021 as Max Verstappen wins title after last-lap drama with Lewis Hamilton', *The Mirror,* December 12. www.mirror.co.uk/sport/formula-1/lewis-hamilton-max-verstappen-formula1-25679394 (accessed June 20, 2023); Ferrari (2022) 'Scuderia Ferrari official partners', *Ferrari.* www.ferrari.com/en-EN/formula1/partners (accessed June 20, 2023); Formula 1 (2021) 'Formula 1 announces TV and digital audience figures for 2020', February 8. www.formula1.com/en/latest/article.formula-1-announces-tv-and-digital-audience-figures-for-2020.3sbRmZm4u5Jf8pagvPoPUQ.html (accessed June 20, 2023); Kanal, S. (2019) 'How F1 technology has supercharged the world', *Formula 1,* November 7. www.formula1.com/en/latest/article.how-f1-technology-has-supercharged-the-world.6Gtk3hBxGyUGbNH0q8vDQK.html (accessed June 20, 2023). Mercedes AMG (2022) 'Our partners', www.mercedesamgf1.com/en/partners (accessed June 20, 2023); Red Bull (2022) 'Partners', *Red Bull.* www.redbullracing.com/int-en/partners (accessed June 20, 2023).

2. Bergmann-Lichtenstein, B.M.B. and Brush, C.G. (2001) 'How Do "resource bundles" develop and change in new ventures? A dynamic model and longitudinal exploration', *Entrepreneurship Theory and Practice*, 25 (3): 37–58; Teece, D.J., Pisano, G.P. and Shuen, A. (1997) 'Dynamic capabilities and strategic management', *Strategic Management Journal*, 18 (7): 509–33.

3. Kogut, B. and Zander, U. (1992) 'Knowledge of the firm, combinative capabilities, and the replication of technology', *Organization Science*, 3 (3): 383–97.

4. Sainato, M. (2022) 'Amazon could run out of workers in US in two years, internal memo suggests', *The Guardian*, June 22. www.theguardian.com/technology/2022/jun/22/amazon-workers-shortage-leaked-memo-warehouse (accessed July 26, 2023).

5. Hannan, M.T. and Freeman, J. (1984) 'Structural inertia and organizational change', *American Sociological Review*, 49 (2): 149–64.

6. Kor, Y.Y. and Mesko, A. (2013) 'Dynamic managerial capabilities: Configuration and orchestration of top executives' capabilities and the firm's dominant logic', *Strategic Management Journal*, 34 (2): 233–44.; Prahalad, C.K. (2004) 'The blinders of dominant logic', *Long Range Planning*, 37 (2): 171–9.

7. Feldman, M.S. and Pentland, B.T. (2003) 'Reconceptualizing organizational routines as a source of flexibility and change', *Administrative Science Quarterly*, 48 (1): 94–118.

8. Argote, L. and Greve, H.R. (2007) 'A Behavioral Theory of the Firm – 40 years and counting: Introduction and impact', *Organization Science*, 18 (3): 337–49; Gavetti, G., Greve, H.R., Levinthal, D.A. and Ocasio, W. (2012) 'The Behavioral Theory of the Firm: Assessment and prospects', *Academy of Management Annals*, 6 (1): 1–40.

9. Gilbert, C.G. (2005) 'Unbundling the structure of inertia: Resource versus routine rigidity', *Academy of Management Journal*, 48 (5): 741–63; Nelson, R.R. and Winter, S.G. (1982) 'The Schumpeterian tradeoff revisited', *The American Economic Review*, 72 (1): 114–32.

10. Feldman, E.R. (2021) 'The corporate parenting advantage, revisited', *Strategic Management Journal*, 42: 114–43.

11. Teece, D.J. (2007) 'Explicating dynamic capabilities: The nature and microfoundations of (sustainable) enterprise performance', *Strategic Management Journal*, 28 (13): 1319–50.

12. Eisenhardt, K.M. and Martin, J.A. (2000) 'Dynamic capabilities: What are they?', *Strategic Management Journal*, 21 (10–11): 1105–21; Grant, R.M. (1996) 'Toward a knowledge-based theory of the firm', *Strategic Management Journal*, 17 (S2): 109–22.

13. Eisenhardt, K.M. and Sull, D. (2001) 'Strategy as simple rules', *Harvard Business Review*, 79 (1): 106–19.

14. Helfat, C.E. and Lieberman, M.B. (2002) 'The birth of capabilities: Market entry and the importance of pre-history', *Industrial and Corporate Change*, 11 (4): 725–60.

15. Helfat, C.E. and Winter, S.G. (2011) 'Untangling dynamic and operational capabilities: Strategy for the (n)ever-changing world', *Strategic Management Journal*, 32 (11): 1243–50.

16. Salvato, C. and Rerup, C. (2011) 'Beyond collective entities: Multilevel research on organizational routines and capabilities', *Journal of Management*, 37 (2): 468–90.

17. Augier, M. and Teece, D.J. (2009) 'Dynamic capabilities and the role of managers in business strategy and economic performance', *Organization Science*, 20 (2): 410–21.

18. Porter, M.E. (1985) *Competitive Advantage: Creating and Sustaining Superior Performance*. New York, NY: The Free Press.

19. Acharyulu, G.V.R.K. and Shekbar, B.R. (2012) 'Role of value chain strategy in healthcare supply chain management: An empirical study in India', *International Journal of Management*, 29 (1): 91–7; Holweg, M. and Helo, P. (2014) 'Defining value chain architectures: Linking strategic value creation to operational supply chain design', *International Journal of Production Economics*, 147: 230–8; Mentzer, J.T., DeWitt, W., Keebler, J.S., Min, S., Nix, N.W., Smith, C.D. and Zacharia, Z.G. (2001) 'Defining supply chain management', *Journal of Business Logistics*, 22 (2): 1–25; Stevenson, M. and Spring, M. (2007) 'Flexibility from a supply chain perspective: Definition and review', *International Journal of Operations & Production Management*, 27 (7): 685–713; Walters, D. and Rainbird, M. (2004) 'The demand chain as an integral component of the value chain', *Journal of Consumer Marketing*, 21 (7): 465–75.

20. Porter (1985)

21. Porter, M.E. (1996) 'What is strategy?', *Harvard Business Review*, (Nov/Dec): 61–78.

22. Porter (1996)

23. Helfat C.E., Finkelstein S., Mitchell W., Peteraf M.A., Singh H., Teece D.J. and Winter S.G. (2007) *Dynamic Capabilities: Understanding Strategic Change in Organizations*. Malden, MA: Blackwell. p. 4.

24. Helfat and Winter (2011)

25. Ambrosini, V. and Bowman, C. (2009) 'What are dynamic capabilities and are they a useful construct in strategic management?', *International Journal of Management*

*Reviews*, 11 (1): 29–49; Helfat, C.E. and Peteraf, M.A. (2009) 'Understanding dynamic capabilities: Progress along a developmental path', *Strategic Organization*, 7 (1): 91–102.

26. Helfat, C.E. and Peteraf, M.A. (2003) 'The dynamic resource-based view: Capability lifecycles', *Strategic Management Journal*, 24 (10): 997–1010.

27. Zollo, M. and Winter, S.G. (2002) 'Deliberate learning and the evolution of dynamic capabilities', *Organization Science*, 13 (3): 339–51.

28. Ambrosini and Bowman (2009); Winter, S.G. (2003) 'Understanding dynamic capabilities', *Strategic Management Journal*, 24 (10): 991–5.

29. Felin, T. and Powell, T.C. (2016) 'Designing organizations for dynamic capabilities', *California Management Review*, 58 (4): 78–96.

30. Bartram, D., Robertson, I.T. and Callinan, M. (2002) 'Introduction: A framework for examining organizational effectiveness', in I.T. Robertson, D. Bartram and M. Callinan (eds), *Organizational Effectiveness: The Role of Psychology*. Chichester: Wiley, 1–10.

31. Hamel, G. and Prahalad, C.K. (1994) 'Competing for the future', *Harvard Business Review*, 72 (4): 122–8.

32. Hamel, G. and Pralahad, C.K. (1990) 'Strategic intent', *McKinsey Quarterly*, 1: 36–61.

33. Tushman, M.L. and Anderson, P. (1986) 'Technological discontinuities and organizational environments', *Administrative Science Quarterly*, 31 (3): 439–65.

34. Leonard-Barton, D. (1992) 'Core capabilities and core rigidities: A paradox in managing new product development', *Strategic Management Journal*, 13 (S1): 111–25.

35. Barney, J.B. (1995) 'Looking inside for competitive advantage', *Academy of Management Executive*, 9(4): 49–61; Barney, J.B. (1991) 'Firm resources and sustained competitive advantage', *Journal of Management*, 17: 99–120.

36. Barney, J.B. and Hesterly, W.S. (2010) 'VRIO framework', in J.B. Barney and W.S. Hesterly (eds), *Strategic Management and Competitive Advantage*. Hoboken, NJ: Pearson, 68–86.

37. Winter (2003)

38. ING (2021) 'ING closes Russia's largest-yet sustainability-linked loan', *ING*. www.ingwb.com/en/insights/news/ing-closes-russias-largest-yet-sustainability-linked-loan (accessed June 20, 2022); ING (2022a) 'ING wholesale banking in Russia', *ING*. www.ingwb.com/en/network/emea/russia (accessed June 20, 2022); ING (2022b) 'ING stands with the people of Ukraine', *ING*. www.ing.com/Newsroom/News/ING-stands-with-the-people-of-Ukraine.htm (accessed June 20, 2022); ING (2022c) 'Values', *ING*. www.ing.com/About-us/Profile/Values.htm (accessed June 20, 2022); Za, V. (2022) 'Explainer: Global banks count cost of Russia exposure', *Reuters*, March 18. www.reuters.com/markets/stocks/which-banks-europe-are-exposed-russia-2022-02-28 (accessed June 20, 2023).

## Acknowledgements

The authors thank Emre Karali for his contribution to this chapter.

## Key terms

**Ad hoc problem solving** – a category of change behaviours that are largely non-repetitious, not highly patterned though intendedly rational

**Capability** – a firm's capacity to deploy resources for a desired end result

**Competencies** – a set of behaviours instrumental in the delivery of desired results

**Core competencies** – elements of behaviour that are imperative for nearly all organizational members to possess and indicate what makes a firm more successful than its competitors

**Dynamic capability** – a firm's capacity to create, extend and modify organizational resources in a repeatable, satisfactory, purposeful and reliable manner

**Intangible resources** – less visible assets that are deeply rooted in a firm's history, have accumulated over time, and are rather difficult for competitors to analyze and imitate

**Resources of the firm** – productive assets that are tied into a firm in a relatively permanent fashion, acting as inputs for its production processes

**Routine** – a pattern of actions, involving multiple actors, that is repetitive and recognizable

**Tangible resources** – assets that can be observed, quantified and may be traded

**Value chain** – a sequential chain of a firm's main value creating activities, consisting of various primary activities and support activities

# 9

# ECOSYSTEMS AND PLATFORMS

## LEARNING OBJECTIVES

After reading this chapter, you should be able to:

- distinguish an ecosystem from other types of value systems and point out its characteristics;
- indicate the difference between generic and nongeneric, unique and supermodular, and uni- and bi-directional complementarities;
- identify whether a particular ecosystem has a central platform and assess the type of platform;
- indicate different ways in which platform owners can kickstart the growth of their platform;
- describe how ecosystems in general and platform-centred ecosystems in particular are typically governed.

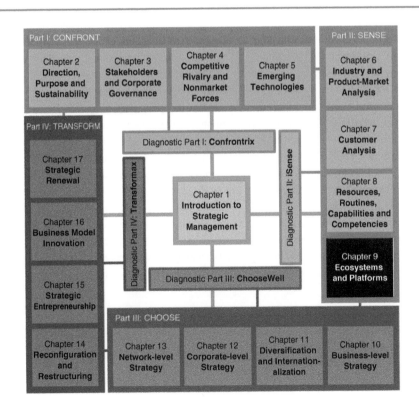

## OPENING CASE

Source: © slyellow (2019) / Shutterstock.

### PayPay: Japan's leading QR code payment application[1]

While in many Western countries a QR code is mainly used to conveniently open lengthy website links, in some other parts of the world, including Japan, people and firms use QR codes for e-payments through applications. The Japanese firm PayPay (not to be confused with PayPal), established in 2018 through a joint venture between SoftBank Corporation and Yahoo Japan, was one of the first to enter this market. PayPay simply provides an alternative way of settling payments to businesses – primarily retail stores – and customers, addressing the needs of these two groups through its platform. Stores have an individualized QR code displayed on their cash register that customers can scan with their smartphone before moving on to manually entering the amount to be paid. The cashier receives a confirmation notification on their app or alternatively just cross-checks by looking at the customer's phone once payment completion is confirmed.

Coinciding with PayPay's launch in 2018, Japan raised consumption tax from 8 to 10% but exempted cashless transactions from the higher rate for eight months. PayPay, already rewarding users with up to 1% of transaction value through cashback rewards, could therefore advertise a 3% discount granted in PayPay balance towards future purchases. Merchants were also incentivized by maintaining low margins on commissions. During repeated campaigns, new members would also enjoy an additional percentage of cashback.

Approximately 95% of PayPay's revenue originates from a single functionality: the e-payment function, of which it keeps a commission similar to credit cards' revenue models. More recently, PayPay added other services, such as savings plans that allow users to put cashback into a fund that can earn additional interest, and further financial services, such as transferring money across user accounts or offering securities investments. PayPay also partners with other services, such as Uber Eats, allowing users that order through the PayPay app to get an additional cashback percentage. One of the latest features added was the ability to scan and pay for utility bills.

PayPay has appealed to Japanese customer preferences, while differentiating themselves from competitors in several ways. One of these ways is that PayPay is free for every customer – as opposed to credit cards, which typically charge an annual membership fee. Furthermore, PayPay shows to its users the amount of cashback earned right after every purchase and lists the day of payout. Also worth mentioning is its step-up program: when reaching different thresholds, the amount of cashback for every purchase increases.

Competition for PayPay, Japan's current market leader in QR code payments, exists on two levels: from within the QR payment industry and from outside. PayPay's main competitors are outside the QR payment industry, namely cash payments, credit cards, debit cards, and smart cards (prepaid-like chargeable cards in credit-card format). QR code payment firms have disrupted the market and have grown fast in Japan. At the end of 2021, the number of cumulative registered PayPay users reached nearly 47 million and the number of payments was 3.6 billion. PayPay's rise from zero to becoming a major player shows how volatile the market is and, moreover, that the threat of new entrants from other payment services is high.

### Questions

1. What are the main two sides of PayPay's platform? What other sides were added later?
2. What is the value proposition of PayPay for each side of its platform? What subsidization and discount strategies were used by the platform to get both sides on board?
3. Who are PayPay's main rivals, and how does PayPay compete with these rivals? Which of these rivals can be considered as competing platforms?

# Introduction

Up until this point, we have mainly focused on how firms strive to achieve and sustain (at least temporarily) a competitive advantage over players that operate in the same industry and that compete for similar resources and customers (Chapter 6). We discussed how firms can realize this by providing superior value to customers through, for instance, product leadership, operational excellence or customer intimacy (Chapter 7). We elaborated on firms' internal value chain, made up of primary and secondary value chain activities, as a basis for materializing customer value propositions (Chapter 8). However, we have not explicitly considered any interdependencies with external entities that may in fact underlie these value propositions. How to describe the successes of firms such as Alibaba, Meta, PayPay, and Uber, which all play a leading role in multilateral value systems wherein different entities are bound together through interdependencies? For this, insights derived from the previous three chapters are insufficient.

The opening case illustrates how technology has created a new way of coordinating and competing in the marketplace. Complex, multilateral systems of interdependent firms have emerged where coordination may take place without turning to any contracts. For instance, convenience stores have affiliated themselves with PayPay's infrastructure without PayPay's active involvement, creating value for these stores, for part of their customers (those who fancy using QR codes for payments) and for PayPay. Such an interdependent, multilateral value system is known as an ecosystem, as discussed in more detail next. Interactions between stores, their customers and PayPay, in this particular QR payment ecosystem, are facilitated through the exchange of data on the PayPay platform, allowing for personalization, rewards and other benefits. This illustrates that platforms can be central to value creation and value capturing in ecosystems. In this chapter, we first discuss ecosystems and then elaborate on platforms and platform-centred ecosystems.

# Ecosystems

As of 2022, seven of the ten biggest firms in the world are hubs in ecosystems.[2] In short, an **ecosystem** denotes a multilateral set of entities whose interactions contribute to joint value creation. These entities depend on one another as a group to enhance their performance over time and to survive and thrive. As we will clarify further below, this implies *nongeneric complementarities*.[3] Understanding how value is created and captured within ecosystems has become a vital piece of knowledge for strategic management in the 21st century.

In the business context, the ecosystem concept first appeared in a 1993 article, *Predators and Prey: A New Ecology of Competition*, by James Moore.[4] As hinted by the article's title, this concept is derived from biology, which distinguishes between biotic (living) and abiotic (nonliving) environments. The biotic environment encompasses organisms, such as animals, plants, algae, fungi and bacteria. The abiotic environment includes factors such as air, minerals, soil, sunlight, and water. A biological ecosystem denotes a community of organisms whose interactions with one another and with their abiotic environment result in cyclic interchanges of matter and energy.[5] These interactions include both feeding interactions (organisms feeding on other organisms) and non-feeding interactions (e.g., providing shelter and competing for food, space, and sunlight). The organisms within an ecosystem, such as a coral reef or rainforest, depend on one another – either directly or indirectly – for obtaining energy and other resources required for their survival and growth. Accordingly, as with the business equivalent of an ecosystem, the entities in a biological ecosystem reciprocally affect each other's evolution, which depends partly on their capability to be flexible and adaptable.

## Ecosystems as a distinct value system

Switching back again to the business context, ecosystems can be perceived as a distinct type of value system.[6] A *value system* is the economic perspective through which we view the process of creating and capturing value. At least three types of value systems can be distinguished besides ecosystems: market-based value systems, integrated value systems, and supplier-mediated value systems (see Figure 9.1). By first briefly examining these other value systems, the notion of an ecosystem-based value system can be grasped more clearly.

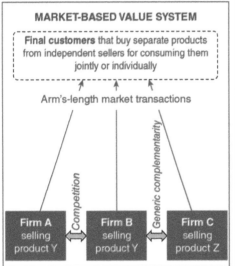

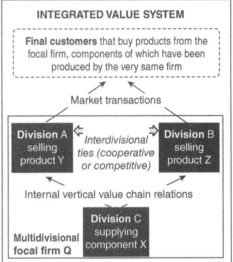

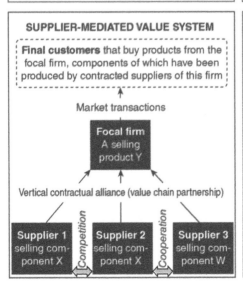

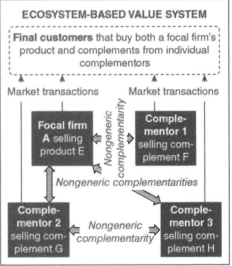

**FIGURE 9.1**    Ecosystems versus alternative types of value systems

Source: Authors, adapted from Jacobides et al. (2018)

A <u>market-based value system</u> implies direct arm's-length market transactions between buyers and sellers of goods or services. These entities at both sides of the market are unrelated and unaffiliated and act independently. The sellers compete for the same buyers (e.g., by all selling variations of tea bags) or they offer complementary products (e.g., tea bags and teacups) that can be created without any coordination between them. You may think of a street market where people buy fish, fruit, vegetables, herbs, and other types of products from merchants that sell these products from small market stalls.

An <u>integrated value system</u> implies economic transactions that take place under the same corporate umbrella. This means that these transactions take between divisions, business units, or subsidiaries that have the same corporate parent (see Chapter 12). For instance, the forest division of the Finland-based multinational firm Stora Enso supplies wood raw material that is used for its packaging materials, processed wood, paper, and biomaterial divisions.[7]

A <u>supplier-mediated value system</u> (also known as a *linear* or *hierarchical buyer-supplier network*) implies that activities in different stages of an industry's value chain are carried out by different firms that are engaged in bilateral contracts. For example, to produce a bicycle, a rubber manufacturer supplies a tire manufacturer with rubber. The tire manufacturer subsequently provides tires to a bicycle manufacturer, which sells the bikes to a retailer that will sell them to customers. Together, these firms form a linear chain enforced through buyer-supplier contracts that result in a single end product: a bicycle. A firm that is positioned downstream of the value chain, whose activities are closer to the final customer, dictates to upstream suppliers what to produce.

Because of the presence of hierarchical linkages in integrated value systems and supplier-mediated value systems, both value systems have been referred to as *hierarchy-based value systems*.[8]

Market-based value systems and hierarchy-based value systems have dominated the economy in the past. However, the competitive landscape has fundamentally changed in the last few decades. Earlier strategic perspectives on gaining competitive advantage that focused on things like supply chain control, operational excellence, economies of scale, contracts, and the market mechanism cannot fully explain the reality of an increasingly digitalized economy. For instance, Apple's iPhone gobbled up a large share of the smartphone market in the 2010s at the expense of LG, Nokia, Motorola, Samsung, and Sony Ericsson, which back in 2007 collectively controlled around 90% of the industry's global profits.[9] Apple, and firms such as PayPay, did not play by the traditional rules of the strategy game. Instead, their competitive successes can be traced back to the way they managed and capitalized ecosystems. Although market- and hierarchy-based value systems remain in existence, ecosystems are becoming increasingly prominent. This growing relevance has been largely the result of a combination of advances in communication technology and digitalization (see Chapter 5), changes in regulatory systems that opened various product markets to a larger number of firms, and – catalyzed by these developments – the blurring of traditional industry boundaries (see Chapter 4).

In contrast to supplier-mediated value systems or integrated value systems, ecosystems do not rely on a linear chain of value-adding activities. Instead, they are characterized by a structure of multilateral, value-creating interactions among interdependent firms or other entities.[10] These interactions, which typically extend beyond industry boundaries,[11] frequently are of a loose and informal nature, as opposed to contractual agreements found in traditional buyer-supplier networks. For instance, PayPay does not have bespoke partnership contracts with each independent convenience store. Instead, PayPay and the stores interdependently work together without formal partnerships. The set of interactions is not two-dimensional – for instance, in the case of PayPay, connectivity providers such as telecom operators play a role in enabling QR-based transactions. Whereas strategic alliances between firms that are part of the same ecosystem are not uncommon,[12] they are not a prerequisite for ecosystem affiliation.

To more fully grasp the structure of an ecosystem-based value system, we need to turn to the notions of modularity and (nongeneric) complementarity, as discussed next.

## Modularity

In most known cases of ecosystems, value creation was enabled by a modular architecture, which allows firms to rely on each other while retaining high levels of autonomy.[13] In general, the term *modularity* indicates the extent to which the components of a particular system, such as a value system, can be separated and recombined.[14] In the case of a **modular architecture**, there are certain 'rules' (i.e., the rules of the system architecture) in place, which may include predefined protocols and standards, that enable the separation, matching and mixing of these components along a production chain.[15] You could think about LEGO bricks, which can be combined and recombined because of their standardized interfaces.

The existence of a modular architecture means that activities or products of multiple producers can be interconnected in predefined ways without the need for customized contractual agreements among these producers. For example, software developers are able to create smartphone applications for Android phones without coordinating the development with producers of these phones. Modularity in ecosystems also provides a unique opportunity for customers, as they can choose which modular components to use.[16] When mobile phones first emerged, the manufacturer decided which applications were available on a phone. Today, users can decide which smartphone and software to combine. The value of an iPhone is not only based on the device, but also on all the third-party applications that you can install on it.

## Complementarity

So far, we have argued that ecosystems comprise multilateral, interdependent interactions among actors that contribute to joint value creation, usually enabled by a modular architecture. However, such an architecture may also be missing, as is the case in, for instance, many industrial ecosystems (communities of players whose interactions result in circulating stocks of raw materials and energy used in production processes, e.g., the Rotterdam chlorine and derivatives cluster – see Chapter 13). Therefore, what can possibly define the scope of an ecosystem? The answer is nongeneric complementarities.

**Complementarity** is when a certain product (in the form of either a good or a service), activity or asset improves or enables the value of another product, activity or asset, or when two or more products, activities or assets improve or enable each other's value.[17] These *complementary* products, activities or assets – such as iPhone applications and the iPhone device – are commonly called *complements*; the firms that provide them to mutual customers are known as *complementors*.[18] Complementors can be of great importance for the success of firms like Apple, however, traditional supply chain thinking ignores complementors that are not linked directly to the supply chain of a focal firm.[19]

Any ecosystem can be seen as a set of complementors. Yet, a certain group of complementors does not necessarily form an ecosystem. Consider manufacturers of trashcans and garbage bags – can we truly say that a trashcan manufacturer and a garbage bag producer form an ecosystem because they sell complementary goods? The answer is 'no', because the complementarity between an ordinary trashcan and garbage bag is of a generic nature. This means that, as with our prior example of tea bags and teacups, these complements can be produced and used independently from each other. *Generic complementarity* refers to when complements that are offered by different firms to mutual customers can be created without any coordination among these firms in specific ways, or without following a standard within a modular architecture.[20] Customers combine these complements, which they buy separately in the market, on their own. There is no specific alignment or collaborative structure between producers of generic complements. Therefore, these complements can be disregarded when defining an ecosystem; **nongeneric complementarity**, or complementarity of a nongeneric nature, is the central determinant of what constitutes an ecosystem.[21] Hence, in a business context, an ecosystem can be defined as 'a set of actors with varying degrees of multilateral, *non*generic complementarities that are not fully hierarchically controlled'.[22] Nongeneric complementarity entails a certain extent of customization.

In an effort to improve their competitiveness, firms can come up with a strategy to turn generic complementarities into nongeneric ones. A case in point is Nestlé Nespresso S.A., an autonomous globally managed division of the Switzerland-based Nestlé Group that was able to make substantial profits by putting its coffee into capsules and by encouraging the design and sale of customized coffee machines, produced by other firms such as Krups, De'Longhi, Magimix, and Sage, that only run on these capsules. The capsules and these coffee machines were heavily branded, with actor George Clooney as 'brand ambassador', contributing to a commercial success story. A 'Nespresso ecosystem' had emerged, made of different complementors all vested in this success.[23]

There are two main categories of nongeneric complementarity: unique and supermodular complementarity.[24] Strictly speaking, **unique complementarity** refers to when a product, activity or asset does not function or is unproductive without another product, activity or asset and thus should be compatible – for instance, a key must be produced in coordination with its lock.[25] Firms producing these complements need to coordinate their production or, at least, follow a standard within a modular architecture. Unique complementarity can also refer to when a particular product, activity or asset functions well only when another product, activity or asset is customized, or when the sum of the value of two or more products, activities or assets is maximized when used together.[26] It can be argued that a trashcan and garbage bag are generally more valuable for buyers when used together compared to using one without the other, however this complementarity is of a generic nature (unless the producers would follow the example of Nespresso). Unique complementarity can be either unidirectional (meaning that a product, activity or asset requires another product, activity or asset, but not the other way around) or bidirectional. Bidirectional unique complementarity that is nongeneric implies co-specialization.[27]

Nongeneric complementarities can also take the form of **supermodular complementarity**, which can be found in both production and consumption sides. In a production context, it refers to when an increased availability (in volume) of a complement or an increased variety of complements leads to a higher production volume or a greater performance of another complement, or when it yields lower costs or higher returns than the sum of costs or returns of the individual complements.[28] In a consumption context, supermodular complementarity refers to when an increased demand for a complement or an increased variety of complements increases the customer-perceived value of other complements. Supermodular complementarity can be uni- or bidirectional. Either way, it implies that an ecosystem's total value is greater than the aggregate value of all ecosystem complements. Put differently, the complementarity between products, activities or assets creates value above and beyond the sum of the individual value of these complements.[29] An example of supermodular complementarity is the relation between a video game console and video games: when there is a broader array of available video games, the value of the console also increases in the customer's eyes. Here, note that in the other direction also another type of complementarity is occurring; video games have a unique complementarity towards consoles as they cannot be used without the console. This example shows that unique and supermodular complementarities may co-exist.

## Ecosystem emergence and governance

Ecosystems are typically the result of deliberate experimentation and engineering involving different parties.[30] After all, the primary prerequisite of an ecosystem is the modularization of the various parts of the ecosystem. Regularly, firms consciously opt for making their product modular by ensuring that they are compatible with other products through standards and protocols. For example, many software firms modularize their products by creating an *application programming interface (API)*, a standardized way other software can interact with a firm's software product. The most common use of APIs is providing an interface for a data-driven service that allows third parties to display that service's data (for instance, a Flickr photo stream) in a proprietary app. Once firms introduce modularization, designing and engineering an ecosystem becomes possible. Ecosystem design and management are an emerging art whereby firms strategize how to maximize their value capture within the ecosystem structure.[31] While ecosystems do not form spontaneously and require firms to enable them, they do not always emerge deliberately. For example, the makers of inkjet printers accidentally created an ecosystem around their printers by modularizing the ink cartridge. Subsequently, an ecosystem emerged when unauthorized producers started selling these standardized ink cartridges.

Once an ecosystem has emerged, how is it then governed? As elaborated earlier in this chapter, an ecosystem is not a hierarchy-based value system whereby there is unilateral hierarchical control by one party and all parties either have the same corporate parent or have contractual relations. Yet, ecosystems often display a certain degree of control. Most ecosystems have what is usually referred to as a *hub* or *hub firm* (or *hub organization*), *keystone actor* or *ecosystem leader*[32], which denotes a firm (or other type of organization) with an outsized influence on the ecosystem. This hub organization tends to leverage its key position to exert its will over other organizations (its 'followers') in this ecosystem. PayPay is an example of an ecosystem hub, whereas convenience stores are mere ecosystem participants. A hub determines the governance rules, the vision of structures, and the roles that others in the ecosystem fill, and enforces the governance rules to the extent it can. For example, you need a paid developer membership to deploy apps to iPhones, and you can only do so through the AppStore or Corporate programme, and apps and their features (such as access to users' data) have to be approved by Apple. Breaking the rules of this hub firm in the iOS ecosystem will lead to developer privileges being revoked. The hub generally sets the protocols, rules, and standards that give shape to an ecosystem's modular architecture. Further, through its position, a hub usually captures the lion's share of the profits in an ecosystem. Its followers agree to the terms of the hub and cede the leadership role. It is difficult to predict which ecosystem player will become the hub, yet traditional metrics such as an organization's size, capital reserves, and capabilities can play an important role in defining the ecosystem leadership.

Even when a powerful hub exists in an ecosystem, this hub lacks a strong hierarchical control as present in hierarchy-based value systems. Apple, with its proprietary iOS operating system, may have substantial control over the iOS ecosystem, yet it lacks hierarchical control over app developers. Apple may set the standards and rules, yet it has no control over parties outside the setting of the protocols under which they collaborate. All members of an ecosystem retain residual control and claims over their assets, with no other party being able to set the terms of their prices or supply. Ecosystems are thus not held together primarily by hierarchical control. Instead, it is co-specialization that holds ecosystem actors together.[33] Interdependencies between ecosystem actors emerge when they enter an ecosystem. It requires an investment to enter the ecosystem, as standards and protocols must be aligned. Complements that a product needs to be compatible with are not fully fungible – meaning that the firm would have to retool this product when it switches to another ecosystem or a standalone system. Because of this, a lock-in effect emerges whereby firms have a direct financial incentive to remain in an ecosystem once they have joined it. Firms tend to leave a certain ecosystem only when the benefits of doing so exceed the associated redeployment costs, as they will have to recoup these costs.

## Competition in and between ecosystems

When it comes to capturing value, competition has always been the name of the game. Much theory on competition that originates from studies conducted in earlier decades remains relevant in an ecosystem context. One of the aspects that has changed most is that competition is no longer defined by industry boundaries: All firms that provide the same interchangeable item in an ecosystem structure are competing with one another. For instance, in the electric vehicle ecosystem, roadside recharging stations compete with household chargers, garage chargers, built-in solar panels on vehicles, and any other source that could recharge an electric vehicle. Industry boundaries have faded in this context. Ecosystems also bring a whole new dimension of competition: Competitiveness no longer exists solely on an interfirm level but now also on an ecosystem level. A firm that takes part in an ecosystem competes against other participants in this ecosystem that can replace its product in the ecosystem and, on top of that, may also have to compete against entire conglomerations of firms that form rival ecosystems.[34] For example, a fitness app developer for iOS competes against other iOS fitness apps *and* against different ecosystems, such as the Android ecosystem (which is dominated by Google). Wearable fitness trackers (such as Fitbit devices) may have apps for both iOS and Android that provide features and functionalities that go beyond what typical fitness apps on these platforms can offer.

A central consideration in examining ecosystem competitiveness is the presence of bottlenecks. *Bottlenecks* are those complements whose performance, cost or scarcity constrain the competitiveness of the entire ecosystem of which they are part.[35] For example, the electric vehicle ecosystem has had various bottlenecks that have constrained its growth over time, such as battery supply and performance constraints and a global shortage in computer chips. The understanding that ecosystem bottlenecks define the competitiveness of a whole ecosystem makes it an essential aspect of ecosystem strategy.[36] Bottlenecks also exist within a traditional supply chain, yet interdependence and the lack of strong hierarchical control makes the issue particularly problematic in ecosystems. Limiting exposure to bottlenecks and resolving existing bottlenecks is therefore an important strategic consideration. Here, approaches such as vertical integration, strategic alliances, and R&D investments may play a role.[37]

## CRACK-THE-CASE

### The accelerating electric mobility ecosystem[38]

The ongoing digitalization of the economy has caused various traditional industry boundaries to fade and set off a wholesale reshuffling of businesses in new competitive structures. The automotive sector, one of the largest sectors of the 20th century, is amidst such transformation. This sector, alongside other sectors such as energy and IT, plays a central role in the nascent electric mobility (or e-mobility) ecosystem (see Figure 9.2). Legacy car manufacturers such as BMW and Volkswagen have faced two major strategic conundrums in the years since e-mobility took off. First, there has been a shift in focal value proposition from internal combustion engine cars to electrified computers on wheels – in other words, the propulsion has shifted to electric, and the most critical components have moved from physical vehicle parts to software. Second, the emergence of an ecosystem structure has blurred industry lines and opened competition along new dimensions. To summarize these challenges, specified further below, car manufacturers are simultaneously tasked with navigating a new value proposition and a shifting competitive structure.

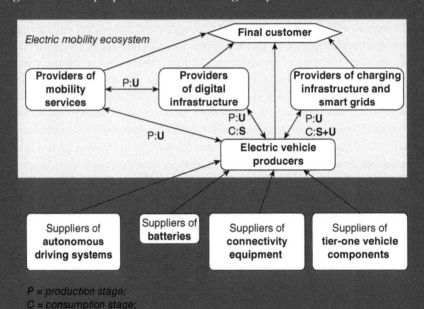

P = production stage;
C = consumption stage;
U = unique complementarity;
S = supermodular complementarity

**FIGURE 9.2**   The e-mobility ecosystem

Source: Goodman et al. (2022)

In the internal combustion engine era, car manufacturers were the primary party who could capitalize on the car value proposition. But will they continue to be in this position? One may look at the computer industry for clues. In the late 20th century, computer manufacturers controlled the markets and took significant profits, however, this shifted when ecosystems started to emerge. Today, the profits in the computer industry are primarily captured by software firms as opposed to computer manufacturers. Legacy car manufacturers have sounded alarm bells regarding their software capabilities. They are highly skilled at producing cars yet have a troubling track record for software development. This has opened the door for firms like Google and Apple to develop software systems that control vehicles. Here, there is a strategic concern. Namely, suppose the controlling position in the industry shifts from producing parts to producing software. This may allow Google and Apple to capture more profit in the mobility ecosystem and leave car manufacturers with empty hands. To counter this, car manufacturers are rapidly investing in software development capabilities and hiring tech talent from established technology firms.

As a gradual shift is taking place from selling cars for individual customers to offering mobility services (which also includes, for instance, ridehailing and car-, moto- or scooter-sharing), catalyzed by increasing digitalization, the boundaries between different mobility solutions fade. To address this, various car manufacturers, such as Ford, increasingly invest in other mobility solutions and have rebranded themselves from car manufacturers to mobility providers. Another milestone in the transition from purchasing mobility products to using mobility services will be the advent of autonomous vehicles, which is set to significantly reduce the cost of taxi services and thereby reduce the appeal of owning and driving a vehicle. Recognizing this threat, car manufacturers are investing heavily in autonomous driving technology, understanding that if they do not, they may be obliterated when competitors develop the technology to a production-level quality.

These two conundrums highlight some of the concerns facing car manufacturers as their business model undergoes unprecedented change. The shift to electric mobility has proven swift and will likely continue to unsettle those active in the mobility ecosystem as progress accelerates.

## Questions

1. The case illustrates that the party who captures most of the profits in an industry can shift from, for example, the car manufacturers to the software developers. What are the causes behind such shift?
2. Who do you believe will be able to appropriate the biggest slice of profit in the autonomous vehicles market? Will it be the car manufacturers, the firms developing the software, or the fleet operators?

## Platforms

Many ecosystems, including the one in which PayPay is the hub, are organized around a central platform that serves as the principal foundation for firms to offer complements.[39] A **platform** comprises an architecture and a set of rules that together enable or facilitate direct interactions between at least two different user groups that are affiliated through the platform (by making use of the platform). Most often, these user groups are platform complementors, who produce products that are offered on the platform, and customers, who buy the platform's offerings, each being at one side of the platform. Although we use the term 'customers' here, the term 'consumers' (users of the offerings) can be equally or more applicable in this context. It may also be the case that the two user groups are complementors and other firms – for instance, there are many business-oriented platform where business entities, and not individuals, are the customers. The user groups could also be customers and different types of complementors, implying more than two user groups – for instance, in a food delivery platform, restaurants and food deliverers are separate complementors that are both required for food delivery to function. Most platforms are embodied as an asset (such as system software or a shopping mall) or a product (such as a printed newspaper or a digital app), but that is not necessarily always the case.

When you use Uber's ridehailing app to get a ride back home, you are in fact directly transacting with a driver while you and the driver are affiliated with the platform. Printed and digital newspapers connect subscribers and advertisers. Shopping malls link merchants and shoppers. And Uber Eats and Just Eat Takeaway.com, two globally operating food delivery marketplaces, connect restaurants and customers. In these and many other instances, platforms help with reducing costs in creating matches between sides, searching for the right product, person, or knowledge, and easily transacting between sides through a set of standardized rules. Due to these 'sides', a platform is also known as a *two-sided* or *multi-sided market* (with the adjective 'multi' often meaning two or more). The different sides of the platform, including complementors and customers (or consumers) that use the platform, collectively form the market or 'network' of the platform.

Many platforms play a central role in how value is created and captured in an ecosystem, in which case we speak about a **platform-centred ecosystem** (or *platform-based ecosystem*). A *complement* in this context is a product, activity or asset that enhances the value users get from using the platform. The entity that owns the platform in a platform-centered ecosystem is usually the hub of that ecosystem. This platform owner sets the platform governance rules and controls the platform's intellectual property. The platform owner may also provide (part of) the digital and/or physical infrastructure that enables the interactions among platform users. Furthermore, in most platform-centred ecosystems there are interface providers that do not own the platform (e.g., a firm such as Samsung that provides devices for the Android platform).

Hence, as depicted in Figure 9.3, there are four types of roles that each player in a platform-centred ecosystem can fill: platform owner, interface provider, producer (i.e., a platform user that creates offerings within that platform), and customer/consumer (i.e., a platform user that buys/consumes these offerings).[40] Each player can fulfill multiple roles and may shift roles rapidly.

At first sight, it may seem that e-commerce platforms such as Airbnb and eBay are not ecosystems. After all, these particular platforms facilitate direct transactions between buyers and independent sellers, with the value being created by the transactions themselves.[41] Airbnb and eBay are essentially online marketplaces that involve the renting of property to travelers and the auction and sale of items, respectively, which can be seen as arm's-length market transactions. Both platforms create and capture value by fulfilling an intermediary

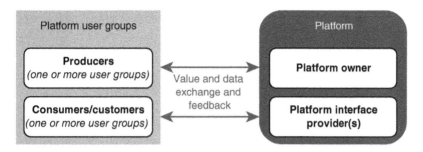

**FIGURE 9.3**  Types of players in a platform-centred ecosystem

Source: adapted from Van Alstyne et al. (2016)

function in what may – because of these arm's-length market transactions – look like a market-based value system. However, in contrast to a market-based value system, the creation of this value depends to at least some extent on the creation of a specific structure of alignment with complementors (such as property owners on Airbnb). Put differently, sellers on these platforms need to make some co-specialized investments with these platforms, and vice versa, which implies nongeneric complementarities. The APIs of Airbnb and eBay facilitate interactions with the complementors. Thus, Airbnb and eBay are firms that each have a multisided platform (carrying their name) that sustains an ecosystem with respectively Airbnb and eBay at its core.

## Types of platforms

As some of our prior examples show, platforms are not a new phenomenon – for instance, printed newspapers have been around for quite a long time. What has changed in the last few decades is that IT-enabled platforms have become increasingly ubiquitous.[42] You are now most likely using a platform daily. Broadly speaking, we can distinguish three types of platforms: transaction platforms, innovation platforms, and hybrid platforms.[43]

Transaction platforms are intermediaries for the direct exchange of a given transaction. Two examples are Uber with riders and drivers, and Twitter where people produce content, and another group of people consume this content. Innovation platforms are technological foundations upon which others develop their complementary products or innovations. It is important to keep in mind this is not an 'either-or' classification; many platforms can have different degrees of traits of either type of platform – and particularly, can be a real hybrid platform where both transaction and innovation platform characteristics are observed. All major gaming consoles (as well as smartphones), for instance, are innovation platforms for which complementary products are developed (such as video games for gaming consoles) but also have their own digital marketplace where users can buy those games (so that the platform acts as an intermediary between the game publishers that sell games and users that buy those games). It is important to identify which type of platform you are dealing with since this determines how to manage the users and complementors on a platform. An innovation platform, for example, needs to be managed in such a way as to allow complementors to develop high-quality complementary products easily for the platform so that customers will value the platform more.

## Platforms versus pipeline businesses

Platforms embody and drive substantial changes in the competitive environment, contributing to the blurring of prior industry boundaries (as discussed in Chapter 4). For instance, Airbnb and Uber have become a force of their own competing with hotels and taxi operators respectively. In the heart of the competitive advantages wielded by firms such as Airbnb and Uber lies the power of platform businesses in comparison with conventional 'pipeline' businesses that have dominated economic society for a long time.[44] A **pipeline business** (as opposed to a platform business) denotes a category of firms that create value by controlling a linear series of activities in a value chain (see Chapter 8).[45] This linear value chain resembles a pipeline, with one or more (vertically related) producers at one end (upstream) and consumers at the other end (downstream). In contrast, a **platform business** creates value by facilitating direct, value-creating interactions among a platform's user groups, which are usually producers and consumers (see Table 9.1). The platform owner sets the standardized governance rules to which these users are bound, and besides may provide the infrastructure for their interactions.

**TABLE 9.1**   Pipeline versus platform business

| Pipeline business | Platform business |
|---|---|
| • Selling products and services to consumers<br>• Value is created upstream<br>• Products have inherent value<br>• Value comes from owning one side of transaction<br>• Focus is solely on converting shoppers into buyers | • Facilitating transactions between multiple parties<br>• Value is co-created on the spot<br>• Platforms create network value<br>• Value comes from owning infrastructure that facilitates transaction<br>• Focus is on attracting both producers and consumers |

Source: Van Alstyne et al. (2016)

Compared to firms that run a pipeline business, such as Nokia back in the day, platform owners are not interested in developing each constituent of a product system (such as developing all the apps as well as the phone), but rather leave the development of complements that can enhance the value of the 'core' of the platform, or at least the majority of these complements, to other actors. For each entry in a traditional encyclopedia, an expert needs to provide content, which then will be carefully edited, curated, and then sold as a product on the market – clearly a pipeline business. Compare this stand-alone product with Wikipedia, a multilingual online encyclopedia launched in 2001, where a community of thousands of volunteers collaborate to create articles on every imaginable topic, and which comes with real-time updates and new topics as events transpire. The curation and fact-checking are done by the same group of people. Wikipedia's articles are the complements to the Wikipedia platform, and the individuals contributing to these articles are the complementors. There is simply little means for a firm to internally produce the same amount of content, given the costs involved and low willingness among potential readers to pay for a general-purpose encyclopedia, given the existence of a freely accessible Wikipedia. Overall, digital platform businesses benefit from several advantages against pipeline businesses and their stand-alone products: (1) reduction of search, matching, monitoring, and transaction costs; (2) leveraging external – and generally underutilized – resources; and (3) rapidly scaling up through less resource needs.[46] These advantages are particularly enabled by the existence of indirect and direct network effects, on which we zoom in next.

## Network effects

A relatively novel thing about platforms is that they can leverage network externality effects – in particular, indirect network effects, in addition to direct network effects, to drive fast adoption and scaling up. **Direct network effects** (also known as *same-side network effects*) occur when an increase in the number of users (usually consumers or producers) at one side of the platform enhances the value that the same group of users derives from their affiliation to the platform (see Figure 9.4). Direct network effects are not exclusive to platforms – telephones, for instance, increased in value over time as more and more people adopted them and hence could be reached by them. **Indirect network effects** (also known as *cross-side network effects*) occur when an increase in the number of users at one side of the platform (such as gamers, riders, or newspaper readers) enhances the value that users at another side of the platform (such as game developers, drivers, or advertisers) derive from this platform (see again Figure 9.4). In other words, as more people or business entities from one group join the platform, the other group (or, when there are three or even more platform sides, one or more of the other groups) perceives a higher value from using the platform. These indirect effects are what sets a platform apart from non-platform entities that benefit from direct network effects.[47] A classic example to illustrate indirect network effects is a video game console such as PlayStation 5: the more games become available for this console, the more it will be valuable for consumers, and the more consumers (gamers) will buy the console (so there will be a higher 'installed base' of the console), the more external parties are willing to develop and sell games on that console.

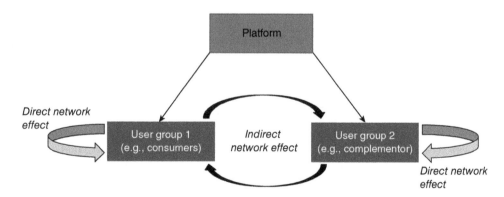

**FIGURE 9.4**   A two-sided platform with its direct and indirect network effects shown

Source: authors

Direct and indirect network effects can be either positive or negative. A hypothetical example of a negative direct network effect is when there is a fixed number of available drivers at a certain point of time on Uber but there are more users looking for a ride, which means these consumers will face surge prices, and hence, negative spillover effects between consumers due to the number of other consumers. In the case of indirect network effects, it can be positive for Side A due to Side B, but negative for Side B due to Side A. One example for this is a website like Facebook, where advertisers value more consumers, but consumers would not necessarily enjoy having more advertisers, and most likely dislike having more advertisements.

## STRATEGIC FOCUS

### Data network effects

Research on network effects focuses increasingly on the value platforms can create by using more data – for example, Spotify improving its recommendations to you by using data from other users, as well as using data from your listening patterns. Data allows platforms to make faster and more accurate predictions, which increases the value users perceive – which is further strengthened if users expect this to make a real difference to them.[48] However, for data to be a source of true network effect, two further conditions need to be met. First, data from one consumer should improve the platform for other consumers, meaning that data should not only bring within-user improvements, but also improvements across users. For instance, listeners should be offered better playlist recommendations in Spotify. And second, such changes and improvements in the product and/or consumer experience should be incorporated fast enough, so current consumers can benefit from the network effects when they are using the platform (as opposed to changes that principally benefit future consumers at a later time).[49]

Although data can become a source of true network effect, its effectiveness could turn out to be less than anticipated – that is, compared to network effects that are based on the virtuous cycle between number of users and number of complementors. The reason is that there are many cases where data may create only limited competitive advantage, such as decreasing returns for data (which means that having more data may have little or no additional benefits), imitation or reverse-engineering of data (which means that competitors can also imitate or mimic the data), or imitation of the improvements in the platform that are achieved via data (which means that competitors can imitate the benefits that can be achieved with data).[50]

## Winner-takes-all outcomes

Due to network effects that create a virtuous cycle of adoption by consumers and the onboarding of complementors, combined with the reduction in various costs enabled by digital platforms, platform owners can scale up quickly and dominate a market, which is known as *winner-takes-all competition* (and sometimes *winner-takes-most competition*). The competitive element here lies in the fact that different platforms try to steal market share from each other. Many platforms that we use are either dominant or, in some other cases, share almost the entire marketplace with only one other platform.

However, not all platform-centred markets are dominated by a single player that takes all or most of the winnings. For example, the video game console market has been shared across three players (Microsoft, Sony, and Nintendo) for two decades. Social media, which was dominated by a single platform (Facebook) is now shared across varied platforms (such as Twitter, TikTok, and Snapchat) that cater to different user bases such as users from different generations – although some of these platforms are eventually acquired by the previously dominant player (for instance, Instagram was acquired by Facebook, which became Meta). What makes winner-takes-all outcomes less likely are the following three factors: multi-homing, differentiation, and crowding.[51]

Multi-homing means that a certain actor at a particular side of the platform participates in two or more platforms simultaneously (e.g., multiple 'homes'). As multi-homing increases, a winner-takes-all outcome becomes less likely. This is because either the complementor or customer is available on both platforms, hence reducing the advantage of a leading platform – for example, if a customer knows that almost all popular apps are available on two competing platforms, then the importance of complement availability decreases in making the decision which platform to join. This issue is even further strengthened if multi-homing is pervasive in the two or more sides of the platform. Think about ride-sharing platforms: both drivers and riders are generally active on multiple platform ridesharing platforms (such as Lyft and Uber) to try to get the 'best deal' possible for their own purposes[52], which makes it difficult for one of these platforms to dominate the market.

Differentiation is a key issue in platform competition (see Chapter 10), since platforms that serve slightly different purposes, user needs, and tastes can relieve a great amount of competitive pressure. In other words, differentiation reduces head-to-head competition. Differentiation also acts as a natural barrier against a dominant platform cornering a market completely. For example, in the mid-90s, Microsoft enjoyed very high market power with its Windows operating system, but it was not able to capture the so-called 'graphics & design' users who strongly preferred Apple's computers and operating systems.

Crowding happens when consumers or complementors on one side of the platform start to impose negative direct network effects on others on the same side, so that there is a limit on how much consumers or complementors can be gathered. As an example, consider Facebook, which younger users are nowadays much less actively using because they are now on the same social media platform where they are connected to their family members. As such, they tend to move to other platforms where they can share more freely. Therefore, Facebook cannot fully unlock winner-takes-all outcomes as the extent of the market is limited by the crowding effect.

## Kickstarting platform growth

Platforms can grow very quickly thanks to direct and indirect network effects. But where to start? Put differently: when a platform is new, how do you make all sides join the platform so that there are enough users to kickstart the network effects? When a rideshare platform (such as Uber) is first introduced, who would come first: the rider, or the driver? Riders prefer to use a platform where there are readily available drivers, and drivers want to earn money by having customers that they hope to find on the platform. This situation, that needs to be solved, is known as the *chicken-and-egg dilemma* or *cold start problem*.

One of the key solutions for this problem – and a critical element for many platforms – is using subsidization correctly. *Subsidization* means that the platform owner covers (part of) the cost of the product or usage for a particular user group (or platform side). People might not be using Gmail for emailing if it required a paid membership – they are subsidized (by allowing them to use Gmail for free), in exchange for attracting more advertisers (who are not subsidized, as they pay to Google), who constitute another side of the platform.

Another example is that many gaming consoles are sold on the market for a price close to the production costs in order to induce people to buy the console. Many platform owners opt to subsidize at least one side of the platform. Early studies on the topic have identified different key principles regarding which side to subsidize:[53]

- If there is no paid transaction between the sides, then subsidize the side that gives more benefits by its presence to the other side (relative to the other way around). A simple example here would be Google's search engine and Gmail users and advertisers, where users are able to use these services for free as advertisers benefit from the presence of users.
- If there is paid transaction between the sides, then subsidize the side that has more value extracted by the other side (i.e., subsidize the side that will end up paying money to the other side) – if you consider the traditional shopping malls, customers can use facilities of the shopping mall (generally) for free, whereas shop owners pay for the rent and the maintenance of the mall since they profit by selling products to customers.
- If only one side of the platform is also a member of (an)other competing platform(s) (that is, if only one side of the platform is multi-homing), then subsidize the single-homing side. When you consider console video games, the users are much less likely to multi-home by owning multiple consoles (although some do) relative to game developers who release their games on multiple platforms. Hence, users of consoles are subsidized instead of game developers.
- Subsidize the quality-sensitive side. Using the console video game industry as an example again, customers are highly sensitive to quality. That is, they try to spend their money and time only on games that they believe are worth it. So, game developers need to be given the right incentives to supply only high-quality products that customers will buy. Platform owners do this by putting the burden of licensing and other fees on game developers.
- Subsidize the price-sensitive side – for example, the PDF file format, which was invented by Adobe Inc., offers a 'free' PDF reader software for Windows and Mac that allows for building a large customer base and capturing market share, whereas the firm also offers highly priced 'pro versions' for content creators and businesses, which contain additional features such as editing, digital signatures, and publishing.

There are other tactics besides subsidization – although a key aspect of launching platforms – to ensure onboarding both sides to the platform and kickstarting its growth.[54] One of these other tactics, *seeding*, implies that a platform owner creates sought-after content, or that it pays another party to provide valuable content on its platform, so as to draw customers and complementors to the platform. Another tactic revolves around the *onboarding of marquee complementors*, which implies that a platform owner engages in one or more partnerships with sought-after complementors (i.e., *marquee complementors*) for their platform when it is launched to signal the platform's quality and to drive its adoption by other complementors and by customers. Furthermore, platform owners can opt for a micro-market launch, the act of which is known as *micro-launching*, which is about leveraging strong network effects within a small group of consumers initially. Yet another tactic for kickstarting a platform's growth is to *offer stand-alone value*, which implies that consumers can be persuaded to onboard even when no complements are yet available. A platform owner may also choose to *leverage open data*, which implies the 'scraping' of publicly available data

**TABLE 9.2** Tactics to kickstart a platform's growth

| Type of tactic | Brief description | Example |
|---|---|---|
| Subsidizing | The platform owner covers (part of) the cost of the product or platform usage for at least one side (i.e., user group) of the platform to drive adoption on that side. | Google's suite of applications (such as Gmail) is free to use by consumers as they are subsidized by Google. This consumer adoption drives advertisers to pay Google to reach its consumers. |
| Seeding | The platform owner provides key complements itself, or pays another party to provide them, to kick-start adoption of the platform. | New generations of Nintendo gaming consoles are almost always released with a new version of high-quality Mario games (developed by Nintendo itself) that drive the adoption of the new gaming console. |
| Onboarding marquee complementors | The platform owner ensures the support of a well-known and/or high quality complementor (e.g., via a partnership deal) to signal the quality of the platform and drive its adoption by other complementors and by consumers. | When Microsoft released the now defunct streaming platform Mixer to compete with Twitch, they partnered with the top Fortnite streamer at the time, 'Ninja' (Richard Tyler Blevins), who switched from Twitch to Mixer to stream his gameplay, aiming to attract his millions of followers, who were avid consumers of streaming content. |
| Micro-launching | The platform is launched restrictively, such that initially it is available only for a small group of consumers, so as to create strong network effects among a tight knit group, and then it can attract other consumers and/or complementors. | Facebook was initially launched only for Harvard students, which then expanded to other Ivy League school students, and then to all university and high school students, and only after this staged adoption became available for everyone. |
| Offering stand-alone value | The platform provides some value to the consumer even if there is no (direct) complement and/or other users available for it yet. | PlayStation 2 was the first gaming console to be released with a DVD drive, which greatly drove its adoption among consumers, as they could use the console as a DVD player and hence use it even without games (direct complements). |
| Leveraging open data | The platform owner scrapes publicly available data to populate the content or complements for a platform to drive its adoption by consumers. | Many platforms that provide data on business leads to call for sales were built by scraping publicly available data on sites such as LinkedIn (this was an issue that has gone to courts due to privacy concerns). |
| Adding users from an existing platform to the new platform | The platform owner transfers users from its existing platform to grow its new platform. | The world's most popular game as of 2022, Fortnite, had its game launcher turned into a game store overnight (Epic Games Store), moving all Fortnite players to the new platform as consumers. |
| Piggybacking | The platform owner persuades users from another platform, which is owned by another entity, to (also) join its new platform. | In its early days, PayPal had bots buying items on eBay, which were requesting to send the money to the PayPal accounts of the sellers, driving consumer adoption through the consumer base of eBay. |

to populate the content or complements for a platform in order to drive its adoption. An alternative tactic can be to *transfer users of an existing platform to the new platform* (both of which are owned by the same entity). This leveraging of an existing user base can also happen by *piggybacking*, which implies that the users of another, larger platform, which has a different owner, are persuaded to join the new platform. See Table 9.2 for an example of each of these different tactics to kickstart a platform's growth.

# CRACK-THE-CASE

## 3DO gaming console[55]

Source: © Bondart Photography (2023) / Shutterstock.

In 1991, Trip Hawkins founded a new firm, 3DO, with the aim of creating the most advanced CD-based multimedia gaming console. 3DO gained a set of investors that formed an alliance around the console: Matsushita/Panasonic, AT&T, Time Warner, and MCA. The idea was original: instead of producing and selling the gaming console, 3DO would license its production, distribution and sale to several other firms, allowing maximum production and distribution of the console. Hawkins' idea was also new regarding which side to subsidize: 3DO aimed to promote developers and give them the chance to develop games as easily as possible, combined with friendly licensing terms and fees. Upon release, 3DO was priced at $699.99 (in 1993 prices, which is today equivalent to approximately $1,400) in the US. Considering the combined forces of the firms supporting the 3DO gaming console, one might have thought this was a potentially highly successful product in the market. However, the reality turned out to be different: 3DO's sales were sluggish, and the console ended up having very low-quality games, also attracting many low-quality developers. The platform had to give up the market within just two years and went on to become a game developer and publisher for other platforms in the market.

## Questions

1.  Why do you think that the 3DO console was highly priced?
2.  Why do you think that the developers for 3DO, who were given tools and better licensing terms compared to competing platforms, did not make better games for the console?

## Beyond the size of the network

Platform success has usually been considered together with the size of the network of customers and complementors – which could be thought of as the correct inference given size is important in driving indirect network effects, and hence will likely drive the success of a platform. However, there is more to this success than the size of the network of user groups. For all user groups (or 'sides'), the particular qualities of the network are as important as the quantity (i.e., the size) of the network. Not all consumers and complements (and complementors) are the same. At the consumer side, it has been highlighted that early adopters of platforms may have different preferences and consumption patterns compared to late adopters. For instance, early adopters tend to spend much more on complements and to seek more novel complements, whereas late adopters are more risk-averse and prefer consuming fewer and more popular complements.[56] Not all complements are equal either. Many platforms, such as mobile operating systems, gaming consoles and platforms for streaming movies and/or music, are highly driven by the demand for superstar complements; the top 2–3% of complements drive the vast majority of consumption by platform users (and sometimes also drive their decision to adopt the platform).[57]

It is also important to note that network effects are dependent on the structure of the network itself (e.g., how closely knit or weakly tied users are)[58] – an idea reflected very clearly in *strong-ties network effects*: for example, in earlier times when mobile phone charges were based on whether the caller and receiver had the same phone operator or not (with higher call prices in the latter case), it was much more important having your frequent contacts to be on the same operator – even if that operator had a smaller user base compared to a competing one.[59] In other words, the 'global network' of each operator mattered less than on which operator your 'local network' (your friends and family) could be found.

**KEY DEBATE**

Big Tech platforms: Monopolies?[60]

Source: © Koshiro (2021) / Shutterstock.

*(Continued)*

The quickly rising power of platform-centred ecosystems – particularly, those in which Google (Alphabet), Amazon, Meta (previously Facebook), and Apple are the respective hubs – has become an important concern to many governments in recent years. These and other influential platforms that have been initiated by very large technology firms are collectively dubbed as *Big Tech platforms*. Governments in Continental Europe, the UK, and the US have started to take action already through legislation.

Google has been fined due to self-preferencing: it favoured (by showing as 'higher ranked' search results) its own comparison-shopping service (and those sellers that used its advertising services) over other comparison-shopping services. Amazon has been proven to enter consistently the market space of its complementors. Meta, besides its role in the Cambridge Analytica scandal, has been under scrutiny due to its strong control over key social media platforms including Facebook (and its Messenger), Instagram and WhatsApp, which it acquired. In addition to this, Meta decided to combine consumer data across these platforms (in addition to the data Facebook collects from third party websites that use its tools), even from users that have no Facebook account. However, this has been considered inappropriate by the Bundeskartellamt, the German competition regulatory agency, which decided that Meta must keep the data separate across platforms – even when the same user is active across these platforms. Apple had been fighting many app developers – with its court case with Epic Games making headlines in late 2020 and in 2021. Apple had the policy of 30% commission on all kinds of (new app or in-app) purchases and subscriptions that are made with its App store (which Google also did with its Google Play Store). Also, Apple had the policy that app developers cannot redirect customers to other places (such as the webpage of the app) through which customers can make the in-app purchase or subscription without the 30% commission to Apple. There have been some remedial actions by Apple (and even more by Google, by reducing its commission to 15%), yet courts in the US have ruled that Apple should allow letting users know they can make in-app purchases or subscriptions with other means (such as websites through a PC, which would not entail the 'Apple tax').

Some of the suggestions on managing Big Tech firms' dominance entail splitting them up into separate firms, which is still on the table in some discussions, but also has been highlighted as a double-edged sword. After all, although this may help to reinvigorate competition, it may lead to less innovation – indeed, the massive scale of the network effects of Big Tech firms helps them to develop cutting edge technologies in particular areas, such as artificial intelligence (see Chapter 5). Moreover, it may not help in changing the situation altogether. These issues become even trickier as Big Tech platforms increasingly enter highly regulated industries including healthcare and education: industries where data privacy is highly important, but also innovation is direly needed.

## Questions

1. Mention and reflect on some trade-offs for consumers of a forced break-up of Big Tech firms.
2. What would be some ways to regulate platforms in such a way that their benefits to users and society is affected minimally, while (potential) harms to users and society are reduced?

## Platform governance

Platform owners need to make decisions beyond pricing. These other decisions, which are equally critical for the platform, most importantly involve setting the main rules of engagement on the platform. These rules of engagement must clarify such things as: Who is allowed to join the platform? What are the different sides of the platform allowed to do? What are the requirements that need to be fulfilled by each side of the platform? In addition to that, a platform owner needs to make decisions about the trade-offs between quality and quantity regarding sides. Some platform owners prefer to have fewer complements and/or customers on their platform as this is more in line with their value proposition – think, for instance, about Toptal, a freelance platform that only aims to have the top 1% of freelancer talents on the platform, and a generalist freelance platform such as Fiverr where everyone can offer services. Governance is a very critical aspect of platforms, with wrong governance ruining even the most dominant of platforms.

## CLOSING CASE
### Epic Games Store[61]

Source: © Cassiano Correia (2021) / Shutterstock.

Epic Games Store was launched in 2018 as a digital video game store for PCs, a market which competes against the long-time dominant Valve's Steam (estimated to have 75%+ of the market), specialist players such as GOG.com (Good Old Games) and Humble Bundle Store, and individual storefronts by major publishers including Electronic Arts (Origin) and Ubisoft (Ubisoft Store). Epic Games Store was launched with a mission to change this market and charges a much lower commission from developers. Steam's commission was 30% at the time of Epic Games Store's launch and Epic Games Store was 12% in comparison. Steam then lowered the commission by creating some tiers, with the lowest being 20% for bestsellers. Epic Games Store's launch is also interesting in that millions of Fortnite players around the world, just in one day, realized that the program to open Fortnite, Epic Games launcher, has been replaced with a game store (Epic Games Store), hence giving a consider- able already-installed base for the platform. In addition, Epic Games started a never-seen aggressive strategy of giving away games for free – which required users to login (and, of

*(Continued)*

course, to create an account if they did not have one) in a window of several days to claim the offer to add the game to their digital library on Epic Games Store. This strategy seems to have cost around 11.6 million dollars during the Epic Games Store's first ten months (which was the 'buyout price' for 35+ game titles that were given away for free). Finally, Epic Games Store has made agreements to become the (limited-time) exclusive distributor to many upcoming expected games. Developers were happy in taking these deals as they were offered a better cut of the profits compared to other platforms (in particular Steam), and also some of the (limited-time) exclusive games were offered minimum pay-out guarantees for the developers. However, the decision of some developers to be exclusive to Epic Games Store (even if for a limited time) has attracted some amount of criticism from gamers – especially in relation to crowdfunded games, with Epic later pledging to refund crowdfunders if there was an existing commitment by the game to be released on other, competing game stores during the crowdfunding campaign.

Bottom line, Epic Games Store had a strategy to close the gap it has against the dominant player in this market by giving away deals for gamers (free games) as well as game developers (much lower commission, good deals for exclusives). Its strategy seems to have started to work, with it reaching 15% market share. But what about the future? The target is 35%+ for 2024. Will this be possible?

## Questions

1. What is the nature of the complementarities between Epic Games Store and its complements?
2. Which launch and growth strategies has Epic Games Store used?
3. What were the main tools Epic Games Store leveraged in competing with the dominant player, Valve, and other players in this market? What insight can we gain from this with regard to platform-versus-platform competition?
4. Do you think that Epic Games Store's strategy of giving away games for free is sustainable in making this platform an enduring, competitive player in the industry?

## Summary

- An ecosystem is a set of actors with varying degrees of multilateral, nongeneric complementarities that are not fully hierarchically controlled.
- Nongeneric complementarities can be unique or supermodular, and uni- or bidirectional.
- Most ecosystems consist of hubs (keystone actors or leaders) that shape the ecosystem and its roles and protocols, and followers, who fill the other ecosystem roles.
- Many ecosystems are organized around a central platform that serves as the principal foundation for firms to offer complements, and which plays a central role in how value is created and captured in the ecosystem.
- A platform comprises an architecture and a set of rules that together enable or facilitate direct interactions between at least two different user groups (for instance, consumers and complementors) that are affiliated with the platform.

- Broadly speaking, a distinction can be made between transaction platforms, innovation platforms, and hybrid platforms.
- Digital platform businesses benefit from several advantages against 'pipeline' businesses and their stand-alone products, such as a reduction of search, matching, monitoring, and transaction costs which are particularly enabled by the existence of network effects.
- Upon launch, most platforms face a 'chicken and egg'-dilemma, which can be handled by adequate subsidization or other ways to get both sides on-board the platform.

## Review questions

- How do ecosystem-based value systems differ from other types of value systems?
- What are the different types of complementarities that can exist between ecosystem players?
- What are common roles of hub firms in ecosystems?
- How do platform businesses differ from pipeline businesses with respect to how value is created?
- What tactics can be used to ensure the onboarding of both sides to a platform?

## Discussion questions

1. Ecosystems have emerged largely because of digitalization. Do you believe ecosystems can also emerge in contexts where digitalization does not play a central role?
2. Many manufacturing firms are now trying to become platform owners, leaving behind their former product-based strategy. What are the main advantages and disadvantages of switching towards becoming a platform owner? When would you think a manufacturing firm should not try to become a platform owner (but maybe instead become a complementor to a platform)?

### EXPERIENTIAL EXERCISES

1. Think of two products that complement each other in a generic way. Would it be feasible for firms to strategize to turn this generic complementarity into specific? What would you advise?
2. Think about two platforms you regularly use. What are the sides of these platforms? Which side was subsidized? Do they compete with other platforms?

## Further reading

Burford, N., Shipilov, A.V. and Furr, N.R. (2022) 'How ecosystem structure affects firm performance in response to a negative shock to interdependencies', *Strategic Management Journal*, 43: 30–57.

Jacobides, M.G., Cennamo, C. and Gawer, A. (2018) 'Towards a theory of ecosystems', *Strategic Management Journal*, 39: 2255–76.

Kapoor, R. (2018) 'Ecosystems: Broadening the locus of value creation', *Journal of Organization Design*, 7 (12): 1–16.

McIntyre, D., Srinivasan, A., Afuah, A., Gawer, A. and Kretschmer, T. (2021) 'Multisided platforms as new organizational forms', *Academy of Management Perspectives*, 35 (4): 566–83.

Rietveld, J. and Schilling, M.A. (2021) 'Platform competition: A systematic and interdisciplinary review of the literature', *Journal of Management*, 47 (6): 1528–63.

## Endnotes (references)

1.  Alpeyev, P. (2021b) 'SoftBank to merge PayPay and Line Pay apps in Japan', *Bloomberg,* March 1. www.bloomberg.com/news/articles/2021-03-01/softbank-is-said-to-merge-paypay-and-line-pay-apps-in-japan (accessed June 21, 2023); Chou, G.J. and Wang, R.Z. (2020) 'The nested QR code', *IEEE Signal Processing Letters,* 27: 1230–4; Koma, K. (2013) 'Kawaii as represented in scientific research: The possibilities of Kawaii cultural studies', *Hemispheres. Studies on Cultures and Societies,* 28: 103–17; Ministry of Finance of Japan (2019) 'Consumption tax rate hike', MOF, October 1. www.mof.go.jp/english/policy/tax_policy/consumption_tax (accessed June 21, 2023); PayPay (2021) 'About PayPay', *PayPay.* https://about.paypay.ne.jp/career/en/about (accessed June 21, 2023); Softbank (2018) 'SoftBank and Yahoo Japan JV to launch "PayPay", barcode-based smartphone payment services in collaboration with India's Paytm in the fall', *Softbank,* July 27. www.softbank.jp/en/corp/news/press/sbkk/2018/20180727_01 (accessed June 21, 2023); Statista (2021) 'Leading incentives to increase the use of cashless payment methods in Japan as of February 2022', *Statista,* April 27. www.statista.com/statistics/1156201/japan-major-incentives-increase-use-cashless-payment (accessed June 21, 2023); Statista (2022) 'Number of merger and acquisition (M&A) transactions worldwide from 2010 to 2021', *Statista,* March 2. www.statista.com/statistics/267368/number-of-mergers-and-acquisitions-worldwide-since-2005 (accessed June 21, 2023); Yamamoto, R. and Endo, M. (2019) 'Consideration of dissemination strategy of mobile payment application "PayPay"', conference paper (in Japanese, with English abstract), Shizuoka: Shizuoka University, www.jstage.jst.go.jp/article/jasmin/201910/0/201910_179/_pdf/-char/en (accessed June 21, 2023).

2.  Davis, M.F., Tse, C. and Foerster, J.-H. (2022) 'Dealmaking slips by almost a third in 2022 marked by volatility, inflation', *Bloomberg,* December 21. www.bloomberg.com/news/articles/2022-12-21/dealmaking-falls-by-30-in-2022-as-inflation-volatility-hit-m-a-volumes (accessed June 21, 2023).

3.  Jacobides, M., Cennamo, C. and Gawer, A. (2018) 'Towards a theory of ecosystems', *Strategic Management Journal*, 39: 2255–76.

4.  Moore, J.F. (1993) 'Predators and prey: A new ecology of competition', *Harvard Business Review*, 71 (3): 75–86.

5.  Tansley, A.G. (1935) 'The use and abuse of vegetational concepts and terms', *Ecology*, 7: 249–73.

6.  Jacobides et al. (2018)

7.  Stora Enso (2020) *Stora Enso Annual Report 2020.* Helsinki: Stora Enso Oyj. https://www.storaenso.com/en/investors/annual-report (accessed June 21, 2023).

8.  Jacobides et al. (2018)

9.  Van Alstyne, M.W., Parker, G.G. and Choudary, S.P. (2016) 'Pipelines, platforms, and the new rules of strategy', *Harvard Business Review*, 94 (4): 54–62.

10. Adner, R. (2017) 'Ecosystem as structure: An actionable construct for strategy', *Journal of Management*, 43 (1): 39–58.
11. Iansiti, M. and Levien, R. (2004) 'Strategy as ecology', *Harvard Business Review*, 82 (3): 68–78.
12. Jacobides et al. (2018)
13. Baldwin, C.Y. and Clark, K.B. (2000) *Design Rules: The Power of Modularity*. Cambridge: MA: The MIT Press.
14. Schilling, M.A. (2000) 'Toward a general modular systems theory and its application to interfirm product modularity', *Academy of Management Review*, 25 (2): 312–34.
15. Jacobides et al. (2018); Schilling (2000)
16. Jacobides et al. (2018)
17. Teece, D.J. (2018) 'Profiting from innovation in the digital economy: Enabling technologies, standards, and licensing models in the wireless world', *Research Policy*, 47 (8): 1367–87.
18. Adner, R. and Lieberman, M. (2021) 'Disruption through complements', *Strategy Science*, 6: 91–109.
19. Adner (2017)
20. Helfat, C.E. and Lieberman, M.B. (2002) 'The birth of capabilities: Market entry and the importance of pre-history', *Industrial and Corporate Change*, 11 (4): 725–60.
21. Jacobides et al. (2018)
22. Jacobides et al. (2018: 2264)
23. Jacobides et al. (2018); Matzler, K., Bailom, F., Von den Eichen, S.F. and Kohler, T. (2013) 'Business model innovation: Coffee triumphs for Nespresso', *Journal of Business Strategy*, 34 (2): 30–7.
24. Jacobides et al. (2018)
25. Hart, O. and Moore, J. (1990) 'Property rights and the nature of the firm', *Journal of Political Economy*, 98: 1119–58.
26. Jacobides et al. (2018)
27. Jacobides et al. (2018); Teece, D.J. (1986) 'Profiting from technological innovation: Implications for integration, collaboration, licensing and public policy', *Research Policy*, 15 (6): 285–305.
28. Arora, A. and Gambardella, A. (1990) 'Complementarity and external linkages: The strategies of the large firms in biotechnology', *Journal of Industrial Economics*, 38 (4): 361–79; Jacobides et al. (2018); Lee, C.H., Venkatraman, N., Tanriverdi, H. and Iyer, B. (2010) 'Complementarity-based hypercompetition in the software industry: Theory and empirical test, 1990–2002', *Strategic Management Journal*, 31: 1431–56.
29. Adner (2017)
30. Jacobides et al. (2018)
31. Parker, G.G., Van Alstyne, M. and Jiang, X. (2017) 'Platform ecosystems: How developers invert the firm', *MIS Quarterly*, 41 (1): 255–66.
32. Adner (2017); Jacobides et al. (2018)
33. Teece (1986)
34. Adner (2017)
35. Baldwin, C.Y. (2015) *Bottlenecks, Modules and Dynamic Architectural Capabilities*, Harvard Business School working paper. #15–028. https://dash.harvard.edu/handle/1/13350434 (accessed June 21, 2023); Hannah, D.P. and Eisenhardt, K.M. (2016) 'Value creation and capture in a world of bottlenecks', working paper, Mack Institute. https://mackinstitute.wharton.upenn.edu/wp-content/uploads/2016/03/Hannah-Douglas-Eisenhardt-Kathleen_Value-Creation-and-Capture-in-a-World-of-Bottlenecks.pdf (accessed June 21, 2023); Kapoor, R. (2018) 'Ecosystems: Broadening the locus of value creation', *Journal of Organization Design*, 7 (12): 1–16.

36. Hannah and Eisenhardt (2016)
37. Adner, R. and Kapoor, R. (2015) 'Innovation ecosystems and the pace of substitution: Re-examining technology S-curves'. *Strategic Management Journal*, 37: 625–48; Ethiraj, S.K. (2007) 'Allocation of inventive effort in complex product systems', *Strategic Management Journal*, 28: 563–84; Hannah and Eisenhardt (2016); Zobel, A., Hoppmann, J. and Núñez Jiménez, A. (2017) 'Unblocking bottlenecks in nascent innovation ecosystems: How bottlenecks impact firm collaboration', *Academy of Management Proceedings*, 2017 (1): article #13336.
38. Goodman, L.O., Hollen, R.M.A. and Volberda, H.W. (2022) 'How political factors shape ecosystems: An analysis of electric mobility policy in China and the EU', *Academy of Management Annual Meeting Proceedings*, 2022 (1). https://doi.org/10.5465/AMBPP.2022.18070abstract
39. Kapoor (2018)
40. Van Alstyne et al. (2016)
41. Shipilov, A. and Gawer, A. (2020) 'Integrating research on interorganizational networks and ecosystems', *Academy of Management Annals*, 14: 92–121.
42. Van Alstyne et al. (2016)
43. Cusumano, M.A., Gawer, A. and Yoffie, D.B. (2019) *The Business of Platforms: Strategy in the Age of Digital Competition, Innovation, and Power.* New York, NY: Harper Business.
44. Van Alstyne et al. (2016)
45. Van Alstyne et al. (2016)
46. Parker et al. (2016)
47. Rysman, M. (2009) 'The economics of two-sided markets', *Journal of Economic Perspectives*, 23 (3): 125–43.
48. Gregory, R.W., Henfridsson, O., Kaganer, E. and Kyriakou, H. (2021) 'The role of artificial intelligence and data network effects for creating user value', *Academy of Management Review*, 46 (3): 534–51.
49. Hagiu, A. and Wright, J. (2020) 'When data creates competitive advantage', *Harvard Business Review*, 98 (1): 94–101.
50. Hagiu and Wright (2020)
51. Boudreau, K.J. and Hagiu, A. (2009) 'Platform rules: Multi-sided platforms as regulators', in A. Gawer (ed.), *Platforms, Markets and Innovation*. Northampton: Edward Elgar, 163–91; Rysman (2009).
52. Zhu, F. and Iansiti, M. (2019) 'Why some platforms thrives… and others don't: What Alibaba, Tencent, and Uber teach us about networks that flourish. The five characteristics that make the difference', *Harvard Business Review*, 97 (1): 118–25.
53. Eisenmann, T., Parker, G.G. and Van Alstyne, M.W. (2006) 'Strategies for two-sided markets', *Harvard Business Review*, 84: 92–101; Hagiu, A. (2014) 'Strategic decisions for multisided platforms', *MIT Sloan Management Review*, 55 (2): 71–9.
54. Edelman, B. (2015) 'How to launch your digital platform', *Harvard Business Review*, 93 (4): 90–7; Parker, G. and Van Alstyne, M.W. (2014) 'Platform strategy', *The Palgrave Encyclopedia of Strategic Management*. http://dx.doi.org/10.2139/ssrn.2439323.
55. Evans, D.S., Hagiu, A. and Schmalensee, R. (2006) *Invisible Engines: How Software Platforms Drive Innovation and Transform Industries*. Boston, MA: The MIT Press.
56. Rietveld, J. and Eggers, J.P. (2018) 'Demand heterogeneity in platform markets: Implications for complementors', *Organization Science*, 29 (2): 304–22.
57. Binken, J.L. and Stremersch, S. (2009) 'The effect of superstar software on hardware sales in system markets', *Journal of Marketing*, 73 (2): 88–104.
58. Afuah, A. (2013) 'Are network effects really all about size? The role of structure and conduct', *Strategic Management Journal*, 34 (3): 257–73.
59. Suarez, F.F. (2005) 'Network effects revisited: The role of strong ties in technology selection', *Academy of Management Journal*, 48 (4): 710–20.

60. Calvano, E. and Polo, M. (2021) 'Market power, competition and innovation in digital markets: A survey', *Information Economics and Policy*, 54: 1–18; Özalp, H., Ozcan, P., Dinckol, D., Zachariadis, M. and Gawer, A. (2022) '"Digital colonization" of highly regulated industries: An analysis of big tech platforms' entry into health care and education', *California Management Review*, 64 (4): 78–107.

61. Orland, K. (2021) 'How long can Epic afford to throw money at the Epic Games Store?', *Arstechnica,* December 4. https://arstechnica.com/gaming/2021/04/how-long-can-epic-afford-to-throw-money-at-the-epic-games-store (accessed June 21, 2023).

## Acknowledgements

The authors thank Hakan Özalp, Liam Goodman and Max Rossmann for their contribution to this chapter.

## Key terms

**Complementarity** – the presence or doing more of one thing (e.g., a product, activity or asset) increases the value of doing more of another thing

**Direct network effects** – an increase in the number of users at one side of the platform increases the value they derive from the platform

**Ecosystem** – a multilateral set of entities with varying degrees of nongeneric complementarities whose non-hierarchical interactions contribute to joint value creation

**Indirect network effects** – an increase in the number of users at one side of the platform increases the value that users at another side of it derive from that platform

**Modular architecture** – a system architecture whose rules enable the separation, matching and mixing of the system's components along a production chain

**Nongeneric complementarity** – a type of complementarity that implies that entities offering certain complements to mutual customers need to coordinate their offerings or follow a standard within a modular architecture

**Pipeline business** – a type of business where value is created by controlling a linear series of activities in a value chain

**Platform** – an architecture and a set of rules enabling or facilitating direct interactions between two or more different user groups

**Platform business** – a type of business where value is created by facilitating direct, value-creating interactions among a platform's user groups

**Platform-centred ecosystem** – an ecosystem where a platform is pivotal for creating and appropriating value

**Supermodular complementarity** – a type of complementarity where an increased demand or variety of complements increases the customer-perceived value of other complements

**Unique complementarity** – a type of complementarity where a product, activity or asset does not work, or not as effectively, without another product, activity or asset

# Diagnostic
# Part II
iSENSE

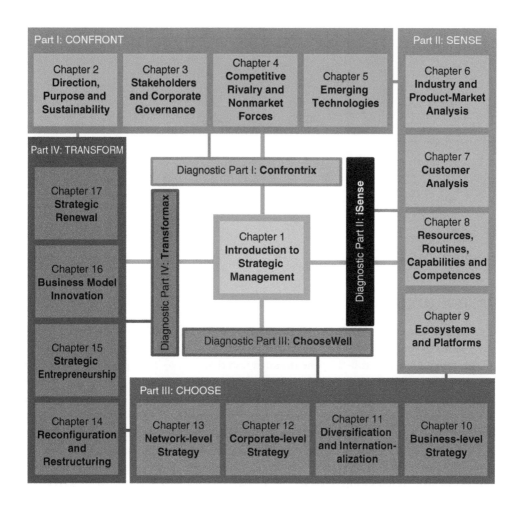

# Introduction

A crucial part of strategy formulation is how you, as an analyst, are able to 'sense' the internal and the external environment surrounding the company. The company's strategic choices should be informed by an analysis that comprises the firm's internal resources, capabilities, and competencies as well as the external environment, including the macro-environment, the industry and product market(s), the customers, and the ecosystem(s) in which the firm is embedded (see Figure B.1). This *iSense* diagnostic chapter builds on the previous four chapters (Chapters 6 to 9) to provide comprehensive sensing of relevant internal and external factors that have to be taken into account before any well-thought-out and reflective strategic choice can be made. In what follows, we present a list of fundamental strategic tools and frameworks that can be used to sense a firm's internal and external environment, some of which have already been discussed in previous chapters.

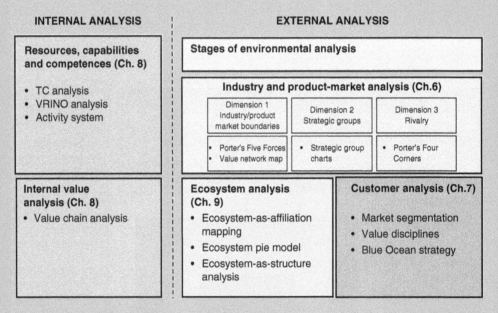

**FIGURE B.1**    iSense aggregate framework

# Internal analysis

The internal environment analysis encompasses the resources and competencies that are used by firms to conceive and implement strategy. Resources comprise tangible and intangible assets owned and controlled by the organization that enable it to operate.[1] Competencies are bundles of integrated and coordinated capabilities, which themselves encompass repetitive routines and processes (see Chapter 8 – Resources, Routines, Capabilities and Competencies). The first step in the internal analysis involves identifying the resources and competencies that firms possess and classifying them as threshold or core (TC analysis). The second step encompasses assessing whether resources and capabilities can bring a temporary or sustained competitive advantage to the firm using the VRINO framework. Activity systems can help to understand how resources and capabilities are linked to each other in order to sustain firms' positioning in the market. The final type of internal analysis that we cover here is the value chain analysis.

# Resources, capabilities and competencies

## TC analysis: Threshold or core

Companies' resources and competencies can be further classified as threshold or core. Threshold resources and competencies are essential for the company to meet minimum requirements and performance demanded by customers and regulators. Such resources and competencies are easier for competitors to imitate, bringing competitive parity. A core, often also called distinctive, resource or competency is typically defined as a firm's enduring and specific ability that leads to above-average economic performance. Competencies allow the organization to differentiate from its main competitors and obtain a sustained (or temporary) competitive advantage.

The analysis of H&M's internal environment allows us to illustrate the difference between threshold and core resources and competencies (see Figure B.2). For instance, organizational culture is a core resource for H&M because it has been crucial for the success of the brand over the years. H&M's culture is based on strong leadership, entrepreneurship, cost consciousness, constant improvement, employee involvement, experimentation, and fast decision-making, allowing the company to build an advantage in the market. H&M's financial resources are an example of a threshold resource. The fact that the majority of the ownership of the company belongs to the Persson family provides a strong financial foundation for H&M. However, other competitors, like Zara, also display a healthy financial situation being able to expand their operations using internal resources. Therefore, strong financial resources only bring competitive *parity* to H&M.

On the competencies side, H&M's supply chain management represents a threshold competency and collaborations with designers a core competency. While in the past, H&M was one of the leading companies in terms of time-to-market speed, nowadays, competitors have already caught up on supply chain management efficiency, being able to have a faster time-to-market and inventory shifts to meet changing demands. Therefore, supply-chain management represents a threshold competency that merely brings competitive parity to H&M. A core competency that through the years has allowed H&M to differentiate itself from competitors is its bundle of partnerships with famous designers, such as Balmain and Vivienne Westwood, which brings a source of competitive advantage for the brand.

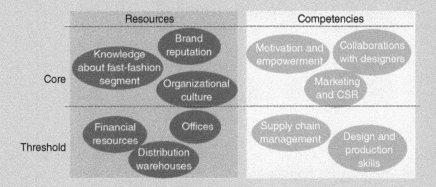

**FIGURE B.2**   H&M TC analysis

Source: authors

## VRINO Framework

Resources and competencies are of greatest value if they can be a source of competitive advantage to companies. The VRINO framework, which builds on Barney's (1991) VRIN framework (1991),[2] can support analysts in evaluating whether a resource or competency can bring a competitive parity, or instead, a temporary or sustained competitive advantage.[3] *VRINO* stands for Valuable (create value to customers), Rare (only one or few companies possess it), Inimitable (difficult or costly to imitate), Non-substitutable (no other resource or capability can replace it), Organized (the company is able to exploit the resource or competency) (see Chapter 8 – Resources, Routines, Capabilities and Competencies for a description of these criteria). An illustrative example of a VRINO analysis is provided in Figure B.3.

| | | Valuable | Rare | Inimitable | Non-substitutable | Organized to exploit | Competitive impact |
|---|---|---|---|---|---|---|---|
| Resources | Store location | No | No | No | No | No | Competitive disadvantage |
| | Capital | Yes | No | No | No | Yes | Competitive parity |
| | Distribution warehouses | Yes | Yes | No | No | Yes | Temporary advantage |
| | Brand | Yes | Yes | Yes | Yes | Yes | Sustained competitive advantage |
| Competencies | Motivate employees | Yes | No | No | No | Yes | Competitive parity |
| | Build reputation | Yes | Yes | Yes | No | Yes | Temporary advantage |
| | Leverage industrial design | Yes | Yes | Yes | Yes | No | Temporary advantage |

**FIGURE B.3**    Illustrative example of a VRINO analysis

According to this framework, a resource or competency can be considered a source of sustainable competitive advantage only when it is valuable, rare, inimitable, non-substitutable, and when the company is sufficiently well-organized to successfully exploit this resource or competency. If one or more of these conditions is not met, then the resource or competency could instead be a source of temporary competitive advantage (if it is valuable and rare), or it brings a competitive parity (if it is valuable but not rare) or even a competitive disadvantage (if it is neither valuable nor rare).

## Activity System

The Activity System model[4] offers an overview of how activities, product features, or resources and competencies interlink, allowing firms to deliver their value proposition to consumers. Figure B.4 shows an example of an activity system of H&M, a fast-fashion company, in which resources (squares) are linked to competencies (circles), explaining how those resources and competencies sustain the firm's positioning in the market (cheap and chic). This Activity

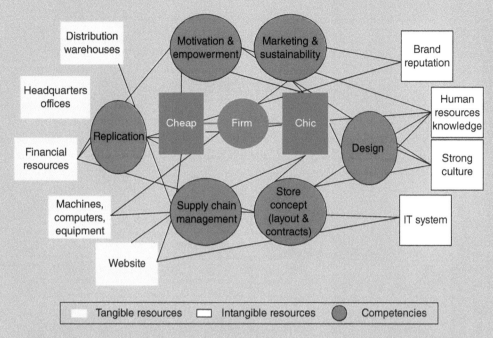

**FIGURE B.4**   Example of an activity system of H&M (fast-fashion company)

Source: authors, based on Porter (1996)[5]

System also illustrates that companies' resources and competencies are interlinked in a complex network that is hard for competitors to imitate.

## Internal value chain analysis

The value chain analysis helps companies identify all the activities undertaken to transform inputs into outputs.[6] It implies mapping the company's primary and support activities (see Chapter 8 – Resources, Routines, Capabilities and Competencies for further details) to spot the activities that add a disproportional amount of value to the final product. The value chain assessment can be combined with the VRINO framework for more in-depth analysis. One can identify the required resources and competencies needed to perform each activity, and whether those provide a competitive advantage to the firm.

Figure B.5 shows the analysis of Dell's value chain, which allows us to identify and locate across the value chain the activities and the resources and competencies that support Dell's competitive positioning. Dell is an American computer technology company whose business model focuses on assembling parts manufactured by other companies, producing at large scale and with low operating margins. In Dell's case, one of the activities that provide sustained competitive advantage is operations, specifically assembly operations. Dell is focused on continuously improving its assembly operations to improve detail, speed, and efficiency to increase quality and decrease costs. Service was another activity that has brought Dell a sustained competitive advantage as they have been widely known for their superior prompt customer service. Providing excellent customer service was a sustainable competitive advantage for the company as it helped build customer loyalty, positive brand reputation, and long-term relationships with their clients. However, Dell faced a significant decline in customer service quality and reputation during the mid-2000s, commonly referred to as the 'Dell Hell' period. Reports of poor customer service experiences, delayed support, and unresolved issues led to widespread dissatisfaction among consumers. Recovering from such a reputation hit can be challenging, and Dell has taken steps to address these issues and improve their customer service, but it takes time to regain trust and credibility. Finally, technology development is a support activity that brings sustained competitive advantage to Dell. Specifically, technology development entails leveraging industrial design competencies, creating and testing product platforms that integrate suppliers' parts effectively at a large scale with low operation margins, which is Dell's central value proposition.

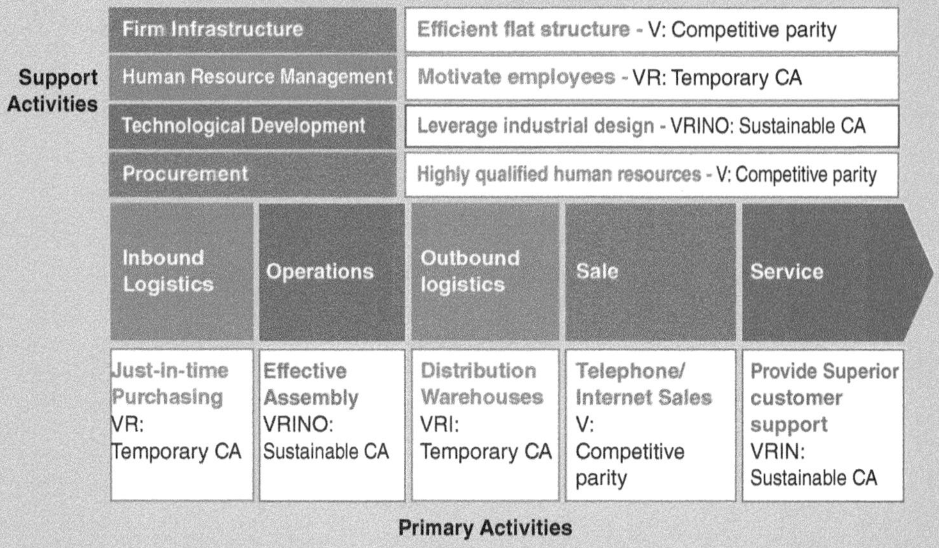

**FIGURE B.5**  Example of Dell's value chain

Source: adapted from Porter (1985)

# External analysis

A strategic investigation of the external environment of a company encompasses different stages and levels of analysis. Companies can produce a clear picture of a company environment through *scanning* (data gathering), *monitoring* (trends identification), *forecasting* (developments anticipation), and *assessing* (events significance analysis). Such stages of analysis can be implemented at several levels, namely the macro-level, in which the analyst looks at the broader geopolitical environment where the organization is inserted (see Diagnostic Part I – *Confrontrix*) or at the micro level, which includes the industry and product market analysis (see Chapter 6), the customer analysis (see Chapter 7) and the ecosystem analysis (see Chapter 9).

## Stages of external analysis

With the rise of globalization and technological advances, most modern firms face turbulent external environments. To address threats and opportunities from the external environment, firms need to actively work to acquire information from their ambiguous and ever changing environment. There are four parts to create a clear picture of a company's environment: Scanning, Monitoring, Forecasting, and Assessing (see Figure B.6). Successful firms establish robust mechanisms to carry out this process consistently and continuously. External cues may present themselves at different levels of the organization. As such, sensing the external environment is not a task that should be assigned exclusively to top management. Instead, strong organizational structures and governance should exist to ensure all levels can contribute and guide the organization through external events.

**FIGURE B.6**   Stages of environmental analysis

Identifying threats and opportunities is a central objective of assessing a firm's external environment. *Threats* in a company's environment are conditions that may impede the company from reaching its strategic goals. When the China/United States trade war started in 2018, American companies faced a tidal wave of threats regarding their operations in China. Eventually, most American companies had to cut their short-term strategic goals for the Chinese market. *Opportunities* are conditions that, if exploited effectively, may help a firm reach its strategic goals. For example, when governments introduced purchase subsidies for electric vehicles, it became more viable for car manufacturers to produce electric vehicles.

## Scanning

Some information from the external environment readily presents itself to a company. Yet most external events and trends do not. Environmental scanning is essential to address the need to understand these unseen activities. Scanning refers to gathering information about events and their relationships within an organization's internal and external environments. Scanning can help detect changes that are imminent or already underway. Further, successful approaches scan all segments of the external environment, such as political events, social events, or economic events. *PESTEL analysis* can be an interesting tool to gather information from the external environment at the macro level, covering Political, Economic, Socio-cultural, Technological, Environmental, and Legal factors (see the *Confrontrix* diagnostic chapter).

In recent years firms have increasingly relied on internet data to scan their environment. Here, firms frequently employ specialist software to acquire a broad spectrum of data from many sources. The uses of these software products alternate between traditional channels, such as news events detection, and advanced data analysis technology that can scan millions of data points concurrently. The Bloomberg Terminal is an example of news events software.[7] Bloomberg, a financial news company, provides financial institutions and businesses worldwide with financial data and high-quality news events shaping the global markets. Companies can automate their scanning procedures by setting alerts when certain events transpire using these software systems.

## Monitoring

After gathering information, the raw data is frequently not immediately usable. But by transforming the data using statistical approaches, long-term trends emerge and, with it, valuable insights. This process is referred to as 'monitoring'. For example, an e-commerce company may analyze their customer data to depict product demand curves. Through this graph, the company may decide to expand a particular product category or discontinue a product. The framework *Key drivers of change* (expanded in the *Confrontrix* diagnostic chapter) can help companies identify and define trends at the macro level, as well as assess if the trend constitutes an opportunity or a threat for the company, and when it will impact the company.

The effectiveness of Monitoring differs depending on a firm's sector, stakeholders, and general environment. Firms need to identify which stakeholders are essential and allocate most monitoring resources to serve their needs to build a strong monitoring capability. Once the relevant data is gathered and analysis of vital stakeholder needs is carried out, a firm will have valuable insights into how it can fulfil its strategic goals.

## Forecasting

Scanning and Monitoring are concerned with understanding what is happening in a company's general environment. Doing this will help firms navigate current events. Yet truly effective environmental analysis does not just look at the recent events and trends but also at those likely to occur in the future. This can be achieved through Forecasting. In this process, analysts produce reasonable estimates of what might happen because of changes and patterns discovered through Scanning and Monitoring. The *General scenario planning framework* (see *Confrontrix*) allows for building future scenarios that can occur at the macro level, making it an excellent framework to support forecasting analysis.

In recent years Forecasting has developed significantly as access to online data proliferated. Modern techniques allow companies to gather data from various sources (including historic data) and store these in large data structures; these are called data warehouses. After studying this data for trends in the monitoring stage, the data and emerging trends are readily used in Forecasting. The online supermarket Picnic collects data throughout its operations and aggregates it in its data warehouse. Data analysts call on this vast data collection to optimize operations, such as speeding up delivery times.

With these new techniques, Forecasting has become significantly more powerful. Yet accurate Forecasting of events and their outcomes remains a challenge. The primary limitation of Forecasting is that it relies on historical data. While it may provide clues on what could happen, practice shows that the past is not an excellent approximation of the future.[8] Another fundamental limitation of Forecasting is that it does not readily consider the company's strategic objectives. However, these limitations are addressed by the *Scenario planning framework* (see *Confrontrix*).

## Assessing

The final step in environmental analysis is Assessing. After gathering data, creating trends, and anticipating potential developments, it is the objective of Assessing to determine the significance of the identified phenomena. In this process, analysts take an expansive view of the phenomenon and consider the implications it has or may have on the firm's strategic goals. In recent years environmental analysis has been transformed through Big Data. In this approach, data analysts, data scientists and other specialists work together to carry out environmental analysis on vast datasets. Arguably the most challenging step in this big-data-based analysis has been Assessing, as this step requires the assessor to have technical expertise, good communication skills, and domain knowledge. Data analysts use visualization tools such as Tableau to condense the entire environmental analysis into an easily understandable set of graphs that management can use to aid in their decision-making.[9] This overview of visualizations is often updated in real-time and referred to as a dashboard.

## Industry and product-market analysis

Industry and product market analysis focuses on a group of companies that produce similar products or services and compete for the same resources and consumers in the marketplace (see Chapter 6 – Industry and product-market analysis). Three dimensions shall be considered to perform an industry and product-market analysis. The first dimension, industry and product-market boundaries, comprises Porter's Five Forces and value network maps frameworks. The second dimension encompasses the analysis of the different strategic groups inside the industry using strategic group charts. Finally, the third dimension looks inside strategic groups to profile the direct rivals, using Porter's Four Corners model (see Figure B.7). All of these frameworks will help analysts assess the industry's landscape and attractiveness.

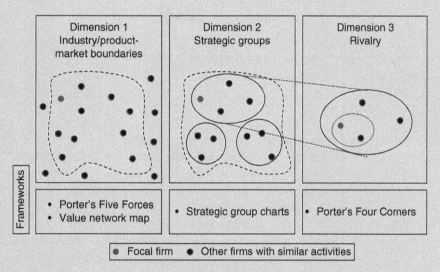

**FIGURE B.7**   Three dimensions of industry and product-market analysis

Source: authors

## Porter's Five Forces framework

*Porter's Five Forces* encompass the main forces impacting business growth across new entrants, substitutes, buyers, suppliers, and rivals.[10] This framework helps collect and structure information about the relevant forces that can influence firms' activities and profitability (see Chapter

6 – Industry and Product Market Analysis for more details). Figure B.8 shows the main dimensions inside each force that can help to determine whether the force has a high or low impact. Sometimes, it might be challenging to understand whether a force might have a low or high impact on a firm's activities and profitability. One tip could be to give a plus (high impact) or minus (low impact) for each dimension inside the force to determine whether the force has a low, medium, or high impact in general (see Figure B.8 for a hypothetical example).

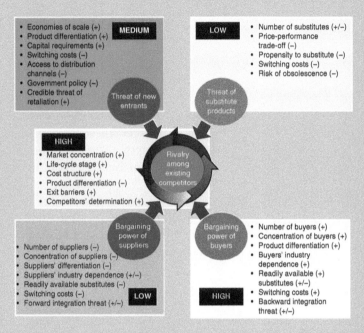

**FIGURE B.8**    Porter's Five Forces analysis applied to a hypothetical industry

Source: based on Porter (2008)

## Value network maps

The *Value network framework* considers a single force of competition: suppliers compete for customers, and customers compete for suppliers.[11] There is always a comparison between the value that is being created with an actor and the value that could be created with an alternative actor. The framework has two levels. In the nucleus of the network, there are the focal firm (for instance, Firm A) and its customers and suppliers. In the periphery, there are alternative customers and suppliers with whom the nuclear network entities can transact with (see Chapter 6 – Industry and Product Market Analysis for more details). An excellent start to understanding the value network is to make a table with network nuclear entities (Focal firm, Customer A and Supplier B) and list the suppliers and customers of Customer A and Supplier B (see Figure B.9).

| Network nucleus | Customers | Suppliers |
|---|---|---|
| Focal firm | Customer A | Supplier B |
| Customer A | Customer X | Supplier N, Supplier M |
| Supplier B | Customer P, Customer U | Supplier L |

**FIGURE B.9**    Value network list of customers and suppliers

## Strategic groups charts

Strategic groups are formed by companies that sell similar products and display similar strategic positioning or/and resources.[12] While theoretically, analysts would pick a single approach to find the strategic groups (theoretical, empirical statistical, or empirical subjective; see Chapter 6 – Industry and Product Market Analysis), in reality, analysts pragmatically mix theoretical and empirical subjective approaches, using pre-existing categories, common sense, and context expert knowledge to find the strategic groups. Such an ad hoc approach may entail three general steps:

1. <u>List the competitors.</u> First, list all relevant competitors in the industry that compete for the same consumers and suppliers, displaying similar value chains (see the table in Figure B.10). Such lists should include all the competitors that the company follows closely and whose market actions are likely to affect the focal company performance in the market.
2. <u>Identify relevant dimensions.</u> Next, identify the relevant dimensions across which competitors are similar or dissimilar. The industry's key success factors can be a good starting point to identify the relevant competitive dimensions for a specific

| Competitors | Competitive positioning | Geographical coverage | R&D investment |
|---|---|---|---|
| Firm A | Cost leadership | High | High |
| Firm B | Cost leadership | High | High |
| Firm C | Differentiation | Low | Low |
| Firm D | Hybrid | Medium | Medium |
| Firm E | Differentiation | Medium | Medium |

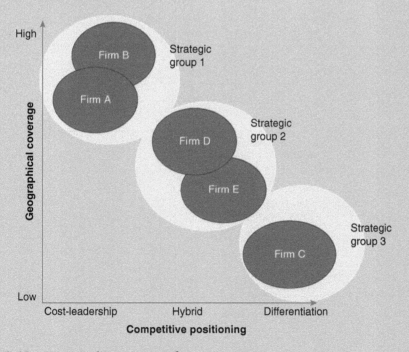

**FIGURE B.10**   Strategic dimensions to form strategic groups

industry. In the hypothetical example in Figure B.10, the pertinent dimensions are competitive positioning (cost-leadership, differentiation, or hybrid), geographical coverage (low, medium, high), and R&D investment (low to high). A good practice is to make a table with the dimensions and assess the competitors for each listed dimension. For the sake of simplicity and to improve readability, it is desirable that strategic group charts are bi-dimensional. In the hypothetical case of Figure B.10, two dimensions seem correlated (geographical coverage and R&D investment); thus, both dimensions provide the same information as larger-scale companies with wider geographical coverage tend to have more resources available to invest in R&D. Looking for correlated dimensions (positive or negative correlation) is a strategy to reduce the number of dimensions by merging the dimensions or abandoning the less important ones. In the example of Figure B.10, the selected dimensions were competitive positioning and geographical coverage.

3. <u>Find the strategic groups.</u> Finally, use the table to position the companies in a bi-dimensional graph. From here, selecting the groups is straightforward. It is often the case that the groups may fall into existing theoretical categories (e.g., Porter's generic strategies of differentiators, cost-leaders, and focus; see Chapter 10) which increases considerably the readability of the framework.

## Porter's Four Corners model

Porter's Four Corners model is a framework used to analyze the competitive behaviour of the main rivals, helping to predict their future course of action. This analysis is composed of four metrics, which are elaborated in detail in Chapter 6: Drivers (what are their goals), Management Motivations (what are their assumptions), Strategy (what are they doing), and Capabilities (what can they do). Figure B.11 suggests a table with guiding questions, so the analyst can quickly identify the different rivals' drivers, motivations, strategies, and capabilities.

| Metrics | Questions | Rival 1 | Rival 2 |
|---|---|---|---|
| Drivers | • What is their goal?<br>• What is their purpose?<br>• What are they pursuing? | | |
| Management motivations | • What are their assumptions?<br>• How do they perceive themselves?<br>• What are their beliefs?<br>• What are they taking for granted? | | |
| Strategy | • What are they doing?<br>• How are their strategies affecting their performance?<br>• Will they continue in the same direction? | | |
| Capabilities | • What can they do?<br>• What are their strengths?<br>• What are their weaknesses? | | |

**FIGURE B.11**   Porter's Four Corners table

Source: authors

## Customer analysis

Customers are the ultimate source of companies' income. Therefore, analyzing market segments (market segmentation) and tailoring a relevant value proposition (value disciplines and Blue Ocean strategy) is essential to succeed in the market (see Chapter 7 – Customer Analysis).

## Market segmentation

Market segmentation implies that a larger market is narrowed down into smaller groups of customers (customer segments), enabling the company to adapt its offers to specific segments.[13] Market segmentation entails understanding who customers are, what they want, when they buy, and how they choose among products (see Chapter 7 for more details on market segmentation). In Figure B.12, a fast-moving consumer good (FMCG) company identifies its main market segment as middle-class young families (socioeconomic and demographic criteria) who are smart shoppers (psychographic criteria).

## Value discipline analysis

Value disciplines is a strategic tool used by companies to communicate how they create value for customers.[14] For instance, through product leadership (the most advanced product in the market), customer intimacy (the most customized solution) or operational excellence (the lowest cost product) (see Chapter 7 – Customer Analysis). This tool basically describes the benefits customers can expect from companies' products and services. In Figure B.12, the FMCG company intends to offer a value proposition that enhances operational efficiency, meaning that they offer the best price-quality value proposition of the market.

## Blue Ocean strategy

Blue Ocean strategy thinking focuses on creating a value proposition that is unique and different from those of competitors.[15] Blue Ocean is about creating uncontested market spaces where competition is nonexistent. In contrast, a Red Ocean value proposition is based on value-cost trade-off, where there is an intense rivalry. The company in Figure B.12 has a Red Ocean value proposition, like most FMCG companies.

| | | Description | Example |
|---|---|---|---|
| **Market segmentation** | | B2B or B2C, geographic, demographic, socioeconomic, psychographic, behavioural, purchasing policies/approach | Middle class young families that are smart shoppers |
| **Value proposition** | **Value discipline** | Product leadership, operational excellence or customer intimacy | Operational excellence |
| | **Blue Ocean strategy** | Red or Blue Ocean | Red Ocean |

**FIGURE B.12**   Market segmentation and value proposition for an FMCG company

## Ecosystem analysis

Companies are often part of a complex network of interdependent organizations involved in delivering a specific product or service. Such an ecosystem can both restrict and enhance companies' activities and add or lower value. Therefore, it is important to understand the main actors in the ecosystem (ecosystem-as-affiliation analysis), how they add value to the ecosystem (Ecosystem Pie model), and how their activities are structured (ecosystem-as-structure analysis).

### Ecosystem-as-affiliation analysis

Ecosystem-as-affiliation[16] allows identifying and mapping all actors affiliated with a specific economic community, such as suppliers, customers, lead producers, competitors, complementors, governments, unions, investors, distributors, and universities (see Chapter 9 – Ecosystems and Platforms). You can list the actors in the ecosystem and name them, as well as represent them in different colors to highlight their level of influence (see Figure B.13).

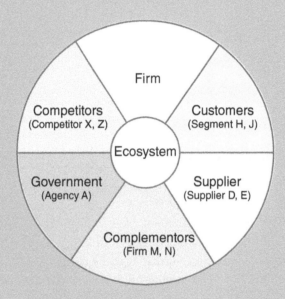

**FIGURE B.13**    Ecosystem affiliates hypothetical example

Source: authors

### Ecosystem Pie model

An Ecosystem Pie model is a strategy tool suggested by Talmar and colleagues[17] with the goal to map, analyze, and design innovation ecosystems. It captures how different actors in an ecosystem interact in creating and capturing value. This tool is complementary to the ecosystem-as-affiliation analysis, adding information about each actor on value capture (how much value is captured by a particular actor), value addition (unique or enhancing contributions of each actor to the final product), activities (mechanisms by which an actor generates its productive contribution), and resources (the basis of each actor-specific value creation). The Ecosystem Pie model helps to visualize simultaneously the ecosystem actors and how they create and capture value (see Figure B.14).

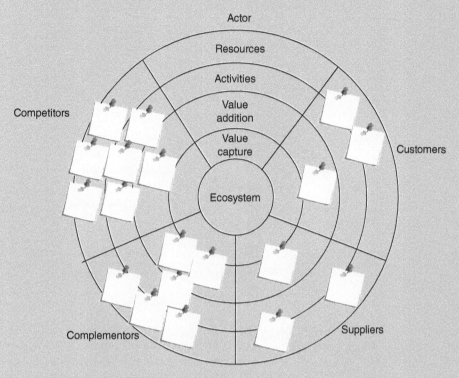

**FIGURE B.14**   Ecosystem Pie model

Source: Talmar et al. (2020: 7)

## Ecosystem-as-structure analysis

The ecosystem-as-structure analysis focuses on the alignment of activities, actors, positions, and transfer links across the ecosystem. This analysis requires several steps. First, identify and specify the discrete *activities* needed for a focal value proposition to be delivered to the final consumer. Second, identify and map all the *actors* (companies and other entities) undertaking these activities. Third, specify the actors' *position* in the activity flow across the system (who hands off to whom). And fourth, specify the *transfer links* between the actors – for instance, the transfer of data, funds, or material (see Figure B.15).[18] Ecosystem-as-structure scholars encourage companies to adopt a 'wide-lens' perspective instead of focusing too much on their innovations and neglecting the ecosystem actors which their product depends on. Therefore, companies should go beyond *execution* (activities, actors, positions, and transfer links) to consider *co-innovation* (the extent to which the success of the innovation depends on the successful commercialization of other innovations) and *adoption* (the extent to which actors need to adopt the focal company innovation before it arrives to the end-consumer) (see Table B.1).[19]

Michelin's PAX run-flat tire system example illustrates how adopting a 'wide lens' towards the ecosystem can determine companies' success when launching a new innovative product. The PAX run-flat tire innovative technology promised to decrease the need for tire changes without sacrificing performance or comfort, integrating a repair system. However, the tire and the repair system technologies were not the only innovations in this case, Michelin also rethought the ecosystem structure, widening its lens. Traditionally the flow of activities, actors, positions and transfer links in the tire market goes as follows: tire makers invent a new tire and convince automakers to install it in their new vehicles; second, the automakers work with dealers to sell new vehicles to end consumers; third, in case of puncture, garages repair

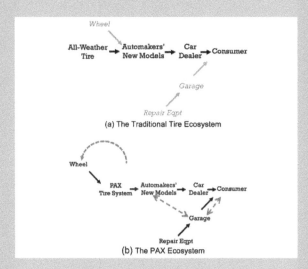

**FIGURE B.15**   Ecosystem structure of traditional tires and the PAX run-flat tire system

Source: Adner (2017: 45)

the tires using standard equipment (see Figure B.15). Michelin decided this time to rethink the tire ecosystem considering multilateral relationships instead of unilateral only. With the new PAX run-flat tire system, Michelin was delivering a new tire-system that required *co-innovation* with the wheel producers (tires and wheels are sold together to the automakers) and the *adoption* by both automakers and garages. If garages were not equipped with the PAX repair equipment, the consumers would not benefit from it, and automakers would not be willing to adopt it as well. This example shows that companies that need co-innovation with and adoption from other actors in the ecosystem need to adopt a *wide-lens ecosystem approach* in order to make sure that the focal innovation reaches the final consumers.

**TABLE B.1**   Assessing three risks of innovation

| Relevant innovation-related risks to consider | Questions to contemplate for assessing these risks |
|---|---|
| *Execution risk* | What challenges does the focal firm face in bringing about its innovation to the required specifications on time? |
| *Co-innovation risk* | To what extent does the success in bringing the focal firm's innovation to the market depend on the success of commercializing other innovations (by other firms or the focal firm itself)? |
| *Adoption chain risk* | To what extent must external parties embrace the focal firm's innovation before end consumers can evaluate the complete value proposition? |

Source: adapted from Adner (2012)

# Sensing external and internal factors

## SWOT overview

SWOT is an abbreviation of Strengths (S), Weaknesses (W), Opportunities (O) and Threats (T). The SWOT overview is a valuable tool to provide analysts with a big picture of the outcomes of your internal analysis (company's strengths and weaknesses) and external analysis (external opportunities and threats). The SWOT overview (different from the SWOT analysis) is a summary of the main points affecting firms' performance resulting from the internal (resources, capabilities, and competencies and internal value analysis) and external analysis (macro-environmental analysis, industry and product-market analysis, ecosystem analysis, and customer analysis) (see Figure B.16).

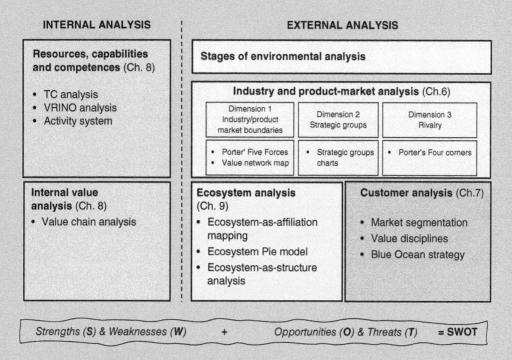

**FIGURE B.16**   iSense framework and SWOT

Source: authors

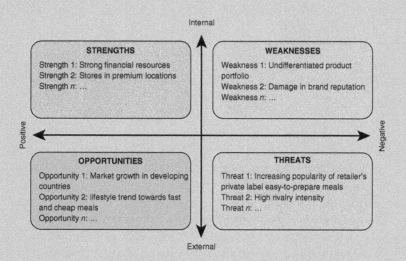

**FIGURE B.17**   Example of a SWOT overview of a fast-food company

Source: authors

The SWOT overview consists of four quadrants (S, W, O, T) that are organized around two bidirectional arrows: internal-external and positive-negative (see Figure B.17). The list of strengths, weaknesses, opportunities, and threats can be as long as desired, but the analyst should not lose the big picture. It is also recommended to rank the factors from the most to the least impactful for the company. SWOT, whose origin is somewhat unclear, has become one of the most widely utilized strategy tools among managers.[20]

## SWOT analysis

Once a SWOT overview has been made, it is time to link the different quadrants (S, W, O, T) with one another (see Figure B.18) by raising and answering questions such as the following:

- How can firms mitigate threats to take advantage of opportunities?
- How can companies use their strength to exploit opportunities (and which)?
- How can firms overcome their weaknesses?
- How are firms' weaknesses inhibiting the exploitation of the opportunities?
- How can a firm's weaknesses exacerbate the threat?
- How can opportunities and threats affect companies' strengths and weaknesses?

These questions invite reflection on how strengths, weaknesses, opportunities and threats relate to each other and how the company can exploit opportunities and mitigate threats;[21] see Figure B.18. This is referred to as a *SWOT analysis*.

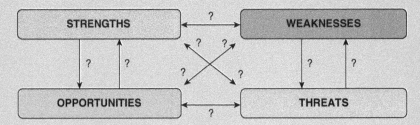

**FIGURE B.18**   SWOT analysis

Source: authors

As part of the SWOT analysis, the analyst could choose to allocate scores to the relationships between the different strengths/weaknesses and environmental changes (opportunities and threats); see Figure B.19 for an illustrative example. In this example, Strength #1 is the most important one to exploit opportunities or mitigate threats in the external environment, and Weakness #3 appears to be the company's weakest point, which may require managerial action. In addition to conducting this analytical exercise for the company, it could also be conducted for the company's main rivals: how do their strengths and weaknesses match the same changes in the external environment?

| | | Changes in external environment (opportunities & threats) | | | | | | |
|---|---|---|---|---|---|---|---|---|
| | | Change #1 | Change #2 | Change #3 | Change #4 | Change #5 | + | - |
| *Strengths* | Strength #1 | +2 | +1 | +5 | +2 | +2 | 12 | n/a |
| | Strength #2 | +5 | +2 | +1 | +1 | 0 | 9 | n/a |
| | Strength #3 | +3 | 0 | 0 | +1 | 0 | 4 | n/a |
| | Strength #4 | 0 | +2 | +1 | +4 | +2 | 9 | n/a |
| | Strength #5 | +1 | +2 | +4 | +3 | 0 | 10 | n/a |
| *Weaknesses* | Weakness #1 | -1 | -1 | -4 | 0 | -1 | n/a | -7 |
| | Weakness #2 | 0 | -2 | 0 | -1 | -1 | n/a | -4 |
| | Weakness #3 | -5 | 0 | -1 | -5 | 0 | n/a | -11 |
| | Weakness #4 | 0 | -3 | -3 | 0 | 0 | n/a | -6 |
| | Weakness #5 | -1 | -4 | 0 | -1 | -1 | n/a | -7 |
| Impact scores of environmental changes <br><br> **(S) = sum of impact** | | +11 <br> -7 <br><br> **(S) + 4** | +7 <br> -10 <br><br> **(S) - 3** | +11 <br> -8 <br><br> **(S) + 3** | +11 <br> -7 <br><br> **(S) + 4** | +4 <br> -3 <br><br> **(S) + 1** | | |

**FIGURE B.19**   Simplified illustrative SWOT analysis with score allocation

Source: authors based on Johnson et al. (2005)[22]

The relatively simplistic classification of environmental circumstances and dynamics into the categories 'opportunities' and 'threats' could be somewhat unsuited for the fast-changing, complex and uncertain environments in which today's firms may operate and compete. Therefore, some scholars have pointed out that instead of this binary threat/opportunity view of the external environment, managers should adopt a 'multiplexed' approach that provides more flexibility in responding to these dynamics.[23] This approach entails that managers cultivate a flexible way of framing or presenting the challenges that the company faces, enabling the company to trial alternate strategic responses to disruptive developments and to reject more quickly those courses of action that did not result in satisfactory outcomes.[24] To apply this approach, it helps to look at the urgency and type of the challenges, coupled with a company's heritage in terms of strengths and weaknesses, and to develop a varied combination of multiple, competing perspectives to respond to these challenges.[25]

# Endnotes (references)

1.  Barney, J.B. (1991) 'Firm resources and sustained competitive advantage', *Journal of Management*, 17: 99–120.
2.  Barney (1991)
3.  Barney, J.B. and Hesterly, W.S. (2010) 'VRIO Framework', in J.B. Barney and W.S. Hesterly (eds) *Strategic Management and Competitive Advantage*. Hoboken, NJ: Pearson, 68–86.

4. Porter, M.E. (1985) *Competitive Advantage: Creating and Sustaining Superior Performance*. New York, NY: The Free Press; Siggelkow, N. (2001) 'Change in the presence of fit: The rise, the fall, and the renaissance of Liz Claiborne', *Academy of Management Journal*, 44: 838–57; Siggelkow, N. (2002) 'Evolution toward fit', *Administrative Science Quarterly*, 47: 125–59.

5. Porter, M.E. (1996) 'What is strategy?', *Harvard Business Review*, Nov/Dec: 61–78.

6. Porter (1985); Porter, M.E. (2001) 'The value chain and competitive advantage', *Understanding Business Processes*, 2: 50–66.

7. Bloomberg (2022) 'Bloomberg Terminal [Software]', *Bloomberg*. www.bloomberg.com/professional/solution/bloomberg-terminal (accessed June 22, 2023).

8. Holopainen, M. and Toivonen, M. (2012) 'Weak signals: Ansoff today', *Futures*, 44 (3): 198–205; Nunes, P. and Breene, T. (2011) 'Reinvent your business before it's too late', *Harvard Business Review*, 89: 80–7.

9. Tableau (2022) 'About Tableau: Helping people see and understand data', *Tableau*. www.tableau.com/about (accessed June 22, 2023).

10. Porter, M.E. (2008) 'The five competitive forces that shape strategy', *Harvard Business Review*, 86 (1): 78–93.

11. Ryall, M.D. (2013) 'The new dynamics of competition', *Harvard Business Review*, 91 (60): 80–7.

12. Hunt, M.S. (1972) *Competition in the Major Home Appliance Industry, 1960–1970*. PhD Thesis, Harvard University, Cambridge MA.

13. Smith, W.R. (1956) 'Product differentiation and market segmentation as alternative marketing strategies', *Journal of Marketing*, 21 (1): 3–8.

14. Treacy, M. and Wiersema, F. (1993) 'Customer intimacy and other value disciplines', *Harvard Business Review*, 71 (1): 84–93.

15. Kim, W.C. and Mauborgne, R. (2014) *Blue Ocean Strategy, Expanded Edition: How to Create Uncontested Market Space and Make the Competition Irrelevant*. Cambridge, MA: Harvard Business Review Press.

16. Adner, R. (2017) 'Ecosystem as structure: An actionable construct for strategy', *Journal of Management*, 43 (1): 39–58.

17. Talmar, M., Walrave, B., Podoynitsyna, K.S., Holmström, J. and Romme, A.G.L. (2020). 'Mapping, analysing and designing innovation ecosystems: The Ecosystem Pie Model', *Long Range Planning*, 53 (4): article #101850.

18. Adner (2017)

19. Adner, R. (2012) *The Wide Lens: A New Strategy for Innovation*. London: Penguin.

20. Kay, J., McKiernan, P. and Faulkner, D. (2006) 'The history of strategy and some thoughts about the future', in D. Faulkner and A. Campbell (eds), *The Oxford Handbook of Strategy*. Oxford: Oxford University Press, 21–46; Madsen, D.Ø. (2016) 'SWOT analysis: A management fashion perspective', *International Journal of Business Research*, 16 (1): 39–56.

21. Kay et al. (2006); Madsen (2016)

22. Johnson, G., Scholes, K. and Whittington, R. (2005) *Exploring Corporate Strategy* (7th ed.). Harlow: Pearson Education

23. Fraser, J. and Ansari, S. (2021) 'Pluralist perspectives and diverse responses: Exploring multiplexed framing in incumbent responses to digital disruption', *Long Range Planning*, 54 (5): article #102016.

24. Scialom, M. (2022) '"End binary threat/opportunity view of economy" says Cambridge Judge study', *Cambridge Independent*, January 5. www.cambridgeindependent.co.uk/business/end-binary-threat-opportunity-view-of-economy-says-cambrid-9233674 (accessed June 22, 2023).

25. Fraser and Ansari (2021)

# PART III
## CHOOSE

This part explains how better decisions about strategies are made. It builds on the analysis conducted in Part 2 and arrives at necessary choices between promising options. Among the classic concepts to develop options, we provide ideas about how to develop a distinctive business strategy (e.g., generic strategies such as focus, differentiation, and cost leadership), how to achieve corporate growth through diversifation (e.g., vertical integration, horizontal diversification, conglomerate diversification) and internationalization (e.g., global, mulitidomestic, transnational), how to build synergies between business (corporate parenting advantages), and how to cooperate with other organizations (e.g., equity alliances, contractual alliances, associational alliances). In this part we also help students in strategic management to craft their own strategies going beyond choosing between generic options; we explain various practical tools and approaches for refining multiple alternatives through iterations and learning. This chapter does not only provide a range of different strategies, the ChooseWell toolkit also helps students develop and internalize the 'algorithm' that helps to process these alternatives and deliver a successful strategy.

# 10
# BUSINESS-LEVEL STRATEGY

## LEARNING OBJECTIVES

After reading this chapter, you should be able to:

- distinguish between differentiation, cost leadership, and focus strategies;
- discuss the three roots of strategic positioning and how they relate to generic strategies;
- recommend when and how leveraging network effects can be an alternative generic strategy;
- articulate the characteristics of competition in different competitive contexts;
- offer suggestions regarding how to respond to disruptive innovations.

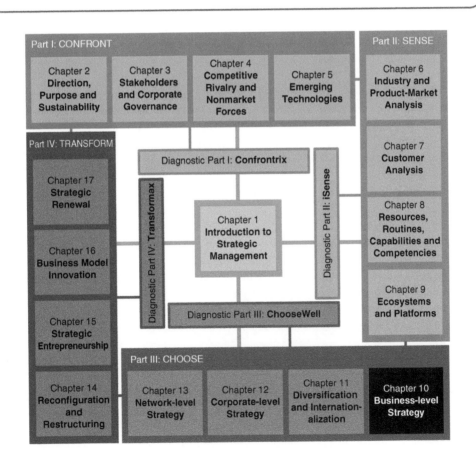

## OPENING CASE

### Tesla versus Volkswagen[1]

Source: © lv-olga (2021) / Shutterstock.

Source: © Monaco (2019) / Shutterstock.

The electric vehicle (EV) market is rapidly developing, and the Volkswagen group has announced that it is after Tesla's crown by 2025. If we unpack this clash, what is eye-catching is how different the two companies are. Tesla, founded in 2003, leads the electric vehicle market in the US with a 55% market share, whereas the Volkswagen group, founded in 1937, leads in Europe with a 34% market share. Tesla has been an electric vehicle manufacturer from inception, whereas Volkswagen has had to turn around its business to accommodate the electric vehicle trend.

Tesla owns only the Tesla car brand but seeks to address different types of customers through different models. Even though all of Tesla's models are electric vehicles, it rapidly increased its market share by means of its Model 3, a relatively cheap model, starting from €48,980. Production started in July 2017 and resulted in it becoming the best selling electric vehicle in the world as well as one of the best selling vehicles overall.

The Volkswagen group, on the other side, holds a multitude of brands, among which are Volkswagen, SEAT, Audi, Porsche and Bugatti (which each in turn comprise a variety of models). The Volkswagen group seeks to penetrate the EV market from a multitude of angles. Porsche and Bugatti will have to conquer the upper side of the market, SEAT the lower side of the market, and Volkswagen and Audi will fight for the respectively lower and higher part of the middle of the market. Volkswagen sparked its fight against Tesla through their ID.3, which starts from €33,490, and ID.4, which starts from €39,190. Though later to the electric vehicle game than Tesla, especially due to its combustion-based legacy, the ID.3 and ID.4 topped the sales charts in Europe.

One of Tesla's concerns amid these recent developments is that it is losing market share. New entrants into the electric vehicle market, especially the Volkswagen group's aggressive stance, have been a major issue. Supply chain problems, particularly in relation to manufacturing, have additionally caused major bottlenecks in supplying customers with Tesla cars. Price hikes have also been of concern, and have caused the more price-conscious customer to look for alternatives.

The Volkswagen group is not free of concerns either. Tesla trumps Volkswagen in China, which by all standards is a massive market. The fast development of the electric vehicle market in China, alongside the emergence of local players, means that Volkswagen has had to shift gears quickly. As Volkswagen Chief

Executive Herbert Diess puts it: 'customers for the EVs are much younger and different to our customer base we are having with the more traditional brands like Volkswagen in China.'[2]

### Questions

1. Which company's generic strategy do you think will be advantageous over time?
2. Do you believe it is a disadvantage that Tesla is focusing solely on upper segments of the car market?

# Introduction

The topics discussed in Part I and II of this book laid out the present-day context, factors, and issues confronting firms and how to analyze these with a view to decide and deploy the right strategy, at the right time, and at the right (market) location. In this third part of the book, we focus on the strategic choices firms must make at the business (unit) level (this chapter), the corporate level (Chapters 11 and 12), and the network level (Chapter 13).

Starting with business-level strategy, which is also known as competitive strategy, this chapter zooms in on decisions regarding how to specifically compete in a particular line of business or industry. First, we discuss three generic competitive-strategy choices available to firms, namely differentiation strategy, cost leadership strategy, and focus strategy. The three generic strategies reflect different ways in which firms can position themselves. The opening case of this chapter illustrates the generic strategies of Tesla and Volkswagen, highlighting the dilemmas they face in choosing between pure and hybrid strategies. A firm's strategic position is typically the outcome of selecting one of three root modes of positioning (or some combination of them): variety-based positioning, needs-based positioning, and access-based positioning. We also discuss how advances in information technology, and especially the emergence of digital platforms, has revealed another type of generic strategy, the leveraging of network effects, which is a strategy that focuses on demand-side economies of scale. This chapter discusses the strategic implications of network effects for competitive strategy and throws light on how to compete using digital platforms.

Furthermore, we consider how the dynamics of competition are affected by an increase in the speed at which developments occur in digital and non-digital industries. The industry's clockspeed is a prime indicator of such competitive dynamics. The final part of this chapter looks at how an industry's clockspeed affects the degree to which firms can rely on their existing strategies and how they can respond to disruptive innovations. Having the right competitive strategy is very important for a firm's competitive advantage. This chapter aims to provide insights that help you as a strategist to make the right strategic choices for a company.

# Generic competitive strategies

Deciding on the strategic target and how to win in the marketplace (the firm's differentiators) are among the central strategic managerial tasks at the business (unit) level. More specifically, business-level executives need to decide whether to target a broad or narrow range of customers, and whether their business differentiates via low-cost competition or by being perceived as unique. Based on these two strategic dimensions, three types of strategic positionings, or generic strategies, can be identified, as indicated in the generic strategies framework[3] (see Figure 10.1):

- Differentiation: the main selling point to customers are desirable, distinctive features.
- Cost leadership ('no frills'): either the main selling point is low prices (while ensuring reasonable profits on sales through the realization of cost reductions) or the company or business unit charges industry-average prices while its cost base is below industry average.
- Focus: differentiation or cost leadership in a narrow target.

As the name of the framework suggests, these strategies are archetypical, meaning that basically any company can select any of these. Generic strategies comprise strategic features that are common across organizations. We will go through each of these three generic strategies in the upcoming paragraphs.

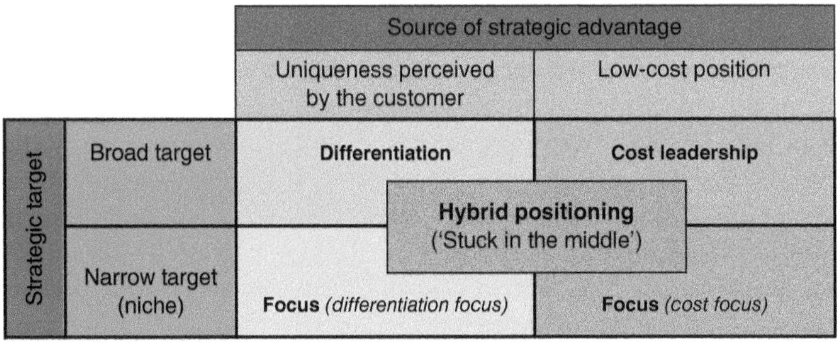

| | | Source of strategic advantage | |
| --- | --- | --- | --- |
| | | Uniqueness perceived by the customer | Low-cost position |
| Strategic target | Broad target | Differentiation | Cost leadership |
| | | Hybrid positioning ('Stuck in the middle') | |
| | Narrow target (niche) | Focus (differentiation focus) | Focus (cost focus) |

**FIGURE 10.1**　Porter's generic strategies framework

Source: adapted from Porter (1980a)

## Differentiation strategy

The **differentiation strategy** rests on a simple yet difficult to execute principle. Differentiators try to offer unique features (e.g., via unique products and services, design, image, quality, after-sales service) to meet the actual and emotional needs of customers in a way that competitors do not. With their unique offering, they can charge a price premium and get loyal customers. This premium should surpass the costs of being unique. Hence, what is important is whether and how much the customer is going to be willing to pay for this uniqueness. This is more difficult than it appears, as the customer will most likely have plenty of alternatives, especially cheaper alternatives, to choose from. Also, the more different you try to be, the steeper the cost curve is likely to be, as differentiation tends to go hand-in-hand with technological requirements. Then there is also the issue of timing. If you try to be different too soon, people may not be receptive to this differentiation, as it may feel too unfamiliar.

Products and services can be unique in terms of their functionality, making these offerings a must-have. They can also be unique in terms of their quality, due to chosen input materials or innovative design, or simply be perceived to be unique. In this case it is vital that you play into the customer's perception. For example, an input material or type of design may not actually enhance quality, but the way in which a product feels, or a service is experienced, may change substantially, and with this, perception may become completely different, leading to a higher willingness to pay.

One of the biggest advantages of the differentiation strategy is that sustaining differentiation over time can lead to higher brand reputation. People continuously experience your unique products and services, such that it becomes a must-have. Brand reputation works as a catalyst for sales, in that it increases willingness to pay beyond what solely the product or service itself can elicit. Brand reputation also temporarily works as an airbag, in case of less successful products and services. The flip side of brand reputation is that counterfeit products may emerge, and if your differentiated products are not cheap and are easy to remake, the business of counterfeits will become more attractive and lucrative. As counterfeit products' sales increase, your products' sales may decline in the absence of substantial benefits from buying the original product. Luxury brands such as LVMH, Cartier, and Prada are struggling with this fact a lot. This has led to the forming of the nonprofit Aura Blockchain Consortium, which has the goal of assuring customers about the authenticity of their luxury purchases through the use of blockchain technology.

## KEY DEBATE

### Moving beyond differentiation: Strategic similarity and frame of reference[4]

The strategic management literature emphasizes that it is important for a firm to be different from others. However, despite managers often tending to (over)emphasize points of differentiation, the literature also recognizes the relevance of similarities between firms. Phrases such as points of parity, strategic conformity, strategic groups, and strategic isomorphism have been coined to express the similarity in strategy between a firm and its competitors. A key advantage of such strategic similarity – for both a focal firm and its competitors – is increased legitimacy. This means that important actors, such as potential customers, suppliers and governmental agencies are more likely to note and acknowledge a group of similar companies and their market offerings. As a result, the similar companies are more likely to be perceived as credible players in the industry. The cryptocurrency market is one of the many markets where such legitimacy and related credibility are a major asset. In 2022, the loss of faith in the cryptocurrency exchange FTX resulted in people rushing to withdraw their money from it. This shows how lack of legitimacy may move a firm towards bankruptcy.

The strategic importance of legitimacy necessitates that a firm pays attention to points of similarity with other companies in its strategic category to be considered a legitimate and credible player. In case of a new solution, lack of similarity with prior solutions can make customers less sure what to expect and why they should buy the new solution. This is also one of the reasons why producers of vegetarian alternatives to meat (e.g., vegan burgers) try to highlight taste, look, and product name similarities of their products with meat-based products. Likewise, Burger King's shift from its original beef burgers to the vegan edition was accompanied by emphasizing the same taste and overlap in product names (e.g., Whopper versus Veggie Whopper).

Underlying the question on strategic differences and similarities is a more fundamental question that is often overlooked: what is the frame of reference? The frame of reference signals what external stakeholders

*(Continued)*

such as customers can expect to achieve when they get in touch with a company, for instance when consuming a (new) product. This frame of reference can be competitors in the same strategic group (with a similar strategy) or broader. In case of vegetarian burgers, the original meat burgers were used as a frame of reference to signal what customers can expect by consuming that product. A broader frame of reference can be advantageous to compare a solution with new and potentially disrupting ones in other categories (and thereby spot the points of similarity and differences with it). Although differentiation has received quite some attention, 'sound competitive positioning requires the identification of an appropriate frame of reference and associated points of parity and points of difference'.[5]

## Questions

1.  What is the importance of a proper frame of reference in strategic positioning?
2.  What are some consequences if firms overemphasize differentiation at the expenses of strategic similarity?
3.  Why do you think Uber headed deliberately for the frame of reference of being a tech company instead of a taxi company?

## Cost leadership strategy

When given the opportunity to choose, the **cost leadership strategy** may not initially sound appealing to most people, but some of the world's most successful companies (including Primark and Walmart) have mastered this generic strategy to get where they currently are. The low-cost strategy is about creating the lowest price in the industry that rivals cannot meet for products and services of roughly the same quality. It can also be about charging industry-average prices while the cost base is below industry-average. While margins per product will be slim, they will either be equal to or higher than those of rivals if you can really manage to be the cost leader. By having lower prices than rivals with at least similar margins, the cost leader will be tremendously profitable through mass sales.

Important for cost leadership is that you are indeed able to suppress costs. This initially requires you to be efficient. Economies of scale are important in this respect, meaning that you are actually able to spread your fixed costs across the many units that you are going to sell. It is also important that you actually utilize all of the capacity you have and do not let anything go to waste, to again maximally utilize economies of scale. Furthermore, cost leadership requires that you substitute more expensive input materials for cheaper ones, that are nevertheless going to deliver decent quality. Finally, it is key to eliminate waste in organizational processes, and any activity that is nonessential should be stopped. Essential activities should be done in the cheapest way possible. If you cannot do this by yourself, you can decide to share costs with alliance partners, or to completely outsource an activity. Pursuing a cost leadership strategy may start or catalyze price competition, potentially leading to situations where succeeding waves of cost reductions are not sufficient anymore for maintaining profit margins at a satisfactory level.

## Focus strategy

The differentiation and cost leadership strategies assume that an organization wants to have a broad appeal. Yet, many companies wish to only focus on a niche. This is where the focus strategy comes in. As opposed to the differentiation and cost leadership strategies with a rather broad target, the **focus strategy** is about addressing a particular need of a rather narrow target (niche), either via differentiation (i.e. focused differentiation strategy) or low costs (i.e. focused cost leadership strategy). Think of IKEA, which focuses mainly on customers who wish to put their own furniture together in exchange for cheaper products. Or think of Fairphone, which differentiates itself as being a phone manufacturer that has a lower environmental impact than rivals and hence caters to the needs of those who value environmental sustainability.

The biggest dilemma with focusing on a subset of the market is that you will potentially sell fewer units. Hence, selecting a focused strategy should be worth the loss of units sold. A niche player should first determine whether their chosen niche is actually big enough to enter into. The chosen market should be worth the entry costs, but also remain sufficiently interesting even after others follow you in. A saturated market is always uninteresting, but saturation is even more of a danger for niche markets due to their smaller size. The presence of multiple niche markets may be a solution, as potential competitors may decide to avoid entering yours in favour of entering another. Also, you need to understand why there is an unfulfilled niche. Has it been overlooked, or has it been avoided on purpose due to lack of lucrativeness? Furthermore, can the heightened focus on the niche market enable the firm to save more costs or increase profit margin more than the loss in terms of potential sales? The answers to these questions will determine whether a firm should become a niche player or not.

## Hybrid positioning: Best cost provider strategy

Not all customers want to have either a low price or a unique solution, but prefer a mixture between them. This would suggest a combination between various generic strategies. For a while, it was thought that the trade-offs of different generic strategies were nearly impossible to combine. It was feared that companies would get 'stuck in the middle', meaning that they would not be able organize their business around the seemingly different needs for different generic strategies. Such a company would get the worst of both generic strategies and consequentially would go bankrupt. A cost leadership strategy requires cost reduction through input substitution, waste reduction, economies of scale and capacity utilization. A differentiation strategy on the other hand tends to lead to a cost increase, due to more expensive input, retention of value adding nonessential activities, unique functionality, and quality design. Hence, combining both generic strategies was argued to bring with it costs and quality that are not competitive. Others could either have cheaper or better products through focusing solely on one generic strategy.

This convention changed with the years. A *hybrid generic strategy*, also called a **best-cost provider strategy**, received increasingly more attention as it proved to be a viable alternative to cost leadership and differentiation.[6] A hybrid generic strategy can be enacted in one of the following two ways:

1. A company can have a better product than a rival for the same costs.
2. They can have a similar product to a rival for less costs.

The difficulty in this is to avoid getting stuck in the middle, requiring that costs and quality need to be balanced in a delicate way. You cannot simply focus on maximally decreasing costs, or maximally increasing quality. While balancing both, quality needs to increase faster than costs do, and costs need to decrease faster than quality does. This is going to require that the people and technology you employ are indeed able to get more out of the same materials, equipment, input, and financial and other resources.

A hybrid strategy lends itself well to being in the middle of the market, if we look at it from a price and quality point of view. Being able to juggle costs and quality well should allow for products that are able to attract both cost conscious and trendy customers. If the middle of the market is a large space, this makes employing a hybrid strategy more attractive. But are there sufficient people that appreciate more modest differentiation? A threat to the hybrid strategy is macroeconomic downturn. Basically, because the hybrid strategy is enacted between the cost leadership and differentiation strategies, it is very receptive to changes in people's purchasing power. In the case of an economic recession, customers who shopped at differentiators may prefer those enacting a hybrid generic strategy, but more people may actually prefer the cost leaders over the hybrid generic strategy enactors. Economic downturn can be problematic if the company that enacts the hybrid generic strategy does not have a sufficiently large target market, has not been able to craft a sufficiently strong brand reputation, and does not especially appeal to less price-sensitive customers. LG's smartphone branch has been struggling for many years with being profitable because of these reasons, leading eventually to an exit.

Another way of combining generic strategies is through structural segregation of units that enact generic strategies. A holding can have different business units, which in turn have different generic strategies to each other. A business unit can then have different business divisions which again can each pursue different generic strategies. As different generic strategies require a different set of resources and capabilities, it is essential that structural segregation enables generic strategies to be carried out independently of each other.

## Strategic positioning

The generic strategies reflect strategic positions that can lead to competitive advantage through different routes. Strategic positions find their roots in different albeit sometimes overlapping sources:[7]

- Variety-based positioning: positioning based on a subset of an industry's products and services.
- Needs-based positioning: positioning based on serving nearly all of the needs of a particular customer group.
- Access-based positioning: positioning based on different ways to reach customers with certain needs.

A central premise of these three ways of positioning is that the essence of strategy is about doing different activities than competitors and/or about doing the same activities differently.[8] Without doing activities differently, competitors can easily do the same thing, making the focal firm's positioning neither unique nor valuable.

In the case of **variety-based positioning**, positioning occurs via product segments instead of customer segments. Such positioning allows a firm to serve a wide range of customers, but in most cases only a subset of their needs is met via that particular product. Many logistical companies, for example, apply this type of positioning, such as by delivering mail or parcels or by shipping chemical cargo. This type of positioning makes sense when a distinctive set of activities are needed to produce a particular set of products and services.

In the case of **needs-based positioning**, the positioning focuses on customers' needs and on a tailored set of activities required to serve those particular needs effectively. According to this positioning source, segmentation can be based on criteria such as price sensitivity, information and services requirements, or product features demanded by customers. Streaming services such as Disney+, HBO Max, Netflix, and Viaplay, for instance, focus on the customer group that is willing to pay for on-demand and/or live access to a wide variety of visual media content, such as movies, series, and sports games.

The third way of positioning – **access-based positioning** – is a less common source of strategic positioning when compared to the other two. In this case, positioning is based on different ways customers with similar needs can be reached. Differences in customer geography (e.g., urban and rural) or size (e.g., large versus small customers), for example, may require a different set of activities to reach those customers with rather similar needs. For example, large customers can be served via account managers, whereas smaller or more remote customers via online or local intermediaries. On-demand grocery delivery companies such as Flink and Getir and providers of shared electric scooters such as Check, Felyx, and Go Sharing are associated with this type of positioning by focusing on customers who are in urban areas.

# Competitive strategies in a digital era

Depending on which generic strategy is adopted, a firm aims to supply an offering that has either low price or unique attributes. To do so, firms need to perform different activities (when compared to competitors' ones) or to perform the same activities differently.[9] With the advent of the digital economy, some companies have been able to compete performing a different range of activities, for which they did not need to own seemingly critical resources. Airbnb, BlaBlaCar, and Booking.com, for example, do not own rooms, apartments, cars, or hotels, respectively, yet they are leading players in their industry (see Chapter 9). The digital economy seems to have enabled new ways of competing through, for instance, reducing the need to own physical infrastructure, connecting two sides of the market, scaling up, and collecting vast amounts of data (see Chapter 9). This seems to contrast with conventional strategic thinking that posits that competitive advantage is based on *possessing and controlling* unique and valuable resources (see Chapter 8).

## Pipeline versus platform strategies: External network effects as main differentiator

The rise of IT has challenged foundational strategy assumptions, with digital firms creating 'new rules of strategy'.[10] Conventional *pipeline businesses* control a linear series of activities to convert various inputs (such as raw materials) into finished products. Pipeline businesses are congruent with the classic value chain view, comprising a series of sequential activities (see Chapter 8). Accordingly, the focus of this type of business commonly lies on supply-side economies of scale, where high fixed costs, low marginal costs and higher sales volumes allow firms to achieve lower costs per unit as the quantity of production increases. The cycle perpetuates as having lower costs allow the firm to set lower prices, which will consequently attract additional volume, enabling the firm to further reduce costs. Hence, in pipeline businesses, competitive advantage is achieved through reaping the advantages of unique resources and activities to achieve economies of scale (and scope).

While supply-side economies of scale dominate in pipeline businesses, *demand-side* economies of scale (referred to in Chapter 9 as *network effects*) are a driving force behind platform businesses, which have proliferated in the digitalized economy (see Chapter 5).

In *platform businesses*, the higher the volume of participants (such as producers and consumers) using the platform, the higher the average value per transaction. This happens because platform businesses intermediate the transactions between user groups (see Chapter 9). Thus, the higher the number of producers and consumers, the better and more accurate is the match between supply and demand, and the richer is the data that can be utilized to refine matching algorithms. In platform businesses, higher volume of participants leads to higher value to participants, which, in turn, attracts even more participants. As with supply-side economies of scale, demand-side economies of scale may generate or reinforce virtuous feedback loops for the firms but may push the market towards a monopolistic structure. For instance, think of how Google, Meta and TikTok utilize vast amounts of data to provide higher average value per transaction via more targeted advertisements and how they (mainly the first movers) were monopolizing the market for long periods of time.

As already becomes clear from the above, platform and pipeline business strategies are different in various ways (see Table 10.1). Pipeline businesses seek to gain advantage by controlling assets (e.g., resources and capabilities) that are valuable, rare, inimitable, non-substitutable and organized (VRINO; see Chapter 8). Whereas in platform strategy, the main asset is the network of producers and consumers (or other user groups), which is combined with the resources that the participants own and contribute towards the network. Hence, the community and their participants' resources are crucial assets for companies such as Airbnb, Alibaba, and Just Eat Takeaway.com.

Pipeline businesses create value by optimizing their chain of production activities, which requires organizing their internal resources including labour. In contrast, platform businesses create value by facilitating or orchestrating interactions between customers and external producers. Whereas internal process optimization is a key skill in pipeline businesses, ecosystem governance and participants attraction become essential skills when following a platform strategy.

**TABLE 10.1**   Differences between pipeline and platform strategy

|  | Pipeline business strategy | Platform strategy |
|---|---|---|
| **Economies of scale:** | Supply-side | Demand-side |
| **Resources:** | Resource control | Resource orchestration |
| **Value creation:** | Internal optimization | External interaction |
| **Likelihood to move into unrelated industries:** | Relatively low: often tends to focus on defending existing positions | Relatively high: can tend to move aggressively into new territories |
| **Value maximization of:** | Customer value | Ecosystem value |
| **Role of producers and consumers:** | Typically fixed | Can vary |
| **Main unit of analysis:** | Goods and services (and their revenues and profit) | Interactions: exchanges of value between producers and consumers |

Source: based on Van Alstyne et al. (2016)

The lack of physical infrastructure and assets also gives platform businesses a competitive edge over pipeline ones, especially related to capital requirements. Platform businesses can use their ecosystem governance skills and their skills in growing networks to enter into new markets without capital-intensive investments, simply by orchestrating the assets of their participants. Firms with a successful platform strategy tend to adopt aggressive market-entry strategies, conquering the markets where they operate. Some examples are Airbnb and Uber that conquered the hospitality and the ride-hailing markets, respectively.

Pipeline businesses aim to generate maximum value for end customers that lie at the end of a linear process through offering a product (good or service). In contrast, platform strategy aims to maximize the ecosystem's value by expanding the network (increasing the number of platform users) in an iterative, feedback-driven, and circular process. The impressive increase of the number of apps on app-stores, participants providing reviews, and influencers and followers on social media are just a few examples of how platform-centred ecosystems (see Chapter 9) can expand. The interactive process associated with a platform strategy can also unfold via roles changing between producers and consumers. A platform user can opt for Uber for requesting a ride, but can also be an Uber driver in different moments in time. Additionally, platform users can be producers and consumers simultaneously – for instance, social media platform users alternate roles between consuming and producing content.

In pipeline businesses, the focus is on selling goods and services to customers, and therefore their primary focus is on their products and respective revenues and profits. In contrast, platform businesses are interested mostly in the exchange of value between platform users. Such focus on interactions require platform businesses to implement metrics on interaction failure (failure to match supply and demand – 'no search results' – which diminish network effects) and user engagement (tracking the degree of involvement of platform users) to monitor and boost the interaction performance. Although a single interaction (e.g., a view on TikTok or YouTube) may involve little or no profit, it is the sheer size of the interactions, combined with the related network effects, that is the main source of competitive advantage for platform businesses.[11]

The different features of platform businesses when compared to those of pipeline businesses challenge foundational assumptions of the traditional (and still dominant) Industrial Organization (I/O) view on strategy and industry structure, as expressed in Porter's Five Forces framework (see Table 10.2). First, there is a shift in focus from firm-level value creation and appropriation, through producing and distributing products, to value creation at the ecosystem level through the exploitation of demand-side economies of scale (instead of supply-side economies of scale). Second, much of existing theory, which mostly derives from pipeline industrial businesses, assumes that firms in an industry compete for a slice of a fixed-size market in a zero-sum game. This implies a battle for a larger slice of a fixed pie – hence, if one player wins, the other loses. However, in the digital economy, market players can jointly increase the total market size in a non-zero-sum game fashion. In this battle for larger slices of a variable pie, all players can win. Third, traditional industry views defend that industry boundaries are well-defined and fixed. However, platform-centred ecosystems often span across multiple industries or product markets, which may be unrelated to each other. Finally, platforms challenge the assumption that market entries can be costly. In a digital economy market, the ease to enter and exit markets due to low sunk costs – as firms do not own all the resources – can lead to *hit-and-run entry* strategies. In this type of entry strategy, firms can quickly grasp a portion of the market share and profit but can also leave those markets fairly easily if they are not successful.

**TABLE 10.2**    Boundary conditions of the Five Forces Framework in a digital economy

| Assumptions in traditional I/O view | Competition in a digital economy |
|---|---|
| An industry is well-defined and its boundaries are fixed | Platforms often span multiple industries and boundaries are fluid |
| Market entry is costly, especially when profits are high | Market entry is cheap; opportunities for hit-and-run entry |
| Zero sum, it's a 'battle' for a variable slice of a fixed pie:<br><br>- Five Forces all compete for the same pie, eating away at firm's share<br>- All firms operating in the same stage of the value chain are competitors<br>- Suppliers and customers are sources of value slippage | Positive sum, it's a 'battle' for a variable slice of a variable pie:<br><br>- Complementors are an important source of value creation<br>- Competitors can help to legitimize and establish an industry<br>- Customers and suppliers can be a source of value creation |
| The best (i.e., differentiated, lowest price) product wins the competition | It is not always the best product that wins the competition |
| First movers are best positioned due to learning and scale advantages | First movers do not always win, learning and scale (at the supply-side) have become less important |
| Macro-level factors (e.g., governments) do not affect value capture | Macro-level factors (e.g., platform governance) strongly affect value capture |

## STRATEGIC FOCUS

### The long tail: Selling less of more[12]

Pursuing a strategy of blockbuster hits for the mass market with the 'winner-takes-it-all' effects might sound attractive, but there is another, opposite strategy that can also be interesting, namely 'selling less of more'. Firms in, for instance, the beer, books and music market have been shown to survive or thrive by operating in fragmented, heterogenous markets. The utilization of IT enabled them to relax the basic constraints of brick-and-mortar businesses (i.e., traditional face-to-face businesses).

Brick-and-mortar businesses have a limited amount of shelve space, requiring firms to make choices between what to put on the shelves and what not. The number of products that fit on the limited shelve space, and the amount of customers in the local geographical area who are willing to pay for those products, are basic constraints for those businesses. Consequently, many firms will put the (potential) top sellers on the shelves.

However, customer demands or preferences often overwhelm the supply of what can be found in a typical brick-and-mortar business. The rise of digital technologies enables businesses to bridge the shortage of supply (on the shelves) to that demand as it enables a tremendous expansion in the variety of products and services that can be made, promoted and sold. For instance, storing a product online is typically much cheaper (e.g., a few lines in a database versus a physical shelf space) and online distribution and promotion enables direct contact with customers (instead of via intermediaries). The lower costs of producing, promoting and selling a solution (e.g., a song) through online platforms makes it more lucrative to invest efforts and time in creating solutions that may appeal to only a small fraction of customers.

Moreover, even if certain customer demands or preferences may be rare in a particular local area, digital technologies aggregate those rare tastes at a national, continental or global scale. Such aggregation may turn into a sufficient or more attractive niche to focus on. Digital technologies thus enable a firm to cater to customer demands for niche offerings which could not have been met via a typical brick-and-mortar business. The sales of niche products that cannot be provided profitably via a brick-and-mortar model are referred to as 'long tail' businesses (i.e., selling low volumes of more specialized products) (see Figure 10.2).

The long tail may also change customer demands and preferences. Markets with increased product variety and information may allow customers to find, evaluate and buy products that otherwise would have been unavailable. This would allow them to cultivate even stronger demands or preferences for those niche products. This suggests that the long tail may change customer tastes, thereby leading to a further lengthening of the long tail.

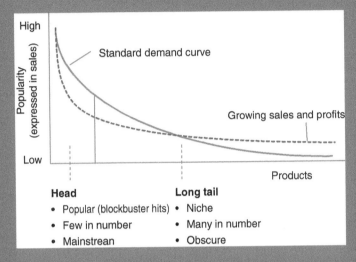

**FIGURE 10.2** The long tail

Source: adapted from Elberse (2008)

## Questions

1. How does the pursuit of a long tail strategy relate to generic strategy choices?
2. How does the pursuit of a long tail strategy affect the chances of disruption?
3. What is the importance of search tools (e.g., on the company website) for firms pursuing a long tail strategy?

## Platform competition

Network effects are a key determinant of a platform's success. This does not, however, mean that a platform can neglect value creation for customers and complementors. A proper competitive position is crucial in that respect. A unique competitive position allows a platform to differentiate itself from other platforms and can result in less head-to-head competition. **Platform identity** delineates a platform's technological and market profile that determines a platform's identity domain and, in doing so, the type and intensity of platform competition.[13] This is shaped by two main factors: the platform architecture and the platform scope (or platform-market scope). The **platform architecture** covers functionalities, capabilities, performance, and the technical structure of a platform, which is especially relevant for innovation platforms. As an example, consider the difference between an iPhone (with its operating system iOS) and an Android-based smartphone (such as a Samsung smartphone): the former is more closed and integrated in its architecture, with far fewer variants of the architecture, whereas the latter has multiple brands and variants across producers using the operating system and is more open in terms of the platform itself. Quite similar to the generic strategies framework (see Figure 10.1), the **platform scope** relates to whether the platform aims to be a niche specialist versus a market generalist. For instance, consider the difference between Toptal, which aims to admit only top freelancers (see Chapter 9), and a generalist freelance platform such as Fiverr where everyone can offer services. Platform scope also relates to how the complements and content of a platform are similar and/or different to other platforms (e.g., a platform having many exclusive complements that are not available on other platforms).

The strategic advantages of a platform strategy in the digital era – compared to a pipeline business – have attracted the attention of firms. This means that firms with a platform strategy face increased chances of competition from firms on a competing platform. How can firms with a platform strategy succeed or thrive with such platform competition?

## Revolutionary functionality versus envelopment

Based on the ideas we highlighted in Chapter 9, there is one simplified way to think about the value a platform provides to a customer: the combination of technological functionality, size of the installed base, and the availability of complements.[14] Unless a new entrant platform can have interoperability with the installed base (customer base) or with the existing complements of a competing platform, they need to offer a big jump in functionality such that different user groups, including complementors, can be persuaded to adopt the platform and allow it to compete with the existing platform. This is also known as providing **revolutionary functionality**.[15]

There is also another way in which a platform can compete with other platforms: **platform envelopment**.[16] A platform (the *enveloping platform*) is said to 'envelop' another platform (the *enveloped platform*) when it enters another platform's market by combining its own functionality with that of the other platform. A classic example is how Internet Explorer won over Netscape, the world's first successful web browser. Microsoft simply started to provide Internet Explorer with newer version of Windows. Customers, most of them first-time buyers of PCs to connect to the internet, therefore tended to use Internet Explorer, eventually causing Netscape's demise – which has been later brought up as an important issue in the antitrust lawsuit case *United States vs. Microsoft Corp.* Envelopment leverages one or more of the following (depending on whether the platforms before envelopment are complements, substitutes, or are functionally unrelated): a substantial overlap in user base between the enveloping and the enveloped platform; economies of scope in production and/or marketing, and pricing the bundle of platform functionalities such that the enveloping platform profits via price discrimination.

## Multidimensional competition

Competition in platform markets resembles a game of multidimensional chess since a platform owner needs to manage competition across three levels:[17] (1) platform versus platform; (2) platform versus complementor; and (3) complementor versus complementor.

Platform-versus-platform competition is the most visible one in many people's minds – for example, the competition between PlayStation and Xbox, or between Android and iOS. The issue is that, in order to manage the platform-versus-platform competition, platform owners usually create their own complements – examples here are Apple's own apps for notes, camera flashlight, or files, or Super Mario games for Nintendo. This however may create an important tension between complementors and the platform owner since a platform owner's entry into the complement space may mean lower sales for the complementor – for instance, customers stopped downloading third-party apps for camera flashlights as built-in controls for the flashlight were directly offered by Apple starting from iOS 7. However, a platform owner's entry into the space of complementors could be also beneficial to these complementors, as the introduction of complements by the platform owner may help the platform to be adopted by more users, which benefits complementors. It may even drive innovation for complementors, as the platform owner's entry may cause customers to focus more on a particular complement category.[18] Finally, although having complements helps platform owners to gain customers and drive indirect network effects, competition between complementors is also an important dilemma a platform needs to manage – some competition helps complementors to bring their best to the platform users, but too much competition may end up discouraging existing and potential complementors to provide complements on the platform altogether.

## CRACK-THE-CASE
### Trendyol's European ambitions

Source: © Schneider (2021) / Shutterstock.

*(Continued)*

Trendyol is one of Turkey's leading e-commerce platforms. Founded by Demet Mutlu in 2010 to fill a gap in the market – the lack of a fashion retail platform – Trendyol has grown to be Turkey's most valuable company. While it has become a very strong player in fashion retail through its brands Trendyolmilla, Trendyol Modest and Trendyol Man, Trendyol has grown its interests over the years and is active in many different, though related fronts. The company launched its own logistics division to both enhance its own customer service as well as to accommodate other companies' needs during the global COVID-19 pandemic. Trendyol has also moved into grocery and meal delivery, taken over and enhanced a platform for second-hand products and initiated its own financial payment and loyalty system within its e-commerce platform. Trendyol still predominantly focuses on fashion retail as the key aspect of its platform, and recently started looking beyond Turkey's borders to enter into the fashion retail industry of 27 other European countries. They have a strong foothold in the Turkish fashion retail industry and seek to combat e-commerce platforms like Amazon and Zalando on the one side, and fashion retail chains such as H&M and Zara on the other. Trendyol hopes to benefit from cost advantages due to a relatively cheap Turkish lira, and with that, cheap labour and materials.

Important in all this has been Trendyol's solid rounds of initial investment. They benefitted from investments from famous firms Tiger Global and Kleiner Perkins, and from the European Bank for Reconstruction and Development. In later years, funding from e-commerce giant Alibaba Group has been especially important.[19] The relationship between Alibaba Group and Trendyol dates back to 2018, when the e-commerce behemoth acquired majority ownership over Trendyol. Alibaba Group has kept on investing and by 2021 it had acquired 87% of the Turkish e-commerce platform, valued at a sizeable $9.3 billion. Trendyol has been able to grow thanks to the Alibaba Group's funds and expertise, but they're just getting started and seek yet another $1 billion in funds to further fuel their international ambitions.[20] Currently Trendyol sells roughly 1 million products a day and the annual value of products sold on its platform is about $10 billion.

## Questions

1.  Do you think Trendyol has what it takes to conquer Europe?
2.  Who are its rivals and who are not?
3.  Do you think it is wise for Trendyol to focus on H&M and Zara?

## STRATEGIC FOCUS

### Digital strategies[21]

Digital strategies are about creating and appropriating value by utilizing digital technologies in order to achieve long-term objectives.[22] The platform strategy may have received quite some attention as a digital strategy, but it is not the only one. There are also a couple of other digital strategies which sometimes can be applied in combination with each other. Those other digital strategies are:

- New marginal supply: tapping into sources of supply at a marginal cost due to the utilization of digital technology. For instance, H&M offers a reseller option for its own customers to sell used brand products to someone else.
- Digital-enabled products and services: creating new products with digital features using digital technology, typically as a way to serve new demand. P&G's Oral-B toothbrush with Bluetooth-enabled digital guidance is an example of that strategy.
- Rebundling and customizing: rebundling existing products with digital technology to better serve existing customers. An example is the *New York Times*' paywall allowing people to organize what they read and to personalize reading lists.
- Digital distribution channels: increase the convenience for customers to access a firm's offering via digital distribution channels. Web shops of retailers would fit into this, as would ordering a pizza online at Domino's or another chain.
- Cost efficiency: improving cost efficiency by using digital technology, typically via cost scaling or automatization. The automatization in greenhouses and warehouses is an illustration of that approach.

The first two digital strategies listed above are, just as a platform strategy, mainly offensive, targeting a new demand or new supply or a combination of them. The other three digital strategies that are listed are primarily defensive: they aim to improve what a firm already does. Over the long run, successful firms tend to apply at least a platform strategy, new marginal supply or digital-enabled products and services, sometimes accompanied by some of the other listed digital strategies.

## Questions

1. Why do you think that the platform strategy, new marginal supply or digital-enabled products and services are associated with successful firms?
2. Identify a firm that mainly applies one of the following three digital strategies: rebundling and customizing, digital distribution channels, or cost efficiency. Discuss how that firm can utilize one of the three digital strategies that are associated with successful firms.

# Competitive dynamics

Selecting a generic competitive strategy and/or defending that particular strategic position is not as simple as it might seem. Competitors may close the gap between a firm's competitive positionings (e.g., via imitation), or surpass it with a different competitive advantage (e.g., via innovation). For instance, the competitors of a firm might have a better cost leadership strategy, which hampers the focal firm's ability to attract a larger audience and achieve economies of scale. Similarly, firms pursuing a differentiation strategy may need to reconsider their positioning if they cannot (any longer) charge a sufficiently high premium able to cover the costs they incur. Customers might, for instance, not be willing to pay for the unique features that the firm's products offer, or competitors have found differentiating factors that are more appealing to customers. If firms do not meet the central requirements of their generic strategy or those requirements become outdated in their market, they need to reconsider their competitive strategy.

## Strategic implications of an industry's clockspeed

Industry competitive rivalry (see Chapter 4) and competitive dynamics are pivotal to assess for how long and to what extent a firm can rely on its existing generic strategy. **Industry clockspeed** is a prominent indicator of the competitive dynamics in an industry. It captures the rate of industry change due to endogenous factors (such as competitive and technological developments). Such industry-level changes reflect the aggregate actions that are initiated by all incumbent firms within an industry on three facets:[23]

- Organizational clockspeed: the rate of change of strategic actions (e.g., mergers or international expansion) and structural changes (e.g., changes in top management) of incumbent firms in an industry.
- Product clockspeed: the rate at which new products are introduced and become obsolete.
- Technological process clockspeed: the rate at which process technologies are being replaced in an industry.

The clockspeed may vary among different industries, just as the rate of change may not be stationary within an industry over time. In industries where the rate of change is rather low ('slow-clockspeed industries'), strategic persistence by maintaining existing sources of competitive advantage related to a specific strategic position for quite a while has its merits. Under those circumstances, firms can rely on, protect and reinforce their existing resources and competitive strategies. In such settings, fewer opportunities may also be available to tap into. The development of new sources of competitive advantage (e.g., via product and process innovations) at a high rate may then even hurt firm performance, because it can cannibalize the sales of rather successful existing solutions.[24] Airline manufacturers such as Boeing and Airbus and oil and gas companies such as BP and Shell have relied for quite a long time on their specific generic strategies, operating in slow-clockspeed industries.

However, relatively stable settings may experience leapfrogging strategies by outsiders that bring disruptive solutions to the market. Google's move into the optic industry via Google glass was just one example of that. This suggests that even in slow-clockspeed industries, firms need to reconsider their existing generic strategy in a timely manner before others force them to do so.

In industries where the rate of change is rather high ('fast-clockspeed industries'), strategic flexibility by fundamentally altering a generic strategy in a timely manner is vital for a firm's success. Firms operating in such environments may find their existing generic strategies to be outdated sooner rather than later. Reconsidering their generic strategies enables them to adapt to those changing circumstances – or even drive those developments – by tapping into emerging strategic opportunities or responding to competitive threats.[25] Such reconsiderations may lead to a shift or extension to a different generic strategy (or the hybrid approach) or a fundamental revision within the same type of generic strategy.

## CRACK-THE-CASE

Under Armour under fire: Time to change strategy?[26]

Source: © Way (2021) / Shutterstock.

Founded in 1996, Under Armour is a firm that has enjoyed a fascinating growth trajectory. There are not many people who will not have heard about its clothing to enhance sports performance. Steeply rising stock and double-digit growth across numerous years made many believe the sky was the limit. At one time Under Armour overtook sports apparel giant Adidas in combined footwear and apparel sales, and approached industry leader Nike. In 2013, Under Armour signed an exclusive sneaker and merchandise deal with NBA athlete Stephen Curry to rival Nike's Jordan line. Later on, seemingly to send a message to Nike and Adidas, the company signed the largest ever college athletics sponsorship deal. Under Armour even moved into technology as it sought to infuse its high-performance athlete base with data-based performance feedback, acquiring apps like 'MapMyFitness' and 'MyFitnessPal'. However, Adidas and Nike are no strangers to digital strategies. Adidas' Runtastic division is known for its Running and Training apps, and Nike's Training Club and Run Club apps are also well known to athletes.

Under Armour's success story began to change only a few years ago. Between September 2015 and March 2020, its share price dropped 86%. Under Armour lost a lot of money from being dependent on large retailers at a time when many were going bankrupt. Nike however was focused increasingly on e-retail and direct sales. Under Armour also faced problems related to ineffective human resource management. New hires were not properly

*(Continued)*

integrated, which resulted in faulty market analyses and failed market launches. At human resource management level, Under Armour failed to craft a culture of trust and inclusion. Another issue related to the firm carrying out investments in areas of sport (particularly college sport) where it lacked expertise. While Under Armour was skilled in understanding the needs of football and basketball players, it was less so in running and volleyball. When its clothing did not live up to the promise to those athletes, they went to the rivals instead. Finally, a big dilemma for Under Armour was around what to do with the expensive digital acquisitions it had made, as it failed to craft a strategy around infusing its clothing with software. To solve this last issue, by the end of 2020, Under Armour had decided to sell MyFitnessPal for a sum lower than its acquisition price in 2015.

In January 2020, Kevin Plank, Under Armour's founder, officially stepped down as CEO, making room for Patrik Frisk to help the firm find its way back to the top. An important area of debate is around the term 'athleisure', which is a combination of athletics and leisure. In recent years, Adidas and Nike have heavily invested in this part of the industry to meet the demands of consumers who wish to wear sporty clothes in daily life. This is a booming market, yet Under Armour has stayed firmly away from this part of the sports industry, and Frisk does not seem willing to change this. According to Plank, who is still executive chairman and brand chief, 'The world did not need another competent apparel or footwear manufacturer'. Rather, he said, 'what the customer needs is a dream'. The question is whether the firm will indeed be able to provide customers with this dream.

## Questions

1. How did the clockspeed of the industry in which Under Armour operates change over time?
2. How did that changing industry clockspeed affect the value of Under Armour's generic strategy?

## Responding to disruptive new ways of competing

New ways of competing may emerge, disrupting a firm's existing generic strategy (i.e., disruptive innovation). In such a scenario, a firm can select from five basic strategic responses (or some combination of these):[27]

1. Focus on and invest in the existing generic strategy.
2. Ignore the disruptive innovation.
3. Attack back: Disrupt the disruptive innovation via a different generic strategy.
4. Adopt the disruptive innovation while continuing with the existing generic strategy.
5. Embrace the disruptive innovation and scale it up.

Although it is hard to predict beforehand, not every disruptive innovation will become superior to already existing ways of competing nor conquer the entire market. A focal firm may decide to not adopt the disruptive innovation and instead invest in making its existing generic strategy even more attractive and competitive. Capitalization of large investments in the past are often a main driver for that decision, as is a focus on important challenges related to the existing business. The entrance of low-cost airliners such as Ryanair and easy-Jet revealed a new dimension on how to compete in the European air travel market. Such low-cost strategies gave airliners such as British Airways the opportunity to accentuate their premium differentiation strategies (e.g., by emphasizing comfort) and to devote even further investments (e.g., in luxurious airport lounges) to make it even more premium.

Firms opting for the first basic response aim to make their existing competitive strategy more attractive relative to the disruptive innovation because they view it as a threat. In the second basic response – ignore– firms do not view it as a threat and continue as if it did not occur. Although a disruptive innovation may enter an industry, it does not per se mean that it hits a firm's market. It might just stay in a different market or niche without severely affecting a firm's main markets. The strategic importance of the disruptive innovation for the focal firm (e.g., to what extent it caters to the same customer demands) and the extent to which the existing resources of a firm can be leveraged if it would adopt that disruptive innovation are key in making the decision whether to ignore the development.[28] If the strategic importance is low and hardly any resources can be leveraged, then the disruptive innovation is apparently rather unrelated to the focal firm's market. This unrelatedness may make it more appealing to ignore the disruptive innovation.

Whereas the first basic response is about making the existing generic strategy even more competitive, the third one – attack back – is about the introduction of a new generic strategy to counter the disruptive innovation. This is also known as 'disrupt the disruptor'. The Apple iMac is a classic case in this respect: by emphasizing the design and style of its product, Apple responded to the rise of cheap alternatives in its business. As with disruptive innovation itself, disrupting the disruptor can take place via different approaches. Figure 10.3 categorizes those approaches on the basis of the performance of the core attribute (lower or higher) and of the new attribute (weak, moderate or strong) of the disruptive innovation compared to the product that is being disrupted. For example, whereas incumbents (Nissan, Toyota) entered in the mid-market with electric and hybrid vehicles, Tesla's high-performance electric sportscar (Roadster) – initially aimed for the small group of people who were able to afford it – is an example of the new-market high-end encroachment.

The fourth basic response to disruptive innovation is about adopting the disruptive innovation while continuing with the existing generic strategy. This happened for instance at Coca-Cola by setting up a generic strategy around bottled water alongside its main strategy. If a firm deems it attractive to adopt the disruptive innovation and develop a new generic strategy accordingly alongside its existing one, then it has to find a solution to manage those two different and potentially conflicting strategies. Firms that consider the size of the conflicts to be manageable are more likely to select this approach as opposed to the ones who view these conflicts as serious risks. Managing the conflicts related to multiple generic strategies within a single firm exceeds the scope of this chapter, but will be discussed in later chapters of this book (Chapters 11, 12 and 17).

Whereas the fourth basic response is to add a new generic strategy on top of the existing ones, the fifth basic response is to implement a new generic strategy which replaces the existing one. This enables a firm to focus on the new competitive strategy and avoid the conflicts of having multiple strategies. Incumbent firms possessing the skills and capabilities for scaling up but not really for inventing new knowledge may have an advantage with this fifth basic response in growing a disruptive innovation into the mass market.

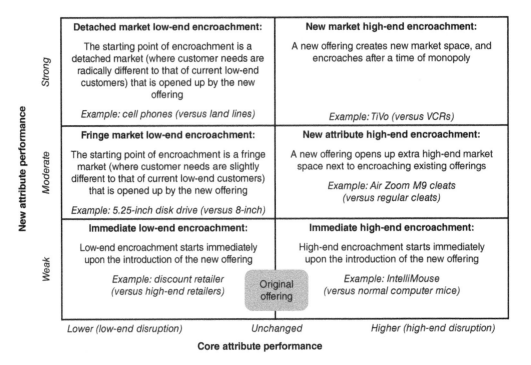

**FIGURE 10.3**  New Various encroachement approaches of disruptive innovation

If none of these five basic responses to disruptive innovation work out or the company is too late to respond properly, then moving away might also be a strategic response. This strategic move may be required to increase the chances of firm survival, especially when the disruptive innovation alters its existing market to such an extent that the firm loses its competitive edge. Firms whose performance is below their aspiration level are more likely to take higher risks in their endeavour to restore their performance. History is full of companies – such as Blackberry and Nokia – that have failed in one domain of business and therefore have chosen to emphasize another. Rather than holding on to a fight you cannot win, pursuing alternative possibilities may generate a greater competitive position for the company overall. In this case, diversification along product and service markets may help firms to opt for a strategic escape. After all, under high time pressure it may be difficult to build and move to a new market position from scratch, and it may be impossible to pull off such a move from an experience, resource and time point of view.

Of course, firms do not have to wait for disruptive innovation to occur and adjust their strategies accordingly. They can also be pioneering firms acting as disruptors themselves. By being among the first to introduce a new offering to a market, a firm may enjoy various first or early mover advantages, for instance because of technological leadership (think of reputational advantages), pre-emption of assets, and buyer switcher costs.[29] Until imitation and competition from followers is starting to take shape, first and early movers have the momentum to gain extra rewards from their new offerings. Although substantial risks are involved in pioneering a new direction, not doing so may lead to complete erosion of a market. The competitive dynamics play a crucial role in the extent it pays off to be a pioneering firm with a disruption strategy.[30]

## CLOSING CASE
### Smartphone industry illuminated

Source: © Ollyy (2023) / Shutterstock.

The smartphone industry is an illustrative example of an industry where competitors adopt different generic strategies. The industry is clearly segmented into lower, middle and higher tiers, with companies competing in one or multiple segments. The fact that phone manufacturers can span across segments and generic strategies adds an important level of dynamism to this industry – smartphone manufacturers can adjust their competitive position over time and across different products.

Plenty of smartphone manufacturers predominantly pursue a certain generic strategy. In terms of the cost leadership strategy, one can think of Alcatel and Motorola, which aim particularly for the lower end of the market. In terms of differentiators, Apple and Samsung come to mind as the most distinguishable actors who are pioneering in terms of smartphone design and technology (we can also count Huawei in this category, considering their performance in recent years). In the middle of the market, we find manufacturers such as Xiaomi, Oppo, and OnePlus, which predominantly pursue a hybrid generic strategy and seek to combine efficiency with elements of uniqueness.

The industry dynamism stems to a large degree from the fact that phone manufacturers can span across segments and generic strategies. Apple is addressing the middle of the market with some of its models, such as its 'SE' line, and even Samsung and Huawei have budget phones in their repertoires, such as the 'A12' and 'Y6P'. Similarly, Motorola also addresses the middle segment through its 'G100'. Xiaomi, Oppo, and OnePlus, in turn, all also

*(Continued)*

have budget and high-end models. Xiaomi's 'Redmi 9A' is a budget phone, but its 'MI1' is a high-end phone. Oppo's 'A15' is a budget phone, but its 'Find X3' is a high-end phone. Finally, OnePlus' 'Nord N100' is a budget phone, whereas the '9 Pro' is a high-end phone.

The competitive position of smartphone manufacturers is by no means static. Xiaomi and Oppo initially focused much more on the lower end of the smartphone industry, and were only able to concentrate on the middle and even higher end of the market later on once they had gained experience and expertise. Apple on the other hand increasingly tries to tap into the middle part of the industry, something it did not consider for many years. Finally, Huawei was known for years as a budget smartphone manufacturer, but in recent years has clearly moved up the ranks in terms of its aspirations and performance – they now predominantly launch handsets for the middle and upper end of the market.

Some smartphone manufacturers get stuck in the middle, causing them to readjust, downsize or even leave the smartphone industry in favour of other adventures. Blackberry was no match for the way in which Apple disrupted the smartphone industry. While Blackberry had more experience and sufficient resources, Apple's approach to design and the internet proved to be more correct. Blackberry hung on for years, but eventually downsized its smartphone business to focus predominantly on the business-to-business market. Similarly, HTC was for a long time a very strong player in the smartphone industry but could not keep up with giants such as Apple and Samsung in the most lucrative high-end market, and saw Google buy a substantial part of its smartphone team in return. Similarly, LG was no match for the emergence of Chinese companies from the lower end of the market and the cost advantages that Samsung had at the higher end of the market. Finding itself squeezed in the middle of the market, it decided to exit the industry.

### Questions

1. Do you think LG could have prevented getting squeezed in the middle of the market?
2. Do you think that Samsung or Apple will have to change their generic strategies anytime soon?

## Summary

- Three main generic competitive strategies are: a strategy based on providing features that are perceived as valuable and unique by customers (differentiation strategy); a strategy where the main selling point is low prices or industry-average prices combined with a below industry-average cost base (cost leadership); and differentiation or cost leadership in a narrow target (focus strategy). A hybrid generic strategy is a combination of those generic strategies.
- Three root modes of strategic positioning are: positioning based on a subset of an industry's products and services (variety-based positioning); positioning based on serving most of the needs of a particular customer group (needs-based positioning); and positioning based on different ways to reach customers with certain customer needs (access-based positioning).

- The advent of information technology was accompanied by an alternative 'generic' strategy: leveraging demand-side economies of scale (network effects).
- In an ecosystem context, competition takes place both within and between ecosystems.
- The platform architecture (functionalities, capabilities, performance, and the technical structure of a platform) and the platform scope (whether the platform aims to be a niche specialist versus a market generalist) shape a platform's identity.
- Platforms that enter a platform market can compete in various ways: a big jump in functionality (revolutionary functionality) or combining its own functionality with that of the target platform (platform envelopment).
- A platform owner must manage multiple levels of competition when competing against other platforms: platform versus platform, platform versus complement, and complement versus complement.
- The rate of change in an industry (i.e., the industry's clockspeed) marks the competitive dynamics, affecting the extent to which firms can rely on their existing generic strategies. In slow-clockspeed industries, there is less urgency for firms to reconsider their generic strategy, while in faster clockspeed industries firms have to frequently change their generic strategy.
- There are five basic strategic to respond to disruption of the focal firm's existing generic strategy: focus on and invest in the existing generic strategy, ignore the development, disrupt the disruptive innovation via a different generic strategy, adopt the disruptive innovation on top of the existing generic strategy, and embrace the disruptive innovation and scale it up.

# Review questions

1. What are the main differences among the three generic strategies?
2. What are the three sources of strategic positioning?
3. How can network effects act as an alternative generic strategy?
4. How can platforms compete with each other?
5. How are generic strategies related to an industry's clockspeed?
6. What are basic strategic responses to disruptive new ways of competing in the market?

# Discussion questions

1. Firms with a pioneering ambition to switch from a brick-and-mortar business to a platform business probably need to reconsider their generic strategy. How does that shift affect their industry's clockspeed and what other competitive dynamics may these firms expect in a platform market?
2. Do you believe bottlenecks are a bigger issue in ecosystems compared to linear supply chains?
3. A brick-and-mortar firm may think that promoting its existing offering via social media will boost its performance. Would you tend to agree with this?

## EXPERIENTIAL EXERCISES

1.  A game developer is facing severe competition from blockbuster hits of other developers. How may a focus strategy help that game developer to counter the success of those blockbuster hits? In answering this question, discuss the differences between a differentiation and focus strategy, include the long tail strategy and one of encroachment approaches to disrupting the disruptor.
2.  How may a platform strategy help that game developer to counter the success of those blockbuster hits?
3.  Think about a platform you regularly use. Does it compete with other platforms, and if so, on what basis does it compete (for instance, revolutionary functionality, envelopment, platform positioning)?

## Further reading

Bingham, C.B., Eisenhardt, K.M. and Furr, N.R. (2015) 'Which strategy when?', *MIT Sloan Management Review*, Top 10 Lessons on Strategy (Special Collection): 20–7.

Cennamo, C. (2021) 'Competing in digital markets: A platform-based perspective', *Academy of Management Perspectives*, 35 (2): 265–291.

Cusumano, M.A., Gawer, A. and Yoffie, D.B. (2019) *The Business of Platforms: Strategy in the Age of Digital Competition, Innovation, and Power.* New York, NY: Harper Business.

Greckhamer, T. and Gur, F.A. (2021) 'Disentangling combinations and contingencies of generic strategies: A set-theoretic configurational approach', *Long Range Planning*, 54 (2): article #101951.

McGrath, R. (2020) 'The new disrupters', *MIT Sloan Management Review* (Spring): 28–33.

## Endnotes (references)

1.  Eddy, N. (2021) 'VW ID4 becomes Europe's top-selling full-electric car', *Automotive News Europe*, May 28. https://europe.autonews.com/sales-segment/vw-id4-becomes-europes-top-selling-full-electric-car); Gibbs, S. (2018) 'First Tesla Model 3 rolls off production line… into the hands of Elon Musk', *The Guardian*, January 4. www.theguardian.com/technology/2017/jul/10/first-tesla-model-3-production-line-hands-elon-musk (accessed June 23, 2023); Meredith, S. (2022) 'Volkswagen chief says German car giant will overtake Tesla on electric vehicle sales by 2025', *CNBC*, May 24. www.cnbc.com/2022/05/24/volkswagen-ceo-says-carmaker-will-overtake-tesla-on-ev-sales-by-2025.html (accessed June 23, 2023); Morris, J. (2021) 'Tesla Model 3 Is now 16th bestselling car in the world', *Forbes,* May 29. www.forbes.com/sites/jamesmorris/2021/05/29/tesla-model-3-is-now-16th-bestselling-car-in-the-world (accessed June 23, 2023); O'Kane, S. (2019) 'Tesla's Model 3 was the best-selling EV in the world last year', *The Verge,* February 22. www.theverge.com/2019/2/22/18236707/tesla-model-3-2018-best-selling-ev-global (accessed June 23, 2023); Volkswagen (2022a) 'De vernieuwde ID.3', *Volkswagen.* www.volkswagen.nl/modellen/id3 (accessed June 23, 2023); Volkswagen (2022b) 'De ID.4', *Volkswagen.* www.volkswagen.nl/modellen/id4 (accessed June 23, 2023).

2. Reuters (2021) 'Volkswagen CEO: We need to change e-car approach in China', *Reuters*, July 29. www.reuters.com/business/autos-transportation/volkswagen-ceo-we-need-change-e-car-approach-china-2021-07-29 (accessed July 26, 2023).

3. Porter, M.E. (1980a) 'Industry structure and competitive strategy: Keys to profitability', *Financial Analysts Journal*, 36 (4): 30–41.

4. Deephouse, D.L. (1996) 'Does isomorphism legitimate?', *Academy of Management Journal*, 39 (4): 1024–39; Haans, R.F. (2019) 'What's the value of being different when everyone is? The effects of distinctiveness on performance in homogeneous versus heterogeneous categories', *Strategic Management Journal*, 40 (1): 3–27; Keller, K.L., Sternthal, B. and Tybout, A. (2002) 'Three questions you need to ask about your brand', *Harvard Business Review*, 80 (9): 80–9.

5. Keller et al. (2002: 81)

6. Thornhill, S. and White, R.E. (2007) 'Strategic purity: A multi-industry evaluation of pure vs. hybrid business strategies', *Strategic Management Journal*, 28 (5): 553–61.

7. Porter, M.E. (1996) 'What is strategy?', *Harvard Business Review*, Nov/Dec: 61–78.

8. Porter (1996)

9. Porter (1996)

10. Van Alstyne, M.W., Parker, G.G. and Choudary, S.P. (2016) 'Pipelines, platforms, and the new rules of strategy', *Harvard Business Review*, 94 (4): 54–62.

11. Van Alstyne et al. (2016)

12. Anderson, C. (2006) *The Long Tail: Why the Future of Business Is Selling Less of More.* London: Hachette; Brynjolfsson, E., Hu, Y.J. and Smith, M.D. (2006) 'From niches to riches: Anatomy of the long tail', *Sloan Management Review*, 47 (4): 67–71; Elberse, A. (2008) 'Should you invest in the long tail?', *Harvard Business Review*, 86 (7/8): 88–96.

13. Cennamo, C. (2021) 'Competing in digital markets: A platform-based perspective', *Academy of Management Perspectives*, 35 (2): 265–91.

14. Schilling, M.A. (2003) 'Technological leapfrogging: Lessons from the US video game console industry', *California Management Review*, 45 (3): 6–32.

15. Eisenmann, T., Parker, G.G. and Van Alstyne, M. (2011) 'Platform envelopment', *Strategic Management Journal*, 32 (12): 1270–85.

16. Eisenmann et al. (2011)

17. Parker, G.G., Van Alstyne, M.W. and Choudary, S.P. (2016) *Platform Revolution: How Networked Markets are Transforming the Economy and How to Make Them Work for You.* New York, NY: WW Norton.

18. Foerderer, J., Kude, T., Mithas, S. and Heinzl, A. (2018) 'Does platform owner's entry crowd out innovation? Evidence from Google photos', *Information Systems Research*, 29 (2): 444–60.

19. Reuters (2021) 'China's Alibaba invests $350 mln in capital increase to Turkey's Trendyol – trade registry', *Reuters,* April 20. www.reuters.com/world/middle-east/chinas-alibaba-invests-350-mln-capital-increase-turkeys-trendyol-trade-registry-2021-04-20 (accessed June 23, 2023).

20. Ersoy, E. and Balezou, M. (2021) 'Trendyol seeks over $1 billion to be largest Turkish startup', *Bloomberg,* April 21. www.bloomberg.com/news/articles/2021-04-26/alibaba-backed-trendyol-seeks-over-1-billion-to-fund-growth (accessed June 23, 2023).

21. Bughin, J. and Van Zeebroeck, N. (2017) 'The best response to digital disruption', *MIT Sloan Management Review,* 58: 80–6.

22. Correani, A., De Massis, A., Frattini, F., Petruzzelli, A.M. and Natalicchio, A. (2020) 'Implementing a digital strategy: Learning from the experience of three digital transformation projects', *California Management Review*, 62 (4): 37–56.

23. Fine, C.H. (1999) *Clockspeed: Winning Industry Control in the Age of Temporary Advantage.* London: Little Brown Publishers; Nadkarni, S., and Narayanan, V.K. (2007) 'Strategic schemas, strategic flexibility, and firm performance: The moderating role of industry clockspeed', *Strategic Management Journal*, 28 (3): 243–70.

24. Bingham, J.B., Gibb Dyer, W., Smith, I. and Adams, G.L. (2011) 'A stakeholder identity orientation approach to corporate social performance in family firms', *Journal of Business Ethics*, 99 (4): 56585; Nadkarni and Narayanan (2007); Volberda, H.W. (1998) *Building the Flexible Firm: How to Remain Competitive.* Oxford: Oxford University Press.

25. Nadkarni and Narayanan (2007); Volberda (1998)

26. Creswell, J. and Draper, K. (2020) 'How Under Armour lost its edge', *The New York Times,* January 26. www.nytimes.com/2020/01/26/business/under-armour-struggles. html (accessed June 23, 2023).

27. Charitou, C.D. and Markides, C.C. (2003) 'Responses to disruptive strategic innovation', *MIT Sloan Management Review*, 44 (2): 55–63; Markides, C. and Oyon, D. (2010) 'What to do against disruptive business models (when and how to play two games at once)', *MIT Sloan Management Review*, 51: 26–32.

28. O'Reilly III, C.A. and Tushman, M.L. (2013) 'Organizational ambidexterity: Past, present, and future', *Academy of Management Perspectives*, 27 (4): 324–38.

29. Lieberman, M.B. and Montgomery, D.B. (1988) 'First-mover advantages', *Strategic Management Journal*, 9(S1): 41–58.

30. Bingham et al. (2011); Suarez, F. and Lanzolla, G. (2005) 'The half-truth of first-mover advantage', *Harvard Business Review*, 83 (4): 121–7.

## Acknowledgements

The authors thank Emre Karali and Hakan Özalp for their contribution to this chapter.

## Key terms

**Access-based positioning** – positioning in the market based on different ways to reach customers whose needs are rather similar

**Best-cost provider strategy** – a hybrid strategy where differentiation, cost leadership and focus strategies are combined

**Cost leadership strategy** – an integrated set of actions taken to produce an offering with features that are acceptable to customers at the lowest cost, relative to that of competitors

**Differentiation strategy** – an integrated set of actions taken to produce an offering that customers perceive as being different in ways that are important to them

**Focus strategy** – an integrated set of actions to produce an offering that serves the needs of a particular competitive segment

**Industry clockspeed** – the rate of industry change reflecting the aggregate actions initiated by firms in that industry

**Needs-based positioning** – positioning based on a substantial part of the needs of a particular customer group

**Platform architecture** – a platform's functionalities, capabilities, performance and technical structure

**Platform envelopment** – a platform (the enveloping platform) enters another platform (the enveloped platform) by combining its own functionality with that of the target platform

**Platform identity** – a platform's competitive identity domain based on its technological and market profile

**Platform scope** – the domain of a platform (niche specialist versus market generalist)

**Revolutionary functionality** – a big jump in functionality of a platform so that different user groups, including complementors, can be persuaded to adopt the platform and allow it to compete with the existing platform

**Variety-based positioning** – positioning based on a subset of products and services in an industry

# 11

# DIVERSIFICATION AND INTERNATIONALIZATION

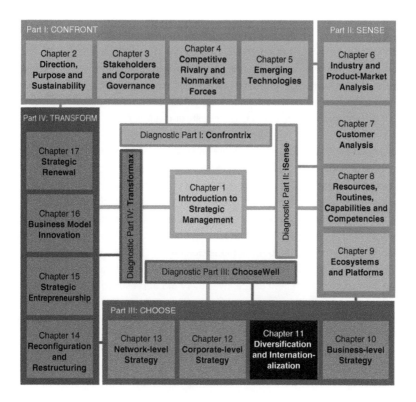

## OPENING CASE

Source: © 8th.creator (2019) / Shutterstock.

### McDonald's Switzerland and the Golden Arch Hotels[1]

McDonald's commercially successful restaurant system is well-known for the uniform methods of fast-food preparation and tight control over suppliers and franchisees. The large majority of McDonald's outlets are run under the firm's franchising model, which also plays a central role in its internationalization. Over time, its franchisees have introduced many menu items, such as the Big Mac, McCroquetas, and the McRaclette burger. The latter item is available only in its country of origin, Switzerland. The McRaclette has not been the only Swiss McDonald's invention. In November 2000, McDonald's Suisse Holding (overseeing 116 outlets at the time) announced that it would open two four-star hotels in the Swiss towns of Rümlang (near Zürich airport) and Lully under the name of Golden Arch Hotels.

The hotel venture was an idea of Urs Hammer, who at the time was the chairman and CEO of 'McDonald's Switzerland', in response to the parent firm's push for innovation and diversification. Ex-hotelier Hammer was a seasoned franchisee with a long history of successful business ventures. By supporting his ideas, McDonald's Corporation reinforced and nurtured its bottom-up innovation culture. In the words of one McDonald's manager: 'We try hundreds of things every year, and only a few turn out to be successful. But those initiatives make our business grow and keep our spirit alive.' The Swiss hotel endeavour fitted into a pattern of McDonald's experiments in Europe. In Germany, it started selling McDonald's tomato ketchup in grocery stores and in Austria and Portugal it had launched coffee-bar concept McCafé, which was introduced later in the US.

The Golden Arch hotels were truly one of a kind. The on-site McDonald's restaurants were open around the clock, which was a rarity in Switzerland. The guest accommodations featured arch-shaped headboards for the adjustable beds, maple floors, high-speed internet access, and a futuristically designed, cylindrical shower stall close to one of the beds. The room decor was brightly colored and sparse, and the hotels offered conference rooms, room service and a revolutionary easy check-in and check-out. A McDonald's spokesman commented that guests 'know they're going to get quality and value. And if it works in our restaurant, as it does, it will work in a hotel'.

The hotels did not deliver the results management had hoped for, however, and consequently closed their doors in 2003. The McDonald's style did not square well with the image and price of a four-star hotel. The worldwide economic downturn and appreciation of the Swiss currency following the 2001 terrorist attacks in the US contributed to the disappointing results. What also did not help was the fact that the 'golden arches' are not associated with McDonald's in German-speaking countries (including part of the Swiss population) and that 'arch' is pronounced as 'arsch' (another word for someone's posterior) by most German speakers.

From a corporate point of view, the demise of the Golden Arch Hotels was not a disaster. By using the name Golden Arch and by publicizing the hotels mainly inside Switzerland, damage to the McDonald's brand was kept to a minimum. The real estate investment did not result in a serious loss, as both hotels were sold to what later became Radisson Hotel Group. The operational losses that were incurred were relatively small and insignificant for the McDonald's business portfolio. Moreover, the hotel adventure offered valuable new insights.

### Questions

1. What lessons can be drawn from McDonald's diversification adventure in the hotel business?
2. To what extent might the Golden Arch concept have been more successful outside Switzerland?

# Introduction

As discussed in Chapter 10, business-level strategy encompasses decisions on how to compete in a certain industry or market. For instance, how can McDonald's compete successfully with other fast-food chains such as Burger King and KFC, resulting in above-average returns, and what strategic choices could have been made to increase the market share of the Golden Arch Hotels in the hotel industry at the expense of other business and family hotels in Switzerland? Before deciding on *how* to compete, however, you first need to decide on *where* to maintain a competitive presence: in what industries and markets? Instead of broadening its competitive focus to the hotel business in the early 2000s, McDonald's Switzerland could also have chosen to remain focused solely on achieving an attractive return on capital in the fast-food industry. An alternative possibility would have been to introduce the Golden Arch Hotels in, for instance, Australia, Egypt or Saudi Arabia, where the conditions of competition may have been different. The question of 'where to compete' is relevant for the smallest venture up to the largest multinational conglomerate. As we will elaborate upon in this chapter, strategic choices with respect to diversification and internationalization lie at the very heart of this question. These choices have in common that they shape a firm's corporate scope. We will first examine this notion, after which we zoom in first on diversification and then on internationalization.

# Corporate scope

Firms' corporate scope can greatly differ from each other, both within across industries. The corporate scope consists of three dimensions that collectively indicate the current boundaries of a firm's activities: horizontal, vertical and geographical (see Figure 11.1). A firm's **horizontal scope** denotes the range of different business areas in which it participates, which can be expressed in terms of either the industries in which it operates (i.e., the industry scope) or the product markets to which it allocates its resources (i.e., the product market scope) (see Chapter 6). Moreover, firms may engage in different types of activities both within and across distinct stages of an industry's overall value chain (see Chapter 8), in which case these activities are said to be aligned 'vertically'. The second dimension of corporate scope, the **vertical scope**, is about the range of vertically aligned activities a firm conducts, which, in turn, denotes its positioning along an industry's overall value chain.[2]

A presence in multiple stages of a certain value chain can come with participation in multiple businesses. Consider, for instance, the Walt Disney Company. The outputs of its film production business function partially as inputs for its theme park business (think about characters featured in Disney franchises such as *Frozen* walking around in its parks) and its licensing business (think about the selling of licensing rights to produce Disney Princess dolls and other merchandise). Hence, activities underlying different businesses can be vertically aligned – put differently, the activities in each value chain stage in which a firm may operate can be focused at least partially on succeeding in a distinct industry or product market. When this is the case, there is overlap between a firm's horizontal scope and vertical scope.

The **geographical scope** (or *geographical market scope*), the third dimension of corporate scope, denotes the range of geographical markets that a firm serves. A *geographical market* is a distinct geographical area in which products are sold and where the conditions of competition are relatively homogeneous.[3]

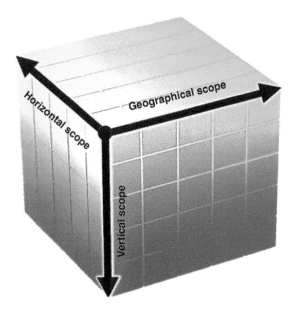

**FIGURE 11.1** Dimensions of corporate scope

# Conceptualizing diversification and internationalization

In a corporate-level strategic context, the term **diversification** (sometimes called *corporate diversification*) can have two meanings.[4] First, diversification can refer to the growth strategy of entering a business area (i.e., industry or product market) outside a firm's current corporate scope. According to this meaning, diversification implies an expansion of a firm's horizontal scope (i.e., its industry scope or product market scope). This expansion may simultaneously result in an expansion of a firm's vertical scope, in which case we can also speak of *vertical integration*. Second, diversification can refer to the degree (or level) to which a firm participates across structurally different industries or product markets – put differently, what does the firm's current horizontal scope look like?

As with diversification, the term internationalization can be used to indicate a growth strategy (i.e., the expansion of a firm's geographical scope), but also to describe a firm's current international profile (i.e., its current geographical scope). Some studies use the term 'international diversification' or 'geographical diversification'.[5] In a strategic context, however, it is more common to use the label '(corporate) diversification' solely to describe industry or product-market diversification.[6]

# Diversification as a growth strategy

Harry Igor Ansoff was among the first to describe diversification as a generic growth alternative open to firms. He introduced a categorization of corporate-level growth strategies along two dimensions: product line (present versus new product line), and the set of market needs that is being catered to (present versus new set of market needs). Figure 11.2 provides a visualization of this categorization, which has become known as the *Ansoff Matrix*. The *product line* refers to the type of products a firm intends to offer to customers in terms of both physical and performance characteristics of those products, whereas the *set of market needs* refers to a certain combination of 'missions' these products are designed to fulfil in terms of, for instance, functionality, design, performance, accessibility, or transparency.

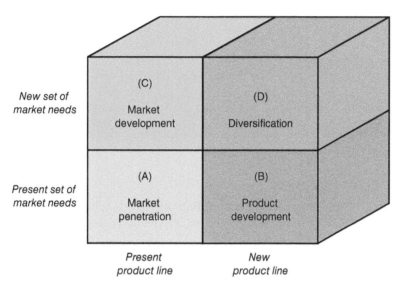

**FIGURE 11.2**   Ansoff Matrix: Four different growth strategies

Source: authors, adapted from Ansoff (1957)

Based on this categorization, one can differentiate four basic growth strategies. Market penetration refers to a firm's efforts to increase its revenues without departing from its present product line(s) and the present set of missions they are designed to fulfil. This can be attained by growing the volume of sales to its present customer base or by attracting new customers (for its present product offering) either within or outside its present market geography. Market development implies that a firm adapts a product line to a new set of market needs with the intention of selling this adapted product line within or outside its present market geography. Product development entails that a firm develops a product that has one or more new and different characteristics compared to its present products, but which is aimed to contribute to the same set of market needs. This product redesign is typically aimed at fulfilling these needs better than its existing products, which the new product line might replace. Finally, diversification, according to this categorization, implies a simultaneous departure from present product lines and present sets of market needs that these products are designed to fulfil.[7]

There has been some criticism of the Ansoff Matrix – see the Strategic Focus below. Over time, most definitions of diversification in the context of growth refer to the act or process of extending the range of industries or product markets in which a firm has a competitive presence by introducing a new type of product.[8]

## Types of diversification

A growth-minded firm can choose among different types (or directions) of diversification (see also Table 11.1). First of all, it may choose to expand its scope of activities to include activities of its suppliers (located upstream in the value chain), which is called <u>upstream diversification</u>. This is also known as *upstream integration* or *backward integration*. The firm will then operate in a business area that provides input for one or more of its existing business units. Inputs can for instance be raw materials, utilities (such as steam, electricity and industrial gas), parts, components, software, or equipment. The new business unit that provides this input may have to compete with outside suppliers that offer the same input. An example of upstream diversification is when in 2021 Red Bull GmbH, owner of the Formula 1 teams Red Bull Racing and AlphaTauri, decided to design and manufacture the engines for both teams for the first time in its history.[11]

A second type of diversification is <u>downstream diversification</u> (also known as *downstream integration* or *forward integration*), which implies expansion into a business area that uses the output (products) of one or more of a firm's existing business units. This means that the firm moves into its distribution channel or customer base. In a business-to-business context, this leads the firm to compete with a (former) customer. A case in point is the 2019 launch of streaming service Disney+ and intense competition with Netflix, to whom The Walt Disney Company previously licensed its films.

Upstream and downstream diversification are two types of *vertical diversification*, which implies not only an extension along a firm's horizontal scope, but also along its vertical scope. Vertical diversification typically results in a (new) corporate-internal market. Firms can also opt for non-vertical types of diversification, however, which include related horizontal diversification, unrelated horizontal diversification, concentric diversification, and conglomerate diversification.

The term 'horizontal diversification', introduced by Ansoff, could be somewhat confusing, as this is only one of multiple ways to expand a firm's horizontal scope. Specifically, growth through *horizontal diversification* implies that a firm comes up with a new type of product that caters primarily to its existing customer base.[12] An example is Apple's launch of the Apple Watch in 2014, which is closely connected to Apple's mobile operating system iOS and synchronizes with other Apple products such as the iPhone. Another example is a local gas station that starts a car wash service. In the first example, the new product is technologically related with the firm's existing product offering, whereas in the latter case it is technologically unrelated.

In the case of <u>concentric diversification</u>, another type of non-vertical diversification, a firm enters a new industry or product market that has some commonality with its current business(es) to serve a new market segment, which can be a similar or a new type of customer. The commonality can for instance be a common technological capability,[13] raw material, by-product, or marketing approach.[14] An example is a producer of packaged coconut water that launches coconut cream or coconut chips or starts selling coconut shell powder to manufacturers of laminated boards and mosquito coils.

When a firm enters an entirely new industry or product market that is unrelated to its current business(es) to cater to a new type of customer, this is called <u>conglomerate diversification</u>. An example is Amazon's expansion into the aerospace manufacturing and spaceflight services business when it founded Blue Origin in 2000.

**TABLE 11.1**  Types of diversification

| The firm chooses to enter a new business (by introducing a new-to-the-firm type of product) that…, | Does the new business have some technical, operational or marketing commonality with one or more of the firm's present businesses? | |
|---|---|---|
| | Yes | No |
| … uses the product output of one or more of the firm's present businesses to move into their distribution channel or customer base | Downstream (forward) diversification | |
| … caters primarily to firm-internal customers (i.e., input for one or more of the firm's present businesses) | Upstream (backward) diversification | |
| … caters primarily to (external) customers that are presently served by the firm | Related horizontal diversification | Unrelated horizontal diversification |
| … caters primarily to a similar (but not the same) or a new type of customer outside the firm's present customer base | Concentric diversification | Conglomerate (lateral) diversification |

Source: authors, adapted from Ansoff (1988); Varadarajan and Rajaratnam (1986)

Rather than diversifying in one of these 'pure' directions (see Table 11.1), expansions of corporate scope can also be of a mixed nature, in which case one can speak of <u>hybrid diversification</u>.[15] Consider, for instance, the diversification of Xiaomi, a Chinese electronics corporation that had focused initially on the smartphone business, into the notebook business in its seventh operational year, using (partly) similar technological and marketing capabilities. Xiaomi's notebooks may have been targeted to the same type of customer the firm already served (related horizontal diversification), but also to a similar or a new type of customer (concentric diversification). There are also instances where it is difficult to distinguish between vertical diversification and other directions of diversification because there is no clear linear sequence of activities, and hence no true value chain.[16] For example, in 2020 Amazon launched its own cloud gaming platform, Luna, to compete with Xbox Cloud and PlayStation Now. Its new cloud gaming business is powered by Amazon Web Services, an Amazon subsidiary that provides cloud computer web services to millions of customers.

In general, as long as competitive conditions are deemed favourable, most growth-minded firms will be inclined to first expand their activities within their current industry scope or product-market scope before embarking on any path of diversification. This enables them to fully exploit the economic potential of these activities while facing lower risks (compared to diversification). To further strengthen their position in their core business(es), upstream or downstream diversification may be required, after which non-vertical types of diversification may follow as a way to create more value.[17]

One may also distinguish solely between *related* (or *synergistic*) *diversification* and *unrelated* (or *lateral*) *diversification* in the context of corporate growth. This dichotomy is based on the notion of 'relatedness', as discussed further in Chapter 12. Related diversification occurs when a firm moves into a new industry or product market in which it will compete by leveraging one or more critical resources (tangible or intangible), skills or activities that it currently employs. In the case of unrelated diversification, there is no such commonality. Having the same type of customers in the new business area does not automatically imply relatedness, as they may need to be approached differently in distinct business areas.[18]

## Modes of diversification

Diversification decisions are not only about the type of diversification and the timing of these decisions, but also about the mode(s) of growth.[19] As with other types of corporate growth, diversification can be achieved in three ways (or a combination thereof): organically (organic growth), through corporate transactions in the form of a merger or acquisition (acquired growth), or through alliances (network-based growth).[20]

Organic growth, also known as *internal growth* or *internal development*, implies that a firm relies on and builds on its own resources and capabilities to achieve growth. When an established firm leverages or recombines (part of) its existing set of resources and capabilities to enter a new business area, this is often called *internal new venturing*. For instance, the Apple Watch, the introduction of which ushered Apple Inc.'s competitive presence in the then-emerging smartwatch market, was developed largely internally.

Acquired growth implies growth through mergers and/or acquisitions. A *merger* means that two firms combine into one firm that then operates as one legal entity under the banner of a single name, whereas an *acquisition* denotes a transaction in which a firm gains full ownership of or a controlling stake in another firm (see Chapter 14). An example of the latter is when the Dutch confectionary company Tony's Chocolonely acquired a chocolate production business. Up until then, it had depended fully on others for producing its chocolate.

Finally, network-based growth implies growth through cooperative arrangements (alliances) with external parties. Such arrangements (see Chapter 13) can be employed to enter a new business area. For instance, the prior diversification of TomTom into the GPS watch business (which they later exited) was enabled by a partnership with Nike in 2011.

## Reasons for diversification

Diversification can be undertaken for various reasons. First, a firm may decide to diversify when its goals or objectives can no longer be met within its current industry scope or product-market scope – for instance, due to market saturation or a decline in demand.[21]

A firm may also choose to diversify when it foresees opportunities in another industry or product market that promise a higher return on capital than other types of growth (such as market penetration), or when it has more financial resources available to leverage its strategic capabilities than needed for its other growth strategies. Diversification can be attractive for firms when it enables them to achieve cost or revenue synergies (in the case of related diversification) or financial economies (in the case of unrelated diversification) (see Chapter 12). Furthermore, firms may decide to diversify in response to an increasing customer demand for integrated or full-service solutions.[22] In order to be able to offer such more holistic solutions, some degree of diversification may be required.

A more value-neutral incentive to diversify is the spreading of risks. For instance, one of the insurance segments of the Dutch insurance group ASR Nederland covers both pension insurance and funeral insurance, which balance each other out in terms of financial risks for the firm: the longer people live, the higher will be the payment of pension benefits to them but the lower will be the funeral-related claims, and vice versa. Also, by diversifying, firms are less vulnerable to unexpected developments in a specific industry, and they may reduce uncertainty about their cash flow.

Another possible reason for a firm to diversify is to increase its *market power* – that is, power in an anti-competitive manner. There are different ways in which diversified firms with a significant competitive presence in their individual markets may yield market power:

- Cross-subsidization, wherein a firm uses (part of) its profits from one market to support predatory pricing activities in one or more other markets where it competes.[23]
- Reciprocal business dealings with other diversified firms, including reciprocal buying ('you buy from me, I will buy from you'), thereby foreclosing the market to less diversified competitors.[24]
- Multipoint competition, which exists when diversified firms compete simultaneously in the same markets.[25] Multipoint competitors tend to compete less aggressively with one another due to possible repercussions ('you attack me here, I attack you there').

Cross-subsidization, reciprocal business dealing, and multipoint competition can be achieved mainly through non-vertical diversification. Vertical diversification can yield market power by foreclosing input (or output) markets to competitors, or at least raising their costs by reducing the number of suppliers (or customers) available to them.[26] Furthermore, vertical diversification can create or exploit market power by raising barriers to entry, in the sense that potential non-integrated entrants may need to enter different stages in the value chain in order for them to compete successfully, which is costly and time-consuming.[27]

Firms can choose vertical diversification for a variety of reasons other than to gain market power. One of the most prominent reasons is vertical market failure. A vertical market (upstream or downstream) 'fails' when market transactions are considered too risky and the contracts that are designed to overcome these risks are too costly to oversee and write.[28] By integrating backward or forward in the value chain, firms can lower the costs and risks associated with transaction challenges within the chain. Another, more contemporary motive for vertical integration is that in many industries, a considerable part of value added has shifted away from production towards service-oriented activities in the consumption stage.[29] By selling directly to consumers, implying forward vertical integration, manufacturing firms place themselves in a better position to gather valuable customer data, the analysis of which may enable them to tailor their products to specific customer needs.

Corporate executives may also pursue diversification objectives that are not in the best interest of the firm. For instance, they may diversify in order to mitigate their own employment risk. Also, they may engage in 'empire building', at the expense of share-holder value, for the sake of having a larger span of control and/or a bigger paycheck.

## To diversify or not to diversify? Some critical questions

Diversification means entering new territory, which comes with a relatively high degree of uncertainty and unpredictability. Failures are not uncommon and can be costly. It is therefore considered a risky growth strategy. To reduce the gamble of diversification, the checklist developed by Markides[30] can be helpful (see Figure 11.3).

As addressed in Chapter 1, the ultimate goal of any organizational strategy is to create and sustain added value for the firm's most relevant stakeholders, such as its shareholders.[31] According to Porter,[32] there are three conditions under which a diversification move will truly create shareholder value. These conditions can be translated into three tests: the attractive-ness test, the cost-of-entry test, and the better-off test. As indicated in Figure 11.4, each of these tests translates into a critical question complementary to the ones listed in Figure 11.3.

**Q1. What can the firm do better than any of its competitors in its current business area(s)?**

This question is about determining what resources, capabilities and competences underlie the firm's success in the business area(s) in which it currently maintains a competitive presence, and how and where the firm can make the best use of these 'strategic assets'.

**Q2. What strategic assets does the firm need in order to succeed in the new business area?**

This question is about determining which of the firm's current strategic assets (see Q1) can be applied in the new business setting, which of these assets are deemed critical to succeed in this setting, and which assets that are deemed critical are not (yet) in the firm's possession.

**Q3. Can the firm catch up to or leapfrog competitors at their own game?**

This question is about determining whether the firm is able to develop, purchase or access all critical strategic assets that it currently lacks (see Q2) for reasonable costs, or whether it is somehow able to render missing assets unnecessary to compete successfully in the new business.

**Q4. Will diversification break up strategic assets that need to be kept together?**

This question is about determining to what extent the assets that are critical for competitive success in the new business (see Q2) and that are in the firm's possession (see Q1) or within its reach (see Q3) can be transported to this business successfully, whilst bearing in mind that this may come with a disadvantageous unbundling, recombination or relocation of interrelated assets.

**Q5. Will the firm be simply a player in the new business area or will it emerge a winner?**

This question is about determining to what extent the strategic assets that the firm intends to introduce into the new business are expected to be a durable source of competitive advantage, based on the VRINO criteria (see Chapter 8) such as rarity, inimitability and non-substitutability.

**Q6. What can the firm learn by diversifying, and is it sufficiently organized to learn from it?**

This question is about thinking some steps ahead in terms of whether the new business allows the firm to learn things that can be reapplied in its current business(es) and whether this new business could be a stepping-stone for entering other new businesses that would otherwise be out of reach.

**FIGURE 11.3**  Markides' diversification risk assessment: Six critical questions

Source: adapted from Markides (1995)

| Attractiveness test | Cost-of-entry test | Better-off test |
|---|---|---|
| Is the business area chosen for diversification structurally attractive or capable of being made attractive? | Is the full cost of entry less than future profits? | Does the new business unit gain competitive advantage from its link with the corporation, or vice versa? |

**FIGURE 11.4** Attractiveness test, cost-of-entry test and better-off test in relation to diversification

Source: Porter (1987)

The *attractiveness test* revolves around the ease with which the average firm in the target business area can earn good profits in the long run. Examples of indicators of industry or market attractiveness are the growth rate and size of the industry or market, its current profitability, and the size of the entry barriers. The *cost-of-entry test* raises the question whether the expected financial returns from competing in this business area exceed the full cost of entry. The *better-off test*, also known as the *added value test*, raises the question whether the presence of the firm in the target business area is expected to improve either the competitiveness of the new business unit or the competitiveness of the firm's current business unit(s) over and above what these units could achieve on their own (i.e., being stand-alone entities).[33] The *ChooseWell* diagnostic chapter provides a list of conditions that are likely to satisfy this test (see Table C.2).

The attractiveness test, cost-of-entry test, and better-off test can be used not only in the context of diversification but also in the context of internationalization.[34]

## CRACK-THE-CASE
### Dyson's electric vehicle adventure[35]

Source: © Mokjc (2020) / Shutterstock.

*(Continued)*

In 2017, self-made billionaire Sir James Dyson announced that his firm was going to make and sell an electric vehicle. His firm, Dyson, is best known for its high-end bagless and cordless vacuum cleaner, but over the last decade they've expanded into the realm of award-winning hand dryers, heaters and other home goods. In September 2019, the firm had a UK patent granted for an electric toothbrush, followed five months later by a patent for air-purifying headphones. An electric vehicle, however, proved to be one step too far.

Dyson planned to spend close to £2 billion ($2.5 billion) – equivalent to two years' earnings – on developing and producing a luxury vehicle that would run on emission-free power, with the deadline set for 2021. However, in October 2019, the firm suddenly announced that it had decided to scrap its ambitious project altogether: 'We are sad to announce a proposal to end our automotive project. The Dyson automotive team has developed a fantastic electric car, but unfortunately it is not commercially viable'.

A few months earlier, Dyson was still filing patents for car vents and vehicle lamps, and plans were being made to hire hundreds of employees at their Singapore factory. Production of the vehicle in Singapore was perceived by James Dyson as a logical step, given that he perceived nearby China as a key sales market. Not only had China decided to impose quotas aimed at a speedier adoption of carbon-free emission vehicles, Dyson's superior air filters were also expected to be of high value in the country's various smog-choked regions. However, there were signs that the vehicle would have struggled to sufficiently differentiate itself, in or outside China. The 'Dysonmobile' prototype reportedly bore 'a striking similarity' to a $40,000-priced SUV that was at the time being road-tested by Chinese auto manufacturer Byton. In January 2019 the firm hired Roland Krueger, the former head of the electric luxury vehicle division of Nissan, to lead Dyson's electric car division but still could not get the project off the ground. The firm's ambition, advanced proprietary electric motor and battery technology, other patented technology, large employee base (around 12,000 employees), and deep financial pockets could not sufficiently change that. When Dyson reached out to a couple of its competitors for help, engineers reportedly came away surprised by how little progress had actually been made.

Part of the explanation for the disappointing progress can possibly be found in Dyson's R&D secrecy, which inhibited collaboration with other firms, and which reportedly made it relatively difficult to attract talented engineers. Its projects are given numbers instead of names. Engineers reportedly work in a series of cramped and windowless test laboratories, and its R&D team operates in a secure laboratory that is covered in reflective cladding. The electric vehicle project (project N526) was no exception. Any information that the firm sent out to auto parts suppliers went into a central 'drop box' in which the information was visible only for one hour before it disappeared. According to one former employee, Dyson tried to impose its own way of working on the automotive industry, but 'You don't build cars the same way you build a vacuum cleaner'.[36] Some suppliers also bristled at what they perceived as Dyson's attempts to gain control of their business – for example, by making minor adjustments to existing car parts and then filing its own patents on these parts. Once, after a heated conversation with engineers from the German automotive parts supplier HELLA, one of Dyson's senior executives reportedly asked: 'Just how big is this firm, anyway?' Bigger than Dyson, was the answer.

In a May 2020 interview with *The Times*, James Dyson decided to show off the seven-seater, electric SUV with a 600+ mile range that was supposed to rival Tesla – he had spent £500 million before scrapping the project.

## Questions

1. How would you describe the diversification strategy (i.e., the type and mode of diversification) used by Dyson when entering the electric vehicle (EV) business?
2. To what extent do you think that this strategy, when it was decided upon, passed the attractiveness test, cost-of-entry test, and better-off test?
3. How would you answer each of Markides' six critical questions in relation to Dyson's expansion into the EV business? Based on your answers, what is your conclusion?
4. What do you see as the main reason(s) why Dyson's eventually failed to succeed in the EV business? What lessons can be learned for Dyson and in general?

# Levels of diversification

Firms that have operations in the same industry can have very different diversification profiles. For instance, consider the following three firms that manufacture and sell footwear. Caleres, a US-based firm, focuses exclusively on manufacturing and selling different brands of footwear. The Spanish fashion group Inditex, through its different retail formats, sells footwear but also offers a variety of other product categories such as garments, accessories, cosmetics, fragrances and furniture. Meanwhile, the Indian conglomerate Action Group competes in industries as diverse as footwear, power, steel, chemicals, computer monitors, and healthcare. Which firm is diversified most?

There are two commonly employed approaches for assessing a firm's level of diversification.[37] A first approach is to use an industry-count measure of diversification. The underlying logic here is that firms are diversified if they are involved in at least two discrete economic activities conforming to the International Standard Industrial Classification (ISIC) or another statistical classification of economic activities, such as SIC, NACE or NAICS. The focus of the count can range from four-digit industry categories (specific industry segments such as 'manufacture of footwear' and 'construction of utility projects') to one-digit categories (major industry groups such as 'manufacturing' and 'construction'). The use of the industry-count measure has been criticized. Montgomery, for instance, commented that 'in industries classified according to manufacturing process, products that are substitutes for one another could be classified in disparate categories if they were produced through different manufacturing processes'.[38]

A second approach to assess a firm's level of diversification is the use of categorical measures based on a classification system originally developed by Leonard Wrigley. This classification (see Table 11.2) distinguishes between four discrete categories of diversification: single business, dominant business, related business and unrelated business. Firms can be assigned to one of these categories based on their specialization ratio and related ratio. The *specialization ratio* is the proportion of a firm's revenues generated by its largest single business unit. If this ratio is 95% or higher, the firm belongs to the <u>single business</u> category, which implies the lowest level of diversification. Caleres is an example, as is Ryanair, Europe's largest airline group that focuses exclusively on the passenger airline business. If the specialization ratio ranges between 70% and 95%, the firm belongs to the <u>dominant business</u> category. An example of this is Heineken, which generates most revenues from its dominant beer business but increasingly also from its flavoured drinks businesses (cider and hard seltzer).

**TABLE 11.2**   Classification of diversified companies

| Diversification category | Specialization ratio (R$_s$) | Related ratio (R$_r$) | Related-core ratio (R$_c$) | Level of diversification |
|---|---|---|---|---|
| Single business | ≥ 95% | | | Very low |
| Dominant business | 95% > R$_s$ ≥ 70% | | | |
| Related constrained | <70% | ≥ 70% | R$_c$ > (R$_s$+R$_r$)/2 | |
| Related linked | <70% | ≥ 70% | R$_c$ < (R$_s$+R$_r$)/2 | |
| Unrelated business | <70% | <70% | | Very high |

**R$_s$**: the proportion of a company's revenues attributable to its largest single business unit;

**R$_r$**: the proportion of a company's revenues attributable to its largest group of somehow related business units;

**R$_c$**: the proportion of a company's revenues attributable to its largest group of business units that share or draw on the same common core skill(s), strength(s) or resource(s).

Source: adapted from Wrigley (1970), Rumelt (1982) and Hitt et al. (2009)

Most diversified firms have a specialization ratio below 70%, which indicates a higher level of diversification. An example is PepsiCo, whose 2020 revenues from its food and beverage businesses was approximately 55% and 45%, respectively.[39] Firms with a specialization ratio below 70% are either in the *related business category* (such as PepsiCo and Inditex) or *unrelated business category* (such as Action Group), depending on the related ratio. The *related ratio* is the proportion of a firm's revenues attributable to its largest group of somehow related business units – 'related' in the sense that each of these business units is related to at least one other unit within this group (which does not necessarily require a single common resource or skill).[40] As detailed further in Chapter 12, relatedness between business units is not about serving the same customers nor about relatedness between the type of products these units cater to a company's customers (although both may give rise to relatedness). Rather, it is about activities, resources, skills and products that are being shared or transferred among these units.[41]

Companies that have a related ratio of at least 70% are classified into the related business category. Based on a third ratio, the related-core ratio, this category can be split into two subcategories: related constrained and related linked.[42] The *related-core ratio* is the proportion of a firm's revenues attributable to its largest group of business units that share or draw on the same common core skill(s), strength(s) or resource(s), which implies that each of these units is related to all other units within this group. A firm whose related-core ratio is higher than half the sum of its specialized ratio and related ratio belongs to the related-constrained category and otherwise it belongs to the related-linked category (see Table 11.2). Although in practice it may be hard for outsiders to get a precise measurement of these ratios, it is usually possible to come up with an acceptable estimate as to whether these ratios fall below or above some critical level.[43] A rough indication of related-constrained diversification is that most business units share technological, production, distribution or marketing linkages. When there are only limited inter-unit linkages, with a dominant focus on the transfer of intangible assets or skills, this is often an indication of related-linked diversification.[44]

Firms whose specialization ratio and related ratio both are less than 70% are classified into the <u>unrelated business</u> category, which implies the highest level of diversification. The component parts of investment firms that focus primarily on buying and selling other companies, often in combination with restructuring efforts (see Chapter 14), are typically unrelated. Examples are private equity firms, hedge funds and real-estate syndicates. Most conglomerates fit the unrelated business category as well. A *conglomerate* is a parent company that owns a controlling stake in multiple subsidiary companies that operate in very different industries. The common thread among these subsidiaries, which typically operate independently from each other, is primarily financial, although there may be some synergistic linkages such as knowledge transfers. The assembly of parent and subsidiary companies is termed a *corporate group*. Examples of conglomerates are 3M, Action Group, CK Hutchison, Siemens, and Tata Group.

## Diversification levels and performance

Firms' preferences for related versus unrelated business diversification strategies seem to have changed over time. An extensive meta-analysis of studies published between 1962 and 2016 shows that levels of unrelated business diversification have decreased in that period, whereas levels of related business diversification have increased since the mid-1990s, following an initial overall decrease in the 1970s and 1980s.[45]

Most strategy textbooks state that performance increases as an undiversified firm shifts to a related (related-linked or related-constrained) diversification strategy and that, on average, performance decreases when a firm shifts to an unrelated business strategy. This inverted U-shape type of relationship between the level of diversification and corporate performance (in terms of rate of return) is based on rich empirical evidence.[46] The underlying theoretical rationale is twofold. First, related diversification enables a firm to reap the benefits of synergies (see Chapter 12), which however can be exploited only up to a certain point. Second, the less related a firm's diversification, the more the costs to the firm may outweigh the benefits.[47]

Other scholars, however, did not find evidence that related business diversification results in better performance than unrelated diversification;[48] some have even found empirical evidence for a consistently positive relationship between the level of diversification and performance[49] or the exact opposite.[50] Scholars that find a consistent positive relationship point out that higher levels of diversification can result in more efficient capital allocation, capital market advantages (such as taxation advantages), market power advantages, and better possibilities to reduce risk or volatility in rates of financial return, whereas scholars that demonstrate an opposite, negative relationship point towards inefficiencies of internal capital markets, inappropriate expansion of the corporate scope due to agency issues, and cost-increasing internal power struggles.[51]

Multibusiness firms are not necessarily more competitive than highly specialized, single-business firms. In fact, there are numerous firms that are successful largely because they focus on relatively few activities that they do very well[52] – for instance because this allows for building a leading reputation in a specific area.[53] When component businesses in a diversified firm outperform stand-alone single-business firms owing to the firm's diversified profile, we talk about a *diversification premium* (or, in the case of conglomerates, a *conglomerate premium*). When the opposite is true, we talk about a *diversification discount* (or *conglomerate discount*).

## Internationalization as a growth strategy

In strategy, *geographical expansion* denotes an expansion of a firm's geographical scope (see Figure 11.1). If we add the 'market geography' dimension to the Ansoff Matrix (see Figure 11.2), the number of generic growth strategies open to firms doubles from four to eight (see Figure 11.5), as each of the four basic growth strategies can be oriented towards either a firm's present geographical market scope (see blocks A, B, C and D in Figure 11.5) or an extended geographical market scope (see blocks E, F, G and H).[62]

Firms can also expand their geographical scope within the country or countries in which they already have a presence – think about a small retail shop that opens a second shop in another city, or a California-based firm that starts selling its products in the neighboring state of Oregon. When a firm's geographical expansion involves entering a new country, we speak of **internationalization**. As visualized in Figure 11.5, internationalization is a growth strategy complementary to diversification.[63] The combination of internationalization and diversification is the riskiest growth strategy, as this involves a double discontinuity from the firm's present situation.[64]

### Types of internationalization

As can be derived partly from Figure 11.5, firms have multiple options at their disposal when it comes to internationalization. One of these options is to offer one or more of their current products to the same type of customers (i.e., with the same needs) in a new market

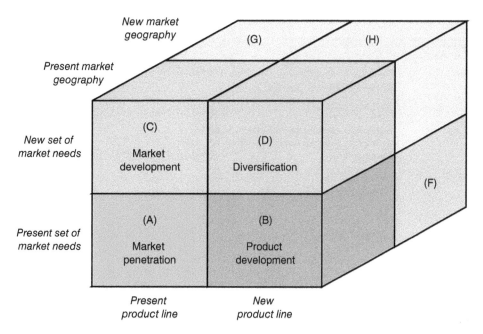

**FIGURE 11.5** Growth strategy cube: Possible directions of corporate expansion

Source: authors, adapted from Ansoff's (1988) Growth Vector framework, which, in turn, is an extension of the Ansoff Matrix (1957)

geography. For instance, Red Bull sells its energy drinks all around the globe to the same type of customers it had learned to serve in its home country of Austria. Other options are to sell the same type of customers an adapted version of these products or a different type of product, to sell the same product to different types of customers, or to sell an adapted or different type of product to a different type of customer in a new market geography.[65]

## Country selection

Besides deciding on the type(s) of internationalization, firms that plan to expand internationally have to make various other choices, such as which country and location to select. One way to make such a decision is by evaluating a firm's compatibility with different countries or locations in terms of how 'distant' or different they are from a firm's current market(s).[66] Some countries or regions might be more different or similar than others in terms of cultural, administrative, geographical, and economic factors (the so-called CAGE factors). The idea behind the CAGE Distance tool (see Table 11.3) is that one can compare potential locations or countries based on their scores on the different CAGE factors (1–very different; 2–different; 3–similar; 4–very similar). The potential market with most points is most similar to a firm's current market(s) and may therefore be the best option.

Differences between countries or regions can provide opportunities for internationalization as well.[67] For instance, several Dutch firms have become international front-runners in coastal and water management and sell their renowned expertise abroad. This expertise was built over time partly because their home country, located on a low-lying delta, has always been

**TABLE 11.3**    CAGE Distance tool: Location (or country) selection

| CAGE factors | | Location 1 | Location 2 |
|---|---|---|---|
| Cultural | Differences in language, ethnicity, religion and social norms, managerial behaviours. | 4 | ... |
| Administrative | Differences in administrative, political, or legal traditions. | 3 | ... |
| Geographical | Geographical distance and differences regarding country size, access, and communication and transportation infrastructures. | 2 | ... |
| Economic | Differences in countries' wealth, GDP, currencies, income level. | 4 | ... |
| Total | | 13 | ... |

Source: adapted from Ghemawat (2007)

highly vulnerable to inundation. Also, differences between countries or regions may enable firms to pursue *location economies*. These economic benefits can be achieved by dispersing some of their value creation activities to one or more locations outside their domestic country or region where these activities can be performed better, faster or cheaper[68] – for instance, because of more favourable factor conditions at these other locations.

Compatibility and differences are not the only criteria that should be taken into account when deciding which country or region to enter, however. Other important criteria may include, for instance, geographical market size, income level, economic instability, corruption, security risks, difficulties to protect intellectual capital, sovereign risks, and competitive rivalry, *independent* of the degree to which the scores on these criteria deviate from what is common within a firm's current geographic scope. The more favourable a country's scores on these or other CAGE-criteria that are relevant to a firm, the more attractive it may be to enter this country.

## Modes of internationalization

How to enter a geographical market is another important choice that needs to be made when internationalizing. Different entry modes correspond to different levels of resource commitment, organizational control, associated risk (such as financial and political risks), and entry speed. The five key entry mode types are:

- Exporting: a firm sells a product that it has produced in its home country to customers in a foreign country.
- Licensing: a partner firm located abroad is granted the permission to use and earn revenue from a firm's assets in exchange for a negotiated payment.
- Joint venture: a firm establishes a jointly owned, independently operating entity in another country with one or more other firms.
- Greenfield investment: a firm constructs a wholly owned subsidiary unit in another country from scratch.
- Brownfield investment: the purchase or lease of a pre-existing firm or facility in another country, or the acquisition of a controlling stake in such a firm or facility.

Joint ventures, greenfield investments and brownfield investments are three types of *foreign direct investment* (or *FDI*).

**TABLE 11.4**   A stylized comparison of characteristics of five modes of internationalization

|  | Export | Licensing | Joint venture | Greenfield investment | Brownfield investment |
|---|---|---|---|---|---|
| **Resource commitment** | Low | Low | Medium | High | High |
| **Organizational control** | Low | Low | Medium | High | High |
| **Entry risk** | Low | Low | Medium | High | High |
| **Entry speed** | High | High | Medium | Low | High |

Source: authors

Exporting and greenfield investments are modes of organic growth. A brownfield investment can be either acquired growth (in the case of a purchase) or network-based growth (in the case of leasing). Licensing and the establishment of a joint venture are considered network-based growth. Table 11.4 provides a concise overview of some characteristics associated to each of the five main entry modes, which can be helpful when choosing how to enter a new country or location. Firms may choose to adopt different entry modes at different stages. For example, a firm can start exporting or licensing, allowing the firm to acquire knowledge about the new market and analyze its potential, and then migrate to a joint venture or greenfield investment.

## Reasons for internationalization

There are a variety of different reasons for firms to internationalize. Some of these reasons are similar to common reasons for (domestic) diversification. For instance, a firm may decide to expand internationally when its objectives can no longer be met within its current geographical scope. It could also be the case that a firm foresees opportunities in new geographical markets that promise a higher return on capital than other types of expansion. Another reason for internationalization is that it can serve to distribute risks across different geographical markets and, in relation to that, stabilize earnings. For firms that operate in a business-to-business environment, another reason to expand internationally can be to follow their customers when these decide to expand their operations abroad. This 'follow-the-customer'-motive is common for service-oriented firms in particular. A case in point is the Swedish industrial services firm Jernbro, which follows its customers abroad to help with assignments and machine deliveries.[69] Furthermore, by entering a certain geographical area that is known to be home to a particular advanced technology, firms based outside this area may be better able to tap into strategically relevant knowledge sources.

Reductions of trade-related obstacles and regulations in other countries facilitate internationalization. Also higher degrees of homogeneity of customer preferences across different parts of the world[70] constitutes a facilitating factor.

## CRACK-THE-CASE

Mindflow: The route of an SME towards internationalization in the EdTech industry

Source: © Ground Picture (2023) / Shutterstock.

Mindflow is an Education Technology (EdTech) SME specialized in mobile learning and gamification that develops learning games for firms and universities. Throughout the years, the firm has developed a gamified learning algorithm. The main selling points of Mindflow mobile games are high knowledge retention, high engagement and high diffusion at low cost. Mindflow started its activities in 2012 as an on-site training and consultancy firm in human resources development. Since the beginning, Mindflow was focused on gamification, developing on-site learning games, and supporting firms to gamify their training programs. From 2012 to 2017, it mainly served the Portuguese market, being one of the first players to step into the gamified learning niche. By then, the corporate training market was embracing the rise of e-learning platforms. Mindflow understood that the future of training and learning would be digital but would involve more sophisticated and engaging techniques and decided to take its first steps towards mobile learning games.

In 2015, Mindflow started a partnership with a mobile game supplier, adding mobile games to its portfolio of services. The experience was satisfactory, however the mobile games focused more on gamification than on the learning and retention side. This led Mindflow in 2017 to decide to internally develop the app Mindflow Academy in which it implemented its vast knowledge in gamified learning, expanding its portfolio of services. One of the first clients that Mindflow attracted in the mobile learning segment was Mercedes Portugal, which was looking for a supplier to train their network of maintenance garages. The initiative was successful, and Mercedes Portugal decided to present this case to Mercedes Global Training, where they were impressed by Mindflow's technology and game results. In March 2017, Mercedes and Mindflow started a journey together all over Europe. To satisfy Mercedes's needs and wants, Mindflow grew internationally, adapting the Mindflow Academy to different languages and legislation (data protection legislation) and developing training and customer support across multiple countries. Together, Mindflow and Mercedes launched four games across 14 countries, and the results were awe-inspiring. Users retained on average 80% of training program knowledge, initiated more than 500,000 one-on-one challenges (users challenge each other to answer sets of questions) and responded to more than 6.5 million questions collectively.

The partnership went successful from 2017 to 2019, but then Mercedes dropped a cold-water bucket on Mindflow: 'The game is a huge success, but we are restructuring Mercedes Global Training, and we decided to develop our learning games internally', they said. While it was difficult for Mindflow to understand such a decision given the partnership's success, they were thankful for Mercedes' role in the firm's internationalization, and they knew that this was also an opportunity to refocus and consolidate their growth path. While COVID-19 brought cuts in training budgets across industries, it also shed light on new ways of training employees and teaching students. This was the race Mindflow wanted to lead. Mindflow knew that its Portuguese home market is a limited market, and scaling would be the name of the game. Mindflow decided to invest in two main strategies to grow its international presence.

The first strategy is through internal growth using online sales channels. Using machine learning and deep learning, Mindflow started to invest in an online platform able to streamline the sales process and to improve customer autonomy in creating and launching learning games. Mindflow's second path to grow is through collaborations with local and foreign training and HR consultancy firms that, through licensing, can re-sell Mindflow Academy to customers in international markets. While in the immediate future, Mindflow's attention is on the business-to-business segment, they imagine a future in which learning games will reach mass-market diffusion. However, diversification is a challenging game to play, and Mindflow knows that the future of learning games shall be built one level at a time.

## Questions

1. Which specific growth strategies did Mindflow implement throughout the years?
2. What were the reasons for Mindflow to grow internationally?
3. State the pros and cons of the two growth options that Mindflow decided to invest in.

## Risks of internationalization

Internationalization may involve drastic departures from a firm's past competencies and experience.[71] Moreover, establishing operations in a new country implies a larger range of political, economic, legal and other macro-environmental factors (see Chapter 4) that have to be dealt with. When there are interdependencies between these new operations and a firm's pre-existing operations, a change in one of these factors may have an impact on the firm as a whole. Particularly in less economically advanced countries, firms may face economic instability, corruption, security risks, difficulties to protect intellectual capital, sovereign risks, and even the effects of economic sanctions. However, in other countries firms run into issues as well (Brexit being one example), some of which may partly derive from unfamiliarity with these countries. When Tesla CEO Elon Musk announced the construction of a massive electric car factory near Berlin, Germany at the end of 2019, little did he know that the firm would have to deal with trade union scrutiny, environmental protests and strict German environmental regulations causing a severe delay in its construction (see Chapter 3).

Multinational firms initially face additional costs relative to their indigenous competitors when they operate in foreign countries, resulting in a competitive disadvantage.[72] These additional costs, which are not the same for each multinational and which differ between countries, are labelled collectively as the *liability of foreignness* and can be divided into:

- Adaptation costs: incurred to identify relevant differences between the host and home country and adapting products to suit local customer demand.
- Discrimination costs: derived from unfavourable treatment by the host country government in the form of stringent requirements, regulations or disapproval of foreign investment.[73]
- Governance costs: incurred due to extra coordination and communication-related efforts[74] – for instance, due to language barriers.
- Appropriation costs: relevant for firms conducting foreign direct investment, and related to the possibility that this investment is expropriated by the host government.[75]

Apart from facing a liability of foreignness, firms that operate outside their home market typically also initially suffer from a *liability of outsidership*. This liability denotes additional costs due to not yet having a relevant network position, which requires the building of trust and commitment with others. Foreignness complicates the process of becoming an 'insider'.

Whether international expansion can be considered as a jump into the unknown or the familiar depends partly on the extent to which customers in the new geographic market have similar or different needs compared to the firm's other customers and on the extent to which the products offered to these new customers are related to the firm's present product portfolio.[76] Moreover, it depends on whether the conditions of competition are structurally different. In some industries, such as the global pharmaceutical industry, expansion to other countries may lead a firm to compete with the same rivals and to rely on largely the same distributors and suppliers.

## Levels of internationalization

Firms tend to differ significantly with respect to the degree to which they participate across distinct geographical areas outside their home country. There are at least three dimensions that should be taken into account when assessing a firm's level of internationalization:[77]

- The intensity of internationalization (or *degree of foreignness*): the dichotomy between foreign versus domestic activities: to what extent are a firm's activities taking place away from its home country? The intensity dimension can be measured by assessing the proportion of revenues attributable to foreign businesses (treating all that is foreign as a black box).

* Geographical spread: the spread of foreign activities in terms of the number of countries in which they take place.
* Geographic concentration: the degree to which these activities are spatially (typically by nation-state) concentrated within specific regions. Put differently, this dimension looks at the worldwide distribution of a firm's foreign operations.[78]

Similar to diversification, research indicates an inverted U-shape relationship between the level of international diversity and corporate performance.[79] Depending on the chosen international strategy, as discussed next, high levels of internationalization enable firms to benefit more from economies of scale and from locational advantages that are present around the globe, however this also comes with increased coordination complexity that may become more costly than these benefits. This complexity becomes even larger when the firm is also highly diversified, although scholars have pointed out that having high levels of diversification may actually help firms to do better from internationalization because they are better equipped to manage internal diversity.[80]

# International strategies

At a business level, firms that operate internationally follow generic strategies as elaborated in Chapter 10, such as cost leadership and differentiation. At the corporate level, firms have three basic international strategies at their disposal: *global*, *multidomestic* or *transnational* (a combination of global and multidomestic). Choosing among these strategies revolves primarily around three broad questions executives need to answer (see Table 11.5).

**TABLE 11.5**  Corporate-level international strategies

| | Global strategy | Multidomestic strategy | Transnational strategy |
|---|---|---|---|
| *Should our products be standardized across national or regional borders, or adapted to different geographical markets?* | Standardized | Adapted | Balanced mix of standardization and adaptation |
| *Should our productive assets and capabilities and our strategic and operational decision-making be concentrated (or centralized) in a limited number of locations, or decentralized across borders?* | Centralized | Decentralized | Partly centralized, partly decentralized |
| *Should our geographical business units (or divisions) be interdependent or independent?* | Interdependent | Independent | Partly interdependent, partly independent |

Source: authors

## STRATEGIC FOCUS

### Switching international strategy[81]

Source: © FotograFFF (2019) / Shutterstock.

Over time, firms may switch from one basic international strategy to another. An example is IKEA. While expanding within Europe between 1963 (opening its first abroad store in Norway) and the 1990s, the firm kept largely the same operational formulas and sold largely the same 'typically Swedish' basic product range in all countries that it entered. This standardization caused serious problems in the US, where IKEA had opened six stores between 1985 and 1990. The large majority of the products offered in these stores were manufactured in Sweden and then exported. Many of these products proved to be a mismatch with the tastes or sometimes the physiques of US customers. For instance, IKEA's glasses were too small for the typical American habit to add substantial quantities of ice to drinks. Its plates were too small for large-sized pizzas. Its bedroom chests were too shallow for the many Americans who tend to store sweaters in chests. And its beds were often considered too narrow and moreover were measured in centimeters instead of inches. As a result of these and other mismatches, the US stores were not as profitable as the European stores. This changed when IKEA started to customize its product offerings in the US. In addition to that, IKEA strongly increased the number of products that were sourced locally, which made the firm less vulnerable to volatility in exchange rates.

A **global strategy** favours cost efficiency over local responsiveness.[82] To realize this cost efficiency, the corporate parent (in the case of a multibusiness firm) continuously strives to achieve integration across the subordinate business units responsible for the different market areas[83] which it coordinates and controls. This integration assumes connectivity and interdependence among these units. Single-business firms can use a global strategy also. Having a high degree of standardization of their product offering across the different geographical markets in which they operate, in combination with a relative centralization of decision-making, assets and capabilities to develop and produce these standardized products, allows firms that adopt a global strategy to achieve and exploit economies of scale. Also, this strategy fosters the transfer of innovations developed through corporate R&D efforts, which otherwise would be dispersed throughout the firm.[84] Furthermore, it enables firms to benefit from locational advantages (such as the availability of a skilled workforce or tax advantages) of the few development and production locations.

In contrast, a **multidomestic strategy** favours local responsiveness over cost efficiency. Firms using this strategy adapt their products to meet the unique requirements of individual national or regional markets they serve. Their value-adding activities are distributed across this international arena.[85] This strategy also implies decentralization of strategic and operational decision-making to units at the country level (or at other geographical levels).[86] This decentralized autonomy is based on the logic that executives in these units are in the best position to decide what competitive strategy is most suitable in a specific country or region, provided that the conditions of competition, regulations, social norms, and customer preferences are not homogeneous across all geographical markets. Compared to a global strategy, a multidomestic strategy enables a higher responsiveness not only to current national or regional needs[87] but also to growth opportunities in each of the countries in which a firm has a competitive presence,[88] which may provide it with a more competitive edge.[89] Also, this strategy allows a firm to benefit from locational advantages available all across its geographical scope.

Finally, a **transnational strategy** combines elements of a global strategy with elements of a multidomestic strategy. Firms that embrace this strategy hence aim to achieve a relatively high level of regional or national responsiveness while simultaneously seeking to achieve efficiency gains through standardization and the integration of geographical market units.[90] This combined (or hybrid) strategy requires flexible coordination: a combination of both 'global' coordination and regional or national flexibility that is built on individual commitment and shared vision through an integrated network.[91] This strategy is more challenging to accomplish than the global and multidomestic strategies due to its contradictory objectives but has been related to a higher performance.[92] A combined strategy that is pursued at a regional level instead of at a global level can be labelled *a regional strategy.*

## CLOSING CASE
### Coca-Cola's booze businesses[93]

Source: © Freer (2021) / Shutterstock.

*(Continued)*

In 2020, hard seltzer (a low-calorie alcoholic beverage) was well on its way to becoming the hottest alcohol trend of the millennium, particularly among more health-conscious millennials. Between 2016 and 2019, the US hard seltzer market grew in revenue from $41 million to $1 billion. In 2020 this had already gone up to $1.8 billion with Goldman Sachs stating that it expected the market to reach $30 billion in sales by 2025. Competition in the hard seltzer category intensified and new rivals decided to enter the arena, including Heineken and… the Coca-Cola Company.

When Coca-Cola decided to diversify into the hard seltzer business, it did not have a rich history in alcoholic beverages. Back in 1977, the firm entered the wine business by acquiring a number of wineries including the US-based Taylor Wine Firm. Coca-Cola was so successful in leveraging its marketing expertise, distribution capabilities and other strengths that Taylor grew to become the country's second-largest wine brand within only a few years. However, in 1983 they decided to sell Taylor and to divest the wine business altogether after top management concluded that it could not make a decent return and realized that there was a misfit between the wine business, where it takes a relatively long time to proceed through the different stages of production, and the nature of Coca-Cola's core business.

Thirty-five years after the wine business divestiture, Coca-Cola introduced Lemon-Do to Japan. Lemon-Do, a spirit made from traditionally distilled Japanese alcohol (shochu), carbonated water and lemon flavouring, is a drink in the chūhai category – this is found almost exclusively in Japan and despite its commercial success there, Coca-Cola has never tried to introduce it elsewhere.

Instead, Coca-Cola has turned to hard seltzer and introduced Topo Chico Hard Seltzer in the US in March 2021, after launching in Mexico, Brazil and various European countries the year before. CEO James Quincey said about the launch: 'The Topo Chico brand has tremendous relevance and resonance with Millennial consumers. So I think this is going to be a great opportunity for us. It's very synergistic for the Coke system globally'.[24] Topo Chico pre-existed as a brand of Mexican sparkling mineral water, which had become increasingly popular across the US after Coca-Cola purchased them for $220 million in 2017. For the US hard seltzer market, Coca-Cola opted for a strategic alliance with Molson Coors Beverage Company, who at the time already had two hard seltzers in stores. According to the agreement, Molson Coors produces, distributes and markets Topo Chico Hard Seltzer in the US. A Coca-Cola representative commented that the alcoholic beverage industry is highly regulated and that the relationship with Molson Coors 'allows the Topo Chico Hard Seltzer product to move forward with a scaled launch with a firm that has generations of experience in the alcoholic beverage industry to responsibly reach consumers in the market'.[25]

In late July 2021, Boston Beer Firm, whose Truly brand, which had been launched in 2016, at that time held nearly 30% of the US hard seltzer market, reported disappointing second-quarter earnings, which according to the firm was mainly due to a slowdown in hard seltzer. Growth in consumption in bars and restaurants had been weaker than anticipated. The once-hot market for hard seltzers seemed to be losing its fizz, media outlets stated. In 2023, the category's rapid slowdown had not yet been halted. Trouble in paradise for Coca-Cola?

## Questions

1. To what extent do you think that it made sense for Coca-Cola to diversify into the wine business, the chūhai spirits business and the hard seltzer business?
2. What type of basic international strategy would you deem most suitable for Coca-Cola's hard seltzer business?

## Summary

- Corporate scope – the perimeter of a firm as a whole – consists of a horizontal dimension (industry scope or product market scope), a vertical dimension (vertical scope), and a geographical dimension (geographical market scope).
- Diversification and internationalization are challenging pathways to corporate growth, yet there are a variety of reasons why it can pay off for firms to choose these paths.
- Growth by diversification can take the form of upstream, downstream, horizontal, concentric, and conglomerate diversification. Alternatively, a distinction can be made between related and unrelated diversification.
- Diversification and internationalization can take place through organic growth, acquired growth, network-based growth, or a combination thereof.
- A firm's state of diversification can be expressed in terms of either the variety of industries or product markets in which it participates or the applicable category of diversification (single, dominant, related-constrained, related-linked, or unrelated business category).
- A firm's state of internationalization can be expressed in terms of the intensity, geographical extensity, and geographical concentration of its foreign activities.
- Multinational firms can use global, multidomestic or transnational corporate-level strategies.
- Overall, moderate levels of diversification and internationalization seem to provide the best corporate performance outcomes, but there are many exceptions.

## Review questions

1. How does unrelated horizontal diversification differ from concentric diversification and conglomerate diversification?
2. How can firms increase their market power through diversification?
3. How to assess a firm's level of diversification and internationalization?
4. Why can diversification and internationalization be beneficial for a firm's performance?
5. What are five different entry modes of internationalization?
6. What are the main differences between a global strategy and a multidomestic strategy?

# Discussion questions

1. To what extent is it appropriate for small-sized firms to compete in multiple business areas?
2. What are the implications of the increasing digitalization of our society on diversification and internationalization?
3. What measures could be taken to minimize the risk that executives opt for diversification or internationalization for reasons that are not in the best interest of shareholders?

## EXPERIENTIAL EXERCISES

1. Select a firm of your choice and identify a diversification option that allows this firm to improve its performance. Mention and explain what industry or product market to enter, the type of diversification, and the mode of diversification and, based on a sound analysis, provide your recommendations.
2. Describe and compare the internationalization (or diversification) paths of three multinational (or diversified) firms of your choice. To what extent are these paths different from one another? What do they have in common, if anything?

# Further reading

Ansoff, H.I. (1988) *Corporate Strategy*. London: Penguin Books.

Cheng, C., Zhong, H. and Cao, L. (2020) 'Facilitating speed of internationalization: The roles of business intelligence and organizational agility', *Journal of Business Research*, 110: 95–103.

Guerras-Martín, L.Á., Ronda-Pupo, G.A., Zúñiga-Vicente, J.Á. and Benito-Osorio, D. (2020) 'Half a century of research on corporate diversification: A new comprehensive framework', *Journal of Business Research*, 114: 124–41.

Penrose, E.T. (1959) *The Theory of the Growth of the Firm*. New York, NY: John Wiley.

Reed, R. and Luffman, G.A. (1986) 'Diversification: The growing confusion', *Strategic Management Journal*, 7: 29–35.

# Endnotes (references)

1. Hospitality Net (2000) 'McDonald's to open Swiss hotels', *hospitalitynet.org*, November 20. www.hospitalitynet.org/news/4006482.html (accessed June 24, 2023); McDonald's (2023a) 'Our history', *McDonalds*. www.mcdonalds.com/us/en-us/about-us/our-history.html (accessed June 24, 2023); McDonald's (2023b) 'Franchising', *McDonalds Switzerland*. www.mcdonalds.com/ch/fr-ch/franchising.html (accessed June 24, 2023); Michel, S. (2007) 'The upside of falling flat', *Harvard Business Review*, April. https://hbr.org/2007/04/the-upside-of-falling-flat (accessed June 24, 2023); Turner, S. (2001) 'In bed with McDonald's', *mcspotlight.org*, March 24. www.mcspotlight.org/media/press/mcds/times240301.html (accessed June 24, 2023); Studer, M. and Ordonez, J. (2000) 'McDonald's plans to open two hotels in Switzerland', *The Wall Street Journal*, November 17. www.wsj.com/articles/SB974411893409831614 (accessed June 24, 2023).

2. Fréry, F. (2006) 'The fundamental dimensions of strategy', *MIT Sloan Management Review*, 48 (1): 71–5.

3. European Commission (1997) 'Commission notice on the definition of relevant market for the purposes of community competition law', *EUR-Lex*. https://eur-lex.europa.eu/legal-content/EN/ALL/?uri=celex%3A31997Y1209%2801%29 (accessed June 24, 2023); Roth, P. and Rose, V. (eds.) (2001) *Bellamy & Child European Community Law of Competition* (5th ed.). Oxford: Oxford University Press.

4. Reed, R. and Luffman, G.A. (1986) 'Diversification: The growing confusion', *Strategic Management Journal*, 7: 29–35.

5. e.g., Jiao, J., Liu, Y. Wu, R. and Xia, J. (2019) 'Corporate strategy and subsidiary performance: The effect of product and geographic diversification', *Management and Organization Review*, 16 (5): 111–43; Mayer, M.C.J., Stadler, C. and Hautz, J. (2015) 'The relationship between product and international diversification: The role of experience', *Strategic Management Journal*, 36: 1458–68.

6. Ansoff, H.I. (1988) *Corporate Strategy* (revised ed.). London: Penguin Books; Sakhartov, A.V. (2017) 'Economies of scope, resource relatedness, and the dynamics of corporate diversification', *Strategic Management Journal*, 38: 2168–88; Schommer, M., Richter, A. and Karna, A. (2019) 'Does the diversification-firm performance relationship change over time? A meta-analytical review', *Journal of Management Studies*, 56 (1): 270–98.

7. Ansoff, H.I. (1957) 'Strategies for diversification', *Harvard Business Review*, 35 (5): 113–24; Ansoff (1988).

8. e.g., De Kluyver, C.A. and Pearce, J.A. (2003) *Strategy: A View From the Top*. Upper Saddle River, NJ: Prentice Hall; Sakhartov (2017); Schommer et al. (2019).

9. Ansoff, H.I. (1957) 'Strategies for diversification', *Harvard Business Review*, 35 (5): 113–24. p. 113.

10. Dawes, J.G. (2018) 'The Ansoff Matrix: A legendary tool, but with two logical problems'. *SSRN*. doi.org/10.2139/ssrn.3130530

11. Richards, G. (2021) 'Red Bull's Horner optimistic after F1 team opt to manufacture own engines', *The Guardian*, February 16. www.theguardian.com/sport/2021/feb/16/red-bulls-horner-optimistic-after-f1-team-opt-to-manufacture-own-engines (accessed June 24, 2023).

12. Ansoff (1988); Varadarajan, P.R. and Rajaratnam, D. (1986) 'Symbiotic marketing revisited', *Journal of Marketing*, 50 (1): 7–17.

13. Kim, H., Hong, S., Kwon, O. and Lee, C. (2017) 'Concentric diversification based on technological capabilities: Link analysis of products and technologies', *Technological Forecasting & Social Change*, 118: 246–57.

14. Carman, J.M. and Langeard, E. (1980) 'Growth strategies for service firms', *Strategic Management Journal*, 1 (1): 7–22.

15. Raynor, M.E. (2000) 'Hidden in plain sight: Hybrid diversification, economic performance, and "real options" in corporate strategy,' in R.K.F. Bresser, M.A. Hitt, R.D. Nixon and D. Heuskel (eds), *Winning Strategies in a Deconstructing World*. Hoboken, NJ: John Wiley & Sons, 77–106.

16. White, C. (2004) *Strategic Management*. New York, NY: Palgrave Macmillan.

17. Hill, C.W. and Jones, G.R. (1989) *Strategic Management: An Integrated Approach*. Boston, MA: Houghton Mifflin.

18. Ansoff (1988)

19. Busija, E.C., O'Neill, H.M. and Zeithaml, C.P. (1997) 'Diversification strategy, entry mode, and performance: Evidence of choice and constraints', *Strategic Management Journal*, 18 (4): 321–27; Malhotra, N.K., Agarwal, J. and Ulgado, F.M. (2003)

'Internationalisation and entry modes: A multitheoretical framework and research propositions', *Journal of International Marketing*, 11 (4): 131; Simmonds, P.G. (1990) 'The combined diversification breadth and mode dimensions and the performance of large diversified firms', *Strategic Management Journal*, 11: 399–410.

20. Peng, M.W. and Heath, P.S. (1996) 'The growth of the firm in planned economies in transition: Institutions, organizations, and strategic choice', *Academy of Management Review*, 21 (2): 492–528; Penrose, E.T. (1959) *The Theory of Growth of the Firm*. New York, NY: Wiley.

21. Ansoff (1988)

22. Osegowitsch, T. and Madhok, A. (2003) 'Vertical integration is dead, or is it?' *Business Horizons*, 46 (2): 25–34.

23. Montgomery, C.A. (1994) 'Corporate diversification', *Journal of Economic Perspectives*, 8 (3): 163–78.

24. Stocking, G.W. and Mueller, W.F. (1957) 'Business reciprocity and the size of firms', *Journal of Business*, 30 (2): 73–95.

25. Fuentelsaz, L. and Gomez, J. (2006) 'Multi-point competition, strategic similarity and entry into geographical markets', *Strategic Management Journal*, 27: 477–99; Gimeno, J. and Woo, C.Y. (1999) 'Multimarket contact, economies of scope, and firm performance', *Academy of Management Journal*, 42: 239–59.

26. Osegowitsch and Madhok (2003)

27. Stuckey, J. and White, D. (1993) 'When and when not to vertically integrate', *MIT Sloan Management Review*, 34 (3): 71–83.

28. Stuckey and White (1993)

29. Osegowitsch and Madhok (2003)

30. Markides, C.C. (1997) 'To diversify or not to diversify', *Harvard Business Review*, 75 (6): 93–9.

31. Fréry (2006)

32. Porter, M.E. (1987) 'From competitive advantage to corporate strategy', *Harvard Business Review*, 65 (3): 43–59.

33. Nanda, A. (2020) 'Corporate strategy', *Harvard Business School Module Note* 720-448, March 2020. https://www.hbs.edu/faculty/Pages/item.aspx?num=57862 (accessed June 24, 2023); Piskorski, M.J. (2006) 'Note on corporate strategy', *Harvard Business School Background Note* 705-449. https://www.hbs.edu/faculty/Pages/item.aspx?num=31932 (accessed June 24, 2023); Porter (1987).

34. Nanda (2020)

35. Turner, G. and Robison, P. (2019) 'What happens when a vacuum company tries to make an electric car', *Bloomberg BusinessWeek*, October 11. www.bloomberg.com/news/features/2019-10-11/dyson-s-expensive-road-from-electric-to-invisible-cars (accessed June 24, 2023); Turner, G. (2020) 'Dyson reveals patents for headphones that purify air around you', *Bloomberg BusinessWeek*, February 4. www.bloomberg.com/news/articles/2020-02-04/dyson-reveals-patents-for-air-purifier-that-s-also-headphones (accessed June 24, 2023); The Times (2020) 'James Dyson interview [by John Arlidge]: How I blew £500m on electric car to rival Tesla', *The Times*, May 16. www.thetimes.co.uk/article/james-dyson-interview-electric-car-tesla-tzls09t5m (accessed June 24, 2023).

36. Quote in Turner, G. and Robison, P. (2019) 'What happens when a vacuum company tries to make an electric car', *Bloomberg BusinessWeek*, October 11. www.bloomberg.com/news/features/2019-10-11/dyson-s-expensive-road-from-electric-to-invisible-cars (accessed July 27, 2023).

37. Montgomery, C.A. (1982) 'The measurement of firm diversification: Some new empirical evidence', *Academy of Management Journal*, 25 (2): 299–307; Pitts, R.A. and

Hopkins, H.D. (1982) 'Firm diversity: Conceptualization and measurement', *Academy of Management Review*, 7(4): 620–9.

38. Montgomery (1982: 300)

39. Ridder, M. (2023), 'PepsiCo's distribution of net revenue worldwide from 2011 to 2022, by food and beverage', *Statista*. www.statista.com/statistics/258121/distribution-of-net-revenue-of-pepsico-worldwide-by-food-and-beverage (accessed July 27, 2023).

40. Rumelt, R.P. (1982) 'Diversification strategy and profitability', *Strategic Management Journal*, 3: 359–69; Wrigley, L. (1970) *Divisional Autonomy and Diversification*, PhD thesis. Cambridge, MA: Harvard Business School.

41. Ansoff (1988); Collis, D.J. and Montgomery, C.A. (1998) 'Creating corporate advantage', *Harvard Business Review*, 76 (3): 71–83; Porter (1987); Rumelt, R.P. (1974) *Strategy, Structure and Economic Performance*. Boston, MA: Harvard Business School.

42. Rumelt (1974, 1982)

43. Rumelt (1982: 360)

44. Hitt, M.A., Ireland, R.D. and Hoskisson, R.E. (2009) *Strategic Management: Competitiveness and Globalization* (8th ed.). Mason, OH: Cengage; Rumelt (1974).

45. Schommer et al. (2019)

46. e.g., Grant, R.M., Jammine, A.P. and Thomas, H. (1988) 'Diversity, diversification, and profitability among British manufacturing companies', *Academy of Management Journal*, 31 (4): 771–801; Hoskisson, R.E. and Hitt, M.A. (1990), 'Antecedents and performance outcomes of diversification: A review and critique of theoretical perspectives', *Journal of Management*, 16 (2): 461–509; Itami, H., Kagono, T., Yoshihara, H. and Sakuma, S. (1982) 'Diversification strategies and economic performance', *Japanese Economic Studies*, 11 (1): 78–110; Palich, L.E., Cardinal, L.B. and Miller, C.C. (2000) 'Curvilinearity in the diversification-performance linkage: An examination of over three decades of research', *Strategic Management Journal*, 21 (2): 155–74; Pitts and Hopkins (1982); Rumelt (1974); Singh, D.A., Gaur, A.S. and Schmid, F.P. (2010) 'Corporate diversification, TMT experience, and performance', *Management International Review*, 50 (1): 35–56.

47. Nippa, M., Pidun, U. and Rubner, H. (2011) 'Corporate portfolio management: Appraising four decades of academic research', *Academy of Management Perspectives*, 25 (4): 50–66.

48. Bettis, R.A. (1981) 'Performance differences in related and unrelated diversified firms', *Strategic Management Journal*, 2: 379–93; Grant, R.M. and Jammine, A.P. (1988) 'Performance differences between the Wrigley/Rumelt strategic categories', *Strategic Management Journal*, 9 (4): 333–46; Hill, C.W.L., Hitt, M.A. and Hoskisson, R.E. (1992) 'Cooperative versus competitive structures in related and unrelated diversified firms', *Organization Science*, 3: 501–21; Montgomery (1982); Palepu, K. (1985) 'Diversification strategy, profit performance and the entropy measure', *Strategic Management Journal*, 6: 239–55.

49. Mathur, I., Singh, M. and Gleason, K.C. (2004) 'Multinational diversification and corporate performance: Evidence from European firms', *European Financial Management*, 10 (3): 439–64; Schoar, A. (2002) 'Effect of corporate diversification on productivity', *Journal of Finance*, 57 (6): 2379–403.

50. Berger, P.G. and Ofek, E. (1995) 'Diversification's effect on firm value', *Journal of Financial Economics*, 37(1): 39–65; Maksimovic, V. and Phillips, G. (2002) 'Do conglomerate firms allocate resources inefficiently across industries? Theory and evidence', *Journal of Finance*, 57 (2): 721–67; Rajan, R., Servaes, H. and Zingales, L. (2000) 'The cost of diversification: The diversification discount and inefficient investment', *Journal of Finance*, 55 (1): 35–80.

51. Nippa et al. (2011)

52. De Kluyver and Pearce (2003)

53. Chatain, O. and Zemsky, P. (2007) 'The horizontal scope of the firm: Organizational tradeoffs vs. buyer-supplier relationships', *Management Science,* 53 (4): 550–65.

54. Rumelt, R.P., Schendel D.E. and Teece, D.J. (1994) *Fundamental Issues in Strategy: A Research Agenda.* Boston, MA: Harvard Business School Press.

55. Argyres, N. (1996b) 'Evidence on the role of firm capabilities in vertical integration decisions', *Strategic Management Journal,* 17: 129–50; Kogut, B. and Zander, U. (1992) 'Knowledge of the firm, combinative capabilities, and the replication of technology', *Organization Science,* 3 (3): 383–97; Penrose (1959); Teece, D.J. (1982) 'Towards an economic theory of the multiproduct firm', *Journal of Economic Behavior and Organization,* 3 (1): 39–63.

56. Ansoff (1988)

57. Hashai, N. (2015) 'Within-industry diversification and firm performance: An S-shaped hypothesis', *Strategic Management Journal,* 36: 1378–400; Wan, W.P., Hoskisson, R.E., Short, J C. and Yiu, D.W. (2011) 'Resource-based theory and corporate diversification: Accomplishments and opportunities', *Journal of Management,* 37: 1335–68; Williamson, O.E. (1985) *The Economic Institutions of Capitalism.* New York, NY: Free Press; Zhou, Y.M. (2011) 'Synergy, coordination costs, and diversification choices', *Strategic Management Journal,* 32 (6): 624–39.

58. Brahm, F., Parmigiani, A. and Tarziján, J. (2021) 'Can firms be both broad and deep? Exploring interdependencies between horizontal and vertical firm scope', *Journal of Management,* 47 (5): 1219–54.

59. Adner, R. and Helfat, C.E. (2003) 'Corporate effects and dynamic managerial capabilities', *Strategic Management Journal,* 24: 1011–25; Helfat, C.E. and Martin, J.A. (2015) 'Dynamic managerial capabilities: Review and assessment of managerial impact on strategic change', *Journal of Management,* 41: 1281–312; Sirmon, D.G., Hitt, M.A., Ireland, R.D. and Gilbert, B.A. (2011) 'Resource orchestration to create competitive advantage breadth, depth, and life cycle effects', *Journal of Management,* 37: 1390–412.

60. Brahm et al. (2021)

61. Brahm et al. (2021)

62. Ansoff (1988)

63. Cantwell, J. (1995) 'The globalization of technology: What remains of the product cycle model?', *Cambridge Journal of Economics,* 19: 155–74; Zander, I. (1997) 'Technological diversification in the multinational corporation-historical evolution and future prospects', *Research Policy,* 26 (2): 209–27.

64. Ansoff (1988)

65. Ansoff (1988)

66. Ghemawat, P. (2007) *Redefining Global Strategy: Crossing Borders in a World Where Differences Still Matter.* Boston, MA: Harvard Business Publishing.

67. Ghemawat, P. (2003) 'The forgotten strategy', *Harvard Business Review,* 18 (11): 76–84.

68. Hill and Jones (1998)

69. Jernbro (2020) *Sustainability Report 2020.* Jernbro. https://jernbro.com/wp-content/uploads/2021/03/Sustainability-Report-2020.pdf (accessed June 24, 2023).

70. Knight, G.A. and Cavusgil, S.T. (2004) 'Innovation, organizational capabilities, and the born-global firm', *Journal of International Business Studies,* 35 (2): 124–41; Madsen, T.K. and Servais, P. (1997) 'The internationalisation of Born Globals: An evolutionary process?', *International Business Review,* 6 (6): 561–83.

71. Ansoff (1988)

72. Elango, B. (2009) 'Minimizing effects of "liability of foreignness": Response strategies of foreign firms in the United States', *Journal of World Business*, 44 (1): 51–62; Hymer, S.H. (1976) *The International Operations of National Firms: A Study of Direct Foreign Investment*. Cambridge, MA: MIT Press; Zaheer, S. (1995) 'Overcoming the liability of foreignness', *Academy of Management Journal*, 38: 341–63.

73. Ambos, T.C. and Ambos, B. (2009) 'The impact of distance on knowledge transfer effectiveness in multinational corporations', *Journal of International Management*, 15: 1–14; Meschi, P.X. (2009) 'Government corruption and foreign stakes in international joint ventures in emerging economies', *Asia Pacific Journal of Management*, 26: 241–61.

74. Hennart, J.F. (2001) 'Theories of the multinational enterprise', in A.M. Rugman and T. Brewer (eds), *Oxford Handbook of International Business*. Oxford: Oxford University Press, 141–70.

75. Zhou, N. and Guillen, M.F. (2016) 'Categorizing the liability of foreignness: Ownership, location, and internalization-specific dimensions', *Global Strategy Journal*, 6: 309–29.

76. Ansoff (1988)

77. Ietto-Gillies, G. (2010) 'Conceptual issues behind the assessment of the degree of internationalisation', *Transnational Corporation*, 18 (3): 59–83.

78. Ietto-Gillies (2010)

79. Geringer, J.M., Tallman, S. and Olsen, D.M. (2000) 'Product and international diversification among Japanese multinational firms', *Strategic Management Journal*, 21: 51–80; Gomes, L. and Ramaswamy, K. (1999) 'An empirical examination of the form of the relationship between multinationality and performance', *Journal of International Business Studies*, 30: 173–88.

80. Hitt, M.A. and Hoskisson, R. (1997) 'International diversification: Effects on innovation and firm performance', *Academy of Management Journal*, 40 (4): 767–98.

81. Carnegy, H. (1995) 'Struggle to save the soul of IKEA', *Financial Times*, March 27: 12; Hill, C.W. and Jones, G.R. (1998) *Strategic Management Theory: An Integrated Approach*. Boston, MA: Houghton Mifflin; The Economist (1994) 'Furnishing the world', *The Economist,* November 19: 79–80; Verbeke, A. (2013) *International Business Strategy* (2nd ed.). Cambridge: Cambridge University Press.

82. Tempel, A. and Walgenbach, P. (2007) 'Global standardisation of organizational forms and management practices? What new institutionalism and business systems approach can learn from each other', *Journal of Management Studies*, 44: 1–24.

83. Moon, H.C. and Kim, M.Y. (2009) 'A new framework for global expansion: A dynamic diversification-coordination (DDC) model', *Management Decision*, 46 (1): 131–51.

84. Connelly, B.L., Hitt, M.A., DeNisi, A.S. and Ireland, R.D. (2007) 'Expatriates and corporate-level international strategy: Governing with the knowledge contract', *Management Decision*, 45: 564–81; Hong, J.F.L., Easterby-Smith, M. and Snell, R.S. (2006) 'Transferring organisational learning systems to Japanese subsidiaries in China', *Journal of Management Studies*, 43: 1027–58.

85. Alfred, B.B. and Swan, K.S. (2004) 'Global versus multidomestic: Culture's consequences on innovation', *Management International Review*, 44: 81–105; Ralston, D.A., Holt, D.H., Terpstra, R.H. and Kai-Cheng, Y. (2008) 'The impact of national culture and economic ideology on managerial work values: A study of the United States, Russia, Japan, and China', *Journal of International Business Studies*, 39 (1): 8–26.

86. Ferner, A., Almond, P., Clark, I., Colling, T. and Edwards, T. (2004) 'The dynamics of central control and subsidiary anatomy in the management of human resources: Case study evidence from U.S. MNCs in the U.K.', *Organization Studies*, 25: 363–92; Grewal,

D., Iyer, G.R., Kamakura, W.A., Mehrotra, A. and Sharma, A. (2009) 'Evaluation of subsidiary marketing performance: Combining process and outcome performance metrics', *Academy of Marketing Science Journal*, 37 (2): 117–20.

87. Connelly et al. (2007); Nachum, L. (2003) 'Does nationality of ownership make any difference and if so, under what circumstances? Professional service MNEs in global competition', *Journal of International Management*, 9: 1–32.

88. Yaprak, A. (2002) 'Globalisation: Strategies to build a great global firm in the new economy', *Thunderbird International Business Review*, 44 (2): 297–302.

89. Hansen, M.W., Pedersen, T. and Petersen, B. (2009) 'MNC strategies and linkage effects in developing countries', *Journal of World Business*, 44 (2): 121–39; Luo, Y. (2001) 'Determinants of local responsiveness: Perspectives from foreign subsidiaries in an emerging market', *Journal of Management*, 27: 451–77.

90. Bartlett, C.A. and Ghoshal, S. (1988) 'Organizing for worldwide effectiveness: The transnational solution', *California Management Review*, 31 (1): 54–74; Bartlett, C.A. and Ghoshal, S. (2002) *Managing Across Borders: The Transnational Solution*. Boston, MA: Harvard Business Press.

91. Hanson, D., Hitt, M.A., Ireland, R.D. and Hoskisson, R.E. (2017) *Strategic Management: Competitiveness and Globalization*. Andover: Cengage.

92. Abbott, A. and Banerji, K. (2003) 'Strategic flexibility and firm performance: The case of U.S. based transnational corporations', *Global Journal of Flexible Systems Management*, 4 (1/2): 1–7; Child, J. and Van, Y. (2001) 'National and transnational effects in international business: Indications from Sino-foreign joint ventures', *Management International Review*, 41 (1): 53–75; Rugman, A.M. and Verbeke, A. (2008) 'A regional solution to the strategy and structure of multinationals', *European Management Journal*, 26 (5): 305–13.

93. Business Wire (2020) 'Molson Coors enters exclusive agreement with The Coca-Cola Company to bring Topo Chico Hard Seltzer to the US', *Business Wire,* September 29. www.businesswire.com/news/home/20200929005637/en/Molson-Coors-Enters-Exclusive-Agreement-Coca-Cola-Company (accessed June 24, 2023); Furnari, C. (2021) 'Topo Chico hard seltzer hits US retailers on March 29', *Forbes,* March 18. www.forbes.com/sites/chrisfurnari/2021/03/18/topo-chico-hard-seltzer-hits-us-retailers-on-march-29 (accessed June 24, 2023); GlobalData Consumer (2020) 'Coca-Cola Japan successfully enters alcohol beverage market', *Drinks Insight Network,* January 30. www.drinks-insight-network.com/digital-disruption/coca-cola-japan-alcohol (accessed June 24, 2023); Kary, T. (2021) 'America's taste for hard seltzer is suddenly starting to wane', *Bloomberg,* July 23. www.bloomberg.com/news/articles/2021-07-23/america-s-taste-for-hard-seltzer-is-suddenly-starting-to-wane (accessed June 24, 2023); Keough, D.R. (2011) *The Ten Commandments for Business Failure.* London: Penguin Books; Lin, M. (n.d.) 'Hard seltzer industry: Unlikely to fizzle out', *Toptal.* www.toptal.com/finance/market-research-analysts/hard-seltzer-industry (accessed June 24, 2023); Lindenberger, H. (2021) 'The hard seltzer market is getting more crowded', *Forbes,* January 12. www.forbes.com/sites/hudsonlindenberger/2021/01/12/the-hard-seltzer-market-is-getting-more-crowded (accessed June 24, 2023); Negishi, M. (2019) 'Coca-Cola cocktails are coming to convenience stores across Japan', *The Wall Street Journal,* July 23. www.wsj.com/articles/coca-cola-to-sell-its-first-alcoholic-drink-nationwide-in-japan-11563874581 (accessed June 24, 2023); Pellechia, T. (2018) 'After more than 35 years away, Coca-Cola is getting back into alcohol', *Forbes,* March 9. www.forbes.com/sites/thomaspellechia/2018/03/09/after-more-than-thirty-five-years-away-from-it-coca-cola-is-getting-back-into-alcohol (accessed June 24, 2023); Rubin, J. (2021) '"Stunning collapse" of hard seltzer sales turn fizzy category flat', *Toronto Star,* September 16. www.thestar.com/business/2021/09/16/stunning-collapse-of-hard-seltzer-

sales-turn-fizzy-category-flat.html (accessed June 24, 2023); Shaw, L. (2020) 'In focus: Hard seltzers', *The Drinks Business,* April 27. www.thedrinksbusiness.com/2020/04/in-focus-hard-seltzers (accessed June 24, 2023); Sozzi, B. (2021) 'Boston Beer stock is crashing because the hard seltzer boom is basically over', *Yahoo! News,* July 23. https://news.yahoo.com/boston-beer-stock-is-crashing-because-the-hard-seltzer-boom-is-basically-over-105544315.html (accessed June 24, 2023); Stone, B. (2021) 'The investment implications of hard seltzer losing its fizz', *Forbes,* September 21. www.forbes.com/sites/bill_stone/2021/09/21/the-investment-implications-of-hard-seltzer-losing-its-fizz (accessed June 24, 2023); T4 (2022) 'US hard seltzer market share, market size and industry growth drivers, 2016–2021', *T4,* December 23. www.t4.ai/industry/hard-seltzer-market-share (accessed June 24, 2023); Taylor, K. (2018) 'Coca-Cola is using a sparkling-water brand with a cult following to take over a \$16 billion industry', *Business Insider Nederland,* June 15. www.businessinsider.nl/coca-cola-secret-weapon-is-topo-chico-2018-6 (accessed June 14, 2023); The Coca Cola Company (2020) 'Topo Chico hard seltzer rolls out in Latin America', *Coca Cola Company,* September 22. www.coca-colacompany.com/news/topo-chico-hard-seltzer-rolls-out-in-latin-america (accessed June 24, 2023).

94. The Coca Cola Company (2020)
95. Furnari, C. (2020) 'Coca-Cola taps Molson Coors to produce and distribute Topo Chico hard seltzer', *Forbes,* September 29. www.forbes.com/sites/chrisfurnari/2020/09/29/coca-cola-taps-molson-coors-to-produce-and-distribute-topo-chico-hard-seltzer (accessed June 24, 2023).

# Key terms

**Diversification** – the growth strategy of entering a business area outside a firm's current industry scope or product-market scope (*act of diversification*) or the level to which a firm participates across structurally different industries or product markets (*state of diversification*)

**Geographical scope** – dimension of corporate scope reflecting the range of different geographical markets in which a firm operates

**Global strategy** – an international strategy favouring cost efficiency over local responsiveness via uniformity and integration across countries

**Horizontal scope** – dimension of corporate scope reflecting the range of different business areas (industries or product markets) in which a firm operates

**Internationalization** – the growth strategy of geographic expansion across national borders (*act of internationalization*) or the level to which a firm participates in geographical markets outside its home market (*state of diversification*)

**Multidomestic strategy** – an international strategy favouring local responsiveness over cost efficiency by adapting a firm's offering to individual national or regional markets and by distributing its activities accordingly

**Transnational strategy** – an international strategy combining elements of a global strategy and a multidomestic strategy

**Vertical scope** – dimension of corporate scope reflecting the range of vertically aligned activities a firm conducts, denoting its positioning along an industry's value chain

# 12
# CORPORATE-LEVEL STRATEGY

## LEARNING OBJECTIVES

After reading this chapter, you should be able to:

- understand what is meant by 'corporate parent' and what its main functions are;
- appreciate the meaning of corporate parenting advantage;
- recognize different ways in which business units within a diversified firm can be related;
- compare synergy management with capital orchestration and identify the underlying value-creating mechanisms of these distinct corporate logics;
- distinguish between different types of corporate parenting activities, approaches to parental involvement, and parental control mechanisms.

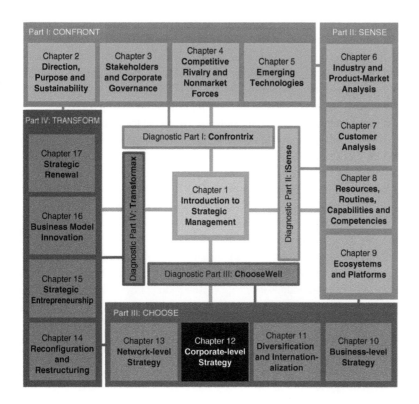

## OPENING CASE

Source: © JHVEPhoto (2020) / Shutterstock.

### Hilton's brand portfolio strategy

Hilton is one of the most famous and recognizable hospitality firms globally, with over 100 years of continued success. Conrad Hilton purchased his first hotel in 1919 in Mobley, Texas, and opened the first Hilton-branded hotel in 1925 in Dallas. What followed was an extraordinary journey leading to managing and operating over 7,100 hotels in 123 countries by 2023. In addition, Hilton shaped the hospitality industry by pioneering innovations like air conditioning in rooms, minibars, and room service. It was also the first lodging firm listed on the NYSE and the first to franchise. Hilton operates in two business segments: Management & Franchise and Ownership & Leasing. Since 2007, the focus has been predominantly on growing the Management & Franchise segment, where third parties own the properties, and Hilton either manages the hotel or collects a fee under a franchise agreement. This strategy reduces the risk for Hilton as they do not physically own the properties, and the owner is obligated to pay Hilton for its services, regardless of external circumstances.

Hilton's brand recognition attracts real estate developers and hotel owners to partner up with the firm, where they supply the building, and Hilton either manages the hotel or franchises it out. Like many firms in the hospitality industry, Hilton Worldwide Holdings, Inc. manages a comprehensive portfolio of hotel brands in different quality segments and price ranges. In mid-2023 there were 17 brands operating in 5 quality segments: Luxury (Waldorf Astoria Hotels & Resorts, LXR Hotels & Resorts, Conrad Hotels & Resorts), Upper upscale (Canopy by Hilton, Signia by Hilton, Hilton Hotels & Resorts, Curio Collection by Hilton, Embassy Suites by Hilton), Upscale (DoubleTree by Hilton, Tapestry Collection by Hilton, Hilton Garden Inn, Homewood Suites), Upper midscale (Motto by Hilton, Hampton by Hilton, Home2 Suites by Hilton), and Midscale (Tru by Hilton). 'Tempo by Hilton' was launched later that year as the 18th brand, while 'Spark by Hilton' was being developed at the time as a new Premium economy offering affordable hotel stays. Additionally, Hilton Grand Vacations offers Timeshare vacation rentals. Hilton tries to be the preferred choice in each segment. Potential disadvantages of having such an extensive portfolio are that brands in the same segments – and perhaps between segments too – compete against each other for market share, and that all the different brand names may dilute Hilton's brand identity: what does 'Hilton' stand for if so many brands carry the name?

Hilton has a high degree of market commonality and resource familiarity with its direct competitors such as Marriott, Accor, IHG, and Hyatt. Hilton tries to counter this by capitalizing on brand loyalty with its customers, as does everyone else. Although this might work in the luxury segment, where wealthy travelers tend to stick to their preferred brand, it is more challenging in lower-quality segments, where the price is often more important than brand loyalty. Hilton keeps the costs down due to its bargaining power with suppliers as they have firm-wide contracts. However, this brings no real competitive advantage as their competitors have similar agreements. The challenge here is keeping the price low while offering higher quality than the competition. But even if Hilton manages this, a new generation of travelers is not loyal to traditional hotel brands and prefers more exciting options like Airbnb and Sonder. Airbnb was the first company to challenge the status quo in the hospitality industry. Instead of staying in a traditional hotel, where the cheaper ones tend to be outside the city center, travelers could stay in a space that reflects the culture of the city they are visiting, giving them more of a 'home-away-from-home' feeling. The tech-driven hospitality firm Sonder went one step further by investing in the digitalization of travel, where guests no longer have to interact face-to-face with others and can use an app for the entire process, which may become a key selling point in the aftermath of the COVID-19 pandemic.

## Questions

1. What do you think are the main activities of corporate parent Hilton Worldwide?
2. To what extent do you expect synergies between Hilton's two business segments, and between its different hotel brands?
3. What are the advantages and disadvantages of intra-portfolio competition?
4. Would you advise consolidating brands within Hilton's quality segments? Why (not)?
5. Do you think Hilton should add boutique, short-term rentals to its portfolio to compete with Airbnb and Sonder? Or should they do something completely different?

# Introduction

Corporate-level strategy – in short, *corporate strategy* (or companywide strategy) – addresses how executives set and oversee their firm's corporate scope. In Chapter 11, we discussed how, as a result of diversification and internationalization, this scope may comprise multiple business areas (i.e., industries or product markets) and geographical markets. Hilton (see the opening case), for instance, operates in the business segments Management & Franchise and Ownership & Leasing, and is present in 123 countries. *Multibusiness firms*, which operate two or more businesses, and *multinational corporations* (MNCs), which have business operations in at least one country other than their home country, play a dominant role in economies around the world and are therefore important to study. Most multibusiness and multinational firms are divided into separate entities (i.e., divisions) that bear responsibility for one or more distinct business areas and/or geographical areas in which the firm engages – hence the name *multidivisional firms*. Multidivisional firms are overseen by executives residing at the corporate parent. The strategic choices that they make to create value for the firm as a whole make up the corporate strategy. After first zooming in on the notion of corporate strategy and how it relates to competitive and functional strategies, this chapter focuses on the characteristics, functions, roles, and activities of corporate parents and how these can create (or destroy) value for the multidivisional setting they oversee.

# Corporate-level, business-level and functional-level strategy

**Corporate-level strategy** concerns the determination of the direction and scope of a firm as a whole, and the creation of value through the coordination and configuration of its component businesses and/or geographical divisions. Most of the corporate strategy literature focuses on multibusiness firms, due to which corporate strategy is occasionally equated to multibusiness strategy. Corporate strategy is also relevant for single-business firms, however. For instance, the corporate-level decision not to diversify is a very important one, which can have a significant effect on the firm's competitive performance – for better or worse. The determination of a firm's direction is covered largely in Chapter 2. Chapter 11 lays out what defines a firm's scope (i.e., its boundaries) and how and why many firms expand their scope. Executives responsible for setting and overseeing this scope have to decide which businesses belong within a firm's boundaries, and which ones do not, which transactions to undertake to achieve that scope, how to coordinate resources within these boundaries, and how to promote which interlinkages (if any) should exist between these businesses.[1]

A successful corporate strategy should reinforce and grow out of business-level strategy[2], which encompasses choices regarding how you employ a particular set of resources and capabilities to deal with a particular set of customers and competitors in relation to a single business area (see Chapter 10). Put differently, business-level strategy is concerned with how to compete in a particular industry or product market with a certain value proposition, and how to deliver this value proposition. Choices at this level should be in harmony with corporate-level strategic decisions. In the case of a single-business firm, the distinction between corporate-level strategy and business-level strategy ranges from minimal to non existent (when the firm is dedicated entirely to a single business), with the latter being more prevalent. Business-level strategies need to be translated into subordinate strategies of departments such as marketing, HR, procurement, logistics and finance – the so-called *functional strategies*. Depending on a firm's organizational structure, one or more of these departments could be part of the corporate layer. In sum, three interrelated levels of organizational strategy can be discerned: corporate-level (i.e., companywide) strategy, business-level (i.e., competitive) strategy, and functional-level strategy (see Figure 12.1). Corporate strategy is the 'highest' of these levels, encapsulating the strategies of all organizational entities that operate under the same corporate umbrella.

**FIGURE 12.1**   Three levels of organizational strategy

## The corporate parent

The divisions of multidivisional firms go by different names, such as *business units*, *business segments*, *corporate divisions*, *profit centers*, or simply *divisions*. There can be multiple layers of divisions, in which case firms often use different labels (e.g., 'business unit' and 'division') to indicate this stratification. This labelling is not always done consistently across firms – for instance, you will find corporate organizational charts depicting 'business units' that consist of 'divisions', but also charts where it is the other way around. In this textbook, these terms are used interchangeably. For now, let's use the term *business unit* to denote a part of a multidivisional firm that bears responsibility for the firm's competitive posture in a distinctive business area (i.e., business line)[3] and, hence, for the firm's performance in this area. This is to say that this entity has a certain level of strategic autonomy and that it carries P&L (profit and loss) responsibility. A multibusiness firm can be thought of as an aggregate of business units – its component businesses – and an over-arching corporate parent. The term **corporate parent** refers to the organizational layer(s) above these business units. Whereas business-level strategy (see Chapter 10) is the domain of a business unit (or of a single-business firm), the overarching corporate-level strategy is corporate parent domain.

The corporate parent includes the *corporate centre*, which is also referred to as the corporate headquarters, HQ unit, corporate office or parent firm, but also any intermediate-level corporate divisions (or divisional offices) that look after these business units. These divisions, which are found in medium- and large-sized firms in particular, typically administer geographical regions or the production and distribution of major product segments, whereas the corporate centre administers the firm as a whole and constitutes the top level of manage-ment.[4] All executives and staff members that are assigned to either the corporate centre or an intermediate-level unit (as opposed to a business unit or a division of that business unit) act in a *corporate parenting role*. The corporate parent of a corporate group (see Chapter 11) is com-monly referred to as the parent company or holding company. This parent typically owns a controlling stake in multiple subsidiary firms, each of which may have multiple business units. Figure 12.2 provides a simplified visualization of a corporate parent of a single multibusiness firm – thus not a corporate group – with two corporate divisions, each of which oversees two individual business units that have been set up to compete in a distinct business area.

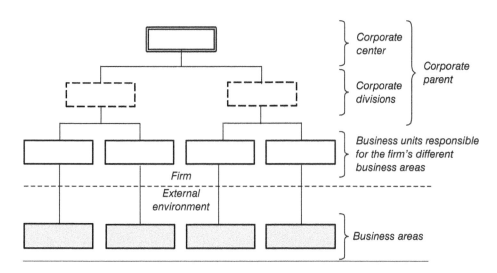

**FIGURE 12.2**   The corporate parent and business units (simplified visualization)

The divisions within a multibusiness firm that operates internationally are not neces-sarily structured around distinctive business areas. Instead, they could, for instance, be structured around certain geographical areas, such as countries, business regions (such as APAC and EMEA) or continents. Another possibility is that a division is responsible for a business area in a defined geographical area. For instance, PepsiCo has three separate divi-sions that focus on the North-American market: PepsiCo Beverages North America, Frito-Lay North America (chips, pretzels, popcorn and other snacks), and Quaker Foods North America (cereals, rice, pasta and other products). Its other four divisions bear responsibility for all

PepsiCo's business lines in respectively the AMESA region (Africa, Middle East, South Asia), the APAC region (Asia, Pacific, Australia/New Zealand, China), Latin America, and Europe. Zooming in, the European division is divided into business units such as PepsiCo North-West Europe and further segmented into regional units (such as the market unit PepsiCo Nordics) and country market units. PepsiCo focuses on achieving integration across its regional and country markets, coordinated by its corporate and divisional headquarters, while tailoring its products to meet the preferences and tastes of customers in these different markets.[5]

## The quest for corporate parenting advantage

Competitive advantage is achieved at an individual business level. Each of the business units that have been brought together in a multibusiness firm could potentially be independent stand-alone firms. Successful corporate strategy enhances the performance of these individual business units over and above what they could achieve otherwise – that is, compared to what they could achieve by being stand-alone firms or by being part of another firm. The extent to which a corporate parent improves the performance of its business units (or, in the context of a corporate group, the performance of its subsidiary companies) is termed **corporate parenting advantage**, also known as *corporate advantage* or *parenting advantage*.[6] Hence, corporate parenting advantage is about the added value that corporate parents are able to create. This 'corporate value' can be created only through the effect that their decisions have on business unit competitiveness – for instance, enabling business units to better serve their customers, to lower their costs, and to deal with competitors more successfully. In that regard, in a business context 'parenting' is synonymous with 'influencing'.[7]

Corporate parents can only truly add value to the business units they oversee if the total benefits of being part of the corporate whole outweigh the inherent costs of not being stand-alone firms.[8] These *costs of ownership* can include bureaucracy costs, incentive costs, capital misallocation and negative outcomes of power play:

- <u>Bureaucracy costs</u> are incurred when business units have to spend significant time complying with corporate-level planning, procedures or policies and explaining decisions to the corporate parent.[9]
- <u>Incentive costs</u> occur when business units have less of an incentive to strive for competitive excellence than if they would be completely independent – for instance, because the corporate parent mandates transfers of economic output between units at prearranged transfer prices.[10]
- <u>Capital misallocation</u> occurs when a business unit find itself with too little capital as a result of potentially biased capital allocation decisions made by the corporate parent. Capital misallocation can also be a result of power struggles in which business unit managers might be involved.[11]
- <u>Power play</u> that undermines inter-unit collaboration may cause corporate parenting advantage to erode.

## Functions of the corporate parent

The corporate parent (i.e., its executives and staff) is there to set and oversee the scope of the firm in such a way that the component business units (or subsidiary companies) benefit from a corporate parenting advantage. This generic responsibility can be broken down into several key functions which are interrelated. One of these functions is to *determine the scope* (i.e., the boundaries) of the firm. As covered in Chapter 11, this encompasses decisions about the industries, product markets, geographical markets and stages of the value chain in which to participate. A second function is to *undertake and implement corporate transactions* that may be required to alter these boundaries – for instance, alliances (see Chapter 13), acquisitions, and divestitures (see Chapter 14). Third, corporate parents *set the firm's overall direction and decide on the purpose and core values* of the firm (see Chapter 2), which should guide decisions regarding its scope. By clearly communicating the unifying vision and mission to subordinate business units and external stakeholders, corporate parents can minimize misalignment between corporate-level and business-level strategic decisions and prevent confusion among investors or shareholders that may affect investment decisions and the share price. Also, by having a vision set outside of the business units there is less chance of mission drift.

The fourth function of corporate parents is to *coordinate how resources are deployed and used*. This function can encompass different actions, including:

- deciding how to allocate capital and other resources, such as managerial and product-specific technical skills and marketing experience, among the firm's business units (and corporate divisions, if any) to productive uses;[12]
- determining whether and how to *cross-subsidize* – that is, to shift capital from one subordinate unit to another, by using profits from the former to financially support the latter;[13]
- moving executives and other personnel between units as a means to transfer knowledge within the firm;[14]
- choosing whether and how to leverage particular activities and resources across units to achieve synergies.[15]

The fifth function is *monitoring*, which is an administrative function that is focused mainly on loss prevention.[16] For instance, corporate parents typically monitor the performance of the firm's business units (and, in the context of a corporate group, its subsidiary companies) and their executives against certain standards, goals and growth paths that have been set. Also, they often monitor these units' use of allocated resources. By measuring progress outside the business units there is less chance of worrying trends not being corrected. Depending on how the units perform and on their resource use, the corporate parent may decide to *intervene* (a sixth function of most corporate parents). For instance, when a business unit's results are disappointing, corporate executives may decide to take action by replacing unit managers, redefining product lines, restructuring, or even divesting a unit (see Chapter 14). Corporate interventions on behalf of the businesses and for the good of the firm as a whole can be the cause of friction between individual business and the corporate parent. The more autonomy a corporate parent has granted to divisions or subsidiaries, the less its tendency to intervene in their strategic conduct.

Seventh, corporate parents may *provide central corporate services and business support* for the business units.[17] Central corporate services, which are shared by the different business units and therefore also referred to as *shared services centers*, may deal with, for instance, human resources (including the hiring and training of personnel), ICT, legal affairs and general counsel. Business support could for instance be provided concerning procurement, logistics, real estate or strategy development. Yet another, closely related, function of corporate parents is to *manage external relations* – that is, to manage relations of the firm with other companies, governmental bodies (such as legislatures), other types of organizations (such as trade associations), and society at large.[18] A corporate communications or corporate responsibility department both have a part in serving this function. Corporate parents might focus on handling relations with the governmental bodies concerning tariffs, taxes or regulation,[19] as well as on managing relationships with alliance partners or on tapping into knowledge from other organizations and networks. However, this is not to say that external relationship management should only be the responsibility of corporate parents – for instance, alliances may primarily be managed by executives at the business-unit level without involvement from the corporate parent.

## CRACK-THE-CASE
### Corporate-level challenges at Philips

Source: © Make More Aerials (2022) / Shutterstock.

Philips is a large Dutch HealthTech firm with a long history that started with the production of light bulbs. As of 2022, the firm comprises four business divisions (segments): Personal Health, Connected Care, Precision Diagnosis, and Image Guided Therapy (IGT). These divisions operate as separate businesses that report individually to a group level, while also being compared against each other and competing to a lesser degree for the available budget being allocated to the businesses from the corporate parent. Although the divisions share their finance, HR, and to some extent development teams, they duplicate their operations teams in each division. The division teams optimize their ways of working among themselves and it can be difficult to share best practices when the governance and role profiles are different. For example, the marketing department in Precision Diagnosis focuses on business-to-business (B2B) strategies and in-person sales, while Personal Health has a much larger digital marketing team focusing on direct-to-consumer (D2C) and e-commerce.

Each division has a Marketing Leader whose job and profile is wildly different as the needs of their business are different. They might share a similar job title but not a similar role. This friction can compound when there is a business segment like Connected Care which touches multiple other business segments in their portfolio of health products. An example would be a software platform that lives on a precision diagnosis machine and an IGT-machine, but the software is made in the Connected Care business. This means three teams whose leaders have similar roles might have different profiles and different understanding of the solution, different timescales to work to, and differing priorities laid out by the business. Such crossovers occur more regularly with acquisitions being made by Philips. This happens when the acquisition comes into alignment with Philips and has to start running Philips Software on their machines. Additionally, not every business division is the same size, or has the same impact on the market. This means that the larger business gets more attention from the corporate parent than the smaller divisions, which can hinder their growth as they compete for the same shared resources.

Philips' transformation from an electronic conglomerate to a HealthTech leader (see the Chapter 14 Closing Case) required an involved change management program, a corporatewide vision uniting its four divisions, and alignment between these divisions on delivery of shared propositions – for instance, Connected Care and IGT routinely collaborate on digital solutions that run on hardware owned by IGT. As Philips was narrowing its focus on health tech and changed into a solution-driven firm, corporate-level executives saw the need to align the experience of all the digital offerings with a common visual expression, especially as more and more software solutions were sitting next to each other in hospital and diagnosis rooms. The Philips Design Language System (DLS) was born as an answer to the diversity of Philips' digital landscape. The DLS was designed to be the consistent colour, spacing, font, visuals, and experience identity of the whole of Philips.

For the DLS to be successful every business division had to come on board and spend their money and energy transforming their very diverse software offering into the DLS global expression. Most of Philips' divisions rejected this idea and did not want to spend part of their AOP (Annual Operating Plan) implementing design that had already been done for their products, which from their point of view meant effectively re-doing what already existed. Few businesses could see that they were part of a greater plan and a larger whole and that the Philips customers were experiencing the Philips brand well beyond their particular business. The short-sightedness of the divisions to only put those items into scope that directly affected their business led to a top-down board KPI to show how far the DLS was implemented inside the business and to explain the progress in implementing the DLS every quarter. While this did help in the uptake of the DLS overall, divisions found ways to stall the DLS implementation, over-report their progress and 'game' the reporting system to make themselves look better than they were. This led to frictions between the enabling

*(Continued)*

function of I&S (Innovation and Strategy) where the DLS originated and the business divisions. Seven years on from its initial release in 2015 DLS is still rolling into the divisions, with varying degrees of success.

## Questions

1. What are the positives for a separate operating structure like the one described in this case? What other benefits can you imagine that are not listed above?
2. How much parental involvement is optimal for a business operational structure like Philips?
3. What are the underlying needs of both Philips Global (the corporate parent) and Philips' individual business divisions, and how do they differ?

# Corporate logics

Corporate parents differ in the way and the degree in which they carry out the parenting functions listed above, and therefore in how they create value. The value-creating roles that a corporate parent adopts can be traced back in part to its dominant **corporate logic** (or *corporate rationale*), which may change over time. Next, we zoom in mainly on two distinct corporate logics in particular, which have been put into practice in multibusiness firms: a *synergy management* logic and a *capital orchestration* logic. These logics rest on different mechanisms by which value is created,[20] however these mechanisms are not necessarily mutually exclusive. Hence, although usually one logic is dominant, both can be at work simultaneously within the same corporate group or single multibusiness firm.

## Synergy management

A dominant **synergy management logic** will imply that corporate-level executives perceive their diversified firm as a set of connections between the component business units, the synergistic potential of which should be maximally exploited. They focus on questions such as where to synergize and how to organize, coordinate, and promote synergistic linkages between these business units.[21] Hence, as implied by its name, this logic revolves around the pursuit of synergy – a term that comes from the ancient Greek word synergós, which translates into 'working together'. In a strategic business context, **synergy** refers to the ability of two or more business units (or firms) to generate more value working together than they could achieve working apart.[22] In this context, working together can take different forms, as described next: sharing activities or resources, transferring skills or intangible resources from one unit to another, and providing input for (or using output of) other units.

### Relationships between business units

To foster synergies, synergy-minded corporate parents focus on building a cluster of related business units that mutually reinforce each other.[23] One way in which this can happen is by having these units *share activities*.[24] This may include both primary activities (e.g., logistics, advertising, sales, and after-sales activities) and support-related activities (e.g., procurement, and recruitment activities) (see Chapter 8). For instance, the different product-market groups of the Dutch shipbuilding firm Royal IHC share activities related to, for example, sales, engineering, procurement, and the development of digital business systems. Another form in which business units can be related is by *sharing resources*. Here, a distinction can be made between sharing inputs (i.e., resources used to create products) and sharing other types of resources. An example of input sharing is that the theme park business, cruise line business, and merchandise business of the Walt Disney Company all make use of the animated characters that are developed in its Imagineering R&D lab. Inputs and other types of resources can be either tangible resources (e.g., raw materials) or, as in the Disney example, intangible resources (e.g., artistic originals). Business units could share a component manufacturing facility, indivisible equipment, warehouses, a sales force, a call center, e-procurement software, etc.[25] All of the abovementioned types of inter-unit relatedness, which can raise differentiation or lower the units' combined operational costs or investments,[26] can be grouped together under the label of *activity and resource sharing*.

A different type of business unit link is the *transferring of skills and intangible resources* from one unit to another. Examples are the transfer of intellectual property rights (e.g., copyrights, patents or trademarks), proprietary technical expertise, sourcing techniques, data security techniques, and other relevant knowledge or ideas on how to perform certain activities that can be applied in different business areas. These inter-unit transfers can be ongoing, occasionally or a one-time occurrence only.[27] A former executive of General Electric illustrated how the transfer of skills and intangible resources can be a catalyst for innovation:

> A breakthrough in GE's Medical Systems business, with relatively little modification, led to a method by which an aircraft engine can transmit continuous information about blade speed, engine heat and other relevant data about its in-flight performance well in advance of any possible safety situation. This innovation, in turn, catalyzed an important new development with respect to a self-monitoring system for use with heart pacemakers.[28]

As this quote illustrates, business units involved in the transfer of skills or intangible resources may not need to have a lot in common.

As explained in the previous chapter, highly diversified firms belong to one of three categories: related constrained, related linked, or unrelated business. In firms with a *related-constrained* diversification profile, most business units share activities and resources and, in addition to that, may engage in the transferring of skills or intangible resources. Business units within firms that have a *related-linked* diversification profile are typically involved in inter-unit transfers of skills or resource transfers, but not in the sharing of activities or resources. Finally, in firms with an *unrelated* diversification profile, such as conglomerates, activity and resource sharing as well as resource and skill transfers are uncommon. Corporate parents of this latter category of firms tend to embrace a capital orchestration logic rather than a synergy management logic.

Another type of relatedness, which has been touched upon also earlier in this textbook when discussing *vertical integration* (see Chapters 8 and 11), is that one or more business units (or divisions) *provide inputs for (or use the output of) other units* within the same multibusiness firm. Hence, they are related via product outputs. Vertical integration has traditionally been defined as the extent to which a firm participates in consecutive stages in the (pre-)production and distribution of a certain type of product.[29] A firm may be engaged in vertically linked activities such as the harvesting or extraction of raw materials, design, component manufacturing, product assembly, distribution, marketing, wholesale, and retail sale. These and other activities, which vary across industries, play a role in bringing a product from its origins to delivery to the final consumer. Firms may also be involved in value-creating activities in the successive *consumption stage*, however. For example, by offering repair services, condition-based or predictive maintenance. Finally, in line with circular economy principles, firms show a growing interest in the *post-consumption stage*, which is directed at recovering products' maximum value after being returned by consumers.[30] IKEA, for instance, buys back used furniture in return for a refund card. In 2020, it opened its first second-hand shop, where all products sold have been refurbished or recycled.[31]

## STRATEGIC FOCUS

### A mathematical explanation of the concept of synergy

The concept of synergy can be clarified through the following mathematical exercise.[32] First, consider the performance of a certain business unit ('BU1', denoted by the subscript $_{BU1}$) in terms of the annual return on investment (*ROI*) on its products in a certain period. We need to divide the difference between the unit's revenues (denoted by the letter *R*) and its operating expenses (denoted by *OE*) during this period by the investments (denoted by *I*) that were needed to put its products on the market:

$$ROI_{BU1} = \frac{(R_{BU1} - OE_{BU1})}{I_{BU1}}$$

*Operating expenses* (or operating costs) are ongoing expenses that are incurred from the day-to-day running of the business. Often abbreviated as OPEX, these expenses can be incurred, for instance, for labour (payroll), materials, marketing, rent, insurance, administration, and overheads. *Investments*, referred to also as capital expenditures or CAPEX, are costs that are incurred from the acquisition, development, maintenance or upgrading of tangible assets (for instance, land, R&D laboratories, warehouses, machinery, and tooling) and intangible assets (for instance, copyrights, patents, trademarks and the training of personnel) that are not consumed during operations.

If all the business units (BU1, BU2, etc.) of a multibusiness firm are unrelated (without any collaboration or interaction), the total revenues of this firm (denoted by $R_U$) will be the sum of the revenues of its component business units (BU1, BU2, etc.). The same reasoning applies to operating expenses and investments. Hence:

$$R_U = R_{BU1} + R_{BU2} + \ldots + R_{BUn}$$

$$OE_U = OE_{BU1} + OE_{BU2} + \ldots + OE_{BUn}$$

$$I_U = I_{BU1} + I_{BU2} + \ldots + I_{BUn}$$

The ROI for this firm as a whole would then be:

$$ROI_U \frac{(R_U - OE_U)}{I_U}$$

Synergy is achieved when relationships between business units (e.g., activity and resource sharing) result in a ROI for the firm as a whole that is higher than would be the case without these links. In other words, there are synergies when the composite return for a firm in which two or more units work together (i.e., a firm with interrelated units, which is denoted by the subscript X is higher than what would be obtained if all component units operated as stand-alone entities (that is, a firm whose business units are all unrelated, denoted by the subscript U):

$$ROI_X > ROI_U$$

The higher the $ROI_X$ in relation to $ROI_U$, the more synergy has been realized. This synergy can imply either higher total revenues ($R_X > R_U$), or lower total operating costs ($OE_X < OE_U$), or lower total investments ($I_X < I_U$), or a combination thereof. Accordingly, we can distinguish three types of synergies from this mathematical illustration: revenue synergies, operating cost synergies, and investment synergies.[33] As discussed later in this chapter, however, there are also managerial and financial synergies.

## Types of synergy

There are different types of synergy that can be achieved between business units. A distinction can be made between revenue synergies and cost synergies, as described next.

**Revenue synergies** (or *sales synergies*) exist where the combined product offering of two or more business units results in higher combined revenues than if these products had been sold separately. By bundling different types of products together, firms can provide a more complete offering. This is often referred to as the creation of a *one-stop shop*.[34] This can be a key differentiator that could attract more buyers (especially when it means higher value for them) or it can allow for charging a price premium. Moreover, it enables the cross-selling of products by different business units. *Cross-selling* (also referred to as *tie-in sales*) to customers implies selling supplementary products based on a customer's purchase of, or interest in, one of the firm's other products. Cross-selling is the revenue synergy used most often by firms when acquiring other firms.[35] Besides cross-selling and the creation of a one-stop shop, opportunities for revenue synergies also exist when, for instance, two or more business units bundle their sales teams to enhance their effectiveness, or when they use common distribution channels in order to achieve a wider customer reach geographically. Another example of the possibilities provided by revenue synergy is when a firm that has built an excellent reputation for quality in one product market sees a higher *willingness to pay* (sometimes abbreviated as *WTP*) for its products in other markets.[36]

Besides or instead of revenue synergies, related diversification may also result in cost synergies. **Cost synergies** exist where the costs of running multiple businesses in one firm are less than the cost of running them separately. Cost synergies denote a firm's ability to exploit *economies of scope*, a term that refers to the cost savings which result from a firm's scope (see Chapter 11).[37] When it would actually be more cost-efficient for connected business units to work separately rather than together, the term *diseconomies of scope* applies. Economies of scope are different from *economies of scale*, which denote cost advantages because of an increased scale of business operations in relation to a single product market.

Cost synergies can be disaggregated into operating cost synergies and investment synergies (see also the Strategic Focus). **Operating cost synergies** exist where the coordination of activities and other forms of collaboration between business units enable these units to lower their aggregate operating costs. This can for instance be achieved through a higher utilization of facilities and personnel, large-scale purchasing of raw materials, and the spreading of overheads.[38] **Investment synergies** exist where inter-unit collaboration enables savings on capital expenditures. For instance, when two business units make use of the same production facility or distribution system, which have high upfront costs, the average production costs will be lower than if they independently ran their own production facility or distribution network. By sharing expensive resources and capabilities, firms can significantly reduce costs.

Another type of synergy that can be achieved between divisions is **managerial synergy** (or *management synergy*). Managers in different business areas typically face different strategic, operating, and organizational problems. Managerial synergies exist when managers are in a position to provide adequate guidance to a business unit that competes in one business area by drawing on their experiences in working in another business area in which the firm competes.[39]

## Downsides of synergy

The sharing of activities and resources across business units and other arrangements that result in synergy requires substantial coordinated efforts. These efforts imply organizational costs, which counterbalance potential synergistic benefits.[40] The more the realization of synergies requires a firm to actively manage the interdependencies between units, the higher the costs of coordination in terms of communication, information processing, and shared decision-making.[41] Depending on the nature and complexity of the interdependencies, the realization of synergies may require joint planning and scheduling, mutual adjustment, setting transfer prices, joint problem solving, and the design of incentive schemes for cross-unit cooperation.[42] In order for revenue and cost synergies to enhance competitiveness of the business units involved, the benefits should outweigh any substantial coordination costs, as well as the costs related to other downsides of having a cluster of related business units. One of these downsides is that to enable resource or activity sharing, compromises may be needed around performance or design, resulting in suboptimal performance outcomes.[43] Furthermore, the use of a shared tangible asset by one business unit may be dependent on its possible use by another unit, and vice versa.[44] This can then affect both units' ability to respond to changing competitive demands in an adequate and timely manner. Therefore, the more synergy across business units, the less their responsiveness could be to market demands, presenting a trade-off decision for executives.[45] This also means that the achievement of cost synergies could simultaneously result in a loss of revenue that could exceed the cost savings, or vice versa.

## STRATEGIC FOCUS

### Mind the gap: Managerial biases regarding synergy

Synergies between a firm's business units can provide a real competitive advantage to these units and to the firm as a whole. However, corporate executives should be aware of several potential managerial biases when it comes to thinking about synergy, which can result in strategic disadvantages.[46] These potential biases include:

- Synergy bias: overestimating the benefits of synergy and underestimating its costs, spurred by the desire corporate executives may have to achieve synergy among the component business units. 'Like wanderers in a desert who see oases where there is only sand',[47] executives may become so entranced by the idea of synergy that they lead their firm to pursue mirages.
- Upside bias: concentrating excessively on the potential benefits of a particular synergy initiative at the expense of taking into account the possible negative consequences of the initiative. These harmful 'knock-on effects' can take many forms. For instance, a corporate-led synergy program may reduce employee motivation, delay innovation or lead to friction between units.
- Parenting bias: the assumption that the only way to capture synergies is by compelling or persuading business units to collaborate with one another, although these units may in fact have good reasons not to do so. This assumption is driven by a belief corporate executives may have that unit managers have the tendency to undervalue or disregard opportunities to collaborate.
- Skills bias: the erroneous belief that all the skills and know-how that is required to achieve the intended synergies will be available within the firm. For instance, a corporate management team that feels compelled to intervene to make synergies among business units happen may lack the facilitative skills, patience, or certain operating knowledge to get things done.

## Questions

1. What antidotes for these managerial biases could you think of?
2. The goals of synergy programs are often expressed in broad and rather vague terms, such as 'leveraging international brands', 'cross-fertilizing ideas' or 'coordinating customer relations'.[48] Could you mention any example? Why is this problematic?

## Capital orchestration

A corporate parent that embraces a **capital orchestration logic** (which is also commonly referred to as a *portfolio management logic*) serves primarily as investment vehicle to and reviewer of a set of typically unrelated, autonomous business units.[49] The contrast with the synergy management logic is stark: while corporate parents with this logic mostly see synergistic linkages between business units as a key source of value creation, these linkages are often close to absent in corporate portfolios that are overseen by parents following a capital orchestration logic. They carry out their capital orchestrator roles with a view to enhance the value attained from the units in their portfolio in a more effective or efficient way than financial markets could.[50] The corporate parent passively serves as an in-house banker by supplying the component businesses capital on favourable terms. Capital allocation to the business units and the compensation of the executives that run them is often based on how well they perform in terms of financial results, which implies a certain degree of internal competition. Instead, however, it may also be based on the bargaining power of poorly performing units.[51]

The corporate parent will often categorize the set of business units in its portfolio by their strength, potential and the attractiveness of the industry or market in which they have a competitive presence. For this, they may use portfolio management frameworks such as the ones we present in the *ChooseWell* diagnostic chapter. The corporate parent typically sets clear targets for the business units and monitors objectively whether these are achieved. Also, it regularly transfers financial capital from one business unit to another, depending on their categorization and cash needs.[52] There is a dominant focus on optimizing cash flows and on balancing risks.[53] The corporate parent typically provides professional management support, reviews, and discipline to businesses once incorporated. The corporate parent does not make significant systematic efforts to achieve synergies across businesses, nor does it tend to participate or intervene in business-level strategy formulation or execution. This permits a relatively small headquarters.

In practice, corporate parents following a dominant capital orchestration logic can create value in different ways. One way is for the corporate parent to acquire undervalued or otherwise attractive firms, which then become part of its portfolio. The analytical resources and expertise of corporate executives provides them with a superior ability to spot attractive acquisition targets. Furthermore, value can be created by endowing the firm's business units with an advantage derived from being part of a professionally managed corporation with an efficient internal capital market. An **internal capital market** means there is firmwide pooling of cash flows, generated by the component business units, with these financial resources allocated across the firm (or corporate group). This allocation can be based on, for instance, the competitive position, risk profile and cash needs of these units and the attractiveness of the markets or industries in which they compete. The more efficient internal capital markets are, the higher the value that a corporate parent creates for its multibusiness portfolio.

An efficient internal capital market can be beneficial relative to an external capital market benchmark – see also this chapter's Key Debate. Business units can benefit from lower interest rates and other financial advantages, such as an enhanced accessibility to necessary funds. Besides cost savings, an efficient corporatewide pooling and allocation of capital in diversified firms usually results in benefits such as an improved ability to balance out risks. The financial advantages of an efficient internal capital market are referred to as **financial synergies** or *financial economies*. Just like revenue and cost synergies, these synergies allow for achieving a consolidated performance that is greater than the sum of what each individual business unit can achieve on its own.[54] Also tax optimization enabled by overseeing a portfolio of multiple businesses, or having a better position to acquire external funding for the same reason, are examples of financial synergies. Whereas revenue and cost synergies are achieved between units, financial synergies are achieved at the level of the multibusiness firm as a whole. The synergy management logic, as discussed earlier, focuses on synergy *between* business units, and thus does *not* imply a focus on achieving financial synergies.

## KEY DEBATE

### The validity of the capital orchestration logic

'Portfolio management is no way to conduct corporate strategy', Harvard Business School professor Michael Porter[55] stated when discussing the corporate logic of capital orchestration (which he referred to as portfolio management). A diversified firm whose corporate strategy is clearly dominated by this logic can be perceived as a collection of (full) business shareholdings.[56] According to Porter, it ceased to be a valid model for corporate strategy in economically advanced countries, where capital markets are well developed, and professional management is not scarce. In these countries, Porter argues, shareholders can readily diversify their own portfolios of stocks, and moreover they may be able to diversify more cheaply than a diversified firm because shareholders can buy shares at market prices and avoid any acquisition premiums. Besides, Porter questions the benefit of granting business units complete autonomy and the concomitant lack of synergistic interlinkages among these units.[57]

Porter's point of view can be debated, however. According to London Business School professor Freek Vermeulen,[58] it is fully acceptable for corporate parents to exist as mere investment vehicles, managed by corporate-level executives, without any need to realize cross-unit synergies and to force business units into an overarching strategy. Vermeulen points out that corporate executives can be superior capital allocators as they know the businesses in the portfolio and their internal dynamics very well and can hence see things external investors, analysts and shareholders miss. Executives have an informational advantage over these external parties, which have to rely on figures and other information provided by the corporation regarding the actual and prospective performance of the component business units. External stakeholders have no guarantee of complete information disclosure.[59] Negative information could well be left out.[60]

Hitt and colleagues[61] point out that the information a firm disseminates to investors may also become available to current and potential competitors, based on which they may attempt to copy a value-creating strategy. Internal capital market allocation reduces the need for external investors and thus the necessity to disseminate strategically sensitive information. Besides, they argue, internal capital markets allow capital to be 'allocated according to more specific criteria than is possible with external market allocations'.[62] On top of that, firms with a clear capital orchestration profile are able to allocate capital more swiftly and based on more sophisticated insights, which can give the component business units a potential advantage.[63]

## CRACK-THE-CASE

### Corporate portfolio choices at KPN

Source: © Dart (2019) / Shutterstock.

*(Continued)*

KPN is a leading telecommunications and IT provider in the Netherlands with more than €5 billion revenues per year. With its fixed and mobile networks for telephony, data and television, the firm serves customers in the Netherlands. KPN focuses on both consumer and business customers. The organization consists of four business units and a Corporate Centre.

- Through its business unit <u>B2C Retail</u>, KPN offers consumers a broad range of services in the area of communication, information, entertainment and commercial services via single-play and multi-play packages. The services include fixed and mobile telephony, mobile data, internet, and TV. In this segment, VodafoneZiggo and Odido are KPN's main competitors.
- Through its business unit <u>B2B Retail</u>, KPN offers its small, medium and large business customers a full range of services. More information on this business unit is presented below.
- Through its business unit <u>wholesale</u>, KPN offers other telecommunications operators access to its widespread mobile and fixed networks on which telecommunications operators and service providers can provide their services under their own brand. Most players do not have an open wholesale policy, so from this perspective KPN has few competitors. Eurofiber is one of the few players that offers wholesale services within the B2B market.
- The business unit <u>Technology & Digital Office</u> is responsible for the network and IT, based on which the business units B2C Retail, B2B Retail and Wholesale provide services to customers. The Technology & Digital Office focuses on, among otherthings, fiber roll-out, copper phase-out, and network maintenance.
- KPN's <u>Corporate Centre</u> acts as corporate parent. Among others, Finance, HR, and Strategy are departments within the Corporate Centre, which support all business units.

KPN has three commercial business units because it allows the firm to leverage its networks to reach all types of customers who all have different needs and expectations. A benefit of serving multiple segments is the synergies that exist between these segments. For example, similar products and services are offered to B2B Small office Home office (SoHo) customers and B2C customers. However, there is also a cannibalization risk between segments with for example the trade-off between an increasing number of customers via wholesale versus a decreasing number of customers via B2C retail (and vice versa).

Let's zoom in further on the business unit B2B Retail, which focuses on the Dutch B2B Information and Communication Technology (ICT) market including all businesses ranging from small (home) offices to large enterprises and corporates (see Table 12.1). ICT services are essential for business users and are vital to many of the Netherlands' critical societal services, such as the Dutch national emergency phone number and Schiphol airport. KPN's B2B Retail business unit has two segments, namely Access & Connectivity and IT Services. The Access & Connectivity segment includes products and services focused on Mobile, Internet, Fixed Voice, Networking and IoT. The IT Services segment focuses on Cloud & Workspace, Security and Consulting. One benefit of providing both Access & Connectivity and IT Services to the B2B market is the synergy in sales. A sales representative can cross-sell IT-services to a customer that buys 'access and connectivity' (and vice versa). A challenge, though, is that for selling IT-services different knowledge is needed – for instance, about

**TABLE 12.1** KPN's B2B portfolio overview (2022)

| Segments and product groups | Product-group description | Current market size NL (in revenue) (in billions) | Current revenue market share KPN | Current revenue market share biggest competitor | Combined revenue market share of top three | Historic average revenue growth market 2019–21 | Historic average revenue growth KPN 2019–21 | Change in revenue market share KPN 201–21 | Expected average market revenue growth 2021–24 | Market profitability |
|---|---|---|---|---|---|---|---|---|---|---|
| **Access & Connectivity** | | €3,5b | 30% | 25% | 80% | -2% | -6% | -3% | +2% | 40–50% |
| **Networking** | Connecting networks of locations, devices among each other. For instance, Internet Protocol-Virtual Private Network (IP-VPN) connects firm sites, datacentres and headquarters through an IP-based Wide Area Network (WAN): a secure and private network. | €1.1b | 10% | 30% | 60% | -4% | -9% | -1% | 0% | |
| **Mobile** | Mobile communication services allow transmission of voice, multimedia data incl. machine-to-machine data without need for a physical link. | €1.0b | 40% | 35% | 95% | -5% | -7% | -1% | -1% | |
| **Fixed Voice & Unified Communications** | Fixed Voice enables voice and/or interactive communication services between two points through the usage of voice equipment. Unified Communications enables communication among colleagues, customers, and partners in the work environment. | €0.7b | 30% | 20% | 70% | -4% | -17% | -10% | +1% | |

*(Continued)*

**TABLE 12.1** (Continued)

| Segments and product groups | Product-group description | Current market size NL (in revenue) (in billions) | Current revenue market share KPN | Current revenue market share biggest competitor | Combined revenue market share of top three | Historic average revenue growth market 2019–21 | Historic average revenue growth KPN 2019–21 | Change in revenue market share KPN 201–21 | Expected average market revenue growth 2021–24 | Market profitability* |
|---|---|---|---|---|---|---|---|---|---|---|
| Access, Internet & Media | Access and connectivity services between locations, things, and the internet. Access to a digital library of content such as films, software, games, images, literature. | €0.5b | 50% | 20% | 85% | +13% | +5% | -8% | +7% | |
| Internet of Things (IoT) | Data-generating hardware that is part of a network. KPN's IoT solutions have six building blocks: Hardware, Connectivity, Data management, Organization, Applications, Security. | €0.3b | 20% | 15% | 45% | +11% | +4% | -3% | +12% | |
| IT Services | | €5.0b | 10% | 12% | 30% | +2% | +3% | +1% | +8% | 5–10% |
| Cloud & Workspace | Supporting organizations in offering a complete workplace for their employees with tools to manage and develop their applications with the right infrastructure for every application (e.g., Public/ Private Cloud). | €3.5b | 5% | 10% | 25% | +4% | +4% | +0% | +10% | |
| Consulting & Service Mgt | Advice, execution and support on IT services. | €1.0b | 20% | 10% | 40% | -5% | -1% | +1% | +3% | |
| Security | Helping organizations ensure increased security of data and applications, such as email traffic, web servers and cloud solutions. KPN offers installation of a central firewall, anti-DDoS protection and network access control. | €0.7b | 10% | 15% | 30% | +6% | +7% | +1% | +6% | |

* Market profitability = EBITDA margin (Earnings Before Interest, Taxes, Depreciation and Amortization)

the primary processes of a customer. An example of a cannibalization risk for KPN in the B2B Retail business unit is the trade-off between pushing for sales in Cloud & Workspace (e.g., on Microsoft Teams) versus a decreasing number of business customers using KPN's Mobile proposition. Within Access & Connectivity, VodafoneZiggo and Odido are KPN's main competitors. The combined market share of these three players is larger than 80%. The IT-services market is very fragmented with many competitors, which have market shares smaller than 10%. Due to KPN's incumbent position, KPN historically had a high market share and a wide reach in the B2B market. Yet while the Access & Connectivity market is relatively stable and saturated, the IT Services market is growing fast and shows a lot of (newly emerging) competitors. KPN has made several acquisitions to keep up and ensure top-notch IT-services capabilities, but it still proves challenging to achieve profitable growth in an IT-services market that is constantly evolving.

## Questions

1. Which metrics would you use to choose the product groups KPN should prioritize investments in?
2. Imagine KPN wants to prioritize investments within its B2B Retail portfolio, which five product groups (out of current eight) would you decide to focus on, and why?
3. If you take synergies and/or cannibalization risks into account, does this lead to another conclusion? Can you explain why? (You are allowed to make some assumptions.)

## Alternative corporate logics

Besides (or complementary to) a synergy management logic and a capital orchestration logic, corporate parents can also embrace a continuous reorganization logic or a parental developer logic, which have received less attention in the literature. A **continuous reorganization logic** implies a dominant focus on ensuring corporate parenting advantage by engaging actively in reconfiguration and restructuring.[64] *Reconfiguration* implies the adding, combining, transferring, splitting or dissolving of business entities (without necessarily modifying their underlying structure). *Restructuring* implies making alterations in the structures around which a firm's resources and activities are grouped and coordinated (organizational restructuring) or in the underlying financial structure (financial restructuring). Chapter 14 discusses both of these types of reorganization[65] and zooms in further on the continuous reorganization logic.

Finally, corporate parents that act in line with a **parental developer logic** employ their in-house competencies and capabilities to add value to the business units in their portfolio without imposing synergies.[66] These so-called 'parental developers' are not restructuring (although this can take place from time to time), but rather supporting business units in their current form and structure to become more successful. In that regard, parental developers could be compared to incubators. Services offered to business units may include brand management support, offering technological or marketing expertise, providing management training, and providing access to relevant networks. This implies a more active role than capital orchestration.

# Parenting strategy composition

A distinction can be made between five primary categories of potentially value-creating parenting activities: [67]

- business direction and development
- utilizing corporate assets and capabilities
- operational engagement
- promoting inter-unit business synergies
- fostering firmwide financial synergies

Each of these categories can be broken down into more specific parenting activities (see Figure 12.3). Corporate parents differ in the degree to which they are involved in each of these activities. The composition of different activities that a corporate parent conducts to add value to the business units that it oversees make up the **parenting strategy composition**.

A *Parenting Strategy Radar* can be used to choose and identify the composition of a firm's parenting strategy. This tool, which is adapted from the parenting strategy spider chart developed by Krühler, Pidun and Rubner,[68] is essentially a radar (spider) chart that plots the different activities of a corporate parent. Figure 12.3 provides an illustrative example for a fictitious corporate parent. This tool can also be used to visualize the changes that ought to be made to migrate to another parenting strategy that may result in a greater parenting

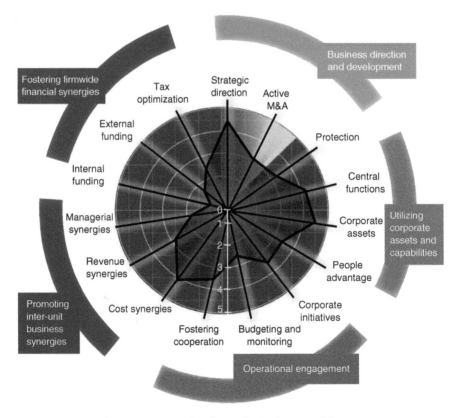

**FIGURE 12.3**   Parenting Strategy Radar (hypothetical example)

Source: adapted from Krühler et al. (2012)

advantage.[69] The importance that is attached to each of the 15 parental foci in this radar can be rated on a scale of zero to five or on a larger scale. Although it is possible for a corporate parent to engage in all types of parenting activities, trade-offs should be made in how much to focus on each of them.

# Parental involvement

Besides deciding on how the corporate parent could add value to its portfolio of businesses in order to enhance parenting advantage, corporate executives also need to decide on how and to what extent they should intervene in the conduct of the business units they oversee. Apart from the dominant corporate logic, this should depend on the capabilities of the corporate centre (or the corporate-level divisions) and the needs of the business units.[70] A distinction can be made between six common approaches that can be taken in this regard, ranging from light to heavy involvement (see Figure 12.4): hands-off owner, financial sponsor, family builder, strategic guide, functional leader, and hands-on manager (the heaviest form of involvement). Corporate-level executives should reflect on what kind of parent the businesses in their portfolio need when choosing among these approaches.

**Common approaches of parental involvement, ranging from light (left) to heavy involvement**
*The corporate parent (of a multi-business firm) . . .*

| . . . puts together a portfolio of highly autonomous business units that it manages as pure financial assets for which high-level financial targets are set. | . . . provides financial advantages to business units (e.g., access to relatively cheap and flexible funding and reduced tax burdens) and offers protection. | . . . assembles a synergistic portfolio of business units to drive cost reductions or revenue growth but limits its interference in business-level issues. | . . . sets a strategic direction for the business units, injects them with strategic insight and experience, and may catalyse M&A initiatives or organic growth. | . . . builds strong corporate functions that allow for establishing central services, standardization and firmwide functional excellence. | . . . influences business-unit level strategic and operating decisions and puts in place comprehensive plans, controls, and procedures. |
|---|---|---|---|---|---|
| **HANDS-OFF OWNER** | **FINANCIAL SPONSOR** | **FAMILY BUILDER** | **STRATEGIC GUIDE** | **FUNCTIONAL LEADER** | **HANDS-ON MANAGER** |

**FIGURE 12.4** Parental Involvement Palette

Source: adapted from Krühler et al. (2012) and Pidun et al. (2019). The direction of the arrow indicates an increase in involvement.

# Parental control

To ensure that the component business units operate in line with the dominant logic of the corporate parent, depending on the extent of parental involvement, different controls usually have to be in place. **Corporate controls** refer to how the execution of tasks and activities by business units and their performance are controlled by the corporate parent. There are two generic types of corporate controls: financial controls and strategic controls.[71] **Financial controls** include budgets and objective criteria used to measure business unit performance (output) against quantitative standards. Examples of such criteria are return on investment, return on assets, economic value added, and aggregate sales growth. Business units and their managers are held accountable for how they score on these criteria. There are typically strong incentives to meet certain outcomes. Corporate parents that rely heavily on financial outcomes, as is typical in firms with an unrelated diversification profile in particular, tend to have standardized financial controls in place to compare performances between units (and between managers).

**Strategic controls** (sometimes called *operating controls*) are criteria – quantitative and qualitative – intended to verify that a firm's business units are using appropriate strategies for the conditions in the external environment and the firm's competitive advantages. Rather than measuring outputs, strategic control is concerned with evaluating managers' decisions and actions. Examples are strategic plans and reports, operating reviews, and capital-budgeting discussions. Strategic controls demand rich communications between the executives that are responsible for using them to judge the units' performance and those with primary responsibility for implementing business-level strategies. Strategic controls are used in particular by firms with a related diversification profile to verify the sharing of appropriate strategic factors such as knowledge, technologies and assets across units.

In times of a crisis, such as an unexpected recession, a dominant focus on financial controls may result in the punishment of managers when profits are below what was expected. In contrast, a dominant focus on strategic controls could result in even rewarding managers for anticipating the downturn and cutting inventories, even though they might have missed their budget targets. Hence, using financial controls may have different implications than using strategic controls. Typically, these two generic controls are used in combination with each other. However, one generic control type may be more dominant than the other. For instance, in firms with a dominant capital orchestration logic, financial controls will be more prevalent than strategic controls.

## CLOSING CASE
### Unilever versus Ben & Jerry's: From star acquisition to problem child[72]

Source: © Egg (2019) / Shutterstock.

When global consumer goods company Unilever acquired Ben & Jerry's in 2000, it agreed to let its subsidiary continue setting its own course, and allowed the giant ice cream producer to retain an independent board to oversee its pioneering social mission. For over 40 years, a hallmark of Ben & Jerry's had been its advocacy and social activism (see the Chapter 2 opening case). Activism is reflected in many of its strategic and marketing decisions. A case in point is when in mid-2021 it published the following announcement on its website:

> 'We believe it is inconsistent with our values for Ben & Jerry's ice cream to be sold in the Occupied Palestinian Territory (OPT). We also hear and recognize the concerns shared with us by our fans and trusted partners. We have a longstanding partnership with our licensee, who manufactures Ben & Jerry's ice cream in Israel and distributes it in the region. We have been working to change this, and so we have informed our licensee that we will not renew the license agreement when it expires at the end of next year. Although Ben & Jerry's will no longer be sold in the OPT, we will stay in Israel through a different arrangement.'[73]

The announcement placed Ben & Jerry's at odds with its parent firm and with the Israeli government, which condemned the decision as 'morally wrong' and threatened Unilever with 'severe consequences'. Israel's economy minister and others filmed themselves throwing out Ben & Jerry's tubs, and Jewish groups accused Unilever and its subsidiary of antisemitism. Following Ben & Jerry's decision, several US states, including Florida, Illinois, New Jersey, New York, and Texas, warned Unilever that they were considering divestment from its stocks and bonds, as they perceived Ben & Jerry's exit from the OPT as a boycott of Israel. But there were not just warnings. Three weeks after the announcement, the state of Arizona had already sold $93 million in Unilever bonds, and said it planned to sell the remaining $50 million it had invested in the company. These divestments were mandated by a 2019 state law prohibiting its government agencies to hold investments in any company that boycotts Israel or its territories. As more than 30 other US states have anti-boycott laws or regulations, this whole situation was highly problematic for Unilever. Doing nothing would result in even more financial and reputational damage for the company, but intervening would violate the acquisition agreement that allowed Ben & Jerry's to continue its social mission independent of decisions made by Unilever. What to do?

Nearly a year after the OPT ice cream announcement, Unilever sold its Ben & Jerry's business interests in Israel to the firm Blue and White Ice Cream, owned by Avi Zinger, for an undisclosed sum. This arrangement meant Ben & Jerry's could be sold throughout the West Bank and Israel under the full ownership of the former licensee. Ben & Jerry's did not agree with the deal, and the members of its Independent Board applied to court for an injunction to stop the sell-off. In its suit, the subsidiary outlined its tradition of social activism and the agreement made with Unilever in 2000, and argued the move by Unilever 'poses a risk' to the brand's integrity. A spokesman said: 'We will not allow our principles to be compromised for the benefit of our parent company'.[74] Yet Unilever emphasized that it had very good reasons for the divestiture, and that its subsidiary had no power to undo or stop the sale. Ben & Jerry's application was refused. In December 2022, almost 18 months after the fractious dispute, Unilever issued a public statement, stating: 'Unilever is pleased to announce that the litigation with Ben & Jerry's Independent Board has been resolved'.[75]

*(Continued)*

## Questions

1. Had you been the CEO of Unilever, would you have made the same decision in response to this situation? If not, what would you have decided and why?
2. To what extent does it make sense for a company like Unilever to acquire firms with a progressive mission? What are the pros and cons of overseeing such businesses?
3. To what extent should parent firms in general be careful with granting autonomy to their divisions or subsidiaries? What are the pros and cons of autonomy?

## Summary

- Corporate-level strategy encompasses decisions about the scope and direction of a firm as a whole and how to configure and manage the set of businesses in which it participates.
- Successful corporate strategy should reinforce and grow out of competitive strategy.
- The corporate parent refers to the organizational layer(s) above the business units in a multibusiness firm. This includes the corporate centre, which constitutes the top level of management, but it may also consist of intermediate-level units such as corporate divisions that look after these business units.
- Business units benefit from a corporate parenting advantage when the parenting strategy enhances the competitive advantage of the individual business units over and above what they could achieve otherwise.
- Typical key functions of corporate parents are to determine the boundaries of the firm, to undertake and implement corporate transactions that may be required to alter these boundaries, to set the overall direction of the firm, to coordinate how resources are deployed and used within these boundaries, to monitor the performance of the constituent business units and their use of allocated resources, to intervene, to provide central corporate services and business support, and to manage external relations.
- How firms set and oversee their scope should be in line with their high-level vision and objectives while taking account of their core values and purpose.
- The value-creating roles that a corporate parent adopts can be traced back in part to its dominant corporate logic, which may change over time. Four corporate logics can be distinguished, which rest on distinctive mechanisms by which value is created: synergy management, capital orchestration, restructuring, and development.
- Synergy refers to the ability of two or more business units (or firms) to generate more value working together than they could achieve working apart.
- Internal capital allocation and restructuring of assets enable multibusiness firms to achieve financial economies.
- Whereas firms with a dominant capital orchestration logic focus on maximizing financial economies, firms with a dominant synergy management logic focus on achieving revenue synergies, operating cost synergies and investment synergies.

- Corporate parents can choose among various approaches to involvement, some of which will be more in line with the needs of the component business units than others.
- A combination of financial controls and strategic controls can be used by corporate parents to achieve alignment between the corporate-level strategy and business-level conduct and outcomes.

## Review questions

1. How do the roles corporate parents play relate to their dominant corporate logic?
2. Why is corporate strategy highly interrelated with competitive strategy?
3. How can companies that exhibit a high degree of inter-business unit relatedness create value?
4. How can companies that use an unrelated diversification strategy obtain financial economies?

## Discussion questions

1. How can corporate strategy strengthen competitive strategy in an era of intense competition, rapid change, and evolving technology?
2. To what extent can different corporate logics successfully co-exist within the same firm?
3. To what extent may a dominant corporate logic impact how wide the corporate scope is, and to what extent may the breadth of the corporate scope impose limitations on the corporate logic?

### EXPERIENTIAL EXERCISES

1. Think about a firm that you have work(ed) for (if any). In how many different business areas does this firm participate? If more than two areas, to what extent are they related?
2. Choose a certain multibusiness firm and, based on information you can find on the internet or based on your own experience, indicate which of the four corporate logics that were discussed in this chapter is most applicable to this firm, and indicate why.
3. For the very same or another firm, map the different component businesses in a growth share matrix and a directional policy matrix (see the *ChooseWell* diagnostic chapter), and provide your recommendations.

## Further reading

Campbell, A., Goold, M. and Alexander, M. (1995) 'The value of the parent firm', *California Management Review*, 38 (1): 79–97.

Collis, D.J. and Montgomery, C.A. (1998) 'Creating corporate advantage', *Harvard Business Review*, 76 (3): 71–83.

Feldman, E.R. (2020) 'Corporate strategy: Past, present, and future', *Strategic Management Review*, 1: 179–206.

Feldman, E.R. (2021) 'The corporate parenting advantage, revisited', *Strategic Management Journal*, 42: 114–43.

Menz, M., Kunisch, S., Birkinshaw, J., Collis, D.J., Foss, N.J., Hoskisson, R.E. and Prescott, J.E. (2021) 'Corporate strategy and the theory of the firm in the digital age', *Journal of Management Studies*, 58: 1695–720.

## Endnotes (references)

1. Feldman, E.R. (2020) 'Corporate strategy: Past, present, and future', *Strategic Management Review*, 1: 179–206.

2. Porter, M.E. (1987) 'From competitive advantage to corporate strategy', *Harvard Business Review*, 65 (3): 43–59.

3. Ansoff, H.I. (1988) *Corporate Strategy* (revised ed.). London: Penguin Books; Buijs, J. (1979) 'Strategic planning and product innovation – Some systematic approaches', *Long Range Planning*, 12: 23–34.

4. Chandler Jr, A.D. (1991) 'The functions of the HQ unit in the multibusiness firm', *Strategic Management Journal*, 12: 31–50.

5. PepsiCo (2021) 'About PepsiCo', *PepsiCo*. www.pepsico.com/about/about-the-company (accessed June 26, 2023).

6. Campbell, A., Goold, M. and Alexander, M. (1995a) 'Corporate strategy: The quest for parenting advantage', *Harvard Business Review*, March/April: 120–32; Feldman, E.R. (2021) 'The corporate parenting advantage, revisited', *Strategic Management Journal*, 42: 114–43.

7. Campbell et al. (1995a)

8. Porter (1987)

9. Porter (1987)

10. Piskorski, M.J. (2006) 'Note on corporate strategy', *Harvard Business School Background Note* 705-449. https://www.hbs.edu/faculty/Pages/item.aspx?num=31932 (accessed June 24, 2023).

11. Argyres, N. (1996a) 'Capabilities, technological diversification and divisionalization', *Strategic Management Journal*, 17: 395–410; Rajan et al. (2000); Scharfstein, D.S. and Stein, J.C. (2000) 'The dark side of internal capital markets: Divisional rent-seeking and inefficient investment', *Journal of Finance*, 55 (6): 2537–64.

12. e.g., Arrfelt, M., Wiseman, R.M., McNamara, G. and Hult, G.T.M. (2015) 'Examining a key corporate role: The influence of capital allocation competency on business unit performance', *Strategic Management Journal*, 36 (7): 1017–34; Bardolet, D., Lovallo, D. and Rumelt, R. (2010) 'The hand of corporate management in capital allocations: Patterns of investment in multi- and single-business firms', *Industrial and Corporate Change*, 19 (2): 591–612; Bower, J.L. (1970) *Managing the Resource Allocation Process*. Boston, MA: Harvard University; Chandler Jr, A.D. (1962) *Strategy and Structure: Chapters in the History of the Industrial Empire*. Cambridge, MA: MIT Press; Chandler (1991); Feldman (2020)

13. e.g., Billett, M.T. and Mauer, D.C. (2003) 'Cross-subsidies, external financing constraints, and the contribution of the internal capital market to firm value', *The Review of Financial Studies*, 16 (4): 1167–201; Khanna, N. and Tice, S. (2001) 'The bright side of internal capital markets', *The Journal of Finance*, 56 (4): 1489–528;

Stein, J.C. (1997) 'Internal capital markets and the competition for corporate resources', *The Journal of Finance*, 52 (1): 111–33.

14. e.g., Karim, S. and Williams, C. (2012) 'Structural knowledge: How executive experience with structural composition affects intrafirm mobility and unit reconfiguration', *Strategic Management Journal*, 33 (6): 681–709; Williams, C. and Mitchell, W. (2004) 'Focusing firm evolution: The impact of information infrastructure on market entry by U.S. telecommunications companies, 1984–1998', *Management Science*, 50 (11): 1561–75.

15. e.g., Penrose, E.T. (1959) *The Theory of Growth of the Firm*. New York, NY: Wiley; Sakhartov, A.V. (2017) 'Economies of scope, resource relatedness, and the dynamics of corporate diversification', *Strategic Management Journal*, 38: 2168–88; Teece, D.J., Rumelt, R., Dosi, G. and Winter, S. (1994) 'Understanding corporate coherence: Theory and evidence', *Journal of Economic Behavior & Organization*, 23 (1): 1–30.

16. Chandler (1991)

17. e.g., Campbell et al. (1995a); Kontes, P. (2004) 'A new look for the corporate center: Reorganizing to maximize value', *Journal of Business Strategy*, 25 (4): 18–24.

18. Feldman (2020)

19. Chandler (1991)

20. Goold, M., Campbell, A. and Alexander, M. (1994) *Corporate-Level Strategy: Creating Value in the Multibusiness Company*. New York, NY: Wiley; Porter (1987).

21. Feldman (2020)

22. Goold, M. and Campbell, A. (1998) 'Desperately seeking synergy', *Harvard Business Review*, 76 (5): 131–43.

23. Porter (1987)

24. Porter (1987)

25. Collis, D.J. and Montgomery, C.A. (1998) 'Creating corporate advantage', *Harvard Business Review*, 76 (3): 71–83; Panzar, J.C. and Willig, R.D. (1981) 'Economies of scope', *The American Economic Review*, 71 (2): 268–72.

26. Hill, C.W.L., Hitt, M.A. and Hoskisson, R.E. (1992) 'Cooperative versus competitive structures in related and unrelated diversified firms', *Organization Science*, 3: 501–21.

27. Porter (1987)

28. Steve Kerr (1997), quoted in Miller, D.J., Fern, M.J. and Cardinal, L.B. (2007) 'The use of knowledge for technological innovation within diversified firms', *Academy of Management Journal*, 50 (2): 308–26.

29. e.g., Buzzell, R.D. (1983) 'Is vertical integration profitable?', *Harvard Business Review*, 61 (1): 92–102; Hale, G.E. (1949) 'Vertical integration: Impact of the antitrust laws upon combinations of successive stages of production and distribution', *Columbia Law Review*, 49 (7): 921–54.

30. Kortmann, S. and Piller, F. (2016) 'Open business models and closed-loop value chains: Redefining the firm-consumer relationship', *California Management Review*, 58 (3): 88–108.

31. Ingka Group (2020) 'The world's first second-hand IKEA store is now open', *Ingka*, November 5. www.ingka.com/news/the-worlds-first-second-hand-ikea-store-is-now-open (accessed June 26, 2022).

32. adapted from Ansoff (1988)

33. Ansoff (1988)

34. Chatain, O. and Zemsky, P. (2007) 'The horizontal scope of the firm: Organizational tradeoffs vs. buyer-supplier relationships', *Management Science*, 53 (4): 550–65.

35. Chartier, J., Liu, A., Raberger, N. and Silva, R. (2018) 'Seven rules to crack the code on revenue synergies in M&A', *McKinsey,* October 15. https://www.mckinsey.com/business-functions/marketing-and-sales/our-insights/seven-rules-to-crack-the-code-on-revenue-synergies-in-ma (accessed June 26, 2023).

36. Piskorski (2006)

37. Panzar and Willig (1981); Teece, D.J. (1980) 'Economies of scope and the scope of the enterprise', *Journal of Economic Behavior and Organization,* 1 (3): 223–47; Teece (1982).

38. Ansoff (1988)

39. Ansoff (1988)

40. Panzar and Willig (1981); Zhou, Y.M. (2011) 'Synergy, coordination costs, and diversification choices', *Strategic Management Journal,* 32 (6): 624–39.

41. Marschak, J. and Radner, R. (1972) *Economic Theory of Teams.* New Haven, CT: Yale University Press; Zhou (2011).

42. Thompson J.D. (1967) *Organizations in Action: Social Science Bases of Administrative Theory.* New Brunswick, NJ: Transaction; Zhou (2011).

43. Porter (1987)

44. Collis and Montgomery (1998)

45. De Wit, B. and Meyer R. (2010) *Strategy Synthesis: Resolving Strategy Paradoxes to Create Competitive Advantage.* Andover: Cengage.

46. Goold and Campbell (1998)

47. Goold and Campbell (1998: 134)

48. Goold and Campbell (1998)

49. Porter (1987)

50. Johnson, G., Scholes, K. and Whittington, R. (2005) *Exploring Corporate Strategy.* Harlow: Financial Times Prentice Hall.

51. Argyres (1996a); Rajan et al. (2000); Scharfstein and Stein (2000)

52. Porter (1987)

53. De Wit and Meyer (2010)

54. e.g., Chatterjee, S. (1986) 'Types of synergy and economic value: The impact of acquisitions on merging and rival firms', *Strategic Management Journal,* 7 (2): 119–39.

55. Porter (1987: 52)

56. De Wit and Meyer (2010)

57. Porter (1987)

58. Vermeulen, F. (2013) 'Corporate strategy is a fool's errand', *Harvard Business Review Digital Articles,* March: 2–4.

59. Aggarwal, R. and Kyaw, N.A. (2009) 'International variations in transparency and capital structure: Evidence from European firms', *Journal of International Financial Management & Accounting,* 20 (1): 1–34; Indjejikian, R.J. (2007) 'Discussion of accounting information, disclosure, and the cost of capital', *Journal of Accounting Research,* 45 (2): 421–6.

60. Hitt, M.A., Ireland, R.D. and Hoskisson, R.E. (2009) *Strategic Management: Competitiveness and Globalization* (8th ed.). Mason, OH: Cengage; Vermeulen (2013).

61. Hitt et al. (2009)

62. Hitt et al. (2009: 165)

63. Vermeulen (2013)

64. Porter (1987)

65. Girod, S.J.G. and Karim, S. (2017) 'Restructure or reconfigure?', *Harvard Business Review,* March/April. https://hbr.org/2017/03/restructure-or-reconfigure (accessed June 26, 2023).

66. Johnson et al. (2005)
67. Krühler, M., Pidun, U. and Rubner, H. (2012) *First, Do no Harm: How to Be a Good Corporate Parent.* Boston, MA: The Boston Consulting Group.
68. Krühler et al. (2012)
69. Krühler et al. (2012)
70. Pidun, U., Richter, A., Schommer, M. and Karna, A. (2019) 'A new playbook for diversified companies', *MIT Sloan Management Review*, 60 (2). https://sloanreview.mit.edu/article/a-new-playbook-for-diversified-companies/ (accessed June 26, 2023).
71. Collis and Montgomery (1998)
72. Associated Press (2021) 'Arizona dumps bonds after Ben & Jerry's stops selling in Israeli-occupied territories', *NPR,* September 10. www.npr.org/2021/09/10/1036180160/arizona-ben-jerrys-israeli-occupied-territories-unilever-ice-cream (accessed June 26, 2023); BBC (2002) 'Ben & Jerry's fails to stop sales in Israeli settlements', *BBC,* August 23. www.bbc.com/news/world-middle-east-62643392 (accessed June 26, 2023); Chacar, H. (2022) 'Unilever sells Ben & Jerry's Israeli business to defuse BDS row', *Reuters,* June 30. www.reuters.com/business/retail-consumer/unilever-sells-ben-jerrys-israeli-business-2022-06-29 (accessed June 26, 2023); Evans, J. (2022) 'Ben & Jerry's vs Unilever: How a star acquisition became a legal nightmare', *Financial Times,* October 11. https://www.ft.com/content/30efd993-8c23-4f1b-9385-132bbba3d863 (accessed June 26, 2023); Gambetta, G. (2022) 'US states with BDS bans respond to Unilever's sale of Ben & Jerry's Israel', *Responsible Investor,* June 30. www.responsible-investor.com/us-states-with-bds-bans-respond-to-unilevers-sale-of-ben-jerrys-israel (accessed June 26, 2023); McGeehan, P. (2021) 'N.J. to pull $182 million out of Unilever over Ben & Jerry's and Israel', *The New York Times,* September 16. www.nytimes.com/2021/09/16/nyregion/ben-and-jerrys-israel-unilever.html (accessed June 26, 2023); Stempel, J. (2022) 'Ben & Jerry's will amend lawsuit against Unilever over Israel ice cream sale', *Reuters,* September 7. www.reuters.com/markets/deals/ben-jerrys-will-amend-lawsuit-against-unilever-over-israel-ice-cream-sale-2022-09-07 (accessed June 26, 2023); Unilever (2022b) 'Unilever statement on Ben & Jerry's', *Unilever,* November 16. www.unilever.com/news/press-and-media/press-releases/2022/unilever-statement-on-ben-jerrys (accessed June 26, 2023); Unilever (2022c) 'Unilever statement on Ben & Jerry's – December 2022', December 15. www.unilever.com/news/press-and-media/press-releases/2022/unilever-statement-on-ben-jerrys-december-2022 (accessed June 26, 2023).
73. Ben & Jerry's (2021) 'Ben & Jerry's will end sales of our ice cream in the Occupied Palestinian Territory', *Ben and Jerry's.* www.benjerry.com/about-us/media-center/opt-statement (accessed June 26, 2023).
74. Neerman, P. (2022) 'Ben & Jerry's tries to prevent Israeli sell-out once more', *RetailDetail,* September 7. www.retaildetail.eu/news/food/ben-jerrys-tries-to-prevent-israeli-sell-out-once-more (accessed June 26, 2023).
75. Unilever (2022c)

# Acknowledgements

The authors thank Jeroen Thorenaar, Luuk op de Weegh, Joeri van der Wees and Chrissy Welsh for their contribution to this chapter.

# Key terms

**Capital orchestration logic** – a corporate parent's logic that perceives a diversified firm as a portfolio of largely unrelated business entities, the performance of which can be improved by serving as investment vehicle and reviewer of these entities

**Continuous reorganization logic** – a corporate parent's logic that perceives a diversified firm as an assembly of largely unrelated business entities whose value can be improved through reconfiguration and restructuring and are then sold off

**Corporate controls** – the oversight mechanisms implemented by the corporate parent to monitor and ensure alignment of business unit activities with corporate objectives

**Corporate logic** – the corporate rationale regarding how to achieve corporate parenting advantage

**Corporate parent** – the business entity (or entities) that oversees and has a controlling interest in multiple other business entities that are part of the same company

**Corporate parenting advantage** – the extent to which a corporate parent improves the performance of the business units that it oversees and controls over and above what they could achieve by being stand-alone firms or by being part of another firm

**Corporate-level strategy** – the determination of the direction and scope of a firm as a whole, and the creation of value through the coordination and configuration of its component divisions

**Cost synergies** – cost savings enabled by running multiple businesses together instead of separately

**Financial controls** – budgets and objective criteria used by the corporate parent to measure business unit performance against quantitative standards

**Financial synergies** – synergies that are achieved at the level of a diversified firm as a whole, allowing for achieving a consolidated performance that is greater than the sum of what each individual business unit can achieve on its own

**Internal capital market** – the firmwide pooling of cash flows and allocation of financial resources across a firm

**Investment synergies** – savings on capital expenditures enabled by running multiple businesses together instead of separately

**Managerial synergies** – revenue gains or cost savings enabled by having one or more managers in a position where they provide adequate guidance to a business unit that competes in one business area by drawing on their experiences in working in another business area in which the firm competes

**Operating cost synergies** – savings on operating expenditures enabled by running multiple businesses together instead of separately

**Parental developer logic** – a corporate parent's logic that perceives a diversified firm as an assembly of business entities whose value it can enhance by employing its in-house competencies and capabilities

**Parenting strategy composition** – the range and degree of different activities that a corporate parent conducts to add value to the business units it oversees

**Revenue synergies** – revenues generated by a combination of two or more product offerings that would not been generated if these products had been sold separately

**Strategic controls** – criteria used by the corporate parent to verify that a firm's business units are using appropriate strategies giving the firm's strategy and the environmental circumstances in which it operates

**Synergy** – the ability of two or more business units (or firms) to generate more value working together than they could achieve working apart as standalone entities

**Synergy management logic** – a corporate parent's logic that perceives a diversified firm as a set of connections between component business entities, the synergistic potential of which should be maximally exploited

# 13
# NETWORK-LEVEL STRATEGY

## LEARNING OBJECTIVES

After reading this chapter, you should be able to:

- distinguish between the different forms that cooperative arrangements can take;
- indicate how firms can simultaneously cooperate and compete with each other;
- point out different reasons for forging cooperative strategies;
- indicate what makes a firm a potentially suitable alliance partner;
- recognize how cooperative arrangements can be managed and indicate which changes may take place in these arrangements over time.

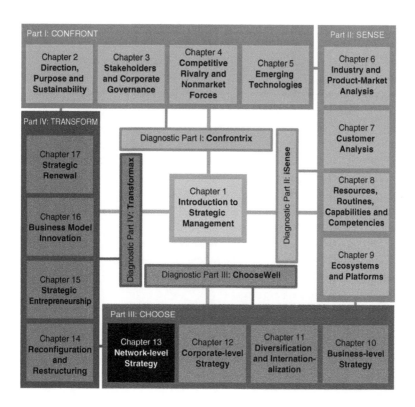

## OPENING CASE

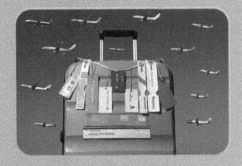

Source: © luirsphoto (2017) / Shutterstock.

### Airline alliances and lobbying in turbulent times

'Last year, we survived the four horsemen of the apocalypse: SARS, conflict in Iraq, terrorism and the economy. This year was meant to be the first profitable year for our industry this century. But a fifth horseman, the price of oil, could add up to $1 billion per month to our costs and deny us profitability yet again'.[1] When the CEO of the International Air Transport Association (IATA) spoke these words in 2004, the outbreak of COVID-19 was still far away, causing an even more severe hit to the global airline industry: in 2020, air travel demand had dropped to about half of its pre-pandemic level and airlines were facing rising costs to comply with health and safety precautions. By then, the airline industry had sort of stabilized after decades of consolidation.[2] This consolidation was characterized by mergers, acquisitions, minority equity participations, joint ventures, codeshare agreements, and the formation and expansion of global airline constellations.

A codeshare agreement essentially means that two or more airlines contractually agree to publish, market and sell the same direct or connecting flight under their own flight code as part of their published flight schedule. The air carrier that operates a certain flight – providing the aircraft and crew – is the operating partner, while its codeshare partner(s) for the same flight are called marketing partners or ticketing carriers. Codesharing partners may agree to sell seats on a block space basis (a marketing partner purchases a fixed number of seats that are kept away from an operating partner's inventory) or on a free flow basis (seats are not locked to any partner). In the case of a connecting flight, codesharing partners may each operate a certain part of the flight itinerary, often based on a hub-and-spoke strategy. Codesharing enables airlines to optimize their networks, offer customers a wider choice of flights, and increase brand exposure without having to expand their fleet size and at a fraction of the cost of operating these flights themselves.

In the wake of waves of deregulation in the European airline industry in the late 1980s and the 1990s, a growing number of airlines formed or joined a global airline alliance. By 2004, the members of Star Alliance (founded by United Airlines, Air Canada, Lufthansa, and Thai Airways in 1997), Oneworld (founded by British Airways, American Airlines, Canadian Airlines, Qantas Airways, and Cathay Pacific in 1999) and SkyTeam (founded by Air France, Delta Air Lines, Korean Airlines, and AeroMexico in 2000) jointly accounted for 60.8% of air passenger traffic.[3] Antitrust legislation does not allow these members to coordinate prices, or provide certain information or share profits, unless done as part of a joint venture agreement.[4] Nonetheless, airlines can benefit from membership while maintaining their independent status. For instance, members in Star Alliance have benefited from its brand identity, an expansion of codesharing practices with fellow members, a common IT platform (allowing them to provide better customer service and to speed up the time-to-market of service offerings while reducing IT and distribution costs), joint product development, the integration of frequent flyer programs, shared facilities (e.g., lounges and self-service kiosks) at the world's major airports, combined training programs, and cost savings through the coordinated purchase of fuel, aircraft, office supplies and advertising services.[5]

To mitigate the impact of the COVID-19 pandemic, individual airlines lobbied for increased government support and funding. By August 2020, governments around the world had already spent over $125 billion to financially support domestic airlines.[6] IATA supported its approximately 290 airline members in their lobbying endeavours. The association said to 'run intensive lobbying campaigns to support many aspects of airline operations'[7] – for instance related to airport slots, emissions trading, and taxation on air transport. During the pandemic, IATA coordinated an extensive global campaign aimed at ensuring that airlines could offer vouchers (rather than cash refunds) to passengers if flights were cancelled and pushing governments to reduce taxes and provide financial support by, for instance, setting up bailout funds and funds to maintain routes.[8] Also Oneworld, SkyTeam and Star Alliance played a role in how the industry responded to the pandemic. The latter, for instance, introduced a set of health and safety procedures for its members to follow and created an information hub for passengers.[9] In July 2020, the three rival alliances jointly released a video message meant to convince future travelers that they can embark on flights with confidence thanks to the measures taken by airlines.

### Questions

1. What type of cooperative arrangements can you distinguish in this case study?
2. To what extent can these arrangements help airlines to cope with a pandemic or another crisis?
3. To what extent is group-based competition peculiar to the airline industry?

## Introduction

In the previous three chapters we have predominantly viewed firms as independently operating entities that strive to enhance their competitive and corporate advantage mainly on their own strength. This view is incomplete in a world where firms are embedded in networks of cooperative relationships with other organizations in their market environment.[10] In the global airline industry, for instance, competition does not only take place between airlines but also between airline alliance constellations.[11] Accordingly, this chapter focuses on making choices with respect to **cooperative strategy**, which is concerned with how to achieve goals at the business level (see Chapter 10) and corporate level (see Chapters 11 and 12) by working together with other organizations at the network level.[12] We zoom in on the different categories, subcategories and types of cooperative arrangements firms can choose from, the benefits that can potentially be gained through these arrangements, and the managerial choices on how to realize these benefits.

## Forms of cooperative arrangements

Interorganizational cooperative arrangements take many forms; see Table 13.1. Also known as *alliances* or *partnerships*, these arrangements include any interorganizational interaction that falls between merger or acquisition activity (see Chapter 14), which results in common corporate ownership and the dissolution of one or more firms, and – at the other extreme of the spectrum – arm's-length market exchanges (such as on a spot market) and discrete, short-term contracts between independent firms that act in their best self-interest.[13] Hence, as visualized in Figure 13.1, alliances are considered as an intermediate or 'hybrid' form of interorganizational interaction.[14] More specifically, an **alliance** is an enduring, voluntary arrangement in which firms or other entities (such as governments[15]), which retain their legal independence and are not bound by common ownership, work together in an effort to accomplish mutually beneficial outcomes. Working together can imply any pooling, sharing, exchange, transfer, alignment, or co-development of resources, capabilities, products (goods or services), skills or activities. An alliance between two organizations can be referred to as a *dyadic alliance* or *bilateral alliance*, while an alliance

**TABLE 13.1**   Overview of different forms of cooperative arrangements

| Category | Subcategory | Type of cooperative arrangement |
|---|---|---|
| **Equity alliance** | *Formation of separate, jointly owned entity* | • Fifty-fifty equity joint venture (50:50 EJV)<br>• Unequal equity joint venture (e.g., 60:40 EJV)<br>• Cooperative (co-op)<br>   ○ Producer and marketing cooperative<br>   ○ Purchasing cooperative<br>   ○ R&D cooperative<br>   ○ Other types of cooperatives<br>• Institutional public-private partnership (iPPP) |
| | *Direct minority equity participation (no new entity formed)* | • Minority equity participation<br>• Cross-shareholding (equity swap)<br>• Keiretsu<br>   ○ Vertical keiretsu<br>   ○ Horizontal keiretsu |
| **Contractual alliance** | *Vertical contractual agreement (buyer-supplier agreement or supply chain partnership)* | • Long-term distribution contract<br>   ○ Distribution outsourcing agreement<br>   ○ Other types of distribution agreements<br>• Long-term supply contract<br>   ○ Procurement outsourcing agreement<br>   ○ Other types of supply agreements<br>• Contractual public-private partnership (cPPP) (special kind of outsourcing agreement) |
| | *Horizontal contractual agreement* | • R&D (co-development) alliance<br>• Joint production (co-production) alliance<br>• Joint distribution (co-distribution) alliance<br>• Joint marketing alliance (incl. affiliate marketing)<br>• Co-branding (brand partnership) alliance<br>• Consortium* or syndicate<br>• Other types of horizontal agreements |
| | *Licensing agreement* | • Classic licensing agreement<br>   ○ Patent licensing agreement<br>   ○ Copyright licensing agreement<br>   ○ Trademark licensing agreement<br>   ○ Other types of licensing agreements<br>• Cross-licensing agreement<br>• Franchising agreement |
| **Associational alliance** | *Separate third entity (membership-based)* | • Trade association (sector or business association)<br>• Confederation |
| | *Separate or no separate third entity* | • Standard-setting alliance<br>• Lobbying coalition |
| | *No separate third entity* | • Community of practice (learning community) |
| **Collusion** | | • Explicit collusion agreement (cartel) |

(*) Sometimes the label 'consortium' is used to refer to an equity-based arrangement.

that is formed by at least three entities can be labelled a *multilateral alliance, multi-firm alliance* or *alliance constellation*[16]. The distinct term *alliance portfolio* is used to indicate a collection of different alliances that a firm has established over time, emphasizing the need for multi-alliance management capabilities and practices.[17] An alliance (or partnership) is called a *strategic alliance* (or *strategic partnership*) when the rationale for its formation is in line with the alliance partners' goals at the business unit or corporate level. As detailed next, (strategic) alliances can broadly be divided into four different categories: equity alliances, contractual alliances, associational alliances, and collusion.

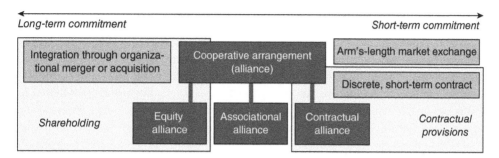

**FIGURE 13.1**   Forms of interorganizational interaction

## Equity alliances

**Equity alliances** constitute a form of interorganizational arrangement that is characterized by shared equity participation, which aligns the incentives of the cooperating organizations. A distinction can be made between two subcategories of equity alliances: alliances that involve the formation of a separate, jointly owned entity (in the form of either an equity joint venture or cooperative), and alliances in which direct minority equity investments are made.

### Equity joint ventures

An **equity joint venture** (or simply *joint venture*) implies that two or more organizations establish a separate, jointly owned and independently operating entity that is governed by a board of directors in which typically each of these partner organizations is represented. As these organizations allocate their residual rights of control – in proportion to their equity participation – to this board, a joint venture arrangement reduces their need to specify all contingencies in their initial agreement. This is also the case with other types of equity alliances.[18] A joint venture coexists with the organizations that incorporated this entity, which share not only the entity's ownership and governance but also the returns and risks of this entity. Profits resulting from the joint venture are allocated in proportion to shareholdings, which sets this type of arrangement apart from a cooperative. It is not uncommon for organizations to set up a joint venture with a purpose that is limited to the completion of a certain project or task with a projected end date. Such an arrangement is called a *project-based joint venture.*

The equity participation of the partners in a joint venture can be equal or unequal. When equity participation is equal, it is often labelled a *fifty-fifty (or 50:50) joint venture.* A *majority-minority joint venture* (for instance, 51:49 or 50:30:20) implies unequal equity participation of the alliance partners. The partner that has the majority share is in a dominant control position. A case in point is when in 2022 France-based Air Liquide and the South Korean firm Lotte Chemical decided to set up a 60:40 equity joint venture focused on developing hydrogen filling units in the latter's home country. A joint venture such as this one, where at least one of the alliance partners is headquartered outside the joint venture's country of operation, is sometimes labelled an *international joint venture*. This label can also be applied to joint ventures that operate in more than one country.[19] The joint venture equity ratio can change over time. For instance, in 2017 Dow Chemical signed an agreement to raise its equity stake in the Sadara Chemical Firm, a joint venture that it had set up in cooperation with Saudi Aramco in 2011 to construct and run a large chemical complex in Saudi Arabia, from 35% to 50%.

Joint ventures can be operating entities or non-operating entities (or a combination of both). In the case of an *operating joint venture*, the joint entity performs a set of activities on behalf of the equity-holding partners, which pool some of their resources and capabilities in this entity and contribute together to its day-to-day operations. Regardless of whether it is a fifty-fifty or a majority-minority joint venture, each partner can be assigned the rights to control certain activities of the joint venture (such as R&D or marketing) or to make certain activity-related decisions. A *nonoperating joint venture*, in contrast, implies that the joint venture does not perform any of its own operations. Instead, it is a purely legal and administrative entity that contracts with each of the participating partners to perform operational activities.[20]

## Cooperatives

Another equity-based alliances option is that firms or other entities collaborate as members of a **cooperative** (abbreviated as *co-op*) that they collectively own and run with the purpose of providing services to each of the members (which could also be individual workers or consumers and even other cooperatives). These members have limited liability and contribute equally to the cooperative's equity capital, from which they benefit in proportion to their 'patronage' or transactions with the cooperative – that is, in proportion to their use of the cooperative's goods or services.[21] Cooperatives operate on a democratic 'one member, one vote'-principle, meaning control is allocated evenly among their members. A cooperative can have many members. A case in point is FrieslandCampina, one of the world's largest dairy cooperatives, whose member base counts over 10,500 dairy farms (and over 15,000 dairy farmers) in the Netherlands, Belgium and Germany. This cooperative owns the firm Royal FrieslandCampina, which oversees manufacturing and sales. All the members have a say in decisions on, for example, quality conditions and changes to milk supply. An example of a much smaller Dutch cooperative is VannoVa, in which seven chrysanthemum growers work together on production and marketing, including the promotion of their cut flowers in Eastern Europe under the VannoVa brand name.

There are different types of cooperatives. FrieslandCampina and VannoVa are examples of a *producer and marketing cooperative*. Other types include *purchasing cooperatives* (such as Norway's Salmon Group), *retail cooperatives* (such as Denmark-based Coop Amba), *credit unions* (such as UK-based Capital Credit Union), *social cooperatives* (such as Gruppo Cooperativo CGM in Italy), and *research and development (R&D) cooperatives* (such as the COVID R&D Alliance).

## Minority equity investments and cross-shareholdings

Equity-based alliances do not necessarily imply that the alliance partners cooperate in a separate entity, as with a joint venture and cooperative. Alternatives are minority equity participations and cross-shareholdings. A **minority equity participation** (or *direct minority equity investment*) implies that an organization takes a non-controlling stake (i.e., less than 50%) in another organization by purchasing equity capital. For instance, Panasonic Corporation, a long-standing industrial partner of Tesla, acquired a substantial minority stake in the latter around the time of its 2010 IPO, which it sold again in 2021 for almost $4 billion.[22] A minority equity participation essentially results in a majority-minority joint venture – but without incorporating a new entity – between a firm's existing owners and the partner firm making the minority equity investment. Firms that take minority equity positions in other firms are usually granted representation on the board of these other firms. A *cross-shareholding* (also known as an *equity swap*) implies that two or more firms take non-controlling stakes in each other. An example is when in 1974 cosmetic firm L'Oréal acquired a small stake in food and beverage firm Nestlé in exchange for a 30% 'white knight'-stake of Nestlé in L'Oréal that helped to protect the latter from possible nationalization by the French government at the time (see Chapter 3). A *keiretsu* refers to a Japanese business structure that is comprised of a set of vertically related firms (*vertical keiretsu*) or horizontally related firms (*horizonal keiretsu*) that are tied together by cross-shareholdings and minority equity investments.[23] Examples as of 2023 are the Fuyo Group, Mitsubishi Group, Mitsui Group and Sumitomo Group.

## CRACK-THE-CASE

McDonald's joint venture struggles in India[24]

Source: © Radiokafka (2015) / Shutterstock.

*(Continued)*

In 1996 McDonald's opened its first outlet in India. In order to tailor its products to local attitudes and tastes, it scaled down on its meat-based patties – selling no beef because of religious objections – in exchange for a menu consisting of a variety of vegetarian options with typical Indian flavours that was developed from scratch. It also ensured low prices in order to be able to compete with the many local street vendors. Between 1996 and 2017, the firm successfully grew to 430 beefless outlets. Many of these outlets, including the first one in Delhi, were established by Connaught Plaza Restaurants Private Limited (CPRL), a 50:50 equity joint venture between Vikram Bakshi and McDonald's Indian subsidiary called McDonald's India Pvt Ltd (MIPL). CPRL had been formed under a 25-year deal between the two partners to set up outlets in the north and east of the country under a franchise model. McDonald's with another partner also formed a second joint venture, Amit Jatia's Hardcastle Restaurants, to run McDonald's business in the west and south.

In May 2019, McDonald's announced that it had bought back Bakshi's entire stake in CPRL, resulting in whole ownership by MIPL and its affiliate McDonald's Global Markets. The settlement put a halt to a legal tussle between CPRL's former partners that started back in 2013. In that year, McDonald's removed Bakshi as CPRL's managing director, accusing him of financial irregularities, only for Bakshi to be reinstalled in 2017 after the case had ended up in the National Company Law Tribunal (NCLT, then the Company Law Board), an authority set up to deal with corporate disputes of a civil nature. The NCLT also judged that McDonald's should no longer interfere in CPRL's operations. The year 2013 was also when Domino's Pizza surpassed McDonald's to become India's largest fast-food chain. Its feud with Bakshi hindered McDonald's plans to catch up. In July 2017, in the same month as NCLT's judgment, McDonald's outlets in Delhi were closed overnight because regulatory health licenses had not been renewed. According to Bakshi, who publicly speculated on the health standards of the McDonald's franchises in northern and western India, he had neglected their renewal on purpose out of quality concerns. One month later, McDonald's terminated Bakshi's franchise rights, accusing the businessman of not paying royalties. Under its notice of termination, CPRL's outlets were no longer allowed to use the McDonald's brand name, trademark, marketing techniques and recipes as of September that year. Bakshi however ignored the notice, resulting in more court cases. By buying out Bakshi in 2019, following two unsuccessful earlier attempts to do so in 2008, McDonald's finally got what it wanted.

## Questions

1. What reasons might have led McDonald's to choose for a joint venture entry mode to India?
2. What lessons could be learned from McDonald's struggles in relation to CPRL?

## Contractual alliances

**Contractual alliances** constitute the most common alliance form. They are a type of arrangement in which two or more firms or other entities work together on the basis of a contractual agreement. These arrangements are not constituted as separate entities and they do not involve short-term arm's-length contracts or equity investments.[25] As described next, partners can rely on different types of contractual alliance agreements, each of which fall into one of the following categories: *vertical contractual agreements, horizontal contractual agreements*, and *licensing agreements*.

## Vertical contractual alliances

Firms that form a contractual alliance with a distributor or supplier are said to engage in a **vertical contractual alliance**, also known as a *buyer-supplier arrangement, supply chain partnership* or *value chain partnership*. This category of alliances, which serve as a substitute for vertical integration, encompasses any type of long-term contractual arrangement, except for licensing agreements, between two or more firms that operate at different stages in a certain extended supply or value chain. A long-term contract is one that lasts for over one year.[26]

A *long-term distribution contract* is a vertical contractual alliance with a distributor. The term *distributor* encompasses any intermediary entity between a contracting firm and one or more other entities (such as a retailer or consumers) downstream in the supply or value chain. Such an intermediary entity, which handles or uses a firm's output either directly or indirectly, can for instance be a system integrator, value-added reseller, wholesaler, retailer, or logistics service provider. The distribution agreement may involve the integration, transport, (re)selling and/or marketing of a product. As with a supply agreement (described next), this agreement could be exclusive, in which case other distributors are excluded from one or more of these activities in one or more geographical regions, or non-exclusive.

The term *supplier* encompasses any provider of input either directly to a certain contracting firm or to another supplier in the extended supply or value chain. This input can be in the form of goods and services. Pursuant to this account, a supplier can be a 'traditional' supplier of goods, examples of which are raw materials and semi-finished products, but also a contractor (which can supply both goods and services), subcontractor, or service provider, such as a consultant. The distinction between some of these supplier categories has become blurred over time. For instance, the increasingly digitalized landscape (see Chapter 5) in which goods-supplying firms operate offers a growing array of opportunities for these firms to increase their level of servitization. *Servitization* means that a producer adds services to its core product offering to create additional customer value.[27] A case in point is Wärtsilä, a Finnish producer of a wide range of engines for marine propulsion, which in 2017 signed a 12-year performance-based contract with cruise firm Carnival Corporation to handle all engine maintenance and monitoring work for many of its cruise vessels.[28] This is an example of a *long-term supply contract*, meaning a vertical contractual alliance with a supplier. Besides a long-term contract, firms may provide their suppliers with leased equipment and technical advice or closely work together with suppliers in upstream activities such as product design. IKEA has worked like that with its suppliers for many years. In return, IKEA demands from these suppliers an exclusive contract and low prices.[29]

The term *outsourcing agreement* is commonly used to denote a contract between two parties in which one party (a distributor or supplier) agrees to perform certain activities that were carried out internally by the other (the outsourcing party) prior to the agreement. Outsourcing agreements that aim to achieve long-term win-win benefits are vertical contractual alliances. A case in point is when Samlink, a financial IT-service provider that was acquired by Kyndryl in 2021, signed a five-year outsourcing contract with global technology firm IBM to manage the IT infrastructure for Samlink's 400+ branch offices across Finland.

A *contractual public-private partnership* (abbreviated as cPPP) is a special kind of long-term outsourcing agreement between a public sector entity (such as a state or local government) and one or more private sector entities (mostly firms). More specifically, these private sector entities agree to take responsibility – and often assume the risks – to deliver public infrastructure goods (such as roads) or services (such as education) during the contract term, for which they are paid by the public sector based on user charges and/or availability-based payments (as per the contract type).[30] A cPPP, which is the most common model for implementing public-private partnership (PPP) projects[31], is different from an *institutional public-private partnership (iPPP)*. In contrast to cPPPs, iPPPs are 'horizontal' rather than vertical in nature and they imply shareholding in a separate entity – that is, both public and private sector entities take responsibility for providing a public asset or service as shareholders in a *special purpose vehicle (SPV)*.[32] Hence, an iPPP constitutes an example of an equity alliance instead of a contractual alliance.

## Horizontal contractual alliances

Firms that cooperate in the form of a **horizontal contractual alliance**, as opposed to a vertical one, operate at the same or a similar stage of the supply or value chain. The alliance partners, which can operate in the same industry or in different industries, are for instance both producers of (different or similar) component parts or they are both providers of advisory services. Partners in a horizontal contractual alliance are usually actual or potential competitors (see Chapter 6) or complementors (see Chapter 9).

A horizontal contractual alliance typically implies that the alliance partners contractually agree to jointly undertake one or more value chain activities, such as research, development, production, distribution, marketing or branding, for their mutual benefit. Partners in a contractual *research and development (R&D) alliance* (or *co-development alliance*), for instance, engage in joint R&D activities.[33] A case in point is when in 2016 Takasago, a Japanese producer of flavours, fragrances, aroma ingredients and fine chemicals, signed a multi-year R&D agreement with Swiss biotech firm Evolva aimed at developing sustainable, cost-effective ingredients by adding Evolva's fermentation technology to its own technologies in flavours and fragrances. An example of a contractual *co-production alliance* is the 1997 agreement between Pixar and The Walt Disney Company – who eventually acquired Pixar nine years later – to collaborate in the creative process of developing and producing five computer-animated feature films for distribution by Disney.[34] This alliance resulted in the blockbusters *A Bug's Life, Monsters, Inc., Finding Nemo, The Incredibles*, and *Cars*. An example of a *co-distribution alliance* (or *joint distribution alliance*) is the 2015 deal between the two publishing firms Elsevier and Bentham Science to distribute Bentham's chemistry titles through ScienceDirect and other global sales channels of Elsevier.

Firms that decide to enter a contractual joint R&D, co-production, or co-distribution alliance keep their own R&D, production or distribution assets largely intact – otherwise it would be considered outsourcing. Similarly, firms that enter into a *contractual joint marketing alliance*, such as MarshBerry and Patra in 2019, keep their own marketing channels.[35] MarshBerry, a firm specialized in rendering consultancy services to insurance firms, agreed to promote and endorse Patra's line of technology-enabled services for the insurance industry to members of its Connect Platform while Patra agreed to provide preferred pricing and exclusive benefits to these members. A contract between a firm and a so-called *affiliate partner* who agrees to market or promote this firm in exchange for a commission is called an *affiliate marketing agreement*. Firms that partner up in a *co-branding alliance*, also known as a *brand partnership*, associate (one of) their brands in a single good or service.[36] For example, Louis Vuitton partnering up with BMW to create a tailor-made set of suitcases and bags crafted in carbon black fiber for the then newly launched BMW i8.

Horizontal contractual alliances in which the alliance partners combine parts of their businesses and operate these parts as if a separate organizational entity was created, without such an entity being actually created, and where the compensation to each alliance partner depends on how much profit is earned, are occasionally referred to as either a *virtual joint venture (VJV)*[37] or a *nonequity joint venture (NEJV)*.[38]

A group of organizations that temporarily participate in a common activity or pool their resources in pursuit of achieving a particular common goal is often referred to as a *consortium*. Consortia are usually disbanded once this goal is attained or put aside. The terms *joint venture* and *consortium* are sometimes used interchangeably, depending partly on the dominant national legislative framework. However, what is more often meant by consortium is an alliance which is formed only by contract (a *consortium agreement*) that delegates responsibilities among the consortium partners, and which is therefore not incorporated as a separate legal entity. This distinguishes consortia from project-based joint ventures.

## Licensing agreements

Licensing agreements constitute a third category of contractual alliances. The word 'licensing' means 'permitting to do something'. A **licensing agreement** between a licensor (i.e., the firm granting the license) and a licensee implies that the latter is authorized to use and earn revenue from certain intellectual properties (e.g., a patented technology or software, copyright, trade secret or trademark) and/or other assets (e.g., real estate) of the licensor in exchange for a negotiated payment. For instance, The Walt Disney Company, the world's largest licensor for over two decades, licenses its brand name and copyrights for its animated film characters to manufacturers of toys, apparel, bedding, accessories, games, and other merchandise. One of these manufacturers is Barbie-producer Mattel, which in 2022 recouped the global licensing rights to produce dolls for the Disney Princess and Frozen lines that it had lost six years earlier to its chief rival Hasbro. Meanwhile, Hasbro renewed its licensing deal with Disney to develop products featuring characters from Star Wars and Indiana Jones. If Mattel or Hasbro would have used the copyrighted characters for their product items without Disney's authorization, this would have constituted an illegal act. A license could therefore be seen as a covenant not to sue.

License payments often consist of an upfront lump-sum fee in conjunction with ongoing, usage-based fees called *royalties* (e.g., 50 cents for each unit sold, or 10% of revenues), but other terms are not uncommon. The licensor and licensee may agree on a certain cap on the amount of royalties payable under the life of the agreement or in any given specific period. They may also agree on certain scaling terms, such that additional royalty fees are incurred for every time the licensed property is used above certain threshold amounts. Cross-licensing agreements are usually royalty-free. A *cross-licensing agreement* implies that two or more firms grant a license to each other, such as patents over different aspects of the same technology or product.

Licenses often revolve around intellectual property (IP). Depending on the type of intellectual property for which the license is granted, a licensing agreement could for instance be a *patent licensing agreement, copyright licensing agreement, trademark licensing agreement* or *trade secret licensing agreement* (or a combination thereof). Licensing agreements can also be categorized based on their level of exclusivity. An *exclusive licensing agreement* implies that a licensee is granted the exclusive rights to use the licensed property. A *sole licensing agreement* gives a licensee the right to use the licensed property to the exclusion of anyone except the licensor. Finally, a *non-exclusive licensing agreement* implies that the licensor is free to use the licensed property and to license it to multiple licensees simultaneously. Another categorization is that a licensing agreement can be *perpetual*, granting the licensee the right to use certain property of the licensor permanently rather than for a fixed period of time.

Besides stipulating compensation and license exclusivity and duration, licensing agreements typically include provisions concerning the field of use of the licensed property (specifying, for example, the range of products that the licensee is allowed to sell utilizing this property and the geographical area of these sales), performance guarantees (such as quality standards and a minimal guaranteed use of the licensed property), license transferability, and dispute settlement.

Franchising is a special, comprehensive form of licensing. While all franchising agreements are licensing agreements, not all licensing agreements include franchising. The term *franchise* should not be confused with a film franchise, such as Disney's Frozen and Star Wars. A **franchising agreement** between a franchisor (that is, the firm granting a franchising license) and a franchisee implies that the latter is granted the right to use a certain franchise formula, typically in a specific geographical area, owned by the franchisor. Such a formula typically consists of a combination of intellectual property (including brand identity elements) and transferable business practices that enable the franchisee to duplicate a certain business model. Franchisors usually provide ongoing guidance, support and training to their franchisees to enable and facilitate this duplication. Franchise rights are often granted in exchange for an upfront fee and royalties along with fees for goods and services such as marketing. Franchisees usually have to abide by a set of rules and core principles as imposed by the franchisor concerning operations and marketing. The level of direction and control exerted by the licensor is more significant than with licensing agreements that do not involve franchising. Franchising takes place in many different business areas but is most pervasive in the fast-food industry, where firms such as Subway, McDonald's, Burger King, KFC, Domino's, and Pizza Hut count over 10,000 franchised outlets each.

## CRACK-THE-CASE
### Adidas sprinting forward[39]

Source: © WR7 (2022) / Shutterstock.

For lifestyle brands, consumer perception is everything. For a long time, the sportswear company Adidas was considered an 'uncool brand'. This had changed by 2016, as Adidas' former North America President Mark King explained: '[Adidas went] from not very popular to being arguably the coolest brand in sport almost overnight. I think it's really because we're focusing on what the consumer wants'. As King notes, Adidas has been very successful in analyzing its environment, focusing on customers, and finding outside opportunities to capitalize on these consumer desires.

In 2016 Kasper Rørsted was elected CEO of Adidas. Under Rørsted's leadership, Adidas undertook an ambitious digital transformation, moving to streamline its operations. Adidas experienced sustained growth and growing brand desirability in the following three years. In 2019, Adidas had its strongest year on record. This success can partly be attributed to the digital transformation initiative. However, it is how Adidas capitalized on opportunities that made the firm stand out most. Where its main competitors focused primarily on consumers, Adidas proactively scanned its environment for opportunities. When these opportunities met Adidas' criteria, the firm worked to secure the opportunity swiftly. This proactive stance led to partnerships with cultural icons such as Pharrell Williams, Rita Ora, Beyoncé, Bad Bunny, and Ye (better known as Kanye West). These partnerships have resulted in a variety of different collections and exclusive releases of Adidas sneakers and sportswear. In particular the fashion partnership with Ye turned out to be a tremendous success, with the brand Yeezy generating significant sales and attention. In April 2020, *Forbes* described Yeezy's rise as 'one of the great retail stories of the century'.[40] Two and a half years later, however, Adidas abruptly ended its partnership with Ye after he made antisemitic remarks in interviews and on social media.

## Questions

1. How would you label the form of cooperative agreement between Adidas and the music artists mentioned in this case study?
2. What are the advantages of collaborating with parties (such as Ye) outside Adidas to capitalize on consumer desires?
3. What are the potential dangers to Adidas for collaborating extensively with outside parties?

## Associational alliances

**Associational alliances** encompass all non-collusive, cooperative arrangements that are neither contractual alliances nor equity alliances. That means that the organizations that form these alliances intentionally combine, transfer or align some of their resources and capabilities or coordinate their actions over an extended period of time without any contractual obligation to do so and without having any equity participation in their alliance partners or in the organizational entity (typically a member-based organization) through which they may cooperate. What binds these organizations is a common purpose or (business) interest. Given this broad definition, there is a large variety in associational alliances. Among the most common examples are communities of practice, standard-setting alliances, lobbying coalitions, trade associations, and confederations.

Organizations that form a *community of practice* (CoP), sometimes called *learning communities*, aim to solve common problems or achieve common goals by sharing and harnessing knowledge, expertise, experience, or best practices on a free-flowing, voluntary basis. Interaction could take place at for instance meetings, events or a shared platform or forum. CoPs are as diverse as the challenges and circumstances that give rise to them. They can be made up of many community members but then usually have a core of participants that provide directional or intellectual leadership. Large CoPs are often subdivided by subject matter or by region in order to encourage participation.[41] An example of a CoP is Réseau Social Professionnel des Achats de l'État (RespAÉ), a professional social network of buyers from French ministries and their public agencies that was launched in 2016. It is aimed at 'fostering cooperation, exchanging of good practices and transferring of skills between buyers, sharing documents and ideas, and allowing buyers to capitalize on their knowledge and know-how'.[42]

Consumers typically show greater interest in products that conform to accepted standards compared to equivalent nonstandard products.[43] A *standard-setting alliance*, or *standard-setting coalition*, denotes a cooperative arrangement in which firms develop one or more technical compatibility standards (i.e., technical norms or requirements) and/or push for adoption of these standards. Standard-setting alliances can compete to establish the dominant standard. A well-documented example is the battle for the next generation digital video disk (DVD) players in the mid-2000s between the Blu-ray Disc Association (BDA) and the HD-DVD Promotion Group. Most members at both sides were either electronic firms (such as Hitachi, Samsung and Sony at the side of BDA, and Fujitsu, Intel and Toshiba at the side of HD-DVD) or movie studios (such as Walt Disney and MGM at the side of BDA, and Universal at the opposing side). Blu-ray eventually became the dominant DVD-standard.

A *lobbying coalition* denotes an alliance between organizations (or between individuals, as in the case of the US-based Business Roundtable, whose members are solely CEOs) that pool some of their resources to coordinate joint lobbying or to hire lobbying firms or individual lobbyists to do so on their behalf. Lobbing is directed at winning influence over legislative processes. Given that directly lobbying legislators may negatively affect a firm's reputation, the lobbying process is often done through trade associations, which masks the firm's role to some extent.

Trade associations and confederations, both of which are member-based organizations, typically participate in lobbying and standard setting, however not exclusively. A *trade association*, such as the International Air Transport Association (IATA), has many other names, including industry trade group, industry association, branch association, sectoral association, and business association. Its members are firms that operate in a certain economic (sub) sector, such as airlines operating scheduled and non-scheduled air services, as in the case of IATA. In contrast, the membership base of a *confederation* consists at least partly of associations, such as trade associations. An example is the Confederation of Netherlands Industry and Employers (known in the Netherlands as VNO-NCW), the largest employers' organization in the Netherlands. More than 160 trade associations – as well as firms – are members, representing over 185,000 firms in almost all sectors of the Dutch economy.[44]

The general purpose of trade associations and confederations is to serve the collective interests of their members, and to represent and promote these interests to external parties, by engaging in activities that contribute to one or more collectively defined, long-term goals.[45] These activities often include lobbying for members' common interests, informing and educating members, setting standards, and facilitating interaction among members.[46] The long-term goals serve as points of reference for collective sensemaking. Trade associations and confederations have a board (elected officials) that decides on the basic policy and sets the agenda, and staff that are empowered to perform secretarial or administrative tasks in the best interests of the members and act or speak on their behalf.[47] Membership decisions range from self-selected membership to being subject to approval by a membership committee, the board, or all members.[48]

## Collusion

In March 2022, the General Court of the European Union ruled that Air France-KLM and its subsidiary Martinair (a cargo airline) had to pay more than €325 million in fines for price-fixing for air freight transport over a six-year period starting just before the beginning of the new millennium. In 1999, Air France, KLM and Martinair were still legally independent firms. These airlines and numerous other carriers, most of which were fined, allegedly engaged in fixing air freight services, fuel and security surcharges. Price-fixing is an act of **collusion**, which implies that two or more firms cooperate with the intention of increasing prices above fully competitive levels, thereby disrupting market equilibrium.[49] In any other situation, these firms would typically compete. Two examples of collusion besides price-fixing are when firms conspire to restrict their collective output or limit customers' knowledge about a certain product to their advantage (and to the customers' disadvantage).

*Explicit collusion*, which is when firms directly communicate with one another concerning collusive practices, is considered illegal in most parts of the world. Groups of firms that engage in explicit collusion are often called *cartels* (e.g., an air cargo cartel). The Organization of the Petroleum Exporting Countries (OPEC), an intergovernmental organization whose members are oil-exporting nations, is considered a cartel (although nations are not firms), however it is not illegal as it does not fall under any jurisdiction. When firms engage in collusive behaviour without actually negotiating and coordinating pricing or output decisions with rivals in a direct manner, we speak about *tacit collusion*. Tacit collusion, which does *not* count as a cooperative arrangement, often results from carefully observing rivals' actions and responses when it comes to price setting or production output.[50]

## STRATEGIC FOCUS

### Make, acquire or ally?

Deciding between either in-house development (i.e., organic growth) or acquiring on the one hand and allying on the other is about organizational boundaries: which businesses and activities should be part of the firm and which should not? When the new resources that a firm needs are similar to its existing resources – or can be developed by the firm relatively fast and easily or in a cost-efficient way without encountering unbridgeable internal conflicts – and, moreover, are considered important for achieving its strategic goals, in-house development ('making') is often the preferred path. If not, it can make most sense to go outside the firm. But in which direction to go? An arm's-length purchase contract could work when a firm and a resource provider are able to craft a transparent agreement that is based on a shared understanding of the resources' value, the firm has the competencies to use purchased resources without any additional contribution by the resource provider, and the level of interdependence is low.[51] If not, either the merger and acquisition path or the alliance path is most probably a better way to go.

*(Continued)*

**TABLE 13.2**   Make, acquire or ally? A simplified checklist

|  | Make | Acquire | Ally |
|---|---|---|---|
| If the firm has relevant knowledge about the market: | X | | |
| If the firm has financial resources available to invest: | X | X | |
| If the synergies with the firm's existing activities is high: | X | X | |
| If the need for control is high: | X | X | |
| If the firm can achieve a high degree of synergy with its existing resource base and activities: | X | X | |
| If there is a substantial risk of opportunistic behaviour of external parties: | X | X | |
| If the firm expects a high degree of coordination complexity in relation to the desired resources: | X | X | |
| If there is M&A competition in the market: | | X | |
| If the firm has sufficiently deep financial pockets for an acquisition: | | X | |
| If speed is important: | | X | X |
| If the market uncertainty is high: | | | X |

Source: authors, partly based on Kale & Singh (2004)

Table 13.2 provides a concise checklist that could be taken into consideration when choosing whether to make, acquire or ally. An equity alliance could in most instances be seen as an intermediate option between an acquisition and a contractual alliance.[52]

# Coopetition

The cooperative orientation of alliances stands in sharp contrast to the competitive focus that dominated our coverage of business-level strategy in Chapter 10, which is rooted in conflicting interests or goals. Yet, cooperation and competition can go hand-in-hand. For example, in order to survive against well-endowed tech giants such as Alphabet, Amazon, Didi Chuxing and Uber, traditional automotive companies are increasingly urged to develop usage-based mobility services. In 2019, two of these companies, the German premium automotive producers Mercedes-Benz Group (Daimler AG at the time) and BMW Group, announced that they would invest one billion euros in an urban mobility alliance. This alliance would encompass the creation of an intelligent network of five 50:50 equity joint ventures in which they would pool their mobility service offerings – marketed mainly to people who may not own a vehicle – and further develop their expertise in this area. The joint ventures would offer apps and services that allow customers to hail rides (the joint venture FREE NOW), charge electric vehicles (CHARGE NOW), share cars (SHARE NOW), book and pay for multimodal transport (REACH NOW), and find parking spots (PARK NOW).

When competing firms, such as Mercedes-Benz and BMW in the example above, choose to enter a cooperative agreement, we speak of **coopetition**: cooperation between competitors. Coopetition often implies that cooperative and competitive interactions take place simultaneously but in distinct product markets (for example, Mercedes-Benz and BMW cooperate in the mobility services market but compete in the market for premium vehicles), geographical markets (for example, probiotic yoghurt drink producers Danone and Yakult cooperate in India but compete in Europe) or stages of the supply chain (for example, Coca-Cola and Pepsi cooperate to foster post-consumption recycling while battling each other in the pre-consumption marketing arena).

## STRATEGIC FOCUS

### The Value Net Model

The *Value Net Model* identifies four type of players (customers, suppliers, complementors and competitors) that have a direct influence on a firm and with whom this firm could create value by collaborating in some way. Any of these players, which collectively form the 'value net', can have multiple roles – for instance, firm A can be both a competitor and supplier to firm B.

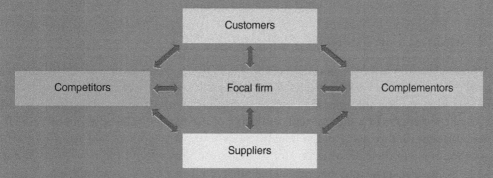

**FIGURE 13.2**   Value Net Model

Source: adapted from Brandenburger and Nalebuff (1996)

Visualizing the value net can be a relevant first step in the process of formulating a cooperative or coopetitive strategy. As a manager, you ought to identify all customers, suppliers, complementors and competitors that are relevant for your business(es) and list these players in the Value Net Model (see Figure 13.2). This is the point of departure for a *value net analysis* that can be broken down into answering the following questions[55]:

- What are the opportunities for (further) cooperation with each of these different players? For example, the focal firm may choose to combine forces with a competitor by purchasing similar production inputs upstream in the value chain, allowing for a better position to negotiate purchasing discounts.
- What is the added value of each of these players in relation to a certain overarching value proposition, what is the focal firm's added value, and how could combining forces enhance aggregate added value?
- In which industries or markets do each of these players (apart from customers in the B2C market) have a competitive presence, which of these industries or markets are outside the focal firm's corporate scope, to what extent and how could the firm create value from pro-actively linking its activities to these industries or markets, and how would that affect the behaviour of the other players?
- Which industry rules, regulations and generally accepted practices could be changed in the focal firm's favour by collaborating with the right players, and what should this collaboration then look like?

A common reason for competing firms to forge an alliance is that this enables them to strengthen their respective competitive positions in their present market vis-à-vis outsiders that operate in the same market or that seek to either get a foothold in this market or disrupt the market altogether. Cooperation may enable them to, for instance, enhance their market reach or to create a more encompassing value proposition vis-à-vis other competitors. Teaming up may also allow competitors to avoid certain investments, share investment risks, and enable or speed up their entry into a new market. Besides these reasons, which may apply to non-competing firms as well, cooperation places a firm in a more favourable position to gain insights in a competitor's strategy, drivers, management motivations and capabilities and, based on these useful insights, to predict this competitor's future course of action. Cooperation can also enable a firm to acquire better benchmarks of a competitor's performance. Mutual long-term gain in the context of coopetition is most feasible when each partner contributes something distinctive and is eager to learn from the other, while limiting access to its proprietary skills.[54]

## Reasons for entering alliances

A firm's first step towards entering an alliance is the decision to do so. Alliances can be forged for a variety of different reasons. A senior director at Lufthansa, founding member of Star Alliance (see the opening case), was quoted saying 'a well-run alliance can offer 80% of the benefits of a merger with only 20% of the hassle'.[55] Likewise, many firms find that alliances capture many of the benefits of in-house development and acquisition while avoiding some of their drawbacks – for instance, the slow speed of in-house development and the large financial and managerial resource requirements of an acquisition.

One of the main reasons for entering an alliance is to manage risks and uncertainties that firms face. Corporate activities such as investing in new technologies, developing new products, entering new geographical markets and diversifying to new business areas can involve substantial financial and reputational risks. By cooperating with others, firms can share these risks. This explains why alliances are forged most during the introduction stage of a certain technological life cycle[56], during which the level of uncertainty is highest.

Firms may also want to work together to overcome funding limitations, as alliance partners can provide part of the financial resources needed to engage in growth-directed endeavours, or to save costs. Furthermore, the forging of alliances can be driven by a firm's quest to improve its economies of scope or scale, as an alliance can result in lower long-term average production costs. Also, alliances may enable a firm to gain (better) access to complementary resources such as new technologies, as alliance partners could bring intellectual properties, technological know-how and competencies. Improved access to new markets is yet another possible reason for initiating an alliance. Alliance partners could bring in a strong market reputation, knowledge of a local or regional market, valuable political contracts, distribution channels, or other assets that can help to access new market areas that would otherwise be out of reach. In some countries, foreign firms are allowed to enter certain 'strategic' sectors (such as defense, energy, telecommunications and banking) only when establishing a joint venture owned partly by the country's government.

Cooperation can be essential for strengthening one's position in the marketplace by, for instance, depending on the alliance form, enabling a firm to enhance economies of scale, leverage its in-house R&D capabilities, ensure a more reliable supply chain, negotiate purchasing discounts, create a more encompassing value proposition, or acquire data based on which it can improve the design of its products. Moreover, forging alliances can allow for greater flexibility, enhanced learning, the closing of certain skill gaps, the generation of additional income streams (as, for instance, with licensing agreements), and more lobbying power. Yet another reason for initiating an alliance is to speed things up – for instance, to speed up the development of a new technology or product or the entry into a new geographical market. In hypercompetitive environments, speed can be crucial for competitive success.

**TABLE 13.3**   Reasons for alliances by market type

| Slow-cycle market | Standard-cycle market | Fast-cycle market |
|---|---|---|
| • Maintain market stability (e.g., establishing standards)<br>• Gain access to a restricted market<br>• Establish a franchise in a new market | • Gain market power<br>• Gain access to complementary resources<br>• Enhance economies of scale<br>• Overcome trade barriers<br>• Pool resources for capital-intensive projects<br>• Learn new business techniques | • Share risky R&D expenses<br>• Overcome uncertainty<br>• Speed up new product development<br>• Speed up new market entry<br>• Maintain market leadership<br>• Form an industry technology standard |

The primary reasons for engaging in cooperative arrangements tend to vary depending on the conditions of the market(s) in which a firm competes.[57] As described in Chapter 10, a distinction can be made in this regard between a *slow-cycle-market* (where competitive advantages can be sustained for a relatively long time period), a *fast-cycle market* (the opposite of a slow-cycle market) and a *standard-cycle market* (an intermediate market condition).[58] Table 13.3 links each of these conditions to certain possible reasons for forging an alliance.

# Choice of alliance partner

Once the decision to enter an alliance has been made, the selection of appropriate alliance partner(s) has to be made. Appropriateness can be defined in terms of contributing to the alliance's intended goals without coming at the expense of a firm's other strategic goals. Research indicates that at least three different partner traits have a positive effect on alliance performance: partner complementarity, partner compatibility, and partner commitment.[59] *Partner complementarity* refers to the degree to which a partner can contribute valuable non-overlapping resources and capabilities to the alliance.[60] *Partner compatibility* denotes the fit between partners in terms of, for instance, their corporate culture, types of resources, decision-making style, and working practices.[61] *Partner commitment* refers to a partner's willingness to contribute the resources required to achieve the alliance goals even when this requires making minor sacrifices.[62] The criticality of these traits in comparison to each other can vary according to factors such as partners' size and longevity[63] and the extent to which it is clear to the partners what is needed during the lifetime of the alliance to achieve its long-term goals.[64]

There are also various other factors that make some firms more attractive as alliance partners than others (depending on the type of alliance). One of these factors is the quality of the alliance-relevant resources and capabilities owned by firms.[65] Another relevant factor to consider, especially when resource endowments are not (easily) accessible prior to or during the alliance formation phase, is the perceived risk of opportunistic behaviour during the course of the alliance.[66] Firms that behave opportunistically are motivated by maximization of their economic self-interest, which may jeopardize the achievement of mutually beneficial outcomes that should be the inherent aim of a cooperative agreement. Ex-ante expected opportunistic hazards thus reduce a firm's attractiveness as an alliance partner.[67] In many ways, goodwill trust is at the opposite of opportunism.[68] Accordingly, trustworthiness enhances alliance partner attractiveness.[69] This is partly because a higher level of goodwill trust reduces the perceived expected costs of monitoring and controlling a partner's behavioural conduct during the alliance post-formation phase.[70] Also competency trust, which is a second type of trust besides goodwill trust, is related positively to partner attractiveness, as higher levels of competency trust reduce the perceived expected costs of controlling a partner's output.[71] Familiarity with a firm because of prior alliance ties[72] enhance trust, as do factors such as a favourable reputation status of both the potential partner firm[73] and its alliance partners[74].

Other factors worthwhile to take into account when choosing an alliance partner are the ex-ante perceived difficulties and complexities in properly managing or coordinating the relationship with a partner throughout the post-formation stage, as discussed next in more detail.[75]

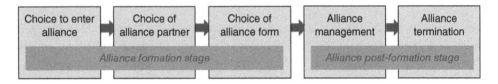

**FIGURE 13.3**  Typical sequence of events in alliances

Source: authors, based on Gulati (1998) and Kale & Singh (2009)

## Alliance management and dynamics in the post-formation stage

At this point we have covered the three main choices of the *alliance formation phase* (see Figure 13.3): the choice to ally (instead of choosing an alternative mode of growth) and for what reason(s), the choice of alliance partner(s) and, earlier in the chapter, the choice of alliance form (and, if applicable, the contractual terms of the alliance). The choice of alliance form determines the principal type of governance used to oversee the alliance: equity ownership (when opting for a type of equity alliance), contractual provisions (when opting for a contractual type of alliance) or self-enforcing governance (when opting for a type of associational alliance). The launch of the alliance marks the beginning of its *post-formation phase*, the duration of which can be undefined or predetermined. During this phrase, alliance partners engage in a cooperative relationship that is negotiated in a continuing communicative process as they contribute towards achieving the goal(s) of their alliance.[76] In most instances, the success of alliances once they are up and running is determined, to an important degree, by how firms manage the interdependencies, operational complexities and uncertainties that exist and arise in these alliances during the post-formation phase.[77] The high alliance failure rate of around 60 to 70%[78] indicates that this can be challenging.

## KEY DEBATE

### Dealing with behavioural manifestations of interdependence

Alliance partners work together in an effort to achieve one or more outcomes that each of these partners could not achieve individually, or at least not as efficiently or effectively. This means that they rely on one another's resources and activities to accomplish these outcomes, which implies mutual dependence – that is, interdependence. In brief, *partner interdependence* means that the choices and actions of one alliance partner are affected by the choices and actions of one or more other partners, and vice versa.[79] The outcomes and the functioning of an alliance is affected by the extent of trade-offs, tensions, and frictions in the alliance, which are all rooted in the partners' interdependence, and how these are dealt with. Hence, in order to avoid or minimize disadvantageous alliance outcomes, alliance partners have to adequately navigate these manifestations of interdependence.[80]

*Trade-offs* are situational challenges of having to choose from two or more competing options. For instance, do you prioritize investments in your firm, or in an alliance in which it participates? Do you exchange data or knowledge with your alliance partner, which would benefit the alliance but at the same time might jeopardize the firm's knowledge-based competitive advantage, or do you constrain and limit this exchange? Do you formalize or standardize roles, procedures and processes in the cooperation, or do you stick to a more informal structure? Do you allocate more resources to one alliance goal, or to another? *Tensions*, which may arise from a trade-off that is left unresolved, can refer to disagreements among alliance partners or to feelings of stress that their managers experience when facing persistence of contradictory choices over time. When alliance partners pull in opposite directions of a persistent trade-off, conflicts may arise. Finally, *frictions* refer to when certain factors or dynamics provide obstacles to achieving an alliance's goals – for instance, resistance by the corporate parent of a subsidiary that participates in the alliance, a clear shift in a partner's priorities, or an adverse event such as a technical breakdown or a strike at the location of one of the partner firms. The extent to which there are trade-offs, tensions and frictions in a strategic alliance often depends on what outcomes are pursued.[81]

What are the positive and negative aspects of trade-offs, tensions, and frictions in alliances? How may these manifestations of interdependence change during the post-formation phase, and how should managers adapt? What if managers experience interdependence differently? These are relevant questions that scholars are still examining.[82]

Building on prior research[83], one can distinguish four dimensions of alliance management: *managing alliance goals or objectives* (which revolves around setting the direction the alliance takes), *managing motivation of the alliance partners* (getting these partners and their people to agree to go in the set direction), *managing across the alliance* (coordinating the interdependent activities of the alliance partners, such as resource allocations), and *managing up and down the alliance* (making and communicating decisions on how work is organized within the alliance). Over the course of an alliance, changes can occur along each of these dimensions, depending on choices managers make, some of which are listed in Table 13.4.[84]

One of these choices concerns the organizational structure of the alliance – that is, the extent of formalization and standardization of roles, procedures, and processes of cooperation, which can increase or decrease over time. For instance, at the time the Star Alliance (see the opening case) was created, there was no formal structure in place. United Airlines' chairman was quoted as saying that the alliance was 'bound together only by four pages of governance, with no formal ownership ties'[85]. In 2019, however, the Star Alliance became

**TABLE 13.4**  Choices and dynamics in relation to types of alliance characteristics

| Characteristics | Choices | Dynamics |
| --- | --- | --- |
| *Goal (or mission)* | What is the goal or mission of our alliance? (What to achieve together?) | Adding a new goal, changing the priority ranking of existing goals, or dropping, modifying or replacing a goal. |
| *Decision-making control* | What is the locus of the interorganizational decision-making? For instance, do we rely on group-based decisions of lower (e.g., operational) level teams that report to corporate executives, or are most decisions made by these executives themselves? | Increasing lower-level team control or increasing top management control. |
| *Organizational structure* | To what extent do we formalize and standardize roles, procedures and processes in our collaboration? | New elements in the structure or more structuration |
| *Interaction style* | Is our interaction style primarily cooperative (as manifested in a high degree of open information sharing without hidden agendas) or primarily competitive (as manifested by a more constrained and limited inter-partner exchange of information)? | From a cooperative to a (more) competitive interaction style or vice versa. |
| *Contract frame* | To what extent is there a focus on transactional approaches to managing our collaboration (such as formal rules, procedures and contractual agreements) versus a focus on relational approaches (socio-psychological agreements, such as mutual adjustment and joint problem solving, which are embedded in an atmosphere of inter-partner trust)? | Increasing reliance on a relational approach or an increasing reliance on a transactional approach. |
| *Actor composition* | Which organizational actors (i.e., firms or other organizations) and which persons (i.e., executives or others) are (or should be) involved? | Adding a new actor or excluding or replacing an existing actor. |

Source: adapted from Majchrzak et al. (2015)

a corporation under German law, headquartered in Frankfurt Airport in Germany.[86] The more the coordination of activities carried out as part of an alliance relies on formal rules, procedures and processes, the more bureaucratic its structure.

The *interaction style* in an alliance can range from competitive to cooperative. An increased emphasis on a cooperative interaction style is manifested in a higher degree of open information sharing or knowledge exchange between alliance partners without hidden agendas[87], whereas a change in opposite direction implies more of a constrained and limited exchange of information and knowledge.[88] Unwanted leakage of intellectual capital can largely be prevented by informing employees at all levels about what information and knowledge are off-limits to a firm's alliance partners and monitor what each of them requests and receives.[89] Multiple interaction style dynamics can occur in parallel at different organizational levels.[90] The extent to which alliance partners (dis)trust each other during the formation phase often leaves a strong imprint on how they interact during the post-formation phase and on the extent to which these interactions rely on a contract frame dominated by transactional rather than relational elements.[91]

The *contract frame* of an alliance, yet another type of alliance characteristic that can change over the course of time[92], denotes the degree to which partners rely on formal (transactional) versus informal (relational) mechanisms in managing their relationship.[93] Transactional mechanisms include formal contractual agreements and other legal matters, such as intellectual property provisions, as well as formal rules and procedures, such as performance standards, standard operating procedures and dispute resolution procedures.[94] Relational mechanisms, in contrast, denote social-psychological types of contracts[95] that translate into mutual adjustment, joint problem solving or other types of joint action.[96] These relational mechanisms are typically embedded in an atmosphere of inter-partner trust, whereas transactional mechanisms do not require such trust.

## CLOSING CASE
### Cooperation in a world of circular pipeline supplies[97]

Source: © uirrii (2023) / Shutterstock.

The port of Rotterdam is home to one of the most highly integrated chlorine and derivates clusters in the world. The heart of this cluster is formed by industrial plants of four multinational firms, which operate in very different product markets: Hexion, Huntsman, Nobian, and Shin-Etsu. The cluster is built around the chlorine production operations of Nobian, which supplies chlorine to nearby derivatives-producing plants of the three other firms by pipelines. The chlorine that Huntsman uses to produce methylene diphenyl isocyanate (MDI) is returned partly to Nobian in the form of hydrogen chloride (HCl). Nobian, in turn, supplies the HCl to Shin-Etsu, where it is used as feedstock for its production of ethylene dichloride (EDC), vinyl chloride monomer (VCM) and polyvinyl chloride (PVC).

*(Continued)*

In addition to that, Huntsman supplies HCl to Shin-Etsu. Shin-Etsu supplies EDC, oxy-waste and wastewater to Nobian. Meanwhile, Hexion uses HCl, which it receives (and later transfers back) by pipeline from Shin-Etsu, and chlorine, which it receives from Nobian, to produce of a range of epoxy resins.

The synergistic coupling of production processes of the entities in this cluster enables them to achieve competitive levels of resource efficiency as residual chemical elements circulate across organizational boundaries. Moreover, their cooperation, embedded in relatively long-term contracts, enables them to avoid undesirable above-ground trans-portation of chlorine and HCl, which have corrosive properties. At the flipside, however, their tight operational quasi-integration has resulted in high levels of interdependence. Relatively small disturbances in any of the plants in the cluster can already cause a shutdown of the production of all four firms for up to multiple days. Because of safety reasons, none of the firms can store chlorine or HCl in large amounts, due to which buffering possibilities – to mitigate against fluctuations in usage or supply – are very limited. How to manage this?

In between 2000 and 2010, the firms relied on bilateral arrangements and mainly stuck to formal contractual terms as part of these arrangements. Operational-level personnel had some informal contact, but only little operational information and knowledge was exchanged as this was against corporate policies. Each of the firms used their own distinct performance indicators and blamed one another for being the biggest efficiency killer when operational performance was below expectations, which happened relatively frequently. Catalyzed by the occurrence of a series of events that caused unacceptable high levels of downtime, three of the four ecosystem partners decided to jointly undertake a project, in which also an independent consultant was involved, to identify the root causes of their operating losses. The project led to better insights in each other's processes and operational interdependen-cies. Based on these new insights, they started to use a newly developed joint performance indicator as of 2011, the monitored outcomes of which were structurally discussed from then on in monthly interorganizational meetings between plant managers and lower-level staff. Hexion, which of all four firms had the least effect on the cluster's performance, only became more involved in the intensified cluster cooperation after some years. Fast forward to 2020 and the firms in the cluster not only keep on using the joint performance indicator and having monthly meetings, but have also started discussing options for joint investments to further improve the cluster's performance, which has improved substantially since 2010.

## Questions

1. How would you describe the cooperation dynamics in this integrated chlorine and derivates cluster in between 2000 and 2020?
2. To what extent do you consider it understandable that the four firms in this cluster are cautious with exchanging operational information and knowledge? What could have been the role of the independent consultant in this regard?
3. What lessons can be drawn from this case regarding how to deal with high levels of interorganizational interdependence?

# Summary

- Firms are typically embedded in networks of cooperative relationships with other organizations in their market environment. These interorganizational relationships influence firms' ability to achieve their business- and corporate-level goals.
- An alliance is an enduring, voluntary arrangement in which two or more organizations, which retain their legal independence and are not bound by common ownership, work together in an effort to accomplish mutually beneficial outcomes.
- Alliances can broadly be divided into four different categories: equity alliances, contractual alliances, associational alliances, and collusive alliances.
- An equity alliance constitutes a form of interorganizational arrangement that is characterized by shared equity participation, which can either imply the formation of a separate, joint owned entity, or direct minority equity investments.
- A contractual alliance constitutes a type of arrangement in which entities work together on the basis of a long-term vertical or horizontal contractual agreement or a licensing agreement.
- An associational alliance is formed by organizations that intentionally combine, transfer or align resources or coordinate their actions without any contractual obligation or equity participation.
- Collusion implies that two or more firms cooperate with the intention of increasing prices above fully-competitive levels, restricting their collective output, or limiting customers' knowledge about a certain product to the firms' advantage.
- Coopetition takes place when competing firms choose to engage in an alliance.
- Entering an alliance may allow firms to, among other things, better manage risks and uncertainties, overcome funding limitations, improve economies of scale, gain access to complementary resources or new markets, close certain skill gaps, increase lobbying power, and speed up market entry or product development.
- Complementarity, compatibility, commitment, and trustworthiness are important traits to look for when selecting an alliance partner.
- The success of alliances once they are up and running is often determined to an important degree by how the alliance partners manage the interdependencies, uncertainties and operational complexities that exist and arise in these alliances during the post-formation phase.

# Review questions

1. What are the differences between a joint venture and a cooperative, between a vertical and a horizontal contractual alliance, and between a confederation and a community of practice?
2. Why is it that all franchising agreements are licensing agreements, but not all licensing agreements include franchising?
3. What are ways in which firms can simultaneously cooperate and compete with each other?
4. What factors contribute to the relatively high failure rate of alliances?

# Discussion questions

1. Does the importance of strategic alliances for enhancing a firm's performance increase when its external environment becomes more volatile, uncertain, complex, and ambiguous?
2. To what extent do the choices that are made during the alliance formation stage determine successful outcomes in the subsequent post-formation stage?
3. Think about your criteria when choosing a life partner – to what extent do these criteria differ from the criteria that you would use when choosing a strategic alliance partner?

## EXPERIENTIAL EXERCISES

1. Choose a firm that is based in your country and provide an overview of its strategic alliances (if any). What is the most prevalent alliance category and type (see Table 13.1)?
2. Search the internet for news on an alliance that was terminated. What was the main reason?

# Further reading

Dyer, J.H., Singh, H. and Hesterly, W.S. (2018) 'The relational view revisited: A dynamic perspective on value creation and value capture', *Strategic Management Journal*, 39: 3140–62.

Klijn, E., Reuer, J.J., Volberda, H.W. and Van den Bosch, F.A.J. (2019) 'Ex-post governance in joint ventures: Determinants of monitoring by JV boards of directors', *Long Range Planning*, 52: 72–85.

Majchrzak, A., Jarvenpaa, S.L. and Bagherzadeh, M. (2015) 'A review of interorganizational collaboration dynamics', *Journal of Management*, 41: 1338–60.

Ryan-Charleton, T., Gnyawali, D.R. and Oliveira, N. (2022) 'Strategic alliance outcomes: Consolidation and new directions', *Academy of Management Annals*, 16 (2): 719–58.

Schilke, O. and Lumineau, F. (2018) 'The double-edged effect of contracts on alliance performance', *Journal of Management*, 44: 2827–58.

# Endnotes (references)

1. Ionides, N. (2004) 'IATA pushes e-ticketing', *FlightGlobal*, June 15. www.flightglobal.com/iata-pushes-e-ticketing/54939.article (accessed June 27, 2023).
2. Gomes-Casseres, B. and Judd, J. (2021a) *Note on the Global Airline Industry in 2020.* London, Ontario: Ivey Publishing.
3. Ariño, A. and Riehl, F. (2004) 'Airline industry alliances in 2004: Improving performance in the beleaguered airline industry', *HBR case* IES115. Barcelona: IESE.
4. Gomes-Casseres, B. and Judd, J. (2021b) *Star Alliance in 2020.* London, Ontario: Ivey Publishing; McDonald, J.B. (2005) 'Antitrust for airlines', *United States Department of Justice,* November 3. www.justice.gov/atr/speech/antitrust-airlines (accessed June 27, 2023).

5. Ariño and Riehl (2004); Gomes-Casseres and Judd (2021b)

6. Gomes-Casseres and Judd (2021b)

7. IATA (2022) 'Home'. https://web.archive.org/web/20230627083233/https://www.iata.org (accessed June 27, 2023).

8. Barratt, L. (2020) 'Documents reveal airline industry plan for tax breaks, subsidies and voucher refunds', *Unearthed,* April 7. https://unearthed.greenpeace.org/2020/04/07/coronavirus-airlines-lobby-for-tax-breaks-subsidies-vouchers-passenger-refunds (accessed June 27, 2023).

9. Gomes-Casseres and Judd (2021b)

10. e.g., Ebers, M. (ed.) (1997) *The Formation of Inter-organizational Networks.* Oxford: Oxford University Press; Gulati, R. (1998) 'Alliances and networks', *Strategic Management Journal*, 19: 293–317; Gulati, R., Nohria, N. and Zaheer, A. (2000) 'Strategic networks', *Strategic Management Journal*, 21: 203–15; Provan, K.G., Fish, A. and Sydow, J. (2007) 'Interorganizational networks at the network level: A review of the empirical literature on whole networks', *Journal of Management*, 33: 479–516; Shipilov A. and Gawer, A. (2020) 'Integrating research on interorganizational networks and ecosystems', *Academy of Management Annals*, 14: 92–121.

11. Gomes-Casseres, B. (1994) 'Group versus group: How alliance networks compete', *Harvard Business Review*, July/August: 62–74; Lazzarini, S.G. (2007) 'The impact of membership in competing alliance constellations: Evidence on the operational performance of global airlines', *Strategic Management Journal*, 28: 345–67.

12. Child, J., Faulkner, D., Tallman, S. and Hsieh, L. (2019) *Cooperative Strategy: Managing Alliances and Networks.* Oxford: Oxford University Press.

13. Contractor, F.J. and Lorange, P. (2002) 'The growth of alliances in the knowledge-based economy', in F.J. Contractor and P. Lorange (eds), *Cooperated Strategies and Alliances.* Kidlington: Elsevier, 3–24.

14. Hardy, C., Phillips, N. and Lawrence, T.B. (2003) 'Resources, knowledge and influence: The organizational effects of interorganizational collaboration', *Journal of Management Studies*, 40: 321–47; Powell, W.W. (1990) 'Neither market nor hierarchy: Network forms of organization', *Research in Organizational Behavior*, 12: 295–336.

15. Richards, M. and Indro, D.C. (2006) 'Government as an alliance partner', in A. Ariño and J.J. Reuer (eds), *Strategic Alliances: Governance and Contracts.* London: Palgrave MacMillan, 53–66.

16. e.g., Das, T.K. and Teng, B. (2002) 'Alliance constellations: A social exchange perspective', *Academy of Management Review*, 27: 445–56.

17. Heimeriks, K.H., Klijn, E. and Reuer, J.J. (2009) 'Building capabilities for alliance portfolios', *Long Range Planning*, 42 (1): 96–114; Hoffmann, W.H. (2005) 'How to manage a portfolio of alliances', *Long Range Planning*, 38: 121–43.

18. Pisano, G.P. (1989) 'Using equity participation to support exchange: Evidence from the biotechnology industry', *Journal of Law, Economics and Organization*, 5 (1): 109–26.

19. Geringer, J.M. and Hebert, L. (1989) 'Control and performance of international joint ventures', *Journal of International Business*, 20 (2): 97–101.

20. Pisano (1989)

21. Lund, M. (2013) *Cooperative Equity and Ownership: An Introduction.* Madison, WI: University of Wisconsin Center for Cooperatives.

22. Ohnsman, A. (2021) 'Panasonic, Tesla's oldest industrial partner, said to have sold off its entire Tesla stake', *Forbes,* June 24. www.forbes.com/sites/alanohnsman/2021/06/24/panasonic-sells-entire-tesla-stake (accessed June 23, 2023).

23. Dyer, J.H. (1996) 'Does governance matter? Keiretsu alliances and asset specificity as sources of Japanese competitive advantage', *Organization Science*, 7: 649–66.

24. Dunseith, B. (2017) 'Joint ventures in India: Learning from McDonald's experience', *India Briefing,* September 14. www.india-briefing.com/news/joint-ventures-india-learning-mcdonalds-experience-15206.html (accessed June 27, 2022); Singh, R. (2019) 'McDonald's buys out estranged JV partner's stake in CPRL', *Forbes India,* May 9. www.forbesindia.com/article/special/mcdonalds-buys-out-estranged-jv-partners-stake-in-cprl/53471/1 (accessed June 27, 2023); The Economic Times (2019) 'Vikram Bakshi is finally out, and McDonald's India is lovin' it', May 14. https://economictimes.indiatimes.com/industry/services/hotels-/-restaurants/vikram-bakshi-is-finally-out-and-mcdonalds-india-is-lovin-it/articleshow/69309704.cms (accessed June 27, 2023).

25. De Man, A.P. (2012) *Alliances: An Executive Guide to Designing Successful Strategic Partnerships.* Chichester: Wiley.

26. Hill, C.W. and Jones, G.R. (1998) *Strategic Management Theory: An Integrated Approach.* Boston, MA: Houghton Mifflin.

27. Raddats, C., Kowalkowski, C., Benedettini, O., Burton, J. and Gebauer, H. (2019) 'Servitization: A contemporary thematic review of four major research streams', *Industrial Marketing Management,* 83: 207–23.

28. Wärtsilä (2017) 'Agreement optimizes fleet lifecycle efficiency – case study: Carnival PBL', Wärtsilä. www.wartsila.com/docs/default-source/services-documents/learning-center/references/wartsila-reference-carnival-pbl.pdf (accessed June 27, 2023).

29. Hill and Jones (1998)

30. Alfen, H. (2010) *Public Private Partnership (PPP) as Part of Infrastructure Management Solutions – A Structural Approach of Delimiting PPP from other Private Sector Participation Models,* 18th CIB World Building Congress. https://www.irbnet.de/daten/iconda/CIB_DC24063.pdf (accessed June 27, 2023); World Bank (2009) *Toolkit for Public-private Partnerships in Roads and Highways,* PPIAF. https://ppiaf.org/sites/ppiaf.org/files/documents/toolkits/highwaytoolkit/6/pdf-version/1-13.pdf (accessed June 27, 2023).

31. Murovec, N. and Kavaš, D. (2021) *Public-private Cooperation in Cultural Heritage Revitalization,* EU Interreg Central Europe. https://programme2014-20.interreg-central.eu/Content.Node/D.T1.2.3-PPC.pdf (accessed June 12, 2023).

32. Alfen (2010); Dong, Z., Wang, M. and Yang, X. (2016) 'Comparative study of China and USA public private partnerships in public transportation', *Journal of Modern Transportation,* 24: 215–23.

33. McGee, J.E. and Dowling, M.J. (1994) 'Using R&D cooperative arrangements to leverage managerial experience: A study of technology-intensive new ventures', *Journal of Business Venturing,* 9: 33–48.

34. FindLaw (1997) 'Co-production agreement – Walt Disney Pictures and Television and Pixar', *FindLaw,* February 24. https://corporate.findlaw.com/contracts/operations/co-production-agreement-walt-disney-pictures-and-television-and.html (accessed June 27, 2023); The Walt Disney Company (2006) 'Disney to acquire Pixar', *The Walt Disney Company,* January 24. https://thewaltdisneycompany.com/disney-to-acquire-pixar (accessed June 27, 2023).

35. Glover, S.I. and Wasserman, C.M. (2003) *Partnerships, Joint Ventures and Strategic Alliances.* New York, NY: Law Journal Press.

36. Pinello, C., Picone, P.M. and Li Destri, A.M. (2022) 'Co-branding research: Where we are and where we could go from here', *European Journal of Marketing,* 56: 584–621.

37. De Man (2012)

38. Glaister, K.W. and Buckley P.J. (1994) 'UK international joint ventures: An analysis of patterns of activity and distribution', *British Journal of Management,* 5: 33–51.

39. Adidas (2022) 'Adidas terminates partnership with Ye immediately', press release October 25. www.adidas-group.com/en/media/news-archive/press-releases/2022/adidas-terminates-partnership-ye-immediately(accessed June 27, 2023); Green, D. (2017) 'How Adidas finally became cool again', *Business Insider,* March 15. www.businessinsider.com/how-adidas-finally-became-cool-again-2017-3 (accessed June 27, 2023); Jhiaile (2021) 'These music artists have collaborated with adidas', *Sneakerjagers,* September 10. www.sneakerjagers.com/en/n/these-music-artists-have-collaborated-with-adidas/25767 (accessed June 27, 2023); Pisani, N. and Lupoi, O. (2020) 'Adidas: How to keep running fast in a post-COVID-19 world?', IMD-7-2222 case study. https://store.hbr.org/product/adidas-how-to-keep-running-fast-in-a-post-covid-19-world/IM1064 (accessed June 27, 2023).

40. O'Malley Greenburg, Z. (2020) 'Kanye West is now officially a billionaire', *Forbes,* April 24. www.forbes.com/sites/zackomalleygreenburg/2020/04/24/kanye-west-is-now-officially-a-billionaireand-he-really-wants-the-world-to-know (accessed June 27, 2023).

41. Wenger, E.C. and Snyder, W.M. (2000) 'Communities of practice: The organizational frontier', *Harvard Business Review*, Jan/Feb: 139–45.

42. European Commission (2017) *Foster a Community of Good Practice,* European Commission. https://web.archive.org/web/20220120081704/https://ec.europa.eu/regional_policy/sources/good_practices/GP_fiche_02.pdf (accessed June 27, 2023).

43. Axelrod, R., Mitchell, W., Thomas, R.E., Bennett, D.S. and Bruderer, E. (1995) 'Coalition formation in standard-setting alliances', *Management Science*, 41: 1493–508.

44. VNO-NCW (2022) 'VNO-NCW in brief', *VNO-NCW.* www.vno-ncw.nl/over-vno-ncw/english (accessed June 27, 2023).

45. Gulati, R., Puranam, P. and Tushman, M. (2012) 'Meta-organization design: Rethinking design in interorganizational and community contexts', *Strategic Management Journal*, 33: 571–86; Reveley, J. and Ville, S. (2010) 'Enhancing industry association theory: A comparative business history contribution', *Journal of Management Studies*, 47: 837–58.

46. Ahrne, G. and Brunsson, N. (2005) 'Organizations and meta-organizations', *Scandinavian Journal of Management*, 21: 429–49; Brunsson, N., Rasche, A. and Seidl, D. (2012) 'The dynamics of standardization: Three perspectives on standards in Organization Studies', *Organization Studies*, 33: 613–32; Oliver, C. (1990) 'Determinants of interorganizational relationships: Integration and future directions', *Academy of Management Review*, 15: 241–65.

47. König, A., Schulte, M. and Enders, A. (2012) 'Inertia in response to non-paradigmatic change: The case of meta-organizations', *Research Policy*, 41: 1325–43; Sako, M. (1996) 'Suppliers' associations in the Japanese automobile industry: Collective action for technology diffusion', *Cambridge Journal of Economics*, 20: 651–71.

48. Gulati et al. (2012)

49. Marshall, R.C., Marx, L.M. and Raiff, M.E. (2008) 'Cartel price announcement: The vitamins industry', *International Journal of Industrial Organization*, 26: 762–802; Sorenson, T.L. (2007) 'Credible collusion in multimarket oligopoly', *Managerial and Decision Economics*, 28: 115–28.

50. D'Aspremont, C., Dos Santos Ferreira, R. and Gérard-Varet, L. (2007) 'Competition for market share or for market size: Oligopolistic equilibria with varying competitive toughness', *International Economic Review*, 48: 761–84; Rees, R. (1993) 'Tacit collusion', *Oxford Review of Economic Policy*, 9 (2): 27–40.

51. Capron, L. and Mitchell, W. (2010) 'Finding the right path', *Harvard Business Review*, 88 (7–8): 102–7.

52. Dyer, J.H., Kale, P. and Singh, H. (2004) 'When to ally and when to acquire', *Harvard Business Review*, 82 (7/8): 108–15.

53. Brandenburger, A.M. and Nalebuff, B.J. (1996) *Co-opetition: A Revolution Mindset that Combines Competition and Cooperation*. New York, NY: Crown.

54. Hamel, G., Doz, Y. and Prahalad, C.K. (1989) 'Collaborate with your competitors – and win', *Harvard Business Review*, 1/2: 133–9.

55. Johnson, K. (2003) 'Air alliances get stronger', *Wall Street Journal,* December 11. www.wsj.com/articles/SB1071089955925043900 (accessed June 27, 2023).

56. Cainarca, G.C., Colombo, M.G. and Mariotti, S. (1992) 'Agreements between firms and the technological life cycle model: Evidence from information technologies', *Research Policy*, 21 (1): 45–62.

57. Volberda, H.W., Morgan, R.E., Reinmoeller, P., Hitt, M.A., Ireland, R.D. and Hoskisson, R.E. (2011) *Strategic Management: Competitiveness and Globalization*. Andover: Cengage.

58. Williams, J.R. (1998) *Renewable Advantage: Crafting Strategy Through Economic Time*. New York, NY: Free Press.

59. Shah, R. and Swaminathan, V. (2008) 'Factors influencing partner selection in strategic alliances: The moderating role of alliance context', *Strategic Management Journal*, 29: 471–94.

60. e.g., Dyer, J.H. and Singh, H. (1998) 'The relational view: Cooperative strategy and sources of interorganizational competitive advantage', *Academy of Management Review*, 23 (4): 660–79; Mowery, D., Oxley, J. and Silverman, B. (1996) 'Strategic alliances and interfirm knowledge transfer', *Strategic Management Journal*, 17 (Winter Special Issue): 77–91.

61. e.g., Mitsuhashi, H. and Greve, H.R. (2017) 'A matching theory of alliance formation and organizational success: Complementarity and compatibility', *Academy of Management Journal*, 52 (5): 975–95.

62. Gundlach, G., Achrol, R. and Mentzer, J. (1995) 'The structure of commitment in exchange', *Journal of Marketing*, 59 (1): 78–92.

63. Rothaermel, F.T. and Boeker, W. (2008) 'Old technology meets new technology: Complementarities, similarities and alliance formation', *Strategic Management Journal*, 29: 47–77.

64. Kale, P. and Singh, H. (2009) 'Managing strategic alliances: What do we know now, and where do we go from here?', *Academy of Management Perspectives*, 23 (3): 45–62.

65. Das, T.K. and Teng, B.-S. (2000) 'a resource-based theory of strategic alliances', *Journal of Management*, 26 (1): 31–61.

66. Castañer, X. and Oliveira, N. (2020) 'Collaboration, coordination, and cooperation among organizations: Establishing the distinctive meanings of these terms through a systematic literature review', *Journal of Management*, 46 (6): 965–1001; Lioukas, C.S. and Reuer, J.J. (2020) 'Choosing between safeguards: Scope and governance decisions in R&D alliances', *Journal of Management*, 46 (3): 359–84.

67. Gulati, R., Lavie, D. and Singh, H. (2009) 'The nature of partnering experience and the gains from alliances', *Strategic Management Journal*, 30 (11): 1213–33; Lioukas and Reuer (2020).

68. Barney, J.B. and Hansen, M.H. (1994) 'Trustworthiness as a source of competitive advantage', *Strategic Management Journal*, 15: 175–90.

69. Ariño, A. and Ring, P.S. (2010) 'The role of fairness in alliance formation', *Strategic Management Journal*, 31 (10): 1054–87.

70. Hoenig, D. and Henkel, J. (2015) 'Quality signals? The role of patents, alliances, and team experience in venture capital financing', *Research Policy*, 44 (5): 1049–64; Robson, M.J., Katsikeas, C.S. and Bello, D.C. (2008) 'Drivers and performance outcomes of trust in international strategic alliances: The role of organizational complexity', *Organization Science*, 19 (4): 647–65.

71. Das, T.K. and Teng, B.-S. (2001) 'Trust, control, and risk in strategic alliances: An integrated framework', *Organization Studies*, 22 (2): 251–83.

72. Gulati, R. (1995) 'Social structure and alliance formation patterns: A longitudinal analysis', *Administrative Science Quarterly*, 40 (4): 619–52.

73. Hubbard, T.D., Pollock, T.G., Pfarrer, M.D. and Rindova, V.P. (2018) 'Safe bets or hot hands? How status and celebrity influence strategic alliance formations by newly public firms', *Academy of Management Journal*, 61 (5): 1976–99; Stern, I., Dukerich, J.M. and Zajac, E. (2014) 'Unmixed signals: How reputation and status affect alliance formation', *Strategic Management Journal*, 35 (4): 512–31.

74. Mukherjee, D., Gaur, A.S., Gaur, S.S. and Schmid, F. (2013) 'External and internal influences on R&D alliance formation: Evidence from German SMEs', *Journal of Business Research*, 66 (11): 2178–85.

75. Castañer and Oliveira (2020); Das and Teng (2001); Gulati, R. and Singh, H. (1998) 'The architecture of cooperation: Managing coordination costs and appropriation concerns in strategic alliances', *Administrative Science Quarterly*, 43 (4): 781–814.

76. Hardy et al. (2003); Klijn, E., Reuer, J.J., Volberda, H.W. and Van den Bosch, F.A.J. (2019), 'Ex-post governance in joint ventures: Determinants of monitoring by JV boards of directors', *Long Range Planning*, 52: 72–85.

77. Draulans, J.A.J., De Man, A.P. and Volberda, H.W. (2003) 'Building alliance capability: Management techniques for superior alliance performance', *Long Range Planning*, 36 (2): 151–66; Dyer and Singh (1998); Schreiner, M., Kale, P. and Corsten, D. (2009) 'What really is alliance management capability and how does it impact alliance outcomes and success?', *Strategic Management Journal*, 30: 1395–419.

78. Hughes, J. and Weiss, J. (2007) 'Simple rules for making alliances work', *Harvard Business Review*, 85: 122–31.

79. Puranam, P., Raveendran, M. and Knudsen, T. (2012) 'Organization design: The epistemic interdependence perspective', *Academy of Management Review*, 37: 419–40; Raveendran, M., Silvestri, L. and Gulati, R. (2020) 'The role of interdependence in the micro-foundations of organization design: Task, goal, and knowledge interdependence', *Academy of Management Annals*, 14: 828–68.

80. Hardy et al. (2003); Ryan-Charleton, T., Gnyawali, D.R. and Oliveira, N. (2022) 'Strategic alliance outcomes: Consolidation and new directions', *Academy of Management Annals*, 16 (2): 719–58; Seidl, D. and Werle, F. (2018) 'Inter-organizational sensemaking in the face of strategic meta-problems: Requisite variety and dynamics of participation', *Strategic Management Journal*, 39: 830–58.

81. Ryan-Charleton et al. (2022)

82. Ryan-Charleton et al. (2022)

83. Birkinshaw, J. (2010) *Reinventing Management: Smarter Choices for Getting Work Done*. Chichester: Wiley; Reuer, J.J., Klijn, E., Van den Bosch, F.A.J. and Volberda, H.W. (2011), 'Bringing corporate governance to international joint ventures', *Global Strategy Journal*, 1 (1): 54–66.

84. Majchrzak, A., Jarvenpaa, S.L. and Bagherzadeh, M. (2015) 'A review of interorganizational collaboration dynamics', *Journal of Management*, 41: 1338–60.

85. Jasper, C. (1999) 'Rising Star', *FlightGlobal*, May 18. www.flightglobal.com/rising-star/26260.article (accessed June 27, 2023).

86. Gomes-Casseres and Judd (2021b)

87. e.g., Faems, D., Janssens, M., Madhok, A. and Van Looy, B. (2008) 'Toward an integrative perspective on alliance governance: Connecting contract design, trust dynamics, and contract application', *Academy of Management Journal*, 51: 1053–78.

88. e.g., Ness, H. (2009) 'Governance, negotiations, and alliance dynamics: Explaining the evolution of relational practice', *Journal of Management Studies*, 46: 451–80.

89. Hamel et al. (1989)

90. e.g., Büchel, B. (2000) 'Framework of joint venture development: Theory-building through qualitative research', *Journal of Management Studies*, 37: 637–61.

91. Klijn, E., Reuer, J.J., Van den Bosch, F.A.J. and Volberda, H.W. (2013) 'Performance implications of IJV boards: A contingency perspective', *Journal of Management Studies*, 50 (7): 1245–6; Vlaar, P.W.L., Van den Bosch, F.A.J. and Volberda, H.W. (2007) 'On the evolution of trust, distrust, and formal coordination and control in interorganizational relationships: Toward an integrative framework', *Group & Organization Management*, 32: 407–29.

92. Majchrzak et al. (2015)

93. e.g., Dyer & Singh (1998); Liu, Y., Li, Y., Shi, L.H. and Liu, T. (2017) 'Knowledge transfer in buyer-supplier relationships: The role of transactional and relational governance mechanisms', *Journal of Business Research*, 78: 285–93; Mahapatra, S.K., Narasimhan, R. and Barbieri, P. (2010) 'Strategic interdependence, governance effectiveness and supplier performance: A dyadic case study investigation and theory development', *Journal of Operations Management*, 28: 537–52; Ring, P.S. and Van de Ven, A.H. (1992) 'Structuring cooperative relationships between organizations', *Strategic Management Journal*, 13: 483–98.

94. e.g., Gulati and Singh (1998); Vlaar et al. (2007)

95. Ring and Van De Ven (1994)

96. Hilbolling, S., Deken, F., Berends, H. and Tuertscher, P. (2022) 'Process-based temporal coordination in multiparty collaboration for societal challenges', *Strategic Organization*, 20 (1): 135–63; Huemer, L. (2006) 'Supply management: Value creation, coordination and positioning in supply relationships', *Long Range Planning*, 39: 133–53; Mesquita, L.F. and Brush, T.H. (2008) 'Untangling safeguard and production coordination effects in long-term buyer-supplier relationships', *Academy of Management Journal*, 51: 785–807; Newell, S., Goussevskaia, A., Swan, J., Bresnen, M. and Obembe, A. (2008) 'Interdependencies in complex project ecologies: The case of biomedical innovation', *Long Range Planning*, 41: 33–54.

97. Authors' own research in combination with Van Wassenhove, L.N., Lebreton, B. and Letizia, P. (2007) *A Paradigm Shift: Supply Chain Collaboration and Competition in and Between Europe's Chemical Clusters*. Rotterdam: Erasmus School of Economics; and Wahyuni, S., Ghauri, P. and Karsten, L. (2007) 'Managing international strategic alliance relationships', *Thunderbird International Business Review*, 49 (6): 671–87.

# Key terms

**Alliance** – an enduring, voluntary cooperative arrangement between legally independent organizational entities aimed at accomplishing mutually beneficial outcomes

**Associational alliance** – a type of non-collusive arrangement in which entities work together without any contractual obligation or equity participation

**Collusion** – a cooperative arrangement between firms aimed to increase prices above fully competitive levels, restrict their collective output, or limit customers' knowledge about a certain product to the firms' advantage

**Contractual alliance** – a type of arrangement in which entities work together on the basis of a long-term vertical or horizontal contractual agreement or a licensing agreement

**Cooperative** – an equity-based alliance in which entities collaborate as members of a separate entity that they collectively own and run with the purpose of providing services to each of the members, who have limited liability and contribute equally to equity capital

**Cooperative strategy** – the determination of how to achieve organizational goals by working together with external entities

**Coopetition** – a cooperative arrangement between business competitors

**Equity alliance** – an interorganizational cooperative arrangement characterized by shared equity participation

**Equity joint venture** (or **joint venture**) – a separate, independently operating economic entity that is jointly owned by two or more organizations

**Franchising agreement** – a special type of licensing agreement where a franchisor grants a franchisee the right to use a certain franchise formula that is owned by the franchisor

**Horizontal contractual alliance** – a contractual alliance between firms that operate at the same or a similar stage of the supply or value chain

**Licensing agreement** – a contractual alliance where a licensor authorizes a licensee to use and earn revenue from one or more assets of the licensor in exchange for a negotiated payment

**Minority equity participation** – non-controlling ownership in another organization

**Vertical contractual alliance** – a contractual alliance between a firm and its distributor or supplier

# Diagnostic Part III
## CHOOSEWELL

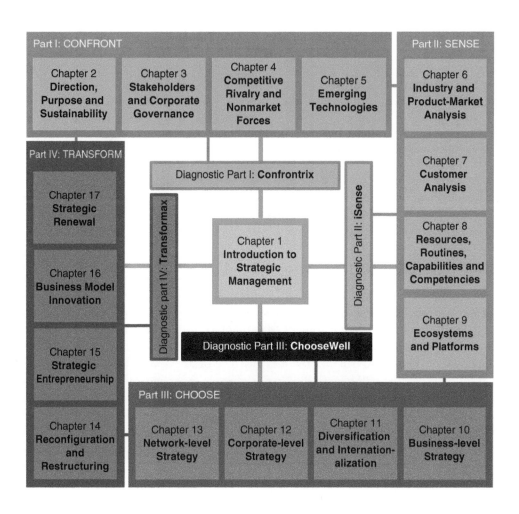

Part I: CONFRONT

Chapter 2
**Direction, Purpose and Sustainability**

Chapter 3
**Stakeholders and Corporate Governance**

Chapter 4
**Competitive Rivalry and Nonmarket Forces**

Chapter 5
**Emerging Technologies**

Part II: SENSE

Chapter 6
**Industry and Product-Market Analysis**

Part IV: TRANSFORM

Diagnostic Part I: **Confrontrix**

Chapter 17
**Strategic Renewal**

Diagnostic part IV: **Transformax**

Chapter 1
**Introduction to Strategic Management**

Diagnostic Part II: **iSense**

Chapter 7
**Customer Analysis**

Chapter 16
**Business Model Innovation**

Chapter 8
**Resources, Routines, Capabilities and Competencies**

Chapter 15
**Strategic Entrepreneurship**

Diagnostic Part III: **ChooseWell**

Chapter 9
**Ecosystems and Platforms**

Part III: CHOOSE

Chapter 14
**Reconfiguration and Restructuring**

Chapter 13
**Network-level Strategy**

Chapter 12
**Corporate-level Strategy**

Chapter 11
**Diversification and Internationalization**

Chapter 10
**Business-level Strategy**

# Introduction

This Diagnostic chapter presents different hands-on approaches to undertake a review of a firm's existing portfolio of business activities. Such a corporate-level review can help in choosing which of a firm's existing businesses (if more than one) it should keep, exit from, or reposition, how to prioritize investments among different business units (each of which is responsible for a certain business area, see Chapter 12), whether and where to cross-subsidize business units in a way that generates the most value, whether the firm should enter any new business areas, and how to achieve a balanced portfolio that can generate sufficient profitability in the long term. This chapter presents six *business portfolio matrices* that can be used for these purposes:

- The Growth Share Matrix (or BCG Matrix)
- The Advantage Matrix (or Strategic Environment Matrix)
- The Life-Cycle Matrix (or ADL Matrix)
- The Directional Policy Matrix (or GE/McKinsey Nine-Box Matrix)
- The Market-Activated Corporate Strategy (MACS) Framework
- The Parental Fit Matrix (Ashridge Matrix)

Most business portfolio matrices do not provide a clear sense of whether there are any synergistic linkages between business units other than financial synergies, which is particularly problematic for corporate parents following a dominant synergy management logic (see Chapter 12). Also, most business portfolio matrices ignore possible negative inter-relationships (such as cannibalization effects) between business units. These two strategic blind spots can be reduced by conducting a *better-off test*, which we present in this chapter as well. Furthermore, we present the *ownership test*, which can be conducted to examine whether common ownership of a certain business unit makes more sense than an alternative option, such as an alliance (see Chapter 13).

# Business portfolio frameworks

*Business portfolio matrices*, also known as *portfolio management matrices* or *portfolio planning matrices*, are tools that can be used to support choices regarding how to prioritize the allocation of resources (capital resources in particular) among the different business units in a multibusiness portfolio, whether and where to cross-subsidize, which businesses to keep, divest or reposition, whether to enter any new business area, and how to achieve a balanced portfolio that will benefit the firm as a whole over time. Most business portfolio matrices are two-dimensional grids that consist of four up to 20 or more square grid boxes, each of which implies a certain challenge or implication relevant for corporate-level strategic decision-making. The placement of business units within the grid provides you with an analytic map for choices concerning capital allocation and other strategic matters, such as divestiture (see Chapter 14). These decisions shall be informed at least partly by the position of the business units within the grid(s) of choice. Table C.1 provides a concise overview of the six business portfolio matrices presented in this chapter. Instead of selecting a matrix from this table, you may also design your own, customized matrix.

Along both the horizontal axis and vertical axis of the chosen matrix there can be a single numeric (qualitative) or categorical (qualitative) criterion, but also an aggregate criterion that is based on multiple criteria with a certain scoring model. Each business unit of a multibusiness firm (or, alternatively, each set of business units), drawn as a circle, is placed within one of the grid boxes or in between boxes. The center of the circle indicates the position within the grid. By relating the radius of the circle to a factor of strategic relevance that is not captured by one of the axes, additional insights can be provided that can play a role in weighing trade-offs. For instance, the radius could be proportional to the relative size of the market (in terms of revenues or volumes) in which a business unit has a competitive presence, which allows to indicate its share of this market in the form of a slice (as illustrated in Figure C.5). Alternatively, the radius could represent the proportion of firmwide revenues attributable to each of the business units that is plotted in the matrix, or it could be proportional to a unit's revenues, profitability, value added, or capital (funds) employed relative to the other business units.

**TABLE C.1**  Selection of business portfolio matrices

| Matrix name (and alternative name) | Structure | Horizontal axis (x-axis) *(from left to right)* | Vertical axis (y-axis) *(from bottom to top)* |
|---|---|---|---|
| Growth-Share Matrix (BCG Matrix) | 2x2 matrix | Relative market share (*high, low*) (or another indicator of a unit's competitive strength) | Yearly market growth (*high, low*) (or alternative indicator of market attractiveness) |
| Advantage Matrix (Strategic Environments Matrix) | 2x2 matrix | Possible size of advantage over competitors (*small, large*) | Number of ways to achieve advantages (*many, very few*) |
| Life-Cycle Matrix (ADL Matrix) | 3x4 or 5x4 matrix or extension | Competitive position (*strong, average, weak*) of business unit (alternative: *dominant, strong, favourable, tenable and weak*). | Industry or product-market life-cycle stages (*emergence, growth, maturity, decline*) (optional to include substages) |
| Directional Policy Matrix (GE/ McKinsey Nine-Box Framework) | 3x3 matrix with diagonal line | Competitive position *(strong, average, weak)* or competitive strength (*high, medium, low*) of business unit | Industry or market attractiveness (*high, medium, low*) |
| Market-Activated Corporate Strategy (MACS) Framework | 3x2 matrix | Business unit's value-creation potential as a stand-alone enterprise (*high, medium, low*) | Corporate parent's ability to extract value from the unit, relative to other potential owners (*one of the pack, natural owner*) |
| Parental Fit Matrix (Ashridge Matrix) | 2x2 matrix | Fit between parenting opportunities and parenting characteristics (*low, high*) | Misfit between CSFs of the business unit and parenting characteristics (*low, high*) |

Source: authors; BU = business unit; CSFs = critical success factors; * Competitive strength = competitive position

Instead of placing all the business units of a firm within a business portfolio matrix, you may also choose to do this for only units that are overseen by one or more particular overarching corporate divisions of the firm. Alternatively, if business units oversee multiple (types of) products, each of these (types of) products could be placed in the matrix. In this chapter, however, we focus on business units.

## Growth-Share Matrix

The original *Growth-Share Matrix* (also known as the *BCG Matrix*), developed in 1968 by the founder of the Boston Consulting Group (BCG), plots business units in a four-box framework that is organized along a horizontal axis that indicates the relative market share of each unit and a vertical axis that indicates the growth rate of the market in which it has a competitive presence. The boxes (or 'quadrants') are labelled *star, question mark, pet* (sometimes called *dog*), and *cash cow* (see Figure C.1). It is up to you to decide which percentages of relative market share and market growth are put along the axes and whether a particular percentage is to be considered 'high' or 'low'. Hence, there is a certain degree of subjectivity involved.

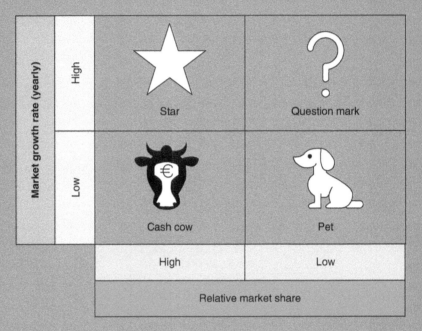

**FIGURE C.1**   Growth Share Matrix

Source: adapted from BCG (2021)

The *market share* of a business unit indicates the percentage of revenues or sales volumes of an entire market that is attributable to this unit. The *relative market share* (horizontal axis), which is another indicator of business unit competitiveness, is the proportion of the market share that is held by this unit (or alternatively its revenues or sales volumes) compared to (that is, divided by) the market share (or revenues or sales volumes) of its largest competitor in that particular market. For instance, when a business unit has a 5% market share while its largest competitor has 25% of the market, then the unit's relative market share would be 0.2.

The yearly *market growth rate* (vertical axis), which is an indicator of market attractiveness, is expressed in percentage terms and is typically assessed by comparing the total revenues or sales volumes in a certain market in the last 12 months compared to the year before. For instance, when the US hard seltzer market grew in revenue from $1 billion in 2019 to $1.8 billion in 2020, the market growth rate was an impressive 80%.

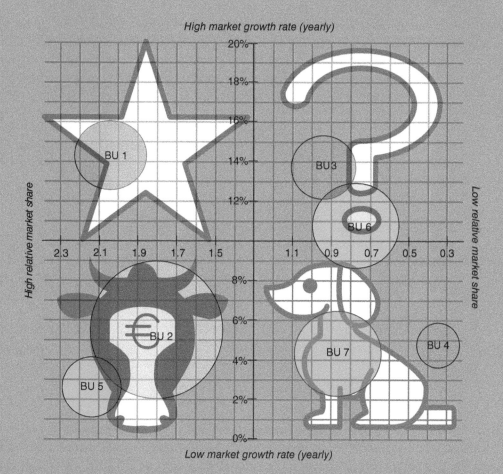

**FIGURE C.2** Growth Share Matrix: Illustrative example

Source: authors based on BCG (2021). Each business unit (BU) is visualized by a circle. The radius of the circle is proportional to its revenues in relation to other business units (but you could also choose another factor of strategic relevance). The colour of the circle (blue or green) indicates the corporate division to which the business unit belongs

An alternative, proxy measure for market growth rate is the average revenue growth of competing firms with a presence in this market.

Figure C.2 illustrates how filling the Growth Share Matrix could look like for a fictitious firm that has seven business units that are divided over two corporate divisions. The size of the circles in this example represents the proportion of firmwide revenues attributable to each of these units, which provides additional insights (but which is not part of the original Growth Share Matrix).

The idea behind the Growth Share Matrix is that business units (ought to) play different roles in a multibusiness portfolio according to their need for growth investment (which depends on industry or market attractiveness) and their ability to generate cash (which depends on their competitiveness), which in turn should determine their financial and strategic targets, and that a balance should be achieved with regard to cash generation and cash consumption.[1] This balance ideally means a mix of high-share, low-growth 'cash cows' (such as BU2 and BU5 in Figure C.2), low-share, high-growth 'question marks' (BU6, BU3) and high-share, high-growth 'stars' (BU1). Cash cows ought to be milked for cash that is redeployed to feed the cash needs of stars (which generate but also use large amounts of cash) and to fuel those question mark businesses that have a clear potential to become stars with a potentially bright future (and otherwise these question marks could be discarded). Both question mark and star business may replace current cash cows later in time, allowing the firm portfolio to generate sufficient profitability in the long term.[2] Low-share, low-growth 'pet' businesses (BU4, BU7) ought to be divested or repositioned, as their current positioning renders it unlikely for these pets to generate significant cash inflows, unless the relatively low cash inflows is compensated by a significant informational value or other strategic advantages (such as synergies) of having these businesses in the corporate portfolio.[3]

This portfolio management technique of rewarding and prioritizing business units based on their relative market share and the market growth rate has received some criticism, that you should take into account. The original Growth Share Matrix was built on the idea that market growth is the main underlying driver of market attractiveness, that relative market share underlies firm competitiveness, and that market leadership leads to sustainably superior returns.[4] However, market growth is not the only indicator of market attractiveness – for instance, especially in an international context, the risk level should also be considered. Also, relative market share does not provide a full picture of how successful business unit currently are and may become. Furthermore, the assumption that market leadership results in sustained superior returns has become less realistic over time as the environments in which most firms compete have become more volatile and uncertain (see in particular Part I of this book). In these rather unpredictable environments, the ability of businesses to adapt to changing environmental demands could be a better predictor of competitive success than their relative market share.[5] According to BCG,[6] in order for the Growth Share Matrix to keep its relevance in this new reality, the horizontal axis needs to be replaced by another (possibly weighted) measure of competitiveness. Also, if the external environment is characterized by a high degree of dynamism and uncertainty, this matrix should be applied with shorter time intervals and with more emphasis on experimentation – for instance, by aiming to raise the number of question marks and by ensuring shorter feedback loops.[7] Also, firms should aim to maximize the information value of their 'pet' businesses to direct further experimentation.[8] Besides this value, 'pets' can also be useful for completing a certain product range, for keeping competitors at bay or for providing a credible market presence.[9]

## Advantage Matrix

The Boston Consulting Group also introduced the *Advantage Matrix* (also known as the *Strategic Environments Matrix*). This business portfolio matrix plots each business unit in a four-quadrant matrix based on the potential size of its advantage over competitors (horizontal axis), which determines its possibilities for gaining economies of scale (cost advantages), and the number of ways through which this advantage can be achieved (vertical axis), which determines possibilities for differentiation. Figure C.3 shows how for a firm with three business units this matrix could look like at a certain point in time.

The idea behind the Advantage Matrix is that the kind of strategic environment in which a certain business unit operates (to be derived from the quadrant in which it is plotted) determines the specific requirements for competitive success,[10] and that corporate

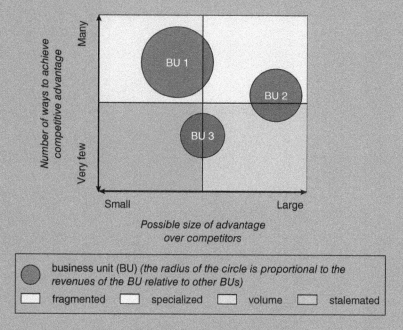

**FIGURE C.3**  Advantage Matrix: Illustrative example

Source: adapted from Lochridge (1981)

executives ought to take these requirements into account when making portfolio choices. In a *fragmented* environment, where there are plenty of opportunities for differentiation but not for gaining economies of scale, a niche-based differentiation focus (see Chapter 10) is preferred. In a *specialized* environment it is feasible to combine differentiation with economies of scale, which means that a unit's competitive success is determined by its ability to be a leader in differentiated products. In a *volume* environment it is all about competing based on a low-cost position that is enabled by a large scale of production. Finally, in a *stalemate* environment a business unit may only be able to compete successfully by locating its production or service activities in countries with favourable factor conditions that allow its labour costs and other costs to be as low as possible.

## Directional Policy Matrix

The *Directional Policy Matrix* (also known as the *GE/McKinsey Nine-Box Matrix* and *GE Business Screen*) was developed in 1971 by McKinsey & Company as part of a consultancy project for General Electric (GE), enabling the latter to better analyze and manage its large business portfolio of roughly 150 business units in a way that suited its requirements.[11] This matrix plots business units in a nine-box framework based on two indicators: the competitive strength of each of these units (horizonal axis) and the attractiveness of the industries or markets in which they compete (vertical axis). A key assumption behind the matrix is that the combination of these two indicators enables you to judge and compare how well each business unit will possibly do in the future.[12] A diagonal line is drawn from bottom left (strong competitive position, low industry attractiveness) to top right (weak competitive position, high industry attractiveness); see Figure C.4.

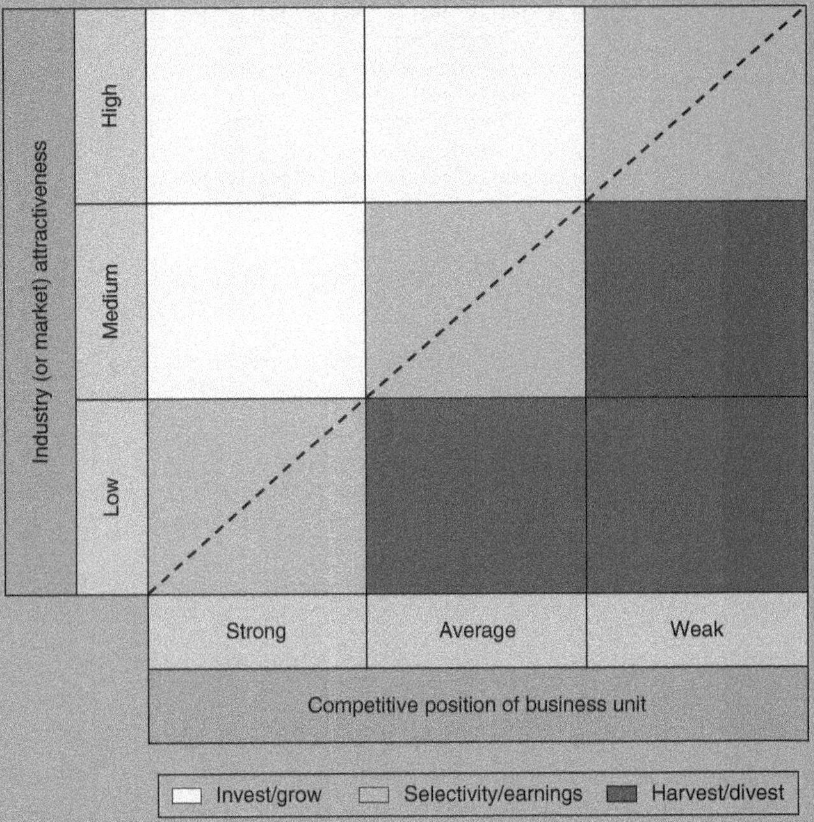


**FIGURE C.4** Directional Policy Matrix

The *competitive position* (that is, the strategic strength) of a business unit is about the degree to which this unit has a powerful advantage over rival firms (or rival business units) and the degree to which this advantage can be sustained over time. Your assessment of this position could for instance be based on (a combination of) proxies for competitiveness such as the absolute or relative market share of business units, the degree to which this market share is growing, the extent to which these units can charge a price premium (an indicator of brand equity strength), and their profitability compared to rivals. The Directional Policy Matrix distinguishes between a strong, average and weak competitive position.

*Industry (or market) attractiveness* is about the ease with which the average firm in this industry is expected to earn good profits in the long run, which is a function of the structure of the industry and the conduct of the industry's players (see Chapter 6). The level of attractiveness can be assessed by, for instance, looking at the yearly or long-run growth rate of the industry or market (see also the Growth Share Matrix), the size of the industry or market, and an industry's or market's current profitability.[13] The Five Forces Framework (see again Chapter 6) could be used for a more sophisticated analysis of industry attractiveness. It is up to you to decide whether a unit's competition position should be labelled 'strong' or 'weak' and whether the level of industry or market attractiveness should be labelled 'low' or 'high'.

The idea behind the Directional Policy Matrix, which for illustrative purposes has been applied to a fictitious firm with five business units in Figure C.5, is as follows. Businesses that are placed in a grid box ('quadrant') above the diagonal (see BU3 and BU4 in Figure C.5) are worth investing in to support their growth. Business units that are placed in one of the grid boxes along the diagonal (see BU1 and BU5) are potential candidates for selective investment (depending on the availability of sufficient capital) that could allow them to move (further) above the diagonal. Finally, units placed in a grid box below the diagonal (see BU2) might be best harvested out of. Instead of divesting these units (see Chapter 14), you could also choose to let them run purely for generating cash. Hence there are three categories (or zones) into which business units are sorted, which have been labeled 'invest/ grow', 'selectivity/earnings', and 'harvest/divest'.

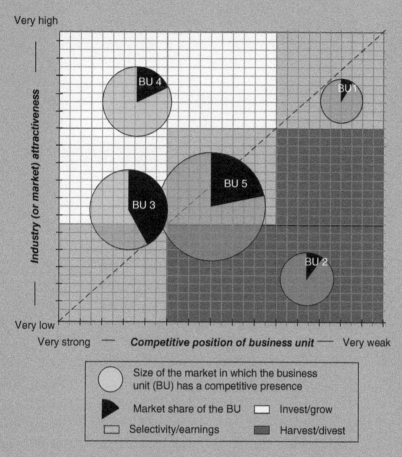

**FIGURE C.5**   Directional Policy Matrix: Illustrative example

Source: authors based on McKinsey

Putting businesses in the matrix and thereby sorting priorities of where to put financial resources should be followed by weighing trade-offs that will likely be involved in deciding where to invest and where to divest. For instance, in relation to the situation shown in Figure C.5, BU1 (weak competitive position in a highly attractive industry) is in a different situation than BU5 (relatively stronger competitive position but active in a less attractive industry): what should be prioritized and why? In making such trade-offs, you need to assess to what extent you would be able to change the position of certain business units in the matrix by investing in them. A second follow-up step to take is to decide how to spend this money to achieve the desired effect.[14]

## Life-Cycle Matrix

The *Life-Cycle Matrix* (also known as the *ADL Matrix* or *Strategic Condition Matrix*), introduced by consultants at Arthur D. Little (ADL), is based on product life-cycle thinking. This type of matrix plots the competitive position (that is, competitive strength) of a firm's different business units along the horizontal axis and the life-cycle stage of the industry or product market in which each of these units has a competitive presence along the vertical axis.[15]

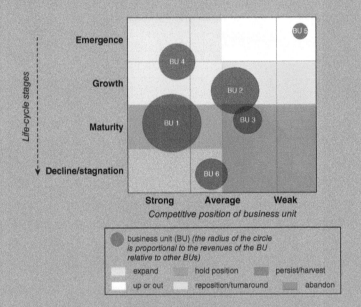

**FIGURE C.6**   Life-Cycle Matrix: Illustrative example

Source: authors based on De Kluyver and Pearce (2003)[16]

    As described earlier (see 'Directional Policy Matrix'), the *competitive position* of a business unit is about the extent to which it has a powerful advantage over competitors and the degree to which this advantage can be sustained. You can distinguish between a strong, average and weak competitive position or opt for a more sophisticated classification – for instance, distinguishing between a dominant, strong, favourable, tenable and weak competitive position. The number of categories on the vertical axis can vary as well, depending on the desired level of sophistication. The main industry (or market) life-cycle stages that can be distinguished include *emergence* (early development), *growth*, *maturity* and *decline/stagnation* (see Chapter 6). The growth stage can be divided into an *industry/market takeoff* stage and a *rapid growth* stage. The maturity stage can be divided into a *competitive shake-out* stage, which implies consolidation of an industry or product market, a *post-shake-out maturity* stage, and a consecutive *market saturation* stage. Figure C.6 indicates how filling a Life-Cycle Matrix with the least refinement on the two axes could look like for a firm with six business units.

The idea behind the Life-Cycle Matrix is that a firm should intend to expand businesses with an above-average competitive position as long as the industry or product market in which they compete is in an embryonic or growth stage and that in following stages the firm ought to try to maintain their position (in the maturity stage) or to persist or harvest (in the decline stage). In contrast, businesses with below-average strength should be divested once the industry or market has reached maturity or decline. In earlier stages, divestiture or repositioning of such businesses should be considered when competitive success seems out of reach.

## Market-Activated Corporate Strategy Framework

From a corporate-level perspective, firms do not only compete in industries or product markets where products are sold to customers, but also in the market for corporate control (that is, the control of business units), where business units are acquired, sold, spun off or split off (see Chapter 14). The main idea behind the so-called *Market-Activated Corporate Strategy (MACS) Framework*, introduced by McKinsey & Company, is that the decision to divest or hold onto a certain business unit ought to be based not only on the value-creation potential of this unit when viewed in isolation but, more importantly, also on the extent to which the corporate parent (see Chapter 12) is suited to run and extract value from this particular unit – that is, is it well-suited compared to other possible corporate parents of that unit.[17] Figure C.7 shows this framework and an illustrative plotting of a fictitious firm's four business units.

Assessing a business unit's potential to create value when viewed in isolation from the rest of the firm to which it belongs (displayed in the horizontal axis of this matrix) requires you to see this unit (for analytical purposes) as an optimally managed stand-alone entity. This intrinsic value-creation potential, which is somewhere on the continuum between (very) high and (very) low, is an aggregate criterion that is based on three factors. Two of these factors are the criteria that make up the Directional Policy Matrix (see Figure C.4. and C.5) – that is, the attractiveness of the industry (or the product market) in which a business unit competes and its competitive position within this industry. The third, complementary factor is the degree to which the firm that owns this business unit has the opportunity to either enhance the attractiveness of that particular industry, or the unit's competitive position within in, or both. This can possibly be achieved by either introducing effective changes in how the unit is managed or by effectuating changes in the industry structure or in the conduct of the industry's players.[18]

The MACS Framework also requires you to assess whether the corporate parent is relatively well-suited to run and extract value from each unit. If, for whatever reason(s), this is indeed the case, the qualification 'natural owner' applies. The corporate parent may, for instance, excel in internal financial control, innovation development, branding, external stakeholder management or the ability to envision and anticipate future market developments. Also, the more a business unit benefits from linkages with a firm's other business units, including vertical interlinkages, knowledge transfers and the sharing of activities or resources with these units, the more natural ownership can be assumed. Alternatively, natural ownership may come from, for instance, embeddedness in certain strategic networks (see Chapter 13), incentives of the firm's owner(s), or technical expertise. If it is concluded

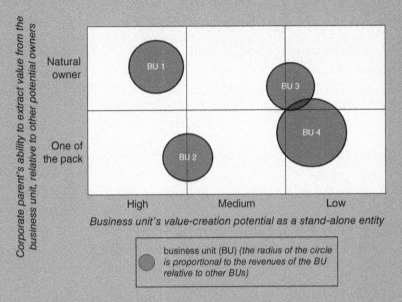

**FIGURE C.7**   MACS Framework: Illustrative example

Source: adapted from Gluck et al. (2000)

instead that one or more other firms would actually be equally or more capable of running and extracting value from a particular business unit (such as BU2 and BU4 in Figure C.7), there is a weak parenting advantage (see Chapter 12) at best, and the qualification in relation to this unit would thus be 'one of the pack'.

The principal strategic prescriptions of the MACS Framework are to:

- divest a structurally attractive business unit by selling it to another firm (see Chapter 14) if it is worth more to this firm or if this other firm is apparently in a better position to run this business unit once it has been brought in excellent shape;
- hold onto a structurally mediocre or even a poor business unit as long as the corporate parent is able to extract more value out of this unit than other potential owners could (unless firmwide performance is affected negatively);
- to give priority to those business units that are plotted towards the left side of the grid – either by strengthening these units (for instance, by investing in them) or, if it is concluded that another firm is the 'natural owner', by selling them as soon as possible.

## Parental Fit Matrix

The *Parental Fit Matrix* (or *Ashridge Matrix*), which has been developed by academics[19] instead of by consultants, essentially zooms in on a corporate parent's ability to run and extract value from each of its business units relative to other potential owners (which is a commonality with the MACS Framework; see Figure C.7). As discussed in Chapter 12, this relative value-creation ability of a corporate parent is referred to alternatively as the *parenting advantage*.[20] The idea behind the Parental Fit Matrix is that parenting advantage should be the leading criterion for considering changes to the corporate portfolio and to the parenting approach in relation to this portfolio. This business portfolio matrix is organized along a horizontal axis that indicates the fit between parenting opportunities and parenting characteristics and a vertical axis that indicates the misfit between these parenting characteristics and the business unit's critical success factors (CSFs). The combination of these two indicators of (mis)fit enables you to assess the potential for parenting advantage for each business unit.

The term *parenting opportunities* refers to the room for improvement within a business unit that the 'natural' corporate owner (which could be either the current corporate parent or any other potential owner of this business unit) should be able to achieve. These opportunities could be identified in different ways. For instance, by identifying and examining strategic challenges facing a business to see whether these challenges contain parenting opportunities, or by learning about other corporate parents that oversee one or more similar businesses, based on which you may discover yet other parenting opportunities.

The term *parenting characteristics* refers to the business unit's current corporate parent. These characteristics fall into five categories (which shown some overlap): (1) the corporate structure, management systems and processes; (2) the central functions, resources and services; (3) the personalities, skills and experience of corporate-level executives; (4) the mental maps (such as values, aspirations, rules of thumb, and biases) that guide these executives as they deal with a business unit; and (5) the degree to which the locus of decision-making authority is delegated to the business-unit level.

A business unit's CSFs set out what needs to be accomplished to ensure competitive success (see Chapter 8) and are commonly derived from a business unit's strategic goals and objectives.

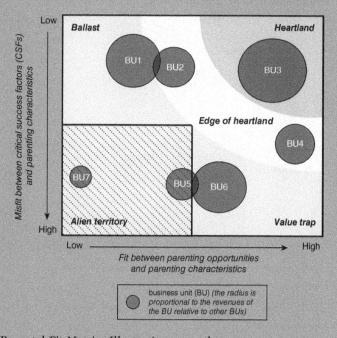

**FIGURE C.8**  Parental Fit Matrix: Illustrative example

Source: adapted from Campbell et al. (1995a)

As shown in Figure C.8, in which seven business units have been plotted for illustrative purposes, the Parental Fit Matrix distinguishes between five zones: 'heartland', 'edge of heartland', 'alien territory', 'ballast', and 'value trap'. *Heartland businesses* – that is, business units plotted in the heartland zone – ought to be at the heart of the corporate portfolio as they have upside potential that the corporate parent knows how to exploit and CSFs that align with the parent's resources, skills, experience, and other characteristics. The opposite is true for businesses that are *alien territory* for their corporate parent (such as BU5 and BU7 in Figure C.8). These businesses should be considered for divestiture, even when making profit, as they would perform better with another corporate parent. In the case of *edge-of-heartland businesses* there are some opportunities to improve these businesses that the corporate parent is able to achieve and at least some of their CSFs align well with the parent's characteristics, but this is accompanied by a value-destroying misfit with some other characteristics. The degree of misalignment between the activities and role of the corporate parent and the needs or opportunities of the portfolio businesses is more significant in the case of *ballast businesses* and *value trap businesses*. Corporate executives should either look for new parenting opportunities for ballast businesses or consider divestiture of these businesses as soon as they can be sold for prices that exceed their expected value of future cash flow. Value trap businesses are called as such because the potential for upside gain may 'trap' executives to accept downside risks as a result of the misfit in relation to CSFs. If these risks cannot be mitigated, their divestiture should be considered.

## Core competencies view

Instead of viewing the multibusiness firm as a portfolio of businesses, as with the business portfolio frameworks presented above, one could also see the firm as a bundle of core competencies[21] (see Figure C.9 for an illustrative example). A *core competency* (see Chapter 8) has the following key characteristics:

- contributes significantly to the perceived customer benefit of a firm's product(s);
- provides potential access to a variety of markets;
- difficult for competitors to imitate.

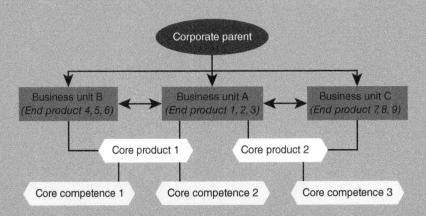

**FIGURE C.9** Core competencies view of a multibusiness firm

Choices with regard to which existing businesses a firm should continue to participate in, which it should exit from, and whether the firm should consider entering any new business areas can be made at least partly based on the firm's core competencies. For instance, if it competes in a business area in which it cannot sufficiently draw on any core competencies, this could be a reason for the firm to divest. And when choosing between two potential diversification options, the one that best allows the firm to draw on its core competencies would possibly be the better choice.

# Better-off test

In Chapter 11, we introduced the better-off test (also known as the added value test) as a tool that, in addition to the attractiveness test and the cost-of-entry test, can support strategic decision-makers in examining whether their firm should diversify into a new business area.[22] The better-off test can also be used, however, to review a firm's existing portfolio of business activities. In the context of business portfolio review, the better-off test raises the following question:

> Does participation in a certain business area (i.e., industry or product market) improve the competitiveness of the firm's other business units over and above what these units could achieve on their own, and vice versa?

This test takes relatedness between business units into account – in contrast to most business portfolio matrices that are presented above – and is therefore particularly relevant for corporate parents following a synergy management logic (see Chapter 12). A positive answer to this question means that the better-off test is satisfied, which indicates that there is a good reason for continuing to participate in that particular business area. A negative answer means that there is a lack of operational synergy or, in some cases, that there is cannibalization, which could be reasons for a firm to divest that business or to invest less resources.[23] Table C.2 lists a couple of conditions that are likely to satisfy the better-off test in this context.

# Ownership test

When a certain business area in which the firm participates passes the better-off test, this does not necessarily imply that the firm should fully own this business. The *ownership test* can be used to identify whether common ownership is the best option, compared to alternative options. Common ownership means that a business entity is part of the same company or corporate group as other business entities (and hence has the same owner). The ownership test raises the following question:[24]

> Does common ownership of the business unit produce a greater competitive advantage than an alternative arrangement would produce?

Conducting this ownership test means that the costs and benefits of ownership should be compared to the costs and benefits of alternative options. There are always alternatives to common ownership. Examples of alternative options are a licensing agreement, other types

**TABLE C.2**   Exemplary conditions likely to satisfy the better-off test when reviewing a firm's business portfolio

| |
|---|
| **Relationship-specific investments** |
| • Two or more of a firm's vertically linked business units have tailored their assets for specific transactions between them, resulting in cost efficiencies, and divesting one could leave these specialized investments vulnerable to exploitation by external parties. |
| **Preventing double marginalization** |
| • By retaining ownership of a focal business unit, the firm can ensure a more streamlined pricing, and more profitability, by preventing double marginalization, which occurs when multiple entities in the supply chain add their own markups. |
| **Downstream or upstream free riding** |
| • By maintaining control of a focal business unit, the firm can thwart downstream or upstream free riding, safeguarding against potential losses stemming from value-reducing behaviour exhibited by suppliers (upstream) or customers (downstream) influenced by opportunistic actions of competitors. |
| **Operating cost synergies** |
| • The combined operating expenditures (i.e., costs incurred from day-to-day operations) for the focal business unit and the firm's other business units are expected to be lower when these units remain together than when the focal business unit stands alone. |
| **Investment cost synergies** |
| • The combined capital expenditures (i.e., costs incurred from the acquisition, development, maintenance or upgrading of assets that are not consumed during operations) for the focal business unit and the firm's other business units are expected to be lower when these units remain together than when the focal business unit stands alone. |
| **Revenue synergies** |
| • The combined product offering of the focal business unit and the firm's other business units is expected to result in higher combined revenues (e.g., owing to a higher customer willingness to pay) when these businesses remain together than when the focal business unit stands alone. |

Source: authors, based on Nanda (2020) and Piskorski (2006)

of contractual alliances, and a joint venture (see Chapter 13). For instance, Tokyo Disneyland is owned by The Oriental Land Company, which licenses the team park from The Walt Disney Company, and the latter owns only 43% of the Shanghai Disney Resort – the remaining 57% is held by a joint venture (Shanghai Shendi Group) of three firms that are owned by the Shanghai government. Hence, instead of fully owning all Disney parks and resorts, The Walt Disney Company has chosen alternative options here. Confronted with changes and challenges in their external and internal environment, firms such as Disney may wish to make different choices in this regard over time.

# Endnotes (references)

1. Pidun, U., Rubner, H., Kruhler, H. and Untiedt, R. (2011) 'Corporate portfolio management: Theory and practice', *Journal of Applied Corporate Finance*, 23(1): 63–76.
2. Reeves, M., Moose, S. and Venema, T. (2014) 'BCG classics revisited: The growth share matrix'. *Boston Consulting Group*, June 4. www.bcg.com/publications/2014/growth-share-matrix-bcg-classics-revisited (accessed June 27, 2023).

3.  BCG (2021) 'What is the growth share matrix', *BCG*. www.bcg.com/about/overview/our-history/growth-share-matrix (accessed June 27, 2023); Reeves et al. (2014).

4.  BCG (2021)

5.  BCG (2021)

6.  Reeves et al. (2014)

7.  BCG (2021); Reeves et al. (2014)

8.  Reeves et al. (2014)

9.  Johnson, G., Scholes, K. and Whittington, R. (2005) *Exploring Corporate Strategy*. Harlow: Financial Times Prentice Hall.

10. Lochridge, R.K. (1981) 'Strategy in the 1980s', *BCG Perspectives*, 241.

11. Coyne, K. (2008) 'Interactive presentation on the GE-McKinsey nine-box matrix as featured on the McKinsey website', *McKinsey Quarterly*, September 1. www.mckinsey.com/business-functions/strategy-and-corporate-finance/our-insights/enduring-ideas-the-ge-and-mckinsey-nine-box-matrix (accessed June 27, 2023).

12. Coyne (2008)

13. Coyne (2008)

14. Coyne (2008)

15. Wright, R.V. (1978) 'A system for managing diversity', in S.H. Britt and H. Boyd (eds), *Marketing Management and Administrative Action*. New York, NY: McGraw-Hill, 46–60.

16. De Kluyver, C.A. and Pearce, J.A. (2003) *Strategy: A View From the Top*. Upper Saddle River, NJ: Prentice Hall.

17. Gluck, F.W., Kaufman, S.P., Walleck, A.S., McLeod, K. and Stuckey, J. (2000) 'Thinking strategically', *McKinsey Quarterly*, June 1. www.mckinsey.com/business-functions/strategy-and-corporate-finance/our-insights/thinking-strategically (accessed June 27, 2023).

18. Gluck et al. (2000)

19. Campbell, A., Goold, M. and Alexander, M. (1995a) 'Corporate strategy: The quest for parenting advantage', *Harvard Business Review*, March/April: 120–32; Goold, M., Campbell, A. and Alexander, M. (1994) *Corporate-Level Strategy: Creating Value in the Multibusiness Company*. New York, NY: Wiley.

20. Campbell, A., Goold, M. and Alexander, M. (1995b) 'The value of the parent company', *California Management Review*, 38 (1): 79–97; Feldman, E.R. (2021) 'The corporate parenting advantage, revisited', *Strategic Management Journal*, 42: 114–43.

21. Prahalad, C.K. and Hamel, G. (1990) 'The core competence of the corporation', *Harvard Business Review*, 68: 79–91.

22. Nanda, A. (2020) 'Corporate strategy', *Harvard Business School Module, Note* 720-448, March 2020. https://www.hbs.edu/faculty/Pages/item.aspx?num=57862 (accessed June 27, 2023); Piskorski, M.J. (2006) 'Note on corporate strategy', *Harvard Business School Background Note*, 705-449. https://www.hbs.edu/faculty/Pages/item.aspx?num=31932 (accessed June 27, 2023); Porter, M.E. (1987) 'From competitive advantage to corporate strategy', *Harvard Business Review*, 65 (3): 43–59.

23. Piskorski (2006)

24. Nanda (2020); Piskorski (2006)

# PART IV
## TRANSFORM

This final part focuses on execution that brings strategy to life by presenting and discussing the concepts and tools that help achieve transformation and, ultimately, enhanced performance with the chosen strategy. We seek to measure and ensure that the strategy comes to life and transforms organizations at risk into those that have better fit with the environment. You will find several ways to master transformation in times of dramatic growth or stagnant growth through reconfiguration or restructuring. Sometimes transformation can be activated by exploiting entrepreneurial opportunities inside the company through intrapreneurship or outside the company by investing in startups. More radical transformations involve a change in business model, or even strategic renewal by exploring new competencies and breaking out of path dependencies. Transformax is our label for the transformation toolkit. It helps to understand the areas, sequence and moves to conclude strategic initiatives (ranging from reconfiguration and restructuring, strategic entrepreneurship, and business model innovation to strategic renewal) with transformation success.

# 14

# RECONFIGURATION AND RESTRUCTURING

## LEARNING OBJECTIVES

After reading this chapter, you should be able to:

- distinguish between different types of acquisitions and between different acquisition motives;
- mention different factors that can explain differences in wealth creation from acquisitions;
- explain the difference between an acquisition, a spin-off, a split-off, a sale-off, and liquidation;
- recognize particular challenges in relation to an adequate carve-out delivery process;
- indicate what is meant with restructuring, and how it relates to acquisition and divestiture.

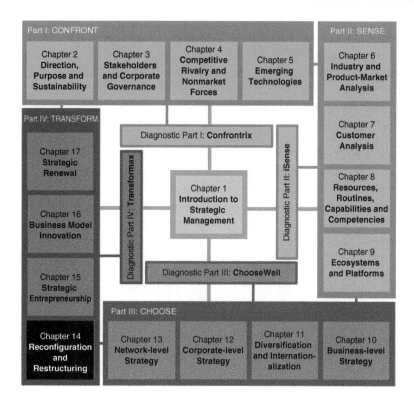

## OPENING CASE

### To split or not to split: Historic recurrence at EY?[1]

EY (formerly Ernst & Young) is one of the world's largest professional services providers. In 2022, EY had over 300,000 employees and a presence in over 150 countries, providing solutions across industries through four integrated service lines: Assurance (which includes audit services), Consulting, Strategy and Transactions, and Tax. Historically, the firm has actively adapted to economic conditions, showcasing not only dogged survival but also market consciousness and renewal. EY was formed in 1989 by a merger of two accounting firms, Ernst & Whinney and Arthur Young & Co. During the 1980s and 1990s, EY heavily expanded its consulting practice, until it decided to spin off this business line from its traditional audit and tax service lines. In 2000, EY Consulting was sold to Capgemini for $11 billion. It would take only a couple of years, however, for EY to expand into consultancy once again, a development that was marked by, among others, EY's acquisition of The Parthenon Group, a global strategy consulting firm, in 2014. In 2021 EY's Assurance practice was the largest contributor to its global revenues (34%) and employed the majority of staff at nearly a third of global employees. Consulting, meanwhile, contributed 28% utilizing just 26% of staff and consistently outgrowing Assurance: FY21 saw 6.4% growth – Assurance 5.8% – with the seven-year compound annual growth rate (CAGR) of Consulting (9.6%) far exceeding Assurance (4.2%).

Together with direct competitors KPMG, PWC, and Deloitte, EY forms the 'Big 4' – the last survivors from the Big 8 accounting firms of the 1980s. For such firms, whilst both Assurance and Consulting services can be offered, both cannot be provided to the same client simultaneously. The two are mutually exclusive at engagement level, and from a firm perspective can only happily coexist to a limited, regulated and highly scrutinized point. For EY, Audit Services comprise the bulk of the Assurance business, and are its absolute strength in market share and reputation; in the firm's own words, audit is its 'bedrock'. Yet, while audit is EY's chief earner it is Consulting that grows more, is less constrained in service possibilities, and generates more opportunity for innovation. As the firm continues to reach revenue milestones – FY22 total revenue grew by 13.5% to a record $45.4bn – Consulting will have to continue building around Assurance if audit remains EY's foundation. This remains particularly problematic in an Assurance environment affected by digitalization, impaired public perceptions and increased scrutiny.

Audit revenue is traditionally built on the model of hours billed. Whether a fixed-cost is charged or the more common billing per-hour, the underlying considerations are principally complexity and time-consumption of the engagement. Loosely translated: the less complex and/or the more time-consuming, the more inexperienced the staff allocated to perform the audit – thus, the cheaper per-hour cost – but the more the hours required. Added to this, a huge amount of audit work requires labour-intensive, high-volume 'ticking and bashing' – which also requires review – expensive work with little ultimate value to the client. As technology begins to play a more fundamental role, firms are no longer willing to pay for expensive manual labour when the same can be performed by technology. Furthermore, complexity is often reduced through computer intervention. Forty years ago, an audit clerk would manually check all entries in a physical ledger line-by-line, contrasted to more recently where this is done in a matter of days in Excel. Nowadays robotic process automation allows execution of repetitive tasks in a matter of hours. Similarly, firms themselves are automating processes and enhancing data mining capabilities, requiring less checking from auditors. Blockchain technology revolutionized financial services by decentralizing the general ledger process. Built into the fabric of blockchain are controls, checks, and balances – so what additional value does an audit have to such technology?

Leaving increasing digitalization aside, auditors are often perceived to be on the 'opposing side' by their clients – in contrast to consultants, who, whilst seen as a luxury expense, are at least viewed as cooperative partners. Additionally, auditors are often deemed by the public to have a key responsibility that is heightening with each major scandal. The 2001 Enron debacle (see the Enron case in Chapter 3) cannot be spoken about without reference to the demise of Arthur Andersen – a trait as relevant now as two decades ago: for example, the 2017 Steinhoff fraud scandal saw Deloitte headline along with Steinhoff, and FinTech giant Wirecard's 2020 insolvency saw several EY Germany partners face criminal investigation.[2] In a 2014 report, the Working Group on Audit Firm Business Model and Incentives, affiliated to the Public Company Accounting Oversight Board, summarized the post-Enron change in audit firm environment,[3] with:

- regulators are now in place that set standards and take action;
- a number of services are increasingly prohibited to auditors;
- the industry has witnessed collapse of firms considered too-large-to-fail;
- audit quality is a required consideration in audit partner compensation;
- audit firms are now required to disclose fees by major category.

This evidences not only a shift in the industry paradigm, but also the increased scrutiny on audit firms. This reaction is not limited to the US. For example, whilst audit firm rotation is not new, in 2016 the EU introduced mandatory reform through ten-year audit firm rotation for all EU public-interest entities. This had a direct impact on firms like EY, who maintained long-term relationships and were required to rotate off significant engagements. Additionally, audit quality – specifically fraud detection – is becoming a spotlighted area. In 2021 EY announced a mammoth $10 billion three-year plan to improve audit quality.[4] Overlaying these regulatory pressures are also market pressure and public probes of auditors. In 2021, for example, the CFA Institute proposed a replacement of the Financial Reporting Council (an agency active in the UK and Republic of Ireland that regulates auditors, accountants, and actuaries) with a regulator more 'empowered' to facilitate audit reform[5] – showing that not only are firms being carefully studied, but the industry at large.

In mid-2022, 22 years after it had sold off its consultancy practice to Capgemini, history seemed to repeat itself as EY announced a possible decoupling of its Assurance and Consulting practices into separate firms. Although the split plan was green lighted by EY's top leaders a few months later, the country-by-country votes on the matter among EY's 13,000 partners were delayed until 2023 as EY 'grapples with the details of which assets, liabilities and people should be retained by its audit business if the split goes ahead in late 2023'.[6] Industry experts speculated that this split plan was in response to regulatory scrutiny of potential conflicts of interest in the profession. Other experts questioned EY's ability to retain talent, and others questioned the cost – least of all exorbitant pay-outs to global partners. But this did not detract from clear upside possibilities, such as the potential to list the new consulting firm – an option previously not available. However, in April 2023 EY called off the split plan. The firm said that the plan faced resistance from some of its partners.[7]

## Questions

1. Considering the developments in the audit environment that EY faces (digitalization, impaired public perceptions, increased scrutiny), what could it do to further grow its assurance business?
2. EY could keep its firm combined but consider its growth prospects by shifting focus to Consulting – or, it could dig further into Assurance with due consideration of the abovementioned external developments. Alternatively, it could attempt the split at a later time. What do you think EY should do?

# Introduction

So far in this textbook, we have discussed a multitude of challenges and choices that you, as a future (or current) strategist will face. This chapter is the first of four that focus on how to transform an organization in the right strategic direction, which implies changes in its structures, systems and operations. In this chapter, we discuss how to accomplish chosen strategies through two different but related types of reorganization[8] (a type of transformation): reconfiguration and restructuring. **Reconfiguration** is a change process that involves the adding, combining, transferring, splitting or dissolving of business entities without necessarily modifying the underlying structure of the firm.[9] We will zoom in on two types of corporate transactions that imply reconfiguration: acquisitions and divestitures. **Restructuring** is a distinct change process that involves alterations in the structures around which a firm's resources and activities are grouped and coordinated or in the underlying financial structure. Reconfiguration and restructuring can go hand-in-hand. For instance, following an acquisition, functions of the buying firm and the acquired business entity are often merged, whereby these functions (and therefore all involved employees) in one way or the other will be restructured immediately or in the future. By altering the corporate composition and structure, reconfiguration and restructuring can contribute significantly to a firm's transformation.

# Acquisition-based reconfiguration

Roughly 60% of successful firms include mergers and acquisitions (M&A) in their growth strategies.[10] M&A is a term that is used often to refer to transactions in which the ownership of firms or part of their assets are consolidated with or transferred to other firms. These transactions enable firms to obtain and incorporate additional resources and capabilities into their organization and to expand the scale or scope of their operations. In a **merger**, the firms agree to the integration of their operations on a relatively coequal basis, which is not very common in today's business world.[11] We therefore focus on acquisitions here. An acquisition is often framed by the acquiring and acquired firm as a 'merger' because of the more positive connotation of this term. An **acquisition** denotes a transaction in which a firm (referred to as the acquiring firm, or 'acquirer') takes full ownership or a controlling stake (that is, >50%) in another firm. The process through which firms evaluate potential acquisition targets is called *due diligence*. The activities that are part of this process, which can be very extensive, are usually performed by investment banks or specialized law, accounting or consultancy firms.

Between 2010 and 2021, over 500,000 M&A deals were completed,[13] with M&A deal value reaching more than $5 trillion in 2021 (see Figure 14.1).[14] One of these deals was the acquisition of Althaea and De Laet International, which ran a joint chocolate production unit in Belgium, by the Dutch confectionary firm Tony's Chocolonely in 2021. For Tony's Chocolonely, the acquisition of these firms was a means to integrate backwards into the industry value chain, as until then it had depended fully on other firms for producing its chocolate.[15] When a firm acquires another firm that operates upstream or downstream (from the perspective of the acquirer) in the value chain, as in the Tony's Chocolonely example, this is called a *vertical integration*.[16] When a firm acquires another

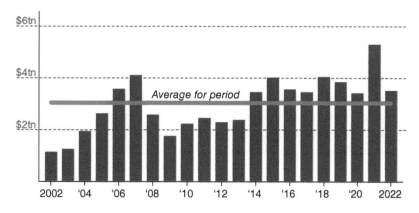

**FIGURE 14.1** Mergers & acquisitions (M&A) worth from 2002 to 2022

Source: Bloomberg (2022)[12]

firm that produces similar goods or services at the same stage of the value chain, such as a rival, this is called a *horizontal integration*. An example is the acquisition of the digital design firm Figma by its rival Adobe in 2022. Horizontal integration typically results in industry consolidation.

Acquisitions do not necessarily have to be instances of either vertical or horizontal integration. A firm may also acquire another firm that operates in a different product market (which dismisses horizontal integration) that is not aligned vertically with one of the acquirer's product markets (which dismisses vertical integration). This implies non-vertical diversification (see Chapter 11). An example of an acquisition-based diversification is the acquisition of the Swiss diagnostic services provider Unilabs by the Denmark-based A.P. Møller Holding.

The above-mentioned acquisitions by Tony's Chocolonely were considered friendly with close collaboration between management teams to ensure a smooth transition.[17] It can also be the case that a firm takes control of a target firm without agreement of the latter, which is formally called a *hostile takeover*.

## Acquisition motives

There are several motives that lead firms to grow through acquisitions. Some motives are focused on value creation, such as (but not limited to) increasing market power, competency building and overcoming entry barriers, whereas other motives may result in value being destroyed, as discussed next.

### Value-creating motives

Increasing market power, achieving market leadership, and consolidating a firm's market share are related motives to justify acquisitions.[18] Market power is achieved through a larger scale and market share.[19] Another motive for acquisition is to acquire new resources (such as a promising technology), capabilities and competencies. The acquisition of startups by established firms, for instance in the high-tech sector, is a popular competency-enhancement growth strategy. When a firm faces significant entry barriers, it may opt for an acquisition to gain immediate access to a certain market, thereby overcoming these barriers. Entry barriers are difficulties that firms encounter when trying to enter in a certain product market or geographical market. For instance, incumbents may benefit from economies of scale that are difficult to achieve for a new entrant, or they have established enduring relationships with customers and distributors that are difficult for new entrants to replicate (see Chapter 6). Acquisitions can be particularly attractive for firms seeking to overcome entry barriers in international markets.[20]

## Value-destroying motives

Some industries witness waves of acquisitions (and mergers), also called the *acquisition bandwagon*. Such waves pressure firms to acquire competitors to consolidate their market position. Firms that are more precautionary are criticized by market analysts for being too conservative and also by stakeholders who fear that a firm will lose its competitive positioning. Also, managers at the firm may worry that if they do not acquire, they will be acquired by a hostile competitor. When firms give in to pressure, they might rush towards acquiring firms without measuring the risks, destroying value along the way. Another common value-destroying motivation is managers' personal ambitions. Managers may have personal interests in leading an acquisition, mainly when their financial incentives are tight to short-term growth targets or stock price increases that can easily be achieved through gaining scale through acquisitions.

## Wealth creation from acquisitions

The antecedents of shareholder wealth creation in acquisitions (and mergers) have long intrigued researchers. Studies highlight that there is a large variance in acquisition performance, as only 35% to 45% of acquirers are able to achieve positive returns in the two to three years after the acquisition.[21] Next, we discuss some factors that can help predict wealth creation or destruction from acquisitions.[22]

- Type of acquisition bid: A firm can make a single or multiple acquisition bids, which can range from friendly to hostile. A 2006 study on 500 acquisitions in the UK shows that, despite the negative press coverage, single hostile bids deliver higher financial returns in the long run than friendly bids and multiple hostile bids.[23] Other studies, however, show that friendly acquisitions facilitate post-acquisition integration plans, as the acquiring and acquired firm work together to find ways to integrate their operations and assets to cut costs and create synergies.[24] In contrast, hostile acquisitions are said to create animosity between firms' management teams that lead inevitably to dysfunctional working relationships, the loss of key personnel in the acquired firm, and resistance from the remaining personnel.[25] Despite the somewhat contradicting results, the dominant view goes for friendly bids as an antecedent of acquisitions' wealth creation.
- Mode of payment: Acquisitions can be financed by cash, stock, or a combination. Shareholders of the acquiring and the acquired firm are both likely to be better off

in cash-financed transactions than in stock-financed ones.[26] Stock-financed bids are generally slower, which increase costs, as regulatory bodies may need to give their approval before shareholders can exchange their shares. Also, the issuance of stock is often viewed negatively by the capital market.[27] Moreover, unlike stock payment, cash payments impose an immediate tax liability on the shareholders of a target firm, for which they seek compensation in the form of a higher acquisition premium.[28]

- <u>Strategic fit:</u> the extent to which the acquiring and acquired firm share attributes that facilitate resource sharing[29] and knowledge transfer.[30] Acquisitions, mainly horizontal ones, result in higher performance when the firms have similar strategies, managerial styles, and resource allocation patterns.[31]

- <u>Asset complementarity</u> between the acquirer and acquired firm also contributes to more successful acquisitions, as this increases the likelihood of creating synergies. The acquirer can maintain its focus on its core business while leveraging the complementary assets of the firm that it acquires, creating a unique set of capabilities and core competencies.[32] When firms display some degree of strategic fit and asset complementarity, the process of integrating activities and assets runs smoother, increasing the odds of wealth creation.

- <u>Cultural fit</u> between the acquiring and acquired firm can play a role in the success of an acquisition. Poor cultural fit, lack of cultural compatibility, or cultural clashes can lower acquisition returns.[33]

## CRACK-THE-CASE

The all-time most expensive acquisition in the beer industry[34]

Source: © Monticello (2021) / Shutterstock.

*(Continued)*

Anheuser-Busch InBev ('AB-InBev') is the world's largest beer brewer. Headquartered in Leuven, Belgium, the firm oversees a portfolio of more than 600 beer brands in 150 countries. In 2016, AB InBev made a bid to buy SABMiller, at that time the world's second largest brewing firm measured by revenues (after AB-InBev), for $107 billion in what would be the biggest consolidation event in the history of the beer industry.

SABMiller, founded in 1895 in South Africa, had started small by selling beers direct to miners around Johannesburg. In the 1990s, however, the firm had embarked on an aggressive growth strategy that eventually culminated in a portfolio of more than 200 beer brands and a presence in 80 countries. AB-InBev predicted that its own market share would decrease in the following years and justified its premium bid over SABMiller by arguing that this acquisition would allow the firm to prevent this projected loss of market share because of various reasons. First of all, acquiring SABMiller would open up ways to cross-sell the firms' products in each other's markets. AB-InBev's strongest markets were Europe, North America, and Brazil, while SABMiller was particularly strong in Africa, Asia, and Central and South America (excluding Brazil). Furthermore, acquiring SABMiller would enable a portfolio expansion into three growing market segments in which the South African brewer was relatively strong: local beer, craft beer, and premium beer. Also, the firms would learn from each other's distinctive capabilities: SABMiller was particularly strong in authentic branding and the streamlining of decentralized operations, while AB-InBev distinguished itself with its focus on achieving a high operating margin (around 33%) and scale efficiencies through a centralized global cost-cutting model. Moreover, AB-InBev expected to save $3 billion by cutting costs in overlapping head offices, distribution channels and production facilities, and to benefit from synergies across production, operations, distribution, and marketing. As the worldwide beer market witnessed a consolidation rush in the last decade, AB-InBev argued that it could choose only from a limited range of acquisition targets.

Despite the evident benefits of such a historical acquisition, analysts were doubting whether this acquisition would live up to AB-InBev's expectations. AB-InBev had promised to keep SABMiller as an independent division, and analysts were not sure how this would enable AB-InBev to realize the indicated cost savings and synergies. Also, as the operations of AB-InBev and SABMiller were largely complementary to each other, with few geographic overlaps, analysts were not convinced about the pool of cost-reduction opportunities. Furthermore, analysts raised concerns about a possible misfit in organizational culture, stressing that the two brewing firms have very different market approaches – for instance, SABMiller's focus on independent local brands and authentic products versus AB-InBev's centralized cost-conscious global model. Moreover, there were some regulatory concerns, as in some markets AB-InBev would gain a near-monopolistic position after the acquisition, which would reduce consumer choice and increase buyer power over suppliers, which would certainly raise the attention of antitrust authorities.

Regardless of these concerns, AB-InBev persisted in its intention to acquire SABMiller for $107 billion, which passed regulatory approval in 2017. SABMiller became a business division of AB-InBev, which resulted in a 30% global market share. The acquisition included SABMiller's hops farming subsidiary SAB Hop Farms. Financially, not everything went as expected: instead of reaching $55 billion in sales and cutting $3 billion in costs, AB-InBev reached $54 billion in sales and was able to cut only $1.75 billion in costs. The firm was also unfortunate with the COVID-19 pandemic that curbed beer consumption in the last few years. However, the future is looking better with beer sales accelerating again.

## Questions

1. What, in your view, were the main motives that led AB-InBev to acquire SABMiller?
2. To what extent are the antecedents of wealth creation in acquisitions present in this case?

## KEY DEBATE

### Integration fixation

The returns of acquirers are often negative or, at best, not statistically significant in the years after they have made the acquisition.[35] And even worse: prior studies indicate that between 70% and 90% of acquisitions fail.[36] What explains this high failure rate? Many managers and scholars point predominantly to integration as the main problem.[37] Once the acquisition transaction has been completed, the acquiring firm needs to integrate the purchased business entity into its own organization. These entities may have a poor cultural fit or a lack of cultural compatibility, among many other potential issues that may be encountered. The post-acquisition integration process can play a role in whether an acquisition will create or destroy value. Many acquisitions do not deliver their projected value because of a deficient post-acquisition integration plan that works around conflicting processes and strategies between acquiring and acquired firms.[38] Firms can learn from their acquisition experiences, enabling them to improve acquisition returns over time.[39] When managers from both the acquired and acquiring firm have post-acquisition integration or divestiture experience, the integration of operations and assets will generally be more successful.[40]

Acquisition-based diversification into unrelated business areas (i.e., unrelated diversification, see Chapter 11) requires relatively little integration. Integration becomes important when a firm acquires another company that operates in either the same business area (i.e., horizontal integration) or in an area that complements the acquirer's core business (i.e., related diversification), theoretically allowing the acquirer to maximize synergies (see Chapter 12). However, in approximately two-thirds of all acquisitions, the acquirer's stock price dropped immediately after announcing the acquisition. This negative response indicates that investors are overall skeptical about acquirers' plans to achieve synergies through acquisitions.[41] Another primary stakeholder group, a firm's customers, is the final arbiter of whether an acquisition will be successful. An interesting observation is that integration problems seem to be particularly severe in cases of related diversification.[42] In these cases, it is important that (key) customers of both the acquirer and acquired entity perceive added value in the broader product range if they are to alter their purchasing behaviour for the goods or services within that range.[43] This raises the question what to focus on most: getting the integration right, or convincing customers about the benefits and logic of the acquisition?

## Divestiture-based reconfiguration

Whilst an acquisition implies adding assets to a firm, a divestiture, also known as a *divestment*, is the contractionary counterpart (the removal of assets). A firm whose assets are partially acquired is in fact divesting these assets. Firms that engage in divestitures can extract knowledge from these transactions that can be useful for completing acquisitions, and vice versa.[44] Although the term **divestiture** can in practice refer to the disposal of any asset, such as staff, a machine or an intellectual property right, it commonly denotes the disposal of a division (that is, a business unit or business line; see Chapter 12) or controlling interest in a subsidiary firm[45] through a sale, exchange or liquidation. Here, the term *corporate divestiture* (or *corporate divestment*) can be used to highlight the difference with other types of divestitures. An example from the opening case is the disposal of EY's consulting service line in 2000. Portfolio management matrices (see the *ChooseWell* diagnostic chapter) can support corporate-level executives in making decisions as to which divisions or group firms to divest. The disposing firm (EY in the previous example) is often referred to as the *divesting firm*, or *divesting parent company* (abbreviated as *ParentCo*); the division or subsidiary that is disposed is usually labelled the *divested entity* or – in the case of a spin-off or a split-off (which we will describe further below) – the *newly established firm*, or *newly established company* (abbreviated as *NewCo*). As with an alliance (see Chapter 13) and an acquisition, a carefully chosen divestiture can potentially optimize a firm's profit potential.[46] Globally, divestitures create more than twice as much shareholder value as mergers and acquisitions.[47]

A divestiture that narrows the firmwide scope can be referred to as a *downscoping divestiture*.[48] This term is most commonly used to denote a reduction in a firm's business scope.[49] For instance, as described in the Closing Case, Philips gradually transformed into a HealthTech firm by divesting its lighting, television, domestic appliances and other businesses that are outside the realm of healthcare. A firm can undertake downscoping divestitures for a variety of different reasons, such as a strategic reorientation (as in the case of Philips), an underperforming division, or a desire to focus on only one or more core business lines (resulting in 'non-core' businesses being divested). Also, a certain business line may no longer be considered sufficiently financially or strategically attractive to maintain a competitive presence. Sometimes firms choose to narrow their business scope once they notice that part of their product offering is not (anymore) in line with their mission, vision, core values, or purpose. For instance, when in late 2021 dermatologists and skin cancer patients petitioned fitness clubs in the Netherlands to stop offering sunbed services to their clients, Fit for Free, a chain of over 90 budget fitness clubs, chose to remove all sunbeds from its clubs. According to a spokesman, the chain had concluded that offering sunbed services was not in line with their core values of promoting a healthy and responsible lifestyle.

A decrease in a firm's geographical market scope has been labelled *de-internationalization*.[50] For instance, in a reaction to the war that Russia raged on Ukraine in 2022, many firms mainly from Europe and the US decided to exit the Russian market. A narrowing in a firm's vertical scope is commonly referred to as *vertical disintegration*.[51] A case in point is SunPower Corporation, which in 2019 announced a spin-off that would lead to its separation into two independent, vertically linked entities: US-based SunPower and Singapore-based Maxeon Solar Technologies. SunPower continues to provide distributed solar and storage services, while Maxeon Solar Technologies, the newly created business entity, focuses on the manufacturing of solar panels. SunPower's CEO commented that this divestiture 'will create two focused businesses, each with unique expertise to excel in their part of the value chain'.[52]

When a divestiture comes with the use of permanent cuts in a firm's resource base, which may include both human resources (think about employee layoffs) and physical resources (think about the closure of a facility), to reduce output while maintaining the corporate scope intact, this can be labelled a *downscaling divestiture*.[53] As with a downscoping divestiture, there can be various reasons for such a divestiture. For instance, it may enable firms to get rid of redundant capacity, obsolete activities or less useful or underperforming assets, thereby eliminating inefficiencies and improving performance. But a downscaling divestiture may also be undertaken to recuperate from paying an acquisition premium or to avert a financial crisis.

## Divestiture transaction formats

Firms can carry out a divestiture in different ways, including a spin-off, split-off, sell-off, equity carve-out, and liquidation. As clarified next, these different transaction formats, which are often referred to as different 'types' of divestitures (see Figure 14.2), differ in terms of transaction nature, cash flow impact, and motivation.[54]

Spin-off        Split-off        Sell-off        Equity carve-out        Liquidation

**FIGURE 14.2**   Divestiture transaction formats

A spin-off and a split-off both imply that a certain division of the firm is turned into a separate, independent firm – in other words, once a spin-off or split-off has been completed, the divested business entity operates independently. The corporate parent of the divesting firm distributes the shares in the division that is being divested to existing shareholders. In the case of a **spin-off**, this allocation of shares is in proportion (or 'pro rata') to shareholdings. An example is when in 2021 IBM completed the spin-off of its managed infrastructure service business to enable a narrower focus on cloud and artificial intelligence (currently operating under the name Kyndryl). In the case of a **split-off**, which is less common, the existing shareholders have to make a choice between owning shares in the divesting parent firm or owning shares in the business entity that is being divested. The choice for either a spin-off or a split-off is usually followed later in time by selling off the newly created business entity, implying a permanent change of ownership.

A **sell-off** implies that a parent firm sells a subsidiary unit (or a controlling interest in this unit), in which it retains no ownership, to another firm. Hence, an existing firm is sold by the divesting parent firm (the seller) to an outside firm (the buyer) who, in turn, incorporates the acquired firm into its own organization. Both the selling and buying entity may be publicly or privately held.[55] An example of a sell-off is when in 2018 AkzoNobel sold its Specialty Chemicals business division to The Carlyle Group and GIC for more than €10 billion, enabling AkzoNobel to fully focus on its paints and coatings business (see the next Crack-the-Case).[56] A sell-off is different from an **equity carve-out**, which implies that a parent firm sells shares of a subsidiary, in which it typically retains considerable ownership, to public investors.[57] In the case that the percentage of ownership remains above 50%,[58] the selling parent firm remains in control, and the corporate scale and scope thus remain intact.

Sell-offs and equity carve-outs have in common that they can generate a cash inflow for the divesting parent firm and that they constitute a clear change in the shareholders' ownership structure. These two characteristics set sell-offs and equity carve-outs apart from spin-offs and split-offs.[59]

The main differences between these transaction formats have to do with the share ownership after the divestiture. In the case of a sell-off, the shares of the divested entity will be owned by a third party – for instance, a private equity firm or a strategic buyer. In the case of an equity carve-out, only part of those shares will be owned by a third party. In the case of a spin-off, the divesting parent firm distributes the shares of the new entity to its current shareholders. While in the case of a split-off, current shareholders of the parent firm will have to choose between keeping shares of the parent firm or exchanging them for shares of the newly established firm.

The reasonings behind these transaction formats differ. A sell-off can be driven by various reasons, such as the wish to raise capital needed by the divesting parent firm (to prevent bankruptcy), to shed a strategic no longer compatible part of its business, to comply with antitrust regulations, to strengthen the parent firm's balance sheet, or to divest a non-performing business. The decision to go for a spin-off can be based on the parent firm's objective to set apart one of its profitable divisions as a separate entity in order to benefit from its profitability. Or in the event of a successful division that does not exactly match the firm's core competencies, a spin-off allows both the divesting parent firm and the division to focus on separate goals and financial performance indicators, while at the same time still being affiliated. Split-offs, however, are generally motivated by the intend to offer more value to shareholders by means of shedding assets and offering them a new, separate firm.

The form of the divestiture (that is, the structure of a specific divestiture) will, to an important degree, be driven by fiscal and legal reasons. For example, if the wish is to split a firm, it can make a multi-million dollar difference whether to divest one part of the parent firm and to leave behind the other, or to execute this operation the other way around. Local, country-specific legal and fiscal regulations therefore make divestments in general complex and very specific operations.

**Liquidation**, which we did not yet discuss, denotes that a certain division or subsidiary ceases to exist, which can be compulsory or voluntary. An example of a liquidation is when in 2019 US-based discount footwear firm Payless filed for bankruptcy and closed all its 2,500 stores in Puerto Rico and in the US, while its stores elsewhere on the globe, belonging to different geographical divisions, continued to operate.[60] Although the terms 'liquidation' and 'dissolution' are often used interchangeably, they do not mean the exact same thing: liquidation means that a firm sells off assets to claimants (owners and creditors) according to priority claims, while dissolution means that the firm deregisters, which implies the end of this firm as a legal entity.

## Implementing divestitures: The carve-out delivery process

The removal of one or more divisions of a firm is usually not something that can be accomplished overnight – instead, it is often a matter of carefully carving out assets, liabilities, rights and obligations. As in archaeology, this requires time, preparation and a detailed eye for internal and external dependencies and intertwining. In the following subsections, we will zoom in on various characteristics of the process of carve-out delivery (not to be confused with an equity carve-out), or *divestiture delivery*. The **carve-out delivery** is about delivering the actual divestiture in practice, by setting apart ('carving out') specific assets (e.g., systems, client and employee contracts, and bank accounts) and liabilities (e.g., loans and supplier contracts) that constitute the newly established or sold entity. Carve-out delivery is often perceived as a reverse integration of a division. Practice shows that this is not exactly the case, however, and in the next few subsections we indicate why.

## Availability of time to deliver the carve-out

To better understand the difference between an integration and a carve-out (apart from the reversed ordering), the time factor is important. When integrating a certain division, there is often no hard deadline. Here, 'hard' denotes a deadline that, if not met, will irrevocably lead to business interruption. When integrating a division into a corporation, the actual integration can be executed over a longer period. Think, for example, of integrating two groups of employees that merge over time into one common culture. The integration of systems can also be spread out over a longer period and there is no real crisis in the short term if this is not delivered as planned. After all, both the divesting parent firm and the purchased entity already operate within the domain of the buyer. In case the business entity to be integrated was bought by a private equity firm, this entity already has its own systems, processes, employees, and management team that take care of the daily operations as they did before. Besides all this, even if an integration has been carefully planned for completion in a short period of time, in practice delivering an integration almost always takes longer than planned. This is mainly because all involved parties are aware of the non-time-critical nature of an integration, and thus consciously or unconsciously take the time to fully realize their own interests and those of their sponsors. In addition to that, consider the power of underlying interests that play a role in integrating two firms. All in all, it is a delicate process that affects people directly in their working and personal lives. As a result, in practice integrations often take a long time to complete, and there is the question whether they will ever be fully delivered.

Divestitures, on the other hand, typically come with strict agreements, including regarding the time of divestiture delivery, between the divesting parent firm and the newly established firm or, in the case of a sell-off, the buyer. Depending on the background of the divestiture, it is in the interest of the divesting firm whether the carve-out is carried out quickly (and maybe partially incomplete) or perfectly and down to the last detail. For example, in the case of an acute capital requirement because of an untenable debt situation, the speed of completion of the divestiture plays an important role – after all, the sooner the divestiture is completed, the sooner the divesting parent firm will have access to the new available financial resources to meet its own financial needs. Time then is the critical factor. But when, for example, the carve-out takes place because of competitive legislation that enforces a divestiture in order to prevent a monopoly position, then a detailed carve-out process, down to the last detail, will often become the modus operandi. Not 'time' but 'meeting the requirements of the competition authority' will then be the critical factor, and time needed will then be a resulting factor. In the end, however, a full split will be the main objective of any carve-out. The ParentCo and the NewCo (in the case of a spin-off or split-off), or the ParentCo and the buyer of a divested entity (in the case of a sale-off), typically adopt a *Transitional Service Agreement (TSA)*, which basically means that the ParentCo agrees to provide certain support services to the NewCo or buyer at a predetermined price. These services, such as in the areas of administration, human resources and IT, are meant to support the NewCo or buyer operationally up until the moment that the carve-out delivery has been finalized.

## Conflicting interests

In practice, overall, the divesting parent firm will be interested in carve-out completion in the shortest amount of time. After all, the sooner the carve-out is completed, the sooner the money from the deal becomes available and the divesting party then can fully focus on optimizing and growing the remaining part of its organization in line with its strategy. While 'the sooner the better' will be the divesting firm's driver for the carve-out approach, the management of the NewCo or buyer may need (much) more time. After all, they must be sure of undisturbed continuity of the newly established or acquired business at the time the carve-out is implemented. And all that is needed for securing continuity cannot be assessed in the blink of an eye, certainly not in the case of a large-scale carve-out. Also consider the difference between a strategic buyer, who already has in-dept knowledge of the type of firm it has bought, versus a private equity investor who, seen from an operational point of view, may have bought a black box. Especially in the latter case, a thorough analysis and detailed preparations for implementing the carve-out will take a considerable amount of time.

In general, a carve-out brings high pressure for all involved. It is important to meet the deadlines the divesting firm and the NewCo's or buyer firm's management have agreed on (in a TSA) with respect to the temporary mutual services until the moment of carve-out completion. These strict deadlines and the time pressure that comes with them often do not exist in integration projects.

## Carve-out delivery: Point of no return

In contrast to an integration process, there is no turning back in the event of a carve-out. For example, if the former parent firm's IT systems have been shut down for use by the carved-out business entity and employees have been assigned to either this former parent firm or this entity (or to its new owner), then their availability is limited to just one of the two organizations. In contrast, with an integration of two already operational firms there is no irreversible issue in case a system integration takes a little longer – after all, none of the parties involved with the integration has an interest in a 'hard' shutdown of systems that causes problems for a business that is part of the same group.

Due to the strict agreements and the hard deadlines that come with a carve-out, meticulous planning, extensive internal and external communication, and accurate execution are often essential for even the simplest separation. Tight control on getting ready to 'switch the button' at the moment of physical split are a mandatory part of the carve-out delivery approach. In short: while strict deadlines are self-imposed in case of an integration, they are mandatory and of vital importance for successfully delivering carve-outs. In practice, this means that specific 'Readiness Checks' must be carried out, in which tests and extensive checks will be done to determine whether specific items are ready for the carve-out to go 'live'. To be successful, an effective carve-out approach must focus on detailed organization, preparation, and delivery, based on an exhaustive plan that is fitted to the situation at hand.

## CRACK-THE-CASE
### Carving out AkzoNobel Specialty Chemicals to Nouryon

Source: © VanderWolf Images (2023) / Shutterstock.

Rewinding to 2018, AkzoNobel is a large worldwide operating firm, which produces and sells all kinds of chemicals. It delivers both semi-finished and finished products to its clients and is organized as two divisions – Paints & Coatings and Specialty Chemicals – that each consist of different business lines. Because of fierce market competition circumstances and shareholder pressure, the firm is highly integrated throughout all functions in order to achieve high levels of economies of scale and efficiency in delivering its products to its clients. Due to the nature of the chemical business, it is highly regulated, dealing with thousands of safety and process auditing certificates, registrations, permits and audit trail related documents. Safety and traceability are a number one priority.

Despite AkzoNobel's relentless efforts to optimize the efficiency of its processes, the share price does not perform in line with the expectations of its shareholders. That is why an activist shareholder forces the management to take action to improve its stock market performance. After assessing all possible scenarios, it is decided to sell-off the Specialty Chemicals division. By this a billion-dollar amount of money will flow into the corporate parent firm, that will be partly paid to its shareholders as a dividend and partly used for a share buyback program. Because of its excellent worldwide reputation, profitable business and promising future perspective, it does not take long before the US-based Carlyle Group and Singaporean GIC show serious interest. After a successful due diligence, they come to an agreement. Now the complex task of carving out the sold division has to be delivered.

*(Continued)*

Following the sale, AkzoNobel will keep its identity, prompting the designated division for divestiture to adopt a new name – Nouryon. The division operates in more than 30 countries and consists of more than 60 legal entities worldwide. Sales, purchasing, production and logistics processes are complex and have become strongly intertwined worldwide over years of optimization and integration. There are a multitude of different products, varying in risk profile from low to very high. Also, there are a multitude of locations where sales activities and production take place. All this has resulted in thousands of (non-)European and local registrations, permits and licenses. For an average delivery, 20 interrelated documents are needed to ensure a successful delivery to the customer. The fundamental baseline is that each registration is related to a specific legal entity and that in practice a specific document can only be drawn up or changed when another document is ready. All in all, a complexity that spans several axes and that results in a tangle of interdependencies. The Carlyle Group and AkzoNobel have decided to change the name of all legal entities involved as soon as possible after 'Day 1' (that is, the day of the legal transfer from seller to buyer). However, the abovementioned dependencies have been unintentionally left out of consideration. As a result, if all legal entities will change their name to Nouryon immediately after Day 1, the vast majority of the documentation required for the production and delivery of products will be invalid at once. In fact, this situation will bring the firm to an emergency stop, resulting in high financial damage.

The program lead, who has recently been commissioned to prepare and deliver this carve-out, raises a red flag. While explaining the dependencies and its consequences to the management team, which had not dealt with this kind and magnitude of operation before, he urges them to postpone the name change of the operating legal entities. His proposal is to change the name on Day 1 only for the fiscal-related legal entities, which are neither registration nor operations related, and to postpone the name change of all other legal entities for eight months. A thorough analysis has shown that this period is needed to make all necessary preparations so that the name change (and thus the actual carve-out) and all updates of applicable items will be in line with each other in such a way that all processes can proceed without interruption. The day-to-day business operations are thus safeguarded both before and after the carve-out, and financial damage will be prevented. This proposal is agreed on just four days before Day 1 and communicated to all worldwide parties involved, such as internal and external lawyers, notaries, and other service providers involved with the name change. The carve-out was indeed delivered in eight months. During this period, all preparations in terms of updating registrations, permits, certificates, IT systems and applications, legal preparations and documents have been completed. The carve-out 'go live' at name change date ran smoothly, with continuous and undisturbed operations and no financial damage. In fact, the smooth transition and all positive communication that goes with it give the now separated operating firm, Nouryon, a kickstart in its markets.

## Questions

1. Why do you think that the 'name' topic was not on the table during the preluding period?
2. During carve-outs a specific management omission, also many times present in regular daily operations nowadays, can be noticed. What omission do you think is meant?
3. What do you think is overall an optimal project structure to deliver a carve-out efficiently and successfully? Explain why.

# Restructuring

So far, we have examined acquisitions and divestitures as two types of corporate transactions that imply reconfiguration. Divestitures and acquisitions usually result in a change in the organizational structure (besides a change in the legal structure) of the divesting entity and, in the case of an acquisition, the acquiring entity. Put differently, reconfiguration often results in restructuring. **Restructuring** is a distinct change process that involves alterations in the structures around which a firm's resources and activities are grouped and coordinated (*organizational restructuring*)[61] or alterations in the underlying financial structure (*financial restructuring*). Restructuring may also occur without any prior reconfiguration (in the form of either an acquisition or divestiture) taking place. If a firm, as part of its restructuring efforts, decides to lay off a certain number of employees in non-core areas, a divestiture of what it considers a non-core division may be one of the outcomes. As this example shows, restructuring may lead to reconfiguration (see Figure 14.3). However, this is not necessarily the case.

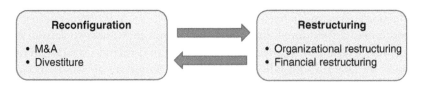

**FIGURE 14.3**   Reconfiguration and restructuring can be intertwined

As indicated above and as detailed next, we can distinguish between organizational and financial restructuring. One can do without the other – for example, changing the lending structure of a firm as part of a financial restructuring does not per se imply a change in organizational structure.

## STRATEGIC FOCUS

### Continuous reorganization

In Chapter 12 we identified four different corporate logics that multibusiness firms have put into practice, each resting on a distinct value-creating mechanism: synergy management, capital orchestration, parental development, and continuous reorganization. Firms whose logic is one of continuous reorganization are engaged actively in reconfiguration and restructuring. They generally use proprietary expertise and insights to seek out firms that are undermanaged or threatened in their existence or that have other problems, such as a lackluster image, or they buy into industry segments that are ripe for transformation. Once acquired, the parent firm intervenes in the new entities (often without having to pay substantial acquisition premiums) in a way that strengthens their competitive position or improves their potential. For instance, the firm may infuse them with new capabilities or new technology, change their business model, and/or replace (part of) their management team. The firm could also opt for follow-up acquisitions to build a certain required critical mass, while selling off those assets that no longer add value.[62]

*(Continued)*

Once a reorganization is complete and market conditions are favourable, the previously acquired entities are typically sold off, as the divesting parent firm can no longer add significant value to these entities. The frequent divestiture of business entities and assets severely limits possibilities for sustainable synergies to exist and would, moreover, be harmful for entities whose competitive strength would be partly derived from these synergies. Therefore, the business entities that are part of a parent firm that focuses predominantly on reorganization are typically unrelated. The firm can generate positive returns on invested capital by making a profit on selling those entities or assets that it previously bought and restructured.[63]

## Organizational restructuring

Simply put, **organizational restructuring** denotes changes in a firm's organizational structure – for instance, changes in how a firm's resources and activities are grouped, how its activities are divided into tasks, and how these different (sets of) resources, activities and tasks are coordinated.[64]

A distinction can be made between three principal types of organizational structures: a simple structure, a functional structure, and a multidivisional structure. The *simple structure* denotes a structure in which a firm's owner or director – which can be the same person – bears the sole responsibility for strategically important decisions and for monitoring the firm's activities. This structure is typically characterized by a limited degree of task specialization and a high degree of informal relationships among employees, who serve as an extension of the owner's or director's authority.[65] In a *functional structure*, the firm is structurally divided into functional departments such as operations, R&D, logistics, marketing, finance and HR, implying a higher degree of task specialization as compared to the simple structure. Each of these departments is headed by a functional line manager who reports to the firm's board, which implies also a higher degree of formalization. Finally, a *multidivisional structure* denotes a structure consisting of at least two corporate divisions, each of which is headed by a division-level management team with profit and loss (P&L) responsibility for one or more distinct product markets, geographical markets, or a combination thereof (see Chapter 12). Functional-level activities can be the direct responsibility of the corporate parent (for instance, a central marketing department), the divisions (for instance, decentralized marketing units that focus on a particular product or geographical market), or both.

Over time, as firms grow larger and become more complex in terms of the scope and number of activities and tasks, as a result of which internal coordination becomes more challenging, they may need to replace their existing simple structure with a functional structure, or to replace their existing functional structure with a multidivisional structure.[66] These are two general examples of organizational restructuring. Another example is a change from a three-region structure with single-product category heads to an alternative structure organized around four product categories, as announced by FMCG multinational Unilever in 2011.[67] By 2021, Unilever had changed this structure into a matrix structure, which in 2022 was replaced by, once again, a simpler, more category-focused structure with distinct business groups, each of which is supported by a corporate division to drive operational excellence.[68] Most firms have organized their resources and activities around business line, function, technology platform, customer segment, geography, or a combination of some of these in the form of a matrix organization. Basically any transformation from one organizational structure to another can be considered *organizational restructuring*. This also includes the splitting of a certain corporate division into two or more divisions that each remain part of the same firm, or the combining of two or more of its divisions into one.

Organizational restructuring is often, but not necessarily, accompanied by layoffs of personnel or the relocation of personnel or other assets. It could, for instance, be the case that fewer people than before are needed to perform specific functions in the new situation to deliver the same or even more output. Also, employees may end up in different positions than before. As with acquisitions and divestitures, implementation of restructuring efforts may be challenging for firms – for instance, there may be strong (hidden) resistance to change from people in affected positions.

## Financial restructuring

The *financial structure* of a firm refers to the way(s) in which its resource base and day-to-day activities are financed. This financing typically consists of a certain mix of funded debt and equity (which together determine a firm's capital structure) and other sources, such as accounts payable and accrued wages that arise from the purchase of labour and other production inputs.[69] Any significant change in a firm's financial structure is referred to as **financial restructuring**. Such a change can be the outcome of, for instance, a buy-out, on which we concentrate here. A **leveraged buyout (LBO)** implies that the assets of a firm or a part of these assets (for instance, a division) are 'bought out' (purchased) by another firm, such as a private equity firm, which uses a considerable sum of borrowed money (commonly known as debt or 'leverage') to finance that transaction. LBOs are often undertaken to make a public firm private, but they can, for instance, also be used to spin off a certain part of a firm. To support debt payments, the new owner of the assets may choose to sell part of the assets right away in order to support debt payments.[70] The label *whole-firm LBO* can be used to refer to cases in which all assets of a firm are bought out (instead of only part of the firm). When all or part of a certain firm is bought out by one or more of its directors (or by the entire management team), this is called a *management buyout*. A case in point is when in 2013 Michael Dell partnered with private equity firm Silver Lake and Microsoft Corp to buy out the firm (Dell Inc.) that he had founded in 1984 for almost $25 billion in order to take it private.[71] Instead of a regular management buyout it could also occur that a firm is bought out by persons from outside the firm, who become the firm's new management once the LBO transaction is completed – this is known as a *buy-in management buyout*.

## Corporate decline and turnaround

Every firm will face decline at some point in time, and for some firms this moment comes sooner or more frequently than for others. The question of why some firms outperform others is central to the field of strategic management (see Chapter 1). In the case of enduring underperformance, firms must come up with a strategy to turn around their core business(es) and additional businesses, if any. Reconfiguration and restructuring, as discussed in this chapter, are commonly an integral part of turnaround efforts. In addition to that, firms may have to look into corporate entrepreneurship (Chapter 15) business model innovation (Chapter 16), and strategic renewal (Chapter 17).

## CLOSING CASE

### Philips: from electronic conglomerate to HealthTech firm[72]

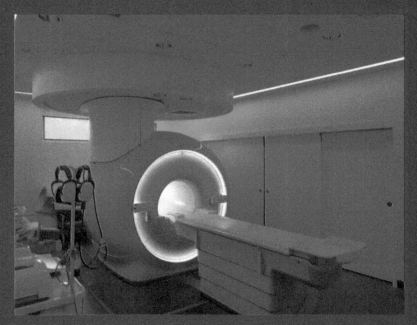

Source: © Sean RhinoPhotography (2019) / Shutterstock.

Light bulbs, lamps, televisions and domestic appliances such as coffee makers and air fryers with a Philips logo were not hard to find for the average consumer in many countries worldwide in 2023. But by then it was no longer Royal Philips ('Philips') that produced and marketed these products. Once a sprawling lighting and consumer electronics conglomerate, the Amsterdam-based firm had gradually transformed into a HealthTech (health technology) firm. In 2010 Philips did not only produce and market lamps, luminaires and lighting, but it had also entered multiple business areas related to consumer lifestyle (including televisions and domestic appliances) and healthcare. In 2012, the firm divested its television business as part of a strategic alliance deal with China-based TPV Technology. Philips retained a 30% stake in TP Vision – part of TPV Technology – until 2014, when it sold this remaining stake to TPV Technology. In the same year, Philips announced that it would sharpen its strategic focus by integrating its Consumer Lifestyle and Healthcare divisions into one operating firm focused on HealthTech business lines, while carving out its Lighting division into a separate legal structure. 'The proposed separation of the Lighting business impacts all businesses and markets as well as all supporting functions and all assets and liabilities of the Group and may require complex and time-consuming disentanglement efforts', as per its 2014 Annual Report. In 2016, Philips Lighting was spun off to become Signify and in 2021 Philips sold its profitable domestic appliances business segment to the Chinese private equity firm Hillhouse Capital. In the meantime, the firm had also sold its audio and video multimedia and accessories businesses. Licensing agreements allowed buyers of these businesses to continue using the Philips brand name, generating a substantial and continuing income stream for Philips.

In 2020, Philips' then CEO Frans van Houten had commented on the firm's plan to carve out its domestic appliances business as 'not a strategic fit for our future as a health technology leader'.[73] Two years later, the firm ended up competing only in the business segments personal health, connected care, precision diagnosis, and image guided therapy. Its purpose became to improve people's health and well-being through meaningful innovation across the health continuum: from healthy living to disease prevention, diagnosis, treatment, and home care. In order to deliver on this purpose and to be able to offer its customers personalized health solutions, the firm significantly increased its expenditures on digital technologies such as artificial intelligence (AI), IoT and sensing technologies. To quickly expand its HealthTech operations, Philips acquired multiple firms. For instance, in 2022 it acquired, among others, Cardiologic, a France-based medical technology firm specialized in transforming cardiac diagnostics using AI and cloud technology.

## Questions

1. What has been the role of reconfiguration and restructuring in realizing Philips' transformation from a lighting and consumer electronics conglomerate into a HealthTech leader?
2. What difficulties might Philips have encountered when carving out its former Lighting division?
3. What are the advantages of having a minority equity stake before full divestment?

## Summary

- Reorganization is a type of transformation that encompasses two distinct change processes: reconfiguration and restructuring.
- Reconfiguration, which can be achieved through acquisition and divestiture, involves adding, combining, transferring, splitting or liquidating business entities without necessarily modifying the underlying structure of the firm.
- An acquisition denotes a transaction in which a firm takes full ownership or a controlling stake in another firm. This firm can operate up- or downstream of the acquirer (vertical integration), in the same stage of the same industry value chain (horizontal integration), or in another value chain.
- Motives for opting for an acquisition may include a desire to increase market power, expand the resource base or capability range, overcome entry barriers, or give in to external pressures (acquisition bandwagon) or personal ambitions. Not all these motives are conducive to creating value for the firm and its shareholders.

- Differences in the type of acquisition bid, mode of payment, asset complementarity, strategic and cultural fit between the acquiring and acquired firm, and the post-acquisition integration process can explain why some acquisitions create more wealth for shareholders than others.
- Although the term divestiture can refer to the disposal of any asset, it commonly denotes the disposal of a division or of a controlling interest in a subsidiary firm through a sale, exchange or liquidation.
- Firms can carry out a divestiture in different ways, including a spin-off, split-off, sell-off, equity carve-out, and liquidation. The main differences between these transaction formats have to do with the share ownership after the divestiture.
- A divestiture transaction is followed by the implementation of the divestiture, which should be seen as a carve-out delivery process in which specific assets and liabilities that constitute the newly established entity (in the case of a spin-off or split-off) or the sold entity (in the case of a sell-off) are set apart ('carved out').
- The characteristics of a carve-out delivery process are partly different from those of a reverse integration process, apart from the reversed ordering.
- Organizational restructuring implies changes in how a firm's resources and activities are grouped, how its activities are divided into tasks, or how these resources, activities and tasks are coordinated.
- Financial restructuring implies changes in the way(s) in which a firm's resources and day-to-day activities are financed.
- Reconfiguration and restructuring can be intertwined, in that reconfiguration can lead directly to restructuring, and vice versa, but they can also take place independently from each other.
- By altering the composition or structure of a firm, acquisition, divestiture, and restructuring strategies can contribute significantly to the firm's transformation and to performance improvements.

## Review questions

1. How could you explain that some acquisitions create more value than others?
2. What is the difference between a spin-off, a split-off, and a sell-off?
3. Why is a carve-out not just simply a mirrored integration?
4. Why can an acquisition or a divestiture result in restructuring efforts, and vice versa?

## Discussion questions

1. Why can acquisitions, divestitures, and restructuring contribute equally to the improvement of a firm's performance?
2. Reorganizations are usually undertaken to improve a firm's performance to the benefit of its owners. Managers should also look after their employees. In practice, reorganizations often result in layoffs. How can managers maximize the safeguarding of both stakeholder groups' interests?

**EXPERIENTIAL EXERCISES**

1.  Select a firm that you find interesting and examine whether it has engaged in acquisitions and divestitures in the last five years. Do the same for its largest rival. To what extent do you see differences and similarities in their choices?
2.  Read an economic newspaper (such as the *Financial Times*) and look for an item on a firm that is in financial trouble. What would be your main suggestions to turn its situation around?

# Further reading

Barkema, H.G. and Schijven, M. (2008) 'Toward unlocking the full potential of acquisitions: The role of organizational restructuring', *Academy of Management Journal*, 51 (4): 696–722.

Doan, T.T., Sahib, P.R. and Van Witteloostuijn, A. (2018) 'Lessons from the flipside: How do acquirers learn from divestitures to complete acquisitions?', *Long Range Planning*, 51 (2): 252–66.

Feldman, E.R. and Sakhartov, A.V. (2022) 'Resource redeployment and divestiture as strategic alternatives', *Organization Science*, 33: 926–45.

Girod, S.J.G. and Whittington, R. (2017) 'Reconfiguration, restructuring and firm performance: Dynamic capabilities and environmental dynamism', *Strategic Management Journal*, 38: 1121–33.

Lee, D.D. and Madhavan, R. (2010) 'Divestiture and firm performance: A meta-analysis', *Journal of Management*, 36: 1345–71.

# Endnotes (references)

1.  Beioley, K. (2021) 'EY to spend $2bn on improving audit quality after scandals', *Financial Times,* September 9. www.ft.com/content/737dd635-dba2-49d7-bcdd-34f467b218ea (accessed June 28, 2023); Consultancy.uk (2022) 'EY's top leaders approve split of audit and consulting business', *Consultancy.uk,* September 9. www.consultancy.uk/news/32281/eys-top-leaders-approve-split-of-audit-and-consulting-business (accessed June 28, 2023); EY (2022) 'EY UK – Home', *EY.* https://web.archive.org/web/20230627224211/https://www.ey.com/en_us (accessed June 28, 2023); Goldstein, M. (2022) 'EY, the accounting and consulting firm, will split into two businesses', *The New York Times,* September 8. www.nytimes.com/2022/09/08/business/ey-ernst-young-split.html (accessed June 28, 2023); Maurer, M. and Eaglesham, J. (2022) 'Accounting firm EY considers split of audit, advisory businesses', *The Wall Street Journal,* May 26. www.wsj.com/articles/accounting-firm-ey-considers-splitting-audit-and-advisory-businesses-11653592588 (accessed June 27, 2023); Peters, S. (2021) 'UK audit reform: Audits of internal controls over financial reporting', CFA Institute, July 27. https://blogs.cfainstitute.org/marketintegrity/2021/07/27/uk-audit-reform-audits-of-internal-controls-over-financial-reporting (accessed June 28, 2023); Reuters (2022) 'EY to report record revenues of $45.4bln for year', *Reuters,* July 28. www.reuters.com/markets/europe/ey-report-record-revenues-454-bln-year-ft-2022-07-28 (accessed June 28, 2023); Storbeck, O. (2021b) 'EY and Wirecard: Anatomy of a

flawed audit', *Financial Times*, October 26. www.ft.com/content/bcadbdcb-5cd7-487e-afdd-1e926831e9b7 (accessed June 28, 2023).

2. Storbek (2021)
3. PCAOB (2014) *Report from the Working Group on Audit Firm Business Model and Incentives.* https://pcaobus.org/News/Events/Documents/10202014_IAG/Audit_Firm_Business_Model.pdf (accessed July 27, 2023).
4. Beioley (2021)
5. Peters (2021)
6. O'Dwyer, M., Foley, S. and White, S. (2022) 'EY attempts to smooth path to vote on radical break-up', *Financial Times,* November 27. www.ft.com/content/810402d4-46aa-4f47-9e8b-2a4d20b3c203 (accessed June 28, 2023).
7. Reuters (2023) 'EY calls off plan to split audit, consulting units', April 11. www.reuters.com/business/ey-scraps-break-up-plan-ft-2023-04-11 (accessed July 27, 2023).
8. Girod, S.J.G. and Karim, S. (2017) 'Restructure or reconfigure?', *Harvard Business Review*, March/April. https://hbr.org/2017/03/restructure-or-reconfigure (accessed June 26, 2023); Girod, S.J.G. and Whittington, R. (2017) 'Reconfiguration, restructuring and firm performance: Dynamic capabilities and environmental dynamism', *Strategic Management Journal*, 38: 1121–33.
9. Girod and Karim (2017)
10. Engert, O. and O'Loughlin, E. (2018) 'How to win at M&A', *McKinsey,* May 28. www.mckinsey.com/capabilities/people-and-organizational-performance/our-insights/the-organization-blog/how-to-win-at-ma (accessed June 28, 2023).
11. Hitt, M.A., Harrison, J.S. and Ireland, R.D. (2001) *Mergers and Acquisitions: A Guide to Creating Value for Stakeholders.* Oxford: Oxford University Press.
12. Davis, M.F., Tse, C. and Foerster, J. (2022) 'Dealmaking slips by almost a third in 2022 marked by volatility, inflation', *Bloomberg,* December 21. www.bloomberg.com/news/articles/2022-12-21/dealmaking-falls-by-30-in-2022-as-inflation-volatility-hit-m-a-volumes (accessed June 28, 2023).
13. Statista (2022) 'Number of merger and acquisition (M&A) transactions worldwide from 2010 to 2021', *Statista,* March 2. www.statista.com/statistics/267368/number-of-mergers-and-acquisitions-worldwide-since-2005 (accessed June 28, 2023).
14. Nishant, N. (2021) 'Global M&A volumes hit record high in 2021, breach $5 trillion for first time', *Reuters,* December 31. www.reuters.com/markets/us/global-ma-volumes-hit-record-high-2021-breach-5-trillion-first-time-2021-12-31 (accessed June 28, 2023).
15. Tony's Chocolonely (2021) 'We're the proud new owners of a choco factory', https://tonyschocolonely.com/us/en/our-mission/news/were-the-proud-new-owners-of-a-choco-factory (accessed June 28, 2023).
16. Gulbrandsen, B., Sandvik, K. and Haugland, S.A. (2009) 'Antecedents of vertical integration: Transaction cost economics and resource-based explanations', *Journal of Purchasing and Supply Management*, 15: 89–102; Rothaermel, F.T., Hitt, M.A. and Jobe, L.A. (2006) 'Balancing vertical integration and strategic outsourcing: Effects on product portfolio, product success, and firm performance', *Strategic Management Journal*, 27: 1033–56.
17. Upshall, E. (2021) 'Tony's Chocolonely acquires Belgian chocolate manufacturer Althaea-De Laet Int', FoodBev Media, April 26. www.foodbev.com/news/tonys-chocolonely-acquires-belgian-chocolate-manufacturer-althaea-de-laet-int (accessed June 28, 2023).
18. Akdogu, E. (2009) 'Gaining a competitive edge through acquisitions: Evidence from the telecommunications industry', *Journal of Corporate Finance*, 15: 99–112; Devos, E., Kadapakkam, P. and Krishnamurthy, S. (2009) 'How do mergers create value?

A comparison of taxes, market power, and efficiency improvements as explanations for synergies', *Review of Financial Studies*, 22: 1179–211.

19. Haleblian, J., Devers, C.E., McNamara, G., Carpenter, M.A. and Davison, R.B. (2009) 'Taking stock of what we know about mergers and acquisitions: A review and research agenda', *Journal of Management*, 35: 469–502; Wright, P., Kroll, M. and Elenkov, D. (2002) 'Acquisition returns, increase in firm size and chief executive officer compensation: The moderating role of monitoring', *Academy of Management Journal*, 45: 599–608.

20. Chen, S.S. and Zeng, M. (2004) 'Japanese investors' choice of acquisitions vs. startups in the U.S.: The role of reputation barriers and advertising outlays', *International Journal of Research in Marketing*, 21 (2): 123–36; Meyer, K.E., Wright, M. and Pruthi, S. (2009) 'Managing knowledge in foreign entry strategies: A resource-based analysis', *Strategic Management Journal*, 30: 557–74.

21. Agrawal, A. and Jaffe, J.F. (2000) 'The post-merger performance puzzle', in C.L. Cooper and S. Finkelstein (eds), *Advances in Mergers and Acquisitions*. Bingley: Emerald, 7–41.

22. Cartwright, S. and Schoenberg, R. (2006) 'Thirty years of mergers and acquisitions research: Recent advances and future opportunities', *British Journal of Management*, 17 (S1): S1–5.

23. Sudarsanam, S. and Mahate, A.A. (2006) 'Are friendly acquisitions too bad for shareholders and managers? Long-term value creation and top management turnover in hostile and friendly acquirers', *British Journal of Management*, 17 (S1): S7–30.

24. Aiello, R.J. and Watkins, M.D. (2000) 'The fine art of friendly acquisition', *Harvard Business Review*, 78 (6): 100–7; Kisgen, D.J., Qian, J. and Song, W. (2009) 'Are fairness opinions fair? The case of mergers and acquisitions', *Journal of Financial Economics*, 91: 179–207.

25. Bergh, D.D. (2001) 'Executive retention and acquisition outcomes: A test of opposing views on the influence of organizational tenure', *Journal of Management*, 27: 603–22; Chatterjee, S. (2009) 'Does increased equity ownership lead to more strategically involved boards?', *Journal of Business Ethics*, 87: 267–77; Walsh, J.P. (1989) 'Doing a deal: Merger and acquisition negotiations and their impact upon target firm top management turnover', *Strategic Management Journal*, 10: 307–22.

26. Datta, D.K., Pinches, G.E. and Narayanan, V.K. (1992) 'Factors influencing wealth creation from mergers and acquisitions: A meta-analysis', *Strategic Management Journal*, 13 (1): 67–84.

27. DeAngelo, H., DeAngelo, L. and Rice, E.M. (1984) 'Going private: Minority freezeouts and stockholder wealth', *The Journal of Law and Economics*, 27 (2): 367–401; Myers, S.C. and Majluf, N.S. (1984) 'Corporate financing and investment decisions when firms have information that investors do not have', *Journal of Financial Economics*, 13 (2): 187–221.

28. Datta et al. (1992); Franks, J.R., Harris, R.S. and Mayer, C. (1988) 'Means of payment in takeovers: Results for the United Kingdom and the United States', in A.J. Auerbach (ed.), *Corporate Takeovers: Causes and Consequences*. Chicago, IL: University of Chicago Press, 221–63; Hayn, C. (1989) 'Tax attributes as determinants of shareholder gains in corporate acquisitions', *Journal of Financial Economics*, 23: 121–53.

29. Capron, L. and Pistre, N. (2002) 'When do acquirers earn abnormal returns?', *Strategic Management Journal*, 23 (9): 781–94.

30. Ahuja, G. and Katila, R. (2001) 'Technological acquisitions and the innovation performance of acquiring firms: A longitudinal study', *Strategic Management Journal*, 22 (3): 197–220.

31. Fee, C.E. and Thomas, S. (2004) 'Sources of gains in horizontal mergers: Evidence from customer, supplier, and rival firms', *Journal of Financial Economics*, 74: 423–60.

32. Porrini, P. (2004) 'Can a previous alliance between an acquirer and a target affect acquisition performance?', *Journal of Management*, 30: 545–62; Reuer, J.J. and Ragozzino, R. (2006) 'Agency hazards and alliance portfolios', *Strategic Management Journal*, 27: 27–43.

33. Cartwright, S. (2005) 'Mergers and acquisitions: An update and appraisal', *International Review of Industrial and Organizational Psychology*, 20: 1–38; Schoenberg, R. (2000) 'The influence of cultural compatibility within cross-border acquisitions: A review', in C.L. Cooper and S. Finkelstein (eds), *Advances in Mergers and Acquisitions*. Bingley: Emerald, 34–59.

34. AB InBev (2016) 'Anheuser-Busch InBev Announces Completion of Combination with SABMiller', *AB InBev,* October 10. www.ab-inbev.com/content/dam/universaltemplate/ ab-inbev/investors/releases/10October2016/Announcement_of_Completion_of_the_ Belgian_Merger.pdf (accessed June 28, 2023); Blenkinsop, P. (2022) 'AB InBev raises 2022 outlook as its beer sales accelerate', *Reuters,* October 27. www.reuters.com/business/ retail-consumer/ab-inbev-pushes-up-2022-outlook-after-solid-third-quarter-2022-10-27 (accessed June 28, 2023); Massoudi, A. and Abboud, L. (2019) 'How deal for SABMiller left AB InBev with lasting hangover', *Financial Times,* July 24. www.ft.com/content/ bb048b10-ad66-11e9-8030-530adfa879c2 (accessed June 28, 2023); Notte, J. (2017) 'Anheuser-Busch InBev shuts out craft beer brewers by hoarding hops', *MarketWatch*, May 12. www.marketwatch.com/story/anheuser-busch-inbev-shuts-out-craft-beer-brewers-by-hoarding-hops-2017-05-11 (accessed June 28, 2023); Ramsay, R. (2017) 'AB InBev South African hops vs. craft breweries (A new drama)', *Beer Street Journal,* May 10. https:// beerstreetjournal.com/ab-inbev-south-african-hops (accessed June 28).

35. Baker et al. (2009); Cool, K. and Van de Laar, M. (2006) 'The performance of acquisitive firms in the U.S.', in L. Renneboog (ed.), *Advances in Corporate Finance and Asset Pricing*. Amsterdam: Elsevier Science, 77–105.

36. Christensen, C.M., Alton, R., Rising, C. and Waldeck, W. (2011) 'The big idea: The new M&A playbook', *Harvard Business Review*, 89 (3): 48–57.

37. Kenny, G. (2020) 'Don't make this common M&A mistake', *Harvard Business Review* (online), March 16. https://hbr.org/2020/03/dont-make-this-common-ma-mistake (accessed June 28, 2023).

38. Coopers & Lybrand (1992) *A Review of the Acquisitions Experience of Major UK Companies*. London: Coopers & Lybrand.

39. Hayward, M.L. (2002) 'When do firms learn from their acquisition experience? Evidence from 1990 to 1995', *Strategic Management Journal*, 23 (1), 21–39.

40. Doan, T.T., Sahib, P.R. and Van Witteloostuijn, A. (2018) 'Lessons from the flipside: How do acquirers learn from divestitures to complete acquisitions?', *Long Range Planning*, 51 (2): 252–66; McDonald, M.L., Westphal, J.D. and Graebner, M.E. (2008) 'What do they know? The effects of outside director acquisition experience on firm acquisition performance', *Strategic Management Journal*, 29: 1155–77; Shaver, J.M. and Mezias, J.M. (2009) 'Diseconomies of managing in acquisitions: Evidence from civil lawsuits', *Organization Science*, 20: 206–22.

41. Baker, M., Pan, X. and Wurgler, J. (2009) 'The psychology of pricing in mergers and acquisitions', Working Paper. https://archive.nyu.edu/bitstream/2451/28091/2/ wpa09001.pdf (accessed June 28, 2023); Cool & Van de Laar (2006).

42. Kenny (2020)

43. Kenny (2020)

44. Doan et al. (2018)

45. Cumming, J. and Mallie, T.Y. (1999) 'Accounting for divestitures: A comparison of sell-offs, spin-offs, split-offs, and split-ups', *Issues in Accounting Education*, 14: 75–97; Feldman, E.R. and McGrath, P.J. (2016) 'Divestitures', *Journal of Organization Design*, 5 (2): 1–16.

46. Lee, D.D. and Madhavan, R. (2010) 'Divestiture and firm performance: A meta-analysis'. *Journal of Management*, 36: 1345–71.

47. Feldman, E.R. (2021) 'The corporate parenting advantage, revisited', *Strategic Management Journal*, 42: 114–43.

48. Anand, R. (2020) *Firm Divestitures in Different Environmental Contexts*. PhD dissertation, Jouy-en Josas: HEC School of Management.

49. Feldman and McGrath (2016)

50. e.g., Benito, G.R.G. and Welch, L.S. (1997) 'De-internationalization', *Management International Review*, 37: 7–25.

51. e.g., Kaiser, F. and Obermaier, R. (2020) 'Vertical (dis-)integration and firm performance: A management paradigm revisited', *Schmalenbach Business Review*, 72: 1–37.

52. Stromsta, K.-E. (2019) 'SunPower to spin off manufacturing business in major strategic shift', *GTM*, November 11. www.greentechmedia.com/articles/read/sunpower-to-spin-off-manufacturing-business-in-major-strategic-shift (accessed June 28, 2023).

53. Dewitt, R. (1998) 'Firm, industry, and strategy influences on choice of downsizing approach', *Strategic Management Journal*, 19 (1): 59–79.

54. Lee and Madhavan (2010)

55. Feldman and McGrath (2016)

56. AkzoNobel (2018) 'AkzoNobel to sell Specialty Chemicals to The Carlyle Group and GIC for €10.1 billion', *AkzoNobel*, March 27. www.akzonobel.com/en/media/latest-news---media-releases-/akzonobel-to-sell-specialty-chemicals-to-the-carlyle-group-and-g (accessed June 28, 2023).

57. Pham, D., Nguyen, T. and Adhikari, H. (2018) 'Determinants of divestiture methods for US firms: Asset sell-off versus equity carve-out', *Review of Accounting and Finance*, 17 (1): 41–57.

58. Allen, J.W. and McConnell, J.J. (1998) 'Equity carve-outs and managerial discretion', *Journal of Finance*, 53 (1): 163–86; Vijh, A. (2002) 'The positive announcement-period returns of equity carveouts: Asymmetric information or divestiture gains?', *The Journal of Business*, 75 (1): 153–90.

59. Pham et al. (2018)

60. del Valle, G. (2019) 'Payless is closing all its US stores', *Vox*, February 19. www.vox.com/the-goods/2019/2/18/18229378/payless-shoesource-liqudation-stores-closing (accessed June 19, 2023).

61. Girod and Karim (2017)

62. Porter, M.E. (1987) 'From competitive advantage to corporate strategy', *Harvard Business Review*, 65 (3): 43–59.

63. Porter (1987)

64. Girod and Karim (2017)

65. Levicki, C. (1999) *The Interactive Strategy Workout* (2nd ed.). London: Prentice Hall.

66. Chandler Jr, A.D. (1962) *Strategy and Structure: Chapters in the History of the Industrial Empire*. Cambridge, MA: MIT Press; Mialon, S.H. (2008) 'Efficient horizontal mergers: The effects of internal capital reallocation and organizational form', *International Journal of Industrial Organization*, 26 (4): 861–77; O'Neill, H.M., Pouder, R.W. and Buchholtz, A.K. (1998) 'Patterns in the diffusion of strategies across organizations: Insights from the innovation diffusion literature', *Academy of Management Review*, 23: 98–114.

67. Reuters (2011) 'Unilever to focus on product categories rather than regions', *Reuters,* June 24. www.reuters.com/article/unilever-reorganisation-idUSL6E7HO0UB20110624 (accessed June 14, 2023).

68. Unilever (2022d) 'Unilever simplifies organisation', *Unilever,* January 25. www.unilever.com/news/press-and-media/press-releases/2022/unilever-simplifies-organisation (accessed June 28, 2023).

69. Belanger, J.P. (2015) 'Firm financial structure', in C.L. Cooper and R.E. McAuliffe (eds), Wiley Encyclopedia of Management, 1–2.

70. Wiersema, M.F. and Liebeskind, J.P. (1995) 'The effects of leveraged buyouts on corporate growth and diversification in large firms', *Strategic Management Journal*, 16: 447–60; Wruck, K.H. (2009) 'Private equity, corporate governance and the reinvention of the market for corporate control', *Journal of Applied Corporate Finance*, 20: 8–21.

71. Roumeliotis, G. and O'Grady, E. (2013) 'Michael Dell closes in on prize with sweeter $25 billion deal', *Reuters*, August 2. www.reuters.com/article/us-dell-buyout-vote-idUSBRE97106220130802 (accessed June 28, 2023).

72. Philips (2015) *Annual Report 2014*. Available from https://www.annualreports.com/Company/koninklijke-philips-nv (accessed June 28, 2023); Philips (2020) 'Philips to review options for its Domestic Appliances business', *Philips,* January 28. www.philips.com/a-w/about/news/archive/standard/news/press/2020/20200128-philips-to-review-options-for-its-domestic-appliances-business.html (accessed June 28, 2023); Philips (2021) 'Philips to further expand its image-guided therapy devices portfolio through acquisition of Vesper Medical', *Philips,* December 14. www.philips.com/a-w/about/news/archive/standard/news/press/2021/20211214-philips-to-further-expand-its-image-guided-therapy-devices-portfolio-through-acquisition-of-vesper-medical.html (accessed June 28, 2023).

73. Philips (2020)

# Acknowledgements

The authors thank Dennis Steur and Naadiya Ismail for their contribution to this chapter.

# Key terms

**Acquisition** – a transaction in which one firm takes full ownership or a controlling stake in another firm

**Carve-out delivery** – the implementation of a divestiture by setting apart specific assets and liabilities that constitute the newly established or sold entity

**Divestiture** – corporate transaction that results in a decrease in corporate size by removing part of a firm's assets and activities

**Equity carve-out** – a type of divestiture where a parent firm sells shares of a subsidiary unit, in which it typically retains considerable ownership, to public investors

**Financial restructuring** – a change process that involves alterations in the underlying financial structure of (part of) a firm

**Leveraged buyout (LBO)** – the purchase of a firm's assets or part of those assets by a firm that uses a considerable sum of borrowed money to finance that transaction

**Liquidation** – a type of divestiture where a parent firm closes down a subsidiary unit or division

**Merger** – a legal consolidation of two firms into one, which then operates as one legal entity

**Organizational restructuring** – a change process that involves alterations in the structures around which a firm's resources and activities are grouped and coordinated

**Reconfiguration** – a change process that involves the adding, combining, transferring, splitting or dissolving of business entities

**Restructuring** – a change process that involves alterations in the structures around which a firm's resources and activities are grouped and coordinated or in the underlying financial structure

**Sell-off** – a type of divestiture where a parent firm sells a subsidiary unit

**Spin-off** – a type of divestiture where the shares in a divested division are distributed to existing shareholders, the allocation of which is in proportion to shareholdings.

**Split-off** – a type of divestiture where the shares in a divested division are distributed to existing shareholders, who have to choose between owning shares in the divesting parent firm or in the divested business entity

# 15

# STRATEGIC ENTREPRENEURSHIP

## LEARNING OBJECTIVES

After reading this chapter, you should be able to:

- appreciate how strategic entrepreneurship is connected to innovation;
- understand the challenges associated with managing corporate entrepreneurship;
- distinguish between different types of innovation and approaches to innovation;
- recognize different avenues available to companies for startup engagement;
- evaluate different methods to promote innovation in a company.

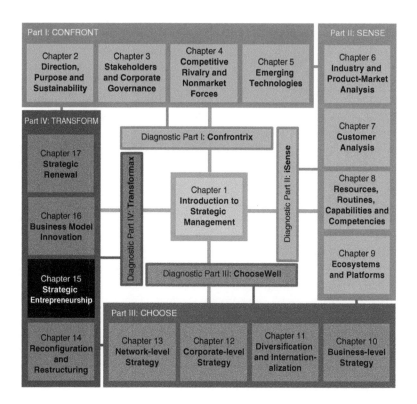

## OPENING CASE

Source: © Gorgev (2023) / Shutterstock.

### Searching for innovations at Google[1]

Imagine being hired by a company, and upon arriving at the office for the first time, you receive a silly hat, are named a 'Noogler', and are encouraged to have a disruptive entrepreneurial mindset. Although for a moment you may be tempted to rethink your decision to join the company, you are likely to be reassured by the fact that it is one of the largest and most successful companies of the 21st century: Google Inc. Much of the company's success is the result of its incredible innovation output – the managerial conviction underwriting this feat is that to optimize a company's innovation potential, all employees need to think and act like entrepreneurs.

Google specializes in internet-related services and products, including online advertising, search engines, cloud computing, hardware, and software. Larry Page and Sergey Brin founded Google on September 4, 1998. Since its founding, Google has grown rapidly by leveraging its partnerships, acquisitions, and new products. It is considered one of the 'Big Five', a term used to refer to the five largest American information technology companies. Because of a 2015 corporate restructuring, Google is a subsidiary company of Alphabet Inc., which is also the parent of many other smaller companies. As of 2022, Google Inc. employs approximately 140,000 employees worldwide.[2]

Since its inception, Google has developed from a Stanford University search-engine startup, to becoming an exceptionally high-growth company, to becoming one of the largest corporations in the world. The demands of managing a small startup company stand in stark contrast to those of running an enormous corporation. As such, Google has had to sacrifice some of its informal entrepreneurial approach in favour of a more structured and controlled management approach. However, it is unlikely Google will ever lose its entrepreneurial culture. This raises the question, what does corporate entrepreneurship look like at Google as it approaches its 25th birthday?

When a company is as immense as Google, it is perhaps not surprising that it would employ different approaches to innovation. At Google, both open innovation (i.e. innovation based on collaboration with external parties) and closed innovation (i.e. innovation based on use of internal knowledge and no outside participation) are the norm. At times, open and closed innovation even feature in a single project, such that the project moves through sequential stages of public testing based on open innovation, and then a closed-innovation stage of 'stealth development'. Furthermore, Google employs top-down as well as bottom-up innovation approaches. The difference between the two is whether the impetus for innovation and the direction of innovation comes from senior managers or from rank-and-file employees empowered to pursue entrepreneurial ideas. Although the top-down approach has created some of Google's most successful products such as Google Translate, it is Google's bottom-up approach that attracts the attention of outsiders most.

Bottom-up innovation has been an obsession of Google since its inception – empowering the workforce and fostering innovative thinking is vital in Google's view. 'We prefer [our engineers] to run rampant', Google's former CEO Schmidt explained in a 2005 interview with InfoWorld. To maximize the effectiveness of its entrepreneurial innovation, Google has organized itself to foster and support unexpected innovations resulting from entrepreneurial employees. Back in 2005, Google did this by employing a flat, data-driven organizational structure; a '20% time' policy, allowing employees to decide how to spend 20% of their time creating the most benefit for Google; accessible and powerful development environments; infrastructure to help launch, test, and improve products; and generous rewards and recognition for successful innovation.

Since 2005, Google has grown into a technology behemoth and has abandoned its flat organizational structure as well as its famous 20% rule. Although it is no longer the disruptive and fast-moving technology company it once was, the essence of its corporate entrepreneurship approach remains intact. Guiding principles in the 2020s include: employees are encouraged to focus on customers, not competitors; ideas can come from anywhere; embrace open innovation by sharing as much information as possible with customers; think big, start small; fail and learn; and use data, not opinions.

As Google ages, it faces significant external pressure from all directions: political, economic, social, technological, environmental, and legal. Furthermore, in contrast to being a young company that promoted risk-taking in largely underdeveloped markets, it has evolved into a mature company operating in developed markets. Yet, as it spends hundreds of millions a year on its corporate entrepreneurship programs, it remains determined to emerge as the winner in the 2020s. As Google moves to a new phase in its history, the question arises: will Google's corporate entrepreneurship activities continue to deliver the type of success the company has experienced in the past?

## Questions

1. Google has abolished many of its corporate entrepreneurship initiatives such as the '20% rule'. Why do you think it did so?
2. With Google now being an established, large-sized corporation, what type of innovation would be most effective: bottom-up or top-down?
3. Is it smart for a large corporation, in contrast to a young technology company, to promote disruptive thinking across its entire organization?

# Introduction

The opening case of this chapter suggests that entrepreneurial behaviour and innovativeness (i.e., a regular stream of innovations) go hand-in-hand. A company's innovativeness is important for building and sustaining competitive advantage for above-average returns over time. Strategic entrepreneurship, indeed, is one of the fundamental vehicles for the transformation of a company. It fuels the future growth of a company, putting it on a stronger footing than less entrepreneurial competitors. An entrepreneurial company confronts and responds to its context through innovations. Innovations depend on identifying opportunities to create new capabilities, technologies, products, processes, and services. In other words, innovations depend on entrepreneurship. As the future unfolds, entrepreneurial behaviour, as exemplified by the Google story, is thus essential for companies wanting to stay ahead of others in their business domain. Indeed, companies that have an entrepreneurial culture, such as Apple and Tesla, may participate in shaping the unfolding future. In this chapter, you will develop your knowledge of strategic entrepreneurship and how this is important for realizing transformation and innovation. You will also build your understanding of the challenges of managing the process of corporate entrepreneurship, and the different entrepreneurial pathways available for a company seeking to become more innovative.

The expression **strategic entrepreneurship** combines the notion of being strategic with the concept of entrepreneurship. It embodies the idea that advantage-seeking strategic intent should guide opportunity-seeking entrepreneurial conduct with a view to attaining above-average performance. Strategic entrepreneurship is thus about transforming the company by identifying and taking advantage of opportunities presented by the business environment to generate and capture value. While the strategic component of strategic entrepreneurship has to do with the mobilization and allocation of resources to exploit opportunities, the entrepreneurship component centers on the search for and the identification of opportunities. This is easier said than done, because opportunities are difficult to spot – they are often wrapped in uncertainty because of changing technologies, customer demands, and patterns of competition. Once an opportunity has been identified, a firm must gauge its future value and take steps to realize this value. This may necessitate the adaptation of administrative practices and organization structures so that there is a better fit between the company and its unfolding environment.[3]

Much of this chapter centers on **corporate entrepreneurship**, which denotes entrepreneurship within a company. Corporate entrepreneurship seeks the organization-wide nurturing of entrepreneurial behaviour with a view to rejuvenate the company through frequent introductions of new innovation-driven businesses.[4] In fast-changing environments, corporate entrepreneurship often holds the key to an established firm's success. As we expand on the above, we concentrate sequentially on several important topics. In the next section, the discussion focuses on the identification of entrepreneurial opportunities. In the section that follows, we turn our attention to innovation, describing how entrepreneurship converts opportunities into innovations, making them an integral part of the firm's future. Thereafter, we examine how firms engage in startup entrepreneurship and how best to manage strategic entrepreneurship.

# Entrepreneurship and opportunity recognition

Entrepreneurship is linked inextricably to identifying and exploiting opportunities that constitute either a totally new or a superior solution to a need in the market. Indeed, **entrepreneurship** is defined as the process of identifying and exploiting entrepreneurial opportunities by an individual, a startup, or an established company.[5] Oftentimes, an **entrepreneurial opportunity** starts as a belief or idea about the possibility of developing a commercially successful product, process, or service that is fundamentally new or an improvement vis-à-vis an existing one. To illustrate, the genesis of Google can be ascribed to the conviction of Larry Page and Sergey Brin, the two entrepreneurs who founded the company, that there was a better way, namely an algorithm, to search for webpages on the internet, and that this better way had commercial value.

An entrepreneurial opportunity need not be limited to a product, process, or service – it could also be related to a new business model (see Chapter 16), new manufacturing technology, new distribution channel, or sales in new markets. There is an important timing element to entrepreneurial opportunities. An opportunity that is not recognized and pursued on a timely basis may disappear. For instance, before a dominant technological design emerges, entrepreneurs have a limited window of opportunity to introduce their new technology into the race before the window closes.[6] Moving quickly on an opportunity can secure a first-mover advantage. It follows from the above that entrepreneurship entails the faculty of seeing and acting on potentially profitable opportunities or ideas that others have not yet seen or cannot act on promptly.[7]

In the case of established companies, entrepreneurship faces two broad cognitive challenges. Firstly, corporate entrepreneurship may be held back by perceptions of potential misalignment between the identified entrepreneurial opportunities and the company's existing business(es). In this case, the company may continue to commit most of its resources to its existing market offerings and customers, such that innovation is curbed. Secondly, corporate entrepreneurship may be held back by uncertainty regarding whether it will lead to successful outcomes that achieve the objectives set by the company. Such uncertainty can be a major impediment to initiating the entrepreneurship process. One way to deal with this is to recognize that even if an entrepreneurial initiative fails, learning from failure can help the company in its future endeavours.[8]

To benefit from corporate entrepreneurship, companies must learn to manage the process. Successful corporate entrepreneurship depends on building an internal climate of relentless focus on innovation as the external environment of the company changes. Firms that exhibit corporate entrepreneurship tend to have a culture that encourages individuals to deviate from the formal policies, practices, and strategies of the company to pursue new avenues. This suggests that firms seeking to internalize corporate entrepreneurship would do well to commit to an overall strategy of ongoing innovation. Such a strategy is, however, difficult to formulate and implement, and even more challenging to maintain. We examine this issue in more detail in the next section of the chapter. To add to the above, senior executives and managers in companies can also seek to weave a corporate-entrepreneurship strategy into the other major strategies of the firm.

Those at the top of the managerial hierarchy can catalyze innovativeness by nurturing entrepreneurial conduct in employees. For this, it is important to prepare the internal environment along multiple dimensions. Employees must have confidence that engaging in entrepreneurial conduct will not backfire and they will not be penalized for the risk they took to be innovative. Employees must also be provided the necessary resources. A critical resource in this regard is time. Employees must have sanctioned unstructured time, besides the structured time for business-as-usual, to identify new opportunities and act upon them. The creation of a safe psychological space for employees, showing of trust, and recognizing and rewarding entrepreneurial effort regardless of success or failure are other actions that can be taken. Organizational design elements, such as work discretion and organizational boundaries, can also facilitate entrepreneurship in companies.

In today's world, as boundaries between many industries fade because of technological convergences, it has also become strategically important for companies to explore opportunities in areas that may only be indirectly connected to their core business and expertise. In this regard, although the knowledge and entrepreneurial initiatives of employees can be very helpful, they are likely to be insufficient for the level of innovativeness required to remain competitive. Firms must therefore also devise other strategies to tap into opportunities that are distant from their core business and markets. Building alliances, creating joint ventures, mergers and acquisitions (see Chapters 13 and 14) and **corporate venture capital** activities are examples of externally-oriented corporate entrepreneurship strategies. In this chapter, we pay particular attention to corporate venture capital activities, which is an exponentially growing practice of corporate entrepreneurship.

## CRACK-THE-CASE

The expanding business of Stripe Inc.[9]

Source: © Schneider (2021) / Shutterstock.

Whether you are booking a hotel, requesting a taxi, or ordering dinner from your favorite restaurant, you could be paying for your purchase through the payment infrastructure of Stripe Inc. Stripe serves many of the largest technology companies and startups and has expanded into other industries through partnerships with the likes of Ford Motor Company. Stripe started by making it easy for companies to send and receive money from around the world, relieving its customers from the chore of creating their own payment infrastructure – a time-consuming task entailing navigating through financial systems, tax regimes, setting up of merchant accounts, data security issues, and multiple currencies. Stripe offered an easy all-in-one solution, enabling its customers to focus on growing their business instead of managing payments.

The Irish brothers Patrick and John Collision founded Stripe Inc. in 2010. With headquarters in San Francisco and Dublin, Stripe boasts an international workforce of over 4,000 employees and annual revenue of $7.4 billion in 2020.[10] The company's initial focus was to create an online payments platform. However, Stripe has expanded far beyond its initial product offering, fueled by a vision that the serving of fast-growing technology startups and scale-ups would drive its revenue growth. As of 2022, Stripe provides 19 products in the payments and business operations categories, and has a card-issuing service as an ancillary activity. The company's starting business model centered on taking a commission on transactions.

Stripe Payments' mission was to make cross-border transactions by companies and merchants seamless. In the early days, Stripe focused its attention on technology startups because unlike large corporations they had limited resources to set up complex international payment infrastructures. For startups, Stripe would be a game-changer, and as these companies rapidly grew, so would Stripe's revenue. Stripe Payments became a run-away success. By July 2012, Stripe had over 100,000 developer accounts on its platform.[11] Unlike

PayPal, a payment platform company established in 1998, Stripe's exclusive focus on technology startups made it familiar with other 'pain points' involved when running a technology company. This knowledge played a key role in the creation of Stripe's future products.

Stripe's first new product came when Shopify requested a white-label payment gateway. After weighing the pros and cons of building this one-off product, Stripe decided to go for it because Shopify was one of their largest customers. The new product launched successfully and soon many other clients asked for the same product. At this point, Stripe decided to launch it as a generally available product: Stripe Connect, which received widespread praise. The Collinson brothers noted a huge opportunity for Stripe beyond its e-commerce payment platform business. Recognizing that the rise in smartphone ownership and social media usage were developments that could be exploited, they envisioned a world where consumers could buy products directly on social media platforms using smartphones.

In 2014, Stripe collaborated with Facebook to experiment with a solution that would allow users to purchase products directly through the social network. After nearly a year of development, Facebook launched its 'buy' button in July 2015 to significant acclaim. With a single click, users could purchase items directly on Facebook without being redirected to an external website, a feature that benefited both retailers and consumers. Building on the popularity of Facebook's buy button, Stripe launched a product named Relay in 2015, which allowed retailers to sell their products in third-party applications.

In 2016, Stripe launched the Atlas platform, which helped entrepreneurs around the globe incorporate their businesses in the United States, open US dollar-denominated business bank accounts, accept payments from customers in more than 100 currencies, and find proper tax and legal guidance. Startups anywhere on the globe could now be up and running in a matter of days, instead of struggling to overcome barriers to entry. Stripe also worked with the US government to enable access to Atlas to entrepreneurs in Cuba.

Stripe next looked for other opportunities to provide services of value to startups. Besides the payments line of business, solutions concerning business operations became Stripe's second business line, which adopted the founding mentality of serving young technology companies. Over the years, Stripe has launched many new products in both business areas. From invoicing and billing products in their payments portfolio, to fraud detection and carbon offsetting products in their business operations portfolio.

In its first decade, Stripe experienced rapid growth and received widespread acclaim for its products. In early 2022, Stripe is one of the world's largest privately held companies with a valuation of $95 billion. It remains to be seen if Stripe can retain its product innovation velocity as it transforms from a scale-up to an established company.

## Questions

1. Stripe's expansion of its product portfolio was connected to one guiding principle. What was this?
2. While Stripe focused on (young) technology companies, its main competitor, Adyen, focused on established corporations. What do you consider as the upsides and downsides of Stripe's strategy?
3. Stripe has been expanding its product portfolio. Is there a risk to expanding extensively?

# Innovation and innovation strategy

**Innovation** can be defined as the creation and commercialization of a new product, process, or service by combining or recombining available knowledge pieces in a novel way valued by customers in the market.[12] Innovations typically follow inventions, in that they involve the turning of inventions into useable products, processes, or services.[13] The conversion of inventions into innovations rests on entrepreneurship, which refers to the process of identifying and exploiting opportunities for innovation.[14] To stay competitive in the 21st century, innovation is a must. Indeed, the key function of corporate entrepreneurship is to enable innovation on a never-ending basis. Research findings suggest that multinationals that invest more in generating innovations tend to have higher returns. Investors also appreciate the ongoing introduction of innovations because they usually increase the value of a firm's stock.

## Corporate innovation

Research and development (R&D) in companies may have as its aim two types of innovation: incremental and radical (see Table 15.1). *Incremental innovation* refers to relatively minor improvements in the details and functionality of a product, process, or service.[15] Such innovations do not require non-local search and learning to develop new capabilities and expertise.[16] Furthermore, because they are path-following innovations that do not lead to fundamentally new product-market combinations, the risk and uncertainty, as well as the value added and profits, generally tend to be lower as compared to radical innovations.[17] Examples include gradual improvements over time in smartphone cameras and the fuel efficiency of car engines.

**TABLE 15.1**   Incremental versus radical innovation

| Incremental innovation | Radical innovation |
| --- | --- |
| Improved products, services and processes | New products, services and processes |
| Existing markets | New markets |
| Local search | Non-local search |
| Path-following | Path-breaking |

*Radical innovations* are new products, processes, or services that serve a market need in a profoundly different and improved way as compared to earlier solutions.[18] They may reflect technological breakthroughs and are based on non-local search and learning requiring the building of new competencies.[19] Examples include the replacement of horse carriages by automobiles and the emergence of smartphones, which replaced earlier products and services serving customers' need for information and communication. Radical innovations are characterized as path breaking because they imply new product-market combinations. While they entail more risk and uncertainty, the value added and profits are higher relative to incremental innovations.

The top management team (TMT) of a company[20] may decide on a strategy called **internal corporate venturing** to produce both incremental and radical innovations within the firm.[21] Internal corporate venturing consists of top-down processes known as **induced strategic behaviour** and bottom-up processes known as **autonomous strategic behaviour** (see Figure 15.1). Whereas induced strategic behaviour often results in incremental innovations, autonomous strategic behaviour generates radical innovations most of the time – both, however, can generate incremental and radical innovations.[22] The TMT must make the decision about the type of innovation that is necessary given their company's competitive context, and accordingly strategize to facilitate top-down and/or bottom-up processes.

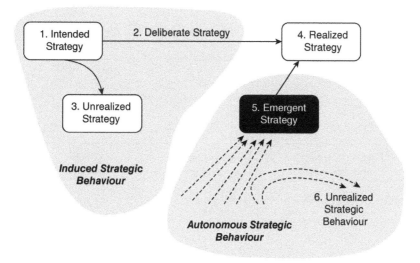

**FIGURE 15.1**   Induced versus autonomous strategic behaviour

Source: Adapted from Mirabeau and Maguire (2014)[23]

In the case of induced strategic behaviour, the attention focus of the TMT and other senior managers is on strategizing about and supporting innovations that reflect and build on the current strategy and structure of the firm. This approach is particularly useful for firms wanting to leverage their existing assets, competencies, and market positions. Thus, BP, Exxon Mobil, and Shell, which have huge asset investments and value-generating competencies related to the processing and distribution of fossil fuels, are likely to favour induced strategic behaviour that produces incremental innovations. Indeed, oil companies tend not to invest much in pursuing renewable-energy based radical innovations. Through induced strategic behaviour, companies seek to preserve their assets and competencies, and outcompete rivals by developing more efficient and effective versions of existing products.

Autonomous strategic behaviour, in contrast, is a good approach for firms operating in dynamic environments characterized by high levels of uncertainty. In such a context, the TMT can delegate innovation-related responsibilities to managers at lower levels of the administrative hierarchy and provide them the support they need.[24] The senior managers should build trust in and give legitimacy to the actions of middle managers and line managers engaged in internal corporate venturing. In the absence of support from senior management, entrepreneurial behaviour is likely to be inhibited because those lower in the hierarchy will be afraid of failures and their actions being rejected.

It is the task of the R&D function or department in firms to envision and pursue ideas leading to innovations. Oftentimes, the R&D function works on innovation projects that have different time horizons (see Figure 15.2): existing products for Horizon 1, incremental innovations for Horizon 2, and radical innovations for Horizon 3. Although many R&D projects may be aimed at improving existing products in the short term, other projects may be focused on long-term radical innovations. Incumbent firms often have difficulties benefitting from their R&D projects for various reasons, including organizational resistance and inertia.[25] Managers must therefore think of ways to ensure the output level of incremental and radical innovations necessary for sustained performance.

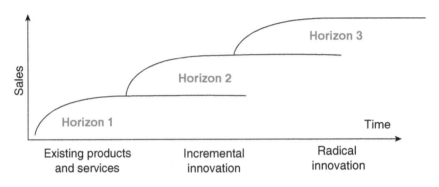

**FIGURE 15.2**  Different time horizons of innovation

Source: adapted from Baghai et al. (2000)[26]

## STRATEGIC FOCUS

### Intrapreneurship

One potential approach to innovation available to managers is **intrapreneurship**. Figure 15.3 illustrates the differences between an entrepreneur and an intrapreneur. Intrapreneurship entails a bottom-up (i.e., employee-led), creative, and proactive development of new ventures within an established company.[27] Examples of intrapreneurship-based innovations include Google's Gmail, 3M's Post-it Notes, and Amazon's Drones. Intrapreneurs are entrepreneurs within an organization. They may be based in either the R&D or some other functional department and have the room to pursue innovation opportunities without having to worry about time and resource constraints. Often, they are boundary-spanning middle and frontline managers with an inquisitive mind. To encourage innovation, in some companies, R&D researchers have the freedom to deviate from the strategic direction set by the top management. Indeed, the strategic direction of a company may be reset to follow intrapreneurial discoveries and innovations.[28]

Whereas intrapreneurship within the scope of a firm's existing business domain, knowledge, and competencies may be labelled as **internal corporate venturing**, intrapreneurship that looks for and invests in opportunities outside the current business domain and capabilities of a firm is referred to as **external corporate venturing**. In the latter case, firms must develop means and pathways to access and utilize external knowledge. They may for this purpose form strategic alliances, enter mergers, acquire other companies, or engage in corporate venture capital activities.[30] This last is important because faced with relentless technological change even innovative firms may not be able to survive by relying solely on internal innovation.

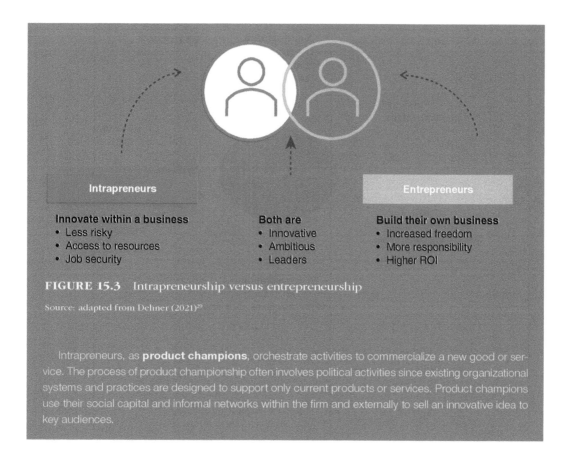

**FIGURE 15.3**  Intrapreneurship versus entrepreneurship

Source: adapted from Dehner (2021)[29]

Intrapreneurs, as **product champions**, orchestrate activities to commercialize a new good or service. The process of product championship often involves political activities since existing organizational systems and practices are designed to support only current products or services. Product champions use their social capital and informal networks within the firm and externally to sell an innovative idea to key audiences.

## Crowdsourcing and open innovation

With advancements in digital technologies the boundaries of the innovation process of companies have changed substantially. Firms are now able to engage those parties in innovation that were traditionally not involved. This is exemplified by **crowdsourcing**, which exposes an organizational problem to a large internal or external crowd, typically via the internet.[31] Crowdsourcing initiatives bring a novel capacity to the firm to use diverse ideas, knowledge, and creative potential available internally in the organization, or externally, worldwide (see Figure 15.4). It has proven to be effective, and sometimes even more effective than the conventional approach to innovation. Examples include crowdsourcing for breakthroughs in drug discovery and designing algorithms that facilitate the diagnosis of diseases.[32] Cisco and Linux use external technology sources to foster innovation.

The most straightforward way of benefitting from a crowds' innovative potential is to arrange a contest that involves a prize, as in the case of LEGO IDEAS. Another form of crowdsourcing-based innovation is collaboration among communities of experts, as in the case of Wikipedia. In a platform business model, a vast array of complementors can provide innovative solutions to the platform, as in the case of iTunes and Google Play.[34] Firms can employ the same strategies for internal and external crowdsourcing. Crowdsourcing exemplifies a mode of **open innovation**, which refers to a distributed innovation process relying on managed knowledge flows across organizational boundaries.[35] Open innovation strategy can complement a firm's traditional R&D. Tesla and Qualcomm have leveraged their internal R&D by creating an open patent system and an open ecosystem, respectively.

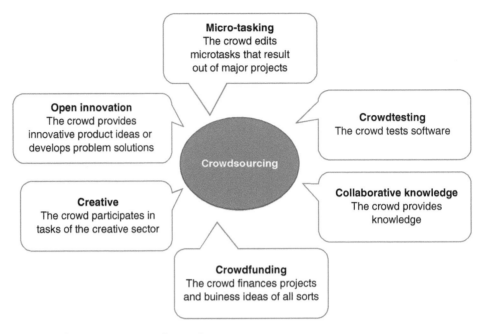

**FIGURE 15.4**   Various ways of crowdsourcing

Source: adapted from Clickworker (2023)[33]

Figure 15.5 shows four different strategies in the Corporate Innovation Strategy Matrix based on the origins of the innovation (internal or external to the firm) and the innovation process (top-down or bottom-up). Most firms attempt to enhance their innovation performance by making significant investments in internal R&D projects, driven by top

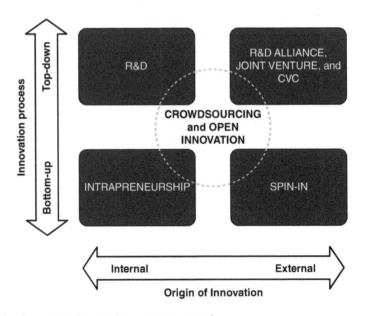

**FIGURE 15.5**   Corporate innovation-strategy matrix

Source: authors

management. Additionally, it is observed that several large firms, including Google (refer to the Opening Case) and Henkel (see Crack-the-Case: Creating an entrepreneurial workforce at Henkel), encourage innovation from within by initiating corporate entrepreneurship programs. However, for many large firms, instilling an entrepreneurial culture within the organization proves to be a challenging task. In such instances, top management is more inclined to boost innovation in these established companies by seeking external options, such as investing in R&D alliances, joint ventures, and corporate venture capital (CVC). Another viable approach involves a bottom-up strategy through the integration of external new ventures, which has the potential to catalyze a transformation in the company's DNA. In practice, the boundaries between these different strategies of corporate innovation are porous, and the strategies overlap.

## CRACK-THE-CASE

### Creating an entrepreneurial workforce at Henkel[36]

Source: © JHVEPhoto (2021) / Shutterstock.

How do you motivate your employees to actively contribute to innovative ideas? Fritz Henkel, the founder of Henkel, had an answer to this question more than a century ago: 'You need employees who work and think independently, and you need to enable them to do so'.[37] The digitalization of the world economy continues at a relentless pace. Driven by both technological advances and other external factors such as the COVID-19 pandemic, companies must continuously ask themselves not only how to survive

*(Continued)*

technological change – but how to capitalize on it. One of the key answers to this is to have an innovative workforce.

Henkel AG & Co. (Henkel) is a German consumer goods and chemicals company. Founded in 1876 in Aachen, the company currently has its headquarters in Düsseldorf and operates globally through its three units (Laundry & Home Care, Beauty Care, and Adhesive Technologies). Henkel boasts a global workforce with over 85% of its 52,950 employees working outside of Germany.[38]

Up until 2008, Henkel had expanded at a steady pace. For over 130 years, Henkel gradually expanded its business while preserving its German, family-owned roots. While less than 20% of its workforce was German, the executive team remained mostly German. The Henkel family also retained an active role on Henkel's shareholder committee. Henkel faced strong competition from firms that were generally far larger than it was. Henkel was the industry leader in their adhesives business, which among other things manufactures the iconic 'Pritt' glue sticks. It was a small player in the laundry and personal care market, competing against the far bigger Unilever and Proctor & Gamble. Many analysts, and some executives within Henkel, perceived the company as complacent and lacking a strong competitive mentality. One of its executives referred to Henkel as 'the happy underperformer': always #2 or #3.[39]

In 2008, Henkel appointed a new CEO, Kasper Rørsted. He was markedly different from his predecessors. Not only was the 46-year-old its youngest CEO ever, but he was also the first who did not hold the German or Austrian nationality. Born in Denmark, Rørsted enjoyed a successful career in the American technology sector before joining Henkel. As its new CEO, his mandate was clear: improve Henkel's competitive position and navigate the adversity of the 2008 financial crisis. Rørsted had a vision for addressing these challenges: Henkel had to become an innovation powerhouse.

Before Rørsted was ready to transform the company's culture, he swiftly moved to restructure the company, divesting low-performing activities while investing heavily in its top-performing products and high-potential markets. After rebalancing the company's operations and optimizing company administration, Henkel's executive team was ready to undertake a cultural transformation. Rørsted's approach consisted of two pillars: (1) redefining Henkel's vision and values, and (2) replacing the performance management system to strengthen its management capabilities.

Henkel reimagined its vision and values by recentering the company around its customers, while also emphasizing its appreciation of employees, financial excellence, and sustainability. Henkel's renewed values were set to build on its foundation as a family business. In 2011, Henkel introduced a new tagline that espoused its values, 'Excellence is our passion'

With its new performance management system, Henkel signaled it would no longer be a 'happy underperformer'. Whereas the old system generally had low targets and limited accountability for each employee, its new system was to drive excellence and innovation within the workforce. In the first years of Rørsted's tenure as CEO, the company introduced various management system tools such as the evaluation grid to assess employee potential; Development Roundtable (DRT), where managers collaboratively evaluated their direct reports; and Frame of Orientation, which provided a global ranking of DRT scores to compel managers to make tough decisions and pursue a high-performing workforce. Further,

Henkel revised its bonus structure, moving to tie bonuses to overall company performance, team performance, and individual performance.

After transforming Henkel's operations and culture, the company gradually moved to boost innovation by bolstering its corporate entrepreneurship activities. Henkel implemented many corporate entrepreneurship approaches that Rørsted undoubtedly experienced during his time in the American technology sector. Building highly autonomous innovation units, organizing hackathons, creating internal 'idea factories' and establishing internal incubator teams.

As Henkel navigates the aftermath of the COVID-19 pandemic in 2022, its new mentality shines through. Based on its view that innovation is more important now than it has ever been, Henkel continues to reimagine how to stay on top. Henkel's answer in 2022 is clear: leadership, diversity, and risk tolerance are the winning ways to encourage innovation. Not showing leadership through autocratic mavericks such as Steve Jobs, but by empowering leadership that makes the entire workforce more entrepreneurial; not by simply tweaking the gender balance, but by creating highly diverse teams across a multitude of characteristics; not by launching highly risky projects championed by top management, but by having the entire workforce embrace experimentation and the principle of 'failing forward'.

As Henkel's 150th birthday approaches, it will have ample reason for celebration. The company that started as a humble German laundry detergent producer has been able to reinvent itself repeatedly. In addition, while its operations now span the globe and its business is diverse, it will hold on to its founder's wisdom: empowered and entrepreneurial employees are the key to innovation.

## Questions

1. Why did Rørsted decide to restructure the company's operations before its culture?
2. Henkel's founding family continues to hold considerable influence over the company. Can you name a positive and a negative of this regarding Henkel's ability to engage with corporate entrepreneurship?
3. Do you believe Henkel's 2022 vision on innovation will be successful?

## STRATEGIC FOCUS

### Corporate entrepreneurship and new innovation practices

In recent years, driven by the fast pace of change in technologies, products, and business models, entrepreneurial companies have started to re-think their innovation practices with a view to accelerate their responses to external changes. The traditional approaches to entrepreneurship may not be effective enough in industries undergoing rapid transformation and those affected by the digital revolution. Instead, in such contexts, defining the right problem rather than the finished product and a commitment to continuous learning and experimentation hold most promise of innovating successfully. To illustrate,

*(Continued)*

according to lean startup methods, innovators would be well advised to develop a minimum viable prototype, and to engage in the testing of the assumptions of the innovation and validating them iteratively before, during, and after launch (see Figure 15.6).

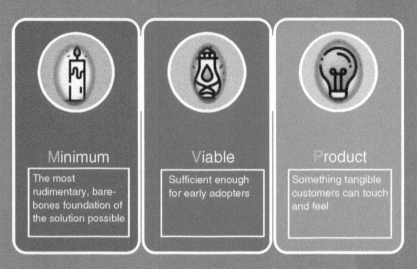

**FIGURE 15.6** Minimum viable product

Source: adapted from Karnes (2019)[40]

An advantage of this is that it enables collective learning at lower costs by reducing uncertainty about the solutions through engagement with stakeholders.[41] Many modern innovation-management practices have been introduced to enable experimentation, including Agile, Design Thinking, Growth Hacking, Scrum, and Sprints.[42] These practices can help overcome resistance to innovation and facilitate corporate entrepreneurship. Firms can employ these practices in their R&D projects as well as in their incubators and accelerator programs and innovation hackathons.

## KEY DEBATE

### The best mix of entrepreneurial initiatives?

Those interested in strategic entrepreneurship wonder what the appropriate mix would be of internal development versus acquisition of startup ventures and venture capital strategies for incumbent firms (see Figure 15.7). Among researchers there seems to be consensus that the acquisition of startups and venture capital strategy are mostly useful in very dynamic environments. However, internal development and keen awareness of environmental changes is necessary to trace and select interesting candidate firms for acquisition and for allocating venture capital to viable projects. The realizing of the right mix may be a chance event that is dependent on market developments and the emerging innovations within an industry. Continuous scanning of the environment and the taking of timely actions would appear vital for either approach to bear fruit.

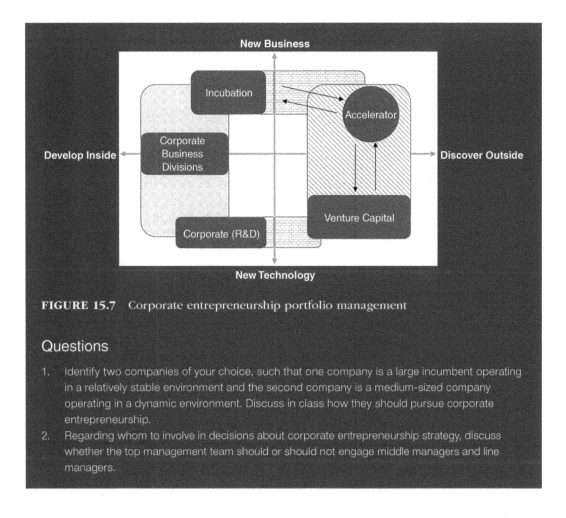

**FIGURE 15.7**   Corporate entrepreneurship portfolio management

## Questions

1. Identify two companies of your choice, such that one company is a large incumbent operating in a relatively stable environment and the second company is a medium-sized company operating in a dynamic environment. Discuss in class how they should pursue corporate entrepreneurship.
2. Regarding whom to involve in decisions about corporate entrepreneurship strategy, discuss whether the top management team should or should not engage middle managers and line managers.

## Corporate startup engagement

A firm can seek to boost innovativeness through **startup engagements** that tap into innovation ideas outside its organizational boundary (see Figure 15.8). Corporate **hackathons** and *incubators* are examples of such startup engagements, in which a company attracts outside entrepreneurs by supporting the initial stages of their idea development. In the case of hackathons, teams of entrepreneurs are invited to solve a corporate innovation problem in a short span of time. In the case of incubators, a company provides the basic facilities needed for startup activities, such as room, legal advice, and marketing support. The aim is to enable startups to launch innovations that are unrelated to the core business of the company.

Corporate accelerators are another form of corporate startup engagement. In this case, a company provides mentoring, education, and resources to a cohort of startups for a limited period. The company may eventually become a customer or a business partner of the startup. The acceleration program can end up in the acquisition of the startup. This form of engagement focuses on strategic aspects of the collaboration rather than any immediate financial benefit. It can help the focal firm identify ventures working on ideas close to the

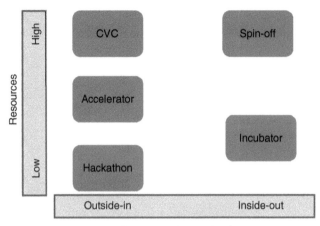

**FIGURE 15.8**  Various forms of startup engagement

Source: adapted from Weiblen and Chesbrough (2015)[43]

business domain of the firm, so that the innovation can be tested in the firm's environment. Accelerators can also function to explore disruptive venture ideas.

*Corporate venture capital* (CVC) is the practice where a firm systematically invests in startups. CVC investments allow large, established firms more flexibility vis-à-vis innovation. The amount invested in startups is relatively low compared to investments in typical R&D projects. Furthermore, CVC investments provide a way around the innovation inertia and resistance difficulties experienced by established firms. Startups are also more agile than established firms in terms of pivoting their strategies and adapting their innovations to emerging market needs. As far as startups are concerned, they can pursue entrepreneurial opportunities better if a corporate investor provides the necessary business network and financial resources.

CVC investments may be motivated by different reasons. The focal firm can learn from advancements in domains that are not directly connected to its core business. When industry boundaries start becoming blurred, it is strategically important to understand the potential effects of innovations in other industries on the focal firm's business. Startups in other industries can provide valuable intelligence, directing managerial attention to emerging technological discontinuities. Additionally, innovative technologies, products, and services of startups can complement the investing firm's products or its internal innovation programs. Another strategic reason for CVC investments is their signaling effect. For example, an oil company may invest in an entrepreneurial business in the renewable-energy sector to send a message to its shareholders, regulators, and competitors.

CVC investors usually select a portfolio of companies for investment. The characteristics of the startups in the portfolio have strategic implications for the investor. The portfolio can be developed to ensure diversity in terms of the stage of the startup lifecycle, the breadth and depth of knowledge in the portfolio, and the technological and cultural distance from the investing company.[44] When a firm invests in startups with the purpose of learning, the ability of the firm to absorb external knowledge is important to the success of the CVC investments. Overall, CVC activities can boost the current strategy of an investing firm by complementing it or by allowing the exploration of new business domains.

# Managing strategic entrepreneurship

Strategic entrepreneurship adds value through identifying opportunities to innovate and converting these into new businesses based on incremental or radical improvements in products, processes, or services. At the same time, strategic entrepreneurship entails risk; a firm's appetite to take that risk may change depending on the circumstances. The financial, human, and time resources a firm allocates to strategic entrepreneurship, thus, can vary over time, affecting the firm's innovations and innovativeness. Financial performance is one important factor that can affect firms' commitment to strategic entrepreneurship. Firms tend to be more willing to take risks and pursue riskier radical innovations when performance falls below their aspiration level; when performing above their aspiration level, however, firms tend to underinvest in radical innovations.[45]

Firms may also be more motivated to pursue riskier innovations when there is industry turbulence and transformation on account of technological advances. For example, in the FinTech and MedTech domains, the strong performance of new entrants may trigger incumbents to invest more in strategic entrepreneurship to improve their own performance. Instead of simply reacting to external factors, however, firms in all industries should mindfully manage their commitment to strategic entrepreneurship to avoid surprises. In other words, firms should be wary of becoming complacent and being blindsided by their current success. Firms that possess a spirit of strategic entrepreneurship continue to engage in venturing activities regardless of their performance. They are on the alert and proactively scout own, adjacent, and distant industries for opportunities and any signs of disruptive changes on the horizon.

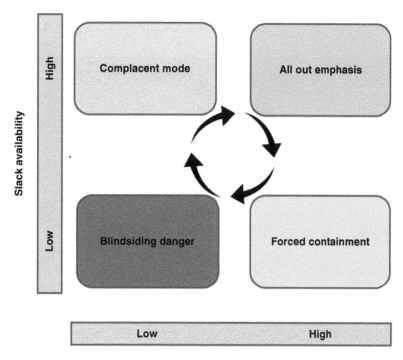

**FIGURE 15.9**  Cyclicity of strategic entrepreneurship

Engaging in venturing activities to improve innovativeness requires the possession of sufficient *slack*,[46] which refers to the availability of excess resources over and above those needed for the operations of a company. Because slack can provide a buffer that allows the firm to absorb costs and take risks,[47] it can be expected to encourage entrepreneurial search for opportunities and their conversion into innovations. One implication of this last is that the amount of slack available may constitute an important contingency that determines firm's investments in strategic entrepreneurship and innovation at a point in time. Figure 15.9 shows possible cyclicity in firms' strategic entrepreneurship because of low or high slack availability and low or high intrinsic drive to innovate. For effectively managing strategic entrepreneurship, it is important for the managerial cadre in a company to understand and manage the underlying factors that can affect it.

In terms of encouraging strategic entrepreneurship, the top management team (TMT) can earmark resources to fuel internal corporate venturing. Moreover, external venturing strategies could be implemented. Intrinsic drive is important in all this. It can take the company from a 'complacent' mode in Figure 15.9 to an 'all out emphasis' mode. Intrinsic drive may lessen though when a firm's performance exceeds its aspirations, so that innovation slips down on the managerial agenda. In this case, a company will move in the opposite direction, from an 'all out emphasis' to a 'complacent' mode. In contrast, when there is high intrinsic drive but decline in the availability of slack, the company may find itself in the 'forced containment' mode. The situation becomes particularly precarious when low slack availability and low intrinsic drive combine to take the company into the 'blindsiding danger' mode. One way for the TMT to guard against this is to have a system in place that supports and recognizes idea and product champions. Such a system can be a catalyst for sparking more autonomous strategic behaviour.

## CLOSING CASE

### Northvolt: From startup to key player in batteries[48]

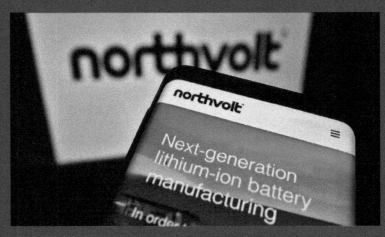

Source: © Schneider (2021) / Shutterstock.

Peter Carlsson did not expect that he would establish one of the world's leading battery producers one day. In 2011, Carlsson worked as a logistics manager at Tesla Inc. in the US. Here he experienced the emerging electric mobility ecosystem. In his role, he was in a perfect position to analyze the development of the electric mobility industry. The industry was rapidly evolving with various new market entrants and legacy automakers starting production of electric vehicles. China had established itself as the leading market early on, yet Europe was keen to catch up. In 2015, Carlsson stepped down from Tesla, as he saw an opportunity in Europe's desire to establish a strong position in the electric vehicle market. European automakers and policy makers emphasized the need for indigenous battery production, viewing battery production and software development as the key competencies that needed further development. Carlsson addressed this demand by founding SGF Energy in 2015.

The company was set to start producing batteries in Carlsson's home country of Sweden. In 2017, the company renamed itself Northvolt and by 2022, it had positioned itself as the world's leader in sustainable battery production, having contracts with leading automakers such as Volkswagen and BMW Group. With seven successful years behind him, what challenges lie ahead for Carlsson and his team? Northvolt has positioned itself in line with the EU Commission's aim of becoming the world's leading sustainable battery producing region. In line with the policy measures the EU has implemented to decarbonize its economy and accelerate the energy transition, Northvolt is developing and manufacturing sustainable, high-quality lithium-ion batteries and energy storage solutions. Its main factory in Skellefteå, Sweden, is operating at 60GWh, with funding secured for a total of 150GWh by 2030 – exceeding the renewable energy capacity of entire nations such as Germany in 2020.[49]

Two developments can explain Northvolt's decision to operate a differentiation strategy of producing 'green batteries'. First, China's battery producing giants continue to hold a firm grip on the global battery market. Unwilling to compete with the Asian competitors head-on in making generic batteries, Northvolt has chosen to develop green batteries, as it views this niche as fertile ground for establishing a battery giant. Considerations such as EU grants and willingness to pay a premium for sustainable components played into this strategy. Second, battery production has exploded since the rise of electric vehicles. With this emergence, the number of exhausted batteries is set to explode. Northvolt has recognized this impending rise in worn-out batteries as an opportunity to cost-effectively extract the raw materials for batteries in local markets instead of South America, Asia, and Africa. Northvolt aims to source half of the raw materials for new cells from recycled cells by 2030.

Despite early success, Northvolt faces several strategic challenges. First, because Northvolt predominantly sources raw materials from Asia, it faces supply-chain risks in raw materials essential to producing lithium-ion batteries. Soaring demand for raw materials can cause future shortages as mining companies struggle to scale up amidst environmental opposition. The Chinese electric vehicle market is expanding rapidly at an expected 24% per year growth until 2030, and local demand for resources takes priority over all else.[50] Moreover, Chinese government regulations have imposed trade barriers that increase costs and restrict Northvolt's primary supply chain. With existing constraints, Northvolt strategists are likely

*(Continued)*

asking themselves: what will happen to our access to raw materials when shortages or supply chain restrictions emerge in Asia?

Another strategic challenge is that battery production and batteries themselves are currently undergoing rapid advancements. With more money pouring into battery development than ever before, new production techniques and battery technology are set to be delivered at a constant rate in the coming years. Northvolt will face immense pressure to efficiently exploit its battery technology to generate profit while, in parallel, investing heavily in R&D for its sustainable production techniques and battery technology. Especially significant advancements towards completely new battery platforms such as solid-state batteries may pose a severe risk to Northvolt's operations.

When Carlsson founded Northvolt in 2015, he was in a perfect position to acquire EU grants and secure large clients. As Northvolt expands its battery production facilities and the electric vehicle market matures, will Northvolt's focus on sustainable batteries provide it with a pathway to becoming a prominent global battery producer?

## Questions

1. What could Northvolt do to strengthen its leading position in the European energy storage industry?
2. Do you believe Northvolt's niche of developing highly sustainable batteries in Europe will be as successful in other regions?

## Summary

- Strategic entrepreneurship can enable the transformation of a company. It requires an advantage-seeking strategic intent to guide the firm's opportunity-seeking entrepreneurial conduct. The timely conversion of identified opportunities into successful innovations is important for competitive advantage.
- Entrepreneurial conduct, whether at the level of an individual or a team, is integral to the entrepreneurship process. The expression 'corporate entrepreneurship' refers to the process of entrepreneurship within an established company. Its goal is to nurture an organization-wide entrepreneurial culture to foster innovativeness.
- Innovation, which is the creation and commercialization of a new product, process, or service, may be of an incremental or radical nature. Whereas incremental innovations are relatively minor improvements in details and functionality that require only local search and limited learning, radical innovations represent fundamentally novel ways to serve a market need.
- Internal corporate venturing is a strategy for producing incremental and radical innovations through induced and autonomous strategic behaviours. Whereas induced strategic behaviour is a top-down process to stimulate innovations consistent with the firm's existing strategy and structure, autonomous strategic behaviour is a bottom-up process that encourages middle managers and line managers to envision and pursue innovations.
- External corporate venturing is a strategy for producing innovations based on pursuing and exploiting opportunities that are beyond the current business domain

and capabilities of the company. It depends on access to external knowledge, for which the firm may form strategic alliances and/or turn to mergers and acquisitions.

- Advancements in digital technologies have made it possible for companies to harness the potential of crowdsourcing, a mode of open innovation. This enables a firm to tap into a vast pool of ideas and knowledge outside the organizational boundaries.
- Corporate accelerators, hackathons, and incubators are forms of startup engagements through which a company attracts external entrepreneurs by providing them the resources needed to develop their ideas into innovations.

# Review questions

1. What is corporate entrepreneurship and how is it related to the idea of strategic entrepreneurship?
2. How is the recognition of entrepreneurial opportunities connected to incremental and radical innovations in companies?
3. What are some of the key challenges to entrepreneurship in established companies and how can these be addressed?
4. In the context of internal corporate venturing, how is induced strategic behaviour different from autonomous strategic behaviour?
5. Identify and distinguish between the different types of startup engagements a company could consider for increasing innovativeness.

# Discussion questions

1. As startups become established companies, and established companies age and become bigger, they tend to become less innovative. Why is this the case and how can this trajectory be avoided?
2. To pursue entrepreneurial opportunities, a company needs slack resources for absorbing costs and taking risks. However, when a company has slack resources, it may become complacent and pay little attention to innovation. How do you propose to resolve this paradox?
3. Discuss the pros and cons of induced strategic behaviour versus autonomous strategic behaviour. Are there industries in which you would favour one much more strongly than the other?

## EXPERIENTIAL EXERCISES

1. Company X is a large multinational in the car manufacturing industry. It has just concluded a three-year project that has resulted in a line of efficient engines that are based on fossil fuels. The cost of the project was more than €300 million. It is time for Company X to start the mass production of a new generation of cars. In the industry, all major competitors of Company X have started investing heavily in hybrid cars that can run on fossil fuel as well as electricity. Other competitors have introduced cars based on bio-fuel engines; also, some competitors have

*(Continued)*

started experimenting with hydrogen-based engines, but the results so far have not been as favourable as was hoped. It seems that while hybrid engines and bio-fuel engines present a viable opportunity in the short term, hydrogen engines present a potentially interesting opportunity in the long term. What strategy would you recommend to Company X, and why?

2.   Do companies really walk the talk when it comes to strategic entrepreneurship? Form a team in the classroom and decide on a company that is covered well on the internet. Looking at the company's annual reports of the last three years, trace its statements on strategic entrepreneurship.

- Provide an overview of the company's announced strategic-entrepreneurship activities.
- Keeping in mind the context of the company's industry, identify what, if anything, is unique about these activities.
- Gather additional information from newspapers, business magazines, industry reports, etc., to determine whether the company has been successful in completing the announced activities.
- If it was successful, map out the company's road to success; if it was not successful, provide an overview of the hurdles it faced.
- Considering your responses to the above exercises, discuss with other teams why some companies are better at corporate entrepreneurship than others.

## Further reading

Barringer, B.R. and Ireland, R.D. (2016). *Entrepreneurship: Successfully Launching New Ventures* (5th ed.). London: Pearson.

Es-Sajjade, A., Pandza, K. and Volberda, H. (2021) 'Growing pains: Paradoxical tensions and vicious cycles in new venture growth', *Strategic Organization*, 19 (1): 37–69.

Khanagha, S., Volberda, H.W., Alexiou, A. and Annosi, M.C. (2022) 'Mitigating the dark side of agile teams: Peer pressure, leader's control, and the innovative output of agile teams', *Journal of Product Innovation Management*, 39: 334–50.

Perra, D.B., Sidhu J.S and Volberda H.W. (2017) 'How do established firms produce breakthrough innovations? Managerial identity-dissemination discourse and the creation of novel product-market solutions', *Journal of Product Innovation Management*, 34: 509–25.

Van Doorn, S., Heyden, M.L.M. and Volberda, H.W. (2017) 'Enhancing entrepreneurial orientation in dynamic environments: The interplay between top management team advice-seeking and absorptive capacity', *Long Range Planning*, 50 (2): 134–44.

## Endnotes (references)

1.  Google (2022) About Google. https://web.archive.org/web/20220101003300/https://about.google (accessed July 20, 2023); McMillan, R. (2005) 'Loosen the reins, says Google CEO', *Infoworld*, May 19. www.infoworld.com/article/2671087/loosen-the-reins--says-google-ceo.html (accessed June 29, 2023); Savoia, A. and Copeland, P. (2011) 'Entrepreneurial Innovation at Google', *IEEE Computer Society*, 44 (4): 56–61.

2.  Google (2022)

3.  Hitt, M.A., Ireland, R.D., Camp, S.M. and Sexton, D.L. (2001) 'Strategic entrepreneurship: Entrepreneurial strategies for wealth creation', *Strategic Management Journal*, 22 (6–7): 479–91.

4.  Ireland, R.D., Covin, J.G. and Kuratko, D.F. (2009) 'Conceptualizing corporate entrepreneurship strategy', *Entrepreneurship Theory and Practice*, 33 (1): 19–46.

5.  Kuratko, D.F. (2016) *Entrepreneurship: Theory, Process, and Practice*. Andover: Cengage.

6.  Suarez, F.F., Grodal, S. and Gotsopoulos, A. (2015) 'Perfect timing? Dominant category, dominant design, and the window of opportunity for firm entry', *Strategic Management Journal*, 36 (3): 437–48.

7.  Shane, S. and Nicolaou, N. (2015) 'Creative personality, opportunity recognition and the tendency to start businesses: A study of their genetic predispositions', *Journal of Business Venturing*, 30 (3): 407–19.

8.  Deichmann, D. and van den Ende, J. (2014) 'Rising from failure and learning from success: The role of past experience in radical initiative taking', *Organization Science*: 25 (3): 670–90.

9.  Rudegeair, P. (2021) 'How payment processor Stripe became Silicon Valley's hottest startup', *The Wall Street Journal*, April 13. www.wsj.com/articles/how-payment-processor-stripe-became-silicon-valleys-hottest-startup-11618306201 (accessed June 29, 2023); Stripe (2016) 'Announcing Stripe Atlas – helping entrepreneurs start a global business from anywhere', February 24. https://stripe.com/nl/newsroom/news/stripe-launches-atlas (accessed June 29, 2023); Stripe (2022) 'Stripe: Payment processing platform for the Internet'. https://web.archive.org/web/20230629000621/https://stripe.com (accessed June 29, 2023); Tsotsis, A. (2012) 'Sexy payments startup Stripe swipes $20M from general Catalyst, Sequoia, Thiel and more', *TechCrunch*, July 10. https://techcrunch.com/2012/07/09/payments-startup-stripe-swipes-20m-from-general-catalyst-sequoia-thiel-and-more (accessed June 29, 2023).

10. Rudegeair (2021)

11. Tsotsis (2012)

12. Heyden, M.L.M., Sidhu, J.S., Van den Bosch, F.A.J. and Volberda, H.W. (2012) 'Top management team search and new knowledge creation: How top management team experience diversity and shared vision influence innovation', *International Studies of Management & Organization*, 42 (4): 27–51.

13. Vinokurova, N. and Kapoor, R. (2020) 'Converting inventions into innovations in large firms: How inventors at Xerox navigated the innovation process to commercialize their ideas', *Strategic Management Journal*, 41 (13): 2372–99.

14. Dutta, D.K. and Crossan, M.M. (2005) 'The nature of entrepreneurial opportunities: Understanding the process using the 4I organizational learning framework', *Entrepreneurship Theory and Practice*, 29 (4): 425–49.

15. Abernathy, W.J. and Clark, K.B. (1985) 'Innovation: Mapping the winds of creative destruction', *Research Policy*, 14 (1): 3–22.

16. Sidhu, J.S., Heyden, M.L., Volberda, H.W. and Van den Bosch, F.A.J. (2020) 'Experience maketh the mind? Top management teams' experiential background and cognitive search for adaptive solutions', *Industrial and Corporate Change*, 29 (2): 333–50.

17. See Banbury, C.M. and Mitchell, W. (1995) 'The effect of introducing important incremental innovations on market share and business survival', *Strategic Management Journal*, 16 (S1): 161–82.

18. Abernathy and Clark (1985)

19. Perra, D.B., Sidhu J.S and Volberda H.W. (2017) 'How do established firms produce breakthrough innovations? Managerial identity-dissemination discourse and the creation of novel product-market solutions', *Journal of Product Innovation*

*Management*, 34 (4): 509–25; Sidhu, J.S., Volberda, H.W. and Commandeur, H.R. (2004) 'Exploring exploration orientation and its determinants: Some empirical evidence', *Journal of Management Studies*, 41 (6): 913–32.

20. Heyden et al. (2012)

21. Burgelman, R.A. (1983) 'A process model of internal corporate venturing in the diversified major firm', *Administrative Science Quarterly*, 28: 223–44.

22. Burgelman, R.A. (2020) *Strategy Is Destiny: How Strategy-making Shapes a Company's Future*. New York, NY: The Free Press.

23. Mirabeau, L. and Maguire, S. (2014) 'From autonomous strategic behavior to emergent strategy', *Strategic Management Journal*, 35 (8): 1202–29.

24. Mirabeau and Maguire (2014)

25. Latham, S.F. and Braun, M. (2009) 'Managerial risk, innovation, and organizational decline', *Journal of Management*, 35 (2): 258–81.

26. Baghai, M., Coley, S. and White, D. (2000) *The Alchemy of Growth: Practical Insights for Building the Enduring Enterprise*. New York, NY: Basic.

27. Kacperczyk, A.J. (2012) 'Opportunity structures in established firms: Entrepreneurship versus intrapreneurship in mutual funds', *Administrative Science Quarterly*, 57 (3): 484–521.

28. Burgelman (1983)

29. Dehner, C. (2021) 'What is intrapreneurship? 4 ways it can supercharge your career', *Intuit Mint Life*. https://mint.intuit.com/blog/relationships-2/what-is-intrapreneurship-5811 (accessed June 29, 2023).

30. Miles, M.P. and Covin, J.G. (2002) 'Exploring the practice of corporate venturing: Some common forms and their organizational implications', *Entrepreneurship Theory and Practice*, 26 (3): 21–40; Narayanan, V.K., Yang, Y. and Zahra, S.A. (2009) 'Corporate venturing and value creation: A review and proposed framework', *Research Policy*, 38 (1): 58–76.

31. Afuah, A. and Tucci, C.L. (2012) 'Crowdsourcing as a solution to distant search', *Academy of Management Review*, 37 (3): 355–75.

32. Lakhani, K.R., Lifshitz-Assaf, H. and Tushman, M.L. (2013) 'Open innovation and organizational boundaries: Task decomposition, knowledge distribution and the locus of innovation' in A. Grandori (ed.), *Handbook of Economic Organization*. Cheltenham: Edward Elgar, 355–82.

33. Clickworker (2023) 'About crowdsourcing', *Clickworker*. www.clickworker.com/about-crowdsourcing (accessed June 29, 2023).

34. Boudreau, K.J. and Lakhani, K.R. (2013) 'Using the crowd as an innovation partner', *Harvard Business Review*, 91 (4): 60–9.

35. Bogers, M., Chesbrough, H., Heaton, S. and Teece, D.J. (2019) 'Strategic management of open innovation: A dynamic capabilities perspective', *California Management Review*, 62 (1): 77–94.

36. Henkel (2022), home page. https://web.archive.org/web/20230629025435/https://www.henkel.com (accessed June 29, 2023); Simons, R. and Kindred, N. (2012) *Henkel: Building a Winning Culture*. Harvard Business School Case Collection. https://www.hbs.edu/faculty/Pages/item.aspx?num=41466 (accessed June 29, 2023).

37. Henkel (2022)

38. Henkel (2022)

39. Simons and Kindred (2012)

40. Karnes, K.C. (2019) 'What is a minimum viable product + methodologies for marketers', *Clevertap*. https://clevertap.com/blog/minimum-viable-product/ (accessed June 29, 2023).

41. Bocken, N. and Snihur, Y. (2020) 'Lean start-up and the business model: Experimenting for novelty and impact', *Long Range Planning*, 53 (4): article #101953.

42. Cavallo, A., D'Angelo, S. and Ghezzi, A. (2020) 'Experimentation and digitalization: Towards a brand-new corporate entrepreneurship?', in A. De Nisco (ed.), *15th European Conference on Innovation and Entrepreneurship, 2020*. Sonning Common: Academic Conferences and Publishing International Limited, 163–9.

43. Weiblen, T. and Chesbrough, H.W. (2015) 'Engaging with startups to enhance corporate innovation', *California Management Review*, 57 (2): 66–90.

44. Wadhwa, A., Phelps, C. and Kotha, S. (2016) 'Corporate venture capital portfolios and firm innovation', *Journal of Business Venturing*, 31 (1): 95–112.

45. Eggers, J.P. and Kaul, A. (2018) 'Motivation and ability? A behavioral perspective on the pursuit of radical invention in multi-technology incumbents', *Academy of Management Journal*, 61 (1): 67–93.

46. Tyler, B.B. and Caner, T. (2016) 'New product introductions below aspirations, slack and R&D alliances: A behavioral perspective', *Strategic Management Journal*, 37 (5): 896–910.

47. Oshri, I., Sidhu, J.S. and Kotlarsky, J. (2019) 'East, west, would home really be best? On dissatisfaction with offshore-outsourcing and firms' inclination to backsource', *Journal of Business Research*, 103: 644–53.

48. International Energy Association (2020) *Germany 2020*. Paris IEA. www.iea.org/reports/germany-2020 (accessed June 29, 2023); Dabelstein, C., Schäfer, P., Schwedhelm, D., Wu, J. and Wu, T. (2021) 'Winning the Chinese BEV market: How leading international OEMs compete', *McKinsey*, May 4. www.mckinsey.com/industries/automotive-and-assembly/our-insights/winning-the-chinese-bev-market-how-leading-international-oems-compete (accessed June 29, 2023); Northvolt (2022) 'Northvolt – the future of energy'. https://web.archive.org/web/20230629011349/https://northvolt.com (accessed June 29, 2023).

49. International Energy Association (IEA) (2020)

50. Dabelstein et al. (2021)

# Acknowledgements

The authors thank Taghi Ramezan Zadeh, Liam Goodman and Hugo Elworthy for their contribution to this chapter.

# Key terms

**Autonomous strategic behaviour** – delegation of responsibilities for innovation to lower levels of the administrative hierarchy and providing them the support they need

**Corporate accelerators** – a startup engagement in which the company provides the basic facilities needed for startup activities, such as room, legal advice, and marketing support

**Corporate entrepreneurship** – entrepreneurship within an established company

**Corporate venture capital** – investment of resources in external startups

**Crowdsourcing** – the obtaining of information from a very large number of people within or outside the company using the internet

**Entrepreneurial opportunity** – possibility of developing a commercially successful product, process, or service that is fundamentally new or an improvement on an existing one

**Entrepreneurship** – the process of identifying and exploiting entrepreneurial opportunities

**External corporate venturing** – the development of capabilities and businesses by acting on opportunities outside the company's existing boundaries

**Hackathons** – a startup engagement in which teams of entrepreneurs are invited to solve a corporate innovation problem in a short span of time

**Induced strategic behaviour** – attention focus of senior management on strategizing about and supporting innovations that reflect and build on the current strategy and structure of the firm

**Innovation** – the creation and commercialization of a new product, process, or service

**Internal corporate venturing** – entrepreneurial initiatives within a company that are intended as new businesses

**Intrapreneurship** – a bottom-up, employee-led, creative and proactive development of new ventures within an established company

**Open innovation** – the sourcing of innovations ideas from external and internal sources

**Product champion** – orchestrators of innovation (mostly middle line managers) who use their social capital and informal networks to sell an innovative idea to key managerial audiences

**Startup engagements** – partnerships with external entrepreneurs with a view to increase innovation

**Strategic entrepreneurship** – advantage-seeking strategic intent guiding opportunity-seeking entrepreneurial conduct in order to attain above-average performance

# 16
# BUSINESS MODEL INNOVATION

## LEARNING OBJECTIVES

After reading this chapter, you should be able to:

- describe what is meant by the business model concept;
- understand the importance of business model innovation and differentiate various types of business model innovation;
- identify the early warning signs of a business model trap;
- understand the different transformation journeys derived from the Business Model Innovation Matrix.

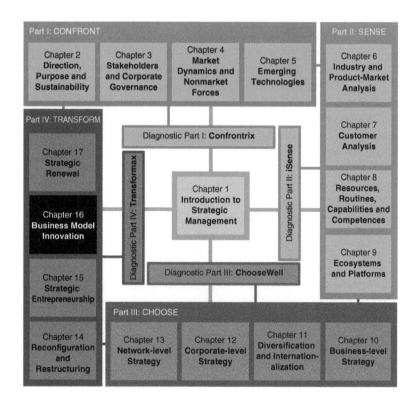

## OPENING CASE

Source: © JPstock (2018) / Shutterstock.

## DSM: Jumping on the next value waves[1]

The Dutch firm DSM has undergone various radical transformations since it started in 1902. It began as a fully state-controlled mining company in the south of The Netherlands, but these days it is positioned as a global science company specializing in solutions for health, nutrition and bioscience. Even though its name (DSM originally stands for Dutch State Mines) is the legacy of its original activities, the abbreviation is assumed to have received a new meaning among its employees recently as Doing Something Meaningful.

The shift from its original to current activities is characterized by a series of intermediate steps. When the mines in The Netherlands were closing down in the 1960s and 1970s, the firm chose to specialize in bulk chemicals. It later shifted to petrochemicals, fine chemicals, and to life sciences and materials respectively. The recent merger with the Swiss flavour and fragrance maker Firmenich points towards yet another development in the course of the firm where it is about to focus purely on ingredients for food and health products. Activities outside that scope are being divested, such as the sale of the protective materials business unit to Avient Corporation and a unit making coatings and resins to Covestro. Nowadays its activities are organized in various product-market combinations: Animal Nutrition & Health, Human Nutrition, Care & Health, and Food & Beverage.

Clearly not every organization survives for over a century, so how did DSM manage to do so? Former CEO Feike Sijbesma claimed that 'it is precisely *because* of this history that we recognize adaptation as being a continual process'.[2] Among the list of elements characterizing DSM is that the company has proven multiple times to be able to jump on the next wave of growth and profitably, as echoed in the previous paragraph. The life sciences and materials markets and currently the food ingredients and health-product markets were and are respectively projected as emerging and substantially growing markets with relatively limited cyclical swings when DSM jumped in. For instance, the expected organic sales growth of DSM-Firmenich, with a combined sales of around €11.5 billion and about 28,000 employees, is 5% to 7% per year.

DSM's standpoint is to add greater value in those markets via anticipating new opportunities for customers as well as challenges that the world will encounter in times to come, for instance in the area of health and sustainability. The shift from chemical activities to life sciences and materials sciences, for instance, was not only because DSM anticipated that the competitive conditions in the industrial chemical sector were going to change substantially. It was also because the company itself wanted to switch to more innovative and sustainable activities which had greater added value. The envisioned co-chief executive officers (co-CEOs) of DSM-Firmenich, currently co-CEOs of DSM, stated that the merger 'creates solutions where we have health, sustainability, and tastes and flavor as being key for the future'[3] and enables 'us to unlock new opportunities for customers as well as position us to deliver enhanced long-term growth and shareholder value, sustainably'.[4] As a science-based company, it aims to be at the frontier of novel ways of value creation for customers and society-at-large in such contexts where it is also able to capture a substantial portion of that created value in terms of profit. Or, as analysts pointed out on the unique position of DSM-Firmenich: it 'create[s] a new giant in the nutrition space, and the only one to combine flavors and fragrances with nutritional benefits'.[5]

### Questions

1. What drove DSM to innovate its activities?
2. What are implications of an increased emphasis on innovation and sustainability for DSM's value proposition(s) and the appropriation of this value?

# Introduction

Choosing the right type of strategy among the list of potential strategies (see also Part III of this book) and deciding how that specific strategy should look are crucial managerial tasks and pivotal for firm success. A business model – i.e., the way a firm creates and captures value – reflects the outcome of a firm's strategic choices and how the firm executes its strategy.[6] As a reflection of a firm's realized strategy, strategy and business models are close cousins, though different concepts.[7] Even if a firm does not have a clear strategy, it does – at least implicitly – have an idea or logic on how it wants to create and capture value.[8] A firm with a better business model may even outperform rivals with a fairly similar strategy, because it is better at creating and capturing value in the execution of that strategy.

Since a business model is a reflection of a firm's chosen strategy, changes in a firm's strategy do also involve changes in its business model, which is referred to as business model innovation. The opening case on DSM illustrates how a company can be successful via a series of business model innovations over time. Business model innovation thus strives towards having a better model – compared to a firm's own model in the past and to that of rivals – as a source of competitive advantage. However, most firms fail to innovate their business model because they continue to do the same things that have made them successful in the past. Managers in these firms listen carefully to customers, invest in existing business, and build distinctive capabilities, but tend to overlook disruptions in markets and technologies.

This chapter seeks to give you a better understanding of 'how' firms can innovate their business model and 'when' management should change the business model. We start with providing the basic elements of a business model. Subsequently, we discuss how successful business models of the past are disrupted and analyze various warning signs that might indicate to management that a change of business model is required. There are actually two ways of changing your business model: through replication of the existing model or through generation of a completely new model. With replication, firms scale up and improve their existing business model over time – as we can see, for instance, with McDonald's and IKEA. With business model generation, firms bring in a new business model that is very different from the previous one. DSM, in particular, has reinvented itself several times as it moved from mining to petrochemicals, then to life sciences and material sciences, and more recently to food and sustainability. These two modes of business model innovation can also be combined in various ways, which is also known as hybrid or dual business models. Finally, we conclude this chapter with the Business Model Innovation Matrix that helps us to derive various transformation trajectories of how to change the business model over time.

# Elements of a business model

With the advent of the internet, the concept of a business model has received a surge of attention.[9] A **business model** describes the set of activities of a firm that contributes to a firm's strategy in creating and capturing value.[10] Essentially, it is about a 'way of doing business'.[11] Three common elements can be distinguished:[12]

- A business model is made up of various <u>components</u> and describes the <u>relationships</u> between them ('architecture').
- A business model embodies how <u>value creation</u> occurs, and for which parties, and how the firm <u>appropriates value</u>.

- A business model provides insights into how the various components and the relationships between them contribute to the <u>competitive strategy</u>.

## The architecture of activities

Business models have been conceptualized as an **architecture** or a template.[13] A business model provides a more holistic view on how a firm conducts business compared to more narrow domains such as individual processes, products and services. Or, as Zott and Amit framed the importance of a business model: 'look at the forest, not the trees – and get the overall design right, rather than concentrating on optimizing details'.[14]

The 'architecture' of an enterprise includes the internal and external actors, information flows, products, and services which the enterprise uses to create value for one or more target groups. In a way, the business model describes the structure of the value chain which is needed to create and distribute a value proposition, as well as the extra assets required for this process.[15] An architecture of this kind is not restricted to the firm: the boundaries of a business model extend beyond those of the enterprise itself. The success of a business model is dependent partly on how it relates to the business models of external players, whether they be partners or rivals.[16]

Over the last couple of years there has been greater emphasis on understanding which components are fundamental to a business model, and how they contribute to competitive advantage and performance. Components that are often mentioned include a firm's value offering, economic model, partner network, internal infrastructure, and target market.[17] The **business model canvas** developed by Osterwalder and Pigneur[18] describes various components of a business model – including both the production side and the market side – and extends to partners, distribution channels, and target groups in the market (see Figure 16.1). Breaking down a business model into its component parts reveals that there are interdependencies between those various components, including some complementary effects.[19]

One element central to a business model is the operational model. This is about how key resources, capabilities, activities, and processes and their interdependencies ranging from a firm's input through to its output are deployed in order to realize operational and process advantages. Some scholars also refer to an operational model as a firm's position in, and its linkages within, its industry value chain.[20] The hub-and-spoke model (organization of routes as a series of 'spokes' to connect outlying points to a central 'hub') deployed by airliners such as British Airways, Delta, Emirates and KLM versus point-to-point transits (travelling directly from source to destination without a hub) utilized by others such as easyJet, Ryanair and Transavia mirror different logics to deliver value in the airline industry.

A proper understanding of both those components and their interdependencies is required to examine them in an integrated and more holistic way, and to assess their effectiveness. However, few companies understand their business model well enough, including its interdependencies, strengths, weaknesses, and underlying assumptions.

## How value is created and how the firm appropriates that value

A second element common to definitions of business model is *value creation* and *value capture*.[21] Although closely related to a firm's technology and its products and services, the famous statement of Harvard Professor Theodore Levitt nicely illustrated their difference with the notion of value: 'people don't want to buy a quarter-inch drill. They want a quarter-inch hole!'[22]

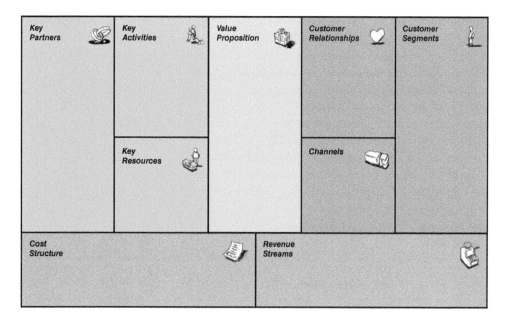

**FIGURE 16.1** Business model canvas

Source: Osterwalder and Pigneur (2010)

The **value proposition** describes how value is realized for specific target groups and markets. A business model can create different kinds of benefits for customers. For example, it can provide cost advantages, meet previously unmet needs with new products and services, offer greater information and choice, or confer status associated with a brand. Some scholars[23] have also described firms as being either 'buses' or 'taxis', depending on whether they provide their customers with more standardized, large-scale, and predesigned solutions, or whether they offer more project-based solutions.

One element that is fundamental to any concept of a business model is the **economic model**: the cost structure and the mechanism by which the firm generates revenue and makes a profit.[24] For whom does the firm create value, and how does it make money? This is also referred to as a 'financial model' or 'monetization', and can be further divided into a 'revenue model' and a cost structure. A firm needs to decide who should pay for the value that is created and which pricing strategy to apply – auctioning, fixed price, or according to delivered value, etc. It also needs to decide how often one should pay. Should it be a one-off payment, as with the sale of a product, or should the payment be spread, as when a product is leased? Additionally, a firm needs to choose when it does and does not charge for the value created. Adobe, for example, uses a so-called 'freemium' model (a combination of 'free' and 'premium'), where certain features are provided for free, and others are charged at a premium rate. In the case of Google and *Metro* it is only the advertisers who are charged for taking up online space. Similarly, traditional firms as Kodak and Polaroid have been in the past very successful with their *razor blade* profit model. The concept springs from the shaving industry, which obtains its profits mainly from the sale of razor blades and much less from the sale of the razors themselves. Kodak and Polaroid were dependent not so much on selling cameras but on selling *consumables*: the rolls of film and, for Polaroid, the instant photographic materials. Senseo and

Nespresso are more recent successful examples of the *razor blade business model*; they made large profits on the coffee pods or capsules, not on the coffee machines. As long as these pods and capsules were patented, they were able to fully capture the value, but when the patent expired many competitors stepped in.

These questions of value creation and value capture are of fundamental importance. After all, without an economic model which delivers revenue, a commercial enterprise cannot exist. A business model should create some level of value for customers and stakeholders, but also 'entices customers to pay for value, and converts those payments to profit through the proper design and operation of the various elements of the value chain'.[25] Capturing enough of the value created is vital (see Figure 16.2). If a firm captures hardly any of the value it creates, the survival of the firm will be threatened as there will be insufficient revenues. However, if a firm captures too much of that value, then customers are unlikely to buy its goods, because the prices, for example, may be too high. This also threatens a firm's survival.

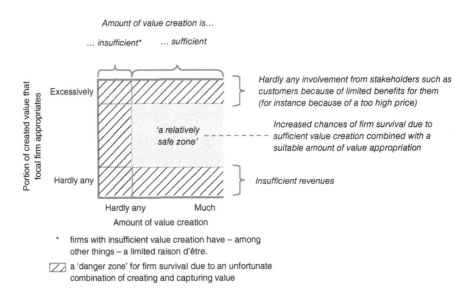

**FIGURE 16.2**    Visualization of creating and capturing a sufficient amount of value

## A business model sets out the competitive strategy

As a reflection of how a firm executes its strategy,[26] a business model provides insights into how business model components and their interdependencies enable value creation and value capture in the realization of a firm's strategy. For instance, a low-cost value proposition and cost structure emphasizing minimization of cost fit with the low-cost strategy (see Chapter 10). Likewise, the choice for an unrelated diversification strategy (see Chapter 11) has implications for the degree of interdependencies, as it likely reduces organization-wide synergies. While firms pursuing a growth strategy start from the right-hand side of the business model canvas, the ones pursuing a profitability strategy start from the left-hand side of that canvas.[27] A business model thus acts as a powerful avenue in the execution of a firm's strategy. This also means that analyzing a business model can reveal a great deal of information on a firm's strategy, including that of rivals.

If a business model does not result in a competitive advantage which is sustainable (at least temporarily), it has no value. That is why the strategy behind business model innovation must make explicit how innovation leads to a position which rivals cannot imitate quickly.[28] It is essential to assess the reaction of rivals; after all, a business model does not work in a vacuum. The success or failure of a business model depends to a large extent on how it compares to business models of other players in the industry. As such, a business model itself also needs to be differentiated from other industry players in order to act as a source of competitive advantage.

## CRACK-THE-CASE

Nintendo's disruptive business model in the gaming industry:
The introduction of *Pokémon Go*[29]

Source: © KeongDaGreat (2016) / Shutterstock.

Sony and Microsoft had introduced the PlayStation and the Xbox, targeting teenagers and young adults, and both were devices with good graphics, functionality, and speed. In response to these disruptive business models, Nintendo introduced the Wii, aimed primarily at families. The emphasis of the Wii is on simplicity, ease of use, family experience, and fitness.

Nowadays, the business model in gaming has moved from game consoles to mobile games that can be accessed at any time, in any place. In this new disruptive business

*(Continued)*

model, firms do not make money by selling consoles, games, and occasionally merchandise. Instead, a game on a smartphone can be downloaded for free or played for free for a trial period. A firm makes money when players make purchases within the game, such as extra lives which allow them to continue playing the game. Nintendo was typically known for video game consoles such as the Wii and Nintendo 64 and for computer games such as Super Mario and Zelda. However, in 1998 Nintendo joined Creatures and Game Freak in establishing The Pokémon Center Company, a privately held company. A third of the shares is owned by Nintendo. With the launch of the *Pokémon Go* app, Nintendo ventured into the realm of smartphones. With augmented reality technology, virtual creatures appear on a smartphone as if they were actually on the street or at other locations.

Within 24 hours after its release in Australia, New Zealand, and the United States, the app was topping the Android and iOS download charts. Only a couple of days after the launch of this app, Nintendo's market value had increased by over 50%. However, the question is to what extent the *Pokémon Go* business model provides Nintendo with a sustainable competitive advantage. Smartphone games are often ephemeral: the hype that surrounds such games immediately after their release typically dies down quite quickly. Thus, while Nintendo may have successfully bridged various developments in the gaming industry (e.g., from game consoles to mobile games) with the introduction of *Pokémon Go*, it is only a matter of time until another wave of disruptions occurs in the gaming industry, meaning that Nintendo may no longer be able to capture the same value from its current business model.

### Questions

1.  What made Nintendo's disruptive business model(s) unique?
2.  How did the other players in the gaming industry respond?

## Disruption and early warning signs

The speed with which technologies and strategies change forces firms to innovate their business model continually. This is true of almost all industries. The introduction of new sharing business models (e.g., Uber, Airbnb, Helpling, Peerby, Taskrabbit) disrupted the existing taxi, hotel, and cleaning sectors and the do-it-yourself (DIY) industry. Many established firms with bricks-and-mortar business models are finding themselves being superseded by new firms whose business models are based on the digital world. Online platforms such as Airbnb, Booking.com, Uber, and perhaps also Google Pay, make it easier for customers to get information about an offering without going through any traditional intermediary.

### Erosion of business models

In the relatively **stable competitive environment** that characterized much of the 20th century, the traditional organizational forms and established strategies for limiting competition were highly satisfactory. They helped well-established firms become large and profitable. During long periods of relatively stable relationships between existing players, firms were able to continually extend and maintain their competitive advantage. The traditional strategies, based on top-down control, formal planning and detailed industrial analysis, guaranteed that their business models would remain both distinctive and sustainable for some time (see Figure 16.3). There is only slow and gradual erosion of the business model and firms can anticipate in advance how to develop a new business model over time.

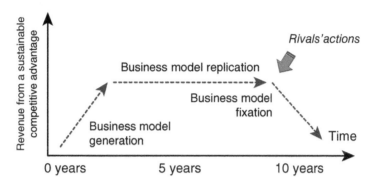

**FIGURE 16.3** Gradual erosion of a business model

Source: Volberda et al. (2018)

Not many enterprises still enjoy this luxury. Instead of long, stable periods with gradual erosion of the dominant business model, competition is now characterized by short periods of competitive advantage, alternating with frequent disturbances and disruption of the business model (see Figure 16.4).[30] Market globalization, rapid technological change, shorter product life cycles, and increasing aggressiveness from competitors have changed the basic rules of competition. Stable competition has become **hypercompetition**, and there does not seem to be a way back.[31] Consequently, no business will survive over the long term without re-inventing itself.[32] Firms will have to cope with frequent disruptions that are either demand-driven (new entrants finding unserved customer needs), supply-driven (emerging technologies that make the firm's business model redundant) or a combination of the two.[33] **Supply-driven disruptions** stem from new entrants introducing a fundamentally new technological architecture that cannot be copied by incumbents by simply improving elements of the existing technology.[34] The iPhone, for example, was an architectural innovation in which software and hardware were integrated in a fundamentally new way that made it difficult for established mobile handset manufacturers to copy. **Demand-driven disruptions** occur when new entrants serve underserved market segments of incumbent firms using technologies that are initially inferior to the mainstream technologies used by incumbents. Although the new entrant's technology may at first underperform, it may do better on particular attributes which are valued by a new customer segment ('new-market foothold') or by a group of mainstream customers who are more price-sensitive ('low-end foothold'). Over time, what was previously an inferior technology retains its initial advantage, but the new entrant also becomes able to meet the needs and demands of mainstream customers of the incumbent firm.[35] There are many examples of industries that were transformed initially by supply-driven disruptions, ranging from steel mills (disrupted by mini-mills), film photography (disrupted by digital imaging technology) to landline telephony (disrupted by smart phones). Industries that have been transformed by demand-driven disruptions include real estate (disrupted by collaborative connected platforms) and travel agencies (disrupted by online platforms).

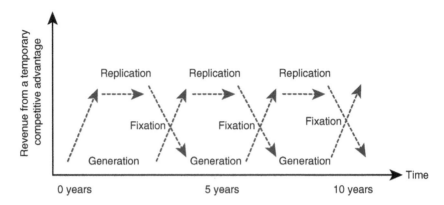

**FIGURE 16.4**   Disruption of business models: Frequent generation of new business models and short periods of replication

Source: Volberda et al. (2018)

Combinations of supply- and demand-driven disruptions often have a great impact on a sector as a whole. The huge growth in the market for smart phones changed the landscape not only for mobile phone manufacturers, but also for infrastructure providers such as KPN. The revenue model that had been the bedrock of the sector since the introduction of commercial telephony – charging people according to the length of the call or later by messages sent – is now on the verge of collapse. Free message traffic via internet telephony using Skype, Teams, Zoom or FaceTime has caused the profits of traditional providers to evaporate.

The decline of Kodak and Polaroid following the advent of digital image technology illustrates how external changes can destroy a successful business model. A salient point is that neither firm was really surprised by the rise of digital image technology. They were both in an excellent position to develop new technological competencies to exploit it. The point was not that the technology changed, but that the entire foundation supporting their growth eroded.

Kodak and Polaroid had for a long time profited from the razor blade business model. The essence of this is that one item (in this case the camera) is offered cheaply, or even for free, and a considerable margin is then achieved on another, related item (rolls of film).[36] In the period up to the Second World War, Kodak sold 25 million cameras, Brownies, for one dollar apiece. The group later introduced another inexpensive, and highly successful model, the Instamatic. The large profits were made on the rolls of film. In the mid-1970s, 90% of all rolls of film sold in the United States were Kodak film. *That* was what Kodak did not dare to let go of. However successful firms may be, business models can be imitated or even improved increasingly swiftly. Products and services quickly turn into commodities; they become less distinctive, and consumers make their purchases more cleverly and cheaply. The result is what Prahalad and Ramaswamy describe as the *'Walmartization'* of everything.[37] This raises the question of how a firm is to stay on its feet in a swiftly changing competitive landscape.

## Warning signs of disruption

But how do you *know* whether you have held on to your existing business model for too long? Retaining an existing business model for too long reduces your chances of developing a new business model in time and competing effectively against the rivals who have done this successfully. Early detection may help a firm to see where its future advantages may lie, which sectors of industry offer the company the most scope to effect disruption, and which business models it needs to build. D'Aveni calls this 'strategic soothsaying',[38] and explains that this involves interpreting the soft signals about how markets and technologies may evolve in ways that offer firms new opportunities to serve current or new customers. In a similar way, Hamel and Prahalad used the word 'industry foresight'[39] to mean an ability to synthesize the collective impact of competitive forces that allows firms to imagine the future and to develop appropriate business models. Early detection of warning signs helps firms to develop viable business models before their rivals have been able to take action. Uber, Airbnb, Google, and Apple are all firms that have created successful first-mover business models based on superior industry foresight, thereby causing disruptive change for their rivals.

**Early warning signs** are relatively easy to detect with hindsight; the value lies in detecting them and assessing their potential impact at the time, and this can be quite difficult. The challenge for managers is to scan the periphery of the market and emergent technology fields just broadly enough, identify alternative business models quickly, and capitalize on those business models.[40] The periphery of a firm's market or industry is where new opportunities for a firm arise, including disruptive ones, and is thus often the place to get foresight information. Or, as Andy Grove from Intel said, 'when spring comes, snow melts first at the periphery, because that is where it is most exposed'.[41] The periphery that may impact on a firm's business models includes not only the intersection between markets or industries, but also the undefined space at the intersection between technologies, mindsets, and industries. However, only a few of the seemingly endless combinations between these dimensions provide interesting and profitable opportunities for a firm. Uber is just one example of a firm that has been successful in exploring new areas at the intersection between a technology (an app) and an industry (the taxi industry). When Apple and Nike joined forces to bring in the Nike+, a running shoe with a sensor which transmits data on the jogger's speed, distance, etc., to an iPod, they were exploiting an opportunity that lay at the intersection between the sports, health, and personal entertainment markets.[42]

Early warning signs of market threats or of disruptive technologies that could harm a firm's existing business model should be given the most attention. Nintendo, for example, was able to develop its successful Wii business model partly because it had spotted several signs of potential disruption to its existing model (passive computer games) at the intersection between the games and fitness market. They recognized, for example, that professional people have only limited time for playing games, that parents are happier when their children play computer games with other children rather than on their own, and that more attention is being paid to sport and to the health of young children. The firm also took note of the blurring of the gaming and fitness markets, and of a strongly held view among non-gamers that video games are a waste of time, and bad for your brain and your health.[43]

Early warning signs of competing markets and disruptive technologies can be many-sided; they can even come from sci-fi movies.[44] For instance, movies such as *Star Wars* and *Back to the Future* have provided many ideas for market and technology-related changes. Management may challenge its employees to detect, understand, and share emerging signs of disruption. For instance, they can facilitate dialogue or organize camp sessions, brainstorming seminars outside the workplace, and even social gatherings. Those signs of potential disruption are often shared in firms via informal networks or during discussions at coffee time. For example, Rabobank challenged its employees to look out for emerging signs of disruption in the financial sector. The Rabobank 'Attack your own Bank' initiative stimulated its employees to spot new opportunities which might form the basis of viable new business models.

Nunes and Breene have identified three **invisible S-curves of strategic performance** which start to decline before a firm's financial performance does (see also point X on the horizontal axis of Figure 16.5):[45] the firm's competitive position curve, its distinctive skills and capabilities curve, and its talent curve. Long before a successful business model hits its revenue peak, its competitive position starts to become eroded. When a new business model is first introduced, the financial performance is initially still relatively low, due to the substantial level of investments made and the low volumes of sales. However, if it is successful there is usually a strong and quite rapid increase in performance. Over time price and turnover pressure occur, partly due to the competition, pushing the financial performance downwards (see Figure 16.5). Any TMTs and CEOs who manage their business from an economic perspective, looking almost exclusively at turnover, costs, and overall financial performance, will perhaps only review the business model for a particular product or service at year T (or even later) in Figure 16.5.

Research has shown that high-performing firms renew their business model much earlier, at around point X in our figure. There is a gap of several years between points X and T, and the number of years will depend on the dynamism and competition in a particular sector. What do these high-performing firms do differently to the firms which pay attention only to the financial S-curve? Research shows that they are much more focused on three invisible S-curves of strategic performance. Those curves reach their peak earlier, sometimes much earlier, than the financial performance S-curve.

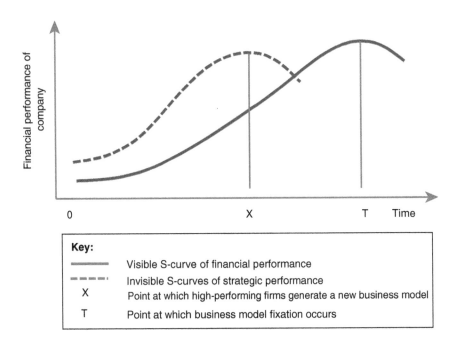

**FIGURE 16.5** S-curves of financial and strategic performance

Source: adapted from Nunes and Breene (2011)

Note: For convenience's sake, the three strategic performance S-curves are represented by a single curve in our figure.

The first of the three invisible S-curves relates to the firm's strategic competitive position. Newcomers and existing rivals can cause that position to be undermined earlier than is shown by the turnover figures of the firm concerned. A second, similarly invisible, S-curve shows the same progression, and concerns the distinctiveness of the firm's core skills and capabilities. The third invisible S-curve relates to the talent within the firm: the employees and managers who possess the capacity to develop new business. In firms that are driven by financial performance, managers will look very closely at costs in order to ramp up the performance of a given business model even more. In this kind of exploitation-oriented context, talented individuals may be let go or may themselves decide to leave the firm.

## STRATEGIC FOCUS

### The invisible S-curves

If a firm wants to change its business model at the appropriate point, it should carefully analyze the three invisible S-curves. The first S-curve may become discernible if top management scans broadly to spot signs of potential disruption from emerging technologies and at the periphery of the market. This allows the firm to identify customer value propositions which have not been attended to, customer needs which have not been recognized, or technology options which have not been considered. Frontline employees, research teams in far-flung parts of the company, and line managers all have a crucial role in detecting important shifts in the market or the emergence of competing technologies. Employees and managers who already have some knowledge of the fringes of the market or some affinity with unknown technologies are often not involved in strategy processes.[46] It is they who form the far corners of the organization, as it were. To reinvent their business models, companies should bring the edges of the market and emerging technologies to the center. In this 'edge-centric' approach, multiple stakeholders are involved in the business model innovation process.[47]

**TABLE 16.1** Actions required by top management to identify invisible S-curves

| Identifying invisible S-curves | | Action required by top management |
|---|---|---|
| 1 | Edge-centric strategy | Investigate the invisible S-curve of a firm's strategic competitive position; take seriously any signals from the furthest corners of the market and furthest periphery of the organization, and incorporate them into strategy formation. |
| 2 | Change at the top | Change the composition of the top management in time, based on the invisible S-curve of distinctive core capabilities; business model generation requires new capabilities and skills. |
| 3 | Surplus talent | Use proactive talent management to stop the invisible S-curve of talent from dipping downwards. |

Source: based on Nunes and Breene (2011)

The second invisible S-curve of distinctiveness of the firm's core skills and capabilities requires that the capacities of the top management itself also have to be reviewed. This will lead to a change at the top (see Table 16.1). Early changes at the top management team gives them time to innovate the business model before it hits the performance peak. CEOs who have just been appointed will take a more

*(Continued)*

critical look at the existing business model, while the ones who have stayed in post for too long are more likely to retain the existing business model for longer than is advisable because it brought their success. Changes at the top to ensure a sufficient balance between long-term and short-term thinking are critical for developing new capabilities.

Top management can tackle the third invisible S-curve of available talent within the firm by trying to cultivate and retain that talent. This kind of policy is aimed at the long term. Talented employees bind themselves to the firm mainly on the basis of intrinsic motivation. They are given the chance to bring promising projects to fruition and develop themselves further through this. Creating a surplus of talent is a necessary condition for completing business model innovation trajectories more rapidly and successfully.

## Questions

1. Take a company that has been disrupted, such as Blockbuster, Kodak, or Nokia. Carefully analyze the firm's visible S-curve of financial performance.
2. Try to find the inflection point of strategic performance by analyzing the invisible S-curve.

# Business model innovation

In disruptive industries, it is no longer relevant to ask *whether* firms should innovate their business model. Continuing to do what you have always done amounts to self-destruction. Many firms fail by doing the very things that have made them successful in the past. Blockbuster, Kodak, Nokia, and Polaroid are all examples of this. Changing the business model is therefore on the agenda of almost every top manager, even if only implicitly. **Business model innovation** occurs not only when the components of the model change, but also when those components are combined in different ways. Such changes in the components and interdependencies may reflect a change in the logic of how a firm conducts business. For instance, the alteration of companies such as Rolls-Royce and ThyssenKrupp from selling a product to customers to a more service-driven logic where customers pay according to a certain leasing model – famously referred to as 'power by the hour' in the case of Rolls-Royce aviation engines – reflects such a shift in logic. We now look in more detail at our two main types of business model innovation: generation, that is, introducing a new business model that is very different from the previous one, and replication, leveraging an existing business model.[48]

## Business model generation

**Business model generation** can be defined as the introduction of new business model components or new interdependencies between the various components which go beyond the framework of an existing model in order to create and capture new value.[49] It involves a radical appraisal of a firm's current business model in order to arrive at a new or more sustainable competitive position for the firm. There are two key characteristics of business model generation (see Table 16.2). First, a firm obtains new business model components, either by developing them itself (making), acquiring them (buying), or accessing external components (e.g., creating alliances). Next, new interdependencies are created among business model components.[50] This is done either by fundamentally revising the existing model, or by developing a new model 'from scratch'.

Business model generation increases a firm's chances of survival in the longer run,[51] but it is a risky process. It requires experimentation, and this can often result in failure as few companies understand their business model well enough, including its interdependencies, strengths, weaknesses, and underlying assumptions.[52] Business model generation also involves more challenges and barriers than replication, due to organizational inertia, political forces, or fear of cannibalization, for example.

Firms that introduce new-to-the-industry business models face particularly high risks, because they have no proof of whether those new models will be viable. The new business model created is not only new for the firm, but also for the sector as a whole.[53] Here we can talk of the reconceptualization of an entire business. Sometimes a new business model of this kind can turn the competitive relationships in a sector completely upside down. This happened when Apple launched iTunes, and when Ryanair and easyJet introduced budget air travel into the European market. Other examples of disruptive business models include Airbnb, Booking.com, Netflix, Peerby, Spotify, and Uber. These online platforms changed the rules within a sector, and resulted in a completely new value proposition. Moves of this kind make it possible for the initiating firm to create a disproportionate level of value and to grow strongly (the 'winner-takes-it-all' effect; see Chapter 9). Business model generation can thus be a powerful means of escaping a competitive race and developing a new and possibly more sustainable competitive advantage.

Radical disruption is essential to business model generation. This is not solely about firms innovating their products as a result of disruptive technologies. Business model generation can enable a firm to make an aggressive move in existing markets or to enter new markets. For instance, Virgin expanded from retail and music into new industries such as airlines and financial services, and Singapore Airlines took on the competition within its own industry by introducing a low-cost carrier airline, SilkAir.[54] Business model generation can also mean the penetration of niche markets which were not being served, the redefinition of customer sectors and customer needs, and new methods of delivery and distribution, or combinations of these. It is not reserved only for small startups or ICT firms. Large corporate groups can also follow totally new avenues. Consider Philips, which has turned to health and lifestyle, or Ricoh, which moved from printing to documents service and 3D printing. DSM is exemplary of a firm able to regenerate its business model various times (see also the Opening Case of this chapter).

**TABLE 16.2** Characteristics of business model generation and business model replication

|  | Business model generation: | Business model replication: |
| --- | --- | --- |
| **Aim** | Reach a new, more sustainable competitive position ('create new success') | Maintain or improve existing competitive position ('leverage success') |
| **Focus** | Generate new methods of value creation and appropriation through radical change of existing business model | Improve current methods of value creation and appropriation through incremental change of the existing business model |
| **Risks** | • (very) high for first movers in industry<br>• high risk for imitators | • limited risk in the short term<br>• high in the longer term |
| **Business model components** | Obtain new business model components | Refine current business model components |
| **Business model complementarities** | Create new complementary effects among business model components | Strengthen complementarities between current business model components |

Source: based on Volberda et al. (2018)

## KEY DEBATE

### Business model generation of small accountancy firms

A recent study carried out in small Dutch accountancy firms who worked mostly with SME clients provides a clear example of business model generation in high-value professional services. Due to competitive pressures from the 'big four' accountancy firms (PwC, Deloitte, EY, and KPMG), smaller accountancy firms were facing decreasing margins. Most of these SME accountants chose the same business model (see the average business model components of 212 SME accountancy firms in Figure 16.6). That is, they all focused on a niche market, and experimented to some extent with digital channels in addition to their traditional physical channels. And they all tried to achieve a balance between advisory and production activities, between people and ICT as key resources, and, in their revenue model, between charging by hourly rate or by subscription. The lack of distinctiveness in their business model led to fierce competition on price and to the closure of many accountancy firms.

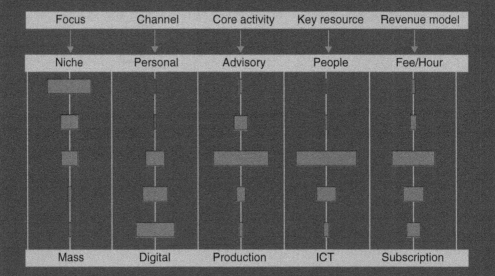

**FIGURE 16.6**  The business model components of SME accountants

Source: Volberda et al. (2018)
Note: the size of each box represents the number of small accountancy firms per column.

More distinctive business models of SME accountants that resulted in more profitable market positions can be clustered into three categories (see Figure 16.7):

- The <u>specialist</u>, which focuses on a specific market niche or specializes in a single service or a small range of services.
- The <u>house of service</u>, which tries to create the best of both worlds: it combines standard services with tailor-made advice.
- The <u>digital accountant</u> (or 'digicountant'), which combines accountancy and automation solutions in a small number of standard online services (administrative support, bookkeeping, and real-time financial dashboard).

Firms in the first two categories focus on a particular niche, use personal rather than digital channels, provide advisory activities, and have people, not ICT, as their key resources. Firms in both these categories use business models in which they still charge an hourly rate rather than a subscription fee.

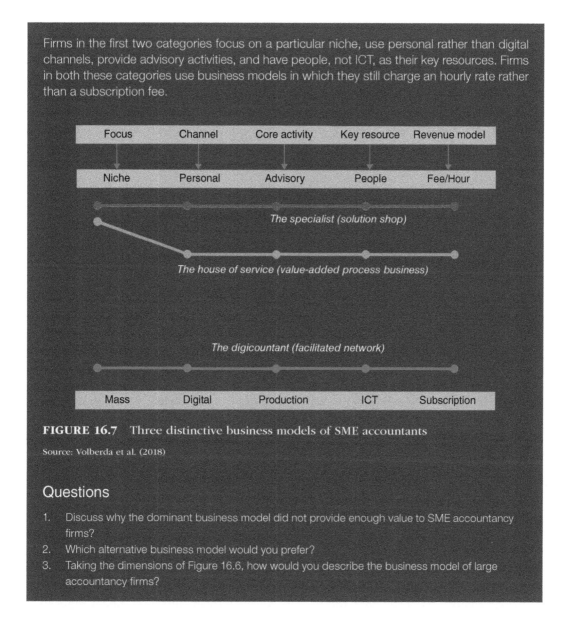

**FIGURE 16.7** Three distinctive business models of SME accountants

Source: Volberda et al. (2018)

## Questions

1. Discuss why the dominant business model did not provide enough value to SME accountancy firms?
2. Which alternative business model would you prefer?
3. Taking the dimensions of Figure 16.6, how would you describe the business model of large accountancy firms?

## Business model replication

As an alternative to radically creating a fundamentally new business model, firms can also employ a strategy of improving or replicating a business model. McDonald's and IKEA have elevated the expansion and perfection of their existing business models to an art, and acquired global success as a result. Since these firms originally worked on the basis of business model generation, they provide powerful examples of how generation and replication can be used effectively in succession.

**Business model replication** can be described as the 're-creation of a successful model'[55] in which a firm develops or upscales components of its existing business model so as to create and capture more value. That is, it leverages those existing components –

and the interdependencies between them – by refining and adjusting its current model,[56] or by using the model more widely across different parts of the firm.[57] Replication is not about cloning the original model, but creating a model that is broadly similar. The focus is on improving existing methods of value creation and appropriation by making incremental changes to an existing business model.[58] It is a dynamic and evolving process that requires the right balance between learning, change, and precise replication. Business model replication offers a comparatively safe route to short-term success, but it lacks variety, and this can threaten a firm's survival in the longer run. The more proficiently a firm replicates a business model elsewhere, the more effectively it can reap the rewards of that replication.

Two key characteristics of business model replication stand out (see Table 16.2). First, business model replication is about leveraging the components of a firm's existing business model. Second, internal fit between business model components is needed to create or reinforce consistency between those components; business model components 'need to be co-specialized to each other, and work together well as a system'[59] so that firms can benefit from the complementary effects of different sources of competitive advantage.

There are various ways to replicate a business model. An existing business model can be applied in a different context. In **geographical replication**, for example, an existing business model is applied in a different country or region. One example of this is the way IKEA continually opens new branches on different continents. Enriched knowledge of operations, products, services, and markets, gathered over time, enables the company to refine its existing business model.

Replication can also be applied over time. In that case, a firm might improve an existing business model over a certain period of time, for instance, and this is known as **longitudinal replication**. Most firms do this: they improve existing business models by enriching their existing knowledge of the market and of production processes.[60]

Improvement in replication takes place using existing knowledge and experience, mainly from within the firm itself. It is a case of exploitative learning, deepening the existing knowledge base of the firm.[61] It is important in this connection to point out that business model replication means not only replicating repeatedly, but also discovering and learning from complex, and partly implicit routines that are interdependent.[62] So, replication does not lead to stagnation: you can learn again from the process itself. Experience of using a particular business model enables a firm to improve on that model by rectifying mistakes and getting rid of inefficiencies. It can also remove particular components or change the priority given to them. Business model replication can increase a firm's profit in two ways. First, it provides cost advantages because it allows the firm to operate more efficiently and exploit economies of scale. Firms with more experience of business model replication can thus replicate at lower cost. Second, replication can also increase revenue, because by increasing its competitive advantage or overcoming previous limitations, the firm is able to capture more value from its existing business model.

Sustained replication also results in stronger interactions, tighter links and more synergies between the various components of a business model. This makes it harder for competitors to identify the precise components of a firm's business model or the source of its success, and the model becomes more difficult for outsiders to imitate.[63] Business model replication is clearly a path-dependent process of learning, in which the strengthening of combinations of components differentiates a firm's business model from those of its competitors. A business model that is more differentiated and more difficult to imitate increases a firm's competitive advantage, and thereby its performance.

## Hybrid business models

We discussed two dominant modes of business model innovation: generation and replication. But can firms also foster both business model replication and generation? In this so-called dual or **hybrid business model**, one part of the firm focuses on the generation of a new business model and creating new added value, and another part focuses on replication and on ensuring that well-established routines and competencies are put to optimal use. For business model generation, the firm uses a separate unit, which has been separated to a certain degree from its mainstream business. For example, the Nestlé Group experimented with its new capsule-based espresso business model in a completely separate unit.[64] Also, when postal operators in various European countries were undertaking new ventures in which they were experimenting with new business models, these were to some extent separated from the companies' mainstream activities.[65] The basic principle behind dual business models is that the parent organization continues to concentrate on business model replication, while a separate sub-unit is tasked with working on business model renewal. This enables a firm to focus on different market segments and customer needs, and gives it multiple ways of commercializing its technologies. One may think of a service-based business model being used alongside a production-based model or a software-based model used alongside a business model relating to a hardware model. The firm's existing models typically remain at arm's length from the new business models so that the focus on existing operations can be maintained.[66]

Having multiple business models within a firm (see Crack-the-Case: Multiple business models at the BMW Group) also provides opportunities for synergies between them – for instance, through the sharing of value chain activities and branding. For managers, it is extremely difficult to determine what the right degree of integration may be between a new business model and existing models.[67] On the one hand, there needs to be sufficient integration between the new business model and the existing business models to ensure adequate coordination between them and to create synergies between them (see Figure 16.8). On the other hand, the integration should not go too far, as the firm needs to ensure that there will be no cannibalization or conflicts between the various models. It is also important to prevent the new business model from losing whatever makes it distinctive from the firm's other business models.

- A different, better way to seize certain opportunities and respond to certain threats
- Less chances for cannibalization and conflicts

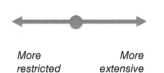

*More restricted*      *More extensive*

- No added value to have different ways (business models) due to substantial overlap
- Increased opportunities for coordination and synergies

Degree of integration between new and existing business model

**FIGURE 16.8** Seemingly opposing forces on the degree of integration between a firm's new and existing business models

# CRACK-THE-CASE

## Multiple business models at the BMW Group[68]

Source: © FooTToo (2020) / Shutterstock.

The BMW Group has three divisions: cars, financial services, and motorbikes. BMW focuses especially on the premium market. The car division designs, builds, and sells passenger cars and off-road vehicles under the BMW, Mini, and Rolls-Royce brands. BMW acquired the Mini brand in 2001. Since then, there has been an explosion in sales. The Mini is even catching on in countries which have their own strong local car industries. The five countries where the Mini sells best are Great Britain, the United States, Germany, Italy, and Japan.

BMW has positioned its Mini as more than just a car: it stands for a lifestyle. The firm offers a wide range of accessories and other items to support this, such as clothing and key fobs. In addition, the Mini has its own online social network or 'urban initiative', called Mini Space. These give the brand more meaning. People who buy a Mini can have their car assembled in the way they want. There are 372 interior and 319 exterior options, making the Mini one of the most customizable cars in its class. Marketing initiatives capitalize on the cheeky image of the brand.

BMW is associated traditionally with larger and premium-priced cars, and ownership of the Mini brand therefore gave the company a completely new way of creating value. With the Mini, BMW entered a very different segment of the car market, one so different that there was very little risk of damage to their existing brand. The takeover also offered opportunities for growth, in both product development and brand development. The Mini enabled BMW to enter the highly competitive small hatchback market and compete with cars such as the Volkswagen Polo, the Audi A1, and the Ford Fiesta. With BMW, Mini, and

Rolls Royce, the BMW Group now has a large market share in the various segments of the car market which the group covers.

## Questions

1. Why does the BMW group have separate business models?
2. To what extent is the Mini brand business model conflicting with BMW's traditional business model and what would be the required level of integration?

# Business model transformation

In this final section, we explore the dynamics of business model innovation. It seems to be almost unavoidable that a period of business model generation will be followed by business model replication. Both generation and replication can be internally driven (by strategy) or externally driven (by customers). Combining types of business model innovation (replication versus generation) with business model orientation (strategy-driven versus customer-driven) gives us four variations (see the Business Model Innovation Matrix in Figure 16.9).

- <u>Strategy-driven business model generation.</u> This is characterized by transformational leadership, a committed top and middle management, an innovative culture, a focus on internal knowledge absorption, a dynamic environment, and an internal organizational identity subject to frequent change. This proactive generation of a new business model entails an organization-wide transformation which involves all levels of management.
- <u>Customer-driven business model generation.</u> This is characterized by transformational leadership, a committed top management, an innovative, customer-driven culture, a focus on external knowledge absorption, a dynamic environment, and an external organizational identity in flux. Business model generation here occurs by upgrading the business model in response to completely new customers.
- <u>Strategy-driven business model replication.</u> This is characterized by transactional leadership, a committed top management, a less innovative culture, a focus on internal knowledge absorption, a competitive environment, and a strong internal organizational identity. In this case, a directive management improves and perfects the existing business model.
- <u>Customer-driven business model replication.</u> This is characterized by transactional leadership, a committed top management, a customer-driven culture, a focus on external knowledge absorption, a high level of competitive pressure, and a strong external organizational identity. In this variation, the business model is improved significantly by being linked more strongly to existing customers. Knowledge combination and exchange are particularly important in this variation.

## The Business Model Innovation Matrix

Firms can be positioned in one of the four quadrants of the **Business Model Innovation Matrix**. DSM, for instance, fits into the upper-left quadrant of strategy-driven business model generation (see Figure 16.9). The firm has fundamentally transformed its business

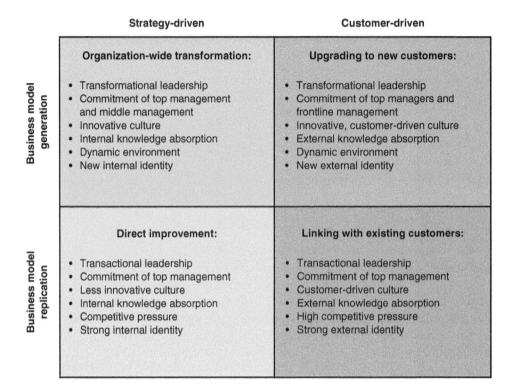

**FIGURE 16.9** The Business Model Innovation Matrix

model several times. It began with coal, then transitioned to bulk chemicals, followed by a shift to fine chemicals. Subsequently, it moved towards life sciences and materials, and most recently, it has ventured into the domains of food and health products. DSM's business model generation to anticipate various strategic opportunities (see Opening Case) arose from corporate strategic dialogues where key figures developed scenarios and future visions, and the group's strategic priorities were established. This proactive generation of the business model entails an organization-wide transformation and requires changes in technology, management and organizational forms. This type of move places a heavy burden on senior managers, and is thus likely to result in some major changes to the top management team. The substantial involvement required from middle managers generally means that this type of trajectory may be more difficult to complete satisfactorily with the firm's existing middle managers still in place. After all, some of those middle managers may have spent a large part of their career focusing on replication. Firms like Apple and Google can also be placed in this quadrant. Apple has changed its initial business model radically within a short period of time. The firm switched from providing personal computers to supplying entirely new devices for new markets, including the iPod (music market), iPad (tablet market), and iPhone (telephony), and services linked to those devices. Google, too, diversified, and stacked up a series of business models. Instead of being purely a search engine, the firm began offering 'business intelligence' to firms, for instance, and developed automated control for cars and activities in the optical industry (Google Glass). At DSM, Apple, and Google, generation of a new business model was driven more from the inside out. The firms saw that there were more attractive returns to be gained by going into unfamiliar territory. In these cases, it was not direct customer needs in the market which led to business model generation (market response), but a proactive strategy of management to create new markets (market creation).

The Port of Rotterdam Authority and Royal IHC fit into the right upper quadrant of customer-driven business model generation (see Figure 16.10). Business model generation here occurs by upgrading the business model in response to completely new customers. It requires changes in management, organizational forms and in collaborations with external actors. The Port of Rotterdam Authority transformed its business model from that of *landlord* to *port developer* by working closely together with customers and attracting new customers. The business model of Royal IHC, which supplies vessels and services for the offshore, dredging, and wet mining markets, changed abruptly from 'if the slipways are full, then it's OK' to a more customer-oriented model. The firm creates value by offering integrated technological solutions. Shell's response towards cleaner energy in which it is working with a set of external partners on hydrogen and wind power also shows characteristics of the right upper quadrant. Or, as its head of global sustainability framed it: 'We keep on emphasizing that we need to be "in step with society", because we cannot go faster than the society allows us to make that transition'.[69] However, Shell's new CEO, Wael Sawan, appears to emphasize shareholder value over societal value with a strong company focus on exploiting fossil energy. He firmly believes that fossil energy will remain Shell's core business and investments in renewable energy will only be made when they are profitable.[70] This seems like a shift back towards a strategy-driven replication of the fossil energy business model.

NXP and Randstad belong in the lower right quadrant of customer-driven business model replication. The drive for business model replication comes mainly from engaging in co-creation with customers, adjusting management practices, and redesigning the organization. The level of involvement required from top management is less than for strategy-driven business model generation, but nevertheless more than for strategy-driven replication. The role of top management is to consider issues such as which types of customer segment to serve or which of the firm's existing customers are most important to invest in. NXP's current business model is considerably more strongly customer-driven, and large customers such as Apple and Samsung are involved early on in the development of customized semiconductors. At the semiconductor company NXP, the customer-driven business model focus is expressed in its mission statement: 'customer-focused passion to win', and even in its name (NXP stands for Next eXPerience). Randstad Netherlands scaled up its business model of providing temporary agency workers to offer 'integrated HR solutions' in which it takes over HR activities from customers such as rostering, planning, outplacement, and recruitment and selection.

The lower left quadrant of strategy-driven replication includes General Motors (GM), IKEA, McDonald's and Vopak. It requires refinement of a firm's technology, management and organizational forms. GM lost ground in the long run by continuing to refine existing models. Being in this quadrant does not necessarily have to be negative, though. IKEA and McDonald's are highly successful at replicating their existing business models in many different countries. Using their experience, they have been able to refine their business models repeatedly over time. Vopak, the world's leading independent tank storage company, has also learned by trial and error that strategy-driven replication of its business model for tank storage (liquid gas, biofuels, and oil) was more likely to provide long-term success.

Over time, most firms move between different quadrants of the Business Model Innovation Matrix. Firms focusing on business model replication for quite a while may over time experience a greater urgency for business model generation to avoid ending up in the

| | Strategy-driven | Customer-driven |
|---|---|---|
| **Business model generation** | *Organization-wide transformation*<br>Examples: DSM, Apple, Google | *Upgrading to new customers*<br>Examples: Port of Rotterdam Authority, Shell |
| **Business model replication** | *Directive improvement*<br>Examples: IKEA, McDonald's, Vopak | *Linking with existing customers*<br>Examples: NXP, Randstad |

**FIGURE 16.10**   Four types of business model innovation and company examples

Source: based on Volberda et al. (2018)

replication trap. An organization which has initially worked on business model generation can be actively replicating just a few years later. Likewise, firms can also move relatively swiftly from replication to generation. In business model innovation it is also possible to be strategy-driven one moment and customer-driven the next. We call this migration from one stage to another **business model transformation**. In the current dynamic context, firms can go extremely rapidly from one stage to the next. In theory, an organization can go through all quadrants of the Business Model Innovation Matrix in a single decade, although what happens more often is that it moves between two or three quadrants.

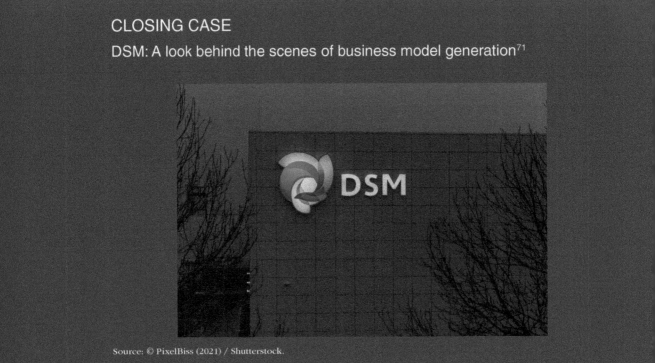

## CLOSING CASE
### DSM: A look behind the scenes of business model generation[71]

Let us return to DSM (opening case of this chapter). It generated several new business models, neither automatically nor overnight. The company already had a periphery technology in place when they chose a new business model. When the government decided to close the local coal mines, DSM already had developed a chemicals arm which it could use to build a new, successful future in the bulk chemicals sector, based on gas and oil. At the early stage of business model generation (life sciences and materials), a special products business unit at DSM already produced components needed for penicillin, among other things. The company noticed that it 'did not earn the money in the penicillin value chain,' thereby sparking the firm's interest in life sciences, with its higher margins. What had at first been a peripheral technology became the core technology, strengthened by acquisitions and collaborative agreements. These days, DSM's innovation center cultivates future growth opportunities across the company and explores adjacent business opportunities located outside of the scope of existing business groups with a current focus on biomedical and bio-based solutions. The lion's share of what is in the innovation pipeline has an eco+ or people+ character. As a science-based company, it devotes substantial attention to technology, with R&D-investments of €438 million in 2020 (4.8% of sales). This should also be a hallmark after the merger with Firmenich, as stated by Thomas Leysen (chairman of DSM): 'DSM-Firmenich will bring together leading creativity and cutting-edge science and innovation'.

A recurring element of business model generation at DSM was the presence of leaders with strong personalities who combined inspiration and charisma with a vision for the future. Management anticipated market developments – for instance via corporate strategic dialogues – and played an important part in driving the innovation. This goes beyond merely making decisions about resetting the firm's scope and related aspects, such as acquisitions, collaborative arrangements, divestments, and innovations. Board chairs sometimes stepped out of their own shadow and were willing to explore new and unfamiliar territory. For instance, the reorientation to life sciences was initiated by CEO Simon de Bree, who came from petrochemicals. To ensure that the transition from petrochemicals to life sciences would be supported across the organization, top management invested heavily in new management practices such as inspiring leadership, exemplary behaviour, and transparent communication. Managers were assigned different roles and had to acquire new competencies, partly because of the diffusion of management practices of the company it acquired (Gist-Brocades) and because of the many joint ventures. In 2005 the company expressed the ambition that €1 billion of its revenue should come from new products by 2010. That corporate target was translated into everyone's targets and meant that the speed of innovation had to be doubled. The company exceeded its target, achieving €1.3 billion in revenue.

The introduction of a separate innovation center – next to a worldwide network of R&D centers – is an example of a structural change to increase and accelerate new activities that may lead to new business models. Another example is the new allocation of activities into the four business units – perfumery and beauty, food and beverage, health and nutrition, and animal nutrition – as part of the merger with Firmenich. At the time that DSM started to emphasize life sciences and materials, the more dynamic market conditions drove the

*(Continued)*

organization from being strongly centralized to more decentralized. This was later adjusted again, when ICT and Purchasing were grouped together, for example.

The innovation center also acts as a hub for co-creation. Among the tasks of this center is to invest in promising startups to create and develop new business and innovation opportunities. Instead of wanting to develop everything itself through closed R&D paths, DSM embraced the 'proudly found elsewhere' philosophy. Since customers can be involved at any stage of the process in realizing tailor-made collaborative solutions, they are considered as a crucial external partner: 'The real key to the success of our Innovation & Application Centers is customer engagement, with the facilities being conveniently located to encourage regular and ongoing dialogue'.

## Questions

1.  Discuss how DSM has been able to detect early warning signs and proactively change its business model.
2.  Discuss the business model transformation paths of DSM, focusing especially on the shift towards life sciences and materials.

## Summary

- A business model (1) is made up of various components and describes the relationship between them ('architecture'), (2) embodies how value creation occurs and how the firm appropriates value, and (3) provides insights into how those components and their relationships add value and thereby contribute to a firm's competitive strategy.
- Disruption makes existing business models obsolete and requires new ones to be developed. There are various early warning signs related to (1) the strategic competitive position of a firm, (2) the core skills and capacities of the firm, and (3) the existing talent.
- Firms can innovate their business models in different ways. They can scale up and improve their existing business model through replication. Firms can also change their business model far more radically, through business model generation.
- If firms are capable of both replicating the existing business model and generating new models (hybrid business models), top managers must ensure that there is adequate separation of the different models and that they are able to manage conflicts.
- Both replication and generation can be either strategy-driven or driven by customers. With strategy-driven business model generation (a transformation of the business model which affects the entire firm), both top management and middle management are involved intensively. With customer-driven replication (strengthening the business model by linking it more to existing customers), the improvement comes mainly from engaging in co-creation with customers, adjusting management practices, and redesigning the organization.

# Review questions

1. What is business model innovation?
2. Describe several early warning signs on the demand and supply side.
3. What are the pros and cons of business model replication?
4. When should firms opt for business model generation?
5. What is a hybrid business model?

# Discussion questions

1. How can the rise of the internet, which was associated with a surge of attention to the business model concept, affect the opportunities for a firm to pursue hybrid business models?
2. Take a well-known public company. What is the typical clockspeed of its industry? What is the clockspeed of change of the company itself? Who are the disruptors (the Airbnbs or Ubers) in its industry? Is the firm's business model fundamentally different from average players in its industry? If the company could start from scratch, what would be the preferred business model of value creation and appropriation?

## EXPERIENTIAL EXERCISES

1. Assume you are a key figure at a firm of your choice. What would be the warning signs that the existing business model becomes outdated?
2. What might a new business model of that firm look like? Describe what particular type of business model innovation (focus on generation, replication, or a specific hybrid approach) you would recommend.

# Further reading

Mihalache, O.R. and Volberda, H.W. (2021) 'Business model innovation in transforming economies: A co-evolutionary perspective for a global and digital world', *Management and Organization Review,* 17 (2): 202–25.

Narayan, S., Sidhu, J.S. and Volberda, H.W. (2021) 'From attention to action: The influence of cognitive and ideological diversity in top management teams on business model innovation', *Journal of Management Studies,* 58 (8): 2082–110.

Osterwalder, A. and Pigneur, Y. (2010) *Business Model Generation: A Handbook for Visionaries, Game changers, and Challengers.* Hoboken, NJ: John Wiley & Sons.

Teece, D.J. (2010) 'Business models, business strategy and innovation', *Long Range Planning,* 43 (2/3): 172–94.

Volberda, H.W., Van den Bosch, F.A.J. and Heij, K. (2018) *Reinventing Business Models: How Firms Cope with Disruption.* Oxford: Oxford University Press.

# Endnotes (references)

1. Burger, L. and Meijer, B.H. (2022) 'DSM forges nutrition and fragrance giant with Firmenich deal', *Reuters,* May 31. www.reuters.com/article/dsm-m-a-firmenich-idUSKBN2NH0CA (accessed June 30, 2023); DSM (2022a) 'About DSM'. https://web.archive.org/web/20230527114147/https://www.dsm.com/corporate/our-company.html (accessed June 30, 2023); DSM (2022b) 'Our businesses & organization: Health, nutrition and materials', *DSM.* https://web.archive.org/web/20230307212907/https://www.dsm.com/corporate/our-businesses.html (accessed June 30, 2023); DSM (2022c) 'DSM completes sale of Protective Materials business', *DSM,* September 1. www.dsm.com/corporate/news/news-archive/2022/dsm-completes-sale-of-protective-materials-business.html (accessed June 30, 2023); Nunes, K. (2022) 'Royal DSM to acquire Firmenich', *Food Business News,* May 31. www.foodbusinessnews.net/articles/21456-royal-dsm-to-acquire-firmenich (accessed June 30, 2023); Volberda, H.W., Van den Bosch, F.A.J. and Heij, K. (2018) *Reinventing Business Models: How Firms Cope with Disruption.* Oxford: Oxford University Press.
2. Volberda et al. (2018)
3. Burger, L. and Meijer, B.H. (2022) 'DSM forges nutrition and fragrance giant with Firmenich deal', *euronews.next,* May 31. www.euronews.com/next/2022/05/31/dsm-m-a-firmenich (accessed July 28, 2023).
4. *PR Newswire* (2022) 'DSM and Firmenich to merge, becoming the leading creation and innovation partner in nutrition, beauty and well-being', May 22. www.prnewswire.com/in/news-releases/dsm-and-firmenich-to-merge-becoming-the-leading-creation-and-innovation-partner-in-nutrition-beauty-and-well-being-852826244.html (accessed July 28, 2023).
5. Burger and Meijer (2022)
6. Casadesus-Masanell, R. and Ricart, J.E. (2010) 'From strategy to business models and onto tactics', *Long Range Planning,* 43: 195–215.
7. Schneckenberg, D., Matzler, K. and Spieth, P. (2022) 'Theorizing business model innovation: An organizing framework of research dimensions and future perspectives', *R&D Management,* 52: 593–609.
8. Teece, D.J. (2010) 'Business models, business strategy and innovation', *Long Range Planning,* 43 (2–3), 172–94.
9. Foss, N.J. and Saebi, T. (2017) 'Fifteen years of research on business model innovation: How far have we come, and where should we go?', *Journal of Management,* 43: 200–27.
10. Volberda et al. (2018)
11. Hamel, G. (2000) *Leading the Revolution.* Boston, MA: Harvard Business School Press.
12. Volberda et al. (2018)
13. Baden-Fuller, C.W.F. and Mangematin, V. (2013) 'Business models: A challenging agenda', *Strategic Organization,* 11: 418–27.
14. Zott, C. and Amit, R. (2010) 'Business model design: An activity system perspective'. *Long Range Planning,* 43 (2–3): 216–226.
15. Foss, N.J. and Saebi, T. (2015) 'Business models and business model innovation: Bringing organization into the discussion', In N.J. Foss and T. Saebi (eds), *Business Model Innovation: The Organizational Dimension.* Oxford: Oxford University Press, 1–23.
16. Casadesus-Masanell, R. and Ricart, J.E. (2011) 'How to design a winning business model', *Harvard Business Review,* 89: 100–7.
17. Cortimiglia, M.N., Ghezzi, A. and Frank, A.G. (2016) 'Business model innovation and strategy making nexus: Evidence from a cross-industry mixed-methods study', *R&D Management,* 46: 414–32.

18. Osterwalder, A. and Pigneur, Y. (2010) *Business Model Generation: A Handbook for Visionaries, Game Changers, and Challengers*. Hoboken, NJ: John Wiley & Sons.

19. Massa, L. and Tucci, C.L. (2014) 'Business model innovation', In M. Dodgson, D.M. Gann and N. Philips (eds), *The Oxford Handbook of Innovation Management*. Oxford: Oxford University Press, 420–41.

20. Baden-Fuller and Mangematin (2013)

21. Kraus, S., Filser, M., Puumalainen, K., Kailer, N. and Thurner, S. (2020) 'Business model innovation: A systematic literature review', *International Journal of Innovation and Technology Management*, 17 (6): article #2050043.

22. Christensen, C.M., Cook, S. and Hall, T. (2005) 'Marketing malpractice: The cause and the cure', *Harvard Business Review*, 83: 74–83.

23. Baden-Fuller, C. and Haefliger, S. (2013) 'Business models and technological innovation', *Long Range Planning*, 46 (6): 419–26.

24. Baden-Fuller and Haefliger (2013)

25. Teece (2010: 179)

26. Casadesus-Masanell and Ricart (2010)

27. Heikkilä, M., Bouwman, H. and Heikkilä, J. (2017) 'From strategic goals to business model innovation paths: An exploratory study', *Journal of Small Business and Enterprise Development*, 25: 107–28.

28. Teece (2010)

29. Volberda et al. (2018)

30. Volberda, H.W., Morgan, R.E., Reinmoeller, P., Hitt, M.A., Ireland, R.D. and Hoskisson, R.E. (2011) *Strategic Management: Competitiveness and Globalization*. Andover: Cengage.

31. McGrath, R.G. (2013) *The End of Competitive Advantage: How to Keep Your Strategy Moving as Fast as Your Business*. Boston, MA: Harvard Business Review Press.

32. Bertolini, M., Bevilacqua, M., Ciarapica, F.E. and Postacchini, L. (2015) 'Business process reengineering of drugs storage and distribution: A case study', *International Journal of Procurement Management*, 8 (1/2): 44–65.

33. Sood, A. and Tellis, G.J. (2011) 'Demystifying disruption: A new model for understanding and predicting disruptive technologies', *Marketing Science*, 30 (2): 339–54.

34. Gans, J. (2016) *The Disruption Dilemma*. Boston, MA: MIT Press.

35. Christensen, C.M., Raynor, M. and McDonald, R. (2015) 'What is disruptive innovation?', *Harvard Business Review*, 93: 44–53.

36. Chesbrough, H. and Rosenbloom, R.S. (2002) 'The role of the business model in capturing value from innovation: Evidence from Xerox Corporation's technology spin-off companies', *Industrial and Corporate Change*, 11: 529–55.

37. Prahalad, C.K. and Ramaswamy, V. (2004) 'Co-creation experiences: The next practice in value creation', *Journal of Interactive Marketing*, 18: 5–14.

38. D'Aveni, R.A. (1994) *Hypercompetition: Managing the Dynamics of Strategic Management*. New York, NY: Free Press.

39. Hamel, G. and Prahalad, C.K. (1994) 'Competing for the future', *Harvard Business Review*, 72 (4): 122–8.

40. Day, G.S. and Schoemaker, P.J. (2016) 'Adapting to fast-changing markets and technologies', *California Management Review*, 58: 59–77.

41. Grove, A.S. (1999) *Only the Paranoid Survive: How to Exploit the Crisis Points That Challenge Every Company*. New York, NY: Bantam/Currency.

42. Ofek, E. and Wathieu, L. (2010) 'Are you ignoring trends that could shake up your business?', *Harvard Business Review*, 88: 124–31.

43. Nonaka, I. and Zhu, Z. (2012) *Pragmatic Strategy: Eastern Wisdom, Global Success*. Cambridge: Cambridge University Press.

44. Hiltunen, E. (2008) 'Good sources of weak signals: A global study of where futurists look for weak signals', *Journal of Futures Studies*, 12: 21–44.

45. Nunes, P. and Breene, T. (2011) 'Reinvent your business before it's too late', *Harvard Business Review*, 89: 80–7.

46. Day and Schoemaker (2016)

47. Nunes and Breene (2011)

48. Velu, C. (2016) 'Evolutionary or revolutionary business model innovation through coopetition? The role of dominance in network markets', *Industrial Marketing Management*, 53: 124–35.

49. Kraus et al. (2020)

50. Johnson, M.W., Christensen, C.M. and Kagermann, H. (2008) 'Reinventing your business model', *Harvard Business Review*, 86: 57–68.

51. Andries, P., DeBackere, K. and Van Looy, B. (2013) 'Simultaneous experimentation as a learning strategy: Business model development under uncertainty', *Strategic Entrepreneurial Journal*, 7: 288–310.

52. Johnson et al. (2008)

53. Casadesus-Masanell, R. and Zhu, F. (2013) 'Business model innovation and competitive imitation: The case of sponsor-based business models', *Strategic Management Journal*, 34: 464–82.

54. Markides, C. and Charitou, C.D. (2004) 'Competing with dual business models: A contingency approach', *Academy of Management Perspectives*, 18(3): 22–36.

55. Szulanski, G. and Jensen, R.J. (2008) 'Growing through copying: The negative consequences of innovation on franchise network growth', *Research Policy*, 37: 1732–41. p. 1738.

56. Schneider, S. and Spieth, P. (2013) 'Business model innovation: Towards an integrated future research agenda', *International Journal of Innovation Management*, 17: 1–34.

57. Jonsson, A. and Foss, N.J. (2011) 'International expansion through flexible replication: Learning from the internationalization experience of IKEA', *Journal of International Business Studies*, 42: 1079–102.

58. Baden-Fuller, C.W.F. and Winter, S. (2007) 'Replicating knowledge practices: Principles or templates', Working paper, *Bayes Business School*. doi.org/10.2139/ssrn.1118013

59. Teece (2010: 180)

60. Baden-Fuller, C.W.F. and Volberda, H.W. (2003) 'Dormant capabilities, complex organizations, and renewal', in R. Sanchez (ed.), *Knowledge Management and Organizational Competence*. Oxford: Oxford University Press, 114–36.

61. Winter, S.G., Szulanski, G., Ringov, D. and Jensen, R.J. (2012) 'Reproducing knowledge: Inaccurate replication and failure in franchise organizations', *Organization Science*, 23: 672–85.

62. Szulanski and Jensen (2008)

63. Teece (2010)

64. Matzler, K., Bailom, F., Von den Eichen, S.F. and Kohler, T. (2013) 'Business model innovation: Coffee triumphs for Nespresso', *Journal of Business Strategy*, 34 (2): 30–7.

65. Bogers, M., Sund, K. and Villarroel Fernandez, J.A. (2014) 'The organizational dimension of business model exploration: Evidence from the European postal industry', in N.J. Foss and T. Saebi (eds), *Business Model Innovation: The Organizational Dimension*. Oxford: Oxford University Press, 269–88.

66. Aspara, J., Lamberg, J.A., Laukia, A. and Tikkanen, H. (2013) 'Corporate business model transformation and inter-organizational cognition: The case of Nokia', *Long Range Planning*, 46: 459–74.

67. Markides, C. and Oyon, D. (2010) 'What to do against disruptive business models (when and how to play two games at once)', *MIT Sloan Management Review*, 51: 26–32.
68. Volberda et al. (2018)
69. Volberda, H.W., Sidhu, J.S., Vishwanathan, P., Heij, K. and Kashanizadeh, Z. (2022) *De winst van purpose: Hoe ondernemingen het verschil kunnen maken*. Amsterdam: Mediawerf.
70. Jack, S. (2023) 'Oil giant Shell warns cutting production "dangerous"', *BBC News*, July 6. www.bbc.com/news/business-66108553 (accessed July 28, 2023).
71. Burger and Meijer (2022); DSM (2018) 'Behind the scenes at DSM's Innovation & Application Centers', *DSM,* November 23. www.dsm.com/human-nutrition/en/talking-nutrition/behind-the-scenes-at-dsm-innovation-application-centers.html (accessed June 30, 2023); DSM (2021) 'DSM integrated annual report 2020', *DSM*. https://annualreport.dsm.com/ar2020/report-by-the-managing-board/profit/key-business-figures.html (accessed June 30, 2023); Nunes (2022); Volberda et al. (2018).

# Acknowledgements

Parts of this chapter are based on Volberda, H. W., Van den Bosch, F. A. J., and Heij, K. (2018) *Reinventing business models: How firms cope with disruption*. Oxford: Oxford University Press.

# Key terms

**Architecture** – the structure of the value chain which is needed to create and distribute a value proposition, as well as the extra assets required for this process

**Business model** – the way a firm creates and captures value via various components and their interdependencies, thereby contributing to realizing a firm's strategy

**Business model canvas** – a model that describes various components of a business model – including both the production side and the market side – and extends to partners, distribution channels, and target groups in the market

**Business model generation** – introduction of new components and new interdependencies beyond the framework of an existing business model to create and capture new value

**Business model innovation** – changes in the business model components and their interdependencies to alter value creation and value capture, either in a more radical way (generation) or a more incremental way (replication)

**Business Model Innovation Matrix** – an overview of business model innovation, based on the basic types (generation and replication) and whether it is more strategy- or customer-driven

**Business model replication** – refinement and upscaling of components and their interdependencies within the framework of an existing business model to create and capture more value from it

**Business model transformation** – the switch from one type of business model innovation to another

**Demand-driven disruptions** – new entrants serving underserved market segments of incumbent firms using technologies that are initially inferior to the mainstream technologies used by incumbents

**Early warning signs** – among the first symptoms that hint towards a potential future development

**Economic model** – the cost structure and the mechanisms by which the firm generates revenue and makes a profit

**Geographical replication** – applying an existing business model in a different country or region

**Hybrid business models** – one part of the firm focuses on the generation of a new business model and another part focuses on replication of the existing business model

**Hypercompetition** – short periods of competitive advantage, alternating with frequent disturbances and disruption of the business model

**Invisible S-curves** – curves that start to decline before a firm's financial performance does based on the firm's competitive position curve, its distinctive skills and capabilities curve, and its talent curve

**Longitudinal replication** – improving an existing business model over a certain period of time

**Stable competitive environment** – long, stable periods with gradual erosion of the dominant business model

**Supply-driven disruptions** – new entrants introducing a fundamentally new technological architecture that cannot be copied by incumbents by simply improving elements of the existing technology

**Value proposition** – describes how value is realized for specific target groups and markets

# 17
# STRATEGIC RENEWAL

## LEARNING OBJECTIVES

After reading this chapter, you should be able to:

- understand path dependence, inertia, and why firms find it difficult to adapt;
- define strategic renewal and explain why it is important for organizational survival;
- understand the concept of ambidexterity and describe different ways of balancing exploration and exploitation;
- describe different strategic renewal journeys and explain the roles of top, middle, and front-line management.

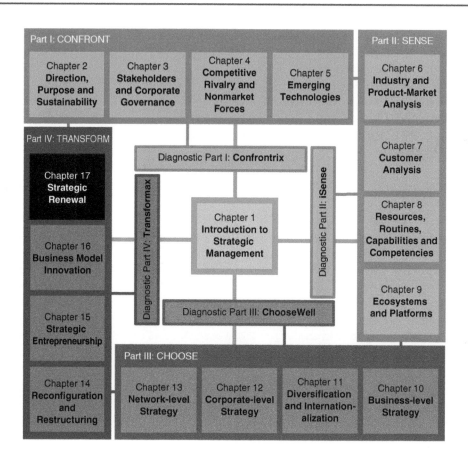

## OPENING CASE

Source: © Nrqemi (2018) / Shutterstock.

### Volkswagen's electrification drive[1]

'Our transformation will be fast … bigger than anything the industry has seen in the past century'. With those words, Volkswagen CEO Herbert Diess described his company's bet on electric cars. As government action against climate change continues to rapidly reshape the competitive environment, Volkswagen is one of the largest industry behemoths undertaking a radical transformation towards an environmentally sustainable business proposition. In Volkswagen's transformation, Diess has been particularly obsessed with the new market entrant that brought electric cars to the masses: Elon Musk's Tesla Inc. It is a peculiar sight: the CEO of a company being obsessed by his rival to such an extent that his employees complain about it. Yet Diess is undeterred: 'Even if I no longer talk about Elon Musk: he'll still be there and revolutionizes our industry and keeps getting more competitive quickly'. For industry watchers, Diess' obsession is not hard to justify. While Volkswagen produces roughly ten times as many vehicles as Tesla, its valuation is only a fifth of Tesla's whopping $1 trillion market capitalization as of early 2022.

Volkswagen's embrace of electric vehicles was not a straightforward decision. The move came on 10 October 2015, when Volkswagen executives convened to discuss a radical shift in Volkswagen's strategy. Volkswagen was set to go full-in on electric and wind-down its internal combustion engine vehicle production. The decision followed a devastating scandal dubbed 'Diesel-gate', where Volkswagen was found to have cheated the emission tests for diesel cars. Before the scandal broke, Volkswagen championed its 'green diesel' cars which they alleged were far more environmentally friendly than the petrol equivalent. However, in 2015 the American Environmental Protection Agency found discrepancies between Volkswagen's touted efficiency and real-world performance. Investigators later found test cheating software installed in Volkswagen cars which led to the discrepancy. In the aftermath of the scandal, Volkswagen was ordered to pay over €27 billion in fines.[2]

Prior to its strategic shift in 2015, Volkswagen was seen to be successfully executing its 'Strategy 2018' which was set a decade earlier. The Strategy 2018 focused on green diesel cars, multi-brand market segmentation, and creating vehicle platforms. The strategy had worked well for Volkswagen before Diesel-gate, with it being on track to becoming the top automobile manufacturer in the world, taking over the coveted position from Toyota.

Diesel-gate cut Strategy 2018 short by three years. Within three days of the infamous meeting that saw Volkswagen dramatically shift its strategy, public announcements were broadcasted that would form the basis for its new strategy. Volkswagen replaced its CEO and, in his place, elected Herbert Diess to lead Volkswagen. A year after Volkswagen declared its new direction, Herbert Diess announced a fully-fledged transformation strategy named 'TOGETHER – Strategy 2025' (Strategy 2025). The strategy aimed to reposition Volkswagen from a traditional automobile producer to a mobility company deploying leading technology and software. Its priority shifted to ensuring it would remain in control of the car mobility value proposition as the automotive sector transitioned into a mobility ecosystem. Fears that power in the car world would shift from car manufacturers towards technology and mobility companies forced Volkswagen to point its crosshairs at the giants in Silicon Valley: Uber, Alphabet, Apple, and Tesla.

The automotive challenge facing Volkswagen is vast: it must fully transform its core business while fighting off Tesla and a slew of new electric vehicle companies. Volkswagen has a long legacy in which it worked to perfect the internal combustion engine (ICE) car, focusing on exploiting this established technology. Now, it must invest heavily in new technology, negotiate with Germany's powerful unions, and convince its almost half-million employees a radical shift is necessary. With this transformation the question remains: how can the firm best balance the exploitation of its ICE technology with the exploration of new electric car technology?

Volkswagen is set on continuing its bet on electrification and aspires to overtake Tesla as the top electric vehicle producer by 2025. Further, Volkswagen is not only protecting its position against other automakers, but is also trying to fend off technology giants entering the emerging mobility ecosystem. Volkswagen's approach is a bold strategy not matched by the other legacy automakers: the world's second-biggest carmaker is putting its future solely in a technology that in 2021 only made up a fraction of vehicles sold. With Volkswagen's big shift to electric mobility, there is one question keeping many awake at night: Will Volkswagen's all-in bet on electrification pay off?

## Questions

1. Why did Volkswagen choose to overpromise on its 'green diesel' technology instead of investing in sustainable transportation technology prior to the Diesel-gate scandal?
2. Unlike Volkswagen, competitors such as Ford are pursuing a more balanced approach between exploiting ICE cars versus developing electric cars. Contrast this strategy with Volkswagen. Which do you believe to be more effective?
3. Unlike Volkswagen's long legacy in car making, Tesla Inc. is a new market entrant. What are the upsides and downsides to Volkswagen's legacy in ICE vehicles?

# Introduction

Modern day organizations operate in extremely challenging environments. Competition forces them to change in a fundamental way. As the Volkswagen case illustrates, renewing incumbent firms is far from straightforward. As organizations grow older, larger and more complex, structures, systems and routines slowly become rooted in the organization. Simultaneously, changing the firm becomes highly dependent on past decisions related to resource allocations and relations with stakeholders. Particular courses of actions, once introduced, can be virtually impossible to reverse. These path dependencies are really problematic as environments change, and can hinder firms in maintaining pace with the environment, or worse, threaten their survival. Surviving under these conditions often requires not only restructuring, strategic entrepreneurship or even changing the business model as discussed in earlier chapters, but a more integrated approach. In these situations, firms have to fundamentally renew by transforming their core activities and seeking new avenues for growth.

Two conflicting forces become apparent when large firms are confronted with internal and external change. On the one hand, there is a need for an efficient, stable structure enabling optimal exploitation of available knowledge and competencies to deal with short-term competitive forces (i.e., *stability*). On the other hand, environmental change forces established firms to be flexible, transform stagnant businesses and explore new sources of wealth through new resource combinations[3] (i.e., *change*). This tension between stability and change is fundamental to understanding organizational survival and strategic renewal.[4] Accordingly, the present chapter focuses on how firms can resolve the tension between stability and change as environments change.

In the first section of this chapter the concept of strategic renewal is introduced. We discuss its importance for firm survival, considering different theoretical perspectives that form the core of the academic debate between managerial intentionality versus environmental selection. We then proceed to explain the distinction between the three dimensions constituting the concept of strategic renewal, and describe generic ways in which the underlying tensions of exploration versus exploitation can be balanced for long-term survival.

Next, we discuss how multiunit firms can balance exploration and exploitation using various forms of ambidexterity as more permanent solutions for strategic renewal. The roles of managers at different levels will be brought to light, and the way they interact in relation to the environment will be linked to several journeys of renewal within multi-unit firms. We close the chapter by returning to the key debate on what matters most for strategic renewal, managerial intentionality or environmental pressures?

# Strategic renewal: Perspectives and dimensions

As environments change over time – because of ever-increasing rates of technological developments, globalization, government interventions, tightening resource constraints, changing customer preferences, new entrants, and shorter product life cycles – organizations need to adapt by changing along. In other words, there should be a fit between the firm and its environment and firms have to continuously renew their strategies to maintain fit. **Strategic renewal** can be understood as the adaptive choices and actions a firm undertakes to alter its **path dependence** and maintain a **dynamic strategic fit** with changing environments over time.[5] This involves the changing, replacing, or refreshing of one or more core organizational attributes which have the potential to affect the firm's long-term performance, and ultimately, survival.[6]

## Selection and adaptation perspectives on strategic renewal

How do firms renew themselves over time? Why do some firms survive for centuries while others cease to exist? Theories explaining organizational renewal and survival abound and still form a core debate in the field of strategy. However, two main perspectives can be distinguished in the body of literature: selection and adaptation perspectives. The key difference between selection and adaptation perspectives relates to the extent to which organizations are believed to be able to renew in the face of environmental change (see Table 17.1). We describe the selection and adaptation perspectives and eight associated theories according to their view on renewal and survival.[7]

### Selection

The selection perspective has a deterministic approach to viewing the interaction between firms and their environment. From a selection perspective, firms are assumed to be limited in their ability and agility for adaptation. The more prominent theories associated with this perspective are population ecology theory, evolutionary theory, the resource-based view and institutional theory.

**TABLE 17.1**   Selection versus adaptation perspectives

| Selection | Adaptation |
|---|---|
| • **Population ecology**<br>Procedural and structural baggage | • **Strategic choice theory**<br>Dynamic process subject to managerial action |
| • **Evolutionary theory**<br>Proliferation of routines | • **Dynamic capability theory**<br>Latent abilities to renew core competencies |
| • **Institutional theory**<br>Industry norms and shared logic | • **Learning theory**<br>Alignment based on learning, unlearning and relearning |
| • **Resource-based theory**<br>Exploitation of core competencies | • **Behavioural theory**<br>Slack and strategic intent |

Population ecology theory views renewal at the level of populations of firms. At this level, environmental factors favour or 'select' organizations that are reliable and specialized. Such firms exhibit unique forms, resources, competencies and routines that match the environmental niche they occupy, and thereby account for competitive advantages.[8] Organizations which survive the selection process gradually build up **structural inertia**. Structural inertia is generated by structures and procedures that organizations accumulate over time. They constrain adaptability to environmental change. Inertia is the opposite of **fitness**, which refers to the capacity to learn and change behavioural characteristics or capabilities to fit to new circumstances in organizational environments.[9] Sources of inertia can stem both from within and outside of the firm (see Table 17.2).

According to some population ecologists, attempts to adapt the organization are futile and can even decrease survival chances.[10] In a simple (stable, uncompetitive) environment, inertia may enable a more effective and economical use of managerial skills and resources and allow managers to focus on the most important decisions.[11] However, when the environment changes, inertia will be difficult to overcome and can result in deteriorating performance, and eventually in 'selecting out' of firms whose competencies have become outdated. These firms will subsequently be replaced by new entrants exhibiting new organizational forms that better match the new environmental conditions, thereby engendering renewal at the population level.

Less radical representations of population ecology recognize that variations and change can occur, yet contend that long-term survival is only feasible when the speed of the organization's response is commensurate with temporal patterns of change in the environment. However, despite the potential to adapt, organizations often respond too slowly to threats and opportunities in their environments. This phenomenon is known as **relative inertia**,[12] referring to the comparison between the organization's internal rate of change and the rate of change in the environment.[13]

**TABLE 17.2**   Internal and external sources of organizational inertia

| | Type of constraint | Locus of constraint | Examples |
|---|---|---|---|
| **Internal** | **Prior investments** | Intra-firm | Sunk costs; investments in property, plant, specialized equipment and personnel; long-term investments; formalized structures and policies |
| | **Behavioural predispositions** | Individual and teams | Commitment to status quo; risk averseness; intolerance for ambiguity; bounded rationality; satisficing behaviour |
| | **Established social structures** | Relation between individuals | Shared identity; organizational culture; strong social ties; organizational politics; shared norms and values; normative contracts; established expectations about roles |
| **External** | **Resource dependencies** | Relation between firms and providers of key resources | Long-term contracts with customers and suppliers; interlocking directorates; established customer base; long-term debts/obligations |
| | **Normative expectations** | Interface of firm with society/stakeholders | Collective rationality; industry recipes; cognitive inertia; normative metrics of reliability; societal expectations; legitimacy-seeking; accreditations and certifications |
| | **Legal and fiscal barriers** | Interface of firm with regulatory agencies | Antitrust regulations; protectionist policies; barriers to entry and exit |

The notion of relative inertia implies that a firm's efforts to adapt to the changing environment are negated by higher levels of environmental change, competition and selection. Competitive advantages are continuously eroded by actions of other players which lead again to higher levels of competition and the need to react faster. In other words, companies adapt faster and faster, but as a consequence of the resulting increase in competition they do not make any progress. In the end, these dynamic interactions between firm adaptation on the one hand and higher levels of competition and selection on the other hand cancel each other out. This condition is known in management theory as hypercompetition, or **'the Red Queen effect'**,[14] after a passage from Lewis Carroll's *Through the Looking Glass* (see Figure 17.1).

Evolutionary theory shares a number of elements with population ecology: (1) a limited role for organizational adaptability, (2) a population level of analysis, and (3) the importance of environmental selection. However, whereas organizational form is the main focus point of population ecology, routines take center stage in evolutionary theory. **Routines** are the regular and predictable behaviour patterns of firms with which day-to-day operations get done. They develop over time as organizations accumulate know-how. In the course of their existence, organizations become repositories of skills that are unique and often difficult to transfer. Routines may therefore create

> "Now! Now!" cried the Queen. "Faster! Faster!" And they went so fast that at last they seemed to skim through the air, hardly touching the ground with their feet till, suddenly, just as Alice was getting quite exhausted, they stopped, and she found herself sitting on the ground, breathless and giddy.
>
> The Queen propped her up against a tree, and said kindly, "You may rest a little now."
>
> Alice looked round her in great surprise. "Why, I do believe we've been under this tree the whole time! Everything's just as it was!"
>
> "Of course it is," said the Queen. "What would you have it?"
>
> "Well, in *our* country," said Alice, still panting a little, "you'd generally get to somewhere else – if you ran very fast for a long time, as we've been doing."
>
> "A slow sort of country!" said the Queen. "Now, *here*, you see, it takes all the running *you* can do to keep in the same place. If you want to get somewhere else, you must run at least twice as fast as that!"
>
> (Lewis Carroll, *Through the Looking Glass*, 1946: 178–9)

**FIGURE 17.1** The Red Queen Effect

opportunities for creating distinctive competitive advantages and further improving organizational know-how (see Chapter 8). The potential benefits include greater reliability in delivering a sound and comprehensible product and economies of efficiency.[15] Yet the same routines limit the firm's capacity to absorb new information and search for new ideas. As organizations age, radical change therefore becomes increasingly difficult. Adaptation occurs either when routines which are not used for some time disappear, or through evolutionary modification.

In a similar way, the resource-based theory[16] views the firm as a bundle of tangible and intangible resources and tacit know-how that must be identified, selected, developed, and deployed to generate superior performance (see Chapter 8 for a detailed discussion of resources, routines, capabilities and competencies). Competitive advantage originates from heterogeneity in the distribution of resources across firms.[17] At the firm-level, firms should therefore seek out resources[18] that are valuable, rare, inimitable and nonsubstitutable (i.e., the so-called VRIN attributes discussed in Chapter 8). These resources, and the unique way they are used – competencies – take time to develop and are complexly intertwined within the organization. In other words, a firm's resource endowments are 'sticky' and difficult to change. When firms lack the capacity to develop new resources and competencies quickly altogether, core competencies can turn into 'core rigidities' or 'competency traps'.[19] Thus, as we saw in population ecology and evolutionary theory, the resource-based theory assumes that, at least for the short term, firms are 'stuck with what they have and have to live with what they lack'.[20] For this reason, the theory has fallen on criticism for being of limited value in explaining how and why certain firms adapt in pursuit of competitive advantage.

Finally, institutional theory focuses on why organizations within a population exhibit **isomorphism**, or similar strategies and characteristics, as the embeddedness of organizations in their institutional context informs the direction of firm adaptation. The core proposition is that firms are inclined or forced to resemble other firms in a population due to isomorphic forces.[21] Firms may for instance mimic the strategic behaviour of competitors that are perceived to be successful or legitimate. Mimetic isomorphism is reflected in the *bandwagon phenomenon*,[22] which is the tendency of firms to follow the behaviour and beliefs of their competitors. Mimicry can for instance be noticed in price wars between supermarkets in, for instance, The Netherlands, France, and the UK, and the internationalization of professional service firms. These isomorphic forces may cause firms to homogenize their strategic choices by conforming to industry rules, norms and shared logics.

## Adaptation

While many companies drift from industry leadership to obscurity, this path is not followed by all companies. Volkswagen (see the Opening Case to this chapter) is an example of a company that has been ranked among the world's top ten automobile companies for almost a century. Such long-lived complex organizations form a major challenge to the pessimistic connotations of the concept of inertia.

Compared to the selection perspective, the adaptation perspective has a more voluntaristic approach to strategic renewal. The intentional actions organizations undertake to adapt to changing environmental conditions take centre stage. Moreover, organizations are considered to be able to change in unfamiliar ways rather than only in familiar ways. Theories associated with this perspective are strategic choice theory, dynamic capabilities theory, organizational learning theory, and behavioural theory (see Table 17.1).

As opposed to most selection theories, strategic choice theory argues that organizations are not always passive recipients of environmental influence, but have the power and opportunity to drive strategic renewal and reshape their environment.[23] Strategic renewal is viewed as a dynamic interaction between managerial action and environmental forces.[24] Decision-makers play an intermediary role between the firm and its environment and have leeway in the choice of strategic renewal actions.

Dynamic capabilities theory is an extension of the resource-based theory of the firm. It focuses on the dynamics of resource deployments within firms over time.[25] As we saw earlier in this chapter, a limited repertoire of available routines severely limits the range of strategic choices when environmental conditions change. Highly specialized resources and core competencies enhance profits, but simultaneously hold the risk of becoming sources of rigidities and inflexibility.[26] Consequently, to remain viable in changing environments, organizations have to repeatedly seek out possibilities to develop and dissipate new skills and capabilities. Organizations should remain in a so-called *dynamic capability-building mode* and continuously renew themselves by exploring opportunities arising in their environment.[27] Accordingly, **dynamic capabilities** are defined as 'the firm's processes that use resources – specifically the processes to integrate, reconfigure, gain and release resources – to match and even create market change. Dynamic capabilities thus are the organizational and strategic routines by which firms achieve new resource configurations as markets emerge, collide, split, evolve, and die'.[28] Organizational learning plays an important role in the development of dynamic capabilities.

Organizational learning theory focuses on how organizational members notice, interpret and use information and knowledge to reconsider the fit of firms with their environment. Organizational learning and the firm's **absorptive capacity** for new external knowledge[29] are considered principal drivers of strategic renewal in strategy research.[30] The balance between the extent to which organizations explore new knowledge domains and their exploitation of existing knowledge domains is of crucial importance to effective learning and survival.[31] 'Where exploration is rooted in variance-increasing activities, learning by doing, and trial and error, exploitation is rooted in variance-decreasing activities and disciplined problem solving. Where exploitation builds on an organization's past, exploration creates futures that may be quite different than the organization's past'.[32] Organizational learning will play a key role in further treatments of renewal in this chapter.

Behavioural theory views organizations as coalitions of individuals with their own objectives that need to be satisfied by balancing resource allocation processes. The theoretical building blocks developed in the book *A Behavioral Theory of the Firm*[33] became the foundations for current research in organizational learning theory and evolutionary theory. For example, the theory's explanation of operating procedures had a strong impact on the development of the theory of routines, central to evolutionary theory.[34] Other important notions of the theory are that decision-makers are boundedly rational and seek to avoid uncertainty by satisficing decision-making, maintaining firm performance within the industry average, and seeking stability. Furthermore, change is considered to be the result of unsatisfactory firm performance in relation to aspiration levels leading to a search for adaptive solutions or *'problemistic search'*. Because of inherent short-sightedness, this search often leads to exploitative rather than explorative adaptive solutions. Finally, the strategic allocation of organizational slack (i.e., excess capacity maintained by an organization) is considered a key aspect of innovativeness.

## CRACK-THE-CASE
### Nokia's weakening reception[35]

Source: © 360b (2013) / Shutterstock.

*(Continued)*

'What? That is our product!' Frank Nuovo, telephone designer at Nokia knows exactly what he thought when Apple introduced the iPhone in 2007. Email, surfing the internet, and downloading apps – Nokia's new phone had been first to include all of these at the same time. But it lay on the shelf for years because Nokia's management did not believe there was a market for 'fun' products. Following Steve Job's introduction of the iPhone, Nokia's downfall was swift. The demise begs the question: How did Nokia go from the world's top phone maker in the early 2000s, to being forced to exit the market a decade later?

Founded in 1865, Nokia has had a long journey that saw it move through many industries. The company started as a pulp mill in Finland. By the late 20th century, Nokia established itself as a titan of the telecommunication industry. During this time, Nokia expanded from telecommunication infrastructure to phone vendor. The move was a success as its phones found global appreciation for their build quality and functionality. By 1998 Nokia became the world's largest vendor of mobile phones. By the year 2000 Nokia soared to new heights, accounting for 4% of Finland's Gross Domestic Product.[36] In 2002 Nokia introduced its Symbian Series 60 device, introducing mobile phones to the general public. Nokia had entered its golden age, retaining the position as the world's top mobile phone vendor for another decade.

During its golden years, Nokia thrived as it became a creative breeding ground for new ideas. 'We made telephones with rounded corners and put a camera in them'. This move exemplified a successful renewal. It was the same with the concept of colored faceplates. This idea emerged following one of many bar sessions enjoyed by Nokia engineers, when they became so drunk that they mixed up their phones. Having customizable fronts was thus a way of ensuring they could better identify their own phone. This was typically Nokia: continuous renewal was part of its DNA.

But with its success came managerial complacency. As Nokia solidified its position as market leader, its leadership shifted focus from creativity, instead focusing on exploiting its existing capabilities. In 2007 a competitor's event heralded Nokia's downfall. On 9 January 2007, Apple Inc.'s founder, Steve Jobs, walked onto the stage and pulled out the first iPhone from his pocket, changing the world forever. On that day, Apple showed how smartphones could be done right. And with the launch of the iPhone and its iOS operating system, The Nokia Symbian line quickly became antiquated.

In 2011, four years after Apple redefined the market, Nokia properly entered the smartphone segment by partnering with Microsoft. The Nokia Lumia line was powered by Microsoft's Windows Phone operating system – an underdog compared to Apple's iOS and Google's Android operating systems.

While Nokia was slow to enter the smartphone market and capitalize on innovation, its main competitor, Samsung, successfully entered the market and overtook Nokia as the world's number one smartphone supplier by units sold. Samsung had a major advantage over Nokia: it was a new market entrant with no legacy business while Nokia had stood as the leader of the pre-smartphone age.

With its mobile phone business in tatters, Nokia turned its attention to its other division: telecommunication infrastructure. In 2021, Nokia could proudly call itself the third-largest supplier of telecommunication equipment in the world and the patent licensor to most mobile phone vendors. Yet Nokia is likely to continue the rest of its existence in the shadow of its former self. At its height in 2000, Nokia hit a market value of €250 billion. Twenty-one years later, only €32 billion remains.[57] Once Finland's pride, Nokia is now viewed by Finns as past glory. Many will ask themselves; how did the world's top mobile phone maker fail to act when nimble and innovative new players entered the market?

## Questions

1. How did path dependence affect the ability of Nokia to adapt to the smartphone?
2. Which adaptation or selection theories are most suitable for describing the challenges Nokia faced?
3. When Nokia entered the smartphone segment it focused on existing capabilities and left the software to Microsoft; how did this move impact Nokia's competitive position?

## Dimensions of strategic renewal

In order to renew, choices have to be made with regard to what needs to be changed to alter path dependencies, where to seek the necessary knowledge, and how to manage the interactions and knowledge flows necessary in the process. Accordingly, three dimensions can be distinguished: the content, context and process of strategic renewal.[38]

The *content* dimension of strategic renewal relates to the question of which core attributes of the current strategy need to be changed, replaced or refreshed.[39] It pertains to whether renewal actions can be thought of as doing more of what is already being done by the organization (exploitation) or doing new things (exploration). Examples include the organization's product market scope, technologies to be applied, organizational design and administrative systems, geographic markets to be considered, and services to be provided. In the case of Volkswagen, the diversification into the environmentally sustainable electric cars market can be considered as a decision relating to the content dimension of strategic renewal.

The *context* dimension in turn relates to the 'where' question, and reflects whether the strategic renewal actions that underlie learning are internally developed through experimental learning or externally acquired through acquisitive learning.[40] *Internal strategic renewal* takes place within the boundaries of the firm and is driven by experience and experimentation with internal resources, (re)combinations of these, and internal development of capabilities. Examples are corporate entrepreneurship initiatives, investments in research and development (R&D), and employee training. *External strategic renewal* involves using external resources and acquiring or cooperating with outside parties. These include mergers, acquisitions, joint ventures, and other forms of cooperative agreements.[41] In the case of Volkswagen, the strategy to seek organic growth rather than engaging in large take-overs (as done by some of its main competitors) is an example of a decision related to the context dimension of strategic renewal.

Finally, the *process* dimension relates to the question of how and when effective strategies are shaped, validated and implemented efficiently within the firm. This dimension incorporates the temporal sequence of events that unfold as organizational change occurs and is fundamentally concerned with the timing, frequency, interaction, and volatility of strategic renewal actions and actors during a particular time period.[42] As becomes evident from the opening case, the number of strategic renewal actions introduced at Volkswagen differs between periods. Such increased internal variety in strategic renewal actions exemplifies a development related to the process dimension of strategic renewal.

## Organizational learning in strategic renewal

For the organization to renew successfully and ensure its long-term survival, it must manage its learning trajectories.[43] Two generic types of learning orientations can be defined: exploratory and exploitative learning.[44]

Exploratory learning ('**exploration**') has a bearing on the long-term renewal of the organization and adds new attributes to the organization's current portfolio of activities and competencies. Outcomes include launching new products and services, starting up new businesses, and entering new markets or new geographic regions. Exploratory learning is the process underlying discontinuous path creations and inevitably entails unlearning of much of what the firm has done before as it replaces previous competencies. Exploitative learning ('**exploitation**') denotes a shorter-term orientation and encompasses those actions that lie in line with the organization's current activities and competencies in existing domains. Exploitative learning is the process underlying more incremental paths of renewal and builds on the cumulative knowledge and capabilities of the firm.

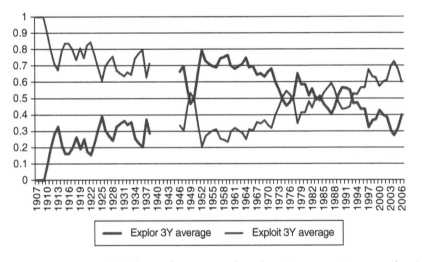

**FIGURE 17.2**   Royal Dutch Shell's exploratory and exploitative strategic renewal trajectories (1907–1938 and 1945–2006) (three year moving average)

Source: content analyses of Shell annual reports, 1907–2006 (Kwee et al., 2011). Adapted with permission of the authors

Figure 17.2 gives a representation of the ratio between Shell's exploratory and exploitative strategic renewal actions over a large part of its history (the gap between 1938 and 1945 is a consequence of missing data due to the Second World War). As becomes evident from this chart, the company oscillated between periods dominated by exploration and periods dominated by exploitation. During the post-war period (1950s throughout the 1970s), Shell's diversification strategy is reflected in the increased attention towards exploration over exploitation. Interestingly, in recent periods – characterized by increased demand and

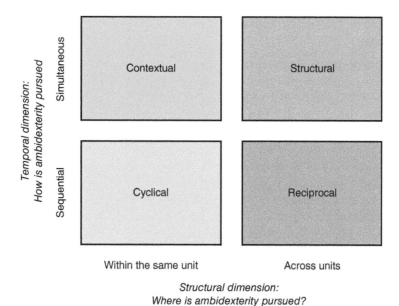

**FIGURE 17.3**   Generic modes of balancing exploration and exploitation

Source: adapted from Simsek et al. (2009)

tight supply of oil – the company has gradually overemphasized exploitation in its strong focus on oil, gas and petrochemicals. This raises the question of whether Shell will still be able to renew in the future, or is slowly on its way to developing detrimental core rigidities threatening its market leadership and survival (see also the closing case of this chapter).

In sum, to remain successful, firms must constantly renew themselves by breaking out of path dependencies and adapting to their environment. To achieve this, they must not only learn new knowledge, but also be able to unlearn redundant or dysfunctional capabilities, relearn, and combine old and partially useful skill sets into novel combinations. This renewed knowledge should then serve to replenish traditional and obsolete systems with life and vigour through new sets of skills and competencies.[45] The challenge confronting the strategist becomes one of a balancing act.

## Towards sustained strategic renewal: Permanent solutions for multiunit firms

Firms have to cope with different levels of competition at the same time and need efficient exploitation as well as superior exploration. What can firms do to reconcile, or at least relax, the seemingly irreconcilable tensions between exploration and exploitation in the long run?

There are various modes in which firms can successfully balance sufficient levels of both exploration and exploitation without having to undergo continuous structural change. This term has been coined **ambidexterity**, as an analogy with reference to the ability of a person to use both hands with equal dexterity. Figure 17.3 provides a framework for understanding different modes of balancing exploration and exploitation by juxtaposing the underlying temporal and structural dimensions.[46]

## Organizational ambidexterity: Balancing exploration and exploitation

Contextual ambidexterity entails managing the tensions of exploration and exploitation concurrently within organizational units. The link between exploration and exploitation is also assumed to be orthogonal – that is, high levels of both types of activities can be achieved simultaneously. To achieve this balancing mode involves 'building a set of processes or systems that enable and encourage individuals to make their own judgments about how to divide their time between conflicting demands [for exploration and exploitation]'.[47] Some large corporations such as 3M and Hewlett Packard have developed structures and cultures to achieve this balancing act. Against their minimal structures, they developed a strong culture dominated by corporate values like trust, respect for individuals, uncompromising integrity, and teamwork.

3M, for example, continually reassesses the barriers to flexibility that tend to develop over time. In order to overcome core rigidities, 3M has a formal goal of having 30% of its sales derived from products that are new or have been substantially modified in the past four years. HP is also pursuing structures and cultures that are more focused on building new competencies. Like 3M, HP has decentralized decision-making at the team and divisional level, and encouraged spin-off projects. In addition, the company constantly seeks ways of making its current technology obsolete in order to push the innovation envelope of its assets. For example, 70% of HP's sales is represented by products introduced or substantially modified in the past two years.

Structural ambidexterity entails designing the organization in such a form that it consists of highly differentiated units with targeted structural integration. It is considered as an interdependent, simultaneous phenomenon, involving the compartmentalizing and synchronizing of exploitation and exploration within different structural units or divisions of an organization. Thus high levels of both exploration and exploitation are possible and each unit exhibits internal consistency in tasks, culture, and organizational arrangements, but across units there is inconsistency in the activities being pursued. The main managerial challenge is to coordinate the integration of the various inputs and outputs between units that, by design, will have the inclination to become disconnected silos. Mechanisms for integration include cross-functional interfaces, informal connectedness between members of different units, job rotation, social integration at senior team level, and periodic reorganizations.[48]

In almost every diversified firm, one sees asymmetry between high-growth businesses and older, mature operations. That is, mature divisions confronted with moderate competition operate in an exploitative mode, whereas some new divisions developed to create or counter hypercompetitive disruption may operate in a more exploratory mode. We can distinguish separation by location in different degrees, varying from the creation of separate project teams or skunk works, corporate ventures, to even completely new venture departments. At the simplest level, we can think of isolating a flexible unit from a rigid operating core. This principle was applied at IBM when the IBM PC was developed, as the mainframe logic was strongly preserved in IBM's culture and prevented entry into the new PC market. While at first IBM was very successful with this isolation strategy, it found that transferring these new capabilities from the flexible mode to the rigid operating core was very difficult. IBM could not exploit these capabilities in its operating core because it lacked communication channels and common mental frames. Similarly, Eastman Kodak, Philips, and Xerox have had only modest success from their internal venturing and new business development programs.

A more complicated form of separation involves the continuous spinning off of groups into separate organizations. Hewlett Packard and Johnson & Johnson are examples of corporations that have developed a system of small, semiautonomous units, and encourage entrepreneurs to pursue their ideas in new separate divisions, while the older, more established divisions provide continuity and stability. Overall, the organization appears to be in a perpetual stage of adaptation, never really rigid as long as new units are being regularly spun off from the older ones. This process is best described as a regular cell fission, characterized by ongoing entrepreneurial revitalization. However, the downside to this cell structure is that such corporations may become overly divisionalized, and have problems with exploiting synergies across certain businesses. Because of continuous fission, these organizations risk losing their identity and becoming uncontrollable.

Cyclical ambidexterity finds the firm focusing the allocation of resources and attention to exploration and exploitation in oscillating fashion. This mode of balancing assumes exploration and exploitation as polar opposites and involves a system of temporal cycling in which organizations alternate between long periods of exploitation and short potent bursts of exploration. It enables organizations to balance exploration and exploitation by shifting from one activity to the other over time. A key challenge in this form is managing the transition between the various states, as the organization is most vulnerable during the transitional phase.

For small entrepreneurial firms, this dynamic alternation between exploration and exploitation is part of their existence and competitive advantage. Their lack of tight commitments and relatively low sunk costs enable them to easily undertake radical change. For large corporations, complete transformations are much more complicated and nearly impossible. However, Microsoft provides an illustration that large organizations can also change. The company frequently initiates a corporate redesign in order to remain competitive, because in the software industry the fully flexible company of today will be the rigid organization of tomorrow. Case histories of large capital-intensive corporations such as DSM Chemicals, Shell, and Unilever that operate in cyclical industries also give us examples of firms that have been successful in managing alternate cycles of convergence and divergence. In the process of frequent change, however, oscillating corporations have to prevent themselves from 'overshooting' and becoming extremely exploitative or exploratory.

Reciprocal ambidexterity requires that organizations strive towards balance across domains of activity. In this mode they do not need to reconcile exploration and exploitation within each domain, as long as an overall balance is maintained across domains. This implies that, for instance, a firm may explore upstream and exploit downstream, or vice versa.[49] This mode is characterized by relationships that embody ongoing information exchange, collaborative problem solving, joint decision-making, and resource flows between the managers in charge of the different domains responsible for exploitation and exploration. An emerging view of this mode is balancing activities by hierarchical separation of explorative and exploitative conditions. Responsibility for exploration can, for instance, increase and decrease with organizational rank.[50]

An example of a hierarchical distinction can be found in the traditional Multidivisional (M-)form, in which top management has a high absorptive capacity for exploring new business opportunities. In this setting, the divisions maximally exploit these business opportunities; they change only as a result of the strategic intent of top management. In most M-forms, exploration of new business opportunities takes place at the top. Yet, we can also think of corporations in which the strategic exploration of new opportunities takes place at the lowest level; interactions with the market and demanding clients cause front-line managers to call into question their norms, objectives, and basic policies. Corporate management operates in the exploitation mode, which permits it to persist in its set policies and achieve formulated objectives, which change as a result of autonomous behaviour of front-line managers. This reversed hierarchy can be found in 3M.

**TABLE 17.3**   Overview of balancing modes

| Balancing mode | Contextual | Structural | Cyclical | Reciprocal |
|---|---|---|---|---|
| **Locus of balance** | Individual and group levels | Organizational level | Organizational level | Aggregate across domains |
| **Mechanisms** | Mutual adjustment and employee empowerment; No buffers between concurrent exploration and exploitation | Separate units dedicated/division of labour and structure dedicated to either exploration or exploitation, simultaneously coordinated at the corporate level | Sequential shifts over time from exploration to exploitation and vice versa | Exploring in one domain while simultaneously exploiting in another |
| **Main challenges** | Managing contradictions within organizational units; Managing conflict; Measuring individual performance/ contribution; Staffing qualified individuals with high tolerance for ambiguity | Coordinating across units and managing contradictions at the senior team level; Determining levels of differentiation and integration necessary between units; Comparability of performance indicators across different units | Managing transitions between exploration and exploitation; Dislodging from inertial pressures | Identifying applicable domains; Deciding whether to explore or exploit in any given domain |
| **Tension between exploration/ exploitation assumed** | Orthogonal | Orthogonal | Continuum | Continuum (within domain); Orthogonal (between domains) |

Source: adapted from Lavie et al. (2010)

Another form of separation, namely by *function*, can be found in nearly all corporations. Usually, production departments operate in an exploitation mode for reasons of efficiency and scale, marketing departments operate in a more exploration mode since they are exposed to various customer demands, while R&D departments that are engaged in highly unpredictable research projects operate in a fully explorative mode. More extreme examples of functional separation for solving the exploration-exploitation paradox can be found in Honda. In order to make functional tensions visible, Honda broke itself apart in a far more radical fashion than had ever occurred in its industry. R&D and Engineering were split into two separate companies. While Honda Motor Company (with sales and manufacturing) is the parent, and primary customer, each of the three companies now has its distinct identity and specific organizational mode. The tensions between these companies, each highly independent, yet interdependent, are not suppressed, but serve as the engine of change and renewal.

In sum, extremity in either exploration or exploitation may create dysfunctions in the form of rigidity (overexploitation) or chaos (overexploration). Only adaptive firms that somehow solve the seemingly paradoxical combination of exploration and exploitation may win the Red Queen race of dynamic competition. Table 17.3 summarizes the core elements of the different balancing modes.

## CRACK-THE-CASE

### Qualcomm: Chipping in on innovation[51]

Source: © Rigo (2020) / Shutterstock.

Founded in 1985 under the leadership of Irwin M. Jacobs, Qualcomm led early research into CDMA wireless cell phone technology. Irwin Jacobs believed CDMA (i.e., Code-Division Multiple Access) had the potential to outperform the GSM standard. Qualcomm invested in R&D for the CDMA technology and after several years held many of the fundamental patents on the technology. Within the wireless industry, CDMA was not seen with much promise. Nonetheless, telecommunications companies agreed to license the technology from Qualcomm to ensure they would not miss out. This initial skepticism towards the technology allowed Qualcomm to sign highly lucrative patent licenses with the telecom companies – after all, the technology would not take off – or so the telecom industry thought.

### A legacy of innovation and legal fights

After years of R&D to address the various technical issues with CDMA and extensive industry lobbying, Qualcomm succeeded in CDMA being included in the 2G wireless standard and later 3G standard. The US, Korea and Japan were top markets opting for CDMA-based 2G wireless networks. This development made Qualcomm one of the key players in wireless

*(Continued)*

technology. By 2005, Qualcomm had cemented its position, holding various fundamental patents for wireless technology, and charging hefty fees for companies licensing its technology.

In the backdrop of the various legal fights with Nokia and Broadcom, Qualcomm's primary industry continued to develop at breakneck pace: in the 21st century, mobile data usage grew astronomically. Between 2000 and 2010, mobile data traffic grew 3,500,000-fold. This change happened under the roll-out of the 3G networks. The next decade saw the roll-out of 4G. Through various acquisitions, Qualcomm was able to obtain a dominant position in the 4G era.

## A new frontier: The 5G-era and intensified competition

By the late 2010s, Qualcomm had established itself as a major player in the chips industry. Yet the competitive pressures it faced in its early years only intensified as legal disputes continued and Chinese rivals matured. Further, Apple Inc., the world's top smartphone manufacturer, is widely rumored to have started producing proprietary wireless connectivity modems for its iPhone line. Qualcomm CFO Akash Palkhiwala has predicted Qualcomm will only be producing 20% of iPhone modems by 2023. While Qualcomm's competitive environment underwent rapid change, the wireless industry also prepared for the 5th generation of its value proposition: 5G connectivity.

By 2019 Qualcomm was preparing for the roll-out of 5G networks. Qualcomm's CEO Mollenkopf likened 5G to 'The new electricity' – emphasizing the importance of this new generation of wireless connectivity. Being a leader in 5G has become imperative for Qualcomm, in its efforts to retain its leading position. Yet Qualcomm's main battleground seems to be taking place elsewhere: Corporate Venturing and Mergers & Acquisitions.

On the corporate venturing angle, Qualcomm decided to invest heavily in complementary technologies to 5G connectivity, including investments in IoT (the internet of things), eHealth, automobiles, and education technology. However, Qualcomm's legacy in corporate venturing had mixed results as its earlier moves into television and display technology failed. As 5G connectivity is rolled-out, many will question: will Qualcomm's corporate venturing bids pay off this time?

In parallel to its corporate venturing initiatives, Qualcomm became more ambitious with Merger & Acquisition (M&A) plans. In October 2016, Qualcomm commenced with an offer to purchase the Dutch company NXP Semiconductors N.V. (NXP) for $47 Billion. With this colossal acquisition attempt, Qualcomm aimed to diversify and gain a strong footing in the chip market for automobiles and IoT. However, at the time, China and the US were waging an increasingly heated trade war. The Chinese government used the NXP acquisition as a bargaining chip by not approving the deal. By 25 July 2018, Qualcomm was forced to kill its acquisition attempt of NXP – having to pay a $2 billion breakup fee to NXP for the failed two-year acquisition attempt. Without NXP, Qualcomm remained limited to its existing portfolio, which faces high levels of competition and legal disputes around the world. Further, any potential synergies Qualcomm would have hoped to capitalize on within the automobile and IoT space were left unrealized.

Still reeling from its unsuccessful merger deal, Qualcomm was confronted by a hostile takeover attempt by Broadcom on 6 November 2017. Qualcomm rejected Broadcom's unsolicited takeover. By 4 March 2018, preliminary polling of Qualcomm's shareholders showed support for Broadcom to join Qualcomm's board. Before the voting could take place, the US government intervened. In an unprecedented move, the government argued the takeover would reduce the US's investment in 5G and as a result endanger its national security. On March 12, President Donald Trump announced he was blocking Broadcom's takeover attempt of Qualcomm.

During the first four generations of wireless connectivity (1G–4G), Qualcomm established a resilient position. However, with growing pressure from competitors, activist investors, geopolitics and legal fights, the question remains: will Qualcomm flourish in the 5th generation of wireless connectivity?

## Questions

1. How can Qualcomm bolster its position besides R&D, M&A, and corporate venturing?
2. What type of ambidexterity does Qualcomm employ, if any?
3. If the NXP acquisition had not failed, how would it have affected Qualcomm's capabilities?

# Mastering strategic renewal: Exploring the different roles of managers

In the previous sections, strategic renewal has been conceptualized as a firm's strategic development path of explorative and exploitative strategic renewal actions to align the company to the changing environment. We discussed various multi-unit forms to deal with the tensions between exploitation and exploration. However, we have not explicitly detailed the various roles of management in these renewal processes. Scholars[52] have argued that these strategic renewal trajectories are conjointly driven by two forces: (1) external selection forces at the industry level and (2) internal forces influenced by managers. We explore how these managerial levels interact, reflecting the tension between forces of environmental selection and intentional adaptation.

## STRATEGIC FOCUS

### Managerial roles of top, middle- and front-line management

Actors at different levels in the renewing organization have different roles that are manifested in different behaviours. Managers face different, and oftentimes inconsistent, behavioural expectations (roles) based on the need to efficiently deploy existing competencies and the need to experiment with new ones. Though any actor is likely to enact several roles at any given point in the renewal process, a distinction can be made between passive or active roles of managers with regard to whether their behaviours are geared towards driving and initiating change in light of changing environments or implementing change directives. Though the roles and behaviours of top managers have by far

*(Continued)*

received the most academic attention, the roles of middle and lower-level managers have been shown to be of crucial importance as well.[53]

## Top management

Within their overarching strategic decision-making role, the more passive roles of top managers in driving renewal include orchestrating,[54] retroactive legitimizing,[55] and judging or arbiting.[56] As orchestrators, top managers influence initiatives for renewal only indirectly, creating the right structures and climate for general innovation and change. As retroactive legitimizers, top managers endorse only those courses of action that are proven successes, and then only after they have established themselves as such. Next to this, they can also act as judges or arbiters between those who champion initiatives for change and those who criticize them.[57]

In a more active role top managers are entrusted to search, direct, and endorse. Top management actively scan the internal and external environment in their *searching* role in an attempt to identify and define what is needed to ensure alignment between the competencies and the environment, for instance, whether exploitative choices are necessary or more diverging explorative ones. In their *directing* roles, top management outlines courses of action, command those involved, and allocate resources accordingly. As *endorsers* they openly advocate change as they provide support, legitimacy, and mentor managers lower down in the hierarchy.

## Middle managers

The term *middle management* refers to managers located below top managers and above supervisors in the hierarchy. The overarching role of middle management is to function as a critical 'vertical link' within the hierarchy of an organization but also an important 'horizontal connector' for disseminating knowledge-based resources throughout the organization.[58] As a nexus for information flows, the distinction between active and passive is more complex for middle managers. Clearly, they play an active role as champions of initiatives for change as they devote their reputation and skills towards selling issues to top management and navigating initiatives for change through the social, cognitive, and political barriers of the organization (see Chapter 15 on autonomous and induced strategic behaviour). A more passive role finds the middle manager as an implementor, enacting mandates for change received from their superiors. However, some of their roles are also contingent on the phase of change. In their roles as facilitators middle managers encourage discourse, new perspectives, and divergence in interpretations of managers across hierarchical levels during early stages of the interpretation process. As synthesizers they guide sensemaking, blend, and articulate the divergent interpretations of managers during later stages.[59]

## Front-line managers

Those who come from the lower levels of the organization are likely both to be closer to the technological and market interfaces and to have the most current specialized knowledge and expertise.[60] They act as reactors to, and extractors of, information from both environments *and* higher-level managers. Because of this they are expected to play an active role in experimenting with new technologies, improve current approaches, propose new initiatives, and identify radically new avenues for change. They also have to observe trends, threats, and opportunities for growth or change that might otherwise go unnoticed by top and middle managers and ensure these get the attention of managers higher up. More passive roles include conforming to prescribed policies and acting in accordance with preset rules and also adjustment of their behaviours and those of their subordinates to the new requirements of the change.

| | Top management is PASSIVE with respect to the environment | Top management is ACTIVE with respect to the environment |
|---|---|---|
| **Frontline and middle management are PASSIVE (stable competition)** | **Emergent Renewal** *'Follow the market'* | **Directed Renewal** *'Top-management should be in control'* |
| **Frontline and middle management are ACTIVE (hypercompetition)** | **Facilitated Renewal** *'Increase variety of renewal initiatives'* | **Transformational Renewal** *'Mobilize company-wide renewal process'* |

**FIGURE 17.4**   Renewal journeys of multi-unit firms

Source: based on Volberda et al. (2001)

## Strategic renewal journeys

By combining the passive and active attitudes of top, middle and front-line managers to change in relation to the environment, four idealized strategic renewal journeys (i.e., patterns of strategic renewal) can be distinguished: emergent, directed, facilitated and transformational journeys (see Figure 17.4). Each of these journeys is relevant to multi-unit firms, but offers different approaches to managing the interactions between the front-line/middle and top management, and between the overall firm and the environment.

### The emergent renewal journey: Follow the market

In the emergent renewal journey, management is essentially passive in regard to the environment. Top managers believe that their role is to amplify market forces and market signals for the benefit of middle and unit management. They often take a trader's attitude, engaging in acquisition and sales of businesses in the firm's portfolio in reaction or anticipation of market trends. At the unit level, meeting profit targets is emphasized and rewarded, while internal processes such as speed, product development, or extensive search for new ideas and business models are discouraged. Existing businesses are evaluated based on a profit-driven, market-orientated approach: those that cannot meet benchmark targets are sold or closed.

The emergent journey is commonly seen in many high-performing conglomerates operating in stable, mature environments. These companies select units based on their ability to achieve synergies and yield high returns in the short run. More often than not, such synergies[61] do not materialize due to a lack of effective coordination across functional and organizational boundaries requiring active management (see Chapter 12 on corporate-level strategy).

### The directed renewal journey: Top management should be in control

The ideal directed journey of renewal assumes that top managers believe they have some form of power over their environment, and that the multi-unit firm is purposeful and adaptive to changes in the competitive environment. Strategy-making is therefore regarded as a rational and intentional process in which management performs extensive analyses before it formulates respectively implements strategy by issuing top-down directives. Top managers explicitly manage the balance of exploration and exploitation by introducing new competencies to some units while utilizing well-developed competencies in others. To this end, top managers should hold a considerable amount of power on the unit level and have access to complete information.

The directed renewal journey is particularly appropriate in firms experiencing steady growth or decline. In these situations the benefits of formal planning and control can be fully realized. The typical tight control and hierarchical style makes this journey less suited for firms in highly turbulent environments. The emergent and directed renewal journeys represent ideal types that are in line with traditional approaches to management thinking in mature environments. Front-line and middle managers are expected to take on a passive, following role in such environments. What to do when following the market is not enough or when top management is not in control? In more hypercompetitive landscapes, front-line and middle managers are required to take a more active stand, creating a more complex and subtle approach to management.

## The facilitated renewal journey: Increase variety of renewal initiatives

In the <u>facilitated renewal journey</u> lower levels of management play an active role in enabling renewal. This approach recognizes that these levels of management have the most current knowledge and expertise as they are closer to the routines and sources of information critical to innovative outcomes. The role of top management is to facilitate front-line and middle management entrepreneurship by creating a strategic context for nurturing and selecting promising renewal initiatives. Top managers should therefore be seen as retrospective legitimizers or judges of renewal actions.

Compared to the emergent renewal journey, the facilitated journey business portfolio exhibits a better balance between exploration and exploitation. Attention is more directed towards frequency of new product and service introductions, rather than pure profit maximization. To this end, top management can intervene in guiding the structure of units, suggesting or directing forms of organizing. This involves splitting innovative units from more rigid parts of the organization, in order to facilitate entrepreneurs to pursue their ideas in separate divisions away from forces of inertia (i.e., structural ambidexterity; see section on generic balancing modes).

The continuous creation of new units from within the firm (i.e., internal selection process) enables a perpetual stage of adaptation, making facilitated renewal journeys particularly appropriate in highly complex and dynamic markets. However, top management's lack of control over the organization may hamper the multi-unit firm to engage in large-scale developments that require some form of central coordination or synergy across units.

## The transformational renewal journey: Mobilize a company-wide renewal process

The <u>transformational renewal journey</u> can be described as a holistic process in which both top management believes it can influence the environment, and lower-level managers are closely involved. Renewal is driven by collective sense-making and the development of shared strategic schemas across organizational levels.[62] Through social interaction, organizational participants socially construct their reality and actively form or enact their environment, which in turn affects future enactments.

This process is best illustrated when applied to a small setting, such as a startup firm. Here, a single entrepreneur drives the innovation process by inspiring and motivating the entire enterprise. The lack of tight commitments and relatively low sunk costs enable these units to undertake radical change easily. Similar processes can be seen in larger firms such as Novotel, one of the largest hotel chains in the world. Novotel's renewal processes were led from the top, but involved close involvement from all organizational levels in the change process itself as well as in shaping the direction of the process. Following this transformational path improved the quality of the result and increased the speed of the process.[63]

Transformational renewal journeys involve the whole multi-unit firm and require systematic rather than piecemeal changes. Consequently, organizations can move in renewal cycles between exploration and exploitation. This journey may therefore prove particularly suitable in evolutionary moving environments punctuated by occasional radical shifts (see Closing Case).

## KEY DEBATE

### What matters most? Managerial intentionality versus environmental selection

Throughout this chapter, we have treated strategic renewal as being driven by either environmental selection or reactive adaptive choices. However, the emerging view of **co-evolution** considers strategic renewal to be jointly influenced by environmental selection forces and managerial intentionality.[64] This perspective acknowledges that environments are not exogenously defined, but must be malleable – at least to some extent – by individual firms. In a population of learning, connected, and mutually influencing interactions between firms, *path-creating* actions of individual firms ahead in the Red Queen Race come to influence the environment.

Combining the previously discussed theoretical perspectives of environmental selection and managerially driven adaptation, from a co-evolution perspective, sustained strategic renewal can be considered to rest on three key principles:[65]

- Self-renewing organizations manage requisite variety by regulating internal rates of change to equal or exceed relevant external rates change (e.g., competitors, technology, customers, etc.).
- Self-renewing organizations optimize self-organization by delegating decision-making to the lowest possible level to maximize search depth and scope throughout the organization.
- Self-renewing organizations synchronize concurrent exploitation and exploration (i.e., ambidexterity).

Figure 17.5 shows these three principles in a three-dimensional space. The red cloud represents firms in the 'denial range'. These are rigid organizations suffering from stunted internal rates of change, over-exploitation and an insufficient ability to self-organize. In contrast, the blue cloud represents firms in the 'chaotic range', which are characterized by internal rates of change that outstrip external rates of change at an unfavourable pace, over-exploration (wasting valuable resources), and self-organizing to an uncontrollable extent. Finally, the green spot represents organizations with a co-evolutionary

*(Continued)*

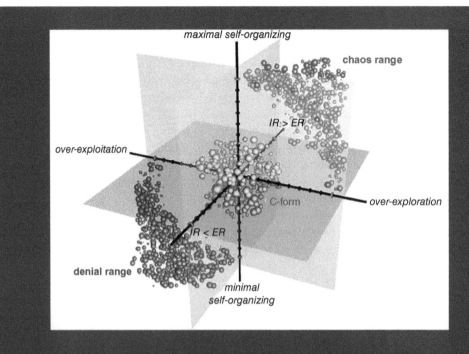

**FIGURE 17.5** Three principles of sustained strategic renewal

(i.e., C-) form. These organizations succeed in the challenge of matching internal rates of change (IR) to external rates of change (ER), balancing exploration and exploitation, and achieving a suitable level of self-organization.

## Questions

1.   If you had to pick one side of the selection versus adaptation debate, which side would you choose, and why?
2.   What do you think are the strengths and weaknesses of a co-evolutionary view of strategic renewal?
3.   To what extent do you personally believe survival to be a matter of chance or 'luck'? If so, how can firms increase their 'luck'?

## Renewal journeys of the future

We have posed four basic journeys of renewal: market selection pressures propelling emergent renewal journeys, top management intentions pushing directed renewal journeys, deliberate variety generation and internal selection driving facilitated renewal journeys, and collective sense-making allowing transformational renewal journeys. These journeys of renewal differ fundamentally, each implying a different solution to the tensions between top, middle-, and front-line management. Although these are ideals, understanding their implications and appreciating the differences between them can be a potent source of understanding for managers of firms in the real world, whose journey of renewal may be hybrid forms of two or more of them. Another reason why firms may be hard to categorize is that they may move through different periods, each characterized by a different renewal journey. Such development journeys of renewal form part of the portfolio of strategic choice.

Consider Shell's corporate transformation, guided by Ben van Beurden; Unilever's corporate change, initiated by Paul Polman; Henkel's transformation, led by Kasper Rørsted; and Volkswagen's renewal, enforced by Herbert Diess. The starting point of these companies seemed to be a period of stasis where both top and front-line managers had been passive and where the financial community was threatening to impose market selection. New CEOs arrived and pushed directed renewal. Typically, they began with a process of competency development led by the CEO, which introduced new concepts, communicated them in an understandable manner through the use of metaphors and analogies, and reiterated them repeatedly. Consequently, new capabilities such as speed, simplicity, and market responsiveness were passed down the organization almost as an order or instruction to be followed. Following these periods of top-down directed renewal, the organizations have moved onto another period, where top management shows more transformational leadership and other management levels are involved in order to create system-wide change (transformational renewal). Finally, top management becomes more of an orchestrator, facilitating decentralized entrepreneurship, and the journey is more like that of facilitated renewal.

Should any of these idealized journeys be preferred over the other? Of course, the emergent renewal journey represents an extreme, where top management amplifies market pressures, often enforcing more rigorous standards than would otherwise be imposed. There is no doubt, however, that for substantial periods of time, firms may benefit by adopting such emergent journeys.

In contrast, in transformational renewal where the cooperation between front-line managers and top managers is the strongest, learning is intense and diversity among levels and groups leads to learning, exploration and rejuvenation. Here, top management sees its role as overcoming market forces of selection, forcing fast-tracked adaptive and learning behaviour. While it sounds ideal as a development model, the resulting path appears to have drawbacks. For instance, it is poor at dealing with technological discontinuities, and the journey may not be sustainable over time because of the effort required from all parties involved. The firm lurches from states of high exploration to high exploitation, placing severe demands on managerial capacity.

Facilitated renewal may be very effective in the future business landscape. Scholars have argued that renewal proceeds most rapidly when top management cause small probes in a characteristic rhythm, recombining the portfolio of units, so that renewal is generated without destroying the best elements of past experience. Top management operates on unit managers indirectly, taking advantage of the tendency for a myriad of local interactions to self-organize into a coherent pattern. Rather than shaping the pattern that constitutes strategic renewal (directed renewal), managers shape the context within which it emerges, speeding up adaptive processes.

Finally, these renewal journeys point to important lessons for practicing strategists. By setting up the benchmark of 'selection' where managers are seen as passive actors driven by path dependencies, these journeys point out that there are real choices that strategists can make. Each of these is distinctive from the other having different competitive advantages and costs. Each may respond differently to different environmental stimuli. Each implies differences in roles of top, middle-line and front-line management.

## CLOSING CASE
### Sustained strategic renewal at Shell[66]

Source: © Pukkato (2018) / Shutterstock.

On 26 May 2021 a remarkable court order was given. The district court of The Hague in The Netherlands ordered Shell plc (formerly Royal Dutch Shell plc) to reduce the carbon dioxide emissions of its activities by 45% by the end of 2030 compared to 2019. The case was celebrated around the world by climate activists as the first time the legal system was used to force a company to address its greenhouse emissions. The verdict, which only applies to Shell's Dutch operations, is currently under appeal by Shell, which has raised eyebrows: the energy transition is happening – with or without such lawsuits. Why is Shell continuing a legal fight to exploit energy sources that will face an imminent and swift decline?

Shell plc was formed in 1907 when two companies, Shell Transport & Trading Company from the UK and the Royal Dutch Petroleum Company agreed to merge, in a move largely driven by the desire to compete more effectively with the US company Standard Oil. The new firm was established as a dual-listed company, whereby each maintained a separate legal identity but operated as a single unit partnership for business purposes. With this merger, the company's stock was split 60/40 in favour of Royal Dutch.

In its early years after the 1907 merger, the combined group thrived in the booming and undeveloped nature of the oil industry by focusing on key success factors such as the development of a vertically integrated business, a broad geographical spread, attention to human resources, and the use of best practice technology. Shell either initiated or funded the introduction of innovations to differentiate its upstream activities of exploration and production (e.g., seismic surveying and new drilling techniques) as well as innovations within its downstream activities of refining (e.g., petroleum cracking and petrochemicals) and product marketing. As a result, the Shell group gradually emerged as a market leader.

The Second World War caused havoc to Shell's operating environment. The company suffered from significant tanker losses, loss of production output, and processing capacity. After the war, the management structure of the parent companies was realigned and the attitude towards staff management changed to increase focus on inhouse selection and training. In the 1950s, Shell established a listing on the New York Stock Exchange and approached McKinsey to review its management structure. This led to the introduction of a matrix-organization structure and decentralized operating companies, to which responsibilities and authorities were delegated.

After 1955, a sharp decline in its return on assets clearly signaled that the Shell group faced increased competition. Shell responded to this situation with a dual strategy, leveraging economies of scale and a focus on product differentiation. In this challenging environment and in line with the business philosophy of that time, Shell also sought to radically diversify its product portfolio. The company began to explore new business sectors to generate growth, in part to address concerns about the longevity of the oil industry.

Shell started the 1960s by strengthening its presence in the Middle East, discovering oil in Yibal, Oman's most prolific field, the Groningen gas field in the Netherlands and then gas under the North Sea. This was also a golden period of research at Shell Chemicals. Around this time, the company decided to strengthen the organization internationally, by placing local people in top positions to make the most of homegrown talent in each country.

Instability in the Middle East at the end of the 1960s and the start of the 1970s led to a quadrupling of oil prices and meant that the era of cheap energy came to an end. In response, Shell sought ways to reduce costs through technology and process efficiency. In parallel, Shell began to diversify, notably into coal, nuclear power, and metals. Shell also began to look beyond the traditional oil-producing countries for supplies and stepped-up exploration in the North Sea and the US.

After the 1973 oil shock, the company diversified into alternative energy sources (e.g., nuclear energy and coal), mining and even forestry. Shell's ease of adoption of new technology was expected to create competitive advantages through a diversified product portfolio. Unfortunately, these new businesses required different approaches and some initially unrealistic expectations about profitability meant that these new business activities generally failed to meet expectations. No diversification could match the performance of crude oil.

When the global economic environment deteriorated in the 1980s and 1990s and competition intensified, Shell stepped back from its diversified and decentralized strategy. Emphasis shifted towards profitability, increasing the return on capital, and delivering shareholder value. Only projects with high-profit potential were allowed to go ahead while underperforming non-core activities such as forestry and mining were gradually disposed of in the 1990s. Shell concentrated its focus on two businesses: energy (mainly oil and gas products) and petrochemicals.

In 2004, Shell's reputation suffered when the value of oil and gas reserves on its balance sheet were perceived to be over-estimated. In Shell's defense, estimating the reserves in oil and gas fields was never an exact science. Partly in response to this scandal, Shell introduced a more simplified corporate structure in 2005, in which the almost century-old partnership between Royal Dutch Petroleum and Shell Transport and Trading was dissolved

*(Continued)*

and replaced by a unified corporate structure under a single new holding company, Royal Dutch Shell plc.

Then, in response to the global recession and a collapse in oil and gas prices, a further reorganization was initiated in 2009 under the leadership of a new CEO (in the same year Shell was ranked first in Fortune's annual ranking of the world's largest corporations, with revenues exceeding €360 billion). 'Transition 2009' was designed to enhance accountability for operating performance and technology development within Shell's organization, thereby improving decision-making and execution speed and reducing costs.

By leveraging its existing skills and the application of innovation, Shell sought to maintain its competitive position against other leading players such as Exxon Mobile, BP, ChevronTexaco, and Total. The downturn within the oil and gas industry also brought opportunities for consolidation. In 2016, Shell completed the acquisition of the BG Group, a UK oil and gas production company, materially expanding the company's oil and gas reserves. Then in 2016, Shell created its New Energies business to focus on exploring and developing commercial opportunities in renewable energy, such as wind and solar.

In the 2020s, Shell faces a new challenge on an unprecedented scale: how to meet the world's growing energy needs while reducing carbon and methane emissions, to satisfy customers, governments, and investors alike that the company is playing its part to address the underlying causes of global warming. Continuing to thrive as the world transitions to a lower-carbon energy system is likely to stretch Shell's business acumen like no other challenge in its long and celebrated history.

### Questions

1. Comment on the different strategies Shell has used over its history to sustain profitable growth.
2. Identify the main changes in Shell's operating environment. How did the company react?
3. Throughout its history, Shell has viewed changes in its operating environment as an opportunity. What should Shell do to ensure a prosperous future, which helps drive the energy transition required to meet the Paris Climate goals?

## Summary

- Strategic renewal refers to the adaptive choices and actions a firm undertakes to overcome path dependence – the firm's attachment to past decisions and actions – and maintain a dynamic strategic fit with changing environments over time.
- Theoretical perspectives differ with regard to the extent to which firms are believed to self-renew. The selection perspective on strategic renewal assumes that firms are limited in their ability to adapt to changing environmental conditions. By contrast, the adaptation perspective assumes that strategic choice enables organizational adaptation to changing environments.
- There are three dimensions of strategic renewal. The content dimension pertains to which core attributes of the current strategy need to be changed. The context dimension reflects whether strategic renewal is internal through experimental

learning or external through acquisitive learning. Finally, the process dimension relates to the question of how and when effective strategies are shaped, validated, and implemented within the firm.

- For the organization to renew successfully and ensure its long-term survival, two generic types of learning can be defined: exploratory and exploitative learning. Too much exploitation drives inertia and conservatism. Similarly, too much exploration drives out efficiencies and prevents gaining economies of scale or learning by doing.

- Multiunit firms can introduce various generic modes to balance sufficient levels of both exploration and exploitation. Four forms of ambidexterity are distinguished: contextual, structural, cyclical, and reciprocal.

- A distinction can be made between an active and a passive role of top, middle-, and front-line managers to change, yielding four idealized strategic renewal journeys: emergent, directed, facilitated, and transformational.

# Review questions

1. What is strategic renewal and how does it relate to organizational learning?
2. What is ambidexterity and what is its role in strategic renewal?
3. Considering the repertoire of passive and active managerial roles, which specific mix of roles is most suitable for each journey of renewal? Justify your choice.

# Discussion questions

1. Describe the relationship between path dependence and inertia and why they can be problematic over time.
2. Explain how the 'Red Queen' metaphor applies to the tension between strategic renewal and survival.
3. Juxtapose the key debate between selection and adaptation and state the strengths, weaknesses, similarities, and differences of both schools of thought.

## EXPERIENTIAL EXERCISES

1. For this exercise find the Global Fortune 500 ranking list (or another similar one) for the year 2000. From this list, select two comparable companies from the *same* primary industry based on at least two attributes (e.g., age, size, rank, revenues, profits, market capitalization). Now look for the same two companies in the last available listing and answer the relevant questions pertaining to the scenario that best describes the companies you chose. *Both* companies are on the latest list, *only one* company is on the latest list, or *neither* company is on the latest list:

   a. Graph their relative ranking and other key financial metrics annually for the period of observation. How did their rank change on the list over this time period? Explain any notable changes in ranking.

   *(Continued)*

b.　What was the rate of industry growth (or decline) during this period and how is this related to the annual rankings? Include this rate in your graph.

c.　Look for at least three other firms in your selected industry on the latest list that were also on the list in 2000. Add these to your graph, as you did for the two previous companies, and identify periods of stability versus periods of change. Consult news archives, annual reports, and other sources to identify how these companies balanced exploration and exploitation during these periods. What are the similarities and differences between their approaches?

d.　Would you attribute survival, as per the list, *primarily* to clever managerial choices or to favourable industry conditions? Explain why in terms of adaptation or selection theories.

## Further reading

Kwee, Z., Van den Bosch, F.A.J. and Volberda, H.W. (2011) 'The influence of top management team's corporate governance orientation on strategic renewal trajectories: A longitudinal analysis of Royal Dutch Shell plc, 1907–2004', *Journal of Management Studies*, 48 (5): 984–1014.

Schmitt, A., Raisch, S., and Volberda, H.W. (2018) 'Strategic renewal: Past research, theoretical tensions and future challenges', *International Journal of Management Reviews*, 20 (1): 81–98.

Sidhu, J.S., Heyden, M.L.M., Volberda, H.W. and Van den Bosch, F.A.J. (2020) 'Experience maketh the mind? Top management teams' experiential background and cognitive search for adaptive solutions', *Industrial and Corporate Change*, 29 (2): 333–50.

Tuncdogan, A., Lindgreen, A., Volberda, H.W. and Van den Bosch, F.A.J. (2019) *Strategic Renewal: Core Concepts, Antecedents, and Micro Foundations*. London: Routledge.

Volberda, H.W. (2017) 'Comments on "Mastering strategic renewal: Mobilising renewal journeys in multi-unit firms"', *Long Range Planning*, 50 (1): 44–7.

## Endnotes (references)

1.　BloombergNEF (2021) 'BloombergNEF's global EV outlook 2021: Commercial vehicles', *Bloomberg*, August 25. www.bloomberg.com/professional/blog/bloombergnefs-global-ev-outlook-2021-commercial-vehicles/ (accessed July 1, 2023); Diess, H. (2021) 'Volkswagen Power Day [Presentation]', *Volkswagen Group*. www.volkswagenag.com/en/events/2021/Volkswagen_Power_Day.html (accessed July 1, 2023); Taylor, E. and Schwartz, E. (2019) 'Bet everything on electric: Inside Volkswagen's radical strategy shift', *Reuters*, February 6. www.reuters.com/article/us-volkswagen-electric-insight-idUSKCN1PV0K4 (accessed July 1, 2023); Volkswagen Group (2022) Volkswagen Group Homepage. https://web.archive.org/web/20230701070700/https://www.volkswagen-group.com/en (accessed July 1, 2023); Volkswagen Group (2021) 'Power Day makes headlines', *Volkswagen News*, March 16. www.volkswagen-newsroom.com/en/stories/power-day-makes-headlines-6888 (accessed July 1, 2023); Davis, R. and Trudell, C. (2022) 'The titans of car making are plotting the overthrow of Elon Musk', *The Sydney Morning Herald*, January 6. www.smh.com.au/business/companies/the-titans-of-carmaking-are-plotting-the-overthrow-of-elon-musk-20220106-p59m8a.html (accessed July 1, 2023).

2. Taylor and Schwartz (2019)

3. Guth, W.D. and Ginsburg, A. (1990) 'Corporate entrepreneurship', *Strategic Management Journal*, 11: 5–15.

4. Volberda, H.W., Baden-Fuller, C.W.F. and Van den Bosch, F.A.J. (2001a) 'Mastering strategic renewal: Mobilising renewal journeys in multi-unit firms', *Long Range Planning*, 34: 159–78.

5. Schmitt, A., Raisch, S. and Volberda, H.W. (2018) 'Strategic renewal: Past research, theoretical tensions and future challenges', *International Journal of Management Reviews*, 20 (1): 81–98.

6. Agarwal, R. and Helfat, C.E. (2009) 'Strategic renewal of organizations', *Organization Science*, 20: 281–93.

7. Volberda, H.W. and Lewin, A.Y. (2003) 'Co-evolutionary dynamics within and between firms: From evolution to co-evolution', *Journal of Management Studies*, 40 (8): 2111–36.

8. Freeman, J., Carroll, G.R. and Hannan, M.T. (1983) 'The liability of newness: Age dependence in organizational death rates', *American Sociological Review*, 48 (5): 692–710.

9. Beer, M., Voelpel, S.C., Leibold, M. and Tekie, E.D. (2005) 'Strategic management as organizational learning: Developing fit and alignment through a disciplined process', *Long Range Planning*, 38: 445–65.

10. Hannan, M.T. and Freeman, J. (1984) 'Structural inertia and organizational change', *American Sociological Review*, 49 (2): 149–64.

11. Miller, D. and Friesen, P.H. (1984) 'A longitudinal study of the corporate life cycle', *Management Science*, 30 (10): 1161–83.

12. Hannan, M.T. and Freeman, J. (1989) *Organizational Ecology*. Cambridge, MA: Harvard.

13. Ben-Menahem, S.M., Van den Bosch, F.A.J., Volberda, H.W. and Kwee, Z. (2013) 'Strategic renewal over time: The enabling role of absorptive capacity in aligning internal and external rates of change – a longitudinal analysis of Royal Dutch Shell (1980–2007)', *Long Range Planning*, 46 (3): 216–35.

14. Van Valen, L. (1973) 'A new evolutionary law', *Evolutionary Theory*, 1: 1–30.

15. Miller, D. and Chen, M. (1994) 'Sources and consequences of competitive inertia: A study of the U.S. airline industry', *Administrative Science Quarterly*, 39: 1–23; Nelson, R.R. and Winter, S.G. (1982) 'The Schumpeterian tradeoff revisited', *The American Economic Review*, 72 (1): 114–32.

16. Penrose, E.T. (1959) *The Theory of Growth of the Firm*. New York, NY: Wiley; Wernerfelt, B. (1984) 'A resource-based view of the firm', *Strategic Management Journal*, 5: 171–80.

17. Peteraf, M.A. (1993) 'The cornerstones of competitive advantage: A resource-based view', *Strategic Management Journal*, 14 (3): 179–91.

18. Barney, J.B. (1991) 'Firm resources and sustained competitive advantage', *Journal of Management*, 17: 99–120.

19. Levinthal, D.A. and March, J.G. (1993) 'The myopia of learning', *Strategic Management Journal*, 14 (Special Issue): 95–112.

20. Teece, D.J., Pisano, G.P. and Shuen, A. (1997) 'Dynamic capabilities and strategic management', *Strategic Management Journal*, 18 (7): 509–33.

21. DiMaggio, P.J. and Powell, W.W. (1983) 'The iron cage revisited: Institutional isomorphism and collective rationality in organizational fields', *American Sociological Review*, 48 (2): 147–60; DiMaggio, P.J. and Powell, W.W. (1991) *The New Institutionalism in Organisational Analysis*. Chigaco, IL: University of Chicago Press.

22. Abrahamson, E. and Rosenkopf, L. (1993) 'Institutional and competitive bandwagons: Using mathematical modeling as a tool to explore innovation diffusion', *Academy of Management Review*, 18: 487–517.

23. Volberda, H.W. (1998) *Building the Flexible Firm: How to Remain Competitive*. Oxford: Oxford University Press.

24. Child, J. (1997) 'Strategic choice in the analysis of action structure, organisations and environment: Retrospect and prospect', *Organization Studies*, 18 (1): 43–76.

25. Sanchez, R. (ed.) (2001) *Building Blocks for Strategy Theory: Resources, Dynamic Capabilities and Competences*. London: Sage.

26. Volberda, H.W. (1996) 'Toward the flexible form: How to remain vital in hypercompetitive environments', *Organization Science*, 7 (4): 359–74.

27. Teece, D.J., Pisano, G.P. and Shuen, A. (1997) 'Dynamic capabilities and strategic management', *Strategic Management Journal*, 18 (7): 509–33.

28. Eisenhardt, K.M. and Martin, J.A. (2000) 'Dynamic capabilities: What are they?', *Strategic Management Journal*, 21 (10–11): 1105–21.

29. Jansen, J.J.P., Van den Bosch, F.A.J. and Volberda, H.W. (2005) 'Managing potential and realized absorptive capacity: How do organizational antecedents matter?' *Academy of Management Journal*, 48 (6): 999–1015.

30. Volberda, H.W., Foss, N.J. and Lyles, M.A. (2010) 'Absorbing the concept of absorptive capacity: How to realize its potential in the organization field', *Organization Science*, 21 (4): 931–51.

31. March, J.G. (1991) 'Exploration and exploitation in organizational learning', *Organization Science*, 2 (1): 71–87.

32. Smith, W.K. and Tushman, M.L. (2005) 'Managing strategic contradictions: A top management team model for managing innovation streams', *Organization Science*, 16: 522–36.

33. Cyert, R.M. and March, J.G. (1963) *A Behavioral Theory of the Firm*. Englewood Cliffs, NJ: Prentice Hall.

34. Argote, L. and Greve, H.R. (2007) 'A Behavioral Theory of the Firm – 40 years and counting: Introduction and impact', *Organization Science*, 18 (3): 337–49.

35. BBC (2013); Chang, A. (2012) '5 Reasons why Nokia lost its handset sales lead and got downgraded to "junk"', *Wired,* April 27. www.wired.com/2012/04/5-reasons-why-nokia-lost-its-handset-sales-lead-and-got-downgraded-to-junk (accessed July 1, 2023); Nokia (2022) 'Nokia Corporation', *Nokia.* https://web.archive.org/web/20230701034828/https://www.nokia.com (accessed July 1); Volberda, H.W., Van den Bosch, F.A.J. and Heij, K. (2018) *Reinventing Business Models: How Firms Cope with Disruption*. Oxford: Oxford University Press.

36. Chang (2012)

37. Nokia (2022)

38. Volberda, H.W. (2017) 'Comments on "Mastering strategic renewal: Mobilising renewal journeys in multi-unit firms"', *Long Range Planning* (Special Issue, Rethinking the Role of the Center in the Multidivisional Firm: A Retrospective), 50 (1): 44–7; Volberda, H.W., Van den Bosch, F.A.J., Flier, B. and Gedajlovic, E.R. (2001b) 'Following the herd or not?: Patterns of renewal in the Netherlands and the UK'. *Long Range Planning*, 34: 209–29.

39. Agarwal, R. and Helfat, C.E. (2009) 'Strategic renewal of organizations', *Organization Science*, 20: 281–93.

40. Sidhu, J.S., Heyden, M.L., Volberda, H.W. and Van den Bosch, F.A.J. (2020) 'Experience maketh the mind? Top management teams' experiential background and cognitive search for adaptive solutions', *Industrial and Corporate Change*, 29 (2): 333–50.

41. Capron, L. and Mitchell, W. (2009) 'Selection capability: How capability gaps and internal social frictions affect internal and external strategic renewal', *Organization Science*, 20 (2): 294–312.

42. Kwee, Z., Van den Bosch, F.A.J. and Volberda, H.W. (2011) 'The influence of top management team's corporate governance orientation on strategic renewal trajectories: A longitudinal analysis of Royal Dutch Shell plc, 19072004', *Journal of Management Studies*, 48 (5): 984–1014.

43. Dess, G.G., Ireland, R.D., Zahra, S.A., Floyd, S.W., Janney, J.J. and Lane, P.J. (2003) 'Emerging issues in corporate entrepreneurship', *Journal of Management*, 29 (3): 351–78.

44. March (1991)

45. Es-Sajjade, A., Pandza, K. and Volberda, H.W. (2021) 'Growing pains: Paradoxical tensions and vicious cycles in new venture growth', *Strategic Organization*, 19 (1): 37–69.

46. Simsek, Z., Heavey, C., Veiga, J.F. and Souder, D. (2009) 'A typology for aligning organizational ambidexterity's conceptualizations, antecedents, and outcomes', *Journal of Management Studies*, 46 (5): 864–94; Lavie, D., Stettner, U. and Tushman, M.I. (2010) 'Exploration and exploitation within and across organizations', *Academy of Management Annals*, 4 (1): 109–55.

47. Gibson, C.B. and Birkinshaw, J. (2004) 'The antecedents, consequences, and mediating role of organizational ambidexterity', *Academy of Management Journal*, 47 (2): 209–26.

48. Jansen, J.J.P., Tempelaar, M.P., Van den Bosch, F.A.J. and Volberda, H.W. (2009) 'Structural differentiation and ambidexterity: The mediating role of integration mechanisms', *Organization Science*, 20 (4): 797–811.

49. Sidhu, J.S., Commandeur, H.R. and Volberda, H.W. (2007) 'The multifaceted nature of exploration and exploitation: Value of supply, demand, and spatial search for innovation', *Organization Science*, 18 (1): 20–38.

50. Mom, T.J.M., Van den Bosch, F.A.J. and Volberda, H.W. (2009) 'Understanding variation in managers' ambidexterity: Investigating direct and interaction effects of formal structural and personal coordination mechanisms', *Organization Science*, 20 (4): 812–28.

51. Qualcomm (2022) 'Wireless technology and innovation | Mobile Technology', *Qualcomm*. www.qualcomm.com (accessed July 1, 2023); Yoffie, D.B. and Choi, A.S. (2018) 'Qualcomm Inc., 2019', *Harvard Business School Case* 718-514. (Revised August 2019). https://www.hbs.edu/faculty/Pages/item.aspx?num=54639 (accessed July 1, 2023).

52. Volberda et al. (2001a)

53. Floyd, S.W. and Lane, P.J. (2000) 'Strategizing throughout the organization: Managing role conflict in strategic renewal', *The Academy of Management Review*, 25 (1): 154–77; Heyden, M.L.M., Sidhu, J.S and Volberda, H.W. (2018) 'The conjoint influence of top and middle management characteristics on management innovation', *Journal of Management*, 44 (4): 1505–29.

54. Galbraith, J.R. (1982) 'Designing the innovating organization', *Organizational Dynamics*, 10: 5–25.

55. Burgelman, R.A. (1983) 'A process model of internal corporate venturing in the diversified major firm', *Administrative Science Quarterly*, 28: 223–44.

56. Angle, H.L. and Van de Ven, A.H. (1989) 'Suggestions for managing the innovation journey', In A.H. Van de Ven, H.L. Angle and M.S. Poole (eds), *Research on the Management of Innovation*. New York, NY: Harper & Row, 663–97.

57. Day, D.L. (1994) 'Raising radicals: Different processes for championing innovative corporate ventures', *Organization Science*, 5 (2): 148–72.

58. Barlett, C.A. and Goshal, S. (1993) 'Toward a managerial theory of the firm', *Strategic Management Journal*, 14: 23–46; Huy, Q.N. (2002) 'Emotional balancing of

organizational continuity and radical change: The contribution of middle managers', *Administrative Science Quarterly*, 47 (1): 31–69.

59. Beck, T.E. and Plowman, D.A. (2009) 'Experiencing rare and unusual events richly: The role of middle managers in animating and guiding organizational interpretation', *Organization Science*, 20 (5): 909–24.

60. Maidique, M.A. (1980) 'Entrepreneurs, champions and technological innovation', *Sloan Management Review*, 21 (2): 59–76.

61. Andrews, A. and Goold, M. (1998) *Synergy: Why Links Between Business Units Often Fail and How to Make Them Work*. Mankato, MN: Capstone.

62. Weick, K.E. (1979) *The Social Psychology of Organizing* (2nd ed.). Reading, MA: Addison-Wesley; Eggers, J.P. and Kaplan, S. (2009) 'Cognition and renewal: Comparing CEO and organizational effects on incumbent adaptation to technical change', *Organization Science*, 20 (2): 461–77.

63. Calori, R., Baden-Fuller, C.W.F. and Hunt, B. (2000) 'Managing change at Novotel: Back to the future', *Long Range Planning*, 33: 779–804.

64. Lewin, A.Y. and Volberda, H.W. (1999) 'Prolegomena on coevolution: A framework for research on strategy and new organizational forms', *Organization Science*, 10 (5): 519–34.

65. Volberda and Lewin (2003)

66. Grant, R.M. (2003) 'Strategic planning in a turbulent environment: Evidence from the oil majors', *Strategic Management*, 24 (6): 491–517; Kwee et al. (2011); Shell (2022a) 'Shell Global', *Shell*. https://web.archive.org/web/20230630230544/http://www.shell.com (accessed July 1, 2023); Van Zanden, J.L., Howarth, S., Jonker, J. and Sluijterman, K. (2007) *A History of Royal Dutch Shell. From Challenger to Joint Industry Leader, 1890–1939, 1939–1973, 1973–2007, 3 volumes and appendices*. New York, NY: Oxford University Press.

## Acknowledgements

The authors thank Liam Goodman for his contribution to this chapter.

## Key terms

**Absorptive capacity** – a firm's ability to value, assimilate, and utilize new external knowledge

**Ambidexterity** – the ability to achieve high levels of exploration and exploitation

**Co-evolution** – the process of reciprocal causation between actors and their environment

**Dynamic capabilities** – the firm's processes to integrate, reconfigure, gain and release resources to match and even create market change

**Dynamic strategic fit** – firm-specific multivariate fit over time between environmental factors and organizational contingencies

**Exploitation** – refinement, choice, production, efficiency, selection, implementation and execution using existing knowledge

**Exploration** – search, variation, risk-taking, experimentation, play, flexibility, discovery, and innovation using new learning

**Fitness** – the organizational capacity to learn and change behavioural characteristics or capabilities to fit to new circumstances in organizational environments

**Isomorphism** – similarity in strategy and behavioural characteristics between firms

**Path dependence** – the (constraining) influence of past stages in organizational development on future decisions and actions

**Red Queen effect** – dynamic interactions between firm adaptation, on the one hand, and higher levels of competition and selection, on the other hand, cancel each other out. Competitive advantages are continuously eroded by the actions of other players, leading to a perpetual cycle of higher competition and the need for faster reactions

**Relative inertia** – the notion that organizations' internal rate of change is too slow to respond to the rate of change in the external environment (e.g., threats and opportunities)

**Routines** – the regular and predictable behaviour patterns of firms with which day-to-day operations get done

**Strategic renewal** – the adaptive choices and actions a firm undertakes to alter its path dependence and maintain a dynamic strategic fit with changing environments over time

**Structural inertia** – generated by structures and procedures that organizations accumulate over time. They constrain adaptability to environmental change

# Diagnostic Part IV

## TRANSFORMAX

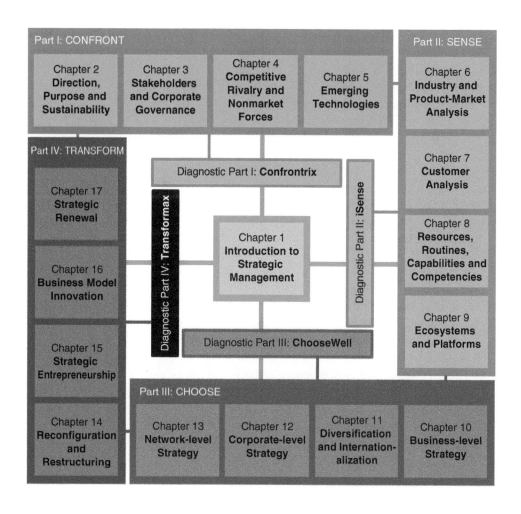

# Introduction

This *Transformax* diagnostic chapter builds on theories and concepts presented in Chapters 14, 15, 16 and 17 to provide you with several diagnostic tools and frameworks that can be employed in pursuit of transforming a company. More specifically, these tools and frameworks may help you to plan for and conduct entrepreneurial activities, conceive of new business models (business model ideation), facilitate business model transformation, and achieve strategic renewal through the revitalization of the organization.

# Fostering corporate entrepreneurship

More than ever, firms engage in entrepreneurial activities to ensure that they stay relevant in a world that experiences frequent technological breakthroughs and other types of innovations. As discussed in Chapter 15, the use or application of these activities within an established company is referred to as *corporate entrepreneurship*, which includes the firm's involvement in internal and external venturing projects. To map out a firm's entire venturing project portfolio, you can categorize its venturing projects into different categories, each of which is represented by a grid, also known as the *Corporate Venturing Matrix*[1] (see Figure D.1). This analytical tool can be employed to plan and manage the allocation of resources to internal and external venturing projects that are associated with different levels of technological and market uncertainty.

The Corporate Venturing Matrix distinguishes between three types of highly uncertain venturing initiatives (or options): positioning initiatives, scouting initiatives, and stepping stone initiatives.

- <u>Positioning initiatives</u> intend to preserve a company's position in one or more certain future technological areas. For these initiatives, a company knows how to manage the market with respect to segmentation and other marketing decisions, but its knowledge about the technological aspects of the initiative is rather poor, resulting in little confidence in its technological feasibility and how certain products will be developed. The development path is ambiguous as well, with different alternative trajectories. The guiding principle is to take only a small number of 'positions' and avoid making a single wrong risky decision. You should, with high certainty, be able to find a superior alternative for the development path or rely on some alternative technology or business designs that can satisfy high-potential market needs.
- <u>Scouting initiatives</u> are used when you believe that you can develop a certain technology, but you are not confident about the combination of specifications the market will expect. These initiatives are chosen to probe the market and test how early adopters receive innovative products, what market segment(s) to focus on, and how to meet the expectations of these market segments. A guideline here is to produce prototype products that incite feedback from customers and assess how they react to their features.
- Finally, when there is high uncertainty not only on the market dimension but also on the technological dimension, an initiative is called a <u>stepping stone</u>, which refers to its role in stepping into an uncertain future. This type of initiative may bring the company on the pathway towards entirely new opportunities.

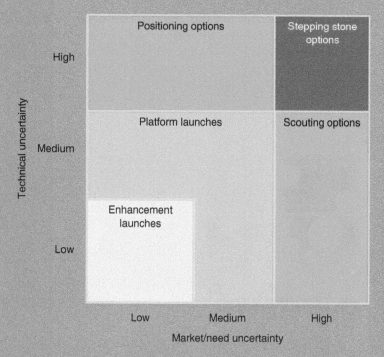

**FIGURE D.1**   Corporate Venturing Matrix

Source: MacMillan and McGrath (2002)

With moderate or low uncertainty with respect to both the market and technological dimensions of entrepreneurial initiatives, it is acceptable to invest in these initiatives immediately – for instance, by launching a new corporate venture. There are two types of launch options: enhancement launches and platform launches (see Figure D.1):

- Enhancements launches are venturing activities to improve existing products. An example is a quality improvement project that is defined according to statistical analysis of operational failures in a production line.
- Platform launches, which commonly need higher investments, can create a base for new competitive advantages in a company's current market(s). For instance, an upgraded central part of a product family's architectural design (such as a new MS Windows version).

To estimate the level of technological and market uncertainty, you could conduct a focus group and guide the discussion on this. The level of *market uncertainty* could be seen as the degree to which a company lacks knowledge about how customers, competitors and other relevant entities will behave in reaction to the outcome of a certain venturing project. To determine this level, you could invite participants to share their assessment of the pricing strategy, future revenue and market size, revenue stability, alternatives of the venturing solutions and the expected impact of regulations on the future business, and conclude by ranking the market uncertainty of the venture as either low, medium or high. The same procedure could be followed with regard to the level of technological uncertainty, which is the degree to which there is a lack of knowledge about the process of a venturing initiative and the innovative outcome of this process. Focus group members could then evaluate this uncertainty from various perspectives, such as the technology development process and time, the availability of human capital and staff, raw materials, complementary technologies, systems and infrastructure, production or operations capacity, and the quality of the products or services.

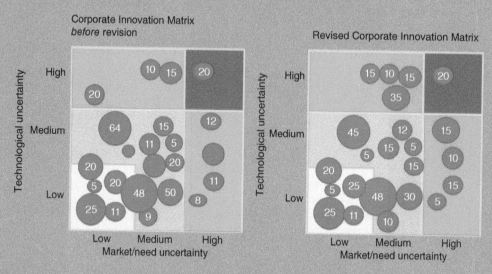

**FIGURE D.2**   Example of a Corporate Venturing Matrix before and after revision

Source: MacMillan and McGrath (2002)

Once you have listed all the internal and external venturing projects that are currently underway in a company and have assigned each project to one of the five categories as described in Figure D.1, you would need to estimate the efforts that are needed for the projects to progress to meet the next budget period. This practice results in an overview of today's venturing projects. Then you would list all the initiatives that are considered for the next period depending on the pace of initiating entrepreneurial activities in the company, which could for instance be a one- or two-year period. You could also calculate the resources needed to get to the next budget period. Then you would need to map the results on a Corporate Innovation Matrix grid, as illustrated in the left part of Figure D.2. Circles with numbers are existing initiatives with allocated resources. Circles without any number represent initiatives for which no resources have currently made available. The size of the circles indicates expected or estimated revenue of the projects, while the numbers indicate the workforce that is allocated to the initiative. For projects that involve equity investment in startups – also known as Corporate Venture Capital (CVC) investments – the investments can be translated into workforce by dividing the value of the investment by an average R&D employee's salary. This exercise would allow you to understand the size of the resources that are allocated to projects and to determine whether this resource allocation is strategically reasonable. You could rethink the resource allocation to serve all near-term and long-term purposes and rearrange things in the venturing project portfolio accordingly (see the right part of Figure D.2).

In the example in Figure D.2, the management team stopped some of the projects and changed resource allocation within the venturing project portfolio (which you can see by comparing the left and right diagrams). The percentage of the resources allocated to the different categories (that is, positioning, scouting, stepping stone and the two types of launches) follows the strategic priority of each of these categories for the company. For example, in a relatively stable business environment, an executive team may allocate 10% of venturing initiatives to scouting options, 10% to positioning options, 5% to stepping stone options, 35% to platform launches, and 30% to enhancement launches. To fully benefit from the application of the Corporate Venturing Matrix it is recommended to form a diverse and inclusive group of managers to discuss the importance of each of the five categories.

# Business model ideation: Designing alternative business models

As discussed in Chapter 16, business models are about the way firms create and capture value. By definition, every company operates at least one business model. The tools presented in this section enable you to describe the existing business model of a company in a structured manner and, from there on, to design alternative business models.

## How to describe your existing business model: The business model canvas

As introduced in Chapter 16, a *business model* describes the logic behind how a company creates, delivers, and captures value. It clarifies not only the building blocks of a company, but also the coherence between these building blocks and how the company is uniquely positioned to compete in the marketplace.

### The building blocks of a business model

To describe the logic of the enterprise, you will need to answer a number of questions. These questions deal with the nine building blocks of a business model.

- Customer Segments – These are all the individuals and organizations a company delivers value to, including paying customers as well as users. Users of Google's search engine, for example, are not paying customers – advertising companies are – but you want to take them into account when considering a business model. Segmenting customer groups is key to determining the way you can differentiate from the competition. Start with studying their needs.
- Value Propositions – What kind of value is delivered to customers? Which customer problems are solved? Which needs are satisfied? When describing the value proposition of a business model, it's all about the combination of products and services delivered to a customer segment and what that means to them.
- Channels – Through which channels does the company communicate with its customers and how does it distribute its products and services? How are these channels connected to each other? How do these channels fit in the daily routines and operational processes of customers? The 'channels' building block describes the various contact points through which the firm interacts with its customers and the distribution channels: it is about communication and (physical or virtual) delivery.

- <u>Customer Relationships</u> – What kind of relationship is maintained with each customer segment? How does the company invest in each relationship, and to what extent? How do these relationships fit with the rest of the business model? Who are the most important customers? The relationship with customers may vary from practically non existent in mass markets (perhaps except for brand identification) to intense, long-term relations in niche markets.

- <u>Revenue Streams</u> – What are customers paying for, and how? How much does each revenue stream contribute to total revenues? Revenue streams clarify how and through which pricing mechanisms the company captures a part of the value added. Basically, it is an analysis of the invoices that are send out: is the total amount based on a price per product, or perhaps a fee per hour, or a monthly subscription? Various pricing models exist and fit with different types of business models.

- <u>Key Resources</u> – Which resources does the company possess that are essential for its value proposition, and for its distribution channels, customer relations, etc.? These include physical resources (such as machines and buildings), intellectual resources (such as intellectual property), financial resources and human capital. Key resources are indispensable for a business model; strategically differentiated resources can be identified by their value and uniqueness.

- <u>Key Activities</u> – Which activities are essential to delivering the value proposition? Activities use resources to produce products and services, but may also pertain to maintaining customer relationships, managing the supply chain or distribution channels, or communicating to customers and other stakeholders. Problem solving and effective decision-making may also be considered key activities, depending on their relevance to the business model.

- <u>Key Partners</u> – Who are the most important partners and suppliers? What resources does the company obtain from them, or which activities do they carry out for the company? Key partners help to realize your business model, as for sure you will not find all the required resources within the firm (it may not even want to own them) and often others will be better equipped to perform certain activities.

- <u>Cost Structure</u> – What are the most important categories of costs that are inherent to a business model? Which firm resources are most expensive, and which activities? Are a company's costs predominantly fixed or variable? Once you understand the infrastructure of a business model, you will also have a better understanding of the cost drivers and their importance. Is the business cost-driven, for example, and oriented towards the leanest costs structure, or is it value-driven and focused on delivering premium value?

## The Business Model Canvas

Understanding the infrastructure of a business model requires more than a plain summary of the nine elements. What you want to do is to sketch and visualize them in a structured scheme. That is the idea of the Business Model Canvas: a schematic representation of the elements of a business model.[2] This schematic representation (see Figure D.3) tells the story of the enterprise: the customer segments it focuses on, the distinctive qualities of the value proposition, the way the company uses its resources and those of its partners, and the costs and revenues brought forward by this model. For example, LinkedIn's multi-sided business model can be captured in one comprehensive overview: see Figure D.4.

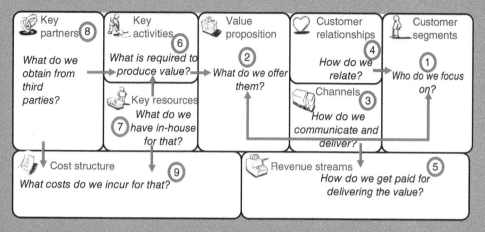

**FIGURE D.3** The nine building blocks of the Business Model Canvas, including linking questions

Source: adapted from Osterwalder and Pigneur (2010)

| Key Partners | Key Activities | Value Propositions | Relationships | Customer Segments |
|---|---|---|---|---|
| | Platform Development | Manage Professional Identity and Build Professional Network | Same-side Network Effects | Internet Users |
| Equinix (for data center facilities) | | Identify and Reach the Right Talent | Cross-side Network Effects | Recruiters |
| | **Key Resources** | Reach the Target Audience | **Channels** | Advertisers and Marketers |
| Content Providers | LinkedIn Platform | Access to LinkedIn Database Content via APIs and Widgets | LinkedIn website, Mobile Apps | Developers |
| | | | Field Sales | |

| Cost Structure | | | Revenue Streams | | |
|---|---|---|---|---|---|
| Web Hostings Cost | Marketing and Sales | Product Development | Free Offerings and Premium Subscriptions | Hiring Solutions | Marketing Solutions |
| General and Administrative | | | | | |

**FIGURE D.4** Business Model Canvas of LinkedIn (2022)

Source: authors using https://www.strategyzer.com

Visualizing a business model helps to communicate your vision even better, as the example of DyeCoo in Figure D.5 illustrates. Through its sustainable business model, DyeCoo revolutionizes the textile dyeing industry by eliminating water consumption and chemicals usage and by reducing energy consumption and the industry's greenhouse gas footprint. Moreover, the Business Model Canvas is an instrument that helps you to discuss a business model, to consider adaptations, and to come up with completely new business models. It works for startups just the same as for incumbents. Furthermore, it can help to analyze business models that are common in an industry and to find out how to disrupt the market. Figure D.6 presents an example of common business models in the technical installations industry.

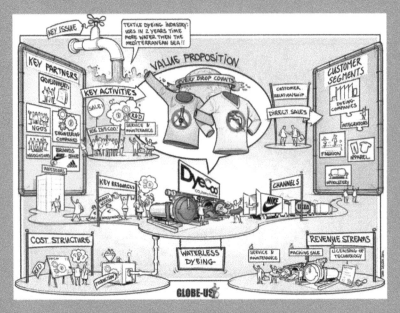

**FIGURE D.5**   DyeCoo's business model explained using a visual representation

Source: Finch & Beak Consulting[3]

| Concierge | Expert | Repairman | Contractor | Subcontractor |
|---|---|---|---|---|
| Maintenance contracts for a specific period. | Specialized in one discipline, in which tailor-made services can be offered to customers. | Ad hoc repair orders come from problems faced by consumers or SMEs without contracts. | Full-service provider of multidisciplinary installation jobs. Jobs can be carried out on their own or with use of subcontractors. | Supplier of human capacity for technical installation jobs. |
| Long-term customer relationships allow for periodic payments for specified period. | The company differentiates itself with specialized knowledge, available inhouse. | Transactional relationship with customers, revenues are based on a tariff per hour, and materials. | Taking on the role of project manager allows the company to act as the linchpin between final customers and subcontractors. | Fluctuations in projects and demand volume are mitigated by the use of a layer of flexible personnel. |
| Multidisciplinary activities are offered to fulfill the needs of the customer (often property owners). | Expert know-how of employees is valued; the company invests in retaining and offers permanent contracts. | Spreading of channels to reach customers. Typical use of lead generators to acquire new customers. | With the project management role comes risk management and responsibility. | Work is carried out under direct supervision of a contractor.

Customer relations are also maintained by the contractor. |

**FIGURE D.6**   Five common business models in the technical installation market

Source: adapted from Techniek Nederland (2023)[4]

## Structured ideation: Conceiving alternative business models

With a Business Model Canvas at hand, you can start developing ideas about whether to replicate or fundamentally change a business model:

- Business model replication is about expanding an existing business model without making actual changes. It's more of the same, either through growth of existing operations or by copying the existing business model to a new market. Fashion conglomerate Zara opening up a new store in another city is an example of the latter. One step further would be what is called a business model upgrade. This will affect some of the building blocks, but its basic infrastructure will remain intact (and hence it is still considered 'replication'). Carrefour supermarkets adding a web shop and delivering to your home is an example of such a business model upgrade, or department store Hema selling notary services.[5]
- Business model generation is about creating a completely new infrastructure and will affect most, if not all of the building blocks. Famous is Apple's move from selling PC hardware, to digital music players (iPod), smart phones, and finally software through its App Store.

Generating ideas for business model replication and generation can be approached from various starting points.[6] Using the existing business model as a basis, you may start from customer needs (working from the outside in) or start with a strategic vision of how the company's core competencies may be used to deliver completely new value (working from inside out). Alterations can be focused on the right-hand side or the left-hand side of the business model, focusing on new customers or new offerings or focusing on developing a new supply chain or activity system, respectively (see Figure D.7).

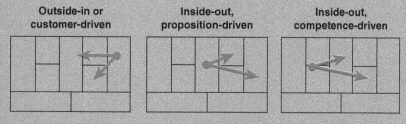

|  Outside-in or | Inside-out, | Inside-out, |
| customer-driven | proposition-driven | competence-driven |

**FIGURE D.7**   Anchor points for business model ideation

Source: adapted from Osterwalder and Pigneur (2010)

## Outside-in approaches

Outside-in approaches can either start by redefining the customer segments or by changing your perception of the business the company is involved in.

- Redefining customers and customer needs – Ask yourself 'who is actually using the products' or 'who would want to use the company's services, but currently cannot'? This requires a deep understanding of customers and their needs and priorities, of course. In a business-to-business context, you may even want to go one step further and consider the needs of the customers' customers. Essentially, the choice of customer becomes a strategic decision: it is you who chooses a customer, and not vice versa. Which customers are good for a company, and which are not? You may identify new customers or segment the existing customer base. With small budgets and a thriving market for second-hand bikes, students were hardly an interesting market for bike retailers. Swapfiets introduced a subscription-based long-term bike rental for only a couple of euro's a week and captured a very large share of the student market.[7]

Here are some tips to get you started:

- Look for customers that competitors are ignoring or underserving (e.g., Swapfiets).
- Identify changing customer needs (Nespresso: barista quality coffee without the hassle).
- Create a new customer need (Swatch: Swiss watches with design. Body Shop: regular cosmetics, but environmentally friendly).
- Redefining the field – 'What business are you in?' The perception of the business a company operates in is perhaps the most dominant mental model any company or executive has. What if you change that perception? That could open up a whole new approach to customers, products and service. Howard Schultz, president of Starbucks, believes he's in the business of consumption experience – of which coffee is a part. A visit to Starbucks is 'romance, theatrics, community – the totality of the coffee experience'.[8] Fashion label Gucci now sells chocolate and even playing cards, because 'We are not in the business of selling handbags. We are in the business of selling dreams'.[9] Thinking of your business in terms of the products may lead to a marketing myopia and a fixed mindset.[10] Thinking in terms of the customer need a company helps to solve may be just the route to discover new business models. Consider how Dutch railway operator NS provides additional services to fulfil its customers' needs to move from door to door: you can hire a bike, a car, or reserve a taxi with their app.

In *Game Changing Strategies*, Markides[11] provides a three-step model to determine what business you want to be in:

1. Generate as many definitions of a business as you can. BMW is in the car business, the prestige business, the mobility business, the engineering business, etc.
2. Evaluate each definition according to a series of criteria. Who are the customers in that definition? Who are the competitors? Can the company satisfy customer needs in a unique way? Can it make a profit, and will this business be a path to growth?
3. Choose one definition and determine the consequences. What does it imply for the business model? Will you change the revenue model? Will the distributors lose business in favour of other channels?

## Inside-out approaches

You may also start generating new business models from what a firm already has – for example, its core competencies and current product offerings. There are different inside-out approaches:

- <u>Proposition-driven business model innovation</u> – When ING bank sought to expand its services to the USA, it lacked the necessary local resources to build a proper bank. Buying or building would be hugely expensive or time consuming. So they ran an experiment: communicating with customers only through the internet or by phone and offering internet banking only. The money saved was used to offer higher interest rates on savings accounts. Another way to innovate from an existing proposition is to think who would want to buy the (new) products offered. When Apple launched the iPad, there was not a market for tablets yet. Apple has the marketing power to make the whole world aware of its new product. But what if you do not? You have to go out and look for customers, often through experimenting and pivoting until you find your niche.

- Another form of proposition-driven innovation is to radically alter some customer value dimensions, which is the core idea of a Blue Ocean Strategy[12] (see Chapter 7). EasyJet provided flights that were 'good enough' in service levels but superior in price. Nintendo developed a gaming console that did not match the computing power and high resolution of competing consoles but by focusing on ease of use and the fun aspect it conquered a whole new group of customers outside of the traditional gamers (see the opening case of Chapter 7).

- Competency-driven business model innovation – Instead of starting with products, look at the competencies of a company. Operating a global network of websites, Amazon developed a core competency in cloud-based hosting. Now, Amazon Web Services (AWS) is one of the world's largest hosting providers. Porsche Consulting and Tata Consulting Services are spin-offs based on their parent companies' capabilities in manufacturing improvement. The Port of Rotterdam Authority now operates a port in Sohar in Oman. A company may also possess certain resources – data is a good example – or operate a supply chain that can be of great value to others. From whatever anchor point, key resources, key activities, and key partners may start your ideation exercise to develop new business models just the same as starting from an outside-in perspective. You do not have to follow customers all the time, sometimes your strategic vision may be a better guide to developing new business.

- Profit model-driven innovation – Changing the revenue model or cost structure may provide alternative venues to develop new business models. An important driver of innovation can be the obstacles purchasers face when buying products or services. Instead of having to buy a complete copy machine, Xerox offered purchasers the option to lease the machine for a monthly fee with an additional small fee per copy. Airbnb does not own any of the apartments it rents to consumers, so by clever marketing and making use of information technology the company was able to disrupt the market for holiday rentals without huge investments in property.

## Creative approaches

Apart from a structured analysis that starts from the existing Business Model Canvas, you may want to use some creative tools for ideation. Here is one that can be very powerful: Imagine how known disruptors of markets would approach a particular business.

- How would IKEA serve that business's customers? By having them do as much as possible themselves.
- How would Uber or Airbnb design a business model for that industry? By refusing to own the assets and act as an intermediary only, focusing on superior (online) customer experience.

- How would Google make money? By providing free information services and selling your attention to advertisers.
- Which disruptor can you think of? As long as it stretches your imagination of new business model configurations, any example will be helpful.

# Business model transformation

Chapter 16 described various drivers of business model transformation and two fundamentally different types of business model innovation. Business model transformation can be externally driven, for example by changing customer needs or new competing offers, or stem from internal drivers such as strategy, vision, or innovation culture. The Business Model Transformation Matrix plots these drivers against the two types of innovation: business model replication and business model generation. Which of these quadrants applies to the organization of your interest? Is there a need to change its approach, and if so, how could it move from one quadrant to another?

The diagnostic tool presented here will help to determine the appropriate transformation journey for an organization. Starting with a diagnosis of the level of competition in its market (the disruption test), it proceeds to plot the organization in the matrix and helps to determine whether a change of position is required. Four levers that support business model transformation will be introduced, as well as a number of enablers and inhibitors. Figure D.8 presents the diagnostic model of business model transformation.[13] Besides the tests that are described in the following sections, an extensive, survey-based test of a business model transformation strategy is available at www.reinventingbusinessmodels.com (free of charge).

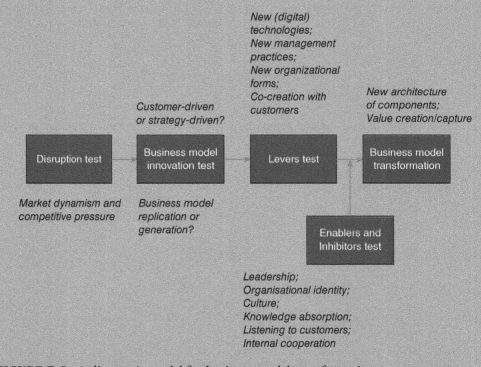

**FIGURE D.8**  A diagnostic model for business model transformation

Source: Volberda et al. (2018)

# Disruption test

Should the company invest in the generation of a completely new or mainly upgraded business model, follow its vision, and go beyond the current needs of customers? The answer is 'yes' if its market is characterized by a high degree of dynamism and competitive pressure and disruption is probably only a matter of time. But perhaps the level of competition in its market is more favourable to business model replication strategies and it should be focusing on existing customers instead. A diagnosis of business model transformation should always start with an assessment of the level of competition, the so-called *disruption test*. Determine which of the four quadrants of Figure D.9 is most applicable to the situation by taking the following two steps:

- Assess the level of market dynamism (either high, moderate, or low): Market dynamism is high when changes in the market are intense and ongoing, demand fluctuates strongly, and customers frequently call for new products and services.
- Assess the degree of competitive pressure (either high, moderate, or low): When competitors are vying with each other in a confined market and the company faces strong competitors, competitive pressure is obviously high. Price competition adds to that.

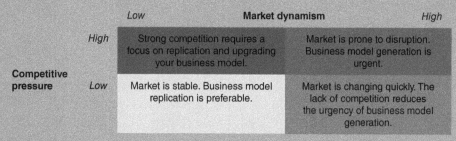

**FIGURE D.9**   Outcomes of the disruption test

Source: authors

# Business model innovation test

The way you transform a business model may be customer-oriented or motivated by strategy and vision. You may focus on replication of the existing business model or on generating new business models. You can find the position of an organization in the Business Model Innovation Matrix by taking the following two steps:

1. Assess the business model innovation focus (replication and/or generation)

   - Business model replication is high if the company regularly modifies its products and services, improves existing distribution channels, increases efficiency and scale of production processes, and strengthens relations with existing customers.
   - Business model generation is high if the company regularly takes on assignments that are beyond the scope of what is currently offered, invents, experiments, and introduces products and services that are new to the market. Or when it often explores new distribution channels or benefits from new opportunities in new markets on a regular basis.

**2.**  <u>Assess the business model innovation orientation (customer- or strategy-driven)</u>

- The orientation is <u>customer-driven</u> when the company lets itself be guided by customers when making investments, its focus is always on customer satisfaction and value, and it is heavily involved in after-sales service, for example.
- The orientation is <u>strategy-driven</u> when investments are guided by a clearly defined and internally aligned strategy, a clear vision of the development of the market, and when the company develops new products and services even if its customers have not asked for them yet.

Based on these two steps, take the outcomes of the business model innovation assessment and plot the company in the extended version of the Business Model Innovation Matrix[14] as shown in Figure D.10 (see also Chapter 16), and assess the fit with market conditions.

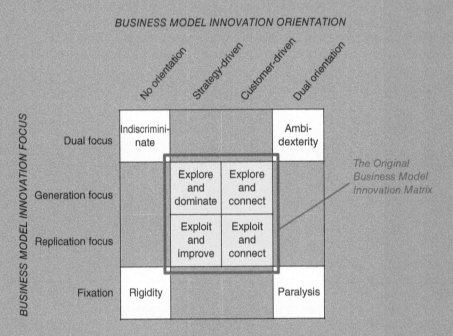

**FIGURE D.10**   Extended Business Model Innovation Matrix

The original (i.e., non-extended) matrix identifies four types of business model innovation:

- 'Explore and dominate' refers to <u>strategy-driven generation</u> and entails organization-wide transformation. This type will probably fit best in a very dynamic market with reasonable levels of competitive pressure. Change is omnipresent and relatively limited competition (or a Blue Ocean, see Chapter 7) creates the potential to develop innovative business models for latent customer needs.
- 'Explore and connect' refers to <u>customer-driven generation</u> and involves upgrading the business model in response to completely new customer demand. This type goes with a very competitive market that is reasonably dynamic, when demanding customers and/or head-on competition in a confined market characterize the business.

- 'Exploit and improve' refers to <u>strategy-driven replication</u> through a directive management approach focused on improving the existing business model. This type goes well in dynamic markets with limited levels of competition, for example when frequently faced with new developments that do not originate from or implicate customers (e.g., new process technologies, changing legislation). This may be applicable to semi-public organizations and monopolists.
- 'Exploit and connect' refers to <u>customer-driven replication</u> where the business model is significantly improved by being linked more strongly to existing customers. This type may fit best when competitive pressure is high, but intensity and frequency of change is relatively low. Competitive moves force firms to react, but within known boundaries. Think of the cola war between Pepsi and Coca-Cola.

If you consider a firm to score high on replication and generation at the same time, choose 'dual focus' and, similarly, choose 'dual orientation' if it's equally customer- and strategy-driven. 'Fixation' is applicable when it scores low both on replication and generation.

In the *extended* part of the matrix, four additional combinations are identified. These are not common, but are theoretical possibilities and may be applicable to a firm. Of these, only the ambidextrous form seems preferable in contemporary markets.

- <u>Ambidexterity</u> refers to a *dual orientation* on strategy and customers in combination with a *dual focus* on business model replication and generation (see Chapter 17). This type is preferable only when the levels of dynamism and competitive pressure are very high, and the market is in a constant state of disruption. Otherwise, the strain and costs of this strategy are too high. Silicon Valley may be just the place for this type of firm, in a manner of speaking.
- <u>Indiscriminate</u> are those firms with a *dual focus* on replication and generation, but without any guiding framework (*no orientation*). Business model upgrading and innovation efforts are incoherent, and luck and coincidence determine the course of the firm. If there is any condition where such undirected innovation and experimentation is feasible, it is in a market that has been disrupted unexpectedly and to the extent that experience is obsolete, and customers are clueless about their needs.
- <u>Paralysis</u> refers to a dual orientation on customers and vision-based strategies without consequent execution of either replication or generation strategies. Executives seem paralyzed by overwhelming choices. This strategy seems completely unfeasible to any situation. But consider when Apple was blown away in the personal computer market by the Wintel-configuration (Windows and Intel), Steve Jobs chose to 'wait for the next big thing'. Instead of expanding and experimenting, he shrunk the company to a minimal size required for survival. When the next window of opportunity opened up, he switched to an explore-and-dominate mode and achieved great successes.[15]
- <u>Rigidity</u> (*business model fixation* and *no orientation*) refers to a singular focus on daily operations and a complete lack of direction. The latter may be intentional if the organization is assigned with a clearly demarcated task from which it is not to deviate. Rigidity is a feasible type of non-business model innovation for organizations that operate in a stable, non-competitive (monopolistic) market, like some state-owned companies in regulated markets in the 20th century.

## Determining the transformation journey

A company may fit into one of the 'ideal types' that are identified in the yellow segments of the matrix – that is, the business model innovation strategy fits neatly with the level of competition. If that is the case and you do not expect a change in competition in the foreseeable future, you may rest for now. If the company's strategy does not fit with the requirements of the environment or you expect a change in the level of competition (either for worse or for better), it may be relevant for you to map out a business model transformation journey. Such a journey will take the company from one position in the matrix to another. Figure D.11 provides some illustrative examples.

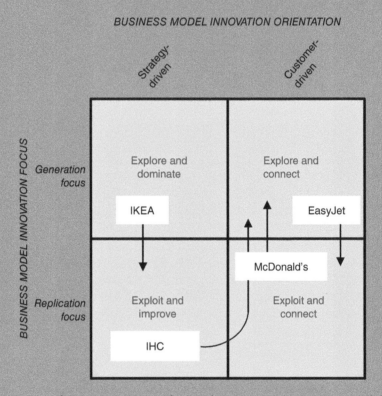

**FIGURE D.11** Transformation journeys of exemplary cases in the Business Model Innovation Matrix

Source: Volberda et al. (2018)

Transformation journeys can involve a natural next step in the evolution of a company, in what is called the oscillating business model journey (see Chapter 16). For example, think about IKEA and easyJet moving from generation towards exploitation once they found out how to make their new business model work. Or conversely, McDonald's entering a stage of customer-driven generation to adapt to changing customer needs. Shipbuilder IHC went through several subsequent transformations. Starting as a strategy-driven replicator with a rather defensive strategic posture ('as long as the yard is fully occupied'), the arrival of a new CEO ushered a transformation journey to become less risk averse and more customer-driven and, eventually, actively exploring new businesses and value propositions (i.e., business model generation).

Once you determine the appropriate transformation journey for a company, you can start to investigate the organizational interventions required to fulfil its journey.

## Levers and enablers test

Switching to another type of business model innovation is not an easy task. Based on various studies and literature reviews, four levers of business model innovation and several enablers and inhibitors can be identified.[16] Below you will find additional assessment tools to determine the extent to which an organization is able to deploy these levers and whether these enablers and inhibitors will facilitate or hinder its progress.

### Levers of business model transformation

Assess the extent to which the company is able to deploy the following four levers of business model transformation:

- <u>Technology</u> is a lever that involves the capacity to encourage technological innovation within the firm itself by acquiring additional knowledge and increasing investment in R&D. On the other hand, it concerns the capacity to absorb new technologies and knowledge from outside the organization. Technology as a lever can be deployed if the company invests heavily in new technologies that can potentially make its existing technologies obsolete and it pays a lot of attention to broadening and deepening its knowledge base.
- <u>Management</u> as a second lever of business model transformation involves the application of new management practices. It covers changes in *what* managers do as well as *how* they do it. These changes reveal themselves through new management practices, processes, or techniques. Indicators of management as a lever for innovation are for example when management set new performance indicators, start rewarding employees for business model innovation success, or introduce new ways of communicating or allocating responsibilities.
- Implementing new <u>organizational forms</u> within a firm is a third lever of business model innovation. Organizational form is about how work is divided into tasks and how those tasks are coordinated. Indicators of facilitating transformation by change in organizational structure may involve the adaptation of job descriptions, control systems, and the delegation of work. Other indicators are the elimination of departments, reconfiguration of teams, and simplification of decision-making processes.
- <u>Co-creation</u> (the fourth lever) will facilitate transformation when the firm collaborates with third parties to develop new business models. Muji, a Japanese retailer of household and consumer goods, for example, is famous for the way its design team works with consumers to develop new products. Co-creation may serve the purpose of a replication focus as well to develop economies of scale. Air France-KLM joining the SkyTeam alliance (see Chapter 13) is an example of the latter. Examples of indicators of the use of co-creation as a lever are the company sharing business

proposals, technical documents, and know-how with partners. Integrated information and communication systems with partners and mutual visits to observe each other in operation are other indicators used to determine the intensity of co-creation efforts.

You may estimate the extent to which the company of your interest deploys these levers for business model transformation. When applied in combination, they will be even more powerful. Depending on the magnitude of transformation efforts, it may need to invest in these levers and make them work in a coherent and reinforcing way.[17]

## Enablers and inhibitors of transformation

The following six different factors have been identified as enablers or inhibitors of business model transformation. Some of these enable business model replication but inhibit business model generation – for instance, listening to customers enables the first, but inhibits the latter.

- Transformational leaders motivate employees to achieve organizational goals by identifying with those goals. In terms of replication, they encourage employees to be fully committed to the company's current activities, and in terms of business model generation they help them to envision a different future.
- Organizational identity is about what the company stands for and how it should operate. It affects how people interpret threats and opportunities. A strong identity is particularly beneficial for replication strategies.
- An innovative culture is characterized by a tendency towards improvisation, absence of a single dominant profession, and typically very few rules. The formal rules that do exist can also be broken. This helps to ensure that talented employees are retained, which is very important for driving business model renewal.
- Absorptive capacity is the ability to identify, take up, process and use knowledge from the environment. A high capacity to absorb external information and identify incipient changes in the market at a very early stage helps to pick up new trends ahead of rivals. It strengthens business model generation, though not as much as replication (possibly because organizations use their knowledge of existing customers and markets as a seedbed for new knowledge).
- Listening to customers can be a major source of new ideas, although it can be dangerous to listen too much. A firm's largest customers are often laggards wary of radical change. Paying a lot of attention to one's largest customers thus usually helps replication (incremental improvements to existing products and services) but hinders generation of new business models.
- Internal cooperation helps employees with different knowledge and experience to exchange ideas and learn from one another, and enables the effective utilization of that knowledge. Connectedness between employees strengthens replication. Having more internal cooperation helps the organization to focus more on its mainstream activities. In settings with a high level of internal cooperation, however, it is more difficult to protect the development of new business models.

Figure D.12 shows which type of business model innovation is enabled or inhibited by each of the six aspects. To complete the series of business model transformation tests, assess a company against these six factors and the extent to which it fits with the type of business model innovation it aspires to.

| | Strategy-driven | Customer-driven |
|---|---|---|
| **Business model generation** | - Transformational leadership: **high**<br>- Identity: **low to moderate** (new internal identity development)<br>- Culture: **low** (innovative, vision oriented)<br>- Knowledge absorption: **high** (internal knowledge)<br>- Listening to customers: **low**<br>- Internal cooperation: **moderate** | - Transformational leadership: **moderate to high**<br>- Identity: **moderate** (external identity development)<br>- Culture: **low** (innovative, customer oriented)<br>- Knowledge absorption: **high** (external knowledge)<br>- Listening to customers: **high**<br>- Internal cooperation: **high** |
| **Business model replication** | - Transformational leadership: **low** (transactional leadership)<br>- Identity: **high** (strong external identity)<br>- Culture: **high** (conservative, inward oriented)<br>- Knowledge absorption: **moderate** (internal knowledge)<br>- Listening to customers: **low**<br>- Internal cooperation: **high** | - Transformational leadership: **low** (transactional leadership)<br>- Identity: **high** (strong external identity)<br>- Culture: **high** (conservative, customer oriented)<br>- Knowledge absorption: **moderate** (external knowledge)<br>- Listening to customers: **high**<br>- Internal cooperation: **moderate** (customer collaboration) |

**FIGURE D.12**   Enablers and inhibitors of the four business model innovation journeys

Source: adapted from Volberda et al. (2018)

# Strategic renewal: Revitalization trajectories

A key question regarding the strategic renewal of firms concerns the adaptive capacity of the organization. Many mature firms face increasing turbulence in their environment and need revitalization. The *Organizational Flexibility Framework* supports you in shaping a revitalization trajectory for your organization. Or – if you are actually too flexible – how to build more routines in your organization and increase efficiency and reliability.

This framework identifies four ideal types of (stylized) organizational forms – see Figure D.13. As shown in the same figure, firms transform from one ideal type into another, either along a natural trajectory of routinization or along a trajectory of revitalization.

## Assessing current and required flexibility

At any point in time, the ideal organizational form depends on the level of environmental turbulence the company faces. The Organizational Flexibility framework supports you in diagnosing '*flexibility fit*': the extent to which an organization's flexible capabilities match the level of turbulence in its industry.[18] The framework identifies four ideal types for four corresponding levels of environmental turbulence:

- The Rigid Form deploys a very limited flexibility mix and has a routine technology, a mechanistic structure and a conservative culture. It operates optimally in a non-competitive environment.

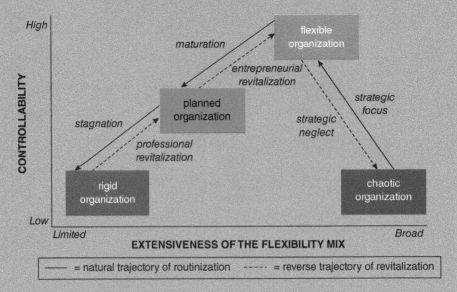

**FIGURE D.13**  Trajectories of renewal derived from the Organizational Flexibility framework

Source: Volberda (1998); Volberda et al. (2011)

- The <u>Planned Form</u> possesses operational flexibility and a non-routine technology, combined with a mechanistic structure and conservative culture. It functions optimally in complex-dynamic environments.
- The <u>Flexible Form</u> deploys a broad flexibility mix with structural and strategic flexibility, has non-routine technology, an organic structure and innovative culture. It operates optimally in a hypercompetitive environment.
- The <u>Chaotic Form</u> does have a high level of strategic flexibility; however, because of its very organic structure and very innovative culture, the responsiveness is low. Such an organization form is only applicable in extremely turbulent environments and for a limited time.

Basically, the framework analyses a company's fitness along three dimensions: (1) the level of environmental turbulence, (2) the flexibility mix, and (3) the potential for flexibility in organization design. Each dimension is described below and includes an assessment that will help you to determine which ideal type fits an organization and which renewal trajectory is appropriate.

## Step 1: The level of environmental turbulence

The intensity and type of change in the business environment determines what kind of flexibility is required, and how much. Firms operating in dynamic markets or in a state of hypercompetition need to be able to develop new competitive advantages quickly and continuously.[19] When markets are stable and predictable, on the other hand, there is less need for flexibility or no need at all.

<u>Assessment of environmental turbulence (ET)</u>: which of the following best describes the business environment of the company under investigation?

1. A static, simple and predictable (i.e., <u>non-competitive</u>) environment. Firms have established positions that enable them to develop absolute sustainable competitive advantages and generate excessive profit potential.
2. A dynamic and considerably complex environment with frequent and/or intense but largely predictable change (<u>moderate competition</u>). Elaborate planning routines enable firms to adapt and maintain their competitive advantages for prolonged periods.
3. A dynamic and complex, but above all unpredictable (<u>hypercompetitive</u>) environment, with changing industry boundaries and new competitors entering the market. Only those firms that are able to change position and adopt new technologies quickly are able to thrive.
4. An extremely fluid, undefined and unpredictable market (<u>extreme competition</u>). These conditions pertain to emerging industries, where industry structures still have to take shape, and customers still have to determine how to make use of new technologies or products. Competitive advantage is temporary by definition.

## Step 2: The flexibility mix to deal with change

Dealing with change – either proactively or reactively – requires management to scan the environment, make decisions in a timely manner, and implement changes effectively. The range of actions may vary, though, from increasing the volume of production, to changing the structure of the organization, or developing new business models, for example. In other words, depending on the level of turbulence the company faces, management needs operational, structural and/or strategic flexibility.[20] *Operational flexibility* enables change in the volume and mix of operational activities. *Structural flexibility* consists of managerial capabilities for adapting the organization structure, and its decision and communication processes. *Strategic flexibility* involves the ability to change strategy and game plans, dismantle current strategies, apply new technologies, or fundamentally renew products.

<u>Assessment of the flexibility mix (FM)</u> of the company: which of the following matches a company's capabilities best?

1. A very restricted flexibility mix dominated by simple procedures (<u>steady-state flexibility</u>). Choice and variation possibilities are limited; improvisation is all but forbidden.
2. A flexibility mix dominated by <u>operational flexibility</u>. Management can activate many sophisticated routines to deal with fluctuations in demand and incremental change. Responses are informed by elaborate environmental scanning and executed through systematically developing business plans.
3. An extensive flexibility mix, dominated by <u>strategic and structural flexibility.</u> Management can effectively and timely alter its strategic course, adapt the organization, and outsource activities to its ecosystem of partners (or, conversely, develop new competencies in-house).
4. <u>Very extensive strategic and structural flexibility</u>, with virtually unlimited options to change course and alter internal and external organizational structures. Solid routines and predictable operational capabilities are non existent, though.

## Step 3: The potential of the organization for flexibility

The ability to initiate any response in the face of market change depends on the adequacy of organizational design. Designing the appropriate organization requires identifying the ideal configuration of technology, organizational structure, and culture.

- Technology concerns the hardware (systems) and the software (knowledge) used in the organization's primary processes. The design of technology can range from routine (specialized) to non-routine (generic) and determines primarily the potential for operational flexibility.
- Organizational structure concerns the division of tasks and responsibilities (basic organizational form), planning and control systems and process regulations. Structures can vary from being highly mechanistic to highly organic, the latter providing the most potential for organizational flexibility.
- Organizational culture concerns the beliefs and values that are present within the organization and which become visible through unwritten rules, leadership style and employees' orientation (inward or outward looking). Corresponding with an increasing potential for strategic flexibility in particular, cultures can vary from highly conservative to highly innovative.

Assessment of organization design (OD) of the organization: which of the following matches the organization best?

1. The organizational design is characterized by a mature, routine technology and a mechanistic (i.e., centralized and hierarchical) structure. The culture is conservative and uniform.
2. The organization operates non-routine technology, meaning it can quickly adjust its volume of operations and utilize various systems (such as information systems and manufacturing technologies) that accommodate variation.
3. The organization design is based on non-routine technologies, and employees operate in an organic organizational structure that can be altered easily. The non-conformist culture values innovation and experimentation, but also acknowledges the value of exploitation and stability.
4. The organization is built on very generic multi-purpose technologies. Moreover, the organization lacks a formal structure and its culture values innovativeness only. Conformist behaviour and routine development are not encouraged.

## Assessment of flexibility fitness

The next step involves positioning the organization in the flexibility framework to determine the fit along the three dimensions and, subsequently, the appropriate renewal journey. The flexibility framework plots the organization on the horizontal axis straightforwardly according to the extensiveness of the *flexibility mix (FM)* (see above). The vertical axis reflects the responsiveness of the *organization design (OD)* (see above). Responsiveness is highest for organizations that operate with non-routine technology, organic structure, and innovative culture. Organizations that combine a non-routine technology with mechanistic structure and conservative culture have a medium-level of responsiveness. A very rigid organization design (that is, routine, mechanistic, conservative) is non-responsive and holds hardly any potential for flexibility. On the other hand, an organization that is extremely innovative, lacks structure and any routine technology base is uncontrollable and therefore just as non-responsive. If Option 1 or Option 4 match the organization best, the level of responsiveness is low. The ultimate judge of flexibility fitness is the environment, though. The level of *environmental turbulence (ET)* (see again above) determines the ideal type of organizational flexibility and is plotted above the framework; see Figure D.14.

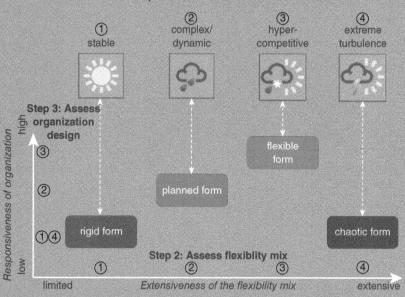

**FIGURE D.14** The Flexibility Framework: Assess an organization's fit in three steps

Source: adapted from Volberda (1998)

The Flexibility Framework identifies four ideal types that match the corresponding level of environmental turbulence. In a static and simple environment, a rigid form is ideal. A dynamic and complex, but largely predictable environment calls for a planned form. Flexible firms thrive best in hypercompetitive markets and even the chaotic firm has its optimum, albeit only temporarily as a startup or temporary organization designed to learn quickly.

## Determining company fitness

Based on your assessments of the environmental turbulence (ET), flexibility mix (FM) and organization design (OD), you are now able to plot the organization in the Flexibility Framework (Figure D.14). Mark the level of environmental turbulence (1 to 4, according to your assessment) and mark where the flexibility mix (your score on the horizontal axis) and the organization design (on the vertical axis) meet each other in the framework. The company may fit within one of the ideal types. For example, when you selected Option 2 for both the flexibility mix and the organization design questions, the company matched the position of the planned form. But you may also find a position somewhere else in the framework, depending on the company's scores in the other two assessments. Is it in the right position? The calculation sheet in Figure D.15 helps you to assess the measure of fitness more accurately. Take the following two steps to calculate the company fitness:

- Subtract the score for Environmental Turbulence (ET) from the Flexibility Mix (FM) score: *FM – ET = ?*

A *negative* score reflects a shortage of flexibility and means the company should invest in developing more flexible capabilities to match the level of turbulence in its environment. A *positive* score reflects a surplus and means it should focus on reducing flexibility and build more routines to increase efficiency. The higher the score, the greater the need to act.

- Subtract the ET-score from the score for Organization Design (OD): *OD – ET = ?*

A *negative* score means the organization design is not sufficiently responsive considering the environment it operates in. It will not be able to deploy the flexible capabilities it needs. A *positive* score means that the organization is possibly too responsive. It has a lot of potential to develop additional flexibility when necessary, though.

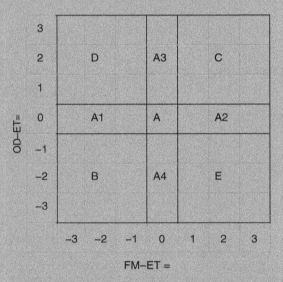

**FIGURE D.15**   Calculation sheet to determine appropriate action to improve flexibility fit

Source: authors

Use the outcomes to determine where the company fits in the calculation sheet in Figure D.15. Each segment is discussed briefly in Figure D.16.

## The appropriate renewal trajectory

Chances are that the company does not have a perfect fit with the level of environmental turbulence as indicated in the flexibility framework (see Figure D.14). But even if it does, a shift in the level of competition may create a misfit in the future. Markets evolve, after all.

| | |
|---|---|
| Segment A: | **Perfect fit.** |
| Segment A1: | **Flexibility deficit**. The organization design has sufficient potential, but management needs to develop its flexibility mix. |
| Segment A2: | **Flexibility surplus**. Management needs to reduce flexibility in order to increase efficiency, but the organization is perfectly fitting the required level. |
| Segment A3: | **Potential surplus**. The organization has a lot of potential for additional flexibility, but it doesn't need it. More stability will increase the effectiveness of the flexibility mix. |
| Segment A4: | **Potential deficit**. The organization design hardly allows for deploying the flexibility mix. Increase the responsiveness of the organization. |
| Segment B: | **Deficit**. Management needs to build a more extensive flexibility mix but work on a more responsive organization to increase the potential for flexibility first. A revitalization trajectory is advised. |
| Segment C: | **Surplus**. Both the flexibility mix and the organization design reflect a surplus in flexibility. Unless you expect the market to be disrupted soon – or you aim to disrupt the market yourself – consider a routinization trajectory. |
| Segment D: | **Flexibility deficit, with high organizational potential**. Management needs to develop additional flexible capabilities to match the level of turbulence. The organization holds sufficient potential, actually too much, which is a very costly situation. |
| Segment E: | **Flexibility surplus with organization deficit**. A bit of a strange combination: the company appears to have a lot of capabilities (too much, actually), but cannot make any use of them with the current organization. It needs to find a better balance. |

**FIGURE D.16**   Recommendations following the flexibility fitness assessment

The framework allows you to map a trajectory for a company to improve its flexibility fitness along two routes: the natural trajectory of routinization, or a trajectory of revitalization (see Figure D.13):

- The <u>natural trajectory of</u> <u>routinization</u> is a process of accumulation of specialized routines and fine-tuning of organizational conditions, typical when companies age and competition decreases. This trajectory is applicable when the company has a surplus of flexibility (that is, when you fit in Segment C). Several sub-trajectories exist: moving away from a chaotic organization requires strategic focus, moving towards a planned organization is a natural form of maturation, but moving even further down the road of routinization results in stagnation and a rigid organization. Routinization can be achieved by building routines, meaning the programming of responses to ever more familiar change. More specialized technology and formalized organizational structure will support the trajectory, as will a culture that values preservation and exploitative learning.

The case of the R&D department of a national gas corporation is illustrative of the need for routinization through strategic focus. The department had unlimited potential for flexibility, it had many initiatives for new research. Management could not capitalize on it, however, as the department had no clear administrative structures or shared values to give direction to these initiatives. Various stakeholders could force the department in any direction. The organization had to build a strategic plan, control systems, and a formal organizational structure that promoted stability and continuity. This also required the development of strong social ties and shared beliefs, and an orientation towards routine-development (i.e., a conserving culture).

- The opposite <u>trajectory of revitalization</u> is all but natural, as it requires the company to overcome inertia and break out of its routine behaviour. It's a trajectory that many mature firms will face when the level of competition increases due to the development of new technologies, deregulation, globalization etc. In other words, when your company has developed a flexibility deficit and you fit in Segment B. For rigid organizations, this entails professional revitalization and the development of operational flexibility as a first step. Planned firms should embark on a trajectory of entrepreneurial revitalization by loosening their structures and developing a culture open to innovation. This will create an organization sufficiently responsive to develop and deploy structural and strategical flexibility. A flexible firm that neglects its routines and focuses solely on innovation enters a state of strategic neglect and will end up in chaos.

Large firms, such as the Dutch airline carrier KLM, have gone through *dual trajectories*. KLM found itself facing increased turbulence while operating a more or less rigid organization. Turning around the whole company would require too much time and would create too much confusion, so it embarked on a dual trajectory. While KLM's Passenger Division was working on a trajectory of professional revitalization (continuously improving service levels, reducing overall costs, and increasing operational flexibility in terms of flight capacity and personnel), its Cargo Division went through a radical transformation from a rigid to an extremely chaotic organizational mode (offering an increased number of value-added services to customers, attracting new customers, and providing non-transport related logistic services). After a temporary state of chaos, it slowly shifted onwards towards a more flexible mode (categorizing the service portfolio, creating a more transparent structure, tightening the strategic vision, and developing 'Cargo values' and a code of conduct).[21]

The site www.reinventingbusinessmodels.com provides access to the Business Model Innovation Scan. After completion of the questionnaire about the firm of your choice, you receive a personalized, automated report containing a comparison of your scores to that of the industry average.

## Endnotes (references)

1. MacMillan, I.C. and McGrath, R.G. (2002) 'Crafting R&D project portfolios', *Research Technology Management*, 45 (5): 48–59.
2. Osterwalder, A. and Pigneur, Y. (2010) *Business Model Generation: A Handbook for Visionaries, Game Changers, and Challengers*. Hoboken, NJ: John Wiley & Sons.
3. Finch & Beak (2023) 'Winning the game of making waterless dyeing mainstream'. www.finchandbeak.com/1066/winning-the-game-making-waterless-dyeing.htm (accessed July 28, 2023).
4. Techniek Nederland (2023) 'Connect 2025'. https://web.archive.org/web/20230327113007/https://www.connect2025.nl/home (accessed July 28, 2023).
5. Volberda, H.W., Van den Bosch, F.A.J. and Heij, C.V. (2018) *Reinventing Business Models: How Firms Cope with Disruption*. Oxford: Oxford University Press.
6. Markides, C.C. (2013) *Game-changing Strategies: How to Create New Market Space in Established Industries by Breaking the Rules*. Hoboken, NJ: John Wiley & Sons.
7. Swapfiets (2022). About https://web.archive.org/web/20220128045348/https://news.swapfiets.com/nl-NL/about (accessed July 20, 2023).

8. Wall Street Journal (1993). The Wall Street Journal Index 1993 https://archive.org/details/wallstreetjourna1993/page/n1085/mode/2up (accessed July 20, 2023).

9. Gumbel, P. (2007) 'Luxury goes mass market', *Fortune*, September 6. https://money.cnn.com/2007/08/30/magazines/fortune/mass_vs_class.fortune/index.htm (accessed July 20, 2023).

10. Levitt, T. (2004) 'Marketing myopia', *Harvard Business Review*, 82 (7/8): 138–149.

11. Markides (2013)

12. Kim, W.C. and Mauborgne, R. (2014) *Blue Ocean Strategy, Expanded Edition: How to Create Uncontested Market Space and Make the Competition Irrelevant.* Cambridge, MA: Harvard Business Review Press.

13. Volberda et al. (2018)

14. Volberda et al. (2018)

15. Rumelt, R.P. (2012) 'Good strategy/bad strategy: The difference and why it matters', *Strategic Direction*, 28 (8). doi.org/10.1108/sd.2012.05628haa.002.

16. Volberda et al. (2018)

17. Volberda et al. (2018)

18. Van der Weerdt, N.P. (2009) *Organizational Flexibility for Hypercompetitive Markets* (No. EPS-2009-173-STR). PhD dissertation, Erasmus Universiteit Rotterdam. https://repub.eur.nl/pub/16182/EPS2009173STR9058922151Weerd.pdf (accessed July 1, 2023); Volberda, H.W. (1996) 'Toward the flexible form: How to remain vital in hypercompetitive environments', *Organization Science*, 7 (4): 359–74.

19. D'Aveni, R.A. (1994) *Hypercompetition: Managing the Dynamics of Strategic Management.* New York, NY: Free Press; Eisenhardt, K.M. and Martin, J.A. (2000) 'Dynamic capabilities: What are they?', *Strategic Management Journal*, 21 (10–11): 1105–21.

20. Volberda, H.W. (1998) *Building the Flexible Firm: How to Remain Competitive.* Oxford: Oxford University Press; Volberda (1996).

21. Volberda (1998)

# Acknowledgements

The authors thank Niels van der Weerdt and Taghi Ramezan Zadeh for their contribution to this chapter.

# INDEX

Note: Page numbers followed by "f" and "t" represents figures and tables respectively.